Investment Banking

Founded in 1807, John Wiley & Sons is the oldest independent publishing company in the United States. With offices in North America, Europe, Australia and Asia, Wiley is globally committed to developing and marketing print and electronic products and services for our customers' professional and personal knowledge and understanding.

The Wiley Finance series contains books written specifically for finance and investment professionals as well as sophisticated individual investors and their financial advisors. Book topics range from portfolio management to e-commerce, risk management, financial engineering, valuation and financial instrument analysis, as well as much more.

For a list of available titles, visit our Web site at www.WileyFinance.com.

Investment Banking

Valuation, Leveraged Buyouts, and Mergers & Acquisitions

SECOND EDITION

JOSHUA ROSENBAUM
JOSHUA PEARL

FOREWORD BY JOSEPH R. PERELLA
AFTERWORD BY JOSHUA HARRIS

WILEY

Cover design: Wiley
Cover image: (Stock Board) © David Pollack / Corbis; (Gold Texture) © Gyro Photography / amanaimagesRF / Jupiter Images; (Arrow) © arahan-Fotolia.com

Copyright © 2013 by Joshua Rosenbaum and Joshua Pearl. All rights reserved.

Published by John Wiley & Sons, Inc., Hoboken, New Jersey.
First Edition published by John Wiley & Sons, Inc. in 2009.
Published simultaneously in Canada.

No part of this publication may be reproduced, stored in a retrieval system, or transmitted in any form or by any means, electronic, mechanical, photocopying, recording, scanning, or otherwise, except as permitted under Section 107 or 108 of the 1976 United States Copyright Act, without either the prior written permission of the Publisher, or authorization through payment of the appropriate per-copy fee to the Copyright Clearance Center, Inc., 222 Rosewood Drive, Danvers, MA 01923, (978) 750-8400, fax (978) 646-8600, or on the Web at www.copyright.com. Requests to the Publisher for permission should be addressed to the Permissions Department, John Wiley & Sons, Inc., 111 River Street, Hoboken, NJ 07030, (201) 748-6011, fax (201) 748-6008, or online at www.wiley.com/go/permissions.

Limit of Liability/Disclaimer of Warranty: While the publisher and author have used their best efforts in preparing this book, they make no representations or warranties with respect to the accuracy or completeness of the contents of this book and specifically disclaim any implied warranties of merchantability or fitness for a particular purpose. No warranty may be created or extended by sales representatives or written sales materials. The advice and strategies contained herein may not be suitable for your situation. You should consult with a professional where appropriate. Neither the publisher nor author shall be liable for any loss of profit or any other commercial damages, including but not limited to special, incidental, consequential, or other damages.

For general information on our other products and services or for technical support, please contact our Customer Care Department within the United States at (800) 762-2974, outside the United States at (317) 572-3993 or fax (317) 572-4002.

Wiley publishes in a variety of print and electronic formats and by print-on-demand. Some material included with standard print versions of this book may not be included in e-books or in print-on-demand. If this book refers to media such as a CD or DVD that is not included in the version you purchased, you may download this material at http://booksupport.wiley.com. For more information about Wiley products, visit www.wiley.com.

ISBN 978-1-118-65621-1 (cloth); ISBN 978-1-118-28125-3 (cloth + models);
ISBN 978-1-118-47220-0 (paper); ISBN 978-1-118-41985-4 (ebk);
ISBN 978-1-118-42161-1 (ebk); ISBN 978-1-118-69505-0 (ebk)

Printed in the United States of America

10 9 8 7 6 5 4 3 2 1

In loving memory of Ronie Rosenbaum, an inspiration for strength and selflessness.

—J.R.

To the memory of my grandfather, Joseph Pearl, a Holocaust survivor, for his inspiration to persevere and succeed.*

—J.P.

---

*A portion of the authors' royalties will be donated to The Blue Card Fund aiding destitute Holocaust survivors—**www.bluecardfund.org**.

Contents

Additional Resources	xiii
About the Authors	xv
Foreword	xvii
Acknowledgments	xix
INTRODUCTION	**1**
Structure of the Book	3
Part One: Valuation (Chapters 1–3)	3
Part Two: Leveraged Buyouts (Chapters 4 & 5)	5
Part Three: Mergers & Acquisitions (Chapters 6 & 7)	6
ValueCo Summary Financial Information	8

PART ONE

Valuation	**11**

CHAPTER 1

Comparable Companies Analysis	**13**
Summary of Comparable Companies Analysis Steps	14
Step I. Select The Universe of Comparable Companies	17
Study the Target	17
Identify Key Characteristics of the Target for Comparison Purposes	18
Screen for Comparable Companies	22
Step II. Locate The Necessary Financial Information	23
SEC Filings: 10-K, 10-Q, 8-K, and Proxy Statements	24
Equity Research	25
Press Releases and News Runs	26
Financial Information Services	26
Summary of Financial Data Primary Sources	27
Step III. Spread Key Statistics, Ratios, and Trading Multiples	28
Calculation of Key Financial Statistics and Ratios	28
Supplemental Financial Concepts and Calculations	42
Calculation of Key Trading Multiples	47

Step IV. Benchmark the Comparable Companies	50
Benchmark the Financial Statistics and Ratios	50
Benchmark the Trading Multiples	50
Step V. Determine Valuation	51
Valuation Implied by EV/EBITDA	52
Valuation Implied by P/E	52
Key Pros and Cons	54
Illustrative Comparable Companies Analysis for ValueCo	55
Step I. Select the Universe of Comparable Companies	55
Step II. Locate the Necessary Financial Information	56
Step III. Spread Key Statistics, Ratios, and Trading Multiples	57
Step IV. Benchmark the Comparable Companies	69
Step V. Determine Valuation	74
Bloomberg Appendix	75

CHAPTER 2
Precedent Transactions Analysis   83

Summary of Precedent Transactions Analysis Steps	84
Step I. Select the Universe of Comparable Acquisitions	87
Screen for Comparable Acquisitions	87
Examine Other Considerations	88
Step II. Locate the Necessary Deal-Related and Financial Information	90
Public Targets	90
Private Targets	93
Summary of Primary SEC Filings in M&A Transactions	93
Step III. Spread Key Statistics, Ratios, and Transaction Multiples	96
Calculation of Key Financial Statistics and Ratios	96
Calculationof Key Transaction Multiples	102
Step IV. Benchmark the Comparable Acquisitions	106
Step V. Determine Valuation	106
Key Pros And Cons	107
Illustrative Precedent Transaction Analysis for ValueCo	108
Step I. Select the Universe of Comparable Acquisitions	108
Step II. Locate the Necessary Deal-Related and Financial Information	108
Step III. Spread Key Statistics, Ratios, and Transaction Multiples	111
Step IV. Benchmark the Comparable Acquisitions	119
Step V. Determine Valuation	121
Bloomberg Appendix	122

CHAPTER 3
Discounted Cash Flow Analysis   125

Summary of Discounted Cash Flow Analysis Steps	126
Step I. Study the Target and Determine Key Performance Drivers	130
Study the Target	130
Determine Key Performance Drivers	130
Step II. Project Free Cash Flow	131
Considerations for Projecting Free Cash Flow	131

Projection of Sales, EBITDA, and EBIT	133
Projection of Free Cash Flow	135
Step III. Calculate Weighted Average Cost of Capital	141
Step III(a): Determine Target Capital Structure	142
Step III(b): Estimate Cost of Debt (r_d)	143
Step III(c): Estimate Cost of Equity (r_e)	144
Step III(d): Calculate WACC	148
Step IV. Determine Terminal Value	148
Exit Multiple Method	149
Perpetuity Growth Method	149
Step V. Calculate Present Value and Determine Valuation	151
Calculate Present Value	151
Determine Valuation	153
Perform Sensitivity Analysis	155
Key Pros and Cons	156
Illustrative Discounted Cash Flow Analysis for ValueCo	157
Step I. Study the Target and Determine Key Performance Drivers	157
Step II. Project Free Cash Flow	157
Step III. Calculate Weighted Average Cost of Capital	164
Step IV. Determine Terminal Value	169
Step V. Calculate Present Value and Determine Valuation	171
Bloomberg Appendix	176

PART TWO

Leveraged Buyouts   183

CHAPTER 4

Leveraged Buyouts   185

Key Participants	187
Financial Sponsors	187
Investment Banks	188
Bank and Institutional Lenders	190
Bond Investors	191
Target Management	191
Characteristics of a Strong LBO Candidate	192
Strong Cash Flow Generation	193
Leading and Defensible Market Positions	193
Growth Opportunities	194
Efficiency Enhancement Opportunities	194
Low Capex Requirements	194
Strong Asset Base	195
Proven Management Team	195
Economics of LBOs	196
Returns Analysis—Internal Rate of Return	196
Returns Analysis—Cash Return	197
How LBOs Generate Returns	197
How Leverage Is Used to Enhance Returns	198

Primary Exit/Monetization Strategies	202
Sale of Business	202
Initial Public Offering	203
Dividend Recapitalization	203
Below Par Debt Repurchase	203
LBO Financing: Structure	204
LBO Financing: Primary Sources	207
Bank Debt	207
High Yield Bonds	211
Mezzanine Debt	213
Equity Contribution	214
LBO Financing: Selected Key Terms	217
Security	217
Seniority	217
Maturity	219
Coupon	219
Call Protection	220
Covenants	221
Term Sheets	224
LBO Financing: Determining Financing Structure	227
Bloomberg Appendix	232

CHAPTER 5
LBO Analysis   235

Financing Structure	235
Valuation	235
Step I. Locate and Analyze the Necessary Information	238
Step II. Build the Pre-LBO Model	238
Step II(a): Build Historical and Projected Income Statement through EBIT	239
Step II(b): Input Opening Balance Sheet and Project Balance Sheet Items	242
Step II(c): Build Cash Flow Statement through Investing Activities	244
Step III. Input Transaction Structure	247
Step III(a): Enter Purchase Price Assumptions	247
Step III(b): Enter Financing Structure into Sources and Uses	249
Step III(c): Link Sources and Uses to Balance Sheet Adjustments Columns	251
Step IV. Complete the Post-LBO Model	256
Step IV(a): Build Debt Schedule	256
Step IV(b): Complete Pro Forma Income Statement from EBIT to Net Income	265
Step IV(c): Complete Pro Forma Balance Sheet	268
Step IV(d): Complete Pro Forma Cash Flow Statement	270
Step V. Perform LBO Analysis	272
Step V(a): Analyze Financing Structure	272
Step V(b): Perform Returns Analysis	274
Step V(c): Determine Valuation	278

Contents   xi

Step V(d): Create Transaction Summary Page	279
Illustrative LBO Analysis for ValueCo	280
Bloomberg Appendix	290

PART THREE
Mergers & Acquisitions   293

CHAPTER 6
Sell-Side M&A   295

Auctions	296
Auction Structure	299
Organization and Preparation	299
Identify Seller Objectives and Determine Appropriate Sale Process	299
Perform Sell-Side Advisor Due Diligence and Preliminary Valuation Analysis	301
Select Buyer Universe	301
Prepare Marketing Materials	302
Prepare Confidentiality Agreement	305
First Round	306
Contact Prospective Buyers	306
Negotiate and Execute Confidentiality Agreement with Interested Parties	306
Distribute Confidential Information Memorandum and Initial Bid Procedures Letter	306
Prepare Management Presentation	308
Set up Data Room	309
Prepare Stapled Financing Package	311
Receive Initial Bids and Select Buyers to Proceed to Second Round	311
Valuation Perspectives—Strategic Buyers vs. Finacial Sponsors	312
Second Round	313
Conduct Management Presentations	313
Facilitate Site Visits	314
Provide Data Room Access	314
Distribute Final Bid Procedures Letter and Draft Definitive Agreement	315
Receive Final Bids	316
Negotiations	320
Evaluate Final Bids	320
Negotiate with Preferred Buyer(s)	320
Select Winning Bidder	320
Render Fairness Opinion	321
Receive Board Approval and Execute Definitive Agreement	321
Closing	322
Obtain Necessary Approvals	322

Shareholder Approval ... 322
Financing and Closing ... 324
Negotiated Sale ... 325
Bloomberg Appendix ... 327

CHAPTER 7
Buy-Side M&A ... **331**
Buyer Motivation ... 332
Synergies ... 333
Cost Synergies ... 334
Revenue Synergies ... 334
Acquisition Strategies ... 335
Horizontal Integration ... 335
Vertical Integration ... 335
Conglomeration ... 336
Form of Financing ... 337
Cash on Hand ... 338
Debt Financing ... 338
Equity Financing ... 339
Debt vs. Equity Financing Summary—Acquirer Perspective ... 340
Deal Structure ... 340
Stock Sale ... 340
Asset Sale ... 343
Stock Sales Treated as Asset Sales for Tax Purposes ... 346
Section 338 Election ... 346
338(h)(10) Election ... 346
Buy-Side Valuation ... 348
Football Field ... 349
Analysis at Various Prices ... 352
Contribution Analysis ... 353
Merger Consequences Analysis ... 355
Purchase Price Assumptions ... 355
Balance Sheet Effects ... 360
Accretion/(Dilution) Analysis ... 365
Acquisition Scenarios—I) 50% Stock / 50% Cash; II) 100% Cash; and III) 100% Stock ... 368
Illustrative Merger Consequences Analysis for the BuyerCo / ValueCo Transaction ... 373
Bloomberg Appendix ... 394

Afterword ... **397**

Bibliography and Recommended Reading ... **399**

Index ... **405**

Additional Resources

Investment Banking, Second Edition is supplemented by a suite of products available for separate purchase that will further enhance your understanding of the material, including:

- Valuation Models
- Investment Banking Workbook
- Investment Banking Focus Notes

Professors can learn more about available instructor and student resources by visiting: http://www.wiley.com/WileyCDA/WileyTitle/productCd-1118472209.html.

VALUATION MODELS

Valuation Models for the methodologies discussed in *Investment Banking, Second Edition* are available with purchase of the book or can be purchased separately at wiley.com. If the models came with your version of the book, go to **www.wiley.com/go/investmentbanking2e** and input the access code found at the back of the book.

There are five model templates as well as five completed models, one for each of the following:

- Comparable Companies
- Precedent Transactions
- DCF Analysis
- LBO Analysis
- Merger Consequences Analysis

WORKBOOK

The *Investment Banking Workbook* is designed for use both as a companion to *Investment Banking, Second Edition*, as well as on a standalone basis. The workbook provides a mix of multi-step problem set exercises, as well as multiple choice and essay questions—over 400 questions in total. It also provides a comprehensive answer key that aims to truly teach and explain as opposed to simply identify the correct answer. Therefore, the answers themselves are an effective learning tool. The completion of this comprehensive guide will help ensure the achievement of your professional and educational milestones.

FOCUS NOTES

Investment Banking Focus Notes provides a comprehensive, yet streamlined, review of the basic skills and concepts discussed in *Investment Banking, Second Edition*. The *Focus Notes* are designed for use as a companion to the main book as well as a standalone study program. This text serves as a one-stop resource in an easy-to-read-and-carry format that serves as a perfect reference material for a quick refresher.

Focus Notes seeks to help solidify knowledge of the core financial topics as true mastery must be tested, honed, and retested over time. It is the ultimate self-help tool for students, job seekers, and existing finance professionals, as well as in formal classroom and training settings.

About the Authors

JOSHUA ROSENBAUM is a Managing Director at UBS Investment Bank in the Global Industrial Group. He originates, structures, and advises on M&A, corporate finance, and capital markets transactions. Previously, he worked at the International Finance Corporation, the direct investment division of the World Bank. He received his AB from Harvard and his MBA with Baker Scholar honors from Harvard Business School.

JOSHUA PEARL is an investment analyst at Brahman Capital Corp. Previously, he structured and executed leveraged loan and high yield bond financings, as well as leveraged buyouts and restructurings as a Director at UBS Investment Bank in Leveraged Finance. Prior to UBS, he worked at Moelis & Company and Deutsche Bank. He received his BS in Business from Indiana University's Kelley School of Business.

CONTACT THE AUTHORS

Please feel free to contact **JOSHUA ROSENBAUM** and **JOSHUA PEARL** with any questions, comments, or suggestions for future editions at **josh@investmentbankingbook.com**.

Foreword

Mark Twain, long known for his critical views of formal education, once wisely noted: "I never let my schooling interfere with my education."

Twain's one-liner strikes at the core of investment banking, where deals must be lived before proper knowledge and understanding can be obtained. Hard time must be spent doing deals, with complexities in valuation, terms, and negotiations unique to every situation. The truly great firms and dealmakers have become so by developing cultures of apprenticeship that transfer knowledge and creativity from one generation to the next. The task of teaching aspiring investment bankers and finance professionals has been further complicated by the all-consuming nature of the trade, as well as its constantly evolving art and science.

Therefore, for me personally, it's exciting to see Joshua Rosenbaum and Joshua Pearl take the lead in training a new generation of investment bankers. Their work in documenting valuation and deal process in an accessible manner is a particularly important contribution as many aspects of investment banking cannot be taught, even in the world's greatest universities and business schools. Rosenbaum and Pearl provide aspiring—and even the most seasoned—investment bankers with a unique real-world education inside Wall Street's less formal classroom, where deals come together at real-time speed.

The school of hard knocks and of learning-by-doing, which was Twain's classroom, demands strong discipline and sound acumen in the core fundamentals of valuation. It requires applying these techniques to improve the quality of deals for all parties, so that deal makers can avoid critical and costly mistakes, as well as unnecessary risks. My own 35+ years of Wall Street education has clearly demonstrated that valuation is at the core of investment banking. Any banker worth his salt must possess the ability to properly value a business in a structured and defensible manner. This logic and rationale must inspire clients and counterparties alike, while spurring strategic momentum and comprehension into the art of doing the deal.

Rosenbaum and Pearl succeed in providing a systematic approach to addressing a critical issue in any M&A, IPO, or investment situation—namely, how much is a business or transaction worth. They also put forth the framework for helping approach more nuanced questions such as how much to pay for the business and how to get the deal done. Due to the lack of a comprehensive written reference material on valuation, the fundamentals and subtlety of the trade are often passed on orally from banker-to-banker on a case-by-case basis. In codifying the art and science of investment banking, the authors convert this oral history into an accessible framework by bridging the theoretical to the practical with user-friendly, step-by-step approaches to performing primary valuation methodologies.

Many seasoned investment bankers commonly lament the absence of relevant and practical "how-to" materials for newcomers to the field. The reality is that most financial texts on valuation and M&A are written by academics. The few books written by practitioners tend to focus on dramatic war stories and hijinks, rather than the nuts-and-bolts of the techniques used to get deals done. Rosenbaum and Pearl fill this heretofore void for practicing and aspiring investment bankers and finance professionals. Their book is designed to prove sufficiently accessible to a wide audience, including those with a limited finance background.

It is true that we live in uncertain and volatile times—times that have destroyed or consumed more than a few of the most legendary Wall Street institutions. However, one thing will remain a constant in the long-term—the need for skilled finance professionals with strong technical expertise. Companies will always seek counsel from experienced and independent professionals to analyze, structure, negotiate, and close deals as they navigate the market and take advantage of value-creating opportunities. Rosenbaum and Pearl promulgate a return to the fundamentals of due diligence and the use of well-founded realistic assumptions governing growth, profitability, and approach to risk. Their work toward instilling the proper skill set and mindset in aspiring generations of Wall Street professionals will help establish a firm foundation for driving a brighter economic future.

JOSEPH R. PERELLA
Chairman and CEO, Perella Weinberg Partners

Acknowledgments

We are deeply indebted to the numerous colleagues and peers who provided invaluable guidance, input, and hard work to help make this book possible.

We would like to highlight the contributions made by **Joseph Gasparro** toward the successful revision and production of the second edition of this book. His contributions were multi-dimensional and his unwavering enthusiasm, insights, and support were nothing short of exemplary. In general, Joe's work ethic, creativity, "can-do" attitude, and commitment to perfection are a true inspiration. We look forward to great things from him in the future.

Joseph Meisner's technical insights on M&A buy-side and sell-side analysis were invaluable for the book's second edition, as was his unique ability to marry the academic with the practical. His technical knowledge and experience is impressive, and he is able to distill the essence of a situation and express himself in layman's terms. He is the consummate M&A professional as well as a true friend and asset to those around him.

Jeffrey Groves provided us with valuable contributions on updating and expanding the leveraged buyouts content. Jeff is a highly skilled and experienced leveraged finance professional with a soft client touch and his pulse on the market. **Daniel Plaxe** was also helpful in enriching our LBO content with his technical and precise approach. **Vijay Kumra** made a valuable contribution to our updated M&A content, providing practical and grounding insights to help preserve the accessibility of a highly complex and technical topic.

We also want to reiterate our thanks to those who were so instrumental in the success of the first edition of *Investment Banking*. The book could never have come to fruition without the sage advice and enthusiasm of **Steve Momper**, Director of Darden Business Publishing at the University of Virginia. Steve believed in our book from the beginning and supported us throughout the entire process. Most importantly, he introduced us to our publisher, John Wiley & Sons, Inc. Special thanks to **Ryan Drook, Michael Lanzarone, Joseph Bress,** and **Benjamin Hochberg** for their insightful editorial contributions. As top-notch professionals in investment banking and private equity, their expertise and practical guidance proved invaluable. Many thanks to **Steven Sherman, Eric Leicht, Greg Pryor, Mark Gordon, Jennifer DiNucci,** and **Ante Vucic** for their exhaustive work in assisting with the legal nuances of our book. As partners at the nation's leading corporate law firms, their oversight helped ensure the accuracy and timeliness of the content.

We'd like to thank the outstanding team at Wiley. **Bill Falloon**, acquisition editor, was always accessible and the consummate professional. He never wavered in his vision and support, and provided strong leadership throughout the entire process.

Our publishers **Joan O'Neil** and **Pamela van Giessen** continue to champion our book both internally and externally. **Meg Freeborn**, development editor, worked alongside Bill on the editorial side. **Tiffany Charbonier**, editorial assistant, worked diligently to ensure all the administrative details were addressed. **Mary Daniello**, production manager, facilitated a smooth production process. **Sharon Polese**, marketing manager, helped us realize our vision through her creativity and foresight.

We also want to express immeasurable gratitude to our families and friends for their encouragement, support, and sacrifice during the weekends and holidays that ordinarily would have been dedicated to them.

This book could not have been completed without the efforts and reviews of the following individuals:

Jonathan Ackerman, *UBS Investment Bank*

Mark Adler, *Piper Jaffray*

Kenneth Ahern, *University of Southern California, Marshall School of Business*

Marc Auerbach, *Standard & Poor's/Leveraged Commentary & Data*

Carliss Baldwin, *Harvard Business School*

Kyle Barker, *Kodiak Building Partners*

Ronnie Barnes, *Cornerstone Research*

Joshua Becker, *Versa Capital Management*

Joseph Bress, *The Carlyle Group*

Stephen Catera, *Siris Capital Group*

Thomas Cole, *Citigroup*

Eric Coghlin, *UBS Investment Bank*

Lawrence Cort

Aswath Damodaran, *New York University, Stern School of Business*

Thomas Davidoff, *University of California Berkeley, Haas School of Business*

Victor Delaglio, *Province Advisors*

Jennifer Fonner DiNucci, *Cooley Godward Kronish LLP*

Wojciech Domanski, *ICENTIS Capital*

Ryan Drook, *Deutsche Bank*

Chris Falk, *Florida State University, College of Business*

Erza Faham, *Baruch College*

Heiko Freitag, *Anschutz Investment Company*

Mark Funk, *EVP & CFO, Mobile Mini, Inc.*

Joseph Gasparro, *Bank of America Merrill Lynch*

Masha Girshin, *Pace University, Lubin School of Business*

Andrew Gladston, *Maquarie Capital*

Peter D. Goodson, *University of California Berkeley, Haas School of Business and Columbia Business School*

Peter M. Goodson, *Eminence Capital*

Acknowledgments

Mark Gordon, *Wachtell, Lipton, Rosen & Katz*
Gary Gray, *Pennsylvania State University, Smeal School of Business*
Jeffrey Groves, *UBS Investment Bank*
David Haeberle, *Indiana University, Kelley School of Business*
John Haynor, *Jefferies & Company*
Milwood Hobbs, *Natixis Securities*
Benjamin Hochberg, *Lee Equity Partners, LLC*
Alec Hufnagel, *Kelso & Company*
Jon Hugo, *Deutsche Bank*
Roger Ibbotson, *Yale School of Management*
Cedric Jarrett, *Deutsche Bank*
John Joliet, *Moelis & Company*
Tamir Kaloti, *Deutsche Bank*
Michael Kamras, *Credit Suisse*
Kenneth Kim, *State University of New York at Buffalo, School of Management*
Eric Klar, *White & Case LLP*
Kenneth Kloner, *UBS Investment Bank*
Philip Konnikov, *UBS Investment Bank*
Vijay Kumra, *UBS Investment Bank*
Alex Lajoux, *National Association of Corporate Directors, Coauthor of "The Art of M&A" Series*
Ian Lampl, *Department of Treasury, Office of Financial Stability*
Michael Lanzarone, CFA, *Société Générale*
Eu-Han Lee, *Indus Capital Advisors (HK) Ltd.*
Franky Lee, *Providence Equity Partners*
Eric Leicht, *White & Case LLP*
Jay Lurie, *International Finance Corporation (IFC)*
David Mayhew, *Deutsche Bank*
Coley McMenamin, *Bank of America Merrill Lynch*
Joseph Meisner, *RBC Capital Markets*
Steve Momper, *University of Virginia, Darden Business Publishing*
Kirk Murphy, *MKM Partners*
Joshua Neren, *J.P. Morgan*
Paul Pai, *BMO Capital Markets*
James Paris, *BMO Capital Markets*
Dan Park, *Foros Group*
Daniel Plaxe, *Pioneer Funding Group, LLC*
Gregory Pryor, *White & Case LLP*
David Ross, *Bank of America Merrill Lynch*

Ashish Rughwani, *Dominus Capital*
David Sanford, *Scout Capital*
Arnold Schneider, *Georgia Tech College of Management*
Mustafa Singaporewalla, *Bank of America Merrill Lynch*
Steven Sherman, *Shearman & Sterling LLP*
Andrew Shogan, *Deutsche Bank*
Emma Smith, *Deutsche Bank*
David Spalding, *Dartmouth College*
Andrew Steinerman, *JP Morgan*
Matthew Thomson
Robb Tretter, *Bracewell & Giuliani LLP*
John Tripodoro, *Cahill Gordon & Reindel LLP*
Ante Vucic, *Wachtell, Lipton, Rosen & Katz*
Siyu Wang, CFA, *TX Investment Consulting (China)*
Chris Wright, *Crescent Capital Group*
Jack Whalen, *Kensico Capital*

Additionally, we would like to highlight the efforts of the students from Baruch College's Investment Management Group who were invaluable in the production of our university ancillary materials:

- Omotola Atolagbe
- Mohammad Awais
- Albert Balasiano
- Ricky Chang
- Dennis Chin
- Lailee Chui
- Shokhrukh Erkinov
- MinYe Feng
- Gregory Flores
- David Hung
- Olgi Kendro
- Dimitris Kouvaros
- Jenny Lee
- Omair Talib Marghoob
- Sharmin Pala
- Vivek Kumar Rohra
- Aleksey Schukin
- Maksim Soshkin
- Isreal Suero
- Svetlana Vileshina
- Antonio Viveros
- Lily Wen
- Hugh Yoon

Introduction

In the constantly evolving world of finance, a solid technical foundation is an essential tool for success. Due to the fast-paced nature of this world, however, no one has been able to take the time to properly codify the lifeblood of the corporate financier's work—namely, valuation. We have responded to this need by writing the book that we wish had existed when we were trying to break into Wall Street. *Investment Banking: Valuation, Leveraged Buyouts, and Mergers & Acquisitions, Second Edition* is a highly accessible and authoritative book written by investment bankers that explains how to perform the valuation work at the core of the financial world. This book fills a noticeable gap in contemporary finance literature, which tends to focus on theory rather than practical application.

In the aftermath of the subprime mortgage crisis and ensuing credit crunch, the world of finance is returning to the fundamentals of valuation and critical due diligence for mergers & acquisitions (M&A), capital markets, and investment opportunities. This involves the use of more realistic assumptions governing approach to risk as well as a wide range of valuation drivers, such as expected financial performance, discount rates, multiples, leverage levels, and financing terms. While valuation has always involved a great deal of "art" in addition to time-tested "science," the artistry is perpetually evolving in accordance with market developments and conditions. *As a result, we have updated the widely adopted first edition of our book with respect to both technical valuation fundamentals as well as practical judgment skills and perspective. We have also added a comprehensive and highly technical chapter on buy-side M&A analysis.*

The genesis for this book stemmed from our personal experiences as students seeking to break into Wall Street. As we both independently went through the rigorous process of interviewing for associate and analyst positions at investment banks and other financial firms, we realized that our classroom experience was a step removed from how valuation and financial analysis are performed in real-world situations. This was particularly evident during the technical portion of the interviews, which is often the differentiator for recruiters trying to select among hundreds of qualified candidates.

Faced with this reality, we searched in vain for a practical how-to guide on the primary valuation methodologies used on Wall Street. At a loss, we resorted to compiling bits and pieces from various sources and ad hoc conversations with friends and contacts already working in investment banking and private equity. Needless to say, we didn't feel as prepared as we would have liked. While we were fortunate enough to secure job offers, the process left a deep impression on us. In fact, we continued to refine the comprehensive preparatory materials we had created as students, which served as the foundation for this book.

Once on Wall Street, we both went through mandatory training consisting of crash courses on finance and accounting, which sought to teach us the skill set necessary to become effective investment bankers. Months into the job, however, even the limitations of this training were revealed. Actual client situations and deal complexities, combined with evolving market conditions, accounting guidelines, and technologies stretched our knowledge base and skills. In these situations, we were forced to consult with senior colleagues for guidance, but often the demands of the job left no one accessible in a timely manner. Given these realities, it is difficult to overstate how helpful a reliable handbook based on years of "best practices" and deal experience would have been.

Consequently, we believe this book will prove invaluable to those individuals seeking or beginning careers on Wall Street—from students at undergraduate universities and graduate schools to "career changers" looking to break into finance. For working professionals, this book is also designed to serve as an important reference material. Our experience has demonstrated that given the highly specialized nature of many finance jobs, there are noticeable gaps in skill sets that need to be addressed. Furthermore, many professionals seek to continuously brush up on their skills as well as broaden and refine their knowledge base. This book will also be highly beneficial for trainers and trainees at Wall Street firms, both within the context of formal training programs and informal on-the-job training.

Our editorial contributors from private equity firms and hedge funds have also identified the need for a practical valuation handbook for their investment professionals and key portfolio company executives. Many of these professionals come from a consulting or operational background and do not have a finance pedigree. Furthermore, the vast majority of buy-side investment firms do not have in-house training programs and rely heavily upon on-the-job training. This book will serve as a helpful reference guide for individuals joining, or seeking jobs at, these institutions.

This book also provides essential tools for professionals at corporations, including members of business development, finance, and treasury departments. These specialists are responsible for corporate finance, valuation, and transaction-related deliverables on a daily basis. They also work with investment bankers on various M&A transactions (including leveraged buyouts (LBOs) and related financings), as well as initial public offerings (IPOs), restructurings, and other capital markets transactions. Similarly, this book is intended to provide greater context for the legions of attorneys, consultants, and accountants focused on M&A, corporate finance, and other transaction advisory services.

Given the increasing globalization of the financial world, this book is designed to be sufficiently universal for use outside of North America. Our work on cross-border transactions—including in rapidly developing markets such as Asia, Latin America, Russia, and India—has revealed a tremendous appetite for skilled resources throughout the globe. Therefore, this book fulfills an important need as a valuable training material and reliable handbook for finance professionals in these markets.

STRUCTURE OF THE BOOK

This book focuses on the primary valuation methodologies currently used on Wall Street, namely comparable companies analysis, precedent transactions analysis, discounted cash flow analysis, and leveraged buyout analysis. These methodologies are used to determine valuation for public and private companies within the context of M&A transactions, LBOs, IPOs, restructurings, and investment decisions. They also form the cornerstone for valuing companies on a standalone basis, including an assessment of whether a given public company is overvalued or undervalued. As such, these fundamental skills are just as relevant for private equity and hedge fund analysis as for investment banking. Using a step-by-step, how-to approach for each methodology, we build a chronological knowledge base and define key terms, financial concepts, and processes throughout the book.

We also provide context for the various valuation methodologies through a comprehensive overview of the fundamentals of LBOs and M&A transactions. For both LBOs and M&A, we discuss process and analytics in detail, including walking through both an illustrative LBO and M&A analysis as would be performed on a live transaction. This discussion also provides detailed information on an organized M&A sale process, including key participants, financing sources and terms, strategies, milestones, and legal and marketing documentation.

Furthermore, we address the importance of rigorous analysis based on trusted and attributable data sources. In this book, we highlight several datasets and investment banking tools from Bloomberg, a leading provider of business and financial data, news, research, and analytics. The Bloomberg Professional® service is a mainstay throughout the investment banking community, as it is an important tool for performing the depth of company and industry due diligence necessary to ensure successful transaction execution.

This body of work builds on our combined experience on a multitude of transactions, as well as input received from numerous investment bankers, investment professionals at private equity firms and hedge funds, attorneys, corporate executives, peer authors, and university professors. By drawing upon our own transaction and classroom experience, as well as that of a broad network of professional and professorial sources, we bridge the gap between academia and industry as it relates to the practical application of finance theory. The resulting product is accessible to a wide audience—including those with a limited finance background—as well as sufficiently detailed and comprehensive to serve as a primary reference tool and training guide for finance professionals.

This book is organized into three primary parts, as summarized below.

Part One: Valuation (Chapters 1-3)

Part One focuses on the three most commonly used methodologies that serve as the core of a comprehensive valuation toolset—comparable companies analysis (Chapter 1), precedent transactions analysis (Chapter 2), and discounted cash flow analysis (Chapter 3). Each of these chapters employs a user-friendly, how-to approach to performing the given valuation methodology while defining key terms, detailing various calculations, and explaining advanced financial concepts. At the end of each chapter, we use our step-by-step approach to determine a valuation range for an illustrative target company, ValueCo Corporation ("ValueCo"), in accordance with the given methodology. The Base Case set of financials for ValueCo that forms the basis for our valuation work throughout the book is provided in Exhibits I.I to I.III. In addition, all of the valuation models and output pages used in this book are separately accessible in electronic format on our website, www.wiley.com/go/investmentbanking2e (if purchased with your edition).

Chapter 1: Comparable Companies Analysis Chapter 1 provides an overview of comparable companies analysis ("comparable companies" or "trading comps"), one of the primary methodologies used for valuing a given focus company, division, business, or collection of assets ("target"). Comparable companies provides a market benchmark against which a banker can establish valuation for a private company or analyze the value of a public company at a given point in time. It has a broad range of applications, most notably for various M&A situations, IPOs, restructurings, and investment decisions.

The foundation for trading comps is built upon the premise that similar companies provide a highly relevant reference point for valuing a given target as they share key business and financial characteristics, performance drivers, and risks. Therefore, valuation parameters can be established for the target by determining its relative positioning among peer companies. The core of this analysis involves selecting a universe of comparable companies for the target. These peer companies are benchmarked against one another and the target based on various financial statistics and ratios. Trading multiples—which utilize a measure of value in the numerator and an operating metric in the denominator—are then calculated for the universe. These multiples provide a basis for extrapolating a valuation range for the target.

Chapter 2: Precedent Transactions Analysis Chapter 2 focuses on precedent transactions analysis ("precedent transactions" or "transaction comps"), which, like comparable companies, employs a multiples-based approach to derive an implied valuation range for a target. Precedent transactions is premised on multiples paid for comparable companies in prior transactions. It has a broad range of applications, most notably to help determine a potential sale price range for a company, or part thereof, in an M&A or restructuring transaction.

The selection of an appropriate universe of comparable acquisitions is the foundation for performing precedent transactions. The best comparable acquisitions typically involve companies similar to the target on a fundamental level. As a general rule, the most recent transactions (i.e., those that have occurred within the previous two to three years) are the most relevant as they likely took place under similar market conditions to the contemplated transaction. Potential buyers and sellers look closely at the multiples that have been paid for comparable acquisitions. As a result, bankers and investment professionals are expected to know the transaction multiples for their sector focus areas.

Chapter 3: Discounted Cash Flow Analysis Chapter 3 discusses discounted cash flow analysis ("DCF analysis" or the "DCF"), a fundamental valuation methodology broadly used by investment bankers, corporate officers, academics, investors, and other finance professionals. The DCF has a wide range of applications, including valuation for various M&A situations, IPOs, restructurings, and investment decisions.

It is premised on the principle that a target's value can be derived from the present value of its projected *free cash flow* (FCF). A company's projected FCF is derived from a variety of assumptions and judgments about its expected future financial performance, including sales growth rates, profit margins, capital expenditures, and net working capital requirements.

The valuation implied for a target by a DCF is also known as its *intrinsic value*, as opposed to its *market value*, which is the value ascribed by the market at a given point in time. Therefore, a DCF serves as an important alternative to market-based valuation techniques such as comparable companies and precedent transactions, which can be distorted by a number of factors, including market aberrations (e.g., the post-subprime credit crunch). As such, a DCF plays a valuable role as a check on the prevailing market valuation for a publicly traded company. A DCF is also critical when there are limited (or no) "pure play" peer companies or comparable acquisitions.

Part Two: Leveraged Buyouts (Chapters 4 & 5)

Part Two focuses on leveraged buyouts, which comprise a large part of the capital markets and M&A landscape due to the proliferation of private investment vehicles (e.g., private equity firms and hedge funds) and their considerable pools of capital, as well as structured credit vehicles. We begin with a discussion in Chapter 4 of the fundamentals of LBOs, including an overview of key participants, characteristics of a strong LBO candidate, economics of an LBO, exit strategies, and key financing sources and terms. Once this framework is established, we apply our step-by-step how-to approach in Chapter 5 to construct a comprehensive LBO model and perform an LBO analysis for ValueCo. LBO analysis is a core tool used by bankers and private equity professionals alike to determine financing structure and valuation for leveraged buyouts.

Chapter 4: Leveraged Buyouts Chapter 4 provides an overview of the fundamentals of leveraged buyouts. An LBO is the acquisition of a target using debt to finance a large portion of the purchase price. The remaining portion of the purchase price is funded with an equity contribution by a financial sponsor ("sponsor"). In this chapter, we provide an overview of the economics of LBOs and how they are used to generate returns for sponsors. We also dedicate a significant portion of Chapter 4 to a discussion of LBO financing sources, particularly the various debt instruments and their terms and conditions.

LBOs are used by sponsors to acquire a broad range of businesses, including both public and private companies, as well as their divisions and subsidiaries. Generally speaking, companies with stable and predictable cash flows as well as substantial asset bases represent attractive LBO candidates. However, sponsors tend to be flexible investors provided the expected returns on the investment meet required thresholds. In an LBO, the disproportionately high level of debt incurred by the target is supported by its projected FCF and asset base, which enables the sponsor to contribute a small equity investment relative to the purchase price. This, in turn, enables the sponsor to realize an acceptable return on its equity investment upon exit, typically through a sale or IPO of the target.

Chapter 5: LBO Analysis Chapter 5 removes the mystery surrounding LBO analysis, the core analytical tool used to assess financing structure, investment returns, and valuation in leveraged buyout scenarios. These same techniques can also be used to assess refinancing opportunities and restructuring alternatives for corporate issuers. LBO analysis is a more complex methodology than those previously discussed as it requires specialized knowledge of financial modeling, leveraged debt capital markets, M&A, and accounting. At the center of LBO analysis is a financial model, which is constructed with the flexibility to analyze a given target under multiple financing structures and operating scenarios.

As with the methodologies discussed in Part One, LBO analysis is an essential component of a comprehensive valuation toolset. On the debt financing side, LBO analysis is used to help craft a viable financing structure for the target on the basis of its cash flow generation, debt repayment, credit statistics, and investment returns over the projection period. Sponsors work closely with financing providers (e.g., investment banks) to determine the preferred financing structure for a particular transaction. In an M&A advisory context, LBO analysis provides the basis for determining an implied valuation range for a given target in a potential LBO sale based on achieving acceptable returns.

Part Three: Mergers & Acquisitions (Chapters 6 & 7)

Part Three provides a comprehensive foundation for M&A, including process, strategies, deal structure, and analytics. M&A is a catch-all phrase for the purchase, sale, and combination of companies and their parts and subsidiaries. M&A facilitates a company's ability to continuously grow, evolve, and re-focus in accordance with ever-changing market conditions, industry trends, and shareholder demands. M&A advisory assignments are core to investment banking, traditionally representing a substantial portion of the firm's annual corporate finance revenues. In addition, most M&A transactions require financing on the part of the acquirer through the issuance of debt and/or equity.

In Chapter 6, we focus on sell-side M&A including the key process points and stages for running an effective M&A sale process, the medium whereby companies are bought and sold in the marketplace. This discussion serves to provide greater context for the topics discussed earlier in the book as theoretical valuation methodologies and analytics are tested based on what a buyer will actually pay for a business or collection of assets. We also describe how valuation analysis is used to frame the seller's price expectations, set guidelines for the range of acceptable bids, evaluate offers received, and, ultimately, guide negotiations of the final purchase price. Chapter 7 focuses on buy-side M&A. It builds upon the fundamental valuation material discussed earlier in the book by performing detailed valuation and merger consequences analysis on ValueCo from an illustrative strategic buyer's perspective, BuyerCo. As the name suggests, merger consequences analysis centers on examining the pro forma effects of a given transaction on the acquirer.

Chapter 6: Sell-Side M&A The sale of a company, division, business, or collection of assets is a major event for its owners (shareholders), management, employees, and other stakeholders. It is an intense, time-consuming process with high stakes, usually spanning several months. Consequently, the seller typically hires an investment bank ("sell-side advisor") and its team of trained professionals to ensure that key objectives are met—namely an optimal mix of value maximization, speed of execution, and certainty of completion, among other deal-specific considerations. Prospective buyers also often hire an investment bank ("buy-side advisor") to perform valuation work, interface with the seller, and conduct negotiations, among other critical tasks.

The sell-side advisor is responsible for identifying the seller's priorities from the onset and crafts a tailored sale process accordingly. From an analytical perspective, a sell-side assignment requires a comprehensive valuation of the target using those methodologies discussed in this book. Perhaps the most basic decision, however, relates to whether to run a broad or targeted auction, or pursue a negotiated sale. Generally, an auction requires more upfront organization, marketing, process points, and resources than a negotiated sale with a single party. Consequently, Chapter 6 focuses primarily on the auction process.

Chapter 7: Buy-Side M&A Chapter 7 begins by discussing M&A strategies and motivations, including deal rationale and synergies. We also discuss form of financing and deal structure, which are critical components for performing detailed buy-side M&A analysis. We then perform a comprehensive valuation and merger consequences analysis for ValueCo from the perspective of a strategic acquirer, BuyerCo. This analysis starts with an overview of the primary valuation methodologies for ValueCo discussed in Chapters 1–3 and 5—namely, comparable companies, precedent transactions, DCF, and LBO analysis. The results of these analyses are displayed on a graphic known as a "football field" for easy comparison and analysis.

The next level of detail in our buy-side M&A work involves analysis at various prices (AVP) and contribution analysis. AVP, also known as a valuation matrix, displays the implied multiples paid at a range of transaction values and offer prices (for public targets) at set intervals. Contribution analysis analyzes the financial "contributions" made by the acquirer and target to the pro forma entity prior to any transaction adjustments. We then conduct a detailed merger consequences analysis for ValueCo in order to fine-tune the ultimate purchase price, deal structure, and financing mix. This analysis examines the pro forma impact of the transaction on the acquirer. The impact on earnings is known as accretion/(dilution) analysis, while the impact on credit statistics is known as balance sheet effects.

VALUECO SUMMARY FINANCIAL INFORMATION

Exhibits I.I through I.III display the historical and projected financial information for ValueCo. These financials—as well as the various valuation multiples, financing terms, and other financial statistics discussed throughout the book—are purely illustrative and designed to represent normalized economic and market conditions.

EXHIBIT I.I ValueCo Summary Historical Operating Data

($ in millions)

ValueCo Summary Historical Operating Data

	Fiscal Year Ending December 31,			LTM
	2009A	2010A	2011A	9/30/2012A
Sales	$2,600.0	$2,900.0	$3,200.0	$3,385.0
% growth	NA	11.5%	10.3%	NA
Cost of Goods Sold	1,612.0	1,769.0	1,920.0	2,030.0
Gross Profit	$988.0	$1,131.0	$1,280.0	$1,355.0
% margin	38.0%	39.0%	40.0%	40.0%
Selling, General & Administrative	496.6	551.0	608.0	655.0
EBITDA	$491.4	$580.0	$672.0	$700.0
% margin	18.9%	20.0%	21.0%	20.7%
Depreciation & Amortization	155.0	165.0	193.0	200.0
EBIT	$336.4	$415.0	$479.0	$500.0
% margin	12.9%	14.3%	15.0%	14.8%
Capital Expenditures	114.4	116.0	144.0	152.3
% sales	4.4%	4.0%	4.5%	4.5%

Note: For modeling purposes (e.g., DCF analysis and LBO analysis), D&A is broken out separately from COGS & SG&A as its own line item.

EXHIBIT I.II ValueCo Summary Projected Operating Data

($ in millions)

ValueCo Summary Projected Operating Data

	Fiscal Year Ending December 31,					
	2012E	2013E	2014E	2015E	2016E	2017E
Sales	$3,450.0	$3,708.8	$3,931.3	$4,127.8	$4,293.0	$4,421.7
% growth	7.8%	7.5%	6.0%	5.0%	4.0%	3.0%
Cost of Goods Sold	2,070.0	2,225.3	2,358.8	2,476.7	2,575.8	2,653.0
Gross Profit	$1,380.0	$1,483.5	$1,572.5	$1,651.1	$1,717.2	$1,768.7
% margin	40.0%	40.0%	40.0%	40.0%	40.0%	40.0%
Selling, General & Administrative	655.0	704.1	746.4	783.7	815.0	839.5
EBITDA	$725.0	$779.4	$826.1	$867.4	$902.1	$929.2
% margin	21.0%	21.0%	21.0%	21.0%	21.0%	21.0%
Depreciation & Amortization	207.0	222.5	235.9	247.7	257.6	265.3
EBIT	$518.0	$556.9	$590.3	$619.8	$644.6	$663.9
% margin	15.0%	15.0%	15.0%	15.0%	15.0%	15.0%
Capital Expenditures	155.3	166.9	176.9	185.8	193.2	199.0
% sales	4.5%	4.5%	4.5%	4.5%	4.5%	4.5%

Introduction

EXHIBIT I.III ValueCo Summary Historical Balance Sheet Data

($ in millions)

ValueCo Summary Historical Balance Sheet Data

	Fiscal Year Ended December 31,			As of	FYE
	2009A	2010A	2011A	9/30/2012A	2012E
Cash and Cash Equivalents	$627.1	$392.8	$219.8	$183.1	$250.0
Accounts Receivable	317.0	365.5	417.4	441.5	450.0
Inventories	441.6	496.8	556.5	588.4	600.0
Prepaid and Other Current Assets	117.0	142.1	162.3	171.7	175.0
Total Current Assets	**$1,502.7**	**$1,397.1**	**$1,356.0**	**$1,384.8**	**$1,475.0**
Property, Plant and Equipment, net	2,571.1	2,565.6	2,564.6	2,501.3	2,500.0
Goodwill	1,000.0	1,000.0	1,000.0	1,000.0	1,000.0
Intangible Assets	1,018.3	974.8	926.8	891.8	875.0
Other Assets	150.0	150.0	150.0	150.0	150.0
Total Assets	**$6,242.1**	**$6,087.5**	**$5,997.4**	**$5,927.8**	**$6,000.0**
Accounts Payable	189.9	189.0	199.4	210.8	215.0
Accrued Liabilities	221.0	237.8	255.1	269.8	275.0
Other Current Liabilities	75.4	84.1	92.8	98.1	100.0
Total Current Liabilities	**$486.3**	**$510.9**	**$547.2**	**$578.8**	**$590.0**
Total Debt	2,500.0	2,150.0	1,800.0	1,500.0	1,500.0
Other Long-Term Liabilities	410.0	410.0	410.0	410.0	410.0
Total Liabilities	**$3,396.3**	**$3,070.9**	**$2,757.2**	**$2,488.8**	**$2,500.0**
Noncontrolling Interest	-	-	-	-	-
Shareholders' Equity	2,845.8	3,016.6	3,240.2	3,439.1	3,500.0
Total Liabilities and Equity	**$6,242.1**	**$6,087.5**	**$5,997.4**	**$5,927.8**	**$6,000.0**
Balance Check	0.000	0.000	0.000	0.000	0.000

PART One

Valuation

CHAPTER 1

Comparable Companies Analysis

Comparable companies analysis ("comparable companies" or "trading comps") is one of the primary methodologies used for valuing a given focus company, division, business, or collection of assets ("target"). It provides a market benchmark against which a banker can establish valuation for a private company or analyze the value of a public company at a given point in time. Comparable companies has a broad range of applications, most notably for various mergers & acquisitions (M&A) situations, initial public offerings (IPOs), restructurings, and investment decisions.

The foundation for trading comps is built upon the premise that similar companies provide a highly relevant reference point for valuing a given target due to the fact that they share key business and financial characteristics, performance drivers, and risks. Therefore, the banker can establish valuation parameters for the target by determining its relative positioning among peer companies. The core of this analysis involves selecting a universe of comparable companies for the target ("comparables universe"). These peer companies are benchmarked against one another and the target based on various financial statistics and ratios. Trading multiples are then calculated for the universe, which serve as the basis for extrapolating a valuation range for the target. This valuation range is calculated by applying the selected multiples to the target's relevant financial statistics.

While valuation metrics may vary by sector, this chapter focuses on the most widely used trading multiples. These multiples—such as enterprise value-to-earnings before interest, taxes, depreciation, and amortization (EV/EBITDA) and price-to-earnings (P/E)—utilize a measure of value in the numerator and a financial statistic in the denominator. While P/E is the most broadly recognized in circles outside Wall Street, multiples based on enterprise value are widely used by bankers because they are independent of capital structure and other factors unrelated to business operations (e.g., differences in tax regimes and certain accounting policies).

Comparable companies analysis is designed to reflect "current" valuation based on prevailing market conditions and sentiment. As such, in many cases it is more relevant than *intrinsic valuation* analysis, such as discounted cash flow analysis (see Chapter 3). At the same time, market trading levels may be subject to periods of irrational investor sentiment that skew valuation either too high or too low. Furthermore, no two companies are exactly the same, so assigning a valuation based on the trading characteristics of similar companies may fail to accurately capture a given company's true value.

As a result, trading comps should be used in conjunction with the other valuation methodologies discussed in this book. A material disconnect between the derived valuation ranges from the various methodologies might be an indication that key assumptions or calculations need to be revisited. Therefore, when performing trading comps (or any other valuation/financial analysis exercise), it is imperative to diligently footnote key sources and assumptions both for review and defense of conclusions.

This chapter provides a highly practical, step-by-step approach to performing trading comps consistent with how this valuation methodology is performed in real world applications (see Exhibit 1.1). Once this framework is established, we walk through an illustrative comparable companies analysis using our target company, ValueCo (see Introduction for reference).

EXHIBIT 1.1   Comparable Companies Analysis Steps

> Step I.   Select the Universe of Comparable Companies
> Step II. Locate the Necessary Financial Information
> Step III. Spread Key Statistics, Ratios, and Trading Multiples
> Step IV. Benchmark the Comparable Companies
> Step V.   Determine Valuation

SUMMARY OF COMPARABLE COMPANIES ANALYSIS STEPS

- **Step I. Select the Universe of Comparable Companies.** The selection of a universe of comparable companies for the target is the foundation for performing trading comps. While this exercise can be fairly simple and intuitive for companies in certain sectors, it can prove challenging for others whose peers are not readily apparent. To identify companies with similar business and financial characteristics, it is first necessary to gain a sound understanding of the target.

    As a starting point, the banker typically consults with peers or senior colleagues to see if a relevant set of comparable companies already exists internally. If beginning from scratch, the banker casts a broad net to review as many potential comparable companies as possible. This broader group is eventually narrowed, and then typically further refined to a subset of "closest comparables." A survey of the target's public competitors is generally a good place to start identifying potential comparable companies.

- **Step II. Locate the Necessary Financial Information.** Once the initial comparables universe is determined, the banker locates the financial information necessary to analyze the selected comparable companies and calculate ("spread"[1]) key financial statistics, ratios, and trading multiples (see Step III). The primary data for calculating these metrics is compiled from various sources, including a

---

[1]The notion of "spreading" refers to performing calculations in a spreadsheet program such as Microsoft Excel.

company's SEC filings,[2] consensus research estimates, equity research reports, and press releases, all of which are available via Bloomberg.

- **Step III. Spread Key Statistics, Ratios, and Trading Multiples.** The banker is now prepared to spread key statistics, ratios, and trading multiples for the comparables universe. This involves calculating market valuation measures such as enterprise value and equity value, as well as key income statement items, such as EBITDA and net income. A variety of ratios and other metrics measuring profitability, growth, returns, and credit strength are also calculated at this stage. Selected financial statistics are then used to calculate trading multiples for the comparables.

  As part of this process, the banker needs to employ various financial concepts and techniques, including the calculation of *last twelve months* (LTM)[3] financial statistics, *calendarization* of company financials, and adjustments for *nonrecurring items*. These calculations are imperative for measuring the comparables accurately on both an absolute and relative basis (see Step IV).

- **Step IV. Benchmark the Comparable Companies.** The next level of analysis requires an in-depth examination of the comparable companies in order to determine the target's relative ranking and closest comparables. To assist in this task, the banker typically lays out the calculated financial statistics and ratios for the comparable companies (as calculated in Step III) alongside those of the target in spreadsheet form for easy comparison (see Exhibits 1.53 and 1.54). This exercise is known as "benchmarking."

  Benchmarking serves to determine the relative strength of the comparable companies versus one another and the target. The similarities and discrepancies in size, growth rates, margins, and leverage, for example, among the comparables and the target are closely examined. This analysis provides the basis for establishing the target's relative ranking as well as determining those companies most appropriate for framing its valuation. The trading multiples are also laid out in a spreadsheet form for benchmarking purposes (see Exhibits 1.2 and 1.55). At this point, it may become apparent that certain outliers need to be eliminated or that the comparables should be further tiered (e.g., on the basis of size, sub-sector, or ranging from closest to peripheral).

- **Step V. Determine Valuation.** The trading multiples of the comparable companies serve as the basis for deriving a valuation range for the target. The banker typically begins by using the means and medians for the relevant trading multiples (e.g., EV/EBITDA) as the basis for extrapolating an initial range. The high and low multiples for the comparables universe provide further guidance in terms of a potential ceiling or floor. The key to arriving at the tightest, most appropriate range, however, is to rely upon the multiples of the closest comparables as guideposts. Consequently, only a few carefully selected companies may serve as the ultimate basis for valuation, with the broader group serving as additional reference points. As this process involves as much "art" as "science," senior bankers are typically consulted for guidance on the final decision. The chosen range is then applied to the target's relevant financial statistics to produce an implied valuation range.

---

[2]The Securities and Exchange Commission (SEC) is a federal agency created by the Securities Exchange Act of 1934 that regulates the U.S. securities industry. SEC filings can be located online at www.sec.gov.
[3]The sum of the prior four quarters of a company's financial performance, also known as trailing twelve months (TTM).

EXHIBIT 1.2 Comparable Companies Analysis—Trading Multiples Output Page

ValueCo Corporation
Comparable Companies Analysis
($ in millions, except per share data)

Company	Ticker	Current Share Price	% of 52-wk. High	Equity Value	Enterprise Value	LTM Sales	2012E Sales	2013E Sales	LTM EBITDA	2012E EBITDA	2013E EBITDA	LTM EBIT	2012E EBIT	2013E EBIT	LTM EBITDA Margin	Total Debt / EBITDA	LTM EPS	2012E EPS	2013E EPS	LT EPS Growth
Tier I: Specialty Chemicals																				
BuyerCo	BUY	$70.00	91%	$9,800	$11,600	1.8x	1.7x	1.6x	8.0x	7.8x	7.3x	9.1x	8.8x	8.2x	22%	1.5x	13.9x	13.5x	12.5x	7%
Sherman Co.	SHR	40.00	76%	5,600	8,101	1.4x	1.4x	1.3x	7.7x	7.7x	7.2x	10.8x	10.7x	10.1x	18%	3.0x	13.4x	12.8x	11.8x	9%
Pearl Corp.	PRL	68.50	95%	5,172	5,856	1.4x	1.4x	1.3x	7.0x	7.0x	6.5x	9.4x	9.4x	8.7x	20%	1.8x	15.9x	14.7x	13.4x	11%
Gasparro Corp.	JDG	50.00	80%	5,000	6,750	1.4x	1.4x	1.3x	7.5x	7.1x	6.6x	9.3x	8.8x	8.2x	19%	2.1x	12.9x	11.2x	10.0x	12%
Kumra Inc.	KUM	52.50	88%	4,852	5,345	1.7x	1.7x	1.5x	8.0x	7.9x	7.4x	10.6x	10.4x	9.7x	21%	1.3x	19.5x	16.6x	14.4x	10%
Mean						1.5x	1.5x	1.4x	7.7x	7.5x	7.0x	9.8x	9.6x	9.0x	20%	1.9x	15.1x	13.8x	12.4x	10%
Median						1.4x	1.4x	1.3x	7.7x	7.7x	7.2x	9.4x	9.4x	8.7x	20%	1.8x	13.9x	13.5x	12.5x	10%
Tier II: Commodity / Diversified Chemicals																				
Falloon Group	FLN	$31.00	87%	$7,480	$11,254	1.0x	1.0x	0.9x	6.9x	7.0x	6.7x	10.8x	11.0x	10.5x	14%	2.5x	16.1x	15.0x	13.1x	5%
Goodson Corp.	GDS	64.00	83%	4,160	5,660	1.2x	1.2x	1.1x	7.4x	7.5x	7.2x	10.8x	11.0x	10.4x	16%	2.9x	19.5x	18.6x	16.3x	9%
Pryor Industries	PRI	79.00	88%	3,926	4,166	1.1x	1.2x	1.1x	7.3x	7.4x	7.1x	9.9x	10.1x	9.6x	15%	1.1x	17.3x	16.9x	15.4x	10%
Lanzarone Global	LNZ	32.25	95%	3,230	3,823	1.0x	1.0x	1.0x	6.6x	6.7x	6.4x	8.9x	9.0x	8.6x	16%	1.3x	13.9x	12.9x	11.7x	8%
McMenamin & Co.	MCM	33.50	80%	3,193	3,193	1.0x	0.9x	0.8x	9.0x	8.4x	7.5x	14.2x	13.1x	11.8x	11%	1.2x	26.8x	23.3x	20.3x	12%
Mean						1.1x	1.1x	1.0x	7.4x	7.4x	7.0x	10.9x	10.8x	10.2x	14%	1.8x	18.7x	17.3x	15.3x	9%
Median						1.0x	1.0x	1.0x	7.3x	7.4x	7.1x	10.8x	11.0x	10.4x	15%	1.3x	17.3x	16.9x	15.4x	9%
Tier III: Small-Cap Chemicals																				
S. Momper & Co.	MOMP	$28.00	95%	$2,240	$2,921	1.4x	1.4x	1.2x	7.7x	7.4x	6.7x	9.9x	9.5x	8.6x	18%	2.6x	17.2x	17.5x	16.2x	5%
Adler Worldwide	ADL	10.50	80%	1,217	1,463	0.9x	1.0x	0.9x	6.0x	6.1x	5.8x	8.0x	8.1x	7.7x	16%	1.6x	13.7x	14.8x	13.7x	7%
Schachter & Sons	STM	4.50	89%	1,125	1,674	1.0x	0.9x	0.8x	7.0x	6.5x	5.7x	9.8x	9.1x	7.9x	14%	2.5x	14.8x	13.6x	12.2x	11%
Girshin Holdings	MGP	50.00	67%	1,035	1,298	0.8x	0.8x	0.7x	7.3x	6.8x	6.1x	11.5x	10.7x	9.7x	11%	1.8x	20.0x	18.9x	17.2x	8%
Crespin International	MCR	27.00	80%	872	1,222	0.8x	0.8x	0.7x	6.4x	6.0x	5.4x	9.2x	8.6x	7.7x	13%	2.1x	14.2x	14.0x	12.7x	6%
Mean						1.0x	1.0x	0.9x	6.9x	6.6x	5.9x	9.7x	9.2x	8.3x	14%	2.1x	16.0x	15.7x	14.4x	7%
Median						0.9x	0.9x	0.8x	7.0x	6.5x	5.8x	9.8x	9.1x	7.9x	14%	2.1x	14.8x	14.8x	13.7x	7%
Overall																				
Mean						1.1x	1.1x	1.0x	7.3x	7.2x	6.7x	10.3x	10.0x	9.3x	16%	1.9x	17.0x	16.0x	14.4x	9%
Median						1.0x	1.0x	1.0x	7.3x	7.4x	6.7x	9.9x	9.8x	9.2x	16%	1.8x	16.6x	15.8x	14.1x	9%
High						1.8x	1.7x	1.6x	9.0x	8.4x	7.5x	14.2x	13.1x	11.8x	22%	3.0x	26.8x	23.3x	20.3x	12%
Low						0.8x	0.8x	0.7x	6.0x	6.0x	5.4x	8.0x	8.1x	7.7x	11%	1.1x	12.9x	11.2x	10.0x	5%

Source: Company filings, Bloomberg, Consensus Estimates
Note: Last twelve months data based on September 30, 2012. Estimated annual financial data based on a calendar year.

Bloomberg provides comparable companies analysis via the "Relative Valuation" function (see Appendix 1.1), which calculates key valuation multiples and other metrics for any public company and its peers. The analysis uses an algorithmic approach to identify comparable companies and calculate metrics, and can be customized to reflect a banker's judgment regarding specific calculations and company peers.

STEP I. SELECT THE UNIVERSE OF COMPARABLE COMPANIES

The selection of a universe of comparable companies for the target is the foundation for performing trading comps. In order to identify companies with similar business and financial characteristics, it is first necessary to gain a sound understanding of the target. At its base, the methodology for determining comparable companies is relatively intuitive. Companies in the same sector (or, preferably, "sub-sector") with similar size tend to serve as good comparables. While this can be a fairly simple exercise for companies in certain sectors, it may prove challenging for others whose peers are not readily apparent.

For a target with no clear, publicly traded comparables, the banker seeks companies outside the target's core sector that share business and financial characteristics on some fundamental level. For example, a medium-sized manufacturer of residential windows may have limited or no truly direct publicly traded peers in terms of products, namely companies that produce windows. If the universe is expanded to include companies that manufacture building products, serve homebuilders, or have exposure to the housing cycle, however, the probability of locating companies with similar business drivers is increased. In this case, the list of potential comparables could be expanded to include manufacturers of related building products such as decking, roofing, siding, doors, and cabinets.

Study the Target

The process of learning the in-depth "story" of the target should be exhaustive as this information is essential for making decisions regarding the selection of appropriate comparable companies. Toward this end, the banker is encouraged to read and study as much company- and sector-specific material as possible. *The actual selection of comparable companies should only begin once this research is completed.*

For targets that are public registrants,[4] annual (10-K) and quarterly (10-Q) SEC filings, consensus research estimates, equity and fixed income research reports, press releases, earnings call transcripts, investor presentations,[5] and corporate

---

[4]Public or publicly traded companies refer to those listed on a public stock exchange where their shares can be traded. Public filers ("public registrants"), however, may include privately held companies that are issuers of public debt securities and, therefore, subject to SEC disclosure requirements.
[5]Presentations at investment conferences or regular performance reports, typically posted on a company's corporate website. Investor presentations may also be released for significant M&A events or as part of Regulation FD requirements. They are typically posted on the company's corporate website under "Investor Relations" and filed in an 8-K (current report). Presentations are also available via Bloomberg using the Events function (EVTS<GO>).

websites provide key business and financial information. Private companies present a greater challenge as the banker is forced to rely upon sources such as corporate websites, sector research reports, news runs, and trade journals for basic company data. Public competitors' SEC filings, research reports, and investor presentations may also serve as helpful sources of information on private companies. In an organized M&A sale process[6] for a private company, however, the banker is provided with detailed business and financial information on the target (see Chapter 6).

Identify Key Characteristics of the Target for Comparison Purposes

A simple framework for studying the target and selecting comparable companies is shown in Exhibit 1.3. This framework, while by no means exhaustive, is designed to determine commonality with other companies by profiling and comparing key business and financial characteristics. Relevant Bloomberg functions for the business and financial framework below are found in Appendix 1.2.

EXHIBIT 1.3 Business and Financial Profile Framework

Business Profile	Financial Profile
- Sector	- Size
- Products and Services	- Profitability
- Customers and End Markets	- Growth Profile
- Distribution Channels	- Return on Investment
- Geography	- Credit Profile

Business Profile

Companies that share core business characteristics tend to serve as good comparables. These core traits include sector, products and services, customers and end markets, distribution channels, and geography.

Sector

Sector refers to the industry or markets in which a company operates (e.g., consumer products, financials, healthcare, industrials, and technology). A company's sector can be further divided into sub-sectors, which facilitates the identification of the target's closest comparables. Within the industrials sector, for example, there are numerous sub-sectors, such as aerospace and defense, automotive, building products, chemicals, and paper and packaging. Even these sub-sectors can be further segmented—for example, chemicals can be divided into specialty and commodity chemicals. For companies with distinct business divisions, the segmenting of comparable companies by sub-sector may be critical for valuation.

A company's sector conveys a great deal about its key drivers, risks, and opportunities. For example, a cyclical sector such as oil & gas will have dramatically different earnings volatility from consumer staples. On the other hand, cyclical or

---

[6] A process through which a target is marketed to prospective buyers, typically run by an investment banking firm. See Chapter 6: Sell-Side M&A for additional information.

highly fragmented sectors may present growth opportunities that are unavailable to companies in more stable or consolidated sectors. The proper identification and classification of the target's sector and sub-sector is an essential step toward locating comparable companies.

Products and Services

A company's products and services are at the core of its business model. Accordingly, companies that produce similar products or provide similar services typically serve as good comparables. Products are commodities or value-added goods that a company creates, produces, or refines. Examples of products include computers, lumber, oil, prescription drugs, and steel. Services are acts or functions performed by one entity for the benefit of another. Examples of common services include banking, consulting, installation, lodging, and transportation. Many companies provide both products and services to their customers, while others offer one or the other. Similarly, some companies offer a diversified product and/or service mix, while others are more focused.

Within a given sector or sub-sector, comparable companies may be tiered according to their products and services. For example, within the chemicals sector, specialty chemicals producers tend to consistently trade at a premium to commodity chemicals producers. Hence, they are often grouped together in a tighter comparables category within the broader chemicals universe. The same holds true for the commodity players.

Customers and End Markets

Customers A company's customers refer to the purchasers of its products and services. Companies with a similar customer base tend to share similar opportunities and risks. For example, companies supplying automobile manufacturers abide by certain manufacturing and distribution requirements, and are subject to the automobile purchasing cycles and trends.

The quantity and diversity of a company's customers are also important. Some companies serve a broad customer base while others may target a specialized or niche market. While it is generally positive to have low customer concentration from a risk management perspective, it is also beneficial to have a stable customer core to provide visibility and comfort regarding future revenues.

End Markets A company's end markets refer to the broad underlying markets into which it sells its products and services. For example, a plastics manufacturer may sell into several end markets, including automotive, construction, consumer products, medical devices, and packaging. End markets need to be distinguished from customers. For example, a company may sell into the housing end market, but to retailers or suppliers as opposed to homebuilders.

A company's performance is generally tied to economic and other factors that affect its end markets. A company that sells products into the housing end market is susceptible to macroeconomic factors that affect the overall housing cycle, such as interest rates and unemployment levels. Therefore, companies that sell products and services into the same end markets generally share a similar performance outlook, which is important for determining appropriate comparable companies.

Distribution Channels

Distribution channels are the avenues through which a company sells its products and services to the end user. As such, they are a key driver of operating strategy, performance, and, ultimately, value. Companies that sell primarily to the wholesale channel, for example, often have significantly different organizational and cost structures from those selling directly to retailers or end users. Selling to a superstore or value retailer requires a physical infrastructure, sales force, and logistics that may be unnecessary for serving the professional or wholesale channels.

Some companies sell at several levels of the distribution chain, such as wholesale, retail, and direct-to-customer. A flooring manufacturer, for example, may distribute its products through selected wholesale distributors and retailers, as well as directly to homebuilders and end users.

Geography

Companies that are based in (and sell to) different regions of the world often differ substantially in terms of fundamental business drivers and characteristics. These may include growth rates, macroeconomic environment, competitive dynamics, path(s)-to-market, organizational and cost structure, and potential opportunities and risks. Such differences—which result from local demographics, economic drivers, regulatory regimes, consumer buying patterns and preferences, and cultural norms—can vary greatly from country to country and, particularly, from continent to continent. Consequently, there are often valuation disparities for similar companies in different global regions or jurisdictions.[7] Therefore, in determining comparable companies, bankers tend to group U.S.-based (or focused) companies in a separate category from European- or Asian-based companies even if their basic business models are the same.

For example, a banker seeking comparable companies for a U.S. retailer would focus primarily on U.S. companies with relevant foreign companies providing peripheral guidance. This geographic grouping is slightly less applicable for truly global industries such as oil and aluminum, for example, where domicile is less indicative than global commodity prices and supply/demand dynamics. Even in these instances, however, valuation disparities by geography are often evident.

Financial Profile

Key financial characteristics must also be examined both as a means of understanding the target and identifying the best comparable companies.

Size

Size is typically measured in terms of market valuation (e.g., equity value and enterprise value), as well as key financial statistics (e.g., sales, gross profit, EBITDA, EBIT, and net income). Companies of similar size in a given sector are more likely to have similar multiples than companies with significant size discrepancies. This reflects the fact that companies of similar size are also likely to be analogous in other respects

---

[7]Other factors, such as the local capital markets conditions, including volume, liquidity, transparency, shareholder base, and investor perceptions, as well as political risk, also contribute to these disparities.

(e.g., economies of scale, purchasing power, pricing leverage, customers, growth prospects, and the trading liquidity of their shares in the stock market).

Consequently, differences in size often map to differences in valuation. Hence, the comparables are often tiered based on size categories. For example, companies with under $5 billion in equity value (or enterprise value, sales) may be placed in one group and those with greater than $5 billion in a separate group. This tiering, of course, assumes a sufficient number of comparables to justify organizing the universe into sub-groups.

Profitability

A company's profitability measures its ability to convert sales into profit. Profitability ratios ("margins") employ a measure of profit in the numerator, such as gross profit, EBITDA, EBIT, or net income, and sales in the denominator.[8] As a general rule, for companies in the same sector, higher profit margins translate into higher valuations, all else being equal. Consequently, determining a company's relative profitability versus its peers' is a core component of the benchmarking analysis (see Step IV).

Growth Profile

A company's growth profile, as determined by its historical and estimated future financial performance, is a critical driver of valuation. Equity investors reward high growth companies with higher trading multiples than slower growing peers. They also discern whether the growth is primarily organic or acquisition-driven, with the former generally viewed as preferable. In assessing a company's growth profile, historical and estimated future growth rates for various financial statistics (e.g., sales, EBITDA, and earnings per share (EPS)) are examined at selected intervals. For mature public companies, EPS growth rates are typically more meaningful. For early stage or emerging companies with little or no earnings, however, sales or EBITDA growth trends may be more relevant.

Return on Investment

Return on investment (ROI) measures a company's ability to provide earnings (or returns) to its capital providers. ROI ratios employ a measure of profitability (e.g., EBIT, NOPAT,[9] or net income) in the numerator and a measure of capital (e.g., invested capital, shareholders' equity, or total assets) in the denominator. The most commonly used ROI metrics are return on invested capital (ROIC), return on equity (ROE), and return on assets (ROA). Dividend yield, which measures the dividend payment that a company's shareholders receive for each share owned, is another type of return metric.

Credit Profile

A company's credit profile refers to its creditworthiness as a borrower. It is typically measured by metrics relating to a company's overall debt level ("leverage")

---

[8]Depending on the sector, profitability may be measured on a per unit basis (e.g., per ton or pound).
[9]Net operating profit after taxes, also known as tax-effected EBIT or earnings before interest after taxes (EBIAT).

as well as its ability to make interest payments ("coverage"), and reflects key company and sector-specific benefits and risks. Moody's Investors Service (Moody's), Standard & Poor's (S&P), and Fitch Ratings (Fitch) are the three primary independent credit rating agencies that provide formal assessments of a company's credit profile.

Screen for Comparable Companies

Once the target's basic business and financial characteristics are researched and understood, the banker uses various resources to screen for potential comparable companies. At the initial stage, the focus is on identifying companies with a similar business profile. While basic financial information (e.g., sales, enterprise value, or equity value) should be assessed early on, more detailed financial benchmarking is performed in Step IV.

Investment banks generally have established lists of comparable companies by sector containing relevant multiples and other financial data, which are updated on a quarterly basis and for appropriate company-specific actions. Often, however, the banker needs to start from scratch. In these cases, an examination of the target's public competitors is usually the best place to begin. Competitors generally share key business and financial characteristics and are susceptible to similar opportunities and risks. Public companies typically discuss their primary competitors in their 10-Ks, annual proxy statement (DEF14A),[10] and, potentially, in investor presentations. Furthermore, equity research reports, especially those known as *initiating coverage*,[11] often explicitly list the research analyst's views on the target's comparables and/or primary competitors. For private targets, public competitors' 10-Ks, proxy statements, investor presentations, research reports, and broader industry reports are often helpful sources.

An additional source for locating comparables is the proxy statement for a relatively recent M&A transaction in the sector ("merger proxy"),[12] as it contains excerpts from a *fairness opinion*. As the name connotes, a fairness opinion opines on the "fairness" of the purchase price and deal terms offered by the acquirer from a financial perspective (see Chapter 6). The fairness opinion is supported by a detailed overview of the methodologies used to perform a valuation of the target, typically including comparable companies, precedent transactions, DCF analysis, and LBO analysis, if applicable.[13] The trading comps excerpt from the fairness opinion generally provides a list of the comparable companies used to

---

[10] A company's annual proxy statement typically provides a suggested peer group of companies that is used for benchmarking purposes.

[11] An initiating coverage equity research report refers to the first report published by an equity research analyst beginning coverage on a particular company. This report often provides a comprehensive business description, sector analysis, and commentary.

[12] A solicitation of shareholder votes in a business combination is initially filed under SEC Form PREM14A (preliminary merger proxy statement) and then DEFM14A (definitive merger proxy statement).

[13] Not all companies are LBO candidates. See Chapter 4: Leveraged Buyouts for an overview of the characteristics of strong LBO candidates.

value the M&A target as well as the selected range of multiples used in the valuation analysis.

The banker may also screen for companies that operate in the target's sector using SIC, NAICS, or other industry codes.[14] Bloomberg provides comprehensive sector classification using such codes as well as proprietary Bloomberg Industry Classification Standard ("BICS") codes (see Appendix 1.3). This type of screen is typically used either to establish a broad initial universe of comparables or to ensure that no potential companies have been overlooked. Sector reports published by the credit rating agencies (e.g., Moody's, S&P, and Fitch) may also provide helpful lists of peer companies.

In addition to the aforementioned, senior bankers are perhaps the most valuable resources for determining the comparables universe. Given their sector knowledge and familiarity with the target, a brief conversation is usually sufficient for them to provide the junior banker with a strong starting point. Toward the end of the process—once the junior banker has done the legwork to craft and refine a robust list of comparables—a senior banker often provides the finishing touches in terms of more nuanced additions or deletions.

At this stage of the process, there may be sufficient information to eliminate certain companies from the group or tier the selected companies by size, business focus, or geography, for example.

STEP II. LOCATE THE NECESSARY FINANCIAL INFORMATION

This section provides an overview of the relevant sources for locating the necessary financial information to calculate key financial statistics, ratios, and multiples for the selected comparable companies (see Step III). The most common sources for public company financial data are SEC filings (such as 10-Ks, 10-Qs, and 8-Ks), as well as earnings announcements, investor presentations, equity research reports, consensus estimates, and press releases, each of which are available via Bloomberg. A summary list of where to locate key financial data is provided in Exhibit 1.4.

In trading comps, valuation is driven on the basis of both historical performance (e.g., LTM financial data) and expected future performance (e.g., consensus estimates for future calendar years). Depending on the sector and point in the cycle, however, financial projections tend to be more meaningful. Estimates for forward-year financial performance are typically sourced from consensus estimates such as Bloomberg BEst estimates (see Appendix 1.4)[15] as well as individual company equity research reports. In the context of an M&A or debt capital raising transaction, by contrast, more emphasis

---

[14]Standard Industrial Classification (SIC) is a system established by the U.S. government for classifying the major business operations of a company with a numeric code. Some bankers use the newer North American Industry Classification System (NAICS) codes in lieu of SIC codes. The SEC, however, still uses SIC codes.

[15]Bloomberg BEst estimates provide consensus figures for leading equity analysts, as followed by the professional investment community.

is placed on LTM financial performance. LTM financial information is calculated on the basis of data obtained from a company's public filings (see Exhibits 1.24 and 1.25).

SEC Filings: 10-K, 10-Q, 8-K, and Proxy Statement

As a general rule, the banker uses SEC filings to source historical financial information for comparable companies. This financial information is used to determine historical sales, gross profit, EBITDA, EBIT, and net income (and EPS) on both an annual and LTM basis. SEC filings are also the primary source for other key financial items such as balance sheet data, capital expenditures ("capex"), basic shares outstanding, stock options/warrants data, and information on non-recurring items. SEC filings can be obtained through numerous mediums, including a company's corporate website (typically through an "Investor Relations" link) as well as EDGAR[16] and other financial information services, such as Bloomberg.

10-K (Annual Report) The 10-K is an annual report filed with the SEC by a public registrant that provides a comprehensive overview of the company and its prior year performance.[17] It is required to contain an exhaustive list of disclosure items including, but not limited to, a detailed business description, management's discussion & analysis (MD&A),[18] audited financial statements[19] and supplementary data, outstanding debt detail, basic shares outstanding, and stock options/warrants data. It also contains an abundance of other pertinent information about the company and its sector, such as business segment detail, customers, end markets, competition, insight into material opportunities (and challenges and risks), significant recent events, and acquisitions.

10-Q (Quarterly Report) The 10-Q is a quarterly report filed with the SEC by a public registrant that provides an overview of the most recent quarter and year-to-date (YTD) period.[20] It is less comprehensive than the 10-K, but provides financial statements as well as MD&A relating to the company's financial performance for the most recent quarter and YTD period versus the prior year periods.[21] The 10-Q also provides the most recent share count information and may also contain the most recent stock options/warrants data. For detailed financial information on a company's final quarter of the fiscal year, the banker refers to the 8-K containing the fourth quarter earnings press release that usually precedes the filing of the 10-K.

---

[16]The Electronic Data Gathering, Analysis, and Retrieval (EDGAR) system performs automated collection, validation, indexing, acceptance, and forwarding of submissions by companies and others who are required to file forms with the SEC.
[17]The deadline for the filing of the 10-K ranges from 60 to 90 days after the end of a company's fiscal year depending on the size of its public float.
[18]A section in a company's 10-K and 10-Q that provides a discussion and analysis of the prior reporting period's financial performance. It also contains forward-looking information about the possible future effects of known and unknown events, conditions, and trends.
[19]The financial statements in a 10-K are audited and certified by a Certified Public Accountant (CPA) to meet the requirements of the SEC.
[20]The deadline for the filing of the 10-Q ranges from 40 to 45 days after the end of a company's fiscal quarter depending on the size of its public float. The 10-K, instead of the 10-Q, is filed after the end of a company's fiscal fourth quarter.
[21]The financial statements in a company's 10-Q are reviewed by a CPA, but not audited.

8-K (Current Report) The 8-K, or current report, is filed by a public registrant to report the occurrence of *material* corporate events or changes ("triggering event") that are of importance to shareholders or security holders.[22] For the purposes of preparing trading comps, key triggering events include, but are not limited to, earnings announcements, entry into a definitive purchase/sale agreement,[23] completion of an acquisition or disposition of assets, capital markets transactions, and Regulation FD disclosure requirements.[24] The corresponding 8-Ks for these events often contain important information necessary to calculate a company's updated financial statistics, ratios, and trading multiples that may not be reflected in the most recent 10-K or 10-Q (see "Adjustments for Recent Events").

Proxy Statement A proxy statement is a document that a public company sends to its shareholders prior to a shareholder meeting containing material information regarding matters on which the shareholders are expected to vote. It is also filed with the SEC on Schedule 14A. For the purposes of spreading trading comps, the annual proxy statement provides a basic shares outstanding count that may be more recent than that contained in the latest 10-K or 10-Q. As previously discussed, the annual proxy statement also typically contains a suggested peer group for benchmarking purposes.

Equity Research

Research Reports Equity research reports provide individual analyst estimates of future company performance, which may be used to calculate forward-looking multiples. They generally include estimates of sales, EBITDA and/or EBIT, and EPS for future quarters and the future two- or three-year period (on an annual basis). More comprehensive reports provide additional estimated financial information from the research analyst's model, including key items from the income statement, balance sheet, and cash flow statement. These reports may also provide segmented financial projections, such as sales and EBIT at the business division level.

Equity research reports often provide commentary on non-recurring items and recent M&A and capital markets transactions, which are helpful for determining pro forma adjustments and normalizing financial data. They may also provide helpful sector and market information, as well as explicitly list the research analyst's view on the company's comparables universe. Initiating coverage research reports tend to be more comprehensive than normal interim reports. As a result, it is beneficial to mine these reports for financial, market, and competitive insights. Research reports can be located through various subscription financial information services such as Bloomberg, where reports are available via function: RES<GO>.

---

[22]Depending on the particular triggering event, the 8-K is typically filed within four business days after occurrence.
[23]The legal contract between a buyer and seller detailing the terms and conditions of an M&A transaction. See Chapter 6: Sell-Side M&A for additional information.
[24]Regulation FD (Fair Disclosure) provides that when a public filer discloses material nonpublic information to certain persons, as defined by the SEC, it must make public disclosure of that information typically through the filing of an 8-K.

Consensus Estimates   Consensus research estimates for selected financial statistics are widely used by bankers as the basis for calculating forward-looking trading multiples in trading comps. Bloomberg BEst consensus estimates are available via several Bloomberg functions, including Earnings Estimates (EEB<GO>), as well as programmatically via Excel.[25]

Press Releases and News Runs

A company issues a press release when it has something important to report to the public. Standard press releases include earnings announcements, declaration of dividends, and management changes, as well as M&A and capital markets transactions. Earnings announcements, which are accompanied by the filing of an 8-K, are typically issued prior to the filing of a 10-K or 10-Q. Therefore, the banker relies upon the financial data provided in the earnings announcement to update trading comps in a timely manner. A company may also release an investor presentation to accompany its quarterly earnings call, which may be helpful in readily identifying key financial data and obtaining additional color and commentary. In the event that certain financial information is not provided in the earnings press release, the banker must wait until the filing of the 10-K or 10-Q for complete information. A company's press releases and recent news articles are available on its corporate website as well as through Bloomberg.

Financial Information Services

As discussed throughout this section, Bloomberg is a key source for obtaining SEC filings, research reports, consensus estimates, and press releases, among other items. Bloomberg is also a primary source for current and historical company share price information, which is essential for calculating equity value and determining a company's current share price as a percentage of its 52-week high. Bloomberg Coverage Dashboard summarizes information for investment bankers to monitor and diligence public companies (see Appendix 1.5).

Financial information services, such as Bloomberg, may also be sourced to provide information on a company's credit ratings. If practical, however, we suggest sourcing credit ratings directly from the official Moody's, S&P, and Fitch websites and attributing such information to its original sources.[26]

---

[25] Once a given consensus estimates source is selected, it is important to screen individual estimates for obsolescent data and outliers. For example, if a company has recently made a transformative acquisition, some analysts may have revised their estimates accordingly, while others may have not. Bloomberg and other sources allow the banker to view individual estimates (and the date when they were posted), which allows for the identification and removal of inconsistent estimates as appropriate.

[26] Access to these websites requires a subscription.

Comparable Companies Analysis

Summary of Financial Data Primary Sources

Exhibit 1.4 provides a summary of the primary sources used to obtain the necessary financial information to perform trading comps.

EXHIBIT 1.4 Summary of Financial Data Primary Sources

Information Item	Source	Bloomberg Function[a]
Income Statement Data		
Sales Gross Profit EBITDA[b] EBIT Net Income / EPS	Most recent 10-K, 10-Q, 8-K, Press Release	Financial Analysis (FA<GO>), Company Filings (CF<GO>)
Research Estimates	Bloomberg BEst estimates, individual equity research reports	Earnings & Estimates (EE<GO>), Research (BRC<GO>)
Balance Sheet Data		
Cash Balance Debt Balance Shareholders' Equity	Most recent 10-K, 10-Q, 8-K, Press Release	Financial Analysis (FA<GO>), Company Filings (CF<GO>)
Cash Flow Statement Data		
Depreciation & Amortization Capital Expenditures	Most recent 10-K, 10-Q, 8-K, Press Release	Financial Analysis (FA<GO>), Company Filings (CF<GO>)
Share Data		
Basic Shares Outstanding	10-K, 10-Q, or Proxy Statement, whichever is most recent	Financial Analysis (FA<GO>), Company Filings (CF<GO>)
Options and Warrants Data	10-K or 10-Q, whichever is more recent	Company Filings (CF<GO>)
Market Data		
Share Price Data	Bloomberg	Quote (BQ<GO>), Description (DES<GO>)
Credit Ratings	Rating agencies' websites	Credit Profile (CRPR<GO>)

[a] Key financial figures are also available via the Bloomberg Excel Add-In.

[b] As a non-GAAP (generally accepted accounting principles) financial measure, EBITDA is not reported on a public filer's income statement. It may, however, be disclosed as supplemental information in the company's public filings.

STEP III. SPREAD KEY STATISTICS, RATIOS, AND TRADING MULTIPLES

Once the necessary financial information for each of the comparables has been located, it is entered into an input page (see Exhibit 1.5).[27] This sample input page is designed to assist the banker in calculating the key financial statistics, ratios, and multiples for the comparables universe.[28] The input page data, in turn, feeds into output sheets that are used to benchmark the comparables (see Exhibits 1.53, 1.54, and 1.55).

In the pages that follow, we discuss the financial data displayed on the sample input sheet, as well as the calculations behind them. We also describe the mechanics for calculating LTM financial statistics, calendarizing company financials, and adjusting for non-recurring items and recent events.

Calculation of Key Financial Statistics and Ratios

In this section, we outline the calculation of key financial statistics, ratios, and other metrics in accordance with the financial profile framework introduced in Step I.

- Size (Market Valuation: equity value and enterprise value; and Key Financial Data: sales, gross profit, EBITDA, EBIT, and net income)

- Profitability (gross profit, EBITDA, EBIT, and net income margins)

- Growth Profile (historical and estimated growth rates)

- Return on Investment (ROIC, ROE, ROA, and dividend yield)

- Credit Profile (leverage ratios, coverage ratios, and credit ratings)

---

[27] For modeling/data entry purposes, manual inputs are typically formatted in blue font and yellow shading, while formula cells (calculations) are in black font.
[28] This template should be adjusted as appropriate in accordance with the specific company/sector (see Exhibit 1.33).

EXHIBIT 1.5 Sample Comparable Company Input Page

Company A (NYSE:AAA)
Input Page
($ in millions, except per share data)

General Information	
Company Name	Company A
Ticker	AAA
Stock Exchange	NYSE
Fiscal Year Ending	Dec-31
Moody's Corporate Rating	NA
S&P Corporate Rating	NA
Predicted Beta	1.00
Marginal Tax Rate	38.0%

Selected Market Data		
Current Price		-
% of 52-week High		NA
52-week High Price	1/1/2000	-
52-week Low Price	1/1/2000	-
Dividend Per Share (MRQ)	1/1/2000	-
Fully Diluted Shares Outstanding		-
Equity Value		**-**
Plus: Total Debt		-
Plus: Preferred Stock		-
Plus: Noncontrolling Interest		-
Less: Cash and Cash Equivalents		-
Enterprise Value		**-**

Trading Multiples

	LTM 9/30/2012	NFY 2012E	NFY+1 2013E	NFY+2 2014E
EV/Sales				
Metric	NA	NA	NA	NA
EV/EBITDA	-	-	-	-
Metric	NA	NA	NA	NA
EV/EBIT	-	-	-	-
Metric	NA	NA	NA	NA
P/E	-	-	-	-
Metric	NA	NA	NA	NA
FCF Yield	-	-	-	-
Metric	NA	NA	NA	NA

LTM Return on Investment Ratios	
Return on Invested Capital	-
Return on Equity	-
Return on Assets	-
Implied Annual Dividend Per Share	NA

LTM Credit Statistics	
Debt/Total Capitalization	-
Total Debt/EBITDA	-
Net Debt/EBITDA	-
EBITDA/Interest Expense	-
(EBITDA-capex)/Interest Expense	-
EBIT/Interest Expense	-

Growth Rates

	Sales	EBITDA	FCF	EPS
Historical				
1-year	-	-	-	-
2-year CAGR	-	-	-	-
Estimated				
1-year	-	-	-	-
2-year CAGR	-	-	-	-
Long-term				NA

Reported Income Statement

	Fiscal Year Ending December 31,			Prior Stub	Current Stub	LTM
	2009A	2010A	2011A	9/30/2011	9/30/2012	9/30/2012
Sales	-	-	-	-	-	-
COGS (incl. D&A)	-	-	-	-	-	-
Gross Profit	**-**	**-**	**-**	**-**	**-**	**-**
SG&A	-	-	-	-	-	-
Other Expense / (Income)	-	-	-	-	-	-
EBIT	**-**	**-**	**-**	**-**	**-**	**-**
Interest Expense	-	-	-	-	-	-
Pre-tax Income	**-**	**-**	**-**	**-**	**-**	**-**
Income Taxes	-	-	-	-	-	-
Noncontrolling Interest	-	-	-	-	-	-
Preferred Dividends	-	-	-	-	-	-
Net Income	**-**	**-**	**-**	**-**	**-**	**-**
Effective Tax Rate	NA	NA	NA	NA	NA	NA
Weighted Avg. Diluted Shares						
Diluted EPS	**NA**	**NA**	**NA**	**NA**	**NA**	**NA**

Adjusted Income Statement

	2009A	2010A	2011A	9/30/2011	9/30/2012	9/30/2012
Reported Gross Profit	-	-	-	-	-	-
Non-recurring Items in COGS	-	-	-	-	-	-
Adj. Gross Profit	**-**	**-**	**-**	**-**	**-**	**-**
% margin	NA	NA	NA	NA	NA	NA
Reported EBIT	-	-	-	-	-	-
Non-recurring Items in COGS	-	-	-	-	-	-
Other Non-recurring Items	-	-	-	-	-	-
Adjusted EBIT	**-**	**-**	**-**	**-**	**-**	**-**
% margin	NA	NA	NA	NA	NA	NA
Depreciation & Amortization	-	-	-	-	-	-
Adjusted EBITDA	**-**	**-**	**-**	**-**	**-**	**-**
% margin	NA	NA	NA	NA	NA	NA
Reported Net Income	-	-	-	-	-	-
Non-recurring Items in COGS	-	-	-	-	-	-
Other Non-recurring Items	-	-	-	-	-	-
Non-operating Non-rec. Items	-	-	-	-	-	-
Tax Adjustment	-	-	-	-	-	-
Adjusted Net Income	**-**	**-**	**-**	**-**	**-**	**-**
% margin	NA	NA	NA	NA	NA	NA
Adjusted Diluted EPS	-	-	-	-	-	-

Cash Flow Statement Data

	2009A	2010A	2011A	9/30/2011	9/30/2012	9/30/2012
Cash From Operations	-	-	-	-	-	-
Capital Expenditures	-	-	-	-	-	-
% sales	NA	NA	NA	NA	NA	NA
Free Cash Flow	**-**	**-**	**-**	**-**	**-**	**-**
% margin	NA	NA	NA	NA	NA	NA
FCF / Share	-	-	-	-	-	-
Depreciation & Amortization	-	-	-	-	-	-
% sales	NA	NA	NA	NA	NA	NA

Notes
(1) [to come]
(2) [to come]
(3) [to come]
(4) [to come]

Business Description
[to come]

Balance Sheet Data

	2011A	9/30/2012
Cash and Cash Equivalents	-	-
Accounts Receivable	-	-
Inventories	-	-
Prepaids and Other Current Assets	-	-
Total Current Assets	**-**	**-**
Property, Plant and Equipment, net	-	-
Goodwill and Intangible Assets	-	-
Other Assets	-	-
Total Assets	**-**	**-**
Accounts Payable	-	-
Accrued Liabilities	-	-
Other Current Liabilities	-	-
Total Current Liabilities	**-**	**-**
Total Debt	-	-
Other Long-Term Liabilities	-	-
Total Liabilities	**-**	**-**
Noncontrolling Interest	-	-
Preferred Stock	-	-
Shareholders' Equity	-	-
Total Liabilities and Equity	**-**	**-**
Balance Check	0.000	0.000

Calculation of Fully Diluted Shares Outstanding

Basic Shares Outstanding
Plus: Shares from In-the-Money Options
Less: Shares Repurchased
Net New Shares from Options
Plus: Shares from Convertible Securities
Fully Diluted Shares Outstanding

Options/Warrants

Tranche	Number of Shares	Exercise Price	In-the-Money Shares	Proceeds
Tranche 1				
Tranche 2				
Tranche 3				
Tranche 4				
Tranche 5				
Total				

Convertible Securities

	Amount	Conversion Price	Conversion Ratio	New Shares
Issue 1				
Issue 2				
Issue 3				
Issue 4				
Issue 5				
Total				

Size: Market Valuation

Equity Value Equity value ("market capitalization") is the value represented by a given company's basic shares outstanding plus "in-the-money" stock options,[29] warrants,[30] and convertible securities—collectively, "fully diluted shares outstanding." It is calculated by multiplying a company's current share price[31] by its fully diluted shares outstanding (see Exhibit 1.6).

EXHIBIT 1.6 Calculation of Equity Value

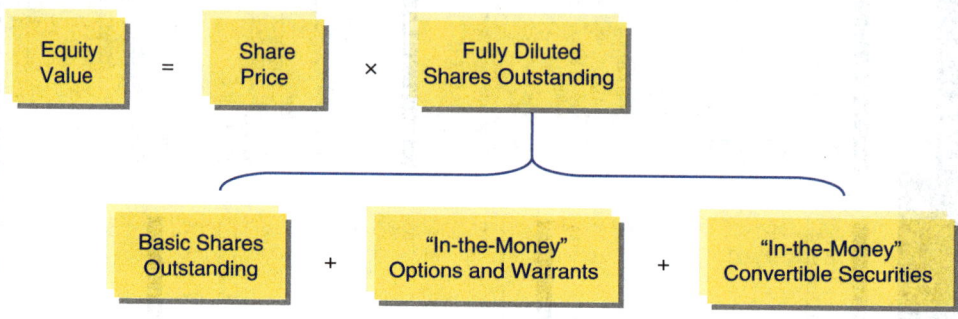

When compared to other companies, equity value only provides a measure of relative size. Therefore, for insight on absolute and relative market performance—which is informative for interpreting multiples and framing valuation—the banker looks at the company's current share price as a percentage of its 52-week high. This is a widely used metric that provides perspective on valuation and gauges current market sentiment and outlook for both the individual company and its broader sector. If a given company's percentage is significantly out of line with that of its peers, it is generally an indicator of company-specific (as opposed to sector-specific) issues. For example, a company may have missed its earnings guidance or underperformed versus its peers over the recent quarter(s). It may also be a sign of more entrenched issues involving management, operations, or specific markets.

---

[29] Stock options are granted to employees as a form of non-cash compensation. They provide the right to buy (call) shares of the company's common stock at a set price ("exercise" or "strike" price) during a given time period. Employee stock options are subject to vesting periods that restrict the number of shares available for exercise according to a set schedule. They become eligible to be converted into shares of common stock once their vesting period expires ("exercisable"). An option is considered "in-the-money" when the underlying company's share price surpasses the option's exercise price.

[30] A warrant is a security typically issued in conjunction with a debt instrument that entitles the purchaser of that instrument to buy shares of the issuer's common stock at a set price during a given time period. In this context, warrants serve to entice investor interest (usually as a detachable equity "sweetener") in riskier classes of securities such as non-investment-grade bonds and mezzanine debt, by providing an increase to the security's overall return.

[31] For trading comps, the banker typically uses the company's share price as of the prior day's close as the basis for calculating equity value and trading multiples.

Calculation of Fully Diluted Shares Outstanding A company's fully diluted shares are calculated by adding the number of shares represented by its in-the-money options, warrants, and convertible securities to its basic shares outstanding.[32] A company's most recent basic shares outstanding count is typically sourced from the first page of its 10-K or 10-Q (whichever is most recent). In some cases, however, the latest proxy statement may contain more updated data and, therefore, should be used in lieu of the 10-K or 10-Q. The most recent stock options/warrants information is obtained from a company's latest 10-K or, in some cases, the 10-Q.

The incremental shares represented by a company's in-the-money options and warrants are calculated in accordance with the treasury stock method (TSM). Those shares implied by a company's in-the-money convertible and equity-linked securities are calculated in accordance with the if-converted method or net share settlement (NSS), as appropriate.

Options and Warrants—The Treasury Stock Method The TSM assumes that all tranches of in-the-money options and warrants are exercised at their weighted average strike price with the resulting option proceeds used to repurchase outstanding shares of stock at the company's current share price. In-the-money options and warrants are those that have an exercise price lower than the current market price of the underlying company's stock. As the strike price is lower than the current market price, the number of shares repurchased is less than the additional shares outstanding from exercised options. This results in a net issuance of shares, which is dilutive.

In Exhibit 1.7, we provide an example of how to calculate fully diluted shares outstanding using the TSM.

EXHIBIT 1.7 Calculation of Fully Diluted Shares Outstanding Using the Treasury Stock Method

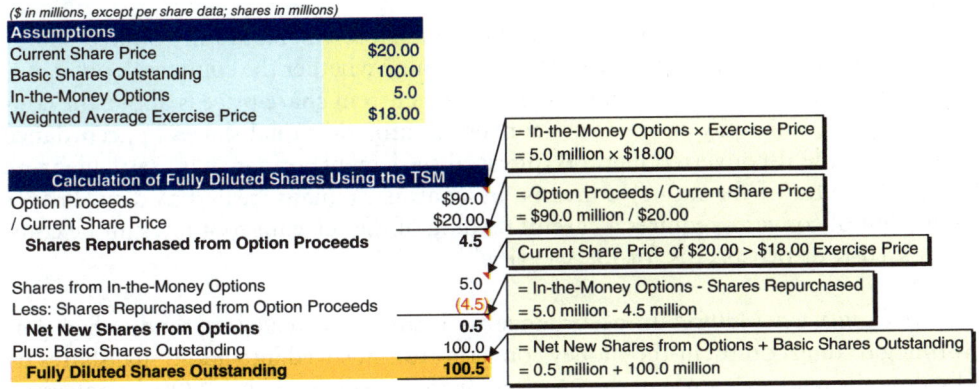

---

[32]Investment banks and finance professionals may differ as to whether they use "outstanding" or "exercisable" in-the-money options and warrants in the calculation of fully diluted shares outstanding when performing trading comps. For conservatism (i.e., assuming the most dilutive scenario), many firms employ all outstanding in-the-money options and warrants as opposed to just exercisable as they represent future claims against the company.

As shown in Exhibit 1.7, the 5 million options are in-the-money as the exercise price of $18.00 is lower than the current share price of $20.00. This means that the holders of the options have the right to buy the company's shares at $18.00 and sell them at $20.00, thereby realizing the $2.00 differential. Under the TSM, it is assumed that the $18.00 of potential proceeds received by the company is used to repurchase shares that are currently trading at $20.00. Therefore, the number of shares repurchased is 90% ($18.00 / $20.00) of the options, or 4.5 million shares in total (90% × 5 million). To calculate net new shares, the 4.5 million shares repurchased are subtracted from the 5 million options, resulting in 0.5 million. These new shares are added to the company's basic shares outstanding to derive fully diluted shares of 100.5 million.

Convertible and Equity-Linked Securities Outstanding convertible and equity-linked securities also need to be factored into the calculation of fully diluted shares outstanding. Convertible and equity-linked securities bridge the gap between traditional debt and equity, featuring characteristics of both. They include a broad range of instruments, such as traditional cash-pay convertible bonds, convertible hybrids, perpetual convertible preferred, and mandatory convertibles.[33]

This section focuses on the traditional cash-pay convertible bond as it is the most "plain-vanilla" and commonly issued structure. A cash-pay convertible bond ("convert") represents a straight debt instrument and an embedded equity call option that provides for the convert to be exchanged into a defined number of shares of the issuer's common stock under certain circumstances. The value of the embedded call option allows the issuer to pay a lower coupon than a straight debt instrument of the same credit. The strike price of the call option ("conversion price"), which represents the share price at which equity would be issued to convertible holders if the bonds were converted, is typically set at a premium to the company's underlying share price at the time of issuance.

For the purposes of performing trading comps, to calculate fully diluted shares outstanding, it is standard practice to first determine whether the company's outstanding converts are in-the-money, meaning that the current share price is above the conversion price. Cash-pay converts are converted into additional shares in accordance with either the if-converted method (physical settlement) or net share settlement, as applicable. Out-of-the-money converts, by contrast, remain treated as debt. Proper treatment of converts requires a careful reading of the relevant footnotes in the company's 10-K or prospectus for the security.

If-Converted Method In accordance with the if-converted method, when performing trading comps, in-the-money converts are converted into additional shares by dividing the convert's amount outstanding by its conversion price.[34] Once converted,

---

[33]While the overall volume of issuance for convertible and equity-linked securities is much less than that for straight debt instruments, they are relatively common in certain sectors.
[34]For GAAP reporting purposes (e.g., for EPS and fully diluted shares outstanding), the if-converted method requires issuers to measure the dilutive impact of the security through a two-test process. First, the issuer needs to test the security as if it were debt on its balance sheet, with the stated interest expense reflected in net income and the underlying shares omitted from the share count. Second, the issuer needs to test the security as if it were converted into equity,

the convert is treated as equity and included in the calculation of the company's fully diluted shares outstanding and equity value. The equity value represented by the convert is calculated by multiplying the new shares outstanding from conversion by the company's current share price. Accordingly, the convert must be excluded from the calculation of the company's total debt.

As shown in Exhibit 1.8, as the company's current share price of $20.00 is greater than the conversion price of $15.00, we determine that the $150 million convert is in-the-money. Therefore the convert's amount outstanding is simply divided by the conversion price to calculate new shares of 10 million ($150 million / $15.00). The new shares from conversion are then added to the company's basic shares outstanding of 100 million and net new shares from in-the-money options of 0.5 million to calculate fully diluted shares outstanding of 110.5 million.

The conversion of in-the-money converts also requires an upward adjustment to the company's net income to account for the foregone interest expense payments associated with the coupon on the convert. This amount must be tax-effected before being added back to net income. Therefore, while conversion is typically EPS dilutive due to the additional share issuance, net income is actually higher on a *pro forma* basis.

EXHIBIT 1.8 Calculation of Fully Diluted Shares Outstanding Using the If-Converted Method

($ in millions, except per share data; shares in millions)

Assumptions	
Company	
Current Share Price	$20.00
Basic Shares Outstanding	100.0
Convertible	
Amount Outstanding	$150.0
Conversion Price	$15.00

If-Converted	
Amount Outstanding	$150.0
/ Conversion Price	$15.00
Incremental Shares	10.0
Plus: Net New Shares from Options	0.5
Plus: Basic Shares Outstanding	100.0
Fully Diluted Shares Outstanding	**110.5**

- = Amount Outstanding / Conversion Price
- = $150.0 million / $15.00
- Calculated in Exhibit 1.7
- = New Shares from Conversion
  + Net New Shares from Options
  + Basic Shares Outstanding
- = 10.0 million + 0.5 million + 100.0 million

---

which involves excluding the interest expense from the convert in net income and including the full underlying shares in the share count. Upon completion of the two tests, the issuer is required to use the more dilutive of the two methodologies.

Net Share Settlement Net share settlement is an increasingly common feature in convertible bonds. For converts issued with a net share settlement accounting feature,[35] the issuer is permitted to satisfy the face (or accreted) value of an in-the-money convert with at least a portion of cash upon conversion. Only the value represented by the excess of the current share price over the conversion price is assumed to be settled with the issuance of additional shares,[36] which results in less share issuance. This serves to limit the dilutive effects of conversion by affording the issuer TSM accounting treatment.

As shown in Exhibit 1.9, the if-converted method results in incremental shares of 10 million shares, while NSS results in incremental shares of only 2.5 million. The NSS calculation is conducted by first multiplying the number of underlying shares in the convert of 10 million by the company's current share price of $20.00 to determine the implied conversion value of $200 million. The $50 million spread between the conversion value and par ($200 million − $150 million) is then divided by the current share price to determine the number of incremental shares from conversion of 2.5 million ($50 million / $20.00).[37] The $150 million face value of the convert remains treated as debt due to the fact that the issuer typically has the right to settle this amount in cash.

EXHIBIT 1.9 Incremental Shares from If-Converted Versus Net Share Settlement

($ in millions, except per share data; shares in millions)

If-Converted		Net Share Settlement	
Amount Outstanding	$150.0	Amount Outstanding	$150.0
/ Conversion Price	$15.00	/ Conversion Price	$15.00
Incremental Shares	**10.0**	**Incremental Shares**	**10.0**
		× Current Share Price	$20.00
		Total Conversion Value	**$200.0**
		Less: Par Value of Amount Outstanding	(150.0)
		Excess Over Par Value	**$50.0**
		/ Current Share Price	$20.00
Incremental Shares – If-Converted	**10.0**	**Incremental Shares – NSS**	**2.5**

= Excess Over Par Value / Current Share Price
= $50.0 million / $20.00

= Total Conversion Value − Par Value of Amt. Out.
= $200.0 million − $150.0 million

= Incremental Shares × Current Share Price
= 10.0 million × $20.00

= Amount Outstanding / Conversion Price
= $150.0 million / $15.00

---

[35]Effective for fiscal years beginning after December 15, 2008, the Financial Accounting Standards Board (FASB) put into effect new guidelines for NSS accounting. These changes effectively bifurcate an NSS convert into its debt and equity components, resulting in higher reported GAAP interest expense due to the higher imputed cost of debt. However, the new guidelines do not change the calculation of shares outstanding in accordance with the TSM. Therefore, one should consult with a capital markets specialist for accounting guidance on in-the-money converts with NSS features.

[36]The NSS feature may also be structured so that the issuer can elect to settle the excess conversion value in cash.

[37]As the company's share price increases, the amount of incremental shares issued also increases as the spread between conversion and par value widens.

Comparable Companies Analysis

Enterprise Value Enterprise value ("total enterprise value" or "firm value") is the sum of all ownership interests in a company and claims on its assets from both debt and equity holders. As the graphic in Exhibit 1.10 depicts, it is defined as equity value + total debt + preferred stock + noncontrolling interest[38] – cash and cash equivalents. The equity value component is calculated on a fully diluted basis.

EXHIBIT 1.10 Calculation of Enterprise Value

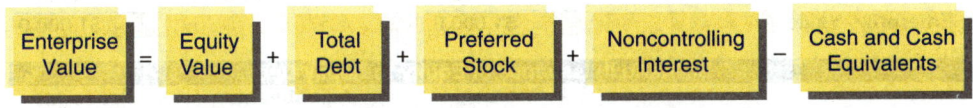

Theoretically, enterprise value is considered independent of capital structure, meaning that changes in a company's capital structure do not affect its enterprise value. For example, if a company raises additional debt that is held on the balance sheet as cash, its enterprise value remains constant as the new debt is offset by the increase in cash (i.e., net debt remains the same, see Scenario I in Exhibit 1.11). Similarly, if a company issues equity and uses the proceeds to repay debt, the incremental equity value is offset by the decrease in debt on a dollar-for-dollar basis (see Scenario II in Exhibit 1.11).[39] Therefore, these transactions are enterprise value neutral.

In both Scenario I and II, enterprise value remains constant despite a change in the company's capital structure. Hence, similar companies would be expected to have consistent enterprise value multiples despite differences in capital structure. One notable exception concerns highly leveraged companies, which may trade at a discount relative to their peers due to the perceived higher risk of financial distress[40] and potential constraints to growth.

---

[38]Formerly known as "minority interest," noncontrolling interest is a significant, but non-majority, interest (less than 50%) in a company's voting stock by another company or an investor. Effective for fiscal years beginning after December 15, 2008, FAS 160 changed the accounting and reporting for minority interest, which is now called noncontrolling interest and can be found in the shareholders' equity section of a company's balance sheet. On the income statement, the noncontrolling interest holder's share of income is subtracted from net income.

[39]These illustrative scenarios ignore financing fees associated with the debt and equity issuance as well as potential breakage costs associated with the repayment of debt. See Chapter 4: Leveraged Buyouts for additional information.

[40]Circumstances whereby a company is unable or struggles to meet its credit obligations, typically resulting in business disruption, insolvency, or bankruptcy. As the perceived risk of financial distress increases, equity value generally decreases accordingly.

EXHIBIT 1.11 Effects of Capital Structure Changes on Enterprise Value

($ in millions)

	Scenario I: Issuance of Debt			
	Actual 2011	Adjustments +	−	Pro forma 2011
Equity Value	$750.0			$750.0
Plus: Total Debt	250.0	100.0		350.0
Plus: Preferred Stock	35.0			35.0
Plus: Noncontrolling Interest	15.0			15.0
Less: Cash and Cash Equivalents	(50.0)		(100.0)	(150.0)
Enterprise Value	**$1,000.0**			**$1,000.0**

	Scenario II: Issuance of Equity to Repay Debt			
	Actual 2011	Adjustments +	−	Pro forma 2011
Equity Value	$750.0	100.0		$850.0
Plus: Total Debt	250.0		(100.0)	150.0
Plus: Preferred Stock	35.0			35.0
Plus: Noncontrolling Interest	15.0			15.0
Less: Cash and Cash Equivalents	(50.0)			(50.0)
Enterprise Value	**$1,000.0**			**$1,000.0**

Size: Key Financial Data

- **Sales** (or revenue) is the first line item, or "top line," on an income statement. Sales represents the total dollar amount realized by a company through the sale of its products and services during a given time period. Sales levels and trends are a key factor in determining a company's relative positioning among its peers. All else being equal, companies with greater sales volumes tend to benefit from scale, market share, purchasing power, and lower risk profile, and are often rewarded by the market with a premium valuation relative to smaller peers.

- **Gross Profit**, defined as sales less cost of goods sold (COGS),[41] is the profit earned by a company after subtracting costs directly related to the production of its products and services. As such, it is a key indicator of operational efficiency and pricing power, and is usually expressed as a percentage of sales for analytical purposes (gross profit margin, see Exhibit 1.12). For example, if a company sells a product for $100, and that product costs $60 in materials, manufacturing, and direct labor to produce, then the gross profit on that product is $40 and the gross profit margin is 40%.

- **EBITDA** (earnings before interest, taxes, depreciation and amortization) is an important measure of profitability. As EBITDA is a non-GAAP financial measure and typically not reported by public filers, it is generally calculated by taking EBIT (or operating income/profit as often reported on the income statement) and adding back the depreciation and amortization (D&A) as sourced from the cash

---

[41]COGS, as reported on the income statement, may include or exclude D&A depending on the filing company. If D&A is excluded, it is reported as a separate line item on the income statement.

flow statement.[42] EBITDA is a widely used proxy for operating cash flow as it reflects the company's total cash operating costs for producing its products and services. In addition, EBITDA serves as a fair "apples-to-apples" means of comparison among companies in the same sector because it is free from differences resulting from capital structure (i.e., interest expense) and tax regime (i.e., tax expense).

- **EBIT** (<u>e</u>arnings <u>b</u>efore <u>i</u>nterest and <u>t</u>axes) is often the same as reported operating income, operating profit, or income from operations[43] on the income statement found in a company's SEC filings. Like EBITDA, EBIT is independent of tax regime and serves as a useful metric for comparing companies with different capital structures. It is, however, less indicative as a measure of operating cash flow than EBITDA because it includes non-cash D&A expense. Furthermore, D&A reflects discrepancies among different companies in capital spending and/or depreciation policy as well as acquisition histories (amortization).

- **Net income** ("earnings" or the "bottom line") is the residual profit after all of a company's expenses have been netted out. Net income can also be viewed as the earnings available to equity holders once all of the company's obligations have been satisfied (e.g., to suppliers, vendors, service providers, employees, utilities, lessors, lenders, state and local treasuries). Wall Street tends to view net income on a per share basis (i.e., earnings per share or EPS).

Profitability

- **Gross profit margin** ("gross margin") measures the percentage of sales remaining after subtracting COGS (see Exhibit 1.12). It is driven by a company's direct cost per unit, such as materials, manufacturing, and direct labor involved in production. These costs are typically largely variable, as opposed to corporate overhead, which is more fixed in nature.[44] Companies ideally seek to increase their gross margin through a combination of improved sourcing/procurement of raw materials and enhanced pricing power, as well as by improving the efficiency of manufacturing facilities and processes.

---

[42]In the event a company reports D&A as a separate line item on the income statement (i.e., broken out separately from COGS and SG&A), EBITDA can be calculated as sales less COGS less SG&A.

[43]EBIT may differ from operating income/profit due to the inclusion of income generated outside the scope of a company's ordinary course business operations ("other income").

[44]*Variable* costs change depending on the volume of goods produced and include items such as materials, direct labor, transportation, and utilities. *Fixed* costs remain more or less constant regardless of volume and include items such as lease expense, advertising and marketing, insurance, corporate overhead, and administrative salaries. These costs are usually captured in the SG&A (or equivalent) line item on the income statement.

EXHIBIT 1.12 Gross Profit Margin

$$\text{Gross Profit Margin} = \frac{\text{Gross Profit (Sales} - \text{COGS)}}{\text{Sales}}$$

- **EBITDA** and **EBIT margin** are accepted standards for measuring a company's operating profitability (see Exhibit 1.13). Accordingly, they are used to frame relative performance both among peer companies and across sectors.

EXHIBIT 1.13 EBITDA and EBIT Margin

$$\text{EBITDA Margin} = \frac{\text{EBITDA}}{\text{Sales}} \qquad \text{EBIT Margin} = \frac{\text{EBIT}}{\text{Sales}}$$

- **Net income margin** measures a company's overall profitability as opposed to its operating profitability (see Exhibit 1.14). It is net of interest expense and, therefore, affected by capital structure. As a result, companies with similar operating margins may have substantially different net income margins due to differences in leverage. Furthermore, as net income is impacted by taxes, companies with similar operating margins may have varying net income margins due to different tax rates.

EXHIBIT 1.14 Net Income Margin

$$\text{Net Income Margin} = \frac{\text{Net Income}}{\text{Sales}}$$

Growth Profile

A company's growth profile is a critical value driver. In assessing a company's growth profile, the banker typically looks at historical and estimated future growth rates as well as compound annual growth rates (CAGRs) for selected financial statistics (see Exhibit 1.15).

EXHIBIT 1.15 Historical and Estimated Diluted EPS Growth Rates

	Fiscal Year Ending December 31,						
	2009A	2010A	2011A	CAGR ('09 - '11)	2012E	2013E	CAGR ('11 - '13)
Diluted Earnings Per Share	$1.00	$1.15	$1.30	14.0%	$1.50	$1.65	12.7%
% growth		15.0%	13.0%		15.4%	10.0%	
Long-term growth rate							12.0%

= (Ending Value / Beginning Value) ^ (1 / Ending Year - Beginning Year) - 1
= ($1.30 / $1.00) ^ (1 / (2011 - 2009)) - 1

Source: Consensus Estimates

Comparable Companies Analysis

Historical annual EPS data is typically sourced directly from a company's 10-K or a financial information service that sources SEC filings, such as Bloomberg. As with the calculation of any financial statistic, historical EPS must be adjusted for non-recurring items to be meaningful. The data that serves as the basis for a company's projected 1-year, 2-year, and long-term[45] EPS growth rates is generally obtained from consensus estimates.

Return on Investment

- **Return on invested capital (ROIC)** measures the return generated by all capital provided to a company. As such, ROIC utilizes a pre-interest earnings statistic in the numerator, such as EBIT or tax-effected EBIT (also known as NOPAT or EBIAT) and a metric that captures both debt and equity in the denominator (see Exhibit 1.16). The denominator is typically calculated on an average basis (e.g., average of the balances as of the prior annual and most recent periods).

EXHIBIT 1.16 Return on Invested Capital

$$\text{ROIC} = \frac{\text{EBIT}}{\text{Average Net Debt + Equity}}$$

- **Return on equity (ROE)** measures the return generated on the equity provided to a company by its shareholders. As a result, ROE incorporates an earnings metric net of interest expense, such as net income, in the numerator and average shareholders' equity in the denominator (see Exhibit 1.17). ROE is an important indicator of performance as companies are intently focused on shareholder returns.

EXHIBIT 1.17 Return on Equity

$$\text{ROE} = \frac{\text{Net Income}}{\text{Average Shareholders' Equity}}$$

- **Return on assets (ROA)** measures the return generated by a company's asset base, thereby providing a barometer of the asset efficiency of a business. ROA typically utilizes net income in the numerator and average total assets in the denominator (see Exhibit 1.18).

EXHIBIT 1.18 Return on Assets

$$\text{ROA} = \frac{\text{Net Income}}{\text{Average Total Assets}}$$

---

[45]Represents a three-to-five-year estimate of annual EPS growth, as reported by equity research analysts.

- **Dividend yield** is a measure of returns to shareholders, but from a different perspective than earnings-based ratios. Dividend yield measures the annual dividends per share paid by a company to its shareholders (which can be distributed either in cash or additional shares), expressed as a percentage of its share price. Dividends are typically paid on a quarterly basis and, therefore, must be annualized to calculate the implied dividend yield (see Exhibit 1.19).[46] For example, if a company pays a quarterly dividend of $0.05 per share ($0.20 per share on an annualized basis) and its shares are currently trading at $10.00, the dividend yield is 2% (($0.05 × 4 payments) / $10.00).

EXHIBIT 1.19 Implied Dividend Yield

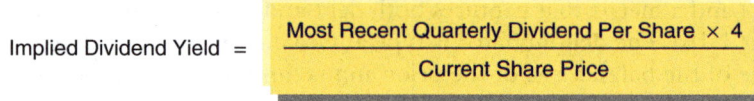

Credit Profile

Leverage Leverage refers to a company's debt level. It is typically measured as a multiple of EBITDA (e.g., debt-to-EBITDA) or as a percentage of total capitalization (e.g., debt-to-total capitalization). Both debt and equity investors closely track a company's leverage as it reveals a great deal about financial policy, risk profile, and capacity for growth. As a general rule, the higher a company's leverage, the higher its risk of financial distress due to the burden associated with greater interest expense and principal repayments.

- **Debt-to-EBITDA** depicts the ratio of a company's debt to its EBITDA, with a higher multiple connoting higher leverage (see Exhibit 1.20). It is generally calculated on the basis of LTM financial statistics. There are several variations of this ratio, including total debt-to-EBITDA, senior secured debt-to-EBITDA, net debt-to-EBITDA, and total debt-to-(EBITDA less capex). As EBITDA is typically used as a rough proxy for operating cash flow, this ratio can be viewed as a measure of how many years of a company's cash flows are needed to repay its debt.

EXHIBIT 1.20 Leverage Ratio

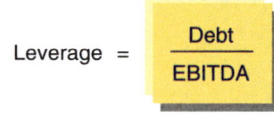

- **Debt-to-total capitalization** measures a company's debt as a percentage of its total capitalization (debt + preferred stock + noncontrolling interest + equity) (see Exhibit 1.21). This ratio can be calculated on the basis of book or market

---

[46] Not all companies choose to pay dividends to their shareholders.

values depending on the situation. As with debt-to-EBITDA, a higher debt-to-total capitalization ratio connotes higher debt levels and risk of financial distress.

EXHIBIT 1.21   Capitalization Ratio

$$\text{Debt-to-Total Capitalization} = \frac{\text{Debt}}{\text{Debt} + \text{Preferred Stock} + \text{Noncontrolling Interest} + \text{Equity}}$$

Coverage   Coverage is a broad term that refers to a company's ability to meet ("cover") its interest expense obligations. Coverage ratios are generally comprised of a financial statistic representing operating cash flow (e.g., LTM EBITDA) in the numerator and LTM interest expense in the denominator. There are several variations of the coverage ratio, including EBITDA-to-interest expense, (EBITDA less capex)-to-interest expense, and EBIT-to-interest expense (see Exhibit 1.22). Intuitively, the higher the coverage ratio, the better positioned the company is to meet its debt obligations and, therefore, the stronger its credit profile.

EXHIBIT 1.22   Interest Coverage Ratio

$$\text{Interest Coverage Ratio} = \frac{\text{EBITDA, (EBITDA – Capex), or EBIT}}{\text{Interest Expense}}$$

Credit Ratings   A credit rating is an assessment[47] by an independent rating agency of a company's ability and willingness to make full and timely payments of amounts due on its debt obligations. Credit ratings are typically required for companies seeking to raise debt financing in the capital markets as only a limited class of investors will participate in a corporate debt offering without an assigned credit rating on the new issue.[48]

The three primary credit rating agencies are Moody's, S&P, and Fitch. Nearly every public debt issuer receives a rating from Moody's, S&P, and/or Fitch. Moody's uses an alphanumeric scale, while S&P and Fitch both use an alphabetic system combined with pluses (+) and minuses (–) to rate the creditworthiness of an issuer. The ratings scales of the primary rating agencies are shown in Exhibit 1.23.

---

[47]Ratings agencies provide opinions, but do not conduct audits.
[48]Ratings are assessed on the issuer (corporate credit ratings) as well as on the individual debt instruments (facility ratings).

EXHIBIT 1.23 Ratings Scales of the Primary Rating Agencies

	Moody's	S&P	Fitch	Definition
Investment Grade	Aaa	AAA	AAA	Highest Quality
	Aa1	AA+	AA+	Very High Quality
	Aa2	AA	AA	
	Aa3	AA-	AA-	
	A1	A+	A+	High Quality
	A2	A	A	
	A3	A-	A-	
	Baa1	BBB+	BBB+	Medium Grade
	Baa2	BBB	BBB	
	Baa3	BBB-	BBB-	
Non-Investment Grade	Ba1	BB+	BB+	Speculative
	Ba2	BB	BB	
	Ba3	BB-	BB-	
	B1	B+	B+	Highly Speculative
	B2	B	B	
	B3	B-	B-	
	Caa1	CCC+	CCC+	Substantial Risk
	Caa2	CCC	CCC	
	Caa3	CCC-	CCC-	
	Ca	CC	CC	Extremely Speculative / Default
	C	C	C	
	–	D	D	

Supplemental Financial Concepts and Calculations

Calculation of LTM Financial Data U.S. public filers are required to report their financial performance on a quarterly basis, including a full year report filed at the end of the fiscal year. Therefore, in order to measure financial performance for the most recent annual or LTM period, the company's financial results for the previous four quarters are summed. This financial information is sourced from the company's most recent 10-K and 10-Q, as appropriate. As previously discussed, however, prior to the filing of the 10-Q or 10-K, companies typically issue a detailed earnings press release in an 8-K with the necessary financial data to help calculate LTM performance. Therefore, it may be appropriate to use a company's earnings announcement to update trading comps on a timely basis.

As the formula in Exhibit 1.24 illustrates, LTM financials are typically calculated by taking the full prior fiscal year's financial data, adding the YTD financial data for the current year period ("current stub"), and then subtracting the YTD financial data from the prior year ("prior stub").

EXHIBIT 1.24 Calculation of LTM Financial Data

Comparable Companies Analysis

In the event that the most recent quarter is the fourth quarter of a company's fiscal year, then no LTM calculations are necessary as the full prior fiscal year (as reported) serves as the LTM period. Exhibit 1.25 shows an illustrative calculation for a given company's LTM sales for the period ending 9/30/2012.

EXHIBIT 1.25 Calculation of LTM 9/30/2012 Sales

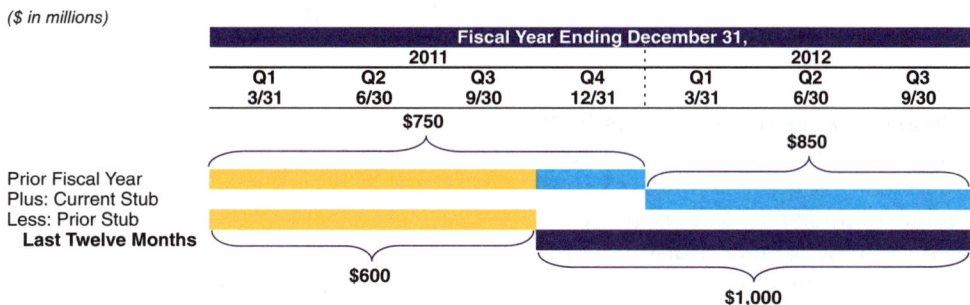

Calendarization of Financial Data The majority of U.S. public filers report their financial performance in accordance with a fiscal year (FY) ending December 31, which corresponds to the calendar year (CY) end. Some companies, however, report on a different schedule (e.g., a fiscal year ending April 30). Any variation in fiscal year ends among comparable companies must be addressed for benchmarking purposes. Otherwise, the trading multiples will be based on financial data for different periods and, therefore, not truly "comparable."

To account for variations in fiscal year ends among comparable companies, each company's financials are adjusted to conform to a calendar year end in order to produce a "clean" basis for comparison, a process known as "calendarization." This is a relatively straightforward algebraic exercise, as illustrated by the formula in Exhibit 1.26, used to calendarize a company's fiscal year sales projection to produce a calendar year sales projection.[49]

EXHIBIT 1.26 Calendarization of Financial Data

$$\text{Next Calendar (CY) Sales} = \frac{(\text{Month \#}) \times (\text{FYA Sales})}{12} + \frac{(12 - \text{Month \#}) \times (\text{NFY Sales})}{12}$$

Note: "Month #" refers to the month in which the company's fiscal year ends (e.g., the Month # for a company with a fiscal year ending April 30 would be 4). FYA = fiscal year actual, and NFY = next fiscal year.

Exhibit 1.27 provides an illustrative calculation for the calendarization of a company's calendar year 2012 estimated (E) sales, assuming a fiscal year ending April 30.

---

[49]If available, quarterly estimates should be used as the basis for calendarizing financial projections.

EXHIBIT 1.27 Calendarization of Sales

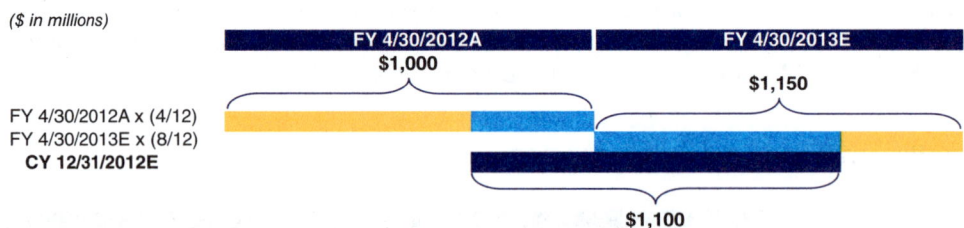

Adjustments for Non-Recurring Items   To assess a company's financial performance on a "normalized" basis, it is standard practice to adjust reported financial data for non-recurring items, a process known as "scrubbing" or "sanitizing" the financials. Failure to do so may lead to the calculation of misleading ratios and multiples, which, in turn, may produce a distorted view of valuation. These adjustments involve the add-back or elimination of one-time charges and gains, respectively, to create a more indicative view of ongoing company performance. Typical charges include those incurred for restructuring events (e.g., store/plant closings and headcount reduction), losses on asset sales, changes in accounting principles, inventory write-offs, goodwill impairment, extinguishment of debt, and losses from litigation settlements, among others. Typical benefits include gains from asset sales, favorable litigation settlements, and tax adjustments, among others.

Non-recurring items are often described in the MD&A section and financial footnotes in a company's public filings (e.g., 10-K and 10-Q) and earnings announcements. These items are often explicitly depicted as "non-recurring," "extraordinary," "unusual," or "one-time." Therefore, the banker is encouraged to comb electronic versions of the company's public filings and earnings announcements using word searches for these adjectives. Often, non-recurring charges or benefits are explicitly broken out as separate line items on a company's reported income statement and/or cash flow statement. Research reports can be helpful in identifying these items, while also providing color commentary on the reason they occurred.

In many cases, however, the banker must exercise discretion as to whether a given charge or benefit is non-recurring or part of normal business operations. This determination is sometimes relatively subjective, further compounded by the fact that certain events may be considered non-recurring for one company, but customary for another. For example, a generic pharmaceutical company may find itself in court frequently due to lawsuits filed by major drug manufacturers related to patent challenges. In this case, expenses associated with a lawsuit should not necessarily be treated as non-recurring because these legal expenses are a normal part of ongoing operations. While financial information services such as Bloomberg provide a breakdown of recommended adjustments that can be helpful in identifying potential non-recurring items, ultimately the banker should exercise professional judgment.

When adjusting for non-recurring items, it is important to distinguish between pre-tax and after-tax amounts. For a pre-tax restructuring charge, for example, the full amount is simply added back to calculate adjusted EBIT and EBITDA. To calculate adjusted net income, however, the pre-tax restructuring charge needs to be tax-effected[50] before being added back. Conversely, for after-tax amounts, the disclosed amount is simply added back to net income, but must be "grossed up" at the company's tax rate (t) (i.e., divided by (1 − t)) before being added back to EBIT and EBITDA.

Exhibit 1.28 provides an illustrative income statement for the fiscal year 2011 as it might appear in a 10-K. Let's assume the corresponding notes to these financials mention that the company recorded one-time charges related to an inventory write-down ($5 million pre-tax) and restructuring expenses from downsizing the sales force ($10 million pre-tax). Provided we gain comfort that these charges are truly non-recurring, we would need to normalize the company's earnings statistics accordingly for these items in order to arrive at adjusted EBIT, EBITDA, and diluted EPS.

EXHIBIT 1.28 Reported Income Statement

($ in millions, except per share data)

Income Statement	Reported 2011
Sales	$1,000.0
Cost of Goods Sold	625.0
Gross Profit	**$375.0**
Selling, General & Administrative	230.0
Restructuring Charges	10.0
Operating Income (EBIT)	**$135.0**
Interest Expense	35.0
Pre-tax Income	**$100.0**
Income Taxes	40.0
Net Income	**$60.0**
Weighted Average Diluted Shares	30.0
Diluted Earnings Per Share	$2.00

As shown in Exhibit 1.29, to calculate adjusted EBIT and EBITDA, we add back the full pre-tax charges of $5 million and $10 million ($15 million in total). This provides adjusted EBIT of $150 million and adjusted EBITDA of $200 million. To calculate adjusted net income and diluted EPS, however, the tax expense on the incremental $15 million pre-tax earnings must be subtracted. Assuming a 40% marginal tax rate, we calculate tax expense of $6 million and additional net income of $9 million ($15 million − $6 million). The $9 million is added to reported net income, resulting in adjusted net income of $69 million. We then divide the $69 million by weighted average fully diluted shares outstanding of 30 million to calculate adjusted diluted EPS of $2.30.

---

[50]In the event the SEC filing's footnotes do not provide detail on the after-tax amounts of such adjustments, the banker typically uses the marginal tax rate. The marginal tax rate for U.S. corporations is the rate at which a company is required to pay federal, state, and local taxes. The highest federal corporate income tax rate for U.S. corporations is 35%, with state and local taxes typically adding another 2% to 5% or more (depending on the state). Most public companies disclose their federal, state, and local tax rates in their 10-Ks in the notes to their financial statements.

EXHIBIT 1.29 Adjusted Income Statement

($ in millions, except per share data)

Income Statement	Reported 2011	Adjustments +	Adjustments −	Adjusted 2011	
Sales	$1,000.0			$1,000.0	
Cost of Goods Sold	625.0		(5.0)	620.0	Inventory write-down
Gross Profit	$375.0			$380.0	
Selling, General & Administrative	230.0			230.0	
Restructuring Charges	10.0		(10.0)	-	Restructuring charge related to severance from downsizing the sales force
Operating Income (EBIT)	$135.0			$150.0	
Interest Expense	35.0			35.0	
Pre-tax Income	$100.0			$115.0	
Income Taxes	40.0	6.0		46.0	= (Inventory write-down + Restructuring charge) × Marginal Tax Rate = ($5 million + $10 million) × 40%
Net Income	$60.0			$69.0	
Operating Income (EBIT)	$135.0	15.0		$150.0	
Depreciation & Amortization	50.0			50.0	D&A is sourced from the company's cash flow statement although it is sometimes broken out on the income statement
EBITDA	$185.0			$200.0	
Weighted Avg. Diluted Shares	30.0			30.0	
Diluted EPS	$2.00			$2.30	

$15 million add-back of total non-recurring items

Adjustments for Recent Events In normalizing a company's financials, the banker must also make adjustments for recent events, such as M&A transactions, financing activities, conversion of convertible securities, stock splits, or share repurchases in between reporting periods. Therefore, prior to performing trading comps, the banker checks company SEC filings (e.g., 8-Ks, registration statements/prospectuses[51]) and press releases since the most recent reporting period to determine whether the company has announced such activities.

For a recently announced M&A transaction, for example, the company's financial statements must be adjusted accordingly. The balance sheet is adjusted for the effects of the transaction by adding the purchase price financing (including any refinanced or assumed debt), while the LTM income statement is adjusted for the target's incremental sales and earnings. Equity research analysts typically update their estimates for a company's future financial performance promptly following the announcement of an M&A transaction. Therefore, the banker can use updated consensus estimates in combination with the *pro forma* balance sheet to calculate forward-looking multiples.[52]

---

[51] A registration statement/prospectus is a filing prepared by an issuer upon the registration/issuance of public securities, including debt and equity. The primary SEC forms for registration statements are S-1, S-3, and S-4; prospectuses are filed pursuant to Rule 424. When a company seeks to register securities with the SEC, it must file a registration statement. Within the registration statement is a preliminary prospectus. Once the registration statement is deemed effective, the company files the final prospectus as a 424 (includes final pricing and other key terms).

[52] As previously discussed, however, the banker needs to confirm beforehand that the estimates have been updated for the announced deal prior to usage. Furthermore, certain analysts may only update NFY estimates on an "as contributed" basis for the incremental earnings from the transaction for the remainder of the fiscal year (as opposed to adding a pro forma full year of earnings).

Calculation of Key Trading Multiples

Once the key financial statistics are spread, the banker proceeds to calculate the relevant trading multiples for the comparables universe. While various sectors may employ specialized or sector-specific valuation multiples (see Exhibit 1.33), the most generic and widely used multiples employ a measure of market valuation in the numerator (e.g., enterprise value, equity value) and a universal measure of financial performance in the denominator (e.g., EBITDA, net income). For enterprise value multiples, the denominator employs a financial statistic that flows to both debt and equity holders, such as sales, EBITDA, and EBIT. For equity value (or share price) multiples, the denominator must be a financial statistic that flows only to equity holders, such as net income (or diluted EPS). Among these multiples, EV/EBITDA and P/E are the most common.

The following sections provide an overview of the more commonly used equity value and enterprise value multiples.

Equity Value Multiples

Price-to-Earnings Ratio / Equity Value-to-Net Income Multiple The P/E ratio, calculated as current share price divided by diluted EPS (or equity value divided by net income), is the most widely recognized trading multiple. Assuming a constant share count, the P/E ratio is equivalent to equity value-to-net income. These ratios can also be viewed as a measure of how much investors are willing to pay for a dollar of a company's current or future earnings. P/E ratios are typically based on forward-year EPS[53] (and, to a lesser extent, LTM EPS) as investors are focused on future growth. Companies with higher P/Es than their peers tend to have higher earnings growth expectations.

The P/E ratio is particularly relevant for mature companies that have a demonstrated ability to consistently grow earnings. However, while the P/E ratio is broadly used and accepted, it has certain limitations. For example, it is not relevant for companies with little or no earnings as the denominator in these instances is *de minimis*, zero, or even negative. In addition, as previously discussed, net income (and EPS) is net of interest expense and, therefore, dependent on capital structure. As a result, two otherwise similar companies in terms of size and operating margins can have substantially different net income margins (and consequently P/E ratios) due to differences in leverage. Similarly, accounting discrepancies, such as for depreciation or taxes, can also produce meaningful disparities in P/E ratios among comparable companies.

The two formulas for calculating the P/E ratio (both equivalent, assuming a constant share count) are shown in Exhibit 1.30.

EXHIBIT 1.30 Equity Value Multiples

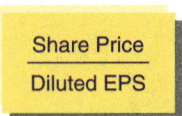

---

[53]Generally, the earnings for the next two calendar years.

Enterprise Value Multiples

Given that enterprise value represents the interests of both debt and equity holders, it is used as a multiple of unlevered financial statistics such as sales, EBITDA, and EBIT. The most generic and widely used enterprise value multiples are EV/EBITDA, EV/EBIT, and EV/sales (see Exhibits 1.31 and 1.32). As with P/E ratios, enterprise value multiples tend to focus on forward estimates in addition to LTM statistics for framing valuation.

Enterprise Value-to-EBITDA and Enterprise Value-to-EBIT Multiples EV/EBITDA serves as a valuation standard for most sectors. It is independent of capital structure and taxes, as well as any distortions that may arise from differences in D&A among different companies. For example, one company may have spent heavily on new machinery and equipment in recent years, resulting in increased D&A for the current and future years, while another company may have deferred its capital spending until a future period. In the interim, this situation would produce disparities in EBIT margins between the two companies that would not be reflected in EBITDA margins.

For the reasons outlined above, as well as potential discrepancies due to acquisition-related amortization, EV/EBIT is less commonly used than EV/EBITDA. However, EV/EBIT may be helpful in situations where D&A is unavailable (e.g., when valuing divisions of public companies) or for companies with high capex.

EXHIBIT 1.31 Enterprise Value-to-EBITDA and Enterprise Value-to-EBIT

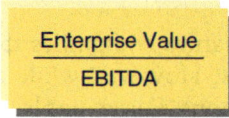 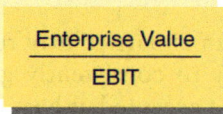

Enterprise Value-to-Sales Multiple EV/sales is also used as a valuation metric, although it is typically less relevant than the other multiples discussed. Sales may provide an indication of size, but it does not necessarily translate into profitability or cash flow generation, both of which are key value drivers. Consequently, EV/sales is used largely as a sanity check on the earnings-based multiples discussed above.

In certain sectors, however, as well as for companies with little or no earnings, EV/sales may be relied upon as a meaningful reference point for valuation. For example, EV/sales may be used to value an early stage technology company that is aggressively growing sales, but has yet to achieve profitability.

EXHIBIT 1.32 Enterprise Value-to-Sales

Comparable Companies Analysis

Sector-Specific Multiples Many sectors employ specific valuation multiples in addition to, or instead of, the traditional metrics previously discussed. These multiples use an indicator of market valuation in the numerator and a key sector-specific financial, operating, or production/capacity statistic in the denominator. Selected examples are shown in Exhibit 1.33. Bloomberg provides many data sets and analyses specific to individual industries via Bloomberg Industries (BI<GO>). Appendix 1.6 displays an example of comparable companies for Basic & Diversified Chemicals, in which P/E, EV/EBITDA, and P/FCF are displayed.

EXHIBIT 1.33 Selected Sector-Specific Valuation Multiples

Valuation Multiple	Sector
Enterprise Value /	
Access Lines/Fiber Miles/Route Miles	▪ Telecommunications
Broadcast Cash Flow (BCF)	▪ Media ▪ Telecommunications
Earnings Before Interest Taxes, Depreciation, Amortization, and Rent Expense (EBITDAR)	▪ Casinos ▪ Restaurants ▪ Retail
Earnings Before Interest Taxes, Depreciation, Depletion, Amortization, and Exploration Expense (EBITDAX)	▪ Natural Resources ▪ Oil & Gas
Population (POP)	▪ Metals & Mining ▪ Natural Resources ▪ Oil & Gas ▪ Paper and Forest Products
Reserves	▪ Metals & Mining ▪ Natural Resources ▪ Oil & Gas
Square Footage	▪ Real Estate ▪ Retail
Subscriber	▪ Media ▪ Telecommunications
Equity Value (Price) /	
Book Value (per share)	▪ Financial Institutions ▪ Homebuilders
Cash Available for Distribution (per share)	▪ Real Estate
Discretionary Cash Flow (per share)	▪ Natural Resources
Funds from Operations (FFO) (per share)	▪ Real Estate
Net Asset Value (NAV) (per share)	▪ Financial Institutions ▪ Mining ▪ Real Estate

STEP IV. BENCHMARK THE COMPARABLE COMPANIES

Once the initial universe of comparable companies is selected and key financial statistics, ratios, and trading multiples are spread, the banker is set to perform benchmarking analysis. Benchmarking centers on analyzing and comparing each of the comparable companies with one another and the target. The ultimate objective is to determine the target's relative ranking so as to frame valuation accordingly. While the entire universe provides a useful perspective, the banker typically hones in on a selected group of closest comparables as the basis for establishing the target's implied valuation range. The closest comparables are generally those most similar to the target in terms of business and financial profile.

We have broken down the benchmarking exercise into a two-stage process. First, we benchmark the key financial statistics and ratios for the target and its comparables in order to establish relative positioning, with a focus on identifying the closest or "best" comparables and noting potential outliers. Second, we analyze and compare the trading multiples for the peer group, placing particular emphasis on the best comparables.

Benchmark the Financial Statistics and Ratios

The first stage of the benchmarking analysis involves a comparison of the target and comparables universe on the basis of key financial performance metrics. These metrics, as captured in the financial profile framework outlined in Steps I and III, include measures of size, profitability, growth, returns, and credit strength. They are core value drivers and typically translate directly into relative valuation. The results of the benchmarking exercise are displayed on spreadsheet output pages that present the data for each company in an easy-to-compare format (see Exhibits 1.53 and 1.54). These pages also display the mean, median, maximum (high), and minimum (low) for the universe's selected financial statistics and ratios.

A thoughtful benchmarking analysis goes beyond a quantitative comparison of the comparables' financial metrics. In order to truly assess the target's relative strength, the banker needs to have a strong understanding of each comparable company's story. For example, what are the reasons for the company's high or low growth rates and profit margins? Is the company a market leader or laggard, gaining or losing market share? Has the company been successful in delivering upon announced strategic initiatives or meeting earnings guidance? Has the company announced any recent M&A transactions or significant ownership/management changes? The ability to interpret these issues, in combination with the above-mentioned financial analysis, is critical to assessing the performance of the comparable companies and determining the target's relative position.

Benchmark the Trading Multiples

The trading multiples for the comparables universe are also displayed on a spreadsheet output page for easy comparison and analysis (see Exhibit 1.55). This enables the banker to view the full range of multiples and assess relative valuation for each of the comparable companies. As with the financial statistics and ratios, the means, medians, highs, and lows for the range of multiples are calculated and displayed, providing a preliminary reference point for establishing the target's valuation range.

Once the trading multiples have been analyzed, the banker conducts a further refining of the comparables universe. Depending on the resulting output, it may become apparent that certain outliers need to be excluded from the analysis or that the comparables should be further tiered (e.g., on the basis of size, sub-sector, or ranging from closest to peripheral). The trading multiples for the best comparables are also noted as they are typically assigned greater emphasis for framing valuation.

STEP V. DETERMINE VALUATION

The trading multiples for the comparable companies serve as the basis for deriving an appropriate valuation range for the target. The banker typically begins by using the means and medians of the most relevant multiple for the sector (e.g., EV/EBITDA or P/E) to extrapolate a defensible range of multiples. The high and low multiples of the comparables universe provide further guidance. The multiples of the best comparables, however, are typically relied upon as guideposts for selecting the tightest, most appropriate range.

Consequently, as few as two or three carefully selected comparables often serve as the ultimate basis for valuation, with the broader group providing reference points. Hence, the selected multiple range is typically tighter than that implied by simply taking the high and low multiples for the universe. As part of this exercise, the banker must also determine which period financial data is most relevant for calculating the trading multiples. Depending on the sector, point in the business cycle, and comfort with consensus estimates, the comparable companies may be trading on the basis of LTM, one-year forward, or even two-year forward financials.

As shown in the illustrative example in Exhibit 1.34, the target has three closest comparables that trade in the range of approximately 6.5x to 7.5x 2012E EBITDA, versus a high/low range of 5.5x to 8.5x, a mean of 7.0x and a median of 6.8x.

EXHIBIT 1.34 Selected Enterprise Value-to-EBITDA Multiple Range

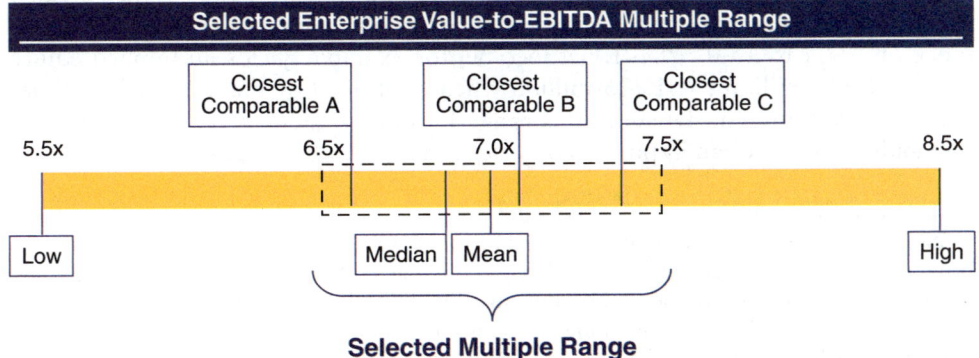

The selected multiple range is then applied to the target's appropriate financial statistics to derive an implied valuation range.

Valuation Implied by EV/EBITDA

Exhibit 1.35 demonstrates how a given EV/EBITDA multiple range translates into an implied range for enterprise value, equity value, and share price. For these calculations, we assume net debt[54] of $500 million and fully diluted shares outstanding of 100 million.[55]

EXHIBIT 1.35 Valuation Implied by EV/EBITDA

($ in millions, except per share data)

EBITDA	Financial Metric	Multiple Range			Implied Enterprise Value	Less: Net Debt	Implied Equity Value	Fully Diluted Shares	Implied Share Price
LTM	$200	7.0x	–	8.0x	$1,400 – $1,600	(500)	$900 – $1,100	100	$9.00 – $11.00
2012E	215	6.5x	–	7.5x	1,398 – 1,613	(500)	898 – 1,113	100	$8.98 – $11.13
2013E	230	6.0x	–	7.0x	1,380 – 1,610	(500)	880 – 1,110	100	$8.80 – $11.10

At a 6.5x to 7.5x multiple range for 2012E EBITDA, the endpoints are multiplied by the target's 2012E EBITDA of $215 million to produce an implied enterprise value range of $1,398 million to $1,613 million.

To calculate implied equity value, we subtract net debt of $500 million from enterprise value, which results in a range of $898 million to $1,113 million. For public companies, the implied equity value is then divided by fully diluted shares outstanding to yield implied share price. Dividing the endpoints of the equity value range by fully diluted shares outstanding of 100 million provides an implied share price range of $8.98 to $11.13. The same methodology can then be performed using the selected multiple range for EV/LTM EBITDA and EV/2013E EBITDA.

Valuation Implied by P/E

Exhibits 1.36 and 1.37 demonstrate how the P/E ratio translates into implied share price and enterprise value ranges. As with the example in Exhibit 1.35, we assume net debt of $500 million and a static fully diluted shares outstanding count of 100 million.

Implied Share Price For a public company, the banker typically begins with net income and builds up to implied equity value. The implied equity value is then divided by fully diluted shares outstanding to calculate implied share price. A P/E multiple range of 12.0x to 15.0x 2012E net income, for example, yields an implied equity value of $900 million to $1,125 million when multiplied by the target's 2012E net income of $75 million. Dividing this range by fully diluted shares outstanding of 100 million produces an implied share price range of $9.00 to $11.25.

---

[54]"Net debt" is often defined to include all obligations senior to common equity.
[55]For illustrative purposes, we assume that the number of fully diluted shares outstanding remains constant for each of the equity values presented. As discussed in Chapter 3: Discounted Cash Flow Analysis, however, assuming the existence of stock options, the number of fully diluted shares outstanding as determined by the TSM is dependent on share price, which in turn is dependent on equity value and shares outstanding (see Exhibit 3.31). Therefore, the target's fully diluted shares outstanding and implied share price vary in accordance with its amount of stock options and their weighted average exercise price.

Comparable Companies Analysis

EXHIBIT 1.36 Valuation Implied by P/E – Share Price

($ in millions, except per share data)

Net Income	Financial Metric	Multiple Range			Implied Equity Value			Fully Diluted Shares	Implied Share Price		
LTM	$70	13.0x	–	16.0x	$910	–	$1,120	100	$9.10	–	$11.20
2012E	75	12.0x	–	15.0x	900	–	1,125	100	$9.00	–	$11.25
2013E	80	11.0x	–	14.0x	880	–	1,120	100	$8.80	–	$11.20

Implied Enterprise Value To calculate an implied enterprise value range using the assumptions above, the same P/E multiple range of 12.0x to 15.0x is multiplied by 2012E net income of $75 million to produce an implied equity value range of $900 million to $1,125 million. Net debt of $500 million is added to the low and high endpoints of the implied equity value range to calculate an implied enterprise value range of $1,400 million to $1,625 million.

EXHIBIT 1.37 Valuation Implied by P/E – Enterprise Value

($ in millions)

Net Income	Financial Metric	Multiple Range			Implied Equity Value			Plus: Net Debt	Implied Enterprise Value		
LTM	$70	13.0x	–	16.0x	$910	–	$1,120	500	$1,410	–	$1,620
2012E	75	12.0x	–	15.0x	900	–	1,125	500	1,400	–	1,625
2013E	80	11.0x	–	14.0x	880	–	1,120	500	1,380	–	1,620

As a final consideration, it is necessary to analyze the extrapolated valuation range for the target and test the key assumptions and conclusions. The banker should also compare the valuation derived from comparable companies to other methodologies, such as precedent transactions, DCF analysis, and LBO analysis (if applicable). Significant discrepancies may signal incorrect assumptions, misjudgment, or even mathematical error, thereby prompting the banker to re-examine the inputs and assumptions used in each technique. Common errors in trading comps typically involve the inclusion or over-emphasis of inappropriate comparable companies, incorrect calculations (e.g., fully diluted equity value, enterprise value, LTM financial data, or calendarization), as well as the failure to accurately scrub the financials for non-recurring items and recent events.

KEY PROS AND CONS

Pros

- *Market-based* – information used to derive valuation for the target is based on actual public market data, thereby reflecting the market's growth and risk expectations, as well as overall sentiment
- *Relativity* – easily measurable and comparable versus other companies
- *Quick and convenient* – valuation can be determined on the basis of a few easy-to-calculate inputs
- *Current* – valuation is based on prevailing market data, which can be updated on a daily (or intraday) basis

Cons

- *Market-based* – valuation that is completely market-based can be skewed during periods of irrational exuberance or bearishness
- *Absence of relevant comparables* – "pure play" comparables may be difficult to identify or even non-existent, especially if the target operates in a niche sector, in which case the valuation implied by trading comps may be less meaningful
- *Potential disconnect from cash flow* – valuation based on prevailing market conditions or expectations may have significant disconnect from the valuation implied by a company's projected cash flow generation (e.g., DCF analysis)
- *Company-specific issues* – valuation of the target is based on the valuation of other companies, which may fail to capture target-specific strengths, weaknesses, opportunities, and risks

ILLUSTRATIVE COMPARABLE COMPANIES ANALYSIS FOR VALUECO

The following section provides a detailed, step-by-step example of how comparable companies analysis is used to establish a valuation range for our illustrative target company, ValueCo. For the purposes of Chapters 1 through 6, we assume that ValueCo is a private company and that the financial statistics and valuation multiples throughout the book represent normalized economic and market conditions.

Step I. Select the Universe of Comparable Companies

Study the Target Our first task was to learn ValueCo's "story" in as much detail as possible so as to provide a frame of reference for locating comparable companies. As ValueCo is a private company, for the purposes of this exercise we assumed that it is being sold through an organized M&A sale process (see Chapter 6). Therefore, we were provided with substantive information on the company, its sector, products, customers, competitors, distribution channels, and end markets, as well as historical financial performance and projections. We sourced this information from the confidential information memorandum (CIM, see Exhibit 6.5), management presentation (see Exhibit 6.6), and data room, such as those provided by Intralinks (see Exhibit 6.7).[56]

Identify Key Characteristics of the Target for Comparison Purposes This exercise involved examining ValueCo's key business and financial characteristics in accordance with the framework outlined in Exhibit 1.3, which provided us with a systematic approach for identifying companies that shared key similarities with ValueCo.

Screen for Comparable Companies Our search for comparable companies began by examining ValueCo's public competitors, which we initially identified by perusing the CIM as well as selected industry reports. We then searched through equity research reports on these public competitors for the analysts' views on comparable companies, which provided us with additional companies to evaluate. We also reviewed the proxy statements for recent M&A transactions involving companies in ValueCo's sector, and found ideas for additional comparable companies from the enclosed fairness opinion excerpts. To ensure that no potential comparables were missed, we screened companies using SIC/NAICS codes corresponding to ValueCo's sector.

These sources provided us with enough information to create a solid initial list of comparable companies (see Exhibit 1.38). We also compiled summary financial information using Bloomberg in order to provide a basic understanding of their financial profiles.

---

[56]See Chapter 6: Sell-Side M&A for an overview of the key documents and sources of information in an organized sale process.

EXHIBIT 1.38 List of Comparable Companies

($ in millions)

List of Comparable Companies

Company	Ticker	Business Description	Equity Value	Enterprise Value	LTM Sales	LTM EBITDA
BuyerCo	BUY	Produces chemicals and advanced materials including acetyl, acetate, vinyl emulsion, and engineered polymers	$9,800	$11,600	$6,560	$1,443
Falloon Group	FLN	Manufactures differentiated and commodity chemical products including those in adhesives, aerospace, automotive, and consumer products	7,480	11,254	11,835	1,636
Sherman Co.	SHR	Produces chemicals and plastics including coatings, adhesives, specialty polymers, inks, intermediates, and performance polymers	5,600	8,101	5,895	1,047
Pearl Corp.	PRL	Supplies specialty chemical, construction, and container products for the food, consumer products, petroleum refinery, and construction industries	5,172	5,856	4,284	839
Gasparro Corp.	JDG	Develops various chemical products for use in crop protection, pharmaceuticals, and electronics applications	5,000	6,750	4,725	900
Kumra Inc.	KUM	Manufactures brominated flame retardants, refinery catalysts, and fine chemistry products	4,852	5,345	3,187	665
Goodson Corp.	GDS	Manufactures and markets basic chemicals, vinyls, polymers, and fabricated products	4,160	5,660	4,769	763
Pryor Industries	PRI	Develops and manufactures specialty chemicals for various end users including aerospace, plastics, coatings, and mining industries	3,926	4,166	3,682	569
Lanzarone Global	LNZ	Manufactures plastics and other chemicals including urethane polymers, flame retardants, seed treatment, and petroleum additives	3,230	3,823	3,712	578
McMenamin & Co.	MCM	Manufactures thermoplastic compounds, specialty resins, specialty polymer formulations, engineered films, and additive systems	3,193	3,193	3,223	355
S. Momper & Co.	MOMP	Manufactures chlorine, caustic soda, sodium hydrosulfite, hydrochloric acid, bleach products, and potassium hydroxide	2,240	2,921	2,077	378
Adler Worldwide	ADL	Produces titanium dioxide pigments for paints, plastics, inks, and cosmetics	1,217	1,463	1,550	245
Schachter & Sons	STM	Manufactures and markets chemical and plastic products including electrochemicals, methanol, and aromatic chemicals	1,125	1,674	1,703	238
Girshin Holdings	MGP	Manufactures carbon compounds and wood treatments	1,035	1,298	1,606	177
Crespin International	MCR	Produces engineered polymers and styrenic block copolymers used in adhesives, coatings, consumer, and personal care products	872	1,222	1,443	190

Step II. Locate the Necessary Financial Information

In Step II, we set out to locate the financial information necessary to spread the key financial statistics and ratios for each of the companies that we identified as being comparable to ValueCo. For Gasparro Corp. ("Gasparro"), one of ValueCo's closest comparables, for example, this information was obtained from its most recent SEC filings, consensus estimates, and equity research. Additional financial information was sourced from Bloomberg.

10-K and 10-Q We used Gasparro's most recent 10-K and 10-Q for the periods ending December 31, 2011, and September 30, 2012, respectively, as the primary sources for historical financial information. Specifically, these filings provided us with the prior year annual as well as current and prior year YTD financial statistics necessary to calculate LTM data. They also served as sources for the most recent basic shares outstanding count, options/warrants data, and balance sheet and cash flow statement information. The MD&A and notes to the financials were key for identifying non-recurring items (see Exhibit 1.47).

Earnings Announcement and Earnings Call Transcript We read through the most recent earnings announcement and earnings call transcript to gain further insight on Gasparro's financial performance and outlook.

8-K/Press Releases We confirmed via a search of Gasparro's corporate website that there were no intra-quarter press releases, 8-Ks, or other SEC filings disclosing new M&A, capital markets, or other activities since the filing of its most recent 10-Q that would affect the relevant financial statistics.

Consensus Estimates and Equity Research Consensus estimates formed the basis for the 2012E and 2013E income statement inputs, namely sales, EBITDA, EBIT, and EPS. We also read individual equity research reports for further color on factors driving Gasparro's growth expectations as well as insights on non-recurring items.

Financial Information Service We used Bloomberg to source Gasparro's closing share price on December 20, 2012 (the day we performed the analysis), as well as its 52-week high and low share price data.

Moody's and S&P Websites We obtained the Moody's and S&P credit ratings for Gasparro from the respective credit rating agencies' websites.

Step III. Spread Key Statistics, Ratios, and Trading Multiples

After locating the necessary financial information for the selected comparable companies, we created input sheets for each company, as shown in Exhibit 1.39 for Gasparro. These input sheets link to the output pages used for benchmarking the comparables universe (see Exhibits 1.53, 1.54, and 1.55).

Below, we walk through each section of the input sheet in Exhibit 1.39.

EXHIBIT 1.39 Comparable Companies Analysis—Trading Multiples Output Page

Gasparro Corp. (NYSE:JDG)
Input Page
($ in millions, except per share data)

Business Description
Develops various chemical products for use in crop protection, pharmaceuticals, and electronics applications

General Information

	Gasparro Corp.
Company Name	JDG
Ticker	NYSE
Stock Exchange	Dec-31
Fiscal Year Ending	Baa3
Moody's Corporate Rating	BBB-
S&P Corporate Rating	1.25
Predicted Beta	38.0%
Marginal Tax Rate	

Selected Market Data

		Gasparro Corp.
Current Price	12/20/2012	$50.00
% of 52-week High		80.0%
52-week High Price	7/20/2012	62.50
52-week Low Price	4/5/2012	40.00
Dividend Per Share (MRQ)		0.25
Fully Diluted Shares Outstanding		100.000
Equity Value		**$5,000.0**
Plus: Total Debt		1,850.0
Plus: Preferred Stock		–
Plus: Noncontrolling Interest		–
Less: Cash and Cash Equivalents		(100.0)
Enterprise Value		**$6,750.0**

Trading Multiples

	LTM 9/30/2012	NFY 2012E	NFY+1 2013E	NFY+2 2014E
EV/Sales Metric	1.4x $4,725.0	1.4x $5,000.0	1.3x $5,350.0	1.2x $5,625.0
EV/EBITDA Metric	7.5x $900.0	7.1x $950.0	6.6x $1,025.0	6.3x $1,075.0
EV/EBIT Metric	9.3x $725.0	8.8x $765.0	8.2x $825.0	7.8x $865.0
P/E Metric	12.9x $3.88	11.2x $4.45	10.0x $5.00	9.1x $5.50
FCF Yield Metric	6.3% $315.0	7.0% $350.0	7.5% $375.0	8.3% $415.0

LTM Return on Investment Ratios
Return on Invested Capital	21.1%
Return on Equity	23.3%
Return on Assets	7.9%
Implied Annual Dividend Per Share	2.0%

LTM Credit Statistics
Debt/Total Capitalization	51.7%
Total Debt/EBITDA	2.1x
Net Debt/EBITDA	1.9x
EBITDA/Interest Expense	9.0x
(EBITDA-capex)/Interest Expense	7.0x
EBIT/Interest Expense	7.3x

Growth Rates

	Sales	EBITDA	FCF	EPS
Historical				
1-year	8.4%	5.1%	13.2%	6.4%
2-year CAGR	9.5%	8.2%	14.2%	11.6%
Estimated				
1-year	11.1%	15.2%	16.7%	31.0%
2-year CAGR	9.0%	11.5%	11.8%	21.3%
Long-term				12.0%

Reported Income Statement

	Fiscal Year Ending December 31,			Prior Stub 9/30/2011	Current Stub 9/30/2012	LTM 9/30/2012
	2009A	2010A	2011A			
Sales	$3,750.0	$4,150.0	$4,500.0	$3,375.0	$3,600.0	$4,725.0
COGS (incl. D&A)	2,450.0	2,700.0	2,925.0	2,200.0	2,350.0	3,075.0
Gross Profit	$1,300.0	$1,450.0	$1,575.0	$1,175.0	$1,250.0	$1,650.0
SG&A	750.0	830.0	900.0	675.0	720.0	945.0
Other Expense / (Income)	–	–	–	–	–	–
EBIT	$550.0	$620.0	$675.0	$500.0	$530.0	$705.0
Interest Expense	110.0	105.0	102.0	75.0	73.0	100.0
Pre-tax Income	$440.0	$515.0	$573.0	$425.0	$457.0	$605.0
Income Taxes	167.2	195.7	217.7	161.5	173.7	229.9
Noncontrolling Interest	–	–	–	–	–	–
Preferred Dividends	–	–	–	–	–	–
Net Income	$272.8	$319.3	$355.3	$263.5	$283.3	$375.1
Effective Tax Rate	*38.0%*	*38.0%*	*38.0%*	*38.0%*	*38.0%*	*38.0%*
Weighted Avg. Diluted Shares	100.0	100.0	100.0	100.0	100.0	100.0
Diluted EPS	$2.73	$3.19	$3.55	$2.64	$2.83	$3.75

Adjusted Income Statement

	2009A	2010A	2011A	Prior Stub 9/30/2011	Current Stub 9/30/2012	LTM 9/30/2012
Reported Gross Profit	$1,300.0	$1,450.0	$1,575.0	$1,175.0	$1,250.0	$1,650.0
Non-recurring Items in COGS	–	–	–	–	30.0	30.0 (1)
Adj. Gross Profit	$1,300.0	$1,450.0	$1,575.0	$1,175.0	$1,280.0	$1,680.0
% margin	*34.7%*	*34.9%*	*35.0%*	*34.8%*	*35.6%*	*35.6%*
Reported EBIT	$550.0	$620.0	$675.0	$500.0	$530.0	$705.0
Non-recurring Items in COGS	–	–	–	–	30.0	30.0
Other Non-recurring Items	–	–	(25.0)*	–	15.0	(10.0) (2), (3)
Adjusted EBIT	$550.0	$620.0	$650.0	$500.0	$575.0	$725.0
% margin	*14.7%*	*14.9%*	*14.4%*	*14.8%*	*16.0%*	*15.3%*
Depreciation & Amortization	155.0	165.0	175.0	125.0	125.0	175.0
Adjusted EBITDA	$705.0	$785.0	$825.0	$625.0	$700.0	$900.0
% margin	*18.8%*	*18.9%*	*18.3%*	*18.5%*	*19.4%*	*19.0%*
Reported Net Income	$272.8	$319.3	$355.3	$263.5	$283.3	$375.1
Non-recurring Items in COGS	–	–	–	–	30.0	30.0
Other Non-recurring Items	–	–	(25.0)*	–	15.0	(10.0)
Non-operating Non-rec. Items	–	–	9.5	–	(17.1)	(7.6)
Tax Adjustment	$272.8	$319.3	$339.8	$263.5	$311.2	$387.5
Adjusted Net Income						
% margin	*7.3%*	*7.7%*	*7.6%*	*7.8%*	*8.6%*	*8.2%*
Adjusted Diluted EPS	$2.73	$3.19	$3.40	$2.64	$3.11	$3.88

Cash Flow Statement Data

	2009A	2010A	2011A	Prior Stub 9/30/2011	Current Stub 9/30/2012	LTM 9/30/2012
Cash From Operations	400.0	450.0	500.0	360.0	380.0	520.0
Capital Expenditures	170.0	185.0	200.0	150.0	155.0	205.0
% sales	*4.5%*	*4.5%*	*4.4%*	*4.4%*	*4.3%*	*4.3%*
Free Cash Flow	$230.0	$265.0	$300.0	$210.0	$225.0	$315.0
% margin	*6.1%*	*6.4%*	*6.7%*	*6.2%*	*6.3%*	*6.7%*
FCF / Share	$2.30	$2.65	$3.00	$2.10	$2.25	$3.15
Depreciation & Amortization	155.0	165.0	175.0	125.0	125.0	175.0
% sales	*4.1%*	*4.0%*	*3.9%*	*3.7%*	*3.5%*	*3.7%*

Notes
(1) In Q2 2012, Gasparro Corp. recorded a $30 million pre-tax inventory valuation charge related to product obsolescence (see Q2 2012 10-Q MD&A, page 14).
(2) In Q4 2011, Gasparro Corp. realized a $25 million pre-tax gain on the sale of a non-core business (see 2011 10-K MD&A, page 45).
(3) In Q3 2012, Gasparro Corp. recognized $15 million of pre-tax restructuring costs in connection with the closure of a manufacturing facility (see Q3 2012 10-Q MD&A, page 15).

Balance Sheet Data

	2011A	9/30/2012
Cash and Cash Equivalents	$75.0	$100.0
Accounts Receivable	625.0	650.0
Inventories	730.0	750.0
Prepaids and Other Current Assets	225.0	250.0
Total Current Assets	**$1,655.0**	**$1,750.0**
Property, Plant and Equipment, net	1,970.0	2,000.0
Goodwill and Intangible Assets	775.0	800.0
Other Assets	425.0	450.0
Total Assets	**$4,825.0**	**$5,000.0**
Accounts Payable	275.0	300.0
Accrued Liabilities	450.0	475.0
Other Current Liabilities	125.0	150.0
Total Current Liabilities	**$850.0**	**$925.0**
Total Debt	1,875.0	1,850.0
Other Long-Term Liabilities	500.0	500.0
Total Liabilities	**$3,225.0**	**$3,275.0**
Noncontrolling Interest	–	–
Preferred Stock	–	–
Shareholders' Equity	1,600.0	1,725.0
Total Liabilities and Equity	**$4,825.0**	**$5,000.0**
Balance Check	0.000	0.000

Calculation of Fully Diluted Shares Outstanding

Basic Shares Outstanding	98.500
Plus: Shares from In-the-Money Options	2.750
Less: Shares Repurchased	(1.250)
Net New Shares from Options	1.500
Plus: Shares from Convertible Securities	–
Fully Diluted Shares Outstanding	**100.000**

Options/Warrants

Tranche	Number of Shares	Exercise Price	In-the-Money Shares	Proceeds
Tranche 1	1.250	$10.00	1.250	$12.5
Tranche 2	1.000	30.00	1.000	30.0
Tranche 3	0.500	40.00	0.500	20.0
Tranche 4	0.250	60.00	–	–
Tranche 5	–	–	–	–
Total	**3.000**		**2.750**	**$62.5**

Convertible Securities

Issue	Amount	Conversion Price	Conversion Ratio	New Shares
Issue 1	–	–	–	–
Issue 2	–	–	–	–
Issue 3	–	–	–	–
Issue 4	–	–	–	–
Issue 5	–	–	–	–
Total				–

Comparable Companies Analysis

General Information In the "General Information" section of the input page, we entered various basic company data (see Exhibit 1.40). Gasparro Corp., ticker symbol JDG, is a U.S.-based company that is listed on the NYSE. Gasparro reports its financial results based on a fiscal year ending December 31 and has corporate credit ratings of Baa3 and BBB– as rated by Moody's and S&P, respectively. Gasparro's predicted levered beta is 1.25, as sourced from Bloomberg (see Chapter 3). We also determined a 38% marginal tax rate from Gasparro's tax rate disclosures in its 10-K.

EXHIBIT 1.40 General Information Section

General Information	
Company Name	Gasparro Corp.
Ticker	JDG
Stock Exchange	NYSE
Fiscal Year Ending	Dec-31
Moody's Corporate Rating	Baa3
S&P Corporate Rating	BBB-
Predicted Beta	1.25
Marginal Tax Rate	38.0%

Selected Market Data Under "Selected Market Data," we entered Gasparro's share price information as well as the most recent quarterly (MRQ) dividend paid of $0.25 per share (as sourced from the latest 10-Q, see Exhibit 1.41). Gasparro's share price was $50.00 as of market close on December 20, 2012, representing 80% of its 52-week high. As the trading multiples benchmarking output page shows (see Exhibit 1.55), this percentage is consistent with that of most of the comparables, which indicates that the market expects Gasparro to perform roughly in line with its peers.

This section also calculates equity value and enterprise value once the appropriate basic shares outstanding count, options/warrants data, and most recent balance sheet data are entered (see Exhibits 1.42, 1.43, 1.44, and 1.45).

EXHIBIT 1.41 Selected Market Data Section

($ in millions, except per share data)

Selected Market Data			
Current Price	12/20/2012	$50.00	= Closing Share Price on December 20, 2012
% of 52-week High		80.0%	
52-week High Price	7/20/2012	62.50	= Closing Share Price / 52-week High Price
52-week Low Price	4/5/2012	40.00	
Dividend Per Share (MRQ)		0.25	
Fully Diluted Shares Outstanding		-	
Equity Value		-	
Plus: Total Debt		-	
Plus: Preferred Stock		-	
Plus: Noncontrolling Interest		-	
Less: Cash and Cash Equivalents		-	
Enterprise Value		-	

Calculation of Fully Diluted Shares Outstanding Gasparro's most recent basic shares outstanding count is 98.5 million, as sourced from the first page of its latest 10-Q. We searched recent press releases and SEC filings to ensure that no stock splits, follow-on offerings, or major share buybacks, for example, took place following the most recent 10-Q filing. We also confirmed that Gasparro does not have convertible securities outstanding. However, Gasparro has several tranches of options, which must be reflected in the calculation of fully diluted shares in accordance with the TSM.

As shown in Exhibit 1.42 under the "Options/Warrants" heading, Gasparro has four tranches of options, each consisting of a specified number of shares and corresponding weighted average exercise price. The first tranche, for example, represents a group of options collectively owning the right to buy 1.25 million shares at a weighted average exercise price of $10.00. This tranche is deemed in-the-money given that Gasparro's current share price of $50.00 is above the weighted average strike price. The exercise of this tranche generates proceeds of $12.5 million (1.25 million × $10.00), which are assumed to repurchase Gasparro shares at the current share price of $50.00.

EXHIBIT 1.42 Calculation of Fully Diluted Shares Outstanding Section

($ in millions, except per share data)

Calculation of Fully Diluted Shares Outstanding

Basic Shares Outstanding	98.500
Plus: Shares from In-the-Money Options	2.750
Less: Shares Repurchased	(1.250)
Net New Shares from Options	1.500
Plus: Shares from Convertible Securities	-
Fully Diluted Shares Outstanding	100.000

- 98.500 = Total In-the-Money Shares
- (1.250) = Total Option Proceeds / Current Share Price = $62.5 million / $50.00

Options/Warrants

Tranche	Number of Shares	Exercise Price	In-the-Money Shares	Proceeds
Tranche 1	1.250	$10.00	1.250	$12.5
Tranche 2	1.000	30.00	1.000	30.0
Tranche 3	0.500	40.00	0.500	20.0
Tranche 4	0.250	60.00	-	-
Tranche 5	-	-	-	-
Total	3.000	-	2.750	$62.5

In-the-Money Shares: = IF(Weighted Average Strike Price < Current Share Price, display Number of Shares, otherwise display 0)
= IF($10.00 < $50.00, 1.250, 0)

Proceeds: = IF(In-the-Money Shares > 0, then In-the-Money Shares x Weighted Average Strike Price, otherwise display 0)
= IF(1.250 > 0, 1.250 x $10.00, 0)

Convertible Securities

	Conversion Amount	Conversion Price	Conversion Ratio	New Shares
Issue 1	-	-	-	-
Issue 2	-	-	-	-
Issue 3	-	-	-	-
Issue 4	-	-	-	-
Issue 5	-	-	-	-
Total	-	-	-	-

We utilized this same approach for the other tranches of options. The fourth tranche, however, has a weighted average exercise price of $60.00 (above the current share price of $50.00) and was therefore identified as out-of-the-money. Consequently, these options were excluded from the calculation of fully diluted shares outstanding.

In aggregate, the 2.75 million shares from the in-the-money options generate proceeds of $62.5 million. At Gasparro's current share price of $50.00, these proceeds are used to repurchase 1.25 million shares ($62.5 million/$50.00). The repurchased shares are then subtracted from the 2.75 million total in-the-money shares to provide net new shares of 1.5 million, as shown under the net new shares from options line item in Exhibit 1.42. These incremental shares are added to Gasparro's basic shares to calculate fully diluted shares outstanding of 100 million.

Equity Value The 100 million fully diluted shares outstanding output feeds into the "Selected Market Data" section, where it is multiplied by Gasparro's current share price of $50.00 to produce an equity value of $5,000 million (see Exhibit 1.43). This calculated equity value forms the basis for calculating enterprise value.

EXHIBIT 1.43 Equity Value

($ in millions, except per share data)

Selected Market Data		
Current Price	12/20/2012	$50.00
% of 52-week High		80.0%
52-week High Price	7/20/2012	62.50
52-week Low Price	4/5/2012	40.00
Dividend Per Share (MRQ)		0.25
Fully Diluted Shares Outstanding		100.000
Equity Value		**$5,000.0**
Plus: Total Debt		-
Plus: Preferred Stock		-
Plus: Noncontrolling Interest		-
Less: Cash and Cash Equivalents		-
Enterprise Value		-

= Current Share Price × Fully Diluted Shares Outstanding
= $50.00 × 100 million

Balance Sheet Data In the "Balance Sheet Data" section, we entered Gasparro's balance sheet data for the prior fiscal year ending 12/31/2011 and the most recent quarter ending 9/30/2012, as sourced directly from its 10-Q (see Exhibit 1.44).

EXHIBIT 1.44 Balance Sheet Data Section

($ in millions)

Balance Sheet Data	2011A	9/30/2012
Cash and Cash Equivalents	$75.0	$100.0
Accounts Receivable	625.0	650.0
Inventories	730.0	750.0
Prepaids and Other Current Assets	225.0	250.0
Total Current Assets	**$1,655.0**	**$1,750.0**
Property, Plant and Equipment, net	1,970.0	2,000.0
Goodwill and Intangible Assets	775.0	800.0
Other Assets	425.0	450.0
Total Assets	**$4,825.0**	**$5,000.0**
Accounts Payable	275.0	300.0
Accrued Liabilities	450.0	475.0
Other Current Liabilities	125.0	150.0
Total Current Liabilities	**$850.0**	**$925.0**
Total Debt	1,875.0	1,850.0
Other Long-Term Liabilities	500.0	500.0
Total Liabilities	**$3,225.0**	**$3,275.0**
Noncontrolling Interest	-	-
Preferred Stock	-	-
Shareholders' Equity	1,600.0	1,725.0
Total Liabilities and Equity	**$4,825.0**	**$5,000.0**
Balance Check	0.000	0.000

Enterprise Value We used selected balance sheet data, specifically total debt and cash, together with the previously calculated equity value to determine Gasparro's enterprise value. As shown in Exhibit 1.45, Gasparro had $1,850 million of total debt outstanding and cash and cash equivalents of $100 million as of 9/30/2012. The net debt balance of $1,750 million was added to equity value of $5,000 million to produce an enterprise value of $6,750 million.

Comparable Companies Analysis

EXHIBIT 1.45 Enterprise Value

($ in millions, except per share data)

Selected Market Data		
Current Price	12/20/2012	$50.00
% of 52-week High		80.0%
52-week High Price	7/20/2012	62.50
52-week Low Price	4/5/2012	40.00
Dividend Per Share (MRQ)		0.25
Fully Diluted Shares Outstanding		100.000
Equity Value		**$5,000.0**
Plus: Total Debt		1,850.0
Plus: Preferred Stock		-
Plus: Noncontrolling Interest		-
Less: Cash and Cash Equivalents		(100.0)
Enterprise Value		**$6,750.0**

= Equity Value + Total Debt - Cash
= $5,000 million + $1,850 million - $100 million

Reported Income Statement In the "Reported Income Statement" section, we entered the historical income statement items directly from Gasparro's most recent 10-K and 10-Q. The LTM column automatically calculates Gasparro's LTM financial data on the basis of the prior annual year, and the prior and current year stub inputs (see Exhibit 1.46).

EXHIBIT 1.46 Reported Income Statement Section

($ in millions, except per share data)

Reported Income Statement				Prior Stub	Current Stub	LTM
	Fiscal Year Ending December 31,			9/30/2011	9/30/2012	9/30/2012
	2009A	2010A	2011A			
Sales	$3,750.0	$4,150.0	$4,500.0	$3,375.0	$3,600.0	$4,725.0
COGS (incl. D&A)	2,450.0	2,700.0	2,925.0	2,200.0	2,350.0	3,075.0
Gross Profit	$1,300.0	$1,450.0	$1,575.0	$1,175.0	$1,250.0	$1,650.0
SG&A	750.0	830.0	900.0	675.0	720.0	945.0
Other Expense / (Income)	-	-	-	-	-	-
EBIT	$550.0	$620.0	$675.0	$500.0	$530.0	$705.0
Interest Expense	110.0	105.0	102.0	75.0	73.0	100.0
Pre-tax Income	$440.0	$515.0	$573.0	$425.0	$457.0	$605.0
Income Taxes	167.2	195.7	217.7	161.5	173.7	229.9
Noncontrolling Interest	-	-	-	-	-	-
Preferred Dividends	-	-	-	-	-	-
Net Income	$272.8	$319.3	$355.3	$263.5	$283.3	$375.1
Effective Tax Rate	38.0%	38.0%	38.0%	38.0%	38.0%	38.0%
Weighted Avg. Diluted Shares	100.0	100.0	100.0	100.0	100.0	100.0
Diluted EPS	$2.73	$3.19	$3.55	$2.64	$2.83	$3.75

= Prior Fiscal Year + Current Stub - Prior Stub
= $4,500 million + $3,600 million - $3,375 million

VALUATION

Adjusted Income Statement After entering the reported income statement, we made adjustments in the "Adjusted Income Statement" section, as appropriate, for those items we determined to be non-recurring (see Exhibit 1.47), namely:

- $25 million pre-tax gain on the sale of a non-core business in Q4 2011
- $30 million pre-tax inventory valuation charge in Q2 2012 related to product obsolescence
- $15 million pre-tax restructuring charge in Q3 2012 related to severance costs

As the adjustments for non-recurring items relied on judgment, we carefully footnoted our assumptions and sources.

EXHIBIT 1.47 Adjusted Income Statement Section

($ in millions, except per share data)

Adjusted Income Statement

	Fiscal Year Ending December 31,			Prior Stub	Current Stub	LTM
	2009A	2010A	2011A	9/30/2011	9/30/2012	9/30/2012
Reported Gross Profit	$1,300.0	$1,450.0	$1,575.0	$1,175.0	$1,250.0	$1,650.0
Non-recurring Items in COGS	-	-	-	-	30.0	30.0 (1)
Adj. Gross Profit	**$1,300.0**	**$1,450.0**	**$1,575.0**	**$1,175.0**	**$1,280.0**	**$1,680.0**
% margin	34.7%	34.9%	35.0%	34.8%	35.6%	35.6%
Reported EBIT	$550.0	$620.0	$675.0	$500.0	$530.0	$705.0
Non-recurring Items in COGS	-	-	-	-	-	30.0
Other Non-recurring Items	-	-	(25.0)	-	15.0	(10.0) (2), (3)
Adjusted EBIT	**$550.0**	**$620.0**	**$650.0**	**$500.0**	**$575.0**	**$725.0**
% margin	14.7%	14.9%	14.4%	14.8%	16.0%	15.3%
Depreciation & Amortization	155.0	165.0	175.0	125.0	125.0	175.0
Adjusted EBITDA	**$705.0**	**$785.0**	**$825.0**	**$625.0**	**$700.0**	**$900.0**
% margin	18.8%	18.9%	18.3%	18.5%	19.4%	19.0%
Reported Net Income	$272.8	$319.3	$355.3	$263.5	$283.3	$375.1
Non-recurring Items in COGS	-	-	-	-	30.0	30.0
Other Non-recurring Items	-	-	(25.0)	-	15.0	(10.0)
Non-operating Non-rec. Items	-	-	-	-	-	-
Tax Adjustment	-	-	9.5	-	(17.1)	(7.6)
Adjusted Net Income	**$272.8**	**$319.3**	**$339.8**	**$263.5**	**$311.2**	**$387.5**
% margin	7.3%	7.7%	7.6%	7.8%	8.6%	8.2%
Adjusted Diluted EPS	$2.73	$3.19	$3.40	$2.64	$3.11	$3.88

Notes
(1) In Q2 2012, Gasparro Corp. recorded a $30 million pre-tax inventory valuation charge related to product obsolescence (see Q2 2012 10-Q MD&A, page 14).
(2) In Q4 2011, Gasparro Corp. realized a $25 million pre-tax gain on the sale of a non-core business (see 2011 10-K MD&A, page 45).
(3) In Q3 2012, Gasparro Corp. recognized $15 million of pre-tax restructuring costs in connection with the closure of a manufacturing facility (see Q3 2012 10-Q MD&A, page 15).

= Negative adjustment for pre-tax gain on asset sale × Marginal tax rate
= - ($25) million × 38%

= Add-back for pre-tax inventory and restructuring charges × Marginal tax rate
= - ($30 million + $15 million) × 38%

As shown in Exhibit 1.47, we entered the $30 million non-recurring product obsolescence charge as an add-back in the non-recurring items in COGS line item under the "Current Stub 9/30/2012" column heading. We also added back the $15 million restructuring charge in the other non-recurring items line under the "Current Stub 9/30/2012" column. The $25 million gain on asset sale, on the other hand, was backed out of reported earnings (entered as a negative value) under the "2011A" column. These calculations resulted in adjusted LTM EBIT and EBITDA of $725 million and $900 million, respectively.

To calculate LTM adjusted net income after adding back the full non-recurring charges of $30 million and $15 million, respectively, and subtracting the full $25 million gain on sale amount, we made tax adjustments in the tax adjustment line item. These adjustments were calculated by multiplying each full amount by Gasparro's marginal tax rate of 38%. This resulted in adjusted net income and diluted EPS of $387.5 million and $3.88, respectively. The adjusted financial statistics then served as the basis for calculating the various LTM profitability ratios, credit statistics, and trading multiples used in the benchmarking analysis (see Exhibits 1.53, 1.54, and 1.55).

Cash Flow Statement Data Gasparro's historical *cash from operations*, D&A, and capex were entered directly into the input page as they appeared in the cash flow statement from its 10-K and 10-Q with adjustments made as necessary for non-recurring items (see Exhibit 1.48). We also calculated free cash flow (FCF) by subtracting capex from cash from operations for each reporting period. This enabled us to calculate a FCF-to-sales margin of 6.7% and FCF per share of $3.15 for LTM 9/30/2012.

EXHIBIT 1.48 Cash Flow Statement Data Section

($ in millions, except per share data)

Cash Flow Statement Data	Fiscal Year Ending December 31,			Prior Stub 9/30/2011	Current Stub 9/30/2012	LTM 9/30/2012
	2009A	2010A	2011A			
Cash From Operations	400.0	450.0	500.0	360.0	380.0	520.0
Capital Expenditures	170.0	185.0	200.0	150.0	155.0	205.0
% sales	4.5%	4.5%	4.4%	4.4%	4.3%	4.3%
Free Cash Flow	**$230.0**	**$265.0**	**$300.0**	**$210.0**	**$225.0**	**$315.0**
% margin	6.1%	6.4%	6.7%	6.2%	6.3%	6.7%
FCF / Share	$2.30	$2.65	$3.00	$2.10	$2.25	$3.15
Depreciation & Amortization	155.0	165.0	175.0	125.0	125.0	175.0
% sales	4.1%	4.0%	3.9%	3.7%	3.5%	3.7%

LTM Return on Investment Ratios

Return on Invested Capital For ROIC, we calculated 21.1% (see Exhibit 1.49) by dividing Gasparro's LTM 9/30/2012 adjusted EBIT of $725 million (as calculated in Exhibit 1.47) by the sum of its average net debt and shareholders' equity balances for the periods ending 12/31/2011 and 9/30/2012 ($725 million / (($1,875 million − $75 million + $1,600 million) + ($1,850 million − $100 million + $1,725 million) / 2)).

Return on Equity For ROE, we calculated 23.3% by dividing Gasparro's LTM 9/30/2012 adjusted net income of $387.5 million (as calculated in Exhibit 1.47) by its average shareholders' equity balance for the periods ending 12/31/2011 and 9/30/2012 (($1,600 million + $1,725 million) / 2).

Return on Assets For ROA, we calculated 7.9% by dividing Gasparro's LTM 9/30/2012 adjusted net income of $387.5 million by its average total assets for the periods ending 12/31/2011 and 9/30/2012 (($4,825 million + $5,000 million) / 2).

Dividend Yield To calculate dividend yield, we annualized Gasparro's dividend payment of $0.25 per share for the most recent quarter (see Exhibit 1.41), which implied an annual dividend payment of $1.00 per share. We checked recent press releases to ensure there were no changes in dividend policy after the filing of the 10-Q. The implied annualized dividend payment of $1.00 per share was then divided by Gasparro's current share price of $50.00 to calculate an implied annual dividend yield of 2%.

EXHIBIT 1.49 LTM Return on Investment Ratios Section

LTM Return on Investment Ratios	
Return on Invested Capital	21.1%
Return on Equity	23.3%
Return on Assets	7.9%
Implied Annual Dividend Per Share	2.0%

= LTM Adjusted EBIT / Average (Total Debt$_{2011}$ - Cash$_{2011}$ + Shareholders' Equity$_{2011}$, Total Debt$_{9/30/2012}$ - Cash$_{9/30/2012}$ + Shareholders' Equity$_{9/30/2012}$)
= $725 million / (($1,875 million - $75 million + $1,600 million) + ($1,850 million - $100 million + $1,725 million) / 2)

= LTM Adjusted Net Income / Average (Shareholders' Equity$_{2011}$, Shareholders' Equity$_{9/30/2012}$)
= $387.5 million / ($1,600 million + $1,725 million) / 2

= LTM Adjusted Net Income / Average (Total Assets$_{2011}$, Total Assets$_{9/30/2012}$)
= $387.5 million / ($4,825 million + $5,000 million) / 2

= (Quarterly Dividend × 4) / Current Share Price
= ($0.25 × 4) / $50.00

LTM Credit Statistics

Debt-to-Total Capitalization For debt-to-total capitalization, we divided Gasparro's total debt of $1,850 million as of 9/30/2012 by the sum of its total debt and shareholders' equity for the same period ($1,850 million + $1,725 million). This provided a debt-to-total capitalization ratio of 51.7% (see Exhibit 1.50).

Total Debt-to-EBITDA For total debt-to-EBITDA, we divided Gasparro's total debt of $1,850 million by its LTM 9/30/2012 adjusted EBITDA of $900 million. This provided a total leverage multiple of 2.1x (1.9x on a net debt basis).

EBITDA-to-Interest Expense For EBITDA-to-interest expense, we divided Gasparro's LTM 9/30/2012 adjusted EBITDA of $900 million by its interest expense of $100 million for the same period. This provided a ratio of 9.0x. We also calculated Gasparro's (EBITDA – capex)-to-interest expense and EBIT-to-interest expense ratios at 7.0x and 7.3x, respectively.

Comparable Companies Analysis

EXHIBIT 1.50 LTM Credit Statistics Section

LTM Credit Statistics	
Debt / Total Capitalization	51.7%
Total Debt / EBITDA	2.1x
Net Debt / EBITDA	1.9x
EBITDA / Interest Expense	9.0x
(EBITDA-capex) / Interest Expense	7.0x
EBIT / Interest Expense	7.3x

= Total Debt$_{9/30/2012}$ / (Total Debt$_{9/30/2012}$ + Shareholders' Equity$_{9/30/2012}$)
= $1,850 million / ($1,850 million + $1,725 million)

= Total Debt$_{9/30/2012}$ / LTM Adjusted EBITDA
= $1,850 million/$900 million

= (Total Debt$_{9/30/2012}$ - Cash$_{9/30/2012}$) / LTM Adjusted EBITDA
= ($1,850 million - $100 million)/$900 million

= LTM Adjusted EBITDA / LTM Interest Expense
= $900 million / $100 million

Trading Multiples

In the "Trading Multiples" section, we entered consensus estimates for Gasparro's 2012E, 2013E, and 2014E sales, EBITDA, EBIT, and EPS (see Exhibit 1.51). These estimates, along with the calculated enterprise and equity values, were used to calculate forward trading multiples. Gasparro's LTM adjusted financial data is also linked to this section and used to calculate trailing trading multiples.

Enterprise Value Multiples For enterprise value-to-LTM EBITDA, we divided Gasparro's enterprise value of $6,750 million by its LTM 9/30/2012 adjusted EBITDA of $900 million, providing a multiple of 7.5x. For EV/2012E EBITDA, we divided the same enterprise value of $6,750 million by Gasparro's 2012E EBITDA of $950 million to calculate a multiple of 7.1x. This same methodology was used for EV/2013E EBITDA and EV/2014E EBITDA, as well as for the trailing and forward sales and EBIT enterprise value multiples.

Price-to-Earnings Ratio The approach for calculating P/E mirrors that for EV/EBITDA. We divided Gasparro's current share price of $50.00 by its LTM, 2012E, 2013E, and 2014E EPS of $3.88, $4.45, $5.00, and $5.50, respectively. These calculations provided P/E ratios of 12.9x, 11.2x, 10.0x, and 9.1x, respectively.

Free Cash Flow Yield Free cash flow (FCF) generation is an important metric for determining valuation. FCF is an indicator of a company's ability to return capital to shareholders or repay debt, which accrues to equity holders. Therefore, many investors focus on FCF yield, calculated as (cash from operations – capex) / market capitalization or FCF per share / share price. Gasparro's FCF yield for LTM, 2012E, 2013E, and 2014E is 6.3%, 7.0%, 7.5%, and 8.3%, respectively.

EXHIBIT 1.51 Trading Multiples Section

($ in millions, except per share data)

Trading Multiples				
	LTM 9/30/2012	NFY 2012E	NFY+1 2013E	NFY+2 2014E
EV/Sales	1.4x	1.4x	1.3x	1.2x
Metric	$4,725.0	$5,000.0	$5,350.0	$5,625.0
EV/EBITDA	7.5x	7.1x	6.6x	6.3x
Metric	$900.0	$950.0	$1,025.0	$1,075.0
EV/EBIT	9.3x	8.8x	8.2x	7.8x
Metric	$725.0	$765.0	$825.0	$865.0
P/E	12.9x	11.2x	10.0x	9.1x
Metric	$3.88	$4.45	$5.00	$5.50
FCF Yield	6.3%	7.0%	7.5%	8.3%
Metric	$315.0	$350.0	$375.0	$415.0

= Enterprise Value / LTM Sales
= $6,750 million / $4,750 million

= Enterprise Value / 2012E EBITDA
= $6,750 million / $950 million

= Current Share Price / 2013E EPS
= $50.00 / $5.00

= 2014E Free Cash Flow / Equity Value
= $415 million / $5,000 million

Growth Rates

In the "Growth Rates" section, we calculated Gasparro's historical and estimated growth rates for sales, EBITDA, and EPS for various periods. For historical data, we used the adjusted income statement financials from Exhibit 1.47. As shown in Exhibit 1.52, Gasparro's EPS grew 6.4% over the past year (1-year historical growth) and at an 11.6% CAGR over the past two years (2-year historical compounded growth).

For the forward growth rates, we used consensus estimates from the "Trading Multiples" section. On a forward year basis, Gasparro's expected EPS growth rate for 2011A to 2012E is 31%, with an expected 2011A to 2013E CAGR of 21.3%. We sourced Gasparro's long-term EPS growth rate of 12%, which is based on equity research analysts' estimates, from consensus estimates.

EXHIBIT 1.52 Growth Rates Section

Growth Rates				
	Sales	EBITDA	FCF	EPS
Historical				
1-year	8.4%	5.1%	13.2%	6.4%
2-year CAGR	9.5%	8.2%	14.2%	11.6%
Estimated				
1-year	11.1%	15.2%	16.7%	31.0%
2-year CAGR	9.0%	11.5%	11.8%	21.3%
Long-term				12.0%

= 2012E Sales / 2011A Sales - 1
= $5,000 million / $4,500 million - 1

= (2013E EBITDA / 2011A Adjusted EBITDA) ^ (1 / (2013E - 2011A)) - 1
= ($1,025 million / $825 million) ^ (1/2) - 1

Step IV. Benchmark the Comparable Companies

After completing Steps I through III, we were prepared to perform the benchmarking analysis for ValueCo.

The first two benchmarking output pages focused on the comparables' financial characteristics, enabling us to determine ValueCo's relative position among its peers for key value drivers (see Exhibits 1.53 and 1.54). This benchmarking analysis, in combination with a review of key business characteristics (outlined in Exhibit 1.3), also enabled us to identify ValueCo's closest comparables—in this case, BuyerCo, Gasparro Corp., and Sherman Co. These closest comparables were instrumental in helping to frame the ultimate valuation range.

Similarly, the benchmarking analysis allowed us to identify outliers, such as McMenamin & Co. and Adler Worldwide among others, which were determined to be less relevant due to their profitability and size, respectively. In this case, we did not eliminate the outliers altogether. Rather, we elected to group the comparable companies into three tiers based on subsector and size—Specialty Chemicals, Commodity/Diversified Chemicals, and Small-Cap Chemicals. The companies in the "Specialty Chemicals" group are more similar to ValueCo in terms of key business and financial characteristics and, therefore, are more relevant in our view. The companies in the "Commodity/Diversified Chemicals" and "Small-Cap Chemicals" groups, however, provided further perspective as part of a more thorough analysis.

We used the output page in Exhibit 1.55 to analyze and compare the trading multiples for ValueCo's comparables. As previously discussed, financial performance typically translates directly into valuation (i.e., the top performers tend to receive a premium valuation to their peers, with laggards trading at a discount). Therefore, we focused on the multiples for ValueCo's closest comparables as the basis for framing valuation.

Exhibit 1.55(a) presents a comparable companies output page in a format preferred by certain equity research analysts and equity investors. Many equity investors focus primarily on free cash flow generation for their valuation and investment decisions.

EXHIBIT 1.53 ValueCo Corporation: Benchmarking Analysis – Financial Statistics and Ratios, Page 1

ValueCo Corporation
Benchmarking Analysis – Financial Statistics and Ratios, Page 1
($ in millions, except per share data)

Company	Ticker	Market Valuation		LTM Financial Statistics					LTM Profitability Margins				Growth Rates							
		Equity Value	Enterprise Value	Sales	Gross Profit	EBITDA	EBIT	Net Income	Gross Profit (%)	EBITDA (%)	EBIT (%)	Net Income (%)	Sales				EBITDA			EPS		
													Hist. 1-year	Est. 1-year	Hist. 1-year	Est. 1-year	Hist. 1-year	Est. 1-year	Hist. 1-year	Est. 1-year	Est. LT
ValueCo Corporation	NA	-	-	$3,385	$1,155	$700	$500	$248	34%	21%	15%	7%	10%	9%	15%	9%	NA	NA	NA	NA
Tier I: Specialty Chemicals																					
BuyerCo	BUY	$9,800	$11,600	$6,560	$2,329	$1,443	$1,279	$705	36%	22%	20%	11%	14%	8%	22%	8%	27%	10%	10%	7%
Sherman Co.	SHR	5,600	8,101	5,895	1,411	1,047	752	419	33%	18%	13%	7%	10%	7%	10%	7%	11%	11%	11%	9%
Pearl Corp.	PRL	5,172	5,856	4,284	1,585	839	625	325	37%	20%	15%	8%	10%	7%	10%	7%	10%	15%	15%	11%
Gasparro Corp.	JDG	5,000	6,750	4,725	1,680	900	725	388	36%	19%	15%	8%	8%	11%	5%	15%	6%	31%	20%	12%
Kumra Inc.	KUM	4,852	5,345	3,187	922	665	506	248	29%	21%	16%	8%	10%	8%	10%	8%	11%	20%	20%	10%
Mean									34%	20%	16%	8%	10%	8%	11%	9%	13%	17%	17%	10%
Median									36%	20%	15%	8%	10%	8%	10%	8%	11%	15%	15%	10%
Tier II: Commodity / Diversified Chemicals																					
Falloon Group	FLN	$7,480	$11,254	$11,835	$3,373	$1,636	$1,044	$465	29%	14%	9%	4%	5%	4%	5%	4%	5%	18%	18%	5%
Goodson Corp.	GDS	4,160	5,660	4,769	1,431	763	525	214	30%	16%	11%	4%	10%	5%	10%	5%	17%	16%	16%	9%
Pryor Industries	PRI	3,926	4,166	3,682	1,178	569	421	227	32%	15%	11%	6%	5%	5%	5%	5%	2%	11%	11%	10%
Lanzarone Global	LNZ	3,230	3,823	3,712	854	578	430	233	23%	16%	12%	6%	5%	5%	4%	5%	4%	16%	16%	8%
McMenamin & Co.	MCM	3,193	3,193	3,223	903	355	226	119	28%	11%	7%	4%	5%	15%	5%	15%	7%	20%	20%	12%
Mean									28%	14%	10%	5%	6%	7%	6%	7%	7%	16%	16%	9%
Median									29%	15%	11%	4%	5%	5%	5%	5%	5%	16%	16%	9%
Tier III: Small-Cap Chemicals																					
S. Momper & Co.	MOMP	$2,240	$2,921	$2,077	$457	$378	$295	$130	22%	18%	14%	6%	5%	11%	5%	11%	7%	8%	8%	5%
Adler Worldwide	ADL	1,217	1,463	1,550	387	245	183	89	25%	16%	12%	6%	5%	5%	5%	5%	7%	8%	8%	7%
Schachter & Sons	STM	1,125	1,674	1,703	426	238	170	76	25%	14%	10%	4%	11%	15%	11%	15%	16%	19%	19%	11%
Girshin Holdings	MGP	1,035	1,298	1,606	273	177	112	52	17%	11%	7%	3%	5%	15%	5%	15%	12%	15%	15%	8%
Crespin International	MCR	872	1,222	1,443	390	190	133	61	27%	13%	9%	4%	5%	15%	4%	14%	5%	10%	10%	6%
Mean									23%	14%	10%	5%	6%	12%	6%	12%	10%	12%	12%	7%
Median									25%	14%	10%	4%	5%	15%	5%	14%	7%	10%	10%	7%
Overall																					
Mean									29%	16%	12%	6%	8%	9%	8%	9%	10%	15%	15%	9%
Median									29%	16%	12%	6%	5%	8%	5%	8%	7%	15%	15%	9%
High									37%	22%	20%	11%	14%	15%	22%	15%	27%	31%	31%	12%
Low									17%	11%	7%	3%	5%	4%	4%	4%	2%	8%	8%	5%

Source: Company filings, Bloomberg, Consensus Estimates
Note: Last twelve months data based on September 30, 2012. Estimated annual financial data based on a calendar year.

EXHIBIT 1.54 ValueCo Corporation: Benchmarking Analysis – Financial Statistics and Ratios, Page 2

ValueCo Corporation
Benchmarking Analysis – Financial Statistics and Ratios, Page 2
($ in millions, except per share data)

		General			Return on Investment				LTM Leverage Ratios			LTM Coverage Ratios			Credit Ratings	
Company	Ticker	FYE	Predicted Beta	ROIC (%)	ROE (%)	ROA (%)	Implied Div. Yield (%)	Debt/ Tot. Cap. (%)	Debt/ EBITDA (x)	Net Debt/ EBITDA (x)	EBITDA/ Int. Exp. (x)	EBITDA - Cpx/Int. (x)	EBIT/ Int. Exp. (x)	Moody's	S&P
ValueCo Corporation	NA	Dec-31	NA	10%	7%	4%	NA	30%	2.1x	1.9x	7.0x	5.5x	5.0x	NA	NA
Tier I: Specialty Chemicals															
Buyer Co	BUY	Dec-31	1.24	30%	29%	9%	0%	47%	1.5x	1.2x	10.1x	8.8x	9.0x	Ba2	BB
Sherman Co.	SHR	Dec-31	1.35	16%	18%	6%	2%	57%	3.0x	2.4x	13.8x	10.7x	9.9x	Baa2	BBB
Pearl Corp.	PRL	Dec-31	1.58	19%	14%	7%	0%	37%	1.8x	0.8x	18.4x	7.1x	6.2x	Baa3	BBB-
Gasparro Corp.	JDG	Dec-31	1.25	21%	23%	8%	2%	52%	2.1x	1.9x	9.0x	7.0x	7.3x	Baa3	BBB-
Kumra Inc.	KUM	Dec-31	1.50	17%	10%	6%	2%	25%	1.3x	0.6x	11.0x	8.7x	8.4x	Baa1	BBB+
Mean			1.38	21%	19%	7%	1%	44%	1.9x	1.4x	10.5x	8.4x	8.2x		
Median			1.35	19%	18%	7%	2%	47%	1.8x	1.2x	10.1x	8.7x	8.4x		
Tier II: Commodity / Diversified Chemicals															
Falloon Group	FLN	Dec-31	1.69	16%	14%	4%	3%	55%	2.5x	2.2x	5.7x	3.8x	3.6x	Ba3	BB
Goodson Corp.	GDS	Dec-31	1.45	15%	11%	5%	1%	52%	2.9x	2.0x	4.2x	3.0x	2.9x	Baa1	BBB-
Pryor, Industries	PRI	Dec-31	1.46	14%	8%	5%	1%	19%	1.1x	0.4x	11.1x	8.9x	8.2x	Baa2	BBB
Lanzarone Global	LNZ	Dec-31	1.68	17%	12%	6%	0%	27%	1.3x	1.0x	10.7x	7.9x	7.9x	Baa3	BB-
McMenamin & Co.	MCM	Dec-31	1.64	12%	7%	4%	1%	18%	1.2x	0.0x	10.6x	8.2x	6.7x	Ba2	BB-
Mean			1.58	15%	10%	5%	1%	34%	1.8x	1.1x	8.5x	6.4x	5.9x		
Median			1.64	15%	11%	5%	1%	27%	1.3x	0.1x	10.6x	7.9x	6.7x		
Tier III: Small-Cap Chemicals															
S. Momper & Co.	MOMP	Dec-31	1.14	15%	9%	6%	4%	40%	2.6x	1.8x	4.5x	3.7x	3.5x	Ba1	BB
Adler Worldwide	ADL	Dec-31	1.46	12%	7%	3%	4%	22%	1.6x	1.0x	6.2x	5.0x	4.7x	Ba2	BB
Schacter & Sons	STM	Dec-31	1.90	12%	8%	3%	1%	38%	2.5x	2.3x	5.0x	3.2x	3.6x	Ba3	BB-
Girshin Holdings	MGP	Dec-31	1.55	13%	9%	4%	3%	34%	1.8x	1.4x	6.3x	4.7x	4.0x	Ba3	BB-
Crespin International	MCR	Dec-31	1.80	10%	6%	4%	0%	28%	2.1x	1.8x	5.7x	4.4x	3.9x	Ba3	BB-
Mean			1.57	12%	8%	4%	2%	33%	2.1x	1.7x	5.5x	4.2x	3.9x		
Median			1.55	12%	8%	4%	3%	34%	2.1x	1.8x	5.7x	4.4x	3.9x		
Overall															
Mean			1.51	16%	12%	5%	1%	37%	2.0x	1.4x	8.2x	6.3x	6.0x		
Median			1.50	15%	10%	5%	1%	37%	1.8x	1.4x	8.4x	7.0x	6.2x		
High			1.90	30%	29%	9%	4%	57%	3.0x	2.4x	13.8x	10.7x	9.9x		
Low			1.14	10%	6%	3%	0%	18%	1.1x	0.0x	4.2x	3.0x	2.9x		

Source: Company filings, Bloomberg, Consensus Estimates
Note: Last twelve months data based on September 30, 2012. Estimated annual financial data based on a calendar year.

EXHIBIT 1.55 ValueCo Corporation: Comparable Companies Analysis—Trading Multiples Output Page

ValueCo Corporation
Comparable Companies Analysis
($ in millions, except per share data)

Company	Ticker	Current Share Price	% of 52-wk. High	Equity Value	Enterprise Value	LTM Sales	2012E Sales	2013E Sales	Enterprise Value / LTM EBITDA	2012E EBITDA	2013E EBITDA	LTM EBIT	2012E EBIT	2013E EBIT	LTM EBITDA Margin	Total Debt / EBITDA	LTM EPS	Price / 2012E EPS	2013E EPS	LT EPS Growth
Tier I: Specialty Chemicals																				
BuyerCo	BUY	$70.00	91%	$9,800	$11,600	1.8x	1.7x	1.6x	8.0x	7.8x	7.3x	9.1x	8.8x	8.2x	22%	1.5x	13.9x	13.5x	12.5x	7%
Sherman Co.	SHR	40.00	76%	5,600	8,101	1.4x	1.4x	1.3x	7.7x	7.7x	7.2x	10.8x	10.7x	10.1x	18%	3.0x	13.4x	12.8x	11.8x	9%
Pearl Corp.	PRL	68.50	95%	5,172	5,856	1.4x	1.4x	1.3x	7.0x	7.0x	6.5x	9.4x	9.4x	8.7x	20%	1.8x	15.9x	14.7x	13.4x	11%
Gasparro Corp.	JDG	50.00	80%	5,000	6,750	1.4x	1.4x	1.3x	7.5x	7.1x	6.6x	9.3x	8.8x	8.2x	19%	2.1x	12.9x	11.2x	10.0x	12%
Kumra Inc.	KUM	52.50	88%	4,852	5,345	1.7x	1.7x	1.5x	8.0x	7.9x	7.4x	10.6x	10.4x	9.7x	21%	1.3x	19.5x	16.6x	14.4x	10%
Mean						1.5x	1.5x	1.4x	7.7x	7.5x	7.0x	9.8x	9.6x	9.0x	20%	1.9x	15.1x	13.8x	12.4x	10%
Median						1.4x	1.4x	1.3x	7.7x	7.7x	7.2x	9.4x	9.4x	8.7x	20%	1.8x	13.9x	13.5x	12.5x	10%
Tier II: Commodity / Diversified Chemicals																				
Falloon Group	FLN	$31.00	87%	$7,480	$11,254	1.0x	1.0x	0.9x	6.9x	7.0x	6.7x	10.8x	11.0x	10.5x	14%	2.5x	16.1x	15.0x	13.1x	5%
Goodson Corp.	GDS	64.00	83%	4,160	5,660	1.2x	1.2x	1.1x	7.4x	7.5x	7.2x	10.8x	11.0x	10.4x	16%	2.9x	19.5x	18.6x	16.3x	9%
Pryor Industries	PRI	79.00	88%	3,926	4,166	1.1x	1.2x	1.1x	7.3x	7.4x	7.1x	9.9x	10.1x	9.6x	15%	1.1x	17.3x	16.9x	15.4x	10%
Lanzarone Global	LNZ	32.25	95%	3,230	3,823	1.0x	1.0x	1.0x	6.6x	6.7x	6.4x	8.9x	9.0x	8.6x	16%	1.8x	13.9x	12.9x	11.7x	8%
McMenamin & Co.	MCM	33.50	80%	3,193	3,193	1.0x	0.9x	0.8x	9.0x	8.4x	7.5x	14.2x	13.1x	11.8x	11%	1.2x	26.8x	23.3x	20.3x	12%
Mean						1.1x	1.1x	1.0x	7.4x	7.4x	7.0x	10.9x	10.8x	10.2x	14%	1.8x	18.7x	17.3x	15.3x	9%
Median						1.0x	1.0x	1.0x	7.3x	7.4x	7.1x	10.8x	11.0x	10.4x	15%	1.3x	17.3x	16.9x	15.4x	9%
Tier III: Small-Cap Chemicals																				
S. Momper & Co.	MOMP	$28.00	95%	$2,240	$2,921	1.4x	1.4x	1.2x	7.7x	7.4x	6.7x	9.9x	9.5x	8.6x	18%	2.6x	17.2x	17.5x	16.2x	5%
Adler Worldwide	ADL	10.50	80%	1,217	1,463	0.9x	1.0x	0.9x	6.0x	6.1x	5.8x	8.0x	8.1x	7.7x	16%	1.6x	13.7x	14.8x	13.7x	7%
Schachter & Sons	STM	4.50	89%	1,125	1,674	0.8x	0.9x	0.8x	7.0x	6.5x	5.7x	9.8x	9.1x	7.9x	14%	2.5x	14.8x	13.6x	12.2x	11%
Girshin Holdings	MGP	50.00	67%	1,035	1,298	0.8x	0.8x	0.7x	7.3x	6.8x	6.1x	11.5x	10.7x	9.7x	11%	1.8x	20.0x	18.9x	17.2x	8%
Crespin International	MCR	27.00	80%	872	1,222	0.8x	0.8x	0.7x	6.4x	6.0x	5.4x	9.2x	8.6x	7.7x	13%	2.1x	14.2x	14.0x	12.7x	6%
Mean						1.0x	1.0x	0.9x	6.9x	6.6x	5.9x	9.7x	9.2x	8.3x	14%	2.1x	16.0x	15.7x	14.4x	7%
Median						0.9x	0.9x	0.8x	7.0x	6.5x	5.8x	9.8x	9.1x	7.9x	14%	2.1x	14.8x	14.8x	13.7x	7%
Overall																				
Mean						1.1x	1.1x	1.0x	7.3x	7.2x	6.7x	10.3x	10.0x	9.3x	16%	1.9x	17.0x	16.0x	14.4x	9%
Median						1.0x	1.0x	1.0x	7.3x	7.4x	6.7x	9.9x	9.8x	9.2x	16%	1.8x	16.6x	15.8x	14.1x	9%
High						1.8x	1.7x	1.6x	9.0x	8.4x	7.5x	14.2x	13.1x	11.8x	22%	3.0x	26.8x	23.3x	20.3x	12%
Low						0.8x	0.8x	0.7x	6.0x	6.0x	5.4x	8.0x	8.1x	7.7x	11%	1.1x	12.9x	11.2x	10.0x	5%

Source: Company filings, *Bloomberg*, *Consensus Estimates*
Note: Last twelve months data based on September 30, 2012. Estimated annual financial data based on a calendar year.

EXHIBIT 1.55(a) ValueCo Corporation: Trading Multiples Output Page for Equity Research Analysts and Equity Investors

ValueCo Corporation
Comparable Companies Analysis
($ in millions, except per share data)

Company	Ticker	Current Share Price	% of 52-wk. High	Equity Value	Enterprise Value	EV / EBITDA 2012E	EV / EBITDA 2013E	2012E EBITDA Margin	LTM Debt / EBITDA	LTM Int Exp / EBITDA	P/E 2012E	P/E 2013E	LT EPS Growth	Div Yield	FCF Yield 2012E	FCF Yield 2013E
Tier I: Specialty Chemicals																
BuyerCo	BUY	$70.00	91%	$9,800	$11,600	7.8x	7.3x	22%	1.5x	10.1x	13.5x	12.5x	7%	0.0%	7.2%	7.8%
Sherman Co.	SHR	$40.00	76%	5,600	8,101	7.7x	7.2x	18%	3.0x	13.8x	12.8x	11.8x	9%	1.8%	8.8%	9.7%
Pearl Corp.	PRL	$68.50	95%	5,172	5,856	7.0x	6.5x	20%	1.8x	8.4x	14.7x	13.4x	11%	0.0%	8.1%	8.9%
Gasparro Corp.	JDG	$50.00	80%	5,000	6,750	7.1x	6.6x	19%	2.1x	9.0x	11.2x	10.0x	12%	2.0%	7.0%	7.5%
Kumra Inc.	KUM	$52.50	88%	4,852	5,345	7.9x	7.4x	21%	1.3x	11.0x	16.6x	14.4x	10%	1.5%	5.8%	6.4%
Mean						7.5x	7.0x	20%	1.9x	10.5x	13.8x	12.4x	10%	1.1%	7.4%	8.1%
Median						7.7x	7.2x	20%	1.8x	10.1x	13.5x	12.5x	10%	1.5%	7.2%	7.8%
Tier II: Commodity / Diversified Chemicals																
Falloon Group	FLN	$31.00	87%	$7,480	$11,254	7.0x	6.7x	14%	2.5x	5.7x	15.0x	13.1x	5%	2.6%	7.0%	7.7%
Goodson Corp.	GDS	$64.00	83%	4,160	5,660	7.5x	7.2x	16%	2.9x	4.2x	18.6x	16.3x	9%	1.0%	5.7%	6.3%
Pryor Industries	PRI	$79.00	88%	3,926	4,166	7.4x	7.1x	15%	1.1x	11.1x	16.9x	15.4x	10%	0.8%	6.9%	7.5%
Lanzarone Global	LNZ	$32.25	95%	3,230	3,823	6.7x	6.4x	16%	1.3x	10.7x	12.9x	11.7x	8%	0.0%	7.3%	8.0%
McMenamin & Co.	MCM	$33.50	80%	3,193	3,193	8.4x	7.5x	11%	1.2x	10.6x	23.3x	20.3x	12%	1.2%	5.4%	5.9%
Mean						7.4x	7.0x	14%	1.8x	8.5x	17.3x	15.3x	9%	1.1%	6.5%	7.1%
Median						7.4x	7.1x	15%	1.3x	10.6x	16.9x	15.4x	9%	1.0%	6.9%	7.5%
Tier III: Small-Cap Chemicals																
S. Momper & Co.	MOMP	$28.00	95%	$2,240	$2,921	7.4x	6.7x	18%	2.6x	4.5x	17.5x	16.2x	5%	3.7%	6.8%	7.4%
Adler Worldwide	ADL	$10.50	80%	1,217	1,463	6.1x	5.8x	16%	1.6x	6.2x	14.8x	13.7x	7%	4.0%	8.2%	8.9%
Schachter & Sons	STM	$4.50	89%	1,125	1,674	6.5x	5.7x	14%	2.5x	5.0x	13.6x	12.2x	11%	0.8%	5.2%	5.7%
Girshin Holdings	MGP	$50.00	67%	1,035	1,298	6.8x	6.1x	11%	1.8x	6.3x	18.9x	17.2x	8%	2.8%	7.1%	7.7%
Crespin International	MCR	$27.00	80%	872	1,222	6.0x	5.4x	13%	2.1x	5.7x	14.0x	12.7x	6%	0.0%	8.9%	9.7%
Mean						6.6x	5.9x	14%	2.1x	5.5x	15.7x	14.4x	7%	2.2%	7.2%	7.9%
Median						6.5x	5.8x	14%	2.1x	5.7x	14.8x	13.7x	7%	2.8%	7.1%	7.7%
Overall																
Mean						7.2x	6.6x	16%	2.0x	8.2x	15.6x	14.0x	9%	1.5%	7.0%	7.7%
Median						7.1x	6.7x	16%	1.8x	8.4x	14.8x	13.4x	9%	1.2%	7.0%	7.7%
High						8.4x	7.5x	22%	3.0x	13.8x	23.3x	20.3x	12%	4.0%	8.9%	9.7%
Low						6.0x	5.4x	11%	1.1x	4.2x	11.2x	10.0x	5%	0.0%	5.2%	5.7%

Source: Company filings, Bloomberg, Consensus Estimates

Step V. Determine Valuation

The means and medians for the Specialty Chemicals comparables universe helped establish an initial valuation range for ValueCo, with the highs and lows providing further perspective. We also looked to the Commodity/Diversified Chemicals and Small-Cap Chemicals comparables for peripheral guidance. To fine-tune the range, however, we focused on those comparables deemed closest to ValueCo in terms of business and financial profile—namely, BuyerCo, Gasparro Corp., and Sherman Co., as well as Goodson Corp. and S. Momper & Co. to a lesser extent.

Companies in ValueCo's sector tend to trade on the basis of forward EV/EBITDA multiples. Therefore, we framed our valuation of ValueCo on the basis of the forward EV/EBITDA multiples for its closest comparables, selecting ranges of 6.75x to 7.75x 2012E EBITDA, and 6.5x to 7.5x 2013E EBITDA. We also looked at the implied valuation based on a range of 7.0x to 8.0x LTM EBITDA.

EXHIBIT 1.56 ValueCo Corporation: Implied Valuation Range – Enterprise Value

ValueCo Corporation
Implied Valuation Range
($ in millions, last twelve months ending 9/30/2012)

EBITDA	Metric	Multiple Range			Implied Enterprise Value		
LTM	$700.0	7.00x	–	8.00x	$4,900.0	–	$5,600.0
2012E	725.0	6.75x	–	7.75x	4,893.8	–	5,618.8
2013E	779.4	6.50x	–	7.50x	5,065.9	–	5,845.3

The chosen multiple ranges in Exhibit 1.56 translated into an implied enterprise value range of approximately $4,900 million to $5,850 million. This implied valuation range is typically displayed in a format such as that shown in Exhibit 1.57 (known as a "football field") for eventual comparison against other valuation methodologies, which we discuss in the following chapters.

EXHIBIT 1.57 ValueCo Football Field Displaying Comparable Companies

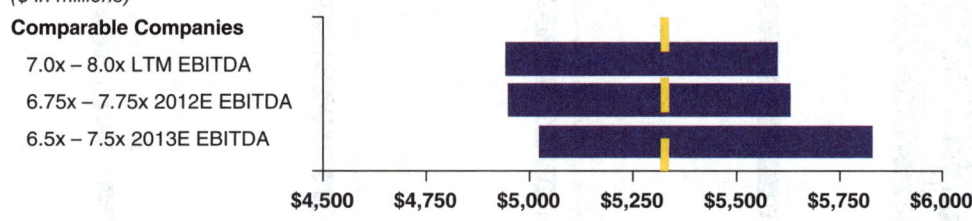

Bloomberg Appendix

APPENDIX 1.1 Bloomberg "Relative Valuation" Comparable Companies Analysis (RV<GO>)

Name	Mkt Cap (USD)	EV	EV/TTM EBITDA	EV/EBITDA FY1	EV/EBITDA FY2	P/E	P/E FY1	P/E FY2	P/FCF	Dividend Yield
Average	14.21B	16.25B	9.22	8.20	7.20	15.48	15.87	12.87	20.56	1.53%
100) BUY CORP	8.46B	9.31B	11.52	10.85	9.75	18.31	17.64	15.42	38.89	0.88%
101) Company A	40.17B	61.97B	9.60	8.27	7.52	18.31	17.49	13.99	20.83	3.80%
102) Company B	1.79B	2.42B	6.87	6.67	5.68	12.11	12.17	10.41	N.A.	3.57%
103) Company C	36.68B	40.26B	10.34	10.04	8.86	14.49	15.08	13.07	34.36	1.99%
104) Company D	887.51M	918.00M	13.48	12.52	9.47	28.24	25.72	19.36	25.99	0.44%
105) Company E	15.57B	16.47B	6.06	6.41	6.27	10.86	10.93	10.67	14.43	1.94%
106) Company F	10.82B	15.57B	11.41	9.33	7.53	14.26	13.11	11.17	16.30	1.70%
107) Company G	53.36B	50.70B	12.61	11.75	10.58	23.32	21.84	19.21	18.55	1.51%
108) Company H	5.65B	5.22B	8.00	7.12	6.74	18.27	15.64	14.88	17.65	0.89%
109) Company I	4.35B	7.73B	5.52	5.53	5.79	9.28	7.98	8.80	8.04	2.20%
110) Company J	25.26B	22.89B	8.16	7.64	6.77	13.49	13.85	12.03	42.81	1.68%
111) Company K	817.44M	1.06B	8.11	6.67	5.95	12.57	12.35	10.57	14.24	2.42%

Metric	BUY	Low	High
P/E	18.31	7.50	28.24
EPS 1 Yr Gr	96.48	−21.28	310.74
Rev 1 Yr Gr	8.39	8.39	53.79
ROE	30.85	12.49	53.55
Chg Pct 1M	16.05	−0.72	16.05

APPENDIX 1.2 Bloomberg Functions for Business and Financial Profile

Information Item	Bloomberg Function
Business Profile	
Sector	Bloomberg Industries (BI <GO>), Company Classification Browser (CCB<GO>)
Products and Services	Description (DES<GO>)
Customers and End Markets	Supply Chain (SPLC<GO>)
Distribution Channels	Supply Chain (SPLC<GO>)
Geography	Financial Analysis (FA<GO>)
Financial Profile	
Size	Description (DES<GO>), Financial Analysis (FA<GO>)
Profitability	Financial Analysis (FA<GO>)
Growth Profile	Financial Analysis (FA<GO>), Earnings & Estimates (EE<GO>)
Return on Investment	Description (DES<GO>), Financial Analysis (FA<GO>)
Credit Profile	Credit Profile (CRPR<GO>)

APPENDIX 1.3 Bloomberg Company Classification Browser (CCB<GO>)

BUY US Equity	1) Settings		2) Actions		Company Classification Browser		
Classification	BICS ▸	Currency	USD ▸	Selected Industry	Agricultural Chemicals ▸	5) Hierarchy (ICS)	
Hierarchy		Rev.	% Rev.	Aggregate Statistics		Value	Count
Materials				Total Market Cap		1.87T	492
└Chemicals				Price/Earnings		12.52	479
├*Agricultural Chemicals				Total Revenue		2.32T	555
│ └Crop Chemicals				Industry Revenue		245.92B	317
│ ├Fungicides		131.81M	3.90%	Industry Rev. 1YR Growth		27.47%	266
│ ├Herbicides		629.74M	18.62%				
│ └Insecticides		702.96M	20.78%	Filter By None ▸		6) Equity Screening	
└Basic & Diversified Chemicals				Public Member Companies ↓	Mkt Cap	Ind. Rev	% Tot. Rev
├Inorganic Base Che...		1.26B	37.35%	11) * BUY CORP	8.14B	1.46B	43.30%
├Alkalis & Chlorine		696.40M	20.59%	12) Company A	66.09B	N.D.	N.D.
├Other Inorganic B...		522.20M	15.44%	13) Company B	148.36M	80.06M	22.85%
└Organic Base Chem...		654.30M	19.35%	14) * Company C	384.18M	25.77M	72.34%
				15) * Company D	1.59B	507.72M	100.00%
				16) Company E	40.65M	32.91M	100.00%
				17) Company F	41.49M	15.85M	6.74%
				18) * Company G	1.90B	2.02B	55.64%
				19) * Company H	1.12M	58.23k	100.00%
				20) Company I	878.80M	624.78M	28.86%
				21) Company J	2.34B	441.33M	9.62%
				22) Company K	23.43M	N.D.	N.D.
				23) * Company L	297.63M	196.05M	100.00%
				24) Company M	65.45M	N.D.	N.D.
				25) * Company N	15.21B	15.16B	92.41%
				* Company's Primary Industry		N.D. Not Disclosed	

APPENDIX 1.4 Bloomberg BEst Consensus Estimates (EEB<GO>)

BUY US Equity	95) Actions	▶	96) Alert			BEst Consensus Detail
Buyer Corp						99) Last Event (Guidance) 12/11/12
Estimate	EPS Adjusted+					
Consensus	● Standard	● 28 Days	● Post Event	● Custom	Period 2012* ▶ - Q4* ▶	USD

Consensus	12/2012	3/2013
Mean Estimate	0.805	1.079
Enhanced Estimate	0.818	1.077
Median Estimate	0.810	1.090
High Estimate	0.840	1.120
Low Estimate	0.770	0.990
Standard Deviation	0.022	0.046
4 Weeks Change	-0.001	-0.003
4 Weeks Up/Down	2/1	1/1
Number of Estimates	12(11)	7(7)
P/E 17.82 Est P/E	15.463	15.078

Historical Mean 12/2012 0.8055
Historical Mean 3/2013   1.0786

	Broker	Analyst	Date	12/2012	Change	3/2013	Change
1)	Broker A	Analyst A	01/07/13	0.790	0.000		↗
2)	Broker B	Analyst B	01/04/13	0.520	NA		↗
3)	Broker C	Analyst C	12/13/12	0.820	0.010		NA ↗
4)	Broker D	Analyst D	12/13/12	0.780	NA	1.050	↗
5)	Broker E	Analyst E	12/12/12	0.790	0.000	0.990	-0.020 ↗
6)	Broker F	Analyst F	12/12/12	0.840	0.020	1.080	NA ↗
7)	Broker G	Analyst G	12/12/12	0.770	0.000	1.120	0.000 ↗
8)	Broker H	Analyst H	12/12/12	0.810	0.000	1.090	0.030 ↗
9)	Broker I	Analyst I	12/12/12	0.820	0.000		↗
10)	Broker J	Analyst J	12/06/12	0.830	0.000	1.110	0.000 ↗
11)	Broker K	Analyst K	11/06/12	0.810	0.000		↗

APPENDIX 1.5 Bloomberg Coverage Dashboard (IBNK<GO>)

BUY Corp (BUY US)						Coverage Dashboard	
						Range 1 Month	CMI
1) Valuation (RV)							
	Price	% Chg	52 Wk Hi	Mkt Cap.	EV	P/E '12E	EV/EBITDA '12	Price/Book
	61.60	14.63	61.83	8.46B	9.31B	15.89	9.88	5.94

2) Price Chart (GP)

Developments

100) EVT	Credit Rating	STANDARD & POOR'S upgrades Rating – LT For...	Dec 17
101)	Credit Rating	STANDARD & POOR'S upgrades Rating – LT Loc...	Dec 17
102)	Conference/Presentation	International CES 2013, Time:13:30	Jan 08
103)	Insider Sell	Daniels, David, Director, 5,500 Shares	Jan 02
104)	Transaction	Acquisition: XYZ Industries China Corp. $500M	Dec 21
105)	Transaction	Acquisition: ABC Technologies, Sought: 19.0%	Dec 19

3) News (CN) Research News

110)	BUY Corp Has Changed Elliott Wave Count	01/09
111)	*BUY REVISES DATES FOR 4Q '12 EARNINGS RELEASE, WEBCAST CALL	01/09
112)	BUY Corporation Revises Dates for Fourth Quarter 2012 Earnings Releas...	01/09
113)	BUY Corp. : 144 12/12/2012	01/08
114)	BUY Corporation Announces Dates for Fourth Quarter 2012 Earnings Rel...	01/07
115)	Chemicals – 2013 Likely to Mirror 2012-Chemicals Should Outperfo	01/07

Company Overview
11) DES   Description
12) MGMT Management
13) RELS Related Secs.
14) HDS   Shareholders
15) FA   Financial
16) PIB   Public Informat...
17) DDIS Debt Distribution

Company Activity
18) CF   Company Filings
19) CACS Corp. Actions
20) EVT   Company Events

Research & Estimates
21) EE   Estimates
22) ANR   Analyst Recs.
23) BRC   Research
24) CRPR Credit Ratings
25) BI   Bloomberg Indu...

Deal Activity
26) MADL M&A Deals

APPENDIX 1.6 Bloomberg Industries Comparable Analysis for Basic & Diversified Chemicals (BI<GO>)

Search BI	91) Actions ▾	92) Contact BI ▾	93) Contributors					Bloomberg Industries	
Basic & Diversified Chemicals (BI BDCHG)		96) Industry Classification (BICS)							Global
Analysis	51) Eq Val	52) Op Stats	53) Profitability	54) Bal Sheet	55) CDS	56) Credit		Curr USD	Zoom 100%
Overview	71) Latest Ratio	72) Latest Data							
Bull & Bear	95) Peer Group BI Americas Basic and Diversified ▸								

	Name	Market Cap	P/E (FY1)	P/E (FY2)	EV/EBITDA (FY1)	EV/EBITDA (FY2)	Dividend Yld (Indic.)	P/FCF (TTM)	P/E (TTM)	P/EBITDA (TTM)
	Median	4.40B	15.37	10.88	8.02	6.62	2.23%	28.67	14.04	7.26
	Average	7.13B	16.64	12.49	8.20	6.71	2.52%	45.74	15.06	8.16
100) Company A		5.74B	16.70	14.55	8.61	7.70	1.24%	N.A.	4.55	N.A.
101) Company B		4.46B	N.A.	19.13	6.52	5.53	4.46%	17.91	N.A.	7.16
102) Company C		7.46B	12.38	10.77	7.85	7.19	0.64%	81.35	13.28	9.49
103) Company D		39.69B	17.28	13.83	8.20	7.46	3.87%	27.72	18.09	8.76
104) Company E		10.66B	12.91	11.00	9.23	7.45	1.73%	32.48	14.04	9.88
105) Company F		1.55B	14.02	10.03	6.54	2.88	0.71%	5.49	18.06	6.29
106) Company G		4.34B	7.94	8.76	5.51	5.78	2.21%	67.89	9.23	4.94
107) Company H		810.04M	12.24	10.47	6.62	5.91	2.40%	16.20	12.46	7.36
108) Company I		810.70M	31.48	10.12	8.41	5.47	N.A.	144.55	N.A.	13.01
109) Company J		3.12B	18.92	11.48	8.42	6.63	2.23%	6.63	18.22	6.69
110) Company K		11.86B	22.52	19.86	12.31	10.72	2.65%	29.62	27.80	10.83
111) Company L		1.78B	12.07	10.32	6.63	5.65	3.60%	104.80	12.01	6.72
112) Company M		1.93B	22.44	9.97	12.96	8.94	6.08%	N.A.	N.A.	N.A.
113) Company N		5.56B	15.37	14.63	6.99	6.61	0.90%	14.31	17.95	6.80

Themes
Key Indicators
Earnings
Valuation
Industry Primer
Data Library
Featured Data
Market Share
Macro
Industry
Company
Cost Analysis
Price/Margin
Value Chains
Monitor
News/Research
Events
Comp Sheets
Markets
Ownership
Coverage

CHAPTER 2

Precedent Transactions Analysis

Precedent transactions analysis ("precedent transactions" or "transaction comps"), like comparable companies analysis, employs a multiples-based approach to derive an implied valuation range for a given company, division, business, or collection of assets ("target"). It is premised on multiples paid for comparable companies in prior M&A transactions. Precedent transactions has a broad range of applications, most notably to help determine a potential sale price range for a company, or part thereof, in an M&A transaction or restructuring.

The selection of an appropriate universe of comparable acquisitions is the foundation for performing precedent transactions. This process incorporates a similar approach to that for determining a universe of comparable companies. The best comparable acquisitions typically involve companies similar to the target on a fundamental level (i.e., sharing key business and financial characteristics such as those outlined in Chapter 1, see Exhibit 1.3).

As with trading comps, it is often challenging to obtain a robust universe of truly comparable acquisitions. This exercise may demand some creativity and perseverance on the part of the banker. For example, it is not uncommon to consider transactions involving companies in different, but related, sectors that may share similar end markets, distribution channels, or financial profiles. As a general rule, the most recent transactions (i.e., those that have occurred within the previous two to three years) are the most relevant as they likely took place under similar market conditions to the contemplated transaction. In some cases, however, older transactions may be appropriate to evaluate if they occurred during a similar point in the target's business cycle or macroeconomic environment.

Under normal market conditions, transaction comps tend to provide a higher multiple range than trading comps for two principal reasons. First, buyers generally pay a "control premium" when purchasing another company. In return for this premium, the acquirer receives the right to control decisions regarding the target's business and its underlying cash flows. Second, strategic buyers often have the opportunity to realize synergies, which supports the ability to pay higher purchase prices. Synergies refer to the expected cost savings, growth opportunities, and other financial benefits that occur as a result of the combination of two businesses.

Potential acquirers look closely at the multiples that have been paid for comparable acquisitions. As a result, bankers and investment professionals are expected to know the transaction multiples for their sector focus areas. As in Chapter 1, this chapter employs a step-by-step approach to performing precedent transactions, as shown in Exhibit 2.1, followed by an illustrative analysis for ValueCo.

EXHIBIT 2.1 Precedent Transactions Analysis Steps

> Step I. Select the Universe of Comparable Acquisitions
> Step II. Locate the Necessary Deal-Related and Financial Information
> Step III. Spread Key Statistics, Ratios, and Transaction Multiples
> Step IV. Benchmark the Comparable Acquisitions
> Step V. Determine Valuation

SUMMARY OF PRECEDENT TRANSACTIONS ANALYSIS STEPS

- **Step I. Select the Universe of Comparable Acquisitions.** The identification of a universe of comparable acquisitions is the first step in performing transaction comps. This exercise, like determining a universe of comparable companies for trading comps, can often be challenging and requires a strong understanding of the target and its sector. As a starting point, the banker typically consults with peers or senior colleagues to see if a relevant set of comparable acquisitions already exists internally. In the event the banker is starting from scratch, we suggest searching through M&A databases (available on Bloomberg via the M&A Analysis function MA<GO>), examining the M&A history of the target and its comparable companies, and reviewing merger proxies of comparable companies for lists of selected comparable acquisitions disclosed in the fairness opinions. Equity and fixed income research reports for the target (if public), its comparable companies, and overall sector may also provide lists of comparable acquisitions, including relevant financial data (for reference purposes only).

    As part of this process, the banker seeks to learn as much as possible regarding the specific circumstances and deal dynamics of each transaction. This is particularly important for refining the universe and, ultimately, honing in on the "best" comparable acquisitions.

- **Step II. Locate the Necessary Deal-Related and Financial Information.** This section focuses on the sourcing of deal-related and financial information for M&A transactions involving both public and private companies. Locating information on comparable acquisitions is invariably easier for transactions involving public companies (including private companies with publicly registered debt securities) due to SEC disclosure requirements. For competitive reasons, however, public acquirers sometimes safeguard these details and only disclose information that is required by law or regulation. For M&A transactions involving private companies, it is often difficult—and sometimes impossible—to obtain complete (or any) financial information necessary to determine their transaction multiples.

- **Step III. Spread Key Statistics, Ratios, and Transaction Multiples.** Once the relevant deal-related and financial information has been located, the banker is prepared to spread each selected transaction. This involves entering the key transaction data relating to purchase price, form of consideration, and target financial statistics into an input page, where the relevant multiples for each transaction are calculated. The key multiples used for precedent transactions mirror those used for comparable companies (e.g., enterprise value-to-EBITDA and equity value-to-net income). As with comparable companies, certain sectors may also rely on additional or other metrics to derive valuation (see Chapter 1, Exhibit 1.33). The notable difference is that multiples for precedent transactions often reflect a premium paid by the acquirer for control and potential synergies. In addition, multiples for precedent transactions are typically calculated on the basis of actual LTM financial statistics (available at the time of deal announcement).

- **Step IV. Benchmark the Comparable Acquisitions.** As with trading comps, the next level of analysis involves an in-depth study of the selected comparable acquisitions so as to identify those most relevant for valuing the target. As part of this benchmarking analysis, the banker examines the key financial statistics and ratios for the acquired companies, with an eye toward those most comparable to the target. Output pages, such as those shown in Exhibits 1.53 and 1.54 in Chapter 1, facilitate this analysis. Other relevant deal circumstances and dynamics are also examined.

    The transaction multiples for each selected acquisition are linked to an output sheet where they can be easily benchmarked against one another and the broader universe (see Exhibit 2.2). Each precedent transaction is closely examined as part of the final refining of the universe, with the best comparable transactions identified and obvious outliers eliminated. Ultimately, an experienced sector banker is consulted to help determine the final universe.

- **Step V. Determine Valuation.** In precedent transactions, the multiples of the selected comparable acquisitions universe are used to derive an implied valuation range for the target. The banker typically uses the mean and median multiples from the universe as a guide to establish a preliminary valuation range for the target, with the high and low ends also serving as reference points. These calculations often serve as the precursor for a deeper level of analysis whereby the banker uses the multiples from the most relevant transactions to anchor the ultimate valuation range. Often, the banker focuses on as few as two or three of the most similar transactions. Once the chosen multiples range is finalized, the endpoints are multiplied by the target's appropriate LTM financial statistics to produce an implied valuation range. As with trading comps, the target's implied valuation range is then given a sanity check and compared to the output from other valuation methodologies.

EXHIBIT 2.2 Precedent Transactions Analysis Output Page

ValueCo Corporation
Precedent Transactions Analysis
($ in millions)

Date Announced	Acquirer	Target	Transaction Type	Purchase Consideration	Equity Value	Enterprise Value	Enterprise Value /			LTM EBITDA Margin	Equity Value / LTM Net Income	Premiums Paid Days Prior to Unaffected		
							LTM Sales	LTM EBITDA	LTM EBIT			1	7	30
11/2/12	Pearl Corp.	Rosenbaum Industries	Public / Public	Cash	$2,500	$3,825	1.6x	8.5x	11.2x	19%	16.6x	35%	33%	37%
7/20/12	Goodson Corp.	Schneider & Co.	Public / Public	Cash / Stock	5,049	6,174	1.4x	8.1x	10.3x	18%	15.3x	29%	32%	31%
6/21/12	Domanski Capital	Ackerman Industries	Sponsor / Public	Cash	8,845	9,995	1.7x	8.0x	10.2x	21%	15.9x	35%	37%	39%
4/15/12	The Hochberg Group	Whalen Inc.	Sponsor / Private	Cash	1,250	1,350	1.9x	7.5x	9.6x	26%	15.2x	NA	NA	NA
8/8/11	Cole Manufacturing	Gordon Inc.	Public / Public	Stock	2,620	3,045	1.5x	9.0x	12.2x	17%	20.4x	47%	44%	49%
7/6/11	Eu-Han Capital	Rughwani International	Sponsor / Public	Cash	3,390	4,340	1.6x	7.8x	9.4x	21%	13.2x	38%	40%	43%
3/20/11	Lanzarone Global	Falk & Sons	Public / Private	Cash	8,750	10,350	1.7x	8.4x	10.5x	21%	16.0x	NA	NA	NA
11/9/10	Meisner Global Management	Kamras Brands	Sponsor / Private	Cash	1,765	2,115	1.5x	7.9x	9.3x	19%	13.8x	NA	NA	NA
6/22/10	Pryor, Inc.	ParkCo	Public / Private	Cash	6,450	8,700	1.1x	7.0x	7.9x	16%	11.8x	NA	NA	NA
4/15/10	Leicht & Co.	Bress Products	Public / Public	Stock	12,431	12,681	1.5x	8.2x	12.1x	19%	19.7x	29%	36%	34%
Mean							1.6x	8.0x	10.3x	19%	15.8x	36%	37%	39%
Median							1.6x	8.0x	10.3x	19%	15.6x	35%	36%	38%
High							1.9x	9.0x	12.2x	26%	20.4x	47%	44%	49%
Low							1.1x	7.0x	7.9x	16%	11.8x	29%	32%	31%

Source: Company filings

STEP I. SELECT THE UNIVERSE OF COMPARABLE ACQUISITIONS

The identification of a universe of comparable acquisitions is the first step in performing transaction comps. This exercise, like determining a universe of comparable companies for trading comps, can often be challenging and requires a strong understanding of the target and its sector. Investment banks generally have internal M&A transaction databases containing relevant multiples and other financial data for focus sectors, which are updated as appropriate for newly announced deals. Often, however, the banker needs to start from scratch.

When practical, the banker consults with peers or senior colleagues with firsthand knowledge of relevant transactions. Senior bankers can be helpful in establishing the basic landscape by identifying the key transactions in a given sector. Toward the end of the screening process, an experienced banker's guidance is beneficial for the final refining of the universe.

Screen for Comparable Acquisitions

The initial goal when screening for comparable acquisitions is to locate as many potential transactions as possible for a relevant, recent time period and then further refine the universe. Below are several suggestions for creating an initial list of comparable acquisitions.

- Search M&A databases using a financial information service such as Bloomberg (see Appendix 2.1), which allows for the screening of M&A transactions through multiple search criteria, including industry, transaction size, form of consideration, time period, and geography, among others

- Examine the target's M&A history and determine the multiples it has paid and received for the purchase and sale, respectively, of its businesses (see Appendix 2.2)

- Revisit the target's universe of comparable companies (as determined in Chapter 1) and examine the M&A history of each comparable company

- Search merger proxies for comparable acquisitions, as they typically contain excerpts from fairness opinion(s) that cite a list of selected transactions analyzed by the financial advisor(s)

- Review equity and fixed income research reports for the target (if public), its comparable companies, and sector as they may provide lists of comparable acquisitions, including relevant financial data (for reference purposes only)

Examine Other Considerations

Once an initial set of comparable acquisitions is selected, it is important for the banker to gain a better understanding of the specific circumstances and context for each transaction. Although these factors generally do not change the list of comparable acquisitions to be examined, understanding the "story" behind each transaction helps the banker better interpret the multiple paid, as well as its relevance to the target being valued. This next level of analysis involves examining factors such as market conditions and deal dynamics.

Market Conditions Market conditions refer to the business and economic environment, as well as the prevailing state of the capital markets, at the time of a given transaction. They must be viewed within the context of specific sectors and cycles (e.g., housing, steel, and technology). These conditions directly affect availability and cost of acquisition financing and, therefore, influence the price an acquirer is willing, or able, to pay. They also affect buyer and seller confidence with respect to undertaking a transaction.

For example, at the height of the technology bubble in the late 1990s and early 2000s, many technology and telecommunications companies were acquired at unprecedented multiples. Equity financing was prevalent during this period as companies used their stock, which was valued at record levels, as acquisition currency. Boardroom confidence was also high, which lent support to contemplated M&A activity. After the bubble burst and market conditions adjusted, M&A activity slowed dramatically, and companies changed hands for fractions of the valuations seen just a couple of years earlier. The multiples paid for companies during this period quickly became irrelevant for assessing value in the following era.

Similarly, during the low-rate debt financing environment of the mid-2000s, acquirers (financial sponsors, in particular) were able to support higher than historical purchase prices due to the market's willingness to supply abundant and inexpensive debt with favorable terms. In the ensuing credit crunch that began during the second half of 2007, however, debt financing became scarce and expensive, thereby dramatically changing value perceptions. Over the subsequent couple of years, the entire M&A landscape changed, with the LBO market grinding to a halt and overall deal volume and valuations falling dramatically.

Deal Dynamics Deal dynamics refer to the specific circumstances surrounding a given transaction. For example:

- Was the acquirer a strategic buyer or a financial sponsor?
- What were the buyer's and seller's motivations for the transaction?
- Was the target sold through an *auction process* or *negotiated sale*? Was the nature of the deal *friendly* or *hostile*?
- What was the purchase consideration (i.e., mix of cash and stock)?

This information can provide insight into factors that may have impacted the price paid by the acquirer.

Strategic Buyer vs. Financial Sponsor Traditionally, strategic buyers have been able to pay higher purchase prices than financial sponsors due to their potential ability to realize synergies from the transaction, among other factors, including lower cost of capital and return thresholds. During periods of robust credit markets, such as the mid-2000s, however, sponsors were able to place higher leverage on targets and, therefore, compete more effectively with strategic buyers on purchase price. In the ensuing credit crunch, the advantage shifted back to strategic buyers as only the strongest and most creditworthy companies were able to source acquisition financing.

Motivations Buyer and seller motivations may also play an important role in interpreting purchase price. For example, a strategic buyer may "stretch" to pay a higher price for an asset if there are substantial synergies to be realized and/or the asset is critical to its strategic plan ("scarcity value"). Similarly, a financial sponsor may be more aggressive on price if synergies can be realized by combining the target with an existing portfolio company. From the seller's perspective, motivations may also influence purchase price. A corporation in need of cash that is selling a non-core business, for example, may prioritize speed of execution, certainty of completion, and other structural considerations, which may result in a lower valuation than a pure value maximization strategy.

Sale Process and Nature of the Deal The type of sale process and nature of the deal should also be examined. For example, auctions, whereby the target is shopped to multiple prospective buyers, are designed to maximize competitive dynamics with the goal of producing the best offer at the highest possible price. Hostile situations, whereby the target actively seeks alternatives to a proposed takeover by a particular buyer, may also produce higher purchase prices. A *merger of equals* (MOE) transaction, on the other hand, is premised on partnership with the target, thereby foregoing a typical takeover premium as both sides collectively participate in the upside (e.g., growth and synergies) over time.

Purchase Consideration The use of stock as a meaningful portion of the purchase consideration tends to result in a lower valuation (measured by multiples and premiums paid) than for an all-cash transaction. The primary explanation for this occurrence is that when target shareholders receive stock, they retain an equity interest in the combined entity and, therefore, expect to share in the upside (driven by growth and realizing synergies). Target shareholders also maintain the opportunity to obtain a control premium at a later date through a future sale of the company. As a result, target shareholders may require less upfront compensation than for an all-cash transaction in which they are unable to participate in value creation opportunities that result from combining the two companies.

STEP II. LOCATE THE NECESSARY DEAL-RELATED AND FINANCIAL INFORMATION

This section focuses on the sourcing of key deal-related and financial information for M&A transactions involving both public and private targets. Locating information on comparable acquisitions is invariably easier for transactions involving public targets (including private companies with publicly registered debt securities) due to SEC disclosure requirements.

For M&A transactions involving private targets, the availability of sufficient information typically depends on whether public securities were used as the acquisition financing. In many cases, it is often challenging and sometimes impossible to obtain complete (or any) financial information necessary to determine the transaction multiples in such deals. For competitive reasons, even public acquirers may safeguard these details and only disclose information that is required by law or regulation. Nonetheless, the resourceful banker conducts searches for information on private transactions via news runs and various databases. In some cases, these searches yield enough data to determine purchase price and key target financial statistics; in other cases, there simply may not be enough relevant information available.

Below, we grouped the primary sources for locating the necessary deal-related and financial information for spreading comparable acquisitions into separate categories for public and private targets.

Public Targets

Proxy Statement In a one-step merger transaction,[1] the target obtains approval from its shareholders through a vote at a shareholder meeting. Prior to the vote, the target provides appropriate disclosure to the shareholders via a proxy statement. The proxy statement contains a summary of the background and terms of the transaction, a description of the financial analysis underlying the fairness opinion(s) of the financial advisor(s), a copy of the definitive purchase/sale agreement ("definitive agreement"), and summary and pro forma financial data (if applicable, depending on the form of consideration). As such, it is a primary source for locating key information used to spread a precedent transaction. The proxy statement is filed with the SEC under the codes PREM14A (preliminary) and DEFM14A (definitive).

In the event that a public acquirer is issuing new shares in excess of 20% of its pre-deal shares outstanding to fund the purchase consideration,[2] it will also need to file a proxy statement for its shareholders to vote on the proposed transaction. In

---

[1] An M&A transaction for public targets where shareholders approve the deal at a formal shareholder meeting pursuant to relevant state law. See Chapter 6: Sell-Side M&A for additional information.

[2] The requirement for a shareholder vote in this situation arises from the listing rules of the New York Stock Exchange and the Nasdaq Stock Market. If the amount of shares being issued is less than 20% of pre-deal levels, or if the merger consideration consists entirely of cash or debt, the acquirer's shareholders are typically not entitled to vote on the transaction.

addition, a registration statement to register the offer and sale of shares must be filed with the SEC if no exemption from the registration requirements is available.[3]

Schedule TO/Schedule 14D-9 In a tender offer, the acquirer offers to buy shares directly from the target's shareholders.[4] As part of this process, the acquirer mails an Offer to Purchase to the target's shareholders and files a Schedule TO. In response to the tender offer, the target files a Schedule 14D-9 within ten business days of commencement. The Schedule 14D-9 contains a recommendation from the target's board of directors to the target's shareholders on how to respond to the tender offer, typically including a fairness opinion. The Schedule TO and the Schedule 14D-9 include the same type of information with respect to the terms of the transaction as set forth in a proxy statement.

Registration Statement/Prospectus (S-4, 424B) When a public acquirer issues shares as part of the purchase consideration for a public target, the acquirer is typically required to file a registration statement/prospectus in order for those shares to be freely tradeable by the target's shareholders. Similarly, if the acquirer is issuing public debt securities (or debt securities intended to be registered)[5] to fund the purchase, it must also file a registration statement/prospectus. The registration statement/prospectus contains the terms of the issuance, material terms of the transaction, and purchase price detail. It may also contain acquirer and target financial information, including on a pro forma basis to reflect the consummation of the transaction (if applicable, depending on the materiality of the transaction).[6]

Schedule 13E-3 Depending on the nature of the transaction, a "going private"[7] deal may require enhanced disclosure. For example, in an LBO of a public company where an "affiliate" (such as a senior company executive or significant shareholder) is part of the buyout group, the SEC requires broader disclosure of information used in the decision-making process on a Schedule 13E-3. Disclosure items on Schedule

---

[3]When both the acquirer and target are required to prepare proxy and/or registration statements, they typically combine the statements in a joint disclosure document.
[4]A tender offer is an offer to purchase shares for cash. An acquirer can also effect an exchange offer, pursuant to which the target's shares are exchanged for shares of the acquirer.
[5]Debt securities are typically sold to qualified institutional buyers (QIBs) through a private placement under Rule 144A of the Securities Act of 1933 initially, and then registered with the SEC within one year after issuance so that they can be traded on an open exchange. This is done to expedite the sale of the debt securities as SEC registration, which involves review of the registration statement by the SEC, can take several weeks or months. Once the SEC review of the documentation is complete, the issuer conducts an exchange offer pursuant to which investors exchange the unregistered bonds for registered bonds.
[6]A joint proxy/registration statement typically incorporates the acquirer's and target's applicable 10-K and 10-Q by reference as the source for financial information.
[7]A company "goes private" when it engages in certain transactions that have the effect of delisting its shares from a public stock exchange. In addition, depending on the circumstances, a publicly held company may no longer be required to file reports with the SEC when it reduces the number of its shareholders to fewer than 300, or fewer than 500, where the company does not have significant assets.

13E-3 include materials such as presentations to the target's board of directors by its financial advisor(s) in support of the actual fairness opinion(s).

8-K In addition to the SEC filings mentioned above, key deal information can be obtained from the 8-K that is filed upon announcement of the transaction. Generally, a public target is required to file an 8-K within four business days of the transaction announcement. In the event a public company is selling a subsidiary or division that is significant in size, the parent company typically files an 8-K upon announcement of the transaction. Public acquirers are also required to file an 8-K upon announcement of material transactions.[8] A private acquirer does not need to file an 8-K as it is not subject to the SEC's disclosure requirements. When filed in the context of an M&A transaction, the 8-K contains a brief description of the transaction, as well as the corresponding press release and definitive agreement as exhibits.

The press release filed upon announcement typically contains a summary of the deal terms, transaction rationale, and a description of the target and acquirer. In the event there are substantial changes to the terms of the transaction following the original announcement, the banker uses the 8-K for the final announced deal (and enclosed press release) as the basis for calculating the deal's transaction multiples. This is a relatively common occurrence in competitive situations where two or more parties enter into a bidding war for a target.

10-K and 10-Q The target's 10-K and 10-Q are the primary sources for locating the information necessary to calculate its relevant LTM financial statistics, including adjustments for non-recurring items and significant recent events. The most recent 10-K and 10-Q for the period ending prior to the announcement date typically serve as the source for the necessary information to calculate the target's LTM financial statistics and balance sheet data. In some cases, the banker may use a filing after announcement if the financial information is deemed more relevant. The 10-K and 10-Q are also relied upon to provide information on the target's shares outstanding and options/warrants.[9]

Equity and Fixed Income Research Equity and fixed income research reports often provide helpful deal insight, including information on pro forma adjustments and expected synergies. Furthermore, research reports typically provide color on deal dynamics and other circumstances.

---

[8]Generally, an acquisition is required to be reported in an 8-K if the assets, income, or value of the target comprise 10% or greater of the acquirer's. Furthermore, for larger transactions where assets, income, or value of the target comprise 20% or greater of the acquirer's, the acquirer must file an 8-K containing historical financial information on the target and pro forma financial information within 75 days of the completion of the acquisition.

[9]The proxy statement may contain more recent share count information than the 10-K or 10-Q.

Private Targets

A private target (i.e., a non-public filer) is not required to publicly file documentation in an M&A transaction as long as it is not subject to SEC disclosure requirements. Therefore, the sourcing of relevant information on private targets depends on the type of acquirer and/or acquisition financing.

When a public acquirer buys a private target (or a division/subsidiary of a public company), it may be required to file certain disclosure documents. For example, in the event the acquirer is using public securities as part of the purchase consideration for a private target, it is required to file a registration statement/prospectus. Furthermore, if the acquirer is issuing shares in excess of 20% of its pre-deal shares, a proxy statement is filed with the SEC and mailed to its shareholders so they can evaluate the proposed transaction and vote. As previously discussed, regardless of the type of financing, the acquirer files an 8-K upon announcement and completion of material transactions.

For LBOs of private targets, the availability of necessary information depends on whether public debt securities (typically high yield bonds) are issued as part of the financing. In this case, the S-4 contains the relevant data on purchase price and target financials to spread the precedent transaction.

Private acquirer/private target transactions (including LBOs) involving nonpublic financing are the most difficult transactions for which to obtain information because there are no SEC disclosure requirements. In these situations, the banker must rely on less formal sources for deal information, such as press releases and news articles. These news pieces can be found by searching a company's corporate website as well as through information services such as Bloomberg. The banker should also search relevant sector-specific trade journals for potential disclosures. Any information provided on these all-private transactions, however, relies on discretionary disclosure by the parties involved. As a result, in many cases it is impossible to obtain even basic deal information that can be relied upon, thus precluding these transactions from being used to derive valuation.

Summary of Primary SEC Filings in M&A Transactions

Exhibit 2.3 provides a list of key SEC filings that can be used to source relevant deal-related data and target financial information for performing precedent transactions. In general, if applicable, the definitive proxy statement or tender offer document should serve as the primary source for deal-related data.

Exhibit 2.4 provides an overview of the sources for transaction information in public and private company transactions.

EXHIBIT 2.3 Primary SEC Filings in M&A Transaction—U.S. Issuers

SEC Filings	Description
Proxy Statements and Other Disclosure Documents	
PREM14A/DEFM14A	Preliminary/definitive proxy statement relating to an M&A transaction
PREM14C/DEFM14C[a]	Preliminary/definitive information statement relating to an M&A transaction
Schedule 13E-3	Filed to report going private transactions initiated by certain issuers or their affiliates
Tender Offer Documents	
Schedule TO	Filed by an acquirer upon commencement of a tender offer
Schedule 14D-9	Recommendation from the target's board of directors on how shareholders should respond to a tender offer
Registration Statement/Prospectus	
S-4	Registration statement for securities issued in connection with a business combination or exchange offer. May include proxy statement of acquirer and/or public target
424B	Prospectus
Current and Periodic Reports	
8-K	When filed in the context of an M&A transaction, used to disclose a material acquisition or sale of the company or a division/subsidiary
10-K and 10-Q	Target company's applicable annual and quarterly reports

[a]In certain circumstances, an *information statement* is sent to shareholders instead of a proxy statement. This occurs if one or more shareholders comprise a majority and can approve the transaction via a written consent, in which case a shareholder vote is not required. An information statement generally contains the same information as a proxy statement.

EXHIBIT 2.4 Transaction Information by Target Type

Information Item	Target Type	
	Public	**Private**
Announcement Date	- 8-K / Press Release	- Acquirer 8-K / Press Release - News Run
Key Deal Terms[a]	- 8-K / Press Release - Proxy - Schedule TO - 14D-9 - Registration Statement / Prospectus (S-4, 424B) - 13E-3	- Acquirer 8-K / Press Release - Acquirer Proxy - Registration Statement / Prospectus (S-4, 424B) - M&A Database - News Run - Trade Publications
Target Description and Financial Data	- Target 10-K / 10-Q - 8-K - Proxy - Registration Statement / Prospectus (S-4, 424B) - 13E-3	- Acquirer 8-K - Acquirer Proxy - Registration Statement / Prospectus (S-4, 424B) - M&A Database - News Run - Trade Publications
Target Historical Share Price Data	- Bloomberg	- NA

[a] Should be updated for amendments to the definitive agreement or a new definitive agreement for a new buyer.

STEP III. SPREAD KEY STATISTICS, RATIOS, AND TRANSACTION MULTIPLES

Once the relevant deal-related and financial information has been located, the banker is prepared to spread each selected transaction. This involves entering the key transaction data relating to purchase price, form of consideration, and target financial statistics into an input page, such as that shown in Exhibit 2.5, where the relevant multiples for each transaction are calculated. An input sheet is created for each comparable acquisition, which, in turn, feeds into summary output sheets used for the benchmarking analysis. In the pages that follow, we explain the financial data displayed on the input page and the calculations behind them.

Calculation of Key Financial Statistics and Ratios

The process for spreading the key financial statistics and ratios for precedent transactions is similar to that outlined in Chapter 1 for comparable companies (see Exhibits 1.53 and 1.54). Our focus for this section, therefore, is on certain nuances for calculating equity value and enterprise value in precedent transactions, including under different purchase consideration scenarios. We also discuss the analysis of premiums paid and synergies.

Equity Value Equity value ("equity purchase price" or "offer value") for public targets in precedent transactions is calculated in a similar manner as that for comparable companies. However, it is based on the announced offer price per share as opposed to the closing share price on a given day. To calculate equity value for public M&A targets, the offer price per share is multiplied by the target's fully diluted shares outstanding at the given offer price. For example, if the acquirer offers the target's shareholders $20.00 per share and the target has 50 million fully diluted shares outstanding (based on the treasury stock method at that price), the equity purchase price would be $1,000 million ($20.00 × 50 million). In those cases where the acquirer purchases less than 100% of the target's outstanding shares, equity value must be grossed up to calculate the implied equity value for the entire company.

In calculating fully diluted shares for precedent transactions, all outstanding in-the-money options and warrants are converted at their weighted average strike prices regardless of whether they are exercisable or not.[10] As with the calculation of fully diluted shares outstanding for comparable companies, out-of-the money options and warrants are not assumed to be converted. For convertible and equity-linked securities, the banker must determine whether they are in-the-money and perform conversion in accordance with the terms and *change of control* provisions as detailed in the registration statement/prospectus.

For M&A transactions in which the target is private, equity value is simply enterprise value less any assumed/refinanced net debt.

---

[10] Assumes that all unvested options and warrants vest upon a change of control (which typically reflects actual circumstances) and that no better detail exists for strike prices than that mentioned in the 10-K or 10-Q.

EXHIBIT 2.5 Precedent Transactions Input Page Template

Acquisition of Target by Acquirer
Input Page
($ in millions, except per share data)

General Information

Target	
Ticker	TRGT
Fiscal Year End	Dec-31
Marginal Tax Rate	

Acquirer	
Ticker	ACOR
Fiscal Year End	Dec-31

Date Announced	1/0/2000
Date Effective	1/0/2000
Transaction Type	NA
Purchase Consideration	NA

Calculation of Equity and Enterprise Value

Offer Price per Share
- Cash Offer Price per Share
- Stock Offer Price per Share
  - Exchange Ratio
  - Acquirer Share Price
- **Offer Price per Share**

- Fully Diluted Shares Outstanding
- **Implied Equity Value**

Implied Enterprise Value
- Plus: Total Debt
- Plus: Preferred Stock
- Plus: Noncontrolling Interest
- Less: Cash and Cash Equivalents
- **Implied Enterprise Value**

LTM Transaction Multiples

	Metric	
EV/Sales		NA
EV/EBITDA		NA
EV/EBIT		NA
P/E		NA

Premiums Paid

Transaction Announcement	Premium
1 Day Prior	

Unaffected Share Price	Premium
1 Day Prior	NA
7 Days Prior	NA
30 Days Prior	NA

Source Documents

	Period	Date Filed
Target 10-K		1/0/2000
Target 10-Q	1/0/2000	1/0/2000
Target 8-K		1/0/2000
Target DEFM14A		1/0/2000
Acquirer 424B		1/0/2000
Acquirer 8-K		1/0/2000

Reported Income Statement

	FYE 1/0/2000	Prior Stub 1/0/2000	Current Stub 1/0/2000	LTM 1/0/2000
Sales				
COGS				
Gross Profit				
SG&A				
Other (Income)/Expense				
EBIT				
Interest Expense				
Pre-tax Income				
Income Taxes				
Noncontrolling Interest				
Preferred Dividends				
Net Income				
Effective Tax Rate	NA	NA	NA	NA
Weighted Avg. Diluted Shares				
Diluted EPS	NA	NA	NA	NA

Adjusted Income Statement

	FYE	Prior Stub	Current Stub	LTM
Reported Gross Profit				
Non-recurring Items in COGS				
Adjusted Gross Profit				
% margin	NA	NA	NA	NA
Reported EBIT				
Non-recurring Items in COGS				
Other Non-recurring Items				
Adjusted EBIT				
% margin	NA	NA	NA	NA
Depreciation & Amortization				
Adjusted EBITDA				
% margin	NA	NA	NA	NA
Reported Net Income				
Non-recurring Items in COGS				
Other Non-recurring Items				
Non-operating Non-rec. Items				
Tax Adjustment				
Adjusted Net Income				
% margin	NA	NA	NA	NA
Adjusted Diluted EPS				

Cash Flow Statement Data

	FYE	Prior Stub	Current Stub	LTM
Depreciation & Amortization				
% sales	NA	NA	NA	NA
Capital Expenditures				
% sales	NA	NA	NA	NA

Notes
(1) [to come]
(2) [to come]
(3) [to come]
(4) [to come]
(5) [to come]

Target Description
[to come]

Acquirer Description
[to come]

Comments
[to come]

Calculation of Fully Diluted Shares Outstanding

Basic Shares Outstanding
Plus: Shares from In-the-Money Options
Less: Shares Repurchased from Option Proceeds
Net New Shares from Options
Plus: Shares from Convertible Securities
Fully Diluted Shares Outstanding

Options/Warrants

Tranche	Number of Shares	Exercise Price	In-the-Money Shares	Proceeds
Tranche 1				
Tranche 2				
Tranche 3				
Tranche 4				
Tranche 5				
Total				

Convertible Securities

	Amount	Conversion Price	Conversion Ratio	New Shares
Issue 1				
Issue 2				
Issue 3				
Issue 4				
Issue 5				
Total				

Purchase Consideration Purchase consideration refers to the mix of cash, stock, and/or other securities that the acquirer offers to the target's shareholders. In some cases, the form of consideration can affect the target shareholders' perception of the value embedded in the offer. For example, some shareholders may prefer cash over stock as payment due to its guaranteed value. On the other hand, some shareholders may prefer stock compensation in order to participate in the upside potential of the combined companies. Tax consequences and other issues may also play a decisive role in guiding shareholder preferences.

The three primary types of consideration for a target's equity are all-cash, stock-for-stock, and cash/stock mix.

All-Cash Transaction As the term implies, in an all-cash transaction, the acquirer makes an offer to purchase all or a portion of the target's shares outstanding for cash (see Exhibit 2.6). This makes for a simple equity value calculation by multiplying the cash offer price per share by the number of fully diluted shares outstanding. Cash represents the cleanest form of currency and certainty of value for all shareholders. However, receipt of such consideration typically triggers a taxable event as opposed to the exchange or receipt of shares of stock, which, if structured properly, is not taxable until the shares are eventually sold.

EXHIBIT 2.6 Press Release Excerpt for All-Cash Transaction

> CLEVELAND, Ohio – June 15, 2012 – AcquirerCo and TargetCo today announced the two companies have entered into a definitive agreement for AcquirerCo to acquire the equity of TargetCo, a publicly held company, in an all-cash transaction at a price of approximately $1 billion, or $20.00 per share. The acquisition is subject to TargetCo shareholder and regulatory approvals and other customary closing conditions, and is expected to close in the fourth quarter of 2012.

Stock-for-Stock Transaction In a stock-for-stock transaction, the calculation of equity value is based on either a *fixed exchange ratio* or a *floating exchange ratio* ("fixed price"). The exchange ratio is calculated as offer price per share divided by the acquirer's share price. A fixed exchange ratio, which is more common than a fixed price structure, is a ratio of how many shares of the acquirer's stock are exchanged for each share of the target's stock. In a floating exchange ratio, the number of acquirer shares exchanged for target shares fluctuates so as to ensure a fixed value for the target's shareholders.

Fixed Exchange Ratio A fixed exchange ratio defines the number of shares of the acquirer's stock to be exchanged for each share of the target's stock. As per Exhibit 2.7, if AcquirerCo agrees to exchange one half share of its stock for every one share of TargetCo stock, the exchange ratio is 0.5.

Precedent Transactions Analysis

EXHIBIT 2.7 Press Release Excerpt for Fixed Exchange Ratio Structure

> CLEVELAND, Ohio – June 15, 2012 – AcquirerCo has announced a definitive agreement to acquire TargetCo in an all-stock transaction valued at $1 billion. Under the terms of the agreement, which has been approved by both boards of directors, TargetCo stockholders will receive, at a fixed exchange ratio, 0.50 shares of AcquirerCo common stock for every share of TargetCo common stock. Based on AcquirerCo's stock price on June 14, 2012 of $40.00, this represents a price of $20.00 per share of TargetCo common stock.

For precedent transactions, offer price per share is calculated by multiplying the exchange ratio by the share price of the acquirer, typically one day prior to announcement (see Exhibit 2.8).

EXHIBIT 2.8 Calculation of Offer Price per Share and Equity Value in a Fixed Exchange Ratio Structure

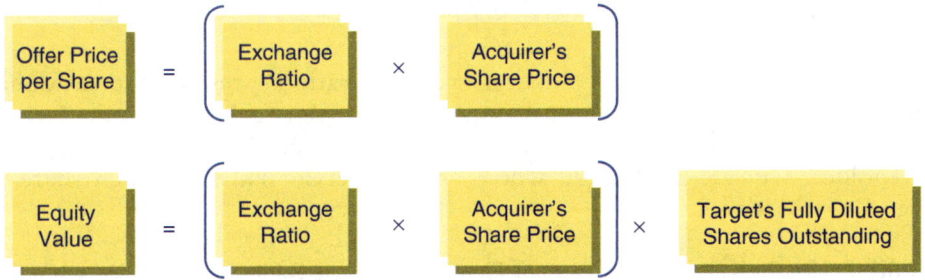

In a fixed exchange ratio structure, the offer price per share (value to target) moves in line with the underlying share price of the acquirer. The amount of the acquirer's shares received, however, is constant (see Exhibit 2.9). For example, assuming TargetCo has 50 million fully diluted shares outstanding, it will receive 25 million shares of AcquirerCo stock. The shares received by the target and the respective ownership percentages for the acquirer and target remain fixed regardless of share price movement between execution of the definitive agreement ("signing") and transaction close (assuming no structural protections for either the acquirer or target, such as a *collar*).[11]

Following a deal's announcement, the market immediately starts to assimilate the publicly disclosed information. In response, the target's and acquirer's share prices begin to trade in line with the market's perception of the transaction.[12] Therefore, the target assumes the risk of a decline in the acquirer's share price, but preserves the potential to share in the upside, both immediately and over time. The fixed exchange ratio is more commonly used than the floating exchange ratio as it "links" both

---

[11] In a fixed exchange ratio deal, a collar can be used to guarantee a certain range of prices to the target's shareholders. For example, a target may agree to a $20.00 offer price per share based on an exchange ratio of 1:2, with a collar guaranteeing that the shareholders will receive no less than $18.00 and no more than $22.00, regardless of how the acquirer's shares trade between signing and closing.

[12] Factors considered by the market when evaluating a proposed transaction include strategic merit, economics of the deal, synergies, and likelihood of closing.

parties' share prices, thereby enabling them to share the risk (or opportunity) from movements post-announcement.

EXHIBIT 2.9   Fixed Exchange Ratio – Value to Target and Shares Received

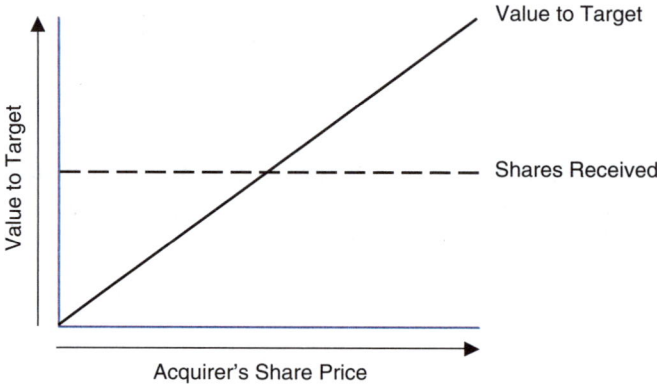

Floating Exchange Ratio   A floating exchange ratio represents the set dollar amount per share that the acquirer has agreed to pay for each share of the target's stock in the form of shares of the acquirer's stock. As per Exhibit 2.10, TargetCo shareholders will receive $20.00 worth of AcquirerCo shares for each share of TargetCo stock they own.

EXHIBIT 2.10   Press Release Excerpt for Floating Exchange Ratio Structure

> CLEVELAND, Ohio – June 15, 2012 – AcquirerCo and TargetCo today announced the execution of a definitive agreement pursuant to which AcquirerCo will acquire TargetCo in an all-stock transaction. Pursuant to the agreement, TargetCo stockholders will receive $20.00 of AcquirerCo common stock for each share of TargetCo common stock they hold. The number of AcquirerCo shares to be issued to TargetCo stockholders will be calculated based on the average closing price of AcquirerCo common stock for the 30 trading days immediately preceding the third trading day before the closing of the transaction.

In a floating exchange ratio structure, as opposed to a fixed exchange ratio, the dollar offer price per share (value to target) is set, and the number of shares exchanged fluctuates in accordance with the movement of the acquirer's share price (see Exhibit 2.11).

The number of shares to be exchanged is typically based on an average of the acquirer's share price for a specified time period prior to transaction close. This structure presents target shareholders with greater certainty in terms of value received as the acquirer assumes the full risk of a decline in its share price (assuming no structural protections for the acquirer). In general, a floating exchange ratio is used when the acquirer is significantly larger than the target. It is justified in these cases on the basis that while a significant decline in the target's business does not materially impact the value of the acquirer, the reciprocal is not true.

Precedent Transactions Analysis

EXHIBIT 2.11 Floating Exchange Ratio – Value to Target and Shares Received

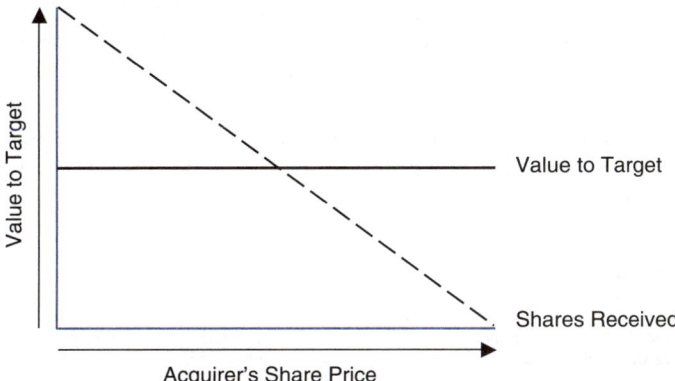

Cash and Stock Transaction In a cash and stock transaction, the acquirer offers a combination of cash and stock as purchase consideration (see Exhibit 2.12).

EXHIBIT 2.12 Press Release Excerpt for Cash and Stock Transaction

> CLEVELAND, Ohio – June 15, 2012 – AcquirerCo and TargetCo announced today that they signed a definitive agreement whereby AcquirerCo will acquire TargetCo for a purchase price of approximately $1 billion in a mix of cash and AcquirerCo stock. Under the terms of the agreement, which was unanimously approved by the boards of directors of both companies, TargetCo stockholders will receive $10.00 in cash and 0.25 shares of AcquirerCo common stock for each outstanding TargetCo share. Based on AcquirerCo's closing price of $40.00 on June 14, 2012, AcquirerCo will issue an aggregate of approximately 12.5 million shares of its common stock and pay an aggregate of approximately $500 million in cash in the transaction.

The cash portion of the offer represents a fixed value per share for target shareholders. The stock portion of the offer can be set according to either a fixed or floating exchange ratio. The calculation of offer price per share and equity value in a cash and stock transaction (assuming a fixed exchange ratio) is shown in Exhibit 2.13.

EXHIBIT 2.13 Calculation of Offer Price per Share and Equity Value in a Cash and Stock Transaction

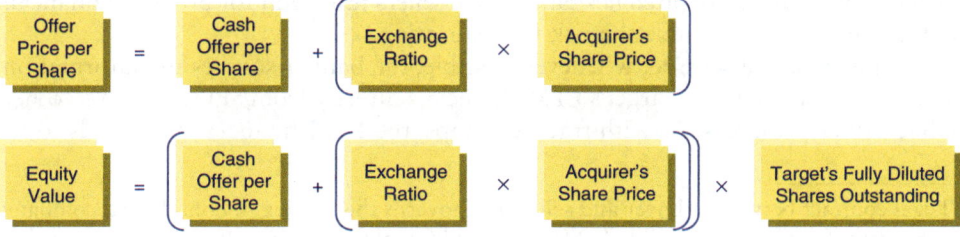

Enterprise Value Enterprise value ("transaction value") is the total value offered by the acquirer for the target's equity interests, as well as the assumption or refinancing of the target's net debt. It is calculated for precedent transactions in the same manner as for comparable companies, comprising the sum of equity, net debt, preferred stock, and noncontrolling interest. Exhibit 2.14 illustrates the calculation of enterprise value, with equity value calculated as offer price per share (the sum of the target's "unaffected" share price and premium paid, see "Premiums Paid") multiplied by the target's fully diluted shares outstanding.

EXHIBIT 2.14 Calculation of Enterprise Value

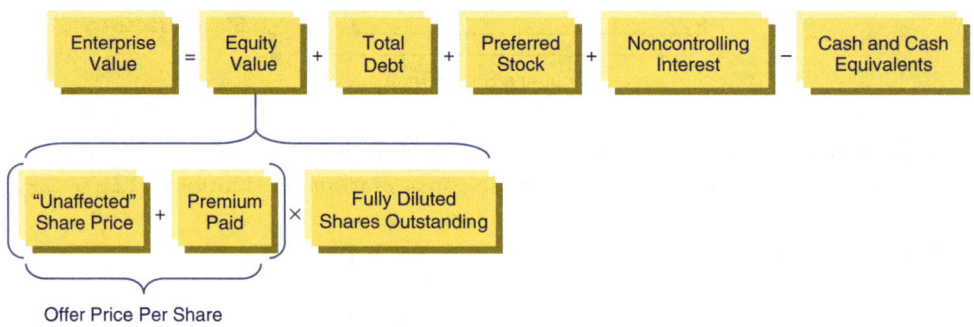

Calculation of Key Transaction Multiples

The key transaction multiples used in transaction comps mirror those used for trading comps. Equity value, as represented by the offer price for the target's equity, is used as a multiple of net income (or offer price per share as a multiple of diluted EPS) and enterprise value (or transaction value) is used as a multiple of EBITDA, EBIT, and, to a lesser extent, sales. In precedent transactions, these multiples are typically higher than those in trading comps due to the premium paid for control and/or synergies.

Multiples for precedent transactions are typically calculated on the basis of actual LTM financial statistics available at the time of announcement. The full projections that an acquirer uses to frame its purchase price decision are generally not public and subject to a confidentiality agreement.[13] Therefore, while equity research may offer insights into future performance for a public target, identifying the actual projections that an acquirer used when making its acquisition decision is typically not feasible. Furthermore, buyers are often hesitant to give sellers full credit for projected financial performance as they assume the risk for realization.

As previously discussed, whenever possible, the banker sources the information necessary to calculate the target's LTM financials directly from SEC filings and other public primary sources. As with trading comps, the LTM financial data needs to be

---

[13]Legal contract between a buyer and seller that governs the sharing of confidential company information. See Chapter 6: Sell-Side M&A for additional information. In the event the banker performing transaction comps is privy to non-public information regarding one of the selected comparable acquisitions, the banker must refrain from using that information in order to maintain client confidentiality.

Precedent Transactions Analysis

adjusted for non-recurring items and recent events in order to calculate clean multiples that reflect the target's normalized performance.

Equity Value Multiples

Offer Price per Share-to-LTM EPS / Equity Value-to-LTM Net Income The most broadly used equity value multiple is the P/E ratio, namely offer price per share divided by LTM diluted earnings per share (or equity value divided by LTM net income, see Exhibit 2.15).

EXHIBIT 2.15 Equity Value Multiples

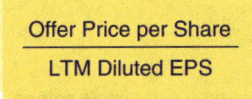
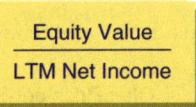

Enterprise Value Multiples

Enterprise Value-to-LTM EBITDA, EBIT, and Sales As in trading comps, enterprise value is used in the numerator when calculating multiples for financial statistics that apply to both debt and equity holders. The most common enterprise value multiples are shown in Exhibit 2.16, with EV/LTM EBITDA being the most prevalent. As discussed in Chapter 1, however, certain sectors may rely on additional or other metrics to drive valuation (see Exhibit 1.33).

EXHIBIT 2.16 Enterprise Value Multiples

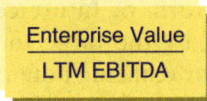

Premiums Paid The *premium paid* refers to the incremental dollar amount per share that the acquirer offers relative to the target's unaffected share price, expressed as a percentage. As such, it is only relevant for public target companies. In calculating the premium paid relative to a given date, it is important to use the target's unaffected share price so as to isolate the true effect of the purchase offer.

The closing share price on the day prior to the official transaction announcement typically serves as a good proxy for the unaffected share price. However, to isolate for the effects of market gyrations and potential share price "creep" due to rumors or information leakage regarding the deal, the banker examines the offer price per share relative to the target's share price at multiple time intervals prior to transaction announcement (e.g., one trading day, seven calendar days, and 30 calendar days or more).[14]

---

[14]60, 90, 180, or an average of a set number of calendar days prior, as well as the 52-week high and low, may also be reviewed.

In the event the seller has publicly announced its intention to pursue "strategic alternatives" or there is a major leak prior to announcement, the target's share price may increase in anticipation of a potential takeover. In this case, the target's share price on the day(s) prior to the official transaction announcement is not truly unaffected. Therefore, it is appropriate to examine the premiums paid relative to the target's share price at various intervals prior to such an announcement or leak in addition to the actual transaction announcement.

The formula for calculating the percentage premium paid, as well as an illustrative example, is shown in Exhibit 2.17. In this example, we calculate a 35% premium assuming that the target's shareholders are being offered $67.50 per share for a stock that was trading at an unaffected share price of $50.00.

EXHIBIT 2.17   Calculation of Premium Paid

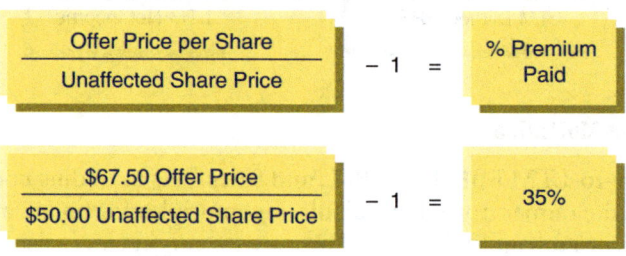

Synergies   Synergies refer to the expected cost savings, growth opportunities, and other financial benefits that occur as a result of the combination of two businesses. Consequently, the assessment of synergies is most relevant for transactions where a strategic buyer is purchasing a target in a related business.

Synergies represent tangible value to the acquirer in the form of future cash flow and earnings above and beyond what can be achieved by the target on a stand-alone basis. Therefore, the size and degree of likelihood for realizing potential synergies play an important role for the acquirer in framing the purchase price for a particular target. Theoretically, higher synergies translate into a higher potential price that the acquirer can pay. In analyzing a given comparable acquisition, the amount of announced synergies provides important perspective on the purchase price and multiple paid.

Upon announcement of a material acquisition, public acquirers often provide guidance on the nature and amount of expected synergies. This information is typically communicated via the press release announcing the transaction (see illustrative press release excerpt in Exhibit 2.18) and potentially an investor presentation.

EXHIBIT 2.18 Press Release Excerpt Discussing Synergies in a Strategic Acquisition

> CLEVELAND, Ohio – June 15, 2012 – AcquirerCo and TargetCo announced today that they have signed a definitive agreement to merge the two companies…The proposed transaction is expected to provide substantial benefits for shareholders of the combined company and significant value creation through identified highly achievable synergies of $25 million in the first year after closing, and $50 million annually beginning in 2014. As facilities and operations are consolidated, a substantial portion of cost synergies and capital expenditure savings are expected to come from increased scale. Additional savings are expected to result from combining staff functions and the elimination of a significant amount of SG&A expenses that would be duplicative in the combined company.

Equity research reports also may provide helpful commentary on the value of expected synergies, including the likelihood of realization. Depending on the situation, investors afford varying degrees of credit for announced synergies, as reflected in the acquirer's post-announcement share price. In precedent transactions, it is helpful to note the announced expected synergies for each transaction where such information is available. However, the transaction multiples are typically shown on the basis of the target's reported LTM financial information (i.e., without adjusting for synergies). For a deeper understanding of a particular multiple paid, the banker may calculate adjusted multiples that reflect expected synergies. This typically involves adding the full effect of expected annual run-rate cost savings synergies (excluding costs to achieve) to an earnings metric in the denominator (e.g., EBITDA and EPS).

Exhibit 2.19 shows the calculation of an EV/LTM EBITDA transaction multiple before and after the consideration of expected synergies, assuming a purchase price of $1,200 million, LTM EBITDA of $150 million, and synergies of $25 million.

EXHIBIT 2.19 Synergies-Adjusted Multiple

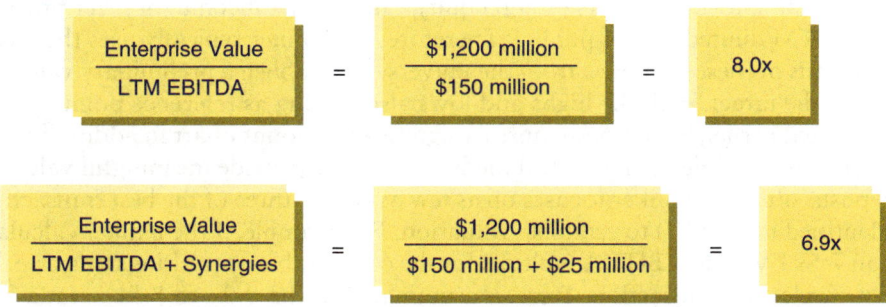

STEP IV. BENCHMARK THE COMPARABLE ACQUISITIONS

As with trading comps, the next level of analysis involves an in-depth study of the selected comparable acquisitions so as to determine those most relevant for valuing the target. As part of this analysis, the banker re-examines the business profile and benchmarks the key financial statistics and ratios for each of the acquired companies, with an eye toward identifying those most comparable to the target. Output sheets, such as those shown in Exhibits 1.53 and 1.54 in Chapter 1, facilitate this analysis.

The transaction multiples and deal information for each selected acquisition are also linked to an output sheet where they can be easily benchmarked against one another and the broader universe (see Exhibit 2.35). Each comparable acquisition is closely examined as part of the final refining of the universe, with the best comparable transactions identified and obvious outliers eliminated. As would be expected, a recently consummated deal involving a direct competitor with a similar financial profile is typically more relevant than, for example, an older transaction from a different point in the business or credit cycle, or for a marginal player in the sector.

A thoughtful analysis weighs other considerations such as market conditions and deal dynamics in conjunction with the target's business and financial profile. For example, a high multiple LBO consummated via an auction process during the credit boom of the mid-2000s would be less relevant for valuing a target in the 2008 to 2009 timeframe.

STEP V. DETERMINE VALUATION

In precedent transactions, the multiples of the selected comparable acquisitions universe are used to derive an implied valuation range for the target. While standards vary by sector, the key multiples driving valuation in precedent transactions tend to be enterprise value-to-LTM EBITDA and equity value-to-net income (or offer price per share-to-LTM diluted EPS, if public). Therefore, the banker typically uses the means and medians of these multiples from the universe to establish a preliminary valuation range for the target, with the highs and lows also serving as reference points.

As noted earlier, valuation requires a significant amount of art in addition to science. Therefore, while the mean and median multiples provide meaningful valuation guideposts, often the banker focuses on as few as two or three of the best transactions (as identified in Step IV) to establish valuation. For example, if the banker calculates a mean 7.5x EV/LTM EBITDA multiple for the comparable acquisitions universe, but the most relevant transactions were consummated in the 8.0x to 8.5x area, a 7.5x to 8.5x range might be more appropriate. This would place greater emphasis on the best transactions. The chosen multiple range would then be applied to the target's LTM financial statistics to derive an implied valuation range for the target, using the methodology described in Chapter 1 (see Exhibits 1.35, 1.36, and 1.37).

As with other valuation methodologies, once a valuation range for the target has been established, it is necessary to analyze the output and test conclusions. A common red flag for precedent transactions is when the implied valuation range is significantly lower than the range derived using comparable companies. In this instance, the banker

Precedent Transactions Analysis

should revisit the assumptions underlying the selection of both the universes of comparable acquisitions and comparable companies, as well as the calculations behind the multiples. However, it is important to note that this may not always represent a flawed analysis. If a particular sector is "in play" or benefiting from a cyclical high, for example, the implied valuation range from comparable companies might be higher than that from precedent transactions. The banker should also examine the results in isolation, using best judgment as well as guidance from a senior colleague to determine whether the results make sense.

KEY PROS AND CONS

Pros

- *Market-based* – analysis is based on actual acquisition multiples and premiums paid for similar companies
- *Current* – recent transactions tend to reflect prevailing M&A, capital markets, and general economic conditions
- *Relativity* – multiples approach provides straightforward reference points across sectors and time periods
- *Simplicity* – key multiples for a few selected transactions can anchor valuation
- *Objectivity* – precedent-based and, therefore, avoids making assumptions about a company's future performance

Cons

- *Market-based* – multiples may be skewed depending on capital markets and/or economic environment at the time of the transaction
- *Time lag* – precedent transactions, by definition, have occurred in the past and, therefore, may not be truly reflective of prevailing market conditions (e.g., the LBO boom in the mid-2000s vs. the ensuing credit crunch)
- *Existence of comparable acquisitions* – in some cases it may be difficult to find a robust universe of precedent transactions
- *Availability of information* – information may be insufficient to determine transaction multiples for many comparable acquisitions
- *Acquirer's basis for valuation* – multiple paid by the buyer may be based on expectations governing the target's future financial performance (which is typically not publicly disclosed) rather than on reported LTM financial information

ILLUSTRATIVE PRECEDENT TRANSACTION ANALYSIS FOR VALUECO

The following section provides a detailed, step-by-step example of how precedent transactions analysis is applied to establish a valuation range for our illustrative target company, ValueCo.

Step I. Select the Universe of Comparable Acquisitions

Screen for Comparable Acquisitions Our screen for comparable acquisitions began by searching M&A databases for past transactions involving companies similar to ValueCo in terms of sector and size. Our initial screen focused on transactions that occurred over the past three years with enterprise value between approximately $1 billion and $15 billion. At the same time, we examined the acquisition history of ValueCo's comparable companies (as determined in Chapter 1) for relevant transactions.

The comparable companies' public filings (including merger proxies) were helpful for identifying and analyzing past acquisitions and sales of relevant businesses. Research reports for individual companies as well as sector reports also provided valuable information. In total, these resources produced a sizeable list of potential precedent transactions. Upon further scrutiny, we eliminated several transactions where the target's size or business model differed significantly from that of ValueCo.

Examine Other Considerations For each of the selected transactions, we examined the specific deal circumstances, including market conditions and deal dynamics. For example, we discerned whether the acquisition took place during a cyclical high or low in the target's sector as well as the prevailing capital markets conditions. We also determined whether the acquirer was a strategic buyer or a financial sponsor and noted whether the target was sold through an auction process or a negotiated/friendly transaction, and if it was contested. The form of consideration (i.e., cash vs. stock) was also analyzed as part of this exercise. While these deal considerations did not change the list of comparable acquisitions, the context helped us better interpret and compare the acquisition multiples and premiums paid.

By the end of Step I, we established a solid initial list of comparable acquisitions to be further analyzed. Exhibit 2.20 displays basic data about the selected transactions and target companies for easy comparison.

Step II. Locate the Necessary Deal-Related and Financial Information

In Step II, we set out to locate the relevant deal-related and financial information necessary to spread each comparable acquisition. To illustrate this task, we highlighted Pearl Corp.'s ("Pearl") acquisition of Rosenbaum Industries ("Rosenbaum"), the most recent transaction on our list.[15] As this transaction involved a public acquirer

---

[15]Pearl is also a comparable company to ValueCo (see Chapter 1, Exhibits 1.53, 1.54, and 1.55).

Precedent Transactions Analysis

and a public target, the necessary information was readily accessible via the relevant SEC filings.

EXHIBIT 2.20 Initial List of Comparable Acquisitions

($ in millions)

Date Announced	Acquirer	Target	Transaction Type	Target Business Description	Equity Value	Enterprise Value	LTM Sales	LTM EBITDA
11/2/12	Pearl Corp.	Rosenbaum Industries	Public / Public	Engages in the manufacture and sale of chemicals, plastics, and fibers	$2,500	$3,825	$2,385	$450
7/20/12	Goodson Corp.	Schneider & Co.	Public / Public	US-based company engaged in providing water treatment and process chemicals	5,049	6,174	4,359	764
6/21/12	Domanski Capital	Ackerman Industries	Sponsor / Public	Specialty chemical company that supplies technologies and produces additives, ingredients, resins, and compounds	8,845	9,995	5,941	1,248
4/15/12	The Hochberg Group	Whalen Inc.	Sponsor / Private	World's largest producer of alkylamines and derivatives	1,250	1,350	700	180
8/8/11	Cole Manufacturing	Gordon Inc.	Public / Public	Provider of cleaning, sanitizing, food safety, and infection prevention products and services	2,620	3,045	1,989	340
7/6/11	Eu-Han Capital	Rughwani International	Sponsor / Public	Supplies products for the manufacturing, construction, automotive, chemical processing, and other industries worldwide	3,390	4,340	2,722	558
3/20/11	Lanzarone Global	Falk & Sons	Public / Private	Manufactures specialty chemicals and functional ingredients for personal care, pharmaceutical, oral care, and institutional cleaning applications	8,750	10,350	5,933	1,235
11/9/10	Meisner Global Management	Kamras Brands	Sponsor / Private	Manufactures and markets basic chemicals, vinyls, polymers, and fabricated building products	1,765	2,115	1,416	269
6/22/10	Pryor, Inc.	ParkCo	Public / Private	Offers a broad range of chemicals and solutions used in consumer products applications	6,450	8,700	7,950	1,240
4/15/10	Leicht & Co.	Bress Products	Public / Public	Engages in the development, production, and sale of food ingredients, enzymes, and bio-based solutions	12,431	12,681	8,250	1,550

8-K/Press Release Our search for relevant deal information began by locating the 8-K filed upon announcement of the transaction. The 8-K contained the press release announcing the transaction as well as a copy of the definitive agreement as an exhibit. The press release provided an overview of the basic terms of the deal, including the offer price per share, enterprise value, and purchase consideration, as well as a description of both the acquirer and target and a brief description of the transaction rationale (see Exhibit 2.21). The definitive agreement contained the detailed terms and conditions of the transaction.

We also checked to see whether the original transaction changed for any new announced terms. As previously discussed, this is a relatively common occurrence in competitive situations where two or more parties enter into a bidding war for a given target.

EXHIBIT 2.21 Press Release Excerpt from the Announcement of the Pearl/Rosenbaum Transaction

> CLEVELAND, Ohio – November 2, 2012 – PEARL CORP. (NYSE: PRL), a producer of specialty chemical products, announced today that it has entered into a definitive agreement to acquire ROSENBAUM INDUSTRIES (NYSE: JNR), a manufacturer of plastics and fibers, for an aggregate consideration of approximately $3.825 billion, including the payment of $20.00 per outstanding share in cash and the assumption of $1.325 billion in net debt. The strategic business combination of Pearl and Rosenbaum will create a leading provider of "best-in-class" chemical products in North America. When completed, Pearl anticipates the combined companies will benefit from a broader product offering, complementary distribution channels, and efficiencies from streamlining its facilities. This is expected to result in $100 million of annual synergies by 2014.

Proxy Statement (DEFM14A) As Rosenbaum is a public company, its board of directors sought approval for the transaction from Rosenbaum's shareholders via a proxy statement. The proxy statement contained Rosenbaum's most recent basic share count, a detailed background of the merger, discussion of the premium paid, and an excerpt from the fairness opinion, among other items. The background described key events leading up to the transaction announcement and provided us with helpful insight into other deal considerations useful for interpreting purchase price, including buyer/seller dynamics (see excerpt in Exhibit 2.22).

EXHIBIT 2.22 Excerpt from Rosenbaum's Proxy Statement

> On June 1, 2012, Rosenbaum's CEO was informed of a financial sponsor's interest in a potential takeover and request for additional information in order to make a formal bid. This unsolicited interest prompted Rosenbaum's Board of Directors to form a special committee and engage an investment bank and legal counsel to explore strategic alternatives. Upon being contacted by Rosenbaum's advisor, the sponsor submitted a written indication of interest containing a preliminary valuation range of $15.00 to $17.00 per share and outlining a proposed due diligence process. Subsequently, certain media outlets reported that a sale of Rosenbaum was imminent, prompting the company to publicly announce its decision to explore strategic alternatives on August 15, 2012.
>
> One week later, Pearl sent Rosenbaum a preliminary written indication of interest with a price range of $17.00 to $18.00. In addition, Rosenbaum's advisor contacted an additional 5 strategic buyers and 10 financial sponsors, although these parties did not ultimately participate in the formal process. Both the bidding financial sponsor and Pearl were then invited to attend a management presentation and perform due diligence, after which the financial sponsor and Pearl presented formal letters with bids of $18.00 and $20.00 per share in cash, respectively. Pearl's offer, as the highest cash offer, was accepted.

This background highlights the competitive dynamics involved in the process, which helped explain why the multiple paid for Rosenbaum is above the mean of the selected comparable acquisitions (see Exhibit 2.35).

Rosenbaum's 10-K and 10-Q   Rosenbaum's 10-K and 10-Q for the period prior to the transaction announcement provided us with the financial data necessary to calculate its LTM financial statistics as well as equity value and enterprise value (based on the offer price per share). We also read through the MD&A and notes to the financials for further insight into Rosenbaum's financial performance as well as for information on potential non-recurring items and recent events. *These public filings provided us with the remaining information necessary to calculate the transaction multiples.*

Research Reports   We also read through equity research reports for Pearl and Rosenbaum following the transaction announcement for further color on the circumstances of the deal, including Pearl's strategic rationale and expected synergies.

Investor Presentation   In addition, Pearl posted an investor presentation to its corporate website under an "Investor Relations" link, which confirmed the financial information and multiples calculated in Exhibit 2.23.

Financial Information Service   We used Bloomberg to source key historical share price information for Rosenbaum. These data points included the share price on the day prior to the actual transaction announcement, the unaffected share price (i.e., on the day prior to Rosenbaum's announcement of the exploration of strategic alternatives), and the share price at various intervals prior to the unaffected share price. This share price information served as the basis for the premiums paid calculations in Exhibit 2.33.

Step III. Spread Key Statistics, Ratios, and Transaction Multiples

After locating the necessary deal-related and financial information for the selected comparable acquisitions, we created input pages for each transaction, as shown in Exhibit 2.23 for the Pearl/Rosenbaum transaction.

EXHIBIT 2.23 Input Page for the Acquisition of Rosenbaum by Pearl

Acquisition of Rosenbaum Industries by Pearl Corp.
Input Page
($ in millions, except per share data)

General Information

Target	
Ticker	Rosenbaum Industries
Fiscal Year End	JNR
Marginal Tax Rate	Dec-31
	38.0%

Acquirer	
Ticker	Pearl Corp.
Fiscal Year End	PRL
	Dec-31

Date Announced	11/2/2012
Date Effective	Pending
Transaction Type	Public / Public
Purchase Consideration	Cash

Calculation of Equity and Enterprise Value

Offer Price per Share	
Cash Offer Price per Share	$20.00
Stock Offer Price per Share	-
Exchange Ratio	-
Pearl Corp. Share Price	-
Offer Price per Share	**$20.00**

Fully Diluted Shares Outstanding	125.000
Implied Equity Value	**$2,500.0**
Plus: Total Debt	1,375.0
Plus: Preferred Stock	-
Plus: Noncontrolling Interest	-
Less: Cash and Cash Equivalents	(50.0)
Implied Enterprise Value	**$3,825.0**

LTM Transaction Multiples

EV/Sales	1.6x
Metric	$2,385.0
EV/EBITDA	8.5x
Metric	$450.0
EV/EBIT	11.2x
Metric	$343.0
P/E	16.6x
Metric	$1.21

Premiums Paid

Transaction Announcement		Premium
1 Day Prior		15.0% (2)

Unaffected Share Price		
1 Day Prior	$14.81	35.0%
7 Days Prior	15.04	33.0%
30 Days Prior	14.60	37.0%

Source Documents

	Period	Date Filed
Rosenbaum Industries 10-K	12/31/2011	2/14/2012
Rosenbaum Industries 10-Q	9/30/2012	10/30/2012
Rosenbaum Industries 8-K		11/2/2012
Rosenbaum Industries DEFM14A		12/15/2012

Reported Income Statement

	FYE 12/31/2011	Prior Stub 9/30/2011	Current Stub 9/30/2012	LTM 9/30/2012
Sales	$2,250.0	$1,687.5	$1,822.5	$2,385.0
COGS	1,500.0	1,125.0	1,215.0	1,590.0
Gross Profit	$750.0	$562.5	$607.5	$795.0
SG&A	450.0	337.5	364.5	477.0
Other (Income)/Expense	-	-	-	-
EBIT	$300.0	$225.0	$243.0	$318.0
Interest Expense	100.0	75.0	75.0	100.0
Pre-tax Income	$200.0	$150.0	$168.0	$218.0
Income Taxes	76.0	57.0	63.8	82.8
Noncontrolling Interest	-	-	-	-
Preferred Dividends	-	-	-	-
Net Income	**$124.0**	**$93.0**	**$104.2**	**$135.2**
Effective Tax Rate	38.0%	38.0%	38.0%	38.0%
Weighted Avg. Diluted Shares	125.0	125.0	125.0	125.0
Diluted EPS	$0.99	$0.74	$0.83	$1.08

Adjusted Income Statement

	FYE 12/31/2011	Prior Stub 9/30/2011	Current Stub 9/30/2012	LTM 9/30/2012
Reported Gross Profit	$750.0	$562.5	$607.5	$795.0
Non-recurring Items in COGS	-	-	-	-
Adjusted Gross Profit	**$750.0**	**$562.5**	**$607.5**	**$795.0**
% margin	33.3%	33.3%	33.3%	33.3%
Reported EBIT	$300.0	$225.0	$243.0	$318.0
Non-recurring Items in COGS	-	-	-	-
Other Non-recurring Items	25.0	-	-	25.0 (1)
Adjusted EBIT	**$325.0**	**$225.0**	**$243.0**	**$343.0**
% margin	14.4%	13.3%	13.3%	14.4%
Depreciation & Amortization	100.0	75.0	82.0	107.0
Adjusted EBITDA	**$425.0**	**$300.0**	**$325.0**	**$450.0**
% margin	18.9%	17.8%	17.6%	18.9%
Reported Net Income	$124.0	$93.0	$104.2	$135.2
Non-recurring Items in COGS	-	-	-	-
Other Non-recurring Items	25.0	-	-	25.0
Non-operating Non-rec. Items	-	-	-	-
Tax Adjustment	(9.5)	-	-	(9.5)
Adjusted Net Income	**$139.5**	**$93.0**	**$104.2**	**$150.7**
% margin	6.2%	5.5%	5.7%	6.3%
Adjusted Diluted EPS	$1.12	$0.74	$0.83	$1.21

Cash Flow Statement Data

	FYE 12/31/2011	Prior Stub 9/30/2011	Current Stub 9/30/2012	LTM 9/30/2012
Depreciation & Amortization	100.0	75.0	82.0	107.0
% sales	4.4%	4.4%	4.5%	4.5%
Capital Expenditures	105.0	75.0	85.0	115.0
% sales	4.7%	4.4%	4.7%	4.8%

Notes
(1) In Q4 2011, Rosenbaum Industries recorded a $25 million pre-tax payment in regards to a litigation settlement (see 2011 10-K MD&A, page 50).
(2) On August 15, 2012, Rosenbaum Industries announced the formation of a special committee to explore strategic alternatives.

Target Description
Engages in the manufacture and sale of chemicals, plastics, and fibers

Acquirer Description
Manufactures and markets performance materials and speciality chemicals

Comments
The combined company will benefit from a broader product offering, complementary distribution channels, and efficiencies from streamlining facilities. The transaction also extends the acquirer's reach into emerging markets. Annual cost saving synergies of approximately $100 million expected by the end of 2014.

Calculation of Fully Diluted Shares Outstanding

Basic Shares Outstanding	123.000
Plus: Shares from In-the-Money Options	3.750
Less: Shares Repurchased from Option Proceeds	(1.750)
Net New Shares from Options	2.000
Plus: Shares from Convertible Securities	-
Fully Diluted Shares Outstanding	**125.000**

Options/Warrants

Tranche	Number of Shares	Exercise Price	In-the-Money Shares	Proceeds
Tranche 1	1.500	$5.00	1.500	$7.5
Tranche 2	1.250	10.00	1.250	12.5
Tranche 3	1.000	15.00	1.000	15.0
Tranche 4				
Tranche 5				
Total			**3.750**	**$35.0**

Convertible Securities

	Amount	Conversion Price	Conversion Ratio	New Shares
Issue 1				
Issue 2				
Issue 3				
Issue 4				
Issue 5				
Total				**-**

Precedent Transactions Analysis

Below, we walk through each section of the input sheet in Exhibit 2.23.

General Information In the "General Information" section of the input page, we entered basic company and transaction information, such as the target's and acquirer's names and fiscal year ends, as well as the transaction announcement and closing dates, transaction type, and purchase consideration. As shown in Exhibit 2.24, Rosenbaum Industries (NYSE:JNR) was acquired by Pearl Corp. (NYSE:PRL) in an all-cash transaction. Both companies have a fiscal year ending December 31. The transaction was announced on November 2, 2012.

EXHIBIT 2.24 General Information Section

General Information	
Target	**Rosenbaum Industries**
Ticker	JNR
Fiscal Year End	Dec-31
Marginal Tax Rate	*38.0%*
Acquirer	**Pearl Corp.**
Ticker	PRL
Fiscal Year End	Dec-31
Date Announced	11/2/2012
Date Effective	Pending
Transaction Type	Public/Public
Purchase Consideration	Cash

Calculation of Equity and Enterprise Value Under "Calculation of Equity and Enterprise Value," we first entered Pearl's offer price per share of $20.00 in cash to Rosenbaum's shareholders, as disclosed in the 8-K and accompanying press release announcing the transaction (see Exhibit 2.25).

EXHIBIT 2.25 Calculation of Equity and Enterprise Value Section

($ in millions, except per share data)

Calculation of Equity and Enterprise Value	
Offer Price per Share	
Cash Offer Price per Share	$20.00
Stock Offer Price per Share	-
Exchange Ratio	-
Pearl Corp. Share Price	-
Offer Price per Share	**$20.00**
Fully Diluted Shares Outstanding	-
Implied Equity Value	-
Implied Enterprise Value	
Plus: Total Debt	-
Plus: Preferred Stock	-
Plus: Noncontrolling Interest	-
Less: Cash and Cash Equivalents	-
Implied Enterprise Value	-

= Cash Offer Price per Share + Stock Offer Price per Share
= $20.00 + $0.00

Calculation of Fully Diluted Shares Outstanding As sourced from the most recent proxy statement, Rosenbaum had basic shares outstanding of 123 million. Rosenbaum also had three "tranches" of options, as detailed in its most recent 10-K (see "Options/Warrants" heading in Exhibit 2.26). At the $20.00 offer price, the three tranches of options are all in-the-money. In calculating fully diluted shares outstanding for precedent transactions, all outstanding in-the-money options and warrants are converted at their weighted average strike prices regardless of whether they are exercisable or not. These three tranches represent 3.75 million shares, which generate total proceeds of $35 million at their respective exercise prices. In accordance with the TSM, these proceeds are assumed to repurchase 1.75 million shares at the $20.00 offer price ($35 million/$20.00), thereby providing net new shares of 2 million. These incremental shares are added to Rosenbaum's basic shares to calculate fully diluted shares outstanding of 125 million.

EXHIBIT 2.26 Calculation of Fully Diluted Shares Outstanding Section

($ in millions, except per share data)

Calculation of Fully Diluted Shares Outstanding

Basic Shares Outstanding	123.000
Plus: Shares from In-the-Money Options	3.750
Less: Shares Repurchased from Option Proceeds	(1.750)
Net New Shares from Options	**2.000**
Plus: Shares from Convertible Securities	-
Fully Diluted Shares Outstanding	**125.000**

- 3.750 = Total In-the-Money Shares
- (1.750) = Total Option Proceeds / Current Share Price = $35.0 million / $20.00

Options/Warrants

Tranche	Number of Shares	Exercise Price	In-the-Money Shares	Proceeds
Tranche 1	1.500	$5.00	1.500	$7.5
Tranche 2	1.250	10.00	1.250	12.5
Tranche 3	1.000	15.00	1.000	15.0
Tranche 4	-	-	-	-
Tranche 5	-	-	-	-
Total	**3.750**		**3.750**	**$35.0**

- In-the-Money Shares: = IF(Weighted Average Strike Price < Current Share Price, display Number of Shares, otherwise display 0) = IF($5.00 < $20.00, 1.500, 0)
- Proceeds: = IF(In-the-Money Shares > 0, then In-the-Money Shares x Weighted Average Strike Price, otherwise display 0) = IF(1.500 > 0, 1.500 x $5.00, 0)

Convertible Securities

	Amount	Conversion Price	Conversion Ratio	New Shares
Issue 1	-	-	-	-
Issue 2	-	-	-	-
Issue 3	-	-	-	-
Issue 4	-	-	-	-
Issue 5	-	-	-	-
Total				**-**

Equity Value The 125 million fully diluted shares outstanding feeds into the "Calculation of Equity and Enterprise Value" section. It is then multiplied by the $20.00 offer price per share to produce an equity value of $2,500 million (see Exhibit 2.27).

Precedent Transactions Analysis

EXHIBIT 2.27 Equity Value

($ in millions, except per share data)

Calculation of Equity and Enterprise Value	
Offer Price per Share	
Cash Offer Price per Share	$20.00
Stock Offer Price per Share	-
Exchange Ratio	-
Pearl Corp. Share Price	-
Offer Price per Share	**$20.00**
Fully Diluted Shares Outstanding	125.000
Implied Equity Value	**$2,500.0**

= Offer Price per Price × Fully Diluted Shares Outstanding
= $20.00 × 125 million

Enterprise Value Rosenbaum's enterprise value was determined by adding net debt to the calculated equity value. We calculated net debt of $1,325 million by subtracting cash and cash equivalents of $50 million from total debt of $1,375 million, as sourced from Rosenbaum's 10-Q for the period ending September 30, 2012. The $1,325 million was then added to the calculated equity value of $2,500 million to derive an enterprise value of $3,825 million (see Exhibit 2.28).

EXHIBIT 2.28 Enterprise Value

($ in millions, except per share data)

Calculation of Equity and Enterprise Value	
Offer Price per Share	
Cash Offer Price per Share	$20.00
Stock Offer Price per Share	-
Exchange Ratio	-
Pearl Corp. Share Price	-
Offer Price per Share	**$20.00**
Fully Diluted Shares Outstanding	125.000
Implied Equity Value	**$2,500.0**
Implied Enterprise Value	
Plus: Total Debt	1,375.0
Plus: Preferred Stock	-
Plus: Noncontrolling Interest	-
Less: Cash and Cash Equivalents	(50.0)
Implied Enterprise Value	**$3,825.0**

= Equity Value + Total Debt - Cash
= $2,500 million + $1,375 million - $50 million

Reported Income Statement Next, we entered Rosenbaum's income statement information for the prior full year 2011 and YTD 2011 and 2012 periods directly from its most recent 10-K and 10-Q, respectively (see Exhibit 2.29). We also made adjustments for non-recurring items, as appropriate (see Exhibit 2.30).

EXHIBIT 2.29 Rosenbaum's Reported Income Statement Section

($ in millions, except per share data)

Reported Income Statement

	FYE 12/31/2011	Prior Stub 9/30/2011	Current Stub 9/30/2012	LTM 9/30/2012
Sales	$2,250.0	$1,687.5	$1,822.5	$2,385.0
COGS	1,500.0	1,125.0	1,215.0	1,590.0
Gross Profit	$750.0	$562.5	$607.5	$795.0
SG&A	450.0	337.5	364.5	477.0
Other (Income)/Expense	-	-	-	-
EBIT	$300.0	$225.0	$243.0	$318.0
Interest Expense	100.0	75.0	75.0	100.0
Pre-tax Income	$200.0	$150.0	$168.0	$218.0
Income Taxes	76.0	57.0	63.8	82.8
Noncontrolling Interest	-	-	-	-
Preferred Dividends	-	-	-	-
Net Income	$124.0	$93.0	$104.2	$135.2
Effective Tax Rate	38.0%	38.0%	38.0%	38.0%
Weighted Avg. Diluted Shares	125.0	125.0	125.0	125.0
Diluted EPS	$0.99	$0.74	$0.83	$1.08

EXHIBIT 2.30 Rosenbaum's Adjusted Income Statement Section

($ in millions, except per share data)

Adjusted Income Statement

	FYE 12/31/2011	Prior Stub 9/30/2011	Current Stub 9/30/2012	LTM 9/30/2012
Reported Gross Profit	$750.0	$562.5	$607.5	$795.0
Non-recurring Items in COGS	-	-	-	-
Adjusted Gross Profit	$750.0	$562.5	$607.5	$795.0
% margin	33.3%	33.3%	33.3%	33.3%
Reported EBIT	$300.0	$225.0	$243.0	$318.0
Non-recurring Items in COGS	-	-	-	-
Other Non-recurring Items	25.0	-	-	25.0
Adjusted EBIT	$325.0	$225.0	$243.0	$343.0
% margin	14.4%	13.3%	13.3%	14.4%
Depreciation & Amortization	100.0	75.0	82.0	107.0
Adjusted EBITDA	$425.0	$300.0	$325.0	$450.0
% margin	18.9%	17.8%	17.8%	18.9%
Reported Net Income	$124.0	$93.0	$104.2	$135.2
Non-recurring Items in COGS	-	-	-	-
Other Non-recurring Items	25.0	-	-	25.0
Non-operating Non-rec. Items	-	-	-	-
Tax Adjustment	(9.5)	-	-	(9.5)
Adjusted Net Income	$139.5	$93.0	$104.2	$150.7
% margin	6.2%	5.5%	5.7%	6.3%
Adjusted Diluted EPS	$1.12	$0.74	$0.83	$1.21

Notes

(1) In Q4 2011, Rosenbaum Industries recorded a $25 million pre-tax payment in regards to a litigation settlement (see 2011 10-K MD&A, page 50).

= Negative Adjustment for Pre-tax Gain on Litigation Settlement × Marginal Tax Rate
= - ($25 million × 38.0%)

Precedent Transactions Analysis

Adjusted Income Statement A review of Rosenbaum's financial statements and MD&A revealed that it made a $25 million pre-tax payment regarding a litigation settlement in Q4 2011, which we construed as non-recurring. Therefore, we added this charge back to Rosenbaum's reported financials, resulting in adjusted EBITDA, EBIT, and EPS of $450 million, $343 million and $1.21, respectively. These adjusted financials served as the basis for calculating Rosenbaum's transaction multiples in Exhibit 2.32.

Cash Flow Statement Data Rosenbaum's D&A and capex information was sourced directly from its cash flow statement, as it appeared in the 10-K and 10-Q (see Exhibit 2.31).

EXHIBIT 2.31 Cash Flow Statement Data Section

($ in millions)

Cash Flow Statement Data	FYE 12/31/2011	Prior Stub 9/30/2011	Current Stub 9/30/2012	LTM 9/30/2012
Depreciation & Amortization	100.0	75.0	82.0	107.0
% sales	4.4%	4.4%	4.5%	4.5%
Capital Expenditures	105.0	75.0	85.0	115.0
% sales	4.7%	4.4%	4.7%	4.8%

LTM Transaction Multiples For the calculation of Rosenbaum's transaction multiples, we applied enterprise value and offer price per share to the corresponding adjusted LTM financial data (see Exhibit 2.32). These multiples were then linked to the precedent transactions output sheet (see Exhibit 2.35) where the multiples for the entire universe are displayed.

EXHIBIT 2.32 LTM Transaction Multiples Section

($ in millions, except per share data)

LTM Transaction Multiples	
EV/Sales	1.6x
Metric	$2,385.0
EV/EBITDA	8.5x
Metric	$450.0
EV/EBIT	11.2x
Metric	$343.0
P/E	16.6x
Metric	$1.21

= Enterprise Value / LTM 9/30/2012 EBITDA
= $3,825 million / $450 million

Adjusted for $100 million of expected synergies, the LTM EV/EBITDA multiple would be approximately 7.0x ($3,825 million / $550 million).

Enterprise Value-to-LTM EBITDA For EV/LTM EBITDA, we divided Rosenbaum's enterprise value of $3,825 million by its LTM 9/30/2012 adjusted EBITDA of $450 million to provide a multiple of 8.5x. We used the same approach to calculate the LTM EV/sales and EV/EBIT multiples.

Offer Price per Share-to-LTM Diluted Earnings per Share For P/E, we divided the offer price per share of $20.00 by Rosenbaum's LTM diluted EPS of $1.21 to provide a multiple of 16.6x.

Premiums Paid The premiums paid analysis for precedent transactions does not apply when valuing private companies such as ValueCo. However, as Rosenbaum was a public company, we performed this analysis for illustrative purposes (see Exhibit 2.33).

EXHIBIT 2.33 Premiums Paid Section

Premiums Paid		
Transaction Announcement		**Premium**
1 Day Prior	$17.39	15.0% (2)
Unaffected Share Price		
1 Day Prior	$14.81	35.0%
7 Days Prior	15.04	33.0%
30 Days Prior	14.60	37.0%
= Offer Price per Price / Share Price One Day Prior to Announcement − 1 = $20.00 / $17.39 − 1		

Notes
(2) On August 15, 2012, Rosenbaum Industries announced the formation of a special committee to explore strategic alternatives.

The $20.00 offer price per share served as the basis for performing the premiums paid analysis, representing a 15% premium to Rosenbaum's share price of $17.39 on the day prior to transaction announcement. However, as shown in Exhibit 2.34, Rosenbaum's share price was directly affected by the announcement that it was exploring strategic alternatives on August 15, 2012 (even though the actual deal wasn't announced until November 2, 2012). Therefore, we also analyzed the unaffected premiums paid on the basis of Rosenbaum's closing share prices of $14.81, $15.04, and $14.60, for the one-, seven-, and 30-calendar-day periods prior to August 15, 2012. This provided us with premiums paid of 35%, 33%, and 37%, respectively, which are more in line with traditional public M&A premiums.

Precedent Transactions Analysis

EXHIBIT 2.34 Rosenbaum's Annotated Price/Volume Graph

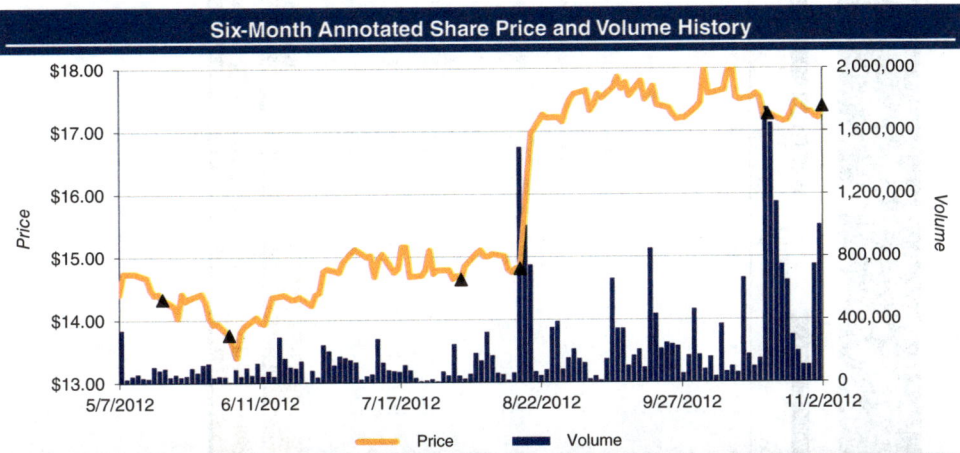

Δ Date	Event
5/15/2012	Rosenbaum Industries reports earnings results for the first quarter ended March 31, 2012
6/01/2012	Rosenbaum's CEO receives unsolicited bid by a financial sponsor
7/31/2012	Media reports that a sale of Rosenbaum Industries is likely
8/15/2012	Rosenbaum reports earnings results for the second quarter ended June 30, 2012
8/15/2012	**Rosenbaum's Board of Directors forms a Special Committee to explore strategic alternatives**
10/20/2012	Media reports that Rosenbaum is close to signing a deal
11/02/2012	Rosenbaum reports earnings results for the third quarter ended September 30, 2012
11/02/2012	**Pearl Corp. enters into a Definitive Agreement to acquire Rosenbaum**

Step IV. Benchmark the Comparable Acquisitions

In Step IV, we linked the key financial statistics and ratios for the target companies (calculated in Step III) to output sheets used for benchmarking purposes (see Chapter 1, Exhibits 1.53 and 1.54, for general templates). The benchmarking sheets helped us determine those targets most comparable to ValueCo from a financial perspective, namely Rosenbaum Industries, Schneider & Co., and Rughwani International. At the same time, our analysis in Step I provided us with sufficient information to confirm that these companies were highly comparable to ValueCo from a business perspective.

The relevant transaction multiples and deal information for each of the individual comparable acquisitions were also linked to an output sheet. As shown in Exhibit 2.35, ValueCo's sector experienced robust M&A activity during the 2010 to 2012 period, which provided us with sufficient relevant data points for our analysis. Consideration of the market conditions and other deal dynamics for each of these transactions further supported our selection of Pearl Corp./Rosenbaum Industries, Goodson Corp./Schneider & Co., and Eu-Han Capital/Rughwani International as the best comparable acquisitions. These multiples formed the primary basis for our selection of the appropriate multiple range for ValueCo.

EXHIBIT 2.35 Precedent Transactions Analysis Output Page

ValueCo Corporation
Precedent Transactions Analysis
($ in millions)

Date Announced	Acquirer	Target	Transaction Type	Purchase Consideration	Equity Value	Enterprise Value	Enterprise Value /			LTM EBITDA Margin	Equity Value / LTM Net Income	Premiums Paid — Days Prior to Unaffected		
							LTM Sales	LTM EBITDA	LTM EBIT			1	7	30
11/2/2012	Pearl Corp.	Rosenbaum Industries	Public/Public	Cash	$2,500	$3,825	1.6x	8.5x	11.2x	19%	16.6x	35%	33%	37%
7/20/2012	Goodson Corp.	Schneider & Co.	Public / Public	Cash / Stock	5,049	6,174	1.4x	8.1x	10.3x	18%	15.3x	29%	32%	31%
6/21/2012	Domanski Capital	Ackerman Industries	Sponsor / Public	Cash	8,845	9,995	1.7x	8.0x	10.2x	21%	15.9x	35%	37%	39%
4/15/2012	The Hochberg Group	Whalen Inc.	Sponsor / Private	Cash	1,250	1,350	1.9x	7.5x	9.6x	26%	15.2x	NA	NA	NA
8/8/2011	Cole Manufacturing	Gordon Inc.	Public / Public	Stock	2,620	3,045	1.5x	9.0x	12.2x	17%	20.4x	47%	44%	49%
7/6/2011	Eu-Han Capital	Rughwani International	Sponsor / Public	Cash	3,390	4,340	1.6x	7.8x	9.4x	21%	13.2x	38%	40%	43%
3/20/2011	Lanzarone Global	Falk & Sons	Public / Private	Cash	8,750	10,350	1.7x	8.4x	10.5x	21%	16.0x	NA	NA	NA
11/9/2010	Meisner Global Management	Kamras Brands	Sponsor / Private	Cash	1,765	2,115	1.5x	7.9x	9.3x	19%	13.8x	NA	NA	NA
6/22/2010	Pryor, Inc.	ParkCo	Public / Private	Cash	6,450	8,700	1.1x	7.0x	7.9x	16%	11.8x	NA	NA	NA
4/15/2010	Leicht & Co.	Bress Products	Public / Public	Stock	12,431	12,681	1.5x	8.2x	12.1x	19%	19.7x	29%	36%	34%
Mean							**1.6x**	**8.0x**	**10.3x**	**19%**	**15.8x**	**36%**	**37%**	**39%**
Median							**1.6x**	**8.0x**	**10.3x**	**19%**	**15.6x**	**35%**	**36%**	**38%**
High							**1.9x**	**9.0x**	**12.2x**	**26%**	**20.4x**	**47%**	**44%**	**49%**
Low							**1.1x**	**7.0x**	**7.9x**	**16%**	**11.8x**	**29%**	**32%**	**31%**

Source: Company filings

Precedent Transactions Analysis

Step V. Determine Valuation

In ValueCo's sector, companies are typically valued on the basis of EV/EBITDA multiples. Therefore, we employed an LTM EV/EBITDA multiple approach in valuing ValueCo using precedent transactions. We placed particular emphasis on those transactions deemed most comparable, namely the acquisitions of Rosenbaum Industries, Schneider & Co., and Rughwani International to frame the range (as discussed in Step IV).

This approach led us to establish a multiple range of 7.5x to 8.5x LTM EBITDA. We then multiplied the endpoints of this range by ValueCo's LTM 9/30/2012 EBITDA of $700 million to calculate an implied enterprise value range of approximately $5,250 million to $5,950 million (see Exhibit 2.36).

EXHIBIT 2.36 ValueCo's Implied Valuation Range

ValueCo Corporation
Implied Valuation Range
($ in millions, LTM 9/30/2012)

EBITDA	Metric	Multiple Range	Implied Enterprise Value
LTM	$700	7.50x – 8.50x	$5,250 – $5,950

As a final step, we analyzed the valuation range derived from precedent transactions versus that derived from comparable companies. As shown in the football field in Exhibit 2.37, the valuation range derived from precedent transactions is relatively consistent with that derived from comparable companies. The slight premium to comparable companies can be attributed to the premiums paid in M&A transactions.

EXHIBIT 2.37 ValueCo Football Field Displaying Comparable Companies and Precedent Transactions

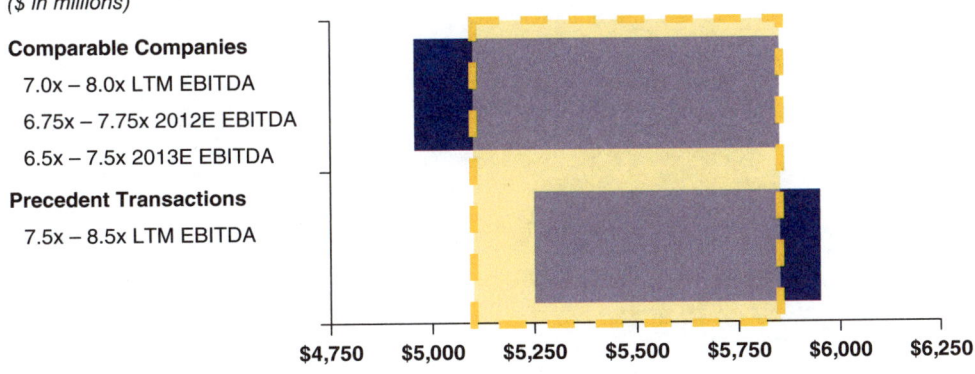

Bloomberg Appendix

APPENDIX 2.1 Example of Custom Transaction Search Criteria using Bloomberg M&A Analysis (MA<GO>)

96) Actions M&A Analysis

41) Build/Edit Search   42) Searches

To search for deals that meet specific criteria, add search criteria using the links below.

Search Criteria | Selected Search Criteria

Deal Criteria
- 11) Date Range
- 12) Deal Size
- 13) Deal Status
- 14) Deal Type
- 15) Payment Type
- 16) Premium
- 17) Other Criteria

Company Universe
- 18) Company List
- 19) Exchange
- 20) Index
- 21) Sector/Industry
- 22) Public/Private
- 23) Region/Country
- 24) SIC Code
- 25) State
- 26) Description
- 27) Product Segment

Deal Terms
- 28) Adviser
- 29) Adviser Type
- 30) Approval
- 31) Deal Multiple
- 32) Fees Disclosed
- 33) Fundamentals
- 34) Nature of Bid

Selected Search Criteria
- 101) Country : Apply to Target, North America
- 102) Dates : Custom(01/01/2000, 01/01/2013) Apply to - Announced Date
- 103) Nature of Bid : Any of These - Friendly
- 104) Payment Type : Cash, Cash & Debt, Debt
- 105) Sector/Industry : Apply to Target or Seller or Acquirer, Media

Note: Media transactions paid for with cash or debt

Display Currency USD   Search Result View Summary   1) Results   2) Save

123

APPENDIX 2.2 List of BuyerCo Acquisitions from 2000–2012, Sorted by Announce Date using Bloomberg M&A Analysis (MA<GO>)

		Deal Type	Announce Date	Target Name	Acquirer Name	Seller Name	Announced Total Value (mil.)	Payment Type	Deal Status
1)	ACQ		08/01/2012	Company A	Buyer Corp		3.45	Undisclo...	Complete
2)	ACQ		06/13/2012	Company B	Buyer Corp		1.00	Undisclo...	Complete
3)	DIV		12/06/2011	Multiple Targets	Buyer Corp	Company C	175.00	Cash	Complete
4)	DIV		11/21/2011	Company D	Buyer Corp	Multiple sellers	34.12	Undisclo...	Complete
5)	ACQ		10/26/2011	Company E	Buyer Corp		15.50	Undisclo...	Complete
6)	JV		09/22/2011	Division F	Company F		575.00	Undisclo...	Pending
7)	DIV		07/27/2011	Target G	Buyer Corp	Company G	75.00	Cash	Complete
8)	DIV		06/25/2009	Target H	Buyer Corp	Company H	19.52	Cash	Complete
9)	DIV		02/20/2009	Target I	Buyer Corp	Company I	45.00	Cash	Complete
10)	ACQ		07/28/2008	Company J	Buyer Corp		44.00	Undisclo...	Complete
11)	DIV		05/20/2008	Target K	Buyer Corp	Company K	100.00	Cash	Complete
12)	DIV		09/01/2005	Target L	Company L		255.00	Cash	Complete
13)	DIV		09/15/2003	Target M	Company M	Buyer Corp	350.00	Undisclo...	Complete
14)	DIV		03/14/2002	Target N	Company N	Buyer Corp	12.50	Undisclo...	Complete
15)	DIV		01/15/2002	Target O	Buyer Corp	Company O	125.00	Undisclo...	Complete
16)	SPIN		10/01/2001	Buyer Division Corp	Shareholders	Buyer Corp	1,204.52		Complete
17)	DIV		07/25/2001	Target P	Buyer Corp	Company P	200.00	Undisclo...	Complete
18)	DIV		02/16/2000	Target Q	Buyer Corp	Company Q	40.00	Cash	Complete

CHAPTER 3

Discounted Cash Flow Analysis

Discounted cash flow analysis ("DCF analysis" or the "DCF") is a fundamental valuation methodology broadly used by investment bankers, corporate officers, university professors, investors, and other finance professionals. It is premised on the principle that the value of a company, division, business, or collection of assets ("target") can be derived from the present value of its projected *free cash flow* (FCF). A company's projected FCF is derived from a variety of assumptions and judgments about its expected financial performance, including sales growth rates, profit margins, capital expenditures, and *net working capital* (NWC) requirements. The DCF has a wide range of applications, including valuation for various M&A situations, IPOs, restructurings, and investment decisions.

The valuation implied for a target by a DCF is also known as its *intrinsic value*, as opposed to its market value, which is the value ascribed by the market at a given point in time. As a result, when performing a comprehensive valuation, a DCF serves as an important alternative to market-based valuation techniques such as comparable companies and precedent transactions, which can be distorted by a number of factors, including market aberrations (e.g., the post-subprime credit crunch). As such, a DCF plays an important role as a check on the prevailing market valuation for a publicly traded company. A DCF is also valuable when there are limited (or no) pure play, peer companies or comparable acquisitions.

In a DCF, a company's FCF is typically projected for a period of five years. The projection period, however, may be longer depending on the company's sector, stage of development, and the underlying predictability of its financial performance. Given the inherent difficulties in accurately projecting a company's financial performance over an extended period of time (and through various business and economic cycles), a *terminal value* is used to capture the remaining value of the target beyond the projection period (i.e., its "going concern" value).

The projected FCF and terminal value are discounted to the present at the target's *weighted average cost of capital* (WACC), which is a discount rate commensurate with its business and financial risks. The present value of the FCF and terminal value are summed to determine an enterprise value, which serves as the basis for the DCF valuation. The WACC and terminal value assumptions typically have a substantial impact on the output, with even slight variations producing meaningful differences in valuation. As a result, a DCF output is viewed in terms of a valuation range based on a range of key input assumptions, rather than as a single value. The impact of these assumptions on valuation is tested using *sensitivity analysis*.

The assumptions driving a DCF are both its primary strength and weakness versus market-based valuation techniques. On the positive side, the use of defensible assumptions regarding financial projections, WACC, and terminal value helps shield the target's valuation from market distortions that occur periodically. In addition, a DCF provides the flexibility to analyze the target's valuation under different scenarios by changing the underlying inputs and examining the resulting impact. On the negative side, a DCF is only as strong as its assumptions. Hence, assumptions that fail to adequately capture the realistic set of opportunities and risks facing the target will also fail to produce a meaningful valuation.

This chapter walks through a step-by-step construction of a DCF, or its science (see Exhibit 3.1). At the same time, it provides the tools to master the art of the DCF, namely the ability to craft a logical set of assumptions based on an in-depth analysis of the target and its key performance drivers. Once this framework is established, we perform an illustrative DCF analysis for our target company, ValueCo.

EXHIBIT 3.1 Discounted Cash Flow Analysis Steps

Step I.	Study the Target and Determine Key Performance Drivers
Step II.	Project Free Cash Flow
Step III.	Calculate Weighted Average Cost of Capital
Step IV.	Determine Terminal Value
Step V.	Calculate Present Value and Determine Valuation

Summary of Discounted Cash Flow Analysis Steps

- **Step I. Study the Target and Determine Key Performance Drivers.** The first step in performing a DCF, as with any valuation exercise, is to study and learn as much as possible about the target and its sector. Shortcuts in this critical area of due diligence may lead to misguided assumptions and valuation distortions later on. This exercise involves determining the key drivers of financial performance (in particular sales growth, profitability, and FCF generation), which enables the banker to craft (or support) a defensible set of projections for the target. Step I is invariably easier when valuing a public company as opposed to a private company due to the availability of information from sources such as SEC filings (e.g., 10-Ks, 10-Qs, and 8-Ks), equity research reports, earnings call transcripts, and investor presentations.

    For private, non-filing companies, the banker often relies upon company management to provide materials containing basic business and financial information. In an organized M&A sale process, this information is typically provided in the form of a CIM (see Chapter 6). In the absence of this information, alternative sources (e.g., company websites, trade journals, and news articles, as well as SEC filings and research reports for public competitors, customers, and suppliers) must be used to learn basic company information and form the basis for developing the assumptions to drive financial projections.

- **Step II. Project Free Cash Flow.** The projection of the target's *unlevered* FCF forms the core of a DCF. Unlevered FCF, which we simply refer to as FCF in this chapter, is the cash generated by a company after paying all cash operating expenses and taxes, as well as the funding of capex and working capital, but prior to the payment of any interest expense.[1] The target's projected FCF is driven by assumptions underlying its future financial performance, including sales growth rates, profit margins, capex, and working capital requirements. Historical performance, combined with third party and/or management guidance, helps in developing these assumptions. The use of realistic FCF projections is critical as it has the greatest effect on valuation in a DCF.

  In a DCF, the target's FCF is typically projected for a period of five years, but this period may vary depending on the target's sector, stage of development, and the predictability of its FCF. However, five years is typically sufficient for spanning at least one business/economic cycle and allowing for the successful realization of in-process or planned initiatives. The goal is to project FCF to a point in the future when the target's financial performance is deemed to have reached a "steady state" that can serve as the basis for a terminal value calculation (see Step IV).

- **Step III. Calculate Weighted Average Cost of Capital.** In a DCF, WACC is the rate used to discount the target's projected FCF and terminal value to the present. It is designed to fairly reflect the target's business and financial risks. As its name connotes, WACC represents the "weighted average" of the required return on the invested capital (customarily debt and equity) in a given company. It is also commonly referred to as a company's *discount rate* or *cost of capital*. As debt and equity components generally have significantly different risk profiles and tax ramifications, WACC is dependent on capital structure.

- **Step IV. Determine Terminal Value.** The DCF approach to valuation is based on determining the present value of future FCF produced by the target. Given the challenges of projecting the target's FCF indefinitely, a terminal value is used to quantify the remaining value of the target after the projection period. The terminal value typically accounts for a substantial portion of the target's value in a DCF. Therefore, it is important that the target's financial data in the final year of the projection period ("terminal year") represents a steady state or normalized level of financial performance, as opposed to a cyclical high or low.

  There are two widely accepted methods used to calculate a company's terminal value—the exit multiple method (EMM) and the perpetuity growth method (PGM). The EMM calculates the remaining value of the target after the projection period on the basis of a multiple of the target's terminal year EBITDA (or EBIT). The PGM calculates terminal value by treating the target's terminal year FCF as a perpetuity growing at an assumed rate.

---

[1]See Chapter 4: Leveraged Buyouts and Chapter 5: LBO Analysis for a discussion of *levered* free cash flow or cash available for debt repayment.

- **Step V. Calculate Present Value and Determine Valuation.** The target's projected FCF and terminal value are discounted to the present and summed to calculate its enterprise value. Implied equity value and share price (if relevant) can then be derived from the calculated enterprise value. The present value calculation is performed by multiplying the FCF for each year in the projection period, as well as the terminal value, by its respective *discount factor*. The discount factor represents the present value of one dollar received at a given future date assuming a given discount rate.[2]

As a DCF incorporates numerous assumptions about key performance drivers, WACC, and terminal value, it is used to produce a valuation range rather than a single value. The exercise of driving a valuation range by varying key inputs is called sensitivity analysis. Core DCF valuation drivers such as WACC, exit multiple or perpetuity growth rate, sales growth rates, and margins are the most commonly sensitized inputs. Once determined, the valuation range implied by the DCF should be compared to those derived from other methodologies such as comparable companies, precedent transactions, and LBO analysis (if applicable) as a sanity check.

Once the step-by-step approach summarized above is complete, the final DCF output page should look similar to the one shown in Exhibit 3.2.

---

[2]For example, assuming a 10% discount rate and a one-year time horizon, the discount factor is 0.91 (1/(1+10%)^1), which implies that one dollar received one year in the future would be worth $0.91 today.

EXHIBIT 3.2 DCF Analysis Output Page

ValueCo Corporation
Discounted Cash Flow Analysis
($ in millions, fiscal year ending December 31)

Operating Scenario: 1 (Base)
Mid-Year Convention: Y

	Historical Period			CAGR	Projection Period					CAGR
	2009	2010	2011	('09 - '11)	2012	2013	2014	2015	2016	2017	('12 - '17)
Sales	$2,600.0	$2,900.0	$3,200.0	10.9%	$3,450.0	$3,708.8	$3,931.3	$4,127.8	$4,293.0	$4,421.7	5.1%
% growth	NA	11.5%	10.3%		7.8%	7.5%	6.0%	5.0%	4.0%	3.0%	
EBITDA	$491.4	$580.0	$672.0	16.9%	$725.0	$779.4	$826.1	$867.4	$902.1	$929.2	5.1%
% margin	18.9%	20.0%	21.0%		21.0%	21.0%	21.0%	21.0%	21.0%	21.0%	
Depreciation & Amortization	155.0	165.0	193.0		207.0	222.5	235.9	247.7	257.6	265.3	
EBIT	$336.4	$415.0	$479.0	19.3%	$518.0	$556.9	$590.3	$619.8	$644.6	$663.9	5.1%
% margin	12.9%	14.3%	15.0%		15.0%	15.0%	15.0%	15.0%	15.0%	15.0%	
Taxes	127.8	157.7	182.0		196.8	211.6	224.3	235.5	244.9	252.3	
EBIAT	$208.6	$257.3	$297.0	19.3%	$321.2	$345.2	$366.0	$384.3	$399.6	$411.6	5.1%
Plus: Depreciation & Amortization	155.0	165.0	193.0		207.0	222.5	235.9	247.7	257.6	265.3	
Less: Capital Expenditures	(114.4)	(116.0)	(144.0)		(155.3)	(166.9)	(176.9)	(185.8)	(193.2)	(199.0)	
Less: Inc./(Dec.) in Net Working Capital						(47.6)	(41.0)	(36.2)	(30.4)	(23.7)	
Unlevered Free Cash Flow						$353.3	$384.0	$410.0	$433.6	$454.2	
WACC	10.0%										
Discount Period						0.5	1.5	2.5	3.5	4.5	
Discount Factor						0.95	0.87	0.79	0.72	0.65	
Present Value of Free Cash Flow						$336.8	$332.8	$323.1	$310.6	$295.8	

Enterprise Value
Cumulative Present Value of FCF	$1,599.2

Terminal Value
Terminal Year EBITDA (2017E)	$929.2
Exit Multiple	7.5x
Terminal Value	$6,969.0
Discount Factor	0.62
Present Value of Terminal Value	$4,327.2
% of Enterprise Value	73.0%
Enterprise Value	**$5,926.4**

Implied Equity Value and Share Price
Enterprise Value	$5,926.4
Less: Total Debt	(1,500.0)
Less: Preferred Stock	-
Less: Noncontrolling Interest	-
Plus: Cash and Cash Equivalents	250.0
Implied Equity Value	**$4,676.4**
Fully Diluted Shares Outstanding	80.0
Implied Equity Value	**$58.45**

Implied Perpetuity Growth Rate
Terminal Year Free Cash Flow (2017E)	$454.2
WACC	10.0%
Terminal Value	$6,969.0
Implied Perpetuity Growth Rate	**3.0%**

Implied EV/EBITDA
Enterprise Value	$5,926.4
LTM 9/30/2012 EBITDA	700.0
Implied EV/EBITDA	**8.5x**

Enterprise Value
WACC	Exit Multiple				
	6.5x	7.0x	7.5x	8.0x	8.5x
9.0%	5,561	5,863	6,165	6,467	6,769
9.5%	5,454	5,749	6,044	6,339	6,634
10.0%	5,349	5,638	**5,926**	6,215	6,503
10.5%	5,248	5,530	5,812	6,094	6,376
11.0%	5,149	5,425	5,700	5,976	6,252

Implied Perpetuity Growth Rate
WACC	Exit Multiple				
	6.5x	7.0x	7.5x	8.0x	8.5x
9.0%	1.1%	1.6%	2.1%	2.5%	2.8%
9.5%	1.5%	2.0%	2.5%	2.9%	3.3%
10.0%	2.0%	2.5%	**3.0%**	3.4%	3.7%
10.5%	2.4%	2.9%	3.4%	3.8%	4.2%
11.0%	2.9%	3.4%	3.9%	4.3%	4.7%

STEP I. STUDY THE TARGET AND DETERMINE KEY PERFORMANCE DRIVERS

Study the Target

The first step in performing a DCF, as with any valuation exercise, is to study and learn as much as possible about the target and its sector. A thorough understanding of the target's business model, financial profile, value proposition for customers, end markets, competitors, and key risks is essential for developing a framework for valuation. The banker needs to be able to craft (or support) a realistic set of financial projections, as well as WACC and terminal value assumptions, for the target. Performing this task is invariably easier when valuing a public company as opposed to a private company due to the availability of information.

For a public company,[3] a careful reading of its recent SEC filings (e.g., 10-Ks, 10-Qs, and 8-Ks), earnings call transcripts, and investor presentations provides a solid introduction to its business and financial characteristics. To determine key performance drivers, the MD&A sections of the most recent 10-K and 10-Q are an important source of information as they provide a synopsis of the company's financial and operational performance during the prior reporting periods, as well as management's outlook for the company. Equity research reports add additional color and perspective while typically providing financial performance estimates for the future two- or three-year period.

For private, non-filing companies or smaller divisions of public companies (for which segmented information is not provided), company management is often relied upon to provide materials containing basic business and financial information. In an organized M&A sale process, this information is typically provided in the form of a CIM. In the absence of this information, alternative sources must be used, such as company websites, trade journals, and news articles, as well as SEC filings and research reports for public competitors, customers, and suppliers. For those private companies that were once public filers, or operated as a subsidiary of a public filer, it can be informative to read through old filings or research reports.

Determine Key Performance Drivers

The next level of analysis involves determining the key drivers of a company's performance (particularly sales growth, profitability, and FCF generation) with the goal of crafting (or supporting) a defensible set of FCF projections. These drivers can be both internal (such as opening new facilities/stores, developing new products, securing new customer contracts, and improving operational and/or working capital efficiency) as well as external (such as acquisitions, end market trends, consumer buying patterns, macroeconomic factors, or even legislative/regulatory changes).

A given company's growth profile can vary significantly from that of its peers within the sector with certain business models and management teams more focused on, or capable of, expansion. Profitability may also vary for companies within a given

---

[3]Including those companies that have outstanding registered debt securities, but do not have publicly traded stock.

sector depending on a multitude of factors including management, brand, customer base, operational focus, product mix, sales/marketing strategy, scale, and technology. Similarly, in terms of FCF generation, there are often meaningful differences among peers in terms of capex (e.g., expansion projects or owned versus leased machinery) and working capital efficiency, for example.

STEP II. PROJECT FREE CASH FLOW

After studying the target and determining key performance drivers, the banker is prepared to project its FCF. As previously discussed, FCF is the cash generated by a company after paying all cash operating expenses and associated taxes, as well as the funding of capex and working capital, but prior to the payment of any interest expense (see Exhibit 3.3). FCF is independent of capital structure as it represents the cash available to all capital providers (both debt and equity holders).

EXHIBIT 3.3 Free Cash Flow Calculation

Earnings Before Interest and Taxes
Less: Taxes (at the Marginal Tax Rate)
Earnings Before Interest After Taxes
Plus: Depreciation & Amortization
Less: Capital Expenditures
Less: Increase/(Decrease) in Net Working Capital
Free Cash Flow

Considerations for Projecting Free Cash Flow

Historical Performance Historical performance provides valuable insight for developing defensible assumptions to project FCF. Past growth rates, profit margins, and other ratios are usually a reliable indicator of future performance, especially for mature companies in non-cyclical sectors. While it is informative to review historical data from as long a time horizon as possible, typically the prior three-year period (if available) serves as a good proxy for projecting future financial performance.

Therefore, as the output in Exhibit 3.2 demonstrates, the DCF customarily begins by laying out the target's historical financial data for the prior three-year period. This historical financial data is sourced from the target's financial statements with adjustments made for non-recurring items and recent events, as appropriate, to provide a normalized basis for projecting financial performance. Reported and adjusted historical financials, as well as consensus estimates are available via Bloomberg Financial Analysis (FA<GO>, see Appendix 3.1).

Projection Period Length Typically, the banker projects the target's FCF for a period of five years depending on its sector, stage of development, and the predictability of its financial performance. As discussed in Step IV, it is critical to project FCF to a point in the future where the target's financial performance reaches a steady state or normalized level. For mature companies in established industries, five years is often sufficient for allowing a company to reach its steady state. A five-year projection period typically spans at least one business cycle and allows sufficient time for the successful realization of in-process or planned initiatives.

In situations where the target is in the early stages of rapid growth, however, it may be more appropriate to build a longer-term projection model (e.g., ten years or more) to allow the target to reach a steady state level of cash flow. In addition, a longer projection period is often used for businesses in sectors with long-term, contracted revenue streams such as natural resources, satellite communications, or utilities.

Alternative Cases Whether advising on the buy-side or sell-side of an organized M&A sale process, the banker typically receives five years of financial projections for the target, which is usually labeled "Management Case." At the same time, the banker must develop a sufficient degree of comfort to support and defend these assumptions. Often, the banker makes adjustments to management's projections that incorporate assumptions deemed more probable, known as the "Base Case," while also crafting upside and downside cases.

The development of alternative cases requires a sound understanding of company-specific performance drivers as well as sector trends. The banker enters the various assumptions that drive these cases into assumptions pages (see Chapter 5, Exhibits 5.52 and 5.53), which feed into the DCF output page (see Exhibit 3.2). A "switch" or "toggle" function in the model allows the banker to move between cases without having to re-input the financial data by entering a number or letter (that corresponds to a particular set of assumptions) into a single cell.

Projecting Financial Performance without Management Guidance In some instances, a DCF is performed without the benefit of receiving an initial set of projections. For publicly traded companies, consensus research estimates for financial statistics such as sales, EBITDA, and EBIT (which are generally provided for a future two- or three-year period) are typically used to form the basis for developing a set of projections. Individual equity research reports may provide additional financial detail, including (in some instances) a full scale two-year (or more) projection model. For private companies, a robust DCF often depends on receiving financial projections from company management. In practice, however, this is not always possible. Therefore, the banker must develop the skill set necessary to reasonably forecast financial performance in the absence of management projections. In these instances, the banker typically relies upon historical financial performance, sector trends, and consensus estimates for public comparable companies to drive defensible projections. The remainder of this section provides a detailed discussion of the major components of FCF, as well as practical approaches for projecting FCF *without the benefit of readily available projections or management guidance*.

Discounted Cash Flow Analysis

Projection of Sales, EBITDA, and EBIT

Sales Projections For public companies, the banker often sources top line projections for the first two or three years of the projection period from consensus estimates. Similarly, for private companies, consensus estimates for peer companies can be used as a proxy for expected sales growth rates, provided the trend line is consistent with historical performance and sector outlook.

As equity research normally does not provide estimates beyond a future two- or three-year period (excluding initiating coverage reports), the banker must derive growth rates in the outer years from alternative sources. Without the benefit of management guidance, this typically involves more art than science. Often, industry reports and consulting studies provide estimates on longer-term sector trends and growth rates. In the absence of reliable guidance, the banker typically steps down the growth rates incrementally in the outer years of the projection period to arrive at a reasonable long-term growth rate by the terminal year (e.g., 2% to 4%).

For a highly cyclical business such as a steel or lumber company, however, sales levels need to track the movements of the underlying commodity cycle. Consequently, sales trends are typically more volatile and may incorporate dramatic peak-to-trough swings depending on the company's point in the cycle at the start of the projection period. Regardless of where in the cycle the projection period begins, it is crucial that the terminal year financial performance represents a normalized level as opposed to a cyclical high or low. Otherwise, the company's terminal value, which usually comprises a substantial portion of the overall value in a DCF, will be skewed toward an unrepresentative level. Therefore, in a DCF for a cyclical company, top line projections might peak (or trough) in the early years of the projection period and then decline (or increase) precipitously before returning to a normalized level by the terminal year.

Once the top line projections are established, it is essential to give them a sanity check versus the target's historical growth rates as well as peer estimates and sector/market outlook. Even when sourcing information from consensus estimates, each year's growth assumptions need to be justifiable, whether on the basis of market share gains/declines, end market trends, product mix changes, demand shifts, pricing increases, or acquisitions, for example. Furthermore, the banker must ensure that sales projections are consistent with other related assumptions in the DCF, such as those for capex and working capital. For example, higher top line growth typically requires the support of higher levels of capex and working capital.

COGS and SG&A Projections For public companies, the banker typically relies upon historical COGS[4] (gross margin) and SG&A levels (as a percentage of sales) and/or sources estimates from research to drive the initial years of the projection period, if available. For the outer years of the projection period, it is common to hold gross margin and SG&A as a percentage of sales constant, although the banker may assume a slight improvement (or decline) if justified by company trends or outlook for the

---

[4]For companies with COGS that can be driven on a unit volume/cost basis, COGS is typically projected on the basis of expected volumes sold and cost per unit. Assumptions governing expected volumes and cost per unit can be derived from historical levels, production capacity, and/or sector trends.

sector/market. Similarly, for private companies, the banker usually relies upon historical trends to drive gross profit and SG&A projections, typically holding margins constant at the prior historical year levels. At the same time, the banker may also examine research estimates for peer companies to help craft/support the assumptions and provide insight on trends.

In some cases, the DCF may be constructed on the basis of EBITDA and EBIT projections alone, thereby excluding line item detail for COGS and SG&A. This approach generally requires that NWC be driven as a percentage of sales as COGS detail for driving inventory and accounts payable is unavailable (see Exhibits 3.9, 3.10, and 3.11). However, the inclusion of COGS and SG&A detail allows the banker to drive multiple operating scenarios on the basis of gross margins and/or SG&A efficiency.

EBITDA and EBIT Projections For public companies, EBITDA and EBIT projections for the future two- or three-year period are typically sourced from (or benchmarked against) consensus estimates, if available.[5] These projections inherently capture both gross profit performance and SG&A expenses. A common approach for projecting EBITDA and EBIT for the outer years is to hold their margins constant at the level represented by the last year provided by consensus estimates (assuming the last year of estimates is representative of a steady state level). As previously discussed, however, increasing (or decreasing) levels of profitability may be modeled throughout the projection period, perhaps due to product mix changes, cyclicality, operating leverage,[6] or pricing power/pressure.

For private companies, the banker looks at historical trends as well as consensus estimates for peer companies for insight on projected margins. In the absence of sufficient information to justify improving or declining margins, the banker may simply hold margins constant at the prior historical year level to establish a baseline set of projections.

---

[5]If the model is built on the basis of COGS and SG&A detail, the banker must ensure that the EBITDA and EBIT consensus estimates dovetail with those assumptions. This exercise may require some triangulation among the different inputs to ensure consistency.
[6]The extent to which sales growth results in growth at the operating income level; it is a function of a company's mix of fixed and variable costs.

Projection of Free Cash Flow

In a DCF analysis, EBIT typically serves as the springboard for calculating FCF (see Exhibit 3.4). To bridge from EBIT to FCF, several additional items need to be determined, including the marginal tax rate, D&A, capex, and changes in net working capital.

EXHIBIT 3.4 EBIT to FCF

EBIT
Less: Taxes (at the Marginal Tax Rate)
EBIAT
Plus: Depreciation & Amortization
Less: Capital Expenditures
Less: Increase/(Decrease) in NWC
FCF

Tax Projections The first step in calculating FCF from EBIT is to net out estimated taxes. The result is tax-effected EBIT, also known as EBIAT or NOPAT. This calculation involves multiplying EBIT by (1 − t), where "t" is the target's marginal tax rate. A marginal tax rate of 35% to 40% is generally assumed for modeling purposes, but the company's actual tax rate (effective tax rate) in previous years can also serve as a reference point.[7]

Depreciation & Amortization Projections Depreciation is a non-cash expense that approximates the reduction of the book value of a company's long-term fixed assets or property, plant, and equipment (PP&E) over an estimated *useful life* and reduces reported earnings. Amortization, like depreciation, is a non-cash expense that reduces the value of a company's *definite life* intangible assets and also reduces reported earnings.[8]

Some companies report D&A together as a separate line item on their income statement, but these expenses are more commonly included in COGS (especially for manufacturers of goods) and, to a lesser extent, SG&A. Regardless, D&A is explicitly disclosed in the cash flow statement as well as the notes to a company's financial statements. As D&A is a non-cash expense, it is added back to EBIAT in the calculation of FCF (see Exhibit 3.4). Hence, while D&A decreases a company's reported earnings, it does not decrease its FCF.

---

[7]It is important to understand that a company's effective tax rate, or the rate that it actually pays in taxes, often differs from the marginal tax rate due to the use of tax credits, nondeductible expenses (such as government fines), deferred tax asset valuation allowances, and other company-specific tax policies.
[8]D&A for GAAP purposes typically differs from that for federal income taxes. For example, federal government tax rules generally permit a company to depreciate assets on a more accelerated basis than GAAP. These differences create deferred tax liabilities (see Chapter 7: Buy-Side M&A for additional detail on deferred tax liabilities). Due to the complexity of calculating tax D&A, the banker typically uses GAAP D&A as a proxy for tax D&A.

Depreciation Depreciation expenses are typically scheduled over several years corresponding to the useful life of each of the company's respective asset classes. The *straight-line depreciation* method assumes a uniform depreciation expense over the estimated useful life of an asset. For example, an asset purchased for $100 million that is determined to have a ten-year useful life would be assumed to have an annual depreciation expense of $10 million per year for ten years. Most other depreciation methods fall under the category of *accelerated depreciation*, which assumes that an asset loses most of its value in the early years of its life (i.e., the asset is depreciated on an accelerated schedule allowing for greater deductions earlier on).

For DCF modeling purposes, depreciation is often projected as a percentage of sales or capex based on historical levels as it is directly related to a company's capital spending, which, in turn, tends to support top line growth. An alternative approach is to build a detailed PP&E schedule[9] based on the company's existing depreciable net PP&E base and incremental capex projections. This approach involves assuming an average remaining life for current depreciable net PP&E as well as a depreciation period for new capex. While more technically sound than the "quick-and-dirty" method of projecting depreciation as a percentage of sales or capex, building a PP&E schedule generally does not yield a substantially different result.

For a DCF constructed on the basis of EBITDA and EBIT projections, depreciation (and amortization) can simply be calculated as the difference between the two. In this scenario however, the banker must ensure that the implied D&A is consistent with historical levels as well as capex projections.[10] Regardless of which approach is used, the banker often makes a simplifying assumption that depreciation and capex are in line by the final year of the projection period so as to ensure that the company's PP&E base remains steady in perpetuity. Otherwise, the company's valuation would be influenced by an expanding or diminishing PP&E base, which would not be representative of a steady state business.

Amortization Amortization differs from depreciation in that it reduces the value of definite life intangible assets as opposed to tangible assets. Definite life intangible assets include contractual rights such as non-compete clauses, copyrights, licenses, patents, trademarks, or other intellectual property, as well as information technology and customer lists, among others. These intangible assets are amortized according to a determined or useful life.[11]

Like depreciation, amortization can be projected as a percentage of sales or by building a detailed schedule based upon a company's existing intangible assets.

---

[9]A schedule for determining a company's PP&E for each year in the projection period on the basis of annual capex (additions) and depreciation (subtractions). PP&E for a particular year in the projection period is the sum of the prior year's PP&E plus the projection year's capex less the projection year's depreciation.

[10]When using consensus estimates for EBITDA and EBIT, the difference between the two may imply a level of D&A that is not defensible. This situation is particularly common when there are a different number of research analysts reporting values for EBITDA than for EBIT.

[11]Indefinite life intangible assets, most notably goodwill (value paid in excess over the book value of an asset), are not amortized. Rather, goodwill is held on the balance sheet and tested annually for impairment.

However, amortization is often combined with depreciation as a single line item within a company's financial statements. Therefore, it is more common to simply model amortization with depreciation as part of one line-item (D&A).

Assuming depreciation and amortization are combined as one line item, D&A is projected in accordance with one of the approaches described under the "Depreciation" heading (e.g., as a percentage of sales or capex, through a detailed schedule, or as the difference between EBITDA and EBIT).

Capital Expenditures Projections Capital expenditures are the funds that a company uses to purchase, improve, expand, or replace physical assets such as buildings, equipment, facilities, machinery, and other assets. Capex is an expenditure as opposed to an expense. It is capitalized on the balance sheet once the expenditure is made and then expensed over its useful life as depreciation through the company's income statement. As opposed to depreciation, capital expenditures represent actual cash outflows and, consequently, must be subtracted from EBIAT in the calculation of FCF (in the year in which the purchase is made).

Historical capex is disclosed directly on a company's cash flow statement under the investing activities section and also discussed in the MD&A section of a public company's 10-K and 10-Q. Historical levels generally serve as a reliable proxy for projecting future capex. However, capex projections may deviate from historical levels in accordance with the company's strategy, sector, or phase of operations. For example, a company in expansion mode might have elevated capex levels for some portion of the projection period, while one in harvest or cash conservation mode might limit its capex.

For public companies, future planned capex is often discussed in the MD&A of its 10-K. Research reports may also provide capex estimates for the future two- or three-year period. In the absence of specific guidance, capex is generally driven as a percentage of sales in line with historical levels due to the fact that top line growth typically needs to be supported by growth in the company's asset base.

Change in Net Working Capital Projections Net working capital is typically defined as non-cash current assets ("current assets") less non-interest-bearing current liabilities ("current liabilities"). It serves as a measure of how much cash a company needs to fund its operations on an ongoing basis. All of the necessary components to determine a company's NWC can be found on its balance sheet. Exhibit 3.5 displays the main current assets and current liabilities line items.

EXHIBIT 3.5 Current Assets and Current Liabilities Components

Current Assets	Current Liabilities
▪ Accounts Receivable (A/R)	▪ Accounts Payable (A/P)
▪ Inventory	▪ Accrued Liabilities
▪ Prepaid Expenses and Other Current Assets	▪ Other Current Liabilities

The formula for calculating NWC is shown in Exhibit 3.6.

EXHIBIT 3.6 Calculation of Net Working Capital

$$\text{NWC} = \frac{(\text{Accounts Receivable} + \text{Inventory} + \text{Prepaid Expenses and Other Current Assets})}{\text{less}}$$
$$(\text{Accounts Payable} + \text{Accrued Liabilities} + \text{Other Current Liabilities})$$

The change in NWC from year to year is important for calculating FCF as it represents an annual source or use of cash for the company. An increase in NWC over a given period (i.e., when current assets increase by more than current liabilities) is a use of cash. This is typical for a growing company, which tends to increase its spending on inventory to support sales growth. Similarly, A/R tends to increase in line with sales growth, which represents a use of cash as it is incremental cash that has not yet been collected. Conversely, an increase in A/P represents a source of cash as it is money that has been retained by the company as opposed to paid out.

As an increase in NWC is a use of cash, it is subtracted from EBIAT in the calculation of FCF. If the net change in NWC is negative (source of cash), then that value is added back to EBIAT. The calculation of a year-over-year (YoY) change in NWC is shown in Exhibit 3.7.

EXHIBIT 3.7 Calculation of a YoY Change in NWC

$$\Delta \text{NWC} = \text{NWC}_n - \text{NWC}_{(n-1)}$$

where: n = the most recent year
(n − 1) = the prior year

A "quick-and-dirty" shortcut for projecting YoY changes in NWC involves projecting NWC as a percentage of sales at a designated historical level and then calculating the YoY changes accordingly. This approach is typically used when a company's detailed balance sheet and COGS information is unavailable and working capital ratios cannot be determined. A more granular and recommended approach (where possible) is to project the individual components of both current assets and current liabilities for each year in the projection period. NWC and YoY changes are then calculated accordingly.

A company's current assets and current liabilities components are typically projected on the basis of historical ratios from the prior year level or a three-year average. In some cases, the company's trend line, management guidance, or sector trends may suggest improving or declining working capital efficiency ratios, thereby impacting FCF projections. In the absence of such guidance, the banker typically assumes constant working capital ratios in line with historical levels throughout the projection period.[12]

---

[12] For the purposes of the DCF, working capital ratios are generally measured on an annual basis.

Current Assets

Accounts Receivable Accounts receivable refers to amounts owed to a company for its products and services sold on credit. A/R is customarily projected on the basis of days sales outstanding (DSO), as shown in Exhibit 3.8.

EXHIBIT 3.8 Calculation of DSO

$$DSO = \frac{A/R}{Sales} \times 365$$

DSO provides a gauge of how well a company is managing the collection of its A/R by measuring the number of days it takes to collect payment after the sale of a product or service. For example, a DSO of 45 implies that the company, on average, receives payment 45 days after an initial sale is made. The lower a company's DSO, the faster it receives cash from credit sales.

An increase in A/R represents a use of cash. Hence, companies strive to minimize their DSO so as to speed up their collection of cash. Increases in a company's DSO can be the result of numerous factors, including customer leverage or renegotiation of terms, worsening customer credit, poor collection systems, or change in product mix, for example. This increase in the cash cycle decreases short-term liquidity as the company has less cash on hand to fund short-term business operations and meet current debt obligations.

Inventory Inventory refers to the value of a company's raw materials, work in progress, and finished goods. It is customarily projected on the basis of days inventory held (DIH), as shown in Exhibit 3.9.

EXHIBIT 3.9 Calculation of DIH

$$DIH = \frac{Inventory}{COGS} \times 365$$

DIH measures the number of days it takes a company to sell its inventory. For example, a DIH of 90 implies that, on average, it takes 90 days for the company to turn its inventory (or approximately four "inventory turns" per year, as discussed in more detail below). An increase in inventory represents a use of cash. Therefore, companies strive to minimize DIH and turn their inventory as quickly as possible so as to minimize the amount of cash it ties up. Additionally, idle inventory is susceptible to damage, theft, or obsolescence due to newer products or technologies.

An alternate approach for measuring a company's efficiency at selling its inventory is the inventory turns ratio. As depicted in Exhibit 3.10, inventory turns measures the number of times a company turns over its inventory in a given year. As with DIH, inventory turns is used together with COGS to project future inventory levels.

EXHIBIT 3.10 Calculation of Inventory Turns

$$\text{Inventory Turns} = \text{COGS / Inventory}$$

Prepaid Expenses and Other Current Assets Prepaid expenses are payments made by a company before a product has been delivered or a service has been performed. For example, insurance premiums are typically paid upfront although they cover a longer-term period (e.g., six months or a year). Prepaid expenses and other current assets are typically projected as a percentage of sales in line with historical levels. As with A/R and inventory, an increase in prepaid expenses and other current assets represents a use of cash.

Current Liabilities

Accounts Payable Accounts payable refers to amounts owed by a company for products and services already purchased. A/P is customarily projected on the basis of days payable outstanding (DPO), as shown in Exhibit 3.11.

EXHIBIT 3.11 Calculation of DPO

$$\text{DPO} = \frac{\text{A/P}}{\text{COGS}} \times 365$$

DPO measures the number of days it takes for a company to make payment on its outstanding purchases of goods and services. For example, a DPO of 45 implies that the company takes 45 days on average to pay its suppliers. The higher a company's DPO, the more time it has available to use its cash on hand for various business purposes before paying outstanding bills.

An increase in A/P represents a source of cash. Therefore, as opposed to DSO, companies aspire to maximize or "push out" (within reason) their DPO so as to increase short-term liquidity.

Accrued Liabilities and Other Current Liabilities Accrued liabilities are expenses such as salaries, rent, interest, and taxes that have been incurred by a company but not yet paid. As with prepaid expenses and other current assets, accrued liabilities and other current liabilities are typically projected as a percentage of sales in line with historical levels. As with A/P, an increase in accrued liabilities and other current liabilities represents a source of cash.

Free Cash Flow Projections Once all of the above items have been projected, annual FCF for the projection period is relatively easy to calculate in accordance with the formula first introduced in Exhibit 3.3. The projection period FCF, however, represents only a portion of the target's value. The remainder is captured in the terminal value, which is discussed in Step IV.

STEP III. CALCULATE WEIGHTED AVERAGE COST OF CAPITAL

WACC is a broadly accepted standard for use as the discount rate to calculate the present value of a company's projected FCF and terminal value. It represents the weighted average of the required return on the invested capital (customarily debt and equity) in a given company. As debt and equity components have different risk profiles and tax ramifications, WACC is dependent on a company's "target" capital structure.

WACC can also be thought of as an opportunity cost of capital or what an investor would expect to earn in an alternative investment with a similar risk profile. Companies with diverse business segments may have different costs of capital for their various businesses. In these instances, it may be advisable to conduct a DCF using a "sum of the parts" approach in which a separate DCF analysis is performed for each distinct business segment, each with its own WACC. The values for each business segment are then summed to arrive at an implied enterprise valuation for the entire company.

The formula for the calculation of WACC is shown in Exhibit 3.12.

EXHIBIT 3.12 Calculation of WACC

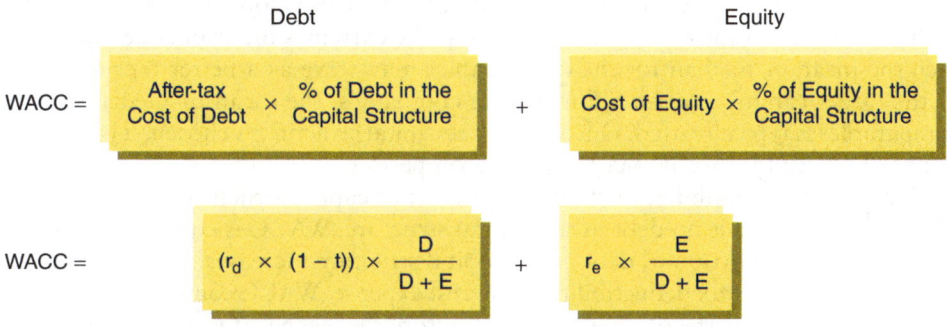

where: r_d = cost of debt
r_e = cost of equity
t = marginal tax rate
D = market value of debt
E = market value of equity

A company's capital structure or total capitalization is comprised of two main components, debt and equity (as represented by D + E). The rates—r_d (return on debt) and r_e (return on equity)—represent the company's market cost of debt and equity, respectively. As its name connotes, the ensuing weighted average cost of capital is simply a weighted average of the company's cost of debt (tax-effected) and cost of equity based on an assumed or "target" capital structure.

Below we demonstrate a step-by-step process for calculating WACC, as outlined in Exhibit 3.13.

EXHIBIT 3.13 Steps for Calculating WACC

> Step III(a):   Determine Target Capital Structure
> Step III(b):   Estimate Cost of Debt (r_d)
> Step III(c):   Estimate Cost of Equity (r_e)
> Step IV(d):   Calculate WACC

Step III(a): Determine Target Capital Structure

WACC is predicated on choosing a target capital structure for the company that is consistent with its long-term strategy. This target capital structure is represented by the debt-to-total capitalization ($D/(D + E)$) and equity-to-total capitalization ($E/(D + E)$) ratios (see Exhibit 3.12). In the absence of explicit company guidance on target capital structure, the banker examines the company's current and historical debt-to-total capitalization ratios as well as the capitalization of its peers. Public comparable companies provide a meaningful benchmark for target capital structure as it is assumed that their management teams are seeking to maximize shareholder value.

In the finance community, the approach used to determine a company's target capital structure may differ from firm to firm. For public companies, existing capital structure is generally used as the target capital structure as long as it is comfortably within the range of the comparables. If it is at the extremes of, or outside, the range, then the mean or median for the comparables may serve as a better representation of the target capital structure. For private companies, the mean or median for the comparables is typically used. Once the target capital structure is chosen, it is assumed to be held constant throughout the projection period.

The graph in Exhibit 3.14 shows the impact of capital structure on a company's WACC. When there is no debt in the capital structure, WACC is equal to the cost of equity. As the proportion of debt in the capital structure increases, WACC gradually decreases due to the tax deductibility of interest expense. WACC continues to decrease up to the point where the *optimal capital structure*[13] is reached. Once this threshold is surpassed, the cost of potential financial distress (i.e., the negative effects of an over-leveraged capital structure, including the increased probability of insolvency) begins to override the tax advantages of debt. As a result, both debt and equity investors demand a higher yield for their increased risk, thereby driving WACC upward beyond the optimal capital structure threshold.

---

[13]The financing mix that minimizes WACC, thereby maximizing a company's theoretical value.

EXHIBIT 3.14 Optimal Capital Structure

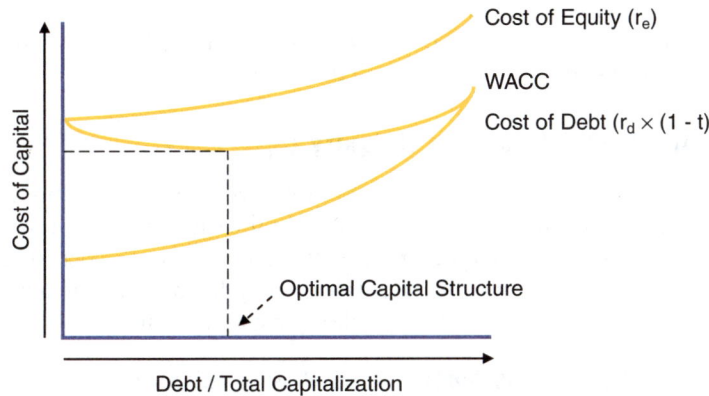

Step III(b): Estimate Cost of Debt (r_d)

A company's cost of debt reflects its credit profile at the target capital structure, which is based on a multitude of factors including size, sector, outlook, cyclicality, credit ratings, credit statistics, cash flow generation, financial policy, and acquisition strategy, among others. Assuming the company is currently at its target capital structure, cost of debt is generally derived from the blended yield on its outstanding debt instruments, which may include a mix of public and private debt. In the event the company is not currently at its target capital structure, the cost of debt must be derived from peer companies.

For publicly traded bonds, cost of debt is determined on the basis of the *current yield*[14] on all outstanding issues. For private debt, such as revolving credit facilities and term loans,[15] the banker typically consults with an in-house debt capital markets (DCM) specialist to ascertain the current yield. Market-based approaches such as these are generally preferred as the current yield on a company's outstanding debt serves as the best indicator of its expected cost of debt and reflects the risk of default. Bond quotes and key terms are available through the Bloomberg Bond Description function DES<GO> (see Appendix 3.2).

In the absence of current market data (e.g., for companies with debt that is not actively traded), an alternative approach is to calculate the company's weighted average cost of debt on the basis of the at-issuance coupons of its current debt maturities. This approach, however, is not always accurate as it is backward-looking and may not reflect the company's cost of raising debt capital under prevailing market conditions. A preferred, albeit more time-consuming, approach in these instances is to approximate a company's cost of debt based on its current (or implied) credit ratings at the target

---

[14]Technically, a bond's current yield is calculated as the annual coupon on the par value of the bond divided by the current price of the bond. However, callable bond yields are typically quoted at the yield-to-worst call (YTW). A callable bond has a call schedule (defined in the bond's indenture) that lists several call dates and their corresponding call prices. The YTW is the lowest calculated yield when comparing all of the possible yield-to-calls from a bond's call schedule given the initial offer price or current trading price of the bond.
[15]See Chapter 4: Leveraged Buyouts for additional information on term loans and other debt instruments.

capital structure and the cost of debt for comparable credits, typically with guidance from an in-house DCM professional.

Once determined, the cost of debt is tax-effected at the company's marginal tax rate as interest payments are tax deductible.

Step III(c): Estimate Cost of Equity (r_e)

Cost of equity is the required annual rate of return that a company's equity investors expect to receive (including dividends). Unlike the cost of debt, which can be deduced from a company's outstanding maturities, a company's cost of equity is not readily observable in the market. To calculate the expected return on a company's equity, the banker typically employs a formula known as the capital asset pricing model (CAPM).

Capital Asset Pricing Model CAPM is based on the premise that equity investors need to be compensated for their assumption of systematic risk in the form of a risk premium, or the amount of market return in excess of a stated risk-free rate. Systematic risk is the risk related to the overall market, which is also known as non-diversifiable risk. A company's level of systematic risk depends on the covariance of its share price with movements in the overall market, as measured by its *beta* (β) (discussed later in this section).

By contrast, unsystematic or "specific" risk is company- or sector-specific and can be avoided through diversification. Hence, equity investors are not compensated for it (in the form of a premium). As a general rule, the smaller the company and the more specified its product offering, the higher its unsystematic risk.

The formula for the calculation of CAPM is shown in Exhibit 3.15.

EXHIBIT 3.15 Calculation of CAPM

Cost of Equity (r_e) = Risk-free Rate + Levered Beta × Market Risk Premium

Cost of Equity (r_e) = $r_f + \beta_L \times (r_m - r_f)$

where:
r_f = risk-free rate
β_L = levered beta
r_m = expected return on the market
$r_m - r_f$ = market risk premium

Risk-Free Rate (r_f) The risk-free rate is the expected rate of return obtained by investing in a "riskless" security. U.S. government securities such as T-bills, T-notes, and T-bonds[16] are accepted by the market as "risk-free" because they are backed by

---

[16]T-bills are non-interest-bearing securities issued with maturities of 3 months, 6 months, and 12 months at a discount to face value. T-notes and bonds, by contrast, have a stated coupon and pay semiannual interest. T-notes are issued with maturities of between one and ten years, while T-bonds are issued with maturities of more than ten years.

Discounted Cash Flow Analysis **145**

the full faith of the U.S. federal government. Interpolated yields[17] for government securities can be located on Bloomberg[18] as well as the U.S. Department of Treasury website,[19] among others. Bloomberg also provides a U.S. Treasury Interpolated Benchmark Monitor which displays yields for 1 month to 30-year treasuries (USTI<GO>, see Appendix 3.3). The actual risk-free rate used in CAPM varies with the prevailing yields for the chosen security.

Investment banks may differ on accepted proxies for the appropriate risk-free rate, with many using the yield on the 10-year U.S. Treasury note and others preferring the yield on longer-term Treasuries. The general goal is to use as long-dated an instrument as possible to match the expected life of the company (assuming a going concern), but practical considerations also need to be taken into account. Due to the moratorium on the issuance of 30-year Treasury bonds[20] and shortage of securities with 30-year maturities, Ibbotson Associates ("Ibbotson")[21] uses an interpolated yield for a 20-year bond as the basis for the risk-free rate.[22,23]

Market Risk Premium ($r_m - r_f$ or mrp)   The market risk premium is the spread of the expected market return[24] over the risk-free rate. Finance professionals, as well as academics, often differ over which historical time period is most relevant for observing the market risk premium. Some believe that more recent periods, such as the last ten years or the post–World War II era are more appropriate, while others prefer to examine the pre–Great Depression era to the present.

Ibbotson tracks data on the equity risk premium dating back to 1926. Depending on which time period is referenced, the premium of the market return over the risk-free rate ($r_m - r_f$) may vary substantially. For the 1926 to 2011 period, Ibbotson calculates a market risk premium of 6.62%.[25]

---

[17] Yields on nominal Treasury securities at "constant maturity" are interpolated by the U.S. Treasury from the daily yield curve for non-inflation-indexed Treasury securities. This curve, which relates the yield on a security to its time-to-maturity, is based on the closing market bid yields on actively traded Treasury securities in the over-the-counter market.
[18] Bloomberg function: ICUR{# years}<GO>. For example, the interpolated yield for a 10-year Treasury note can be obtained from Bloomberg by typing "ICUR10," then pressing <GO>.
[19] Located under "Daily Treasury Yield Curve Rates."
[20] The 30-year Treasury bond was discontinued on February 18, 2002, and reintroduced on February 9, 2006.
[21] Morningstar acquired Ibbotson Associates in March 2006. Ibbotson Associates is a leading authority on asset allocation, providing products and services to help investment professionals obtain, manage, and retain assets. Morningstar's annual *Ibbotson® SBBI® (Stocks, Bonds, Bills, and Inflation) Valuation Yearbook* is a widely used reference for cost of capital input estimations for U.S.-based businesses.
[22] Bloomberg function: ICUR20<GO>.
[23] While there are currently no 20-year Treasury bonds issued by the U.S. Treasury, as long as there are bonds being traded with at least 20 years to maturity, there will be a proxy for the yield on 20-year Treasury bonds.
[24] The S&P 500 is typically used as the proxy for the return on the market.
[25] Expected risk premium for equities is based on the difference of historical arithmetic mean returns for the 1926 to 2011 period. Arithmetic annual returns are independent of one another. Geometric annual returns are dependent on the prior year's returns.

Many investment banks have a firm-wide policy governing market risk premium in order to ensure consistency in valuation work across their various projects and departments. The equity risk premium employed on Wall Street typically ranges from approximately 5% to 8%. Consequently, it is important for the banker to consult with senior colleagues for guidance on the appropriate market risk premium to use in the CAPM formula. For shorter duration calculations of market risk premium, Bloomberg provides functionality via function: EQRP<GO>.

Beta (β) Beta is a measure of the covariance between the rate of return on a company's stock and the overall market return (systematic risk), with the S&P 500 traditionally used as a proxy for the market. As the S&P 500 has a beta of 1.0, a stock with a beta of 1.0 should have an expected return equal to that of the market. A stock with a beta of less than 1.0 has lower systematic risk than the market, and a stock with a beta greater than 1.0 has higher systematic risk. Mathematically, this is captured in the CAPM, with a higher beta stock exhibiting a higher cost of equity; and vice versa for lower beta stocks.

A public company's historical beta may be sourced from financial information resources such as Bloomberg via function: BETA<GO> (see Appendix 3.4). Recent historical equity returns (i.e., over the previous two to five years), however, may not be a reliable indicator of future returns. Therefore, many bankers prefer to use a predicted beta such as the Bloomberg "Adjusted Beta" whenever possible as it is meant to be forward-looking.

The exercise of calculating WACC for a private company involves deriving beta from a group of publicly traded peer companies that may or may not have similar capital structures to one another or the target. To neutralize the effects of different capital structures (i.e., remove the influence of leverage), the banker must *unlever* the beta for each company in the peer group to achieve the *asset beta* ("unlevered beta").

The formula for unlevering beta is shown in Exhibit 3.16.

EXHIBIT 3.16   Unlevering Beta

$$\beta_U = \frac{\beta_L}{\left(1 + \frac{D}{E} \times (1 - t)\right)}$$

where: β_U = unlevered beta
β_L = levered beta
D/E = debt-to-equity[26] ratio
t = marginal tax rate

---

[26]Market value of equity.

Discounted Cash Flow Analysis

After calculating the unlevered beta for each company, the banker determines the average unlevered beta for the peer group.[27] This average unlevered beta is then *relevered* using the company's target capital structure and marginal tax rate. The formula for relevering beta is shown in Exhibit 3.17.

EXHIBIT 3.17 Relevering Beta

$$\beta_L = \beta_U \times \left(1 + \frac{D}{E} \times (1-t)\right)$$

where: D/E = target debt-to-equity ratio

The resulting levered beta serves as the beta for calculating the private company's cost of equity using the CAPM. Similarly, for a public company that is not currently at its target capital structure, its asset beta must be calculated and then relevered at the target D/E.

Size Premium (SP) The concept of a size premium is based on empirical evidence suggesting that smaller-sized companies are riskier and, therefore, should have a higher cost of equity. This phenomenon, which to some degree contradicts the CAPM, relies on the notion that smaller companies' risk is not entirely captured in their betas given limited trading volumes of their stock, making covariance calculations inexact. Therefore, the banker may choose to add a size premium to the CAPM formula for smaller companies to account for the perceived higher risk and, therefore, expected higher return (see Exhibit 3.18). Ibbotson provides size premia for companies based on their market capitalization, tiered in deciles.

EXHIBIT 3.18 CAPM Formula Adjusted for Size Premium

$$r_e = r_f + \beta_L \times (r_m - r_f) + SP$$

where: SP = size premium

---

[27] Average unlevered beta may be calculated on a market-cap weighted basis.

Step III(d): Calculate WACC

Once all of the above steps are completed, the various components are entered into the formula in Exhibit 3.19 to calculate the company's WACC. In addition, Bloomberg provides a WACC analysis via function: WACC<GO> (see Appendix 3.5). Given the numerous assumptions involved in determining a company's WACC and its sizeable impact on valuation, its key inputs are typically sensitized to produce a WACC range (see Exhibit 3.49). This range is then used in conjunction with other sensitized inputs, such as exit multiple, to produce a valuation range for the target.

EXHIBIT 3.19 WACC Formula

$$WACC = \left(r_d \times (1-t)\right) \times \frac{D}{D+E} + r_e \times \frac{E}{D+E}$$

STEP IV. DETERMINE TERMINAL VALUE

The DCF approach to valuation is based on determining the present value of all future FCF produced by a company. As it is infeasible to project a company's FCF indefinitely, the banker uses a terminal value to capture the value of the company beyond the projection period. As its name suggests, terminal value is typically calculated on the basis of the company's FCF (or a proxy such as EBITDA) in the final year of the projection period.

The terminal value typically accounts for a substantial portion of a company's value in a DCF, sometimes as much as three-quarters or more. Therefore, it is important that the company's terminal year financial data represents a steady state level of financial performance, as opposed to a cyclical high or low. Similarly, the underlying assumptions for calculating the terminal value must be carefully examined and sensitized.

There are two widely accepted methods used to calculate a company's terminal value—the exit multiple method and the perpetuity growth method. Depending on the situation and company being valued, the banker may use one or both methods, with each serving as a check on the other.

Exit Multiple Method

The EMM calculates the remaining value of a company's FCF produced after the projection period on the basis of a multiple of its terminal year EBITDA (or EBIT). This multiple is typically based on the current LTM trading multiples for comparable companies. As current multiples may be affected by sector or economic cycles, it is important to use both a normalized trading multiple and EBITDA. The use of a peak or trough multiple and/or an un-normalized EBITDA level can produce a skewed result. This is especially important for companies in cyclical industries.

As the exit multiple is a critical driver of terminal value, and hence overall value in a DCF, the banker subjects it to sensitivity analysis. For example, if the selected exit multiple range based on comparable companies is 7.0x to 8.0x, a common approach would be to create a valuation output table premised on exit multiples of 6.5x, 7.0x, 7.5x, 8.0x, and 8.5x (see Exhibit 3.32). The formula for calculating terminal value using the EMM is shown in Exhibit 3.20.

EXHIBIT 3.20 Exit Multiple Method

$$\text{Terminal Value} = \text{EBITDA}_n \times \text{Exit Multiple}$$

where: n = terminal year of the projection period

Perpetuity Growth Method

The PGM calculates terminal value by treating a company's terminal year FCF as a perpetuity growing at an assumed rate. As the formula in Exhibit 3.21 indicates, this method relies on the WACC calculation performed in Step III and requires the banker to make an assumption regarding the company's long-term, sustainable growth rate ("perpetuity growth rate"). The perpetuity growth rate is typically chosen on the basis of the company's expected long-term industry growth rate, which generally tends to be within a range of 2% to 4% (i.e., nominal GDP growth). As with the exit multiple, the perpetuity growth rate is also sensitized to produce a valuation range.

EXHIBIT 3.21 Perpetuity Growth Method

$$\text{Terminal Value} = \frac{\text{FCF}_n \times (1 + g)}{(r - g)}$$

where: FCF = unlevered free cash flow
  n = terminal year of the projection period
  g = perpetuity growth rate
  r = WACC

The PGM is often used in conjunction with the EMM, with each serving as a sanity check on the other. For example, if the implied perpetuity growth rate, as derived from the EMM is too high or low (see Exhibits 3.22(a) and 3.22(b)), it could be an indicator that the exit multiple assumptions are unrealistic.

EXHIBIT 3.22(a) Implied Perpetuity Growth Rate (End-of-Year Discounting)

$$\text{Implied Perpetuity Growth Rate} = \frac{(\text{Terminal Value}^{(a)} \times \text{WACC}) - \text{FCF}_{\text{Terminal Year}}}{\text{Terminal Value}^{(a)} + \text{FCF}_{\text{Terminal Year}}}$$

EXHIBIT 3.22(b) Implied Perpetuity Growth Rate (Mid-Year Discounting, see Exhibit 3.26)

$$\text{Implied Perpetuity Growth Rate} = \frac{(\text{Terminal Value}^{(a)} \times \text{WACC}) - \text{FCF}_{\text{Terminal Year}} \times (1 + \text{WACC})^{0.5}}{\text{Terminal Value}^{(a)} + \text{FCF}_{\text{Terminal Year}} \times (1 + \text{WACC})^{0.5}}$$

[a] Terminal Value calculated using the EMM.

Similarly, if the implied exit multiple from the PGM (see Exhibits 3.23(a) and 3.23(b)) is not in line with normalized trading multiples for the target or its peers, the perpetuity growth rate should be revisited.

EXHIBIT 3.23(a) Implied Exit Multiple (End-of-Year Discounting)

$$\text{Implied Exit Multiple} = \frac{\text{Terminal Value}^{(a)}}{\text{EBITDA}_{\text{Terminal Year}}}$$

EXHIBIT 3.23(b) Implied Exit Multiple (Mid-Year Discounting, see Exhibit 3.26))

$$\text{Implied Exit Multiple} = \frac{\text{Terminal Value}^{(a)} \times (1 + \text{WACC})^{0.5}}{\text{EBITDA}_{\text{Terminal Year}}}$$

[a] Terminal Value calculated using the PGM.

STEP V. CALCULATE PRESENT VALUE AND DETERMINE VALUATION

Calculate Present Value

Calculating present value centers on the notion that a dollar today is worth more than a dollar tomorrow, a concept known as the time value of money. This is due to the fact that a dollar earns money through investments (capital appreciation) and/or interest (e.g., in a money market account). In a DCF, a company's projected FCF and terminal value are discounted to the present at the company's WACC in accordance with the time value of money.

The present value calculation is performed by multiplying the FCF for each year in the projection period and the terminal value by its respective discount factor. The discount factor is the fractional value representing the present value of one dollar received at a future date given an assumed discount rate. For example, assuming a 10% discount rate, the discount factor for one dollar received at the end of one year is 0.91 (see Exhibit 3.24).

EXHIBIT 3.24 Discount Factor

$$\text{Discount Factor} = \frac{1}{(1 + \text{WACC})^n}$$

$$0.91 = \frac{\$1.00}{(1 + 10\%)^1}$$

where: n = year in the projection period

The discount factor is applied to a given future financial statistic to determine its present value. For example, given a 10% WACC, FCF of $100 million at the end of the first year of a company's projection period (Year 1) would be worth $91 million today (see Exhibit 3.25).

EXHIBIT 3.25 Present Value Calculation Using a Year-End Discount Factor

$$\text{PV of FCF}_n = \text{FCF}_n \times \text{Discount Factor}_n$$

$$\$91 \text{ million} = \$100 \text{ million} \times 0.91$$

where: n = year in the projection period

Mid-Year Convention To account for the fact that annual FCF is usually received throughout the year rather than at year-end, it is typically discounted in accordance with a *mid-year convention*. Mid-year convention assumes that a company's FCF is received evenly throughout the year, thereby approximating a steady (and more realistic) FCF generation.[28]

The use of a mid-year convention results in a slightly higher valuation than year-end discounting due to the fact that FCF is received sooner. As Exhibit 3.26 depicts, if one dollar is received evenly over the course of the first year of the projection period rather than at year-end, the discount factor is calculated to be 0.95 (assuming a 10% discount rate). Hence, $100 million received throughout Year 1 would be worth $95 million today in accordance with a mid-year convention, as opposed to $91 million using the year-end approach in Exhibit 3.25.

EXHIBIT 3.26 Discount Factor Using a Mid-Year Convention

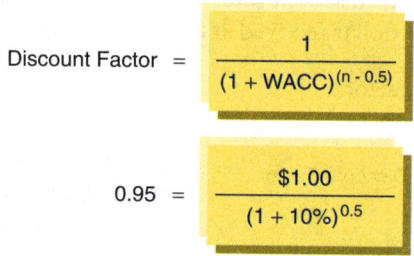

where: n = year in the projection period
0.5 = is subtracted from n in accordance with a mid-year convention

Terminal Value Considerations When employing a mid-year convention for the projection period, mid-year discounting is also applied for the terminal value under the PGM, as the banker is discounting perpetual future FCF assumed to be received throughout the year. The EMM, however, which is typically based on the LTM trading multiples of comparable companies for a calendar year end EBITDA (or EBIT), uses year-end discounting.

---

[28] May not be appropriate for highly seasonal businesses.

Discounted Cash Flow Analysis

Determine Valuation

Calculate Enterprise Value   A company's projected FCF and terminal value are each discounted to the present and summed to provide an enterprise value. Exhibit 3.27 depicts the DCF calculation of enterprise value for a company with a five-year projection period, incorporating a mid-year convention and the EMM.

EXHIBIT 3.27   Enterprise Value Using Mid-Year Discounting

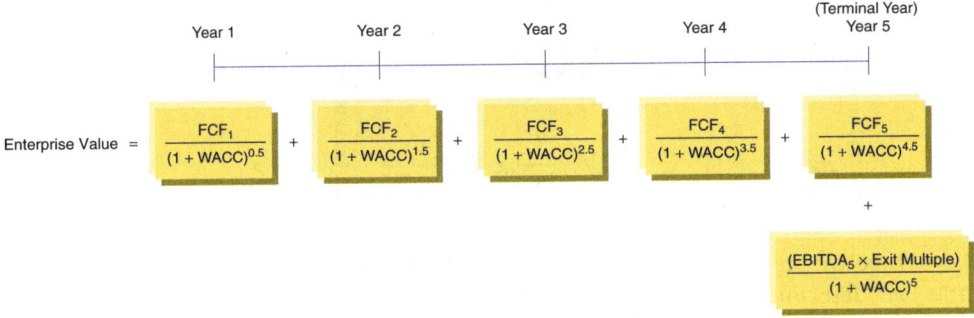

Derive Implied Equity Value   To derive implied equity value, the company's net debt, preferred stock, and noncontrolling interest are subtracted from the calculated enterprise value (see Exhibit 3.28).

EXHIBIT 3.28   Equity Value

Derive Implied Share Price   For publicly traded companies, implied equity value is divided by the company's fully diluted shares outstanding to calculate an implied share price (see Exhibit 3.29).

EXHIBIT 3.29   Share Price

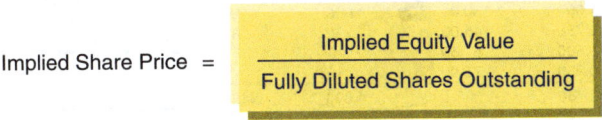

The existence of in-the-money options and warrants, however, creates a *circular reference* in the basic formula shown in Exhibit 3.29 between the company's fully diluted shares outstanding count and implied share price. In other words, equity value per share is dependent on the number of fully diluted shares outstanding, which, in turn, is dependent on the implied share price. This is remedied in the model by activating the *iteration* function in Microsoft Excel (see Exhibit 3.30).

EXHIBIT 3.30 Iteration Function in Microsoft Excel

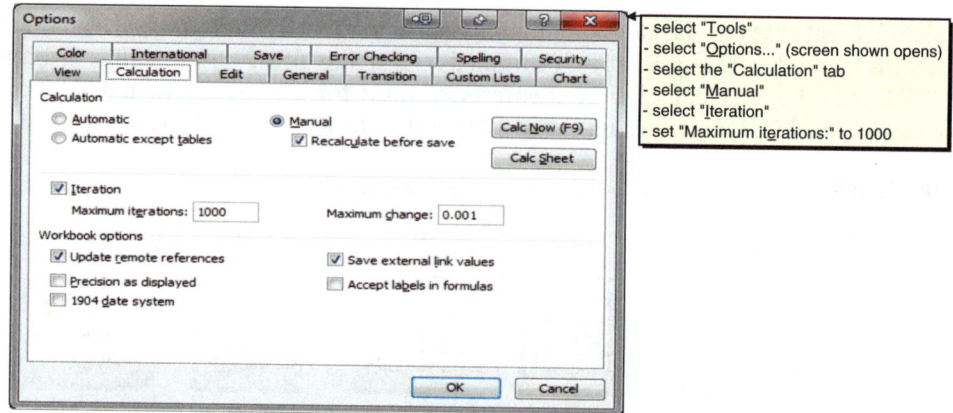

Once the iteration function is activated, the model is able to iterate between the cell determining the company's implied share price (see shaded area "A" in Exhibit 3.31) and those cells determining whether each option tranche is in-the-money (see shaded area "B" in Exhibit 3.31). At an assumed enterprise value of $6,000 million, implied equity value of $4,500 million, 80 million basic shares outstanding, and the options data shown in Exhibit 3.31, we calculate an implied share price of $55.00.

EXHIBIT 3.31 Calculation of Implied Share Price

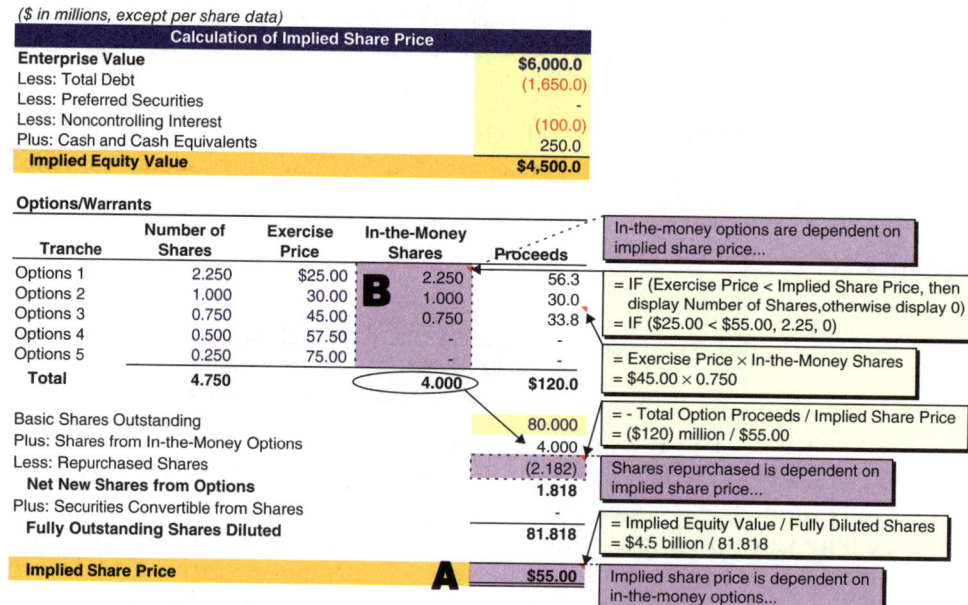

Discounted Cash Flow Analysis

Perform Sensitivity Analysis

The DCF incorporates numerous assumptions, each of which can have a sizeable impact on valuation. As a result, the DCF output is viewed in terms of a valuation range based on a series of key input assumptions, rather than as a single value. The exercise of deriving a valuation range by varying key inputs is called sensitivity analysis.

Sensitivity analysis is a testament to the notion that valuation is as much an art as a science. Key valuation drivers such as WACC, exit multiple, and perpetuity growth rate are the most commonly sensitized inputs in a DCF. The banker may also perform additional sensitivity analysis on key financial performance drivers, such as sales growth rates and profit margins (e.g., EBITDA or EBIT). Valuation outputs produced by sensitivity analysis are typically displayed in a data table, such as that shown in Exhibit 3.32.

The center shaded portion of the sensitivity table in Exhibit 3.32 displays an enterprise value range of $5,598 million to $6,418 million assuming a WACC range of 9.5% to 10.5% and an exit multiple range of 7x to 8x. As the exit multiple increases, enterprise value increases accordingly; conversely, as the discount rate increases, enterprise value decreases.

EXHIBIT 3.32   Sensitivity Analysis

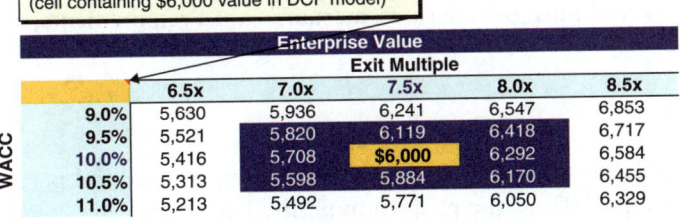

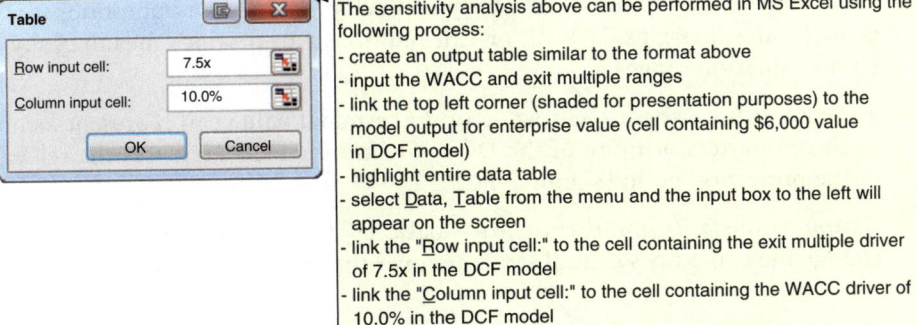

As with comparable companies and precedent transactions, once a DCF valuation range is determined, it should be compared to the valuation ranges derived from other methodologies. If the output produces notably different results, it is advisable to revisit the assumptions and fine-tune, if necessary. Common missteps that can skew the DCF valuation include the use of unrealistic financial projections (which generally has the largest impact),[29] WACC, or terminal value assumptions. A substantial difference in the valuation implied by the DCF versus other methodologies, however, does not necessarily mean the analysis is flawed. Multiples-based valuation methodologies may fail to account for company-specific factors that may imply a higher or lower valuation.

KEY PROS AND CONS

Pros

- *Cash flow-based* – reflects value of projected FCF, which represents a more fundamental approach to valuation than using multiples-based methodologies

- *Market independent* – more insulated from market aberrations such as bubbles and distressed periods

- *Self-sufficient* – does not rely entirely upon truly comparable companies or transactions, which may or may not exist, to frame valuation; a DCF is particularly important when there are limited or no "pure play" public comparables to the company being valued

- *Flexibility* – allows the banker to run multiple financial performance scenarios, including improving or declining growth rates, margins, capex requirements, and working capital efficiency

Cons

- *Dependence on financial projections* – accurate forecasting of financial performance is challenging, especially as the projection period lengthens

- *Sensitivity to assumptions* – relatively small changes in key assumptions, such as growth rates, margins, WACC, or exit multiple, can produce meaningfully different valuation ranges

- *Terminal value* – the present value of the terminal value can represent as much as three-quarters or more of the DCF valuation, which decreases the relevance of the projection period's annual FCF

- *Assumes constant capital structure* – basic DCF does not provide flexibility to change the company's capital structure over the projection period

---

[29]This is a common pitfall in the event that management projections (Management Case) are used without independently analyzing and testing the underlying assumptions.

ILLUSTRATIVE DISCOUNTED CASH FLOW ANALYSIS FOR VALUECO

The following section provides a detailed, step-by-step construction of a DCF analysis and illustrates how it is used to establish a valuation range for our target company, ValueCo. As discussed in the Introduction, ValueCo is a private company for which we are provided detailed historical financial information. However, for our illustrative DCF analysis, we assume that no management projections were provided in order to cultivate the ability to develop financial projections with limited information. We do, however, assume that we were provided with basic information on ValueCo's business and operations.

Step I. Study the Target and Determine Key Performance Drivers

As a first step, we reviewed the basic company information provided on ValueCo. This foundation, in turn, allowed us to study ValueCo's sector in greater detail, including the identification of key competitors (and comparable companies), customers, and suppliers. Various trade journals and industry studies, as well as SEC filings and research reports of public comparables, were particularly important in this respect.

From a financial perspective, ValueCo's historical financials provided a basis for developing our initial assumptions regarding future performance and projecting FCF. We used consensus estimates of public comparables to provide further guidance for projecting ValueCo's Base Case growth rates and margin trends.

Step II. Project Free Cash Flow

Historical Financial Performance

We began the projection of ValueCo's FCF by laying out its income statement through EBIT for the three-year historical and LTM periods (see Exhibit 3.33). We also entered ValueCo's historical capex and working capital data. The historical period provided important perspective for developing defensible Base Case projection period financials.

As shown in Exhibit 3.33, ValueCo's historical period includes financial data for 2009 to 2011 as well as for LTM 9/30/2012. The company's sales and EBITDA grew at a 10.9% and 16.9% CAGR, respectively, over the 2009 to 2011 period. In addition, ValueCo's EBITDA margin was in the approximately 19% to 21% range over this period, and average capex as a percentage of sales was 4.3%.

The historical working capital levels and ratios are also shown in Exhibit 3.33. ValueCo's average DSO, DIH, and DPO for the 2009 to 2011 period were 46.0, 102.8, and 40.0 days, respectively. For the LTM period, ValueCo's EBITDA margin was 20.7% and capex as a percentage of sales was 4.5%.

EXHIBIT 3.33 ValueCo Summary Historical Operating and Working Capital Data

($ in millions, fiscal year ending December 31)

ValueCo Summary Historical Operating and Balance Sheet Data

	Historical Period			CAGR	LTM
	2009A	2010A	2011A	('09 - '11)	9/30/2012A
Operating Data					
Sales	$2,600.0	$2,900.0	$3,200.0	10.9%	$3,385.0
% growth	NA	11.5%	10.3%		NA
Cost of Goods Sold	1,612.0	1,769.0	1,920.0		2,035.0
% sales	62.0%	61.0%	60.0%		60.1%
Gross Profit	**$988.0**	**$1,131.0**	**$1,280.0**	13.8%	**$1,350.0**
% margin	38.0%	39.0%	40.0%		39.9%
Selling, General & Administrative	496.6	551.0	608.0		650.0
% sales	19.1%	19.0%	19.0%		19.2%
EBITDA	**$491.4**	**$580.0**	**$672.0**	16.9%	**$700.0**
% margin	18.9%	20.0%	21.0%		20.7%
Depreciation	116.0	121.5	145.0		150.0
% sales	4.5%	4.2%	4.5%		4.4%
Amortization	39.0	43.5	48.0		50.0
% sales	1.5%	1.5%	1.5%		1.5%
EBIT	**$336.4**	**$415.0**	**$479.0**	19.3%	**$500.0**
% margin	12.9%	14.3%	15.0%		14.8%
				3-year Average	
Capex	114.4	116.0	144.0		152.3
% sales	4.4%	4.0%	4.5%	4.3%	4.5%
Balance Sheet Data					
Current Assets					
Accounts Receivable	317.0	365.5	417.4		
DSO	44.5	46.0	47.6	46.0	
Inventory	441.6	496.8	556.5		
DIH	100.0	102.5	105.8	102.8	
Prepaid Expenses and Other	117.0	142.1	162.3		
% sales	4.5%	4.9%	5.1%	4.8%	
Current Liabilities					
Accounts Payable	189.9	189.0	199.4		
DPO	43.0	39.0	37.9	40.0	
Accrued Liabilities	221.0	237.8	255.1		
% sales	8.5%	8.2%	8.0%	8.2%	
Other Current Liabilities	75.4	84.1	92.8		
% sales	2.9%	2.9%	2.9%	2.9%	

Discounted Cash Flow Analysis

Projection of Sales, EBITDA, and EBIT

Sales Projections   We projected ValueCo's top line growth for the first three years of the projection period on the basis of consensus research estimates for public comparable companies. Using the average projected sales growth rate for ValueCo's closest peers, we arrived at 2013E, 2014E, and 2015E YoY growth rates of 7.5%, 6%, and 5%, respectively, which are consistent with its historical rates.[30] These growth rate assumptions (as well as the assumptions for all of our model inputs) formed the basis for the Base Case financial projections and were entered into an assumptions page that drives the DCF model (see Chapter 5, Exhibits 5.52 and 5.53).

As the projections indicate, Wall Street expects ValueCo's peers (and, by inference, we expect ValueCo) to continue to experience steady albeit declining growth through 2015E. Beyond 2015E, in the absence of additional company-specific information or guidance, we decreased ValueCo's growth to a sustainable long-term rate of 3% for the remainder of the projection period.

EXHIBIT 3.34   ValueCo Historical and Projected Sales

($ in millions, fiscal year ending December 31)

	Historical Period			CAGR		Projection Period					CAGR
	2009	2010	2011	('09 - '11)	2012	2013	2014	2015	2016	2017	('12 - '17)
Sales	$2,600.0	$2,900.0	$3,200.0	10.9%	$3,450.0	$3,708.8	$3,931.3	$4,127.8	$4,293.0	$4,421.7	5.1%
% growth	NA	11.5%	10.3%		7.8%	7.5%	6.0%	5.0%	4.0%	3.0%	

COGS and SG&A Projections   As shown in Exhibit 3.35, we held COGS and SG&A constant at the prior historical year levels of 60% and 19% of sales, respectively. Accordingly, ValueCo's gross profit margin remains at 40% throughout the projection period.

EXHIBIT 3.35   ValueCo Historical and Projected COGS and SG&A

($ in millions, fiscal year ending December 31)

	Historical Period			CAGR		Projection Period					CAGR
	2009	2010	2011	('09 - '11)	2012	2013	2014	2015	2016	2017	('12 - '17)
Sales	$2,600.0	$2,900.0	$3,200.0	10.9%	$3,450.0	$3,708.8	$3,931.3	$4,127.8	$4,293.0	$4,421.7	5.1%
% growth	NA	11.5%	10.3%		7.8%	7.5%	6.0%	5.0%	4.0%	3.0%	
COGS	1,612.0	1,769.0	1,920.0		2,070.0	2,225.3	2,358.8	2,476.7	2,575.8	2,653.0	
% sales	62.0%	61.0%	60.0%		60.0%	60.0%	60.0%	60.0%	60.0%	60.0%	
Gross Profit	$988.0	$1,131.0	$1,280.0	13.8%	$1,380.0	$1,483.5	$1,572.5	$1,651.1	$1,717.2	$1,768.7	5.1%
% margin	38.0%	39.0%	40.0%		40.0%	40.0%	40.0%	40.0%	40.0%	40.0%	
SG&A	496.6	551.0	608.0		655.0	704.1	746.4	783.7	815.0	839.5	
% sales	19.1%	19.0%	19.0%		19.0%	19.0%	19.0%	19.0%	19.0%	19.0%	

EBITDA Projections   In the absence of guidance or management projections for EBITDA, we simply held ValueCo's margins constant throughout the projection period at prior historical year levels. These constant margins fall out naturally due to the fact that we froze COGS and SG&A as a percentage of sales at 2011 levels. As shown in Exhibit 3.36, ValueCo's EBITDA margins remain constant at 21% throughout the projection period. We also examined the consensus estimates for ValueCo's peer

---

[30]We also displayed ValueCo's full year 2012E financial data, for which we have reasonable comfort given its proximity at the end of Q3 2012. For the purposes of the DCF valuation, we used 2013E as the first full year of projections. An alternative approach is to include the "stub" period FCF (i.e., for Q4 2012E) in the projection period and adjust the discounting for a quarter year.

group, which provided comfort that the assumption of constant EBITDA margins was justifiable.

EXHIBIT 3.36 ValueCo Historical and Projected EBITDA

($ in millions, fiscal year ending December 31)

	Historical Period			CAGR		Projection Period					CAGR
	2009	2010	2011	('09 - '11)	2012	2013	2014	2015	2016	2017	('12 - '17)
Sales	$2,600.0	$2,900.0	$3,200.0	10.9%	$3,450.0	$3,708.8	$3,931.3	$4,127.8	$4,293.0	$4,421.7	5.1%
% growth	NA	11.5%	10.3%		7.8%	7.5%	6.0%	5.0%	4.0%	3.0%	
COGS	1,612.0	1,769.0	1,920.0		2,070.0	2,225.3	2,358.8	2,476.7	2,575.8	2,653.0	
% sales	62.0%	61.0%	60.0%		60.0%	60.0%	60.0%	60.0%	60.0%	60.0%	
Gross Profit	$988.0	$1,131.0	$1,280.0	13.8%	$1,380.0	$1,483.5	$1,572.5	$1,651.1	$1,717.2	$1,768.7	5.1%
% margin	38.0%	39.0%	40.0%		40.0%	40.0%	40.0%	40.0%	40.0%	40.0%	
SG&A	496.6	551.0	608.0		655.0	704.1	746.4	783.7	815.0	839.5	
% sales	19.1%	19.0%	19.0%		19.0%	19.0%	19.0%	19.0%	19.0%	19.0%	
EBITDA	$491.4	$580.0	$672.0	16.9%	$725.0	$779.4	$826.1	$867.4	$902.1	$929.2	5.1%
% margin	18.9%	20.0%	21.0%		21.0%	21.0%	21.0%	21.0%	21.0%	21.0%	

EBIT Projections To drive EBIT projections, we held D&A as a percentage of sales constant at the 2011 level of 6%. We gained comfort that these D&A levels were appropriate as they were consistent with historical data as well as our capex projections (see Exhibit 3.39). EBIT was then calculated in each year of the projection period by subtracting D&A from EBITDA (see Exhibit 3.37). As previously discussed, an alternative approach is to construct the DCF on the basis of EBITDA and EBIT projections, with D&A simply calculated by subtracting EBIT from EBITDA.

EXHIBIT 3.37 ValueCo Historical and Projected EBIT

($ in millions, fiscal year ending December 31)

	Historical Period			CAGR		Projection Period					CAGR
	2009	2010	2011	('09 - '11)	2012	2013	2014	2015	2016	2017	('12 - '17)
Sales	$2,600.0	$2,900.0	$3,200.0	10.9%	$3,450.0	$3,708.8	$3,931.3	$4,127.8	$4,293.0	$4,421.7	5.1%
% growth	NA	11.5%	10.3%		7.8%	7.5%	6.0%	5.0%	4.0%	3.0%	
COGS	1,612.0	1,769.0	1,920.0		2,070.0	2,225.3	2,358.8	2,476.7	2,575.8	2,653.0	
% sales	62.0%	61.0%	60.0%		60.0%	60.0%	60.0%	60.0%	60.0%	60.0%	
Gross Profit	$988.0	$1,131.0	$1,280.0	13.8%	$1,380.0	$1,483.5	$1,572.5	$1,651.1	$1,717.2	$1,768.7	5.1%
% margin	38.0%	39.0%	40.0%		40.0%	40.0%	40.0%	40.0%	40.0%	40.0%	
SG&A	496.6	551.0	608.0		655.0	704.1	746.4	783.7	815.0	839.5	
% sales	19.1%	19.0%	19.0%		19.0%	19.0%	19.0%	19.0%	19.0%	19.0%	
EBITDA	$491.4	$580.0	$672.0	16.9%	$725.0	$779.4	$826.1	$867.4	$902.1	$929.2	5.1%
% margin	18.9%	20.0%	21.0%		21.0%	21.0%	21.0%	21.0%	21.0%	21.0%	
D&A	155.0	165.0	193.0		207.0	222.5	235.9	247.7	257.6	265.3	
% of sales	6.0%	5.7%	6.0%		6.0%	6.0%	6.0%	6.0%	6.0%	6.0%	
EBIT	$336.4	$415.0	$479.0	19.3%	$518.0	$556.9	$590.3	$619.8	$644.6	$663.9	5.1%
% margin	12.9%	14.3%	15.0%		15.0%	15.0%	15.0%	15.0%	15.0%	15.0%	

Projection of Free Cash Flow

Tax Projections We calculated tax expense for each year at ValueCo's marginal tax rate of 38%. This tax rate was applied on an annual basis to EBIT to arrive at EBIAT (see Exhibit 3.38).

EXHIBIT 3.38 ValueCo Projected Taxes

($ in millions, fiscal year ending December 31)

	Historical Period			CAGR		Projection Period					CAGR
	2009	2010	2011	('09 - '11)	2012	2013	2014	2015	2016	2017	('12 - '17)
EBIT	$336.4	$415.0	$479.0	19.3%	$518.0	$556.9	$590.3	$619.8	$644.6	$663.9	5.1%
% margin	12.9%	14.3%	15.0%		15.0%	15.0%	15.0%	15.0%	15.0%	15.0%	
Taxes @ 38%						211.6	224.3	235.5	244.9	252.3	
EBIAT						$345.2	$366.0	$384.3	$399.6	$411.6	5.1%

Capex Projections We projected ValueCo's capex as a percentage of sales in line with historical levels. As shown in Exhibit 3.39, this approach led us to hold capex constant throughout the projection period at 4.5% of sales. Based on this assumption, capex increases from $166.9 million in 2013E to $199 million in 2017E.

EXHIBIT 3.39 ValueCo Historical and Projected Capex

($ in millions, fiscal year ending December 31)

	Historical Period			CAGR		Projection Period					CAGR
	2009	2010	2011	('09 - '11)	2012	2013	2014	2015	2016	2017	('12 - '17)
Sales	$2,600.0	$2,900.0	$3,200.0	10.9%	$3,450.0	$3,708.8	$3,931.3	$4,127.8	$4,293.0	$4,421.7	5.1%
% growth	NA	11.5%	10.3%		7.8%	7.5%	6.0%	5.0%	4.0%	3.0%	
Capex	114.4	116.0	144.0		155.3	166.9	176.9	185.8	193.2	199.0	
% sales	4.4%	4.0%	4.5%		4.5%	4.5%	4.5%	4.5%	4.5%	4.5%	

Change in Net Working Capital Projections As with ValueCo's other financial performance metrics, historical working capital levels normally serve as reliable indicators of future performance. The direct prior year's ratios are typically the most indicative provided they are consistent with historical levels. This was the case for ValueCo's 2011 working capital ratios, which we held constant throughout the projection period (see Exhibit 3.40).

For A/R, inventory, and A/P, respectively, these ratios are DSO of 47.6, DIH of 105.8, and DPO of 37.9. For prepaid expenses and other current assets, accrued liabilities, and other current liabilities, the percentage of sales levels are 5.1%, 8.0%, and 2.9%, respectively. For ValueCo's Base Case financial projections, we conservatively did not assume any improvements in working capital efficiency during the projection period.

As depicted in the callouts in Exhibit 3.40, using ValueCo's 2011 ratios, we projected 2012E NWC to be $635 million. To determine the 2013E YoY change in NWC, we then subtracted this value from ValueCo's 2013E NWC of $682.6 million. The $47.6 million difference is a use of cash and is, therefore, subtracted from EBIAT, resulting in a reduction of ValueCo's 2013E FCF. Hence, it is shown in Exhibit 3.41 as a negative value.

EXHIBIT 3.40 ValueCo Historical and Projected Net Working Capital

ValueCo Corporation
Working Capital Projections
($ in millions, fiscal year ending December 31)

	Historical Period				Projection Period					
	2009	2010	2011	2012	2013	2014	2015	2016	2017	
Sales	$2,600.0	$2,900.0	$3,200.0	$3,450.0	$3,708.8	$3,931.3	$4,127.8	$4,293.0	$4,421.7	
Cost of Goods Sold	1,612.0	1,769.0	1,920.0	2,070.0	2,225.3	2,358.8	2,476.7	2,575.8	2,653.0	
Current Assets										
Accounts Receivable	317.0	365.5	417.4	450.0	483.8	512.8	538.4	560.0	576.7	= (Sales$_{2013E}$ / 365) × DSO = ($3,708.8 million / 365) × 47.6
Inventories	441.6	496.8	556.5	600.0	645.0	683.7	717.9	746.6	769.0	= (COGS$_{2013E}$ / 365) × DIH = ($2,225.3 million / 365) × 105.8
Prepaid Expenses and Other	117.0	142.1	162.3	175.0	188.1	199.4	209.4	217.8	224.3	= Sales$_{2013E}$ × % of Sales = $3,708.8 million × 5.1%
Total Current Assets	$875.6	$1,004.4	$1,136.2	$1,225.0	$1,316.9	$1,395.9	$1,465.7	$1,524.3	$1,570.0	
Current Liabilities										
Accounts Payable	189.9	189.0	199.4	215.0	231.1	245.0	257.2	267.5	275.6	= (COGS$_{2013E}$ / 365) × DPO = ($2,225.3 million / 365) × 37.9
Accrued Liabilities	221.0	237.8	255.1	275.0	295.6	313.4	329.0	342.2	352.5	= Sales$_{2013E}$ × % of Sales = $3,708.8 million × 8%
Other Current Liabilities	75.4	84.1	92.8	100.0	107.5	114.0	119.6	124.4	128.2	= Sales$_{2013E}$ × % of Sales = $3,708.8 million × 2.9%
Total Current Liabilities	$486.3	$510.9	$547.2	$590.0	$634.3	$672.3	$705.9	$734.2	$756.2	
Net Working Capital	$389.4	$493.5	$589.0	$635.0	$682.6	$723.6	$759.8	$790.2	$813.9	= Total CA$_{2013E}$ - Total CL$_{2013E}$ = $1,316.9 million - $634.3 million
% sales	15.0%	17.0%	18.4%	18.4%	18.4%	18.4%	18.4%	18.4%	18.4%	
(Increase)/Decrease in NWC		($104.1)	($95.5)	($46.0)	($47.6)	($41.0)	($36.2)	($30.4)	($23.7)	= NWC$_{2012E}$ - NWC$_{2013E}$ = $635 million - $682.6 million
Assumptions										
Current Assets										
Days Sales Outstanding	44.5	46.0	47.6	47.6	47.6	47.6	47.6	47.6	47.6	= (A/R$_{2011}$ / Sales$_{2011}$) × 365 = ($417.4 million / $3,200 million) × 365
Days Inventory Held	100.0	102.5	105.8	105.8	105.8	105.8	105.8	105.8	105.8	= (Inventories$_{2011}$ / COGS$_{2011}$) × 365 = ($556.5 million / $1,920 million) × 365
Prepaids and Other CA (% of sales)	4.5%	4.9%	5.1%	5.1%	5.1%	5.1%	5.1%	5.1%	5.1%	= Prepaids and Other Current Assets$_{2011}$ / Sales$_{2011}$ = $162.3 million / $3,200 million
Current Liabilities										
Days Payable Outstanding	43.0	39.0	37.9	37.9	37.9	37.9	37.9	37.9	37.9	= (A/P$_{2011}$ / COGS$_{2011}$) × 365 = ($199.4 million / $1,920 million) × 365
Accrued Liabilities (% of sales)	8.5%	8.2%	8.0%	8.0%	8.0%	8.0%	8.0%	8.0%	8.0%	= Accrued Liabilities$_{2011}$ / Sales$_{2011}$ = $255.1 million / $3,200 million
Other Current Liabilities (% of sales)	2.9%	2.9%	2.9%	2.9%	2.9%	2.9%	2.9%	2.9%	2.9%	= Other Current Liabilities$_{2011}$ / Sales$_{2011}$ = $92.8 million / $3,200 million

Discounted Cash Flow Analysis

EXHIBIT 3.41 ValueCo's Projected Changes in Net Working Capital

($ in millions, fiscal year ending December 31)

	2012	Projection Period				
		2013	2014	2015	2016	2017
Total Current Assets	$1,225.0	$1,316.9	$1,395.9	$1,465.7	$1,524.3	$1,570.0
Less: Total Current Liabilities	590.0	634.3	672.3	705.9	734.2	756.2
Net Working Capital	**$635.0**	**$682.6**	**$723.6**	**$759.8**	**$790.2**	**$813.9**
(Increase)/Decrease in NWC		($47.6)	($41.0)	($36.2)	($30.4)	($23.7)

= Total Current Assets$_{2012E}$ - Total Current Liabilities$_{2012E}$
= $1,225 million - $590 million

= Net Working Capital$_{2012E}$ - Net Working Capital$_{2013E}$
= $635 million - $682.6 million

The methodology for determining ValueCo's 2013E NWC was then applied in each year of the projection period. Each annual change in NWC was added to the corresponding annual EBIAT (with increases in NWC expressed as negative values) to calculate annual FCF.

A potential shortcut to the detailed approach outlined in Exhibits 3.40 and 3.41 is to bypass projecting individual working capital components and simply project NWC as a percentage of sales in line with historical levels. For example, we could have used ValueCo's 2011 NWC percentage of sales ratio of 18.4% to project its NWC for each year of the projection period. We would then have simply calculated YoY changes in ValueCo's NWC and made the corresponding subtractions from EBIAT.

Free Cash Flow Projections Having determined all of the above line items, we calculated ValueCo's annual projected FCF, which increases from $353.3 million in 2013E to $454.2 million in 2017E (see Exhibit 3.42).

EXHIBIT 3.42 ValueCo Projected FCF

($ in millions, fiscal year ending December 31)

	Historical Period			CAGR	2012	Projection Period					CAGR
	2009	2010	2011	('09 - '11)		2013	2014	2015	2016	2017	('12 - '17)
Sales	$2,600.0	$2,900.0	$3,200.0	10.9%	$3,450.0	$3,708.8	$3,931.3	$4,127.8	$4,293.0	$4,421.7	5.1%
% growth	NA	11.5%	10.3%		7.8%	7.5%	6.0%	5.0%	4.0%	3.0%	
COGS	1,612.0	1,769.0	1,920.0		2,070.0	2,225.3	2,358.8	2,476.7	2,575.8	2,653.0	
% sales	62.0%	61.0%	60.0%		60.0%	60.0%	60.0%	60.0%	60.0%	60.0%	
Gross Profit	**$988.0**	**$1,131.0**	**$1,280.0**	**13.8%**	**$1,380.0**	**$1,483.5**	**$1,572.5**	**$1,651.1**	**$1,717.2**	**$1,768.7**	**5.1%**
% margin	38.0%	39.0%	40.0%		40.0%	40.0%	40.0%	40.0%	40.0%	40.0%	
SG&A	496.6	551.0	608.0		655.0	704.1	746.4	783.7	815.0	839.5	
% sales	19.1%	19.0%	19.0%		19.0%	19.0%	19.0%	19.0%	19.0%	19.0%	
EBITDA	**$491.4**	**$580.0**	**$672.0**	**16.9%**	**$725.0**	**$779.4**	**$826.1**	**$867.4**	**$902.1**	**$929.2**	**5.1%**
% margin	18.9%	20.0%	21.0%		21.0%	21.0%	21.0%	21.0%	21.0%	21.0%	
D&A	155.0	165.0	193.0		207.0	222.5	235.9	247.7	257.6	265.3	
% of sales	6.0%	5.7%	6.0%		6.0%	6.0%	6.0%	6.0%	6.0%	6.0%	
EBIT	**$336.4**	**$415.0**	**$479.0**	**19.3%**	**$518.0**	**$556.9**	**$590.3**	**$619.8**	**$644.6**	**$663.9**	**5.1%**
% margin	12.9%	14.3%	15.0%		15.0%	15.0%	15.0%	15.0%	15.0%	15.0%	
Taxes						211.6	224.3	235.5	244.9	252.3	
EBIAT						**$345.2**	**$366.0**	**$384.3**	**$399.6**	**$411.6**	**5.1%**
Plus: D&A						222.5	235.9	247.7	257.6	265.3	
Less: Capex						(166.9)	(176.9)	(185.8)	(193.2)	(199.0)	
Less: Inc./(Dec.) in NWC						(47.6)	(41.0)	(36.2)	(30.4)	(23.7)	
Unlevered Free Cash Flow						**$353.3**	**$384.0**	**$410.0**	**$433.6**	**$454.2**	

Step III. Calculate Weighted Average Cost of Capital

Below, we demonstrate the step-by-step calculation of ValueCo's WACC, which we determined to be 10%.

Step III(a): Determine Target Capital Structure Our first step was to determine ValueCo's target capital structure. For private companies, the target capital structure is generally extrapolated from peers. As ValueCo's peers have an average (mean) D/E of 42.9%—or debt-to-total capitalization (D/(D+E)) of 30%—we used this as our target capital structure (see Exhibit 3.45).

Step III(b): Estimate Cost of Debt We estimated ValueCo's long-term cost of debt based on the current yields on its existing term loan and senior notes (see Exhibit 3.43).[31] The term loan, which for illustrative purposes we assumed is trading at par, is priced at a spread of 350 basis points (bps)[32] to LIBOR[33] (L+350 bps) with a LIBOR floor of 1% (see Chapter 4). The senior notes are also assumed to be trading at par and have a coupon of 8%. Based on the rough average cost of debt across ValueCo's capital structure, we estimated ValueCo's cost of debt at 6% (or approximately 3.7% on an after-tax basis).

EXHIBIT 3.43 ValueCo Capitalization

($ in millions)

	Amount	% of Total Capitalization	Term	Coupon / LIBOR Floor
Cash and Cash Equivalents	$250.0			
Revolving Credit Facility	-	- %	6 years	L+325 bps / 1%
Term Loan	1,000.0	20.0%	7 years	L+350 bps / 1%
Senior Secured	**$1,000.0**	**20.0%**		
Senior Notes	500.0	10.0%	8 years	8.000%
Total Debt	**$1,500.0**	**30.0%**		
Shareholders' Equity	3,500.0	70.0%		
Total Capitalization	**$5,000.0**	**100.0%**		
Net Debt	$1,250.0			
Debt / Equity	42.9%			
Debt / Total Capitalization	30.0%			

---

[31] Alternatively, ValueCo's cost of debt could be extrapolated from that of its peers. We took comfort with using the current yield on ValueCo's existing debt instruments because its current capital structure is in line with peers.
[32] A basis point is a unit of measure equal to 1/100th of 1% (100 bps = 1%).
[33] The London Interbank Offered Rate (LIBOR) is the rate of interest at which banks can borrow funds from other banks, in marketable size, in the London interbank market.

Discounted Cash Flow Analysis

Step III(c): Estimate Cost of Equity We calculated ValueCo's cost of equity in accordance with the CAPM formula shown in Exhibit 3.44.

EXHIBIT 3.44 CAPM Formula

$$r_e = r_f + \beta_L \times (r_m - r_f) + SP$$

Determine Risk-free Rate and Market Risk Premium We assumed a risk-free rate (r_f) of 3% based on the interpolated yield of the 20-year Treasury bond. For the market risk premium ($r_m - r_f$), we used the arithmetic mean of 6.62% (for the 1926–2011 period) in accordance with Ibbotson.

Determine the Average Unlevered Beta of ValueCo's Comparable Companies As ValueCo is a private company, we extrapolated beta from its closest comparables (see Chapter 1). We began by sourcing predicted levered betas for each of ValueCo's closest comparables.[34] We then entered the market values for each comparable company's debt[35] and equity, and calculated the D/E ratios accordingly. This information, in conjunction with the marginal tax rate assumptions, enabled us to unlever the individual betas and calculate an average unlevered beta for the peer group (see Exhibit 3.45).

EXHIBIT 3.45 Average Unlevered Beta

($ in millions)

= Predicted Levered Beta / (1 + (Debt/Equity) × (1 - t))
= 1.25 / (1 + (56.3%) × (1 - 38%))

Company	Predicted Levered Beta	Market Value of Debt	Market Value of Equity	Debt/ Equity	Marginal Tax Rate	Unlevered Beta
BuyerCo	1.24	$2,200.0	$9,800.0	22.4%	38.0%	1.09
Sherman Co.	1.35	3,150.0	5,600.0	56.3%	38.0%	1.00
Gasparro Corp.	1.25	1,850.0	5,000.0	37.0%	38.0%	1.02
Goodson Corp	1.45	2,250.0	4,160.0	54.1%	38.0%	1.09
S. Momper & Co.	1.14	1,000.0	2,240.0	44.6%	38.0%	0.89
Mean	**1.29**			**42.9%**		**1.02**
Median	**1.25**			**44.6%**		**1.02**

For example, based on Sherman Co.'s predicted levered beta of 1.35, D/E of 56.3%, and a marginal tax rate of 38%, we calculated an unlevered beta of 1.00. We performed this calculation for each of the selected comparable companies and then calculated an average unlevered beta of 1.02 for the group.

---

[34] An alternate approach is to use historical betas (e.g., from Bloomberg), or both historical and predicted betas, and then show a range of outputs.

[35] For simplicity, we assumed that the market value of debt was equal to the book value.

Relever Average Unlevered Beta at ValueCo's Capital Structure We then relevered the average unlevered beta of 1.02 at ValueCo's previously determined target capital structure of 42.9% D/E, using its marginal tax rate of 38%. This provided a levered beta of 1.29 (see Exhibit 3.46).

EXHIBIT 3.46 ValueCo Relevered Beta

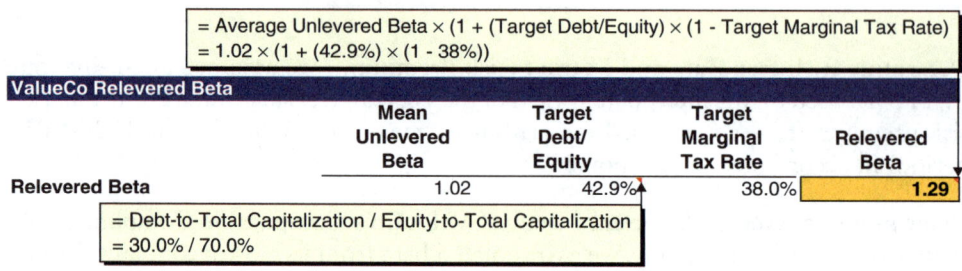

Calculate Cost of Equity Using the CAPM, we calculated a cost of equity for ValueCo of 12.7% (see Exhibit 3.47), which is higher than the expected return on the market (calculated as 9.6% based on a risk-free rate of 3% and a market risk premium of 6.62%). This relatively high cost of equity was driven by the relevered beta of 1.29, versus 1.0 for the market as a whole, as well as a size premium of 1.14%.[36]

EXHIBIT 3.47 ValueCo Cost of Equity

Cost of Equity	
Risk-free Rate	3.0%
Market Risk Premium	6.62%
Levered Beta	1.29
Size Premium	1.14%
Cost of Equity	**12.7%**

= Risk-free Rate + (Levered Beta × Market Risk Premium) + Size Premium
= 3% + (1.29 × 6.62%) + 1.14%

---

[36]Ibbotson estimates a size premium of approximately 1.14% for companies in the Mid-Cap Decile for market capitalization.

Discounted Cash Flow Analysis

Step III(d): Calculate WACC We now have determined all of the components necessary to calculate ValueCo's WACC. These inputs were entered into the formula in Exhibit 3.12, resulting in a WACC of 10%. Exhibit 3.48 displays each of the assumptions and calculations for determining ValueCo's WACC.

As previously discussed, the DCF is highly sensitive to WACC, which itself is dependent on numerous assumptions governing target capital structure, cost of debt, and cost of equity. Therefore, a sensitivity analysis is typically performed on key WACC inputs to produce a WACC range. In Exhibit 3.49, we sensitized target capital structure and pre-tax cost of debt to produce a WACC range of approximately 9.5% to 10.5% for ValueCo.

EXHIBIT 3.48 ValueCo WACC Calculation

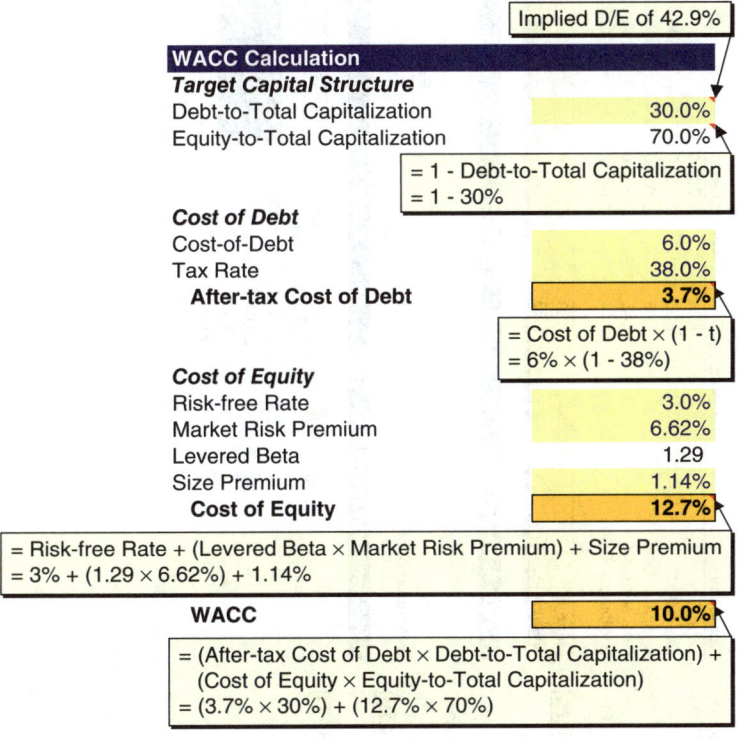

EXHIBIT 3.49 ValueCo Weighted Average Cost of Capital Analysis

ValueCo Corporation
Weighted Average Cost of Capital Analysis
($ in millions)

WACC Calculation

Target Capital Structure
Debt-to-Total Capitalization	30.0%
Equity-to-Total Capitalization	70.0%

Cost of Debt
Cost-of-Debt	6.0%
Tax Rate	38.0%
After-tax Cost of Debt	**3.7%**

Cost of Equity
Risk-free Rate (1)	3.0%
Market Risk Premium (2)	6.62%
Levered Beta	1.29
Size Premium (3)	1.14%
Cost of Equity	**12.7%**

WACC | **10.0%**

Comparable Companies Unlevered Beta

Company	Predicted Levered Beta (4)	Market Value of Debt	Market Value of Equity	Debt/ Equity	Marginal Tax Rate	Unlevered Beta
BuyerCo	1.24	$2,200.0	$9,800.0	22.4%	38.0%	1.09
Sherman Co.	1.35	3,150.0	5,600.0	56.3%	38.0%	1.00
Gasparro Corp.	1.25	1,850.0	5,000.0	37.0%	38.0%	1.02
Goodson Corp	1.45	2,250.0	4,160.0	54.1%	38.0%	1.09
S. Momper & Co.	1.14	1,000.0	2,240.0	44.6%	38.0%	0.89
Mean	**1.29**			**42.9%**		**1.02**
Median	**1.25**			**44.6%**		**1.02**

ValueCo Relevered Beta

	Mean Unlevered Beta	Target Debt/ Equity	Target Marginal Tax Rate	Relevered Beta
Relevered Beta	1.02	42.9%	38.0%	**1.29**

WACC Sensitivity Analysis

		Pre-tax Cost of Debt				
		5.00%	5.50%	6.00%	6.50%	7.00%
Debt-to-Total Capitalization	10.0%	11.7%	11.8%	11.8%	11.8%	11.9%
	20.0%	10.8%	10.8%	10.9%	11.0%	11.0%
	30.0%	9.8%	9.9%	**10.0%**	10.1%	10.2%
	40.0%	8.9%	9.0%	9.1%	9.2%	9.4%
	50.0%	7.9%	8.1%	8.2%	8.4%	8.5%

(1) Interpolated yield on 20-year U.S. Treasury, sourced from *Bloomberg*
(2) Obtained from *Ibbotson SBBI Valuation Yearbook*
(3) Mid-Cap Decile size premium based on market capitalization, per Ibbotson
(4) Sourced from *Bloomberg*

Discounted Cash Flow Analysis

Step IV. Determine Terminal Value

Exit Multiple Method We used the LTM EV/EBITDA trading multiples for ValueCo's closest public comparable companies as the basis for calculating terminal value in accordance with the EMM. These companies tend to trade in a range of 7.0x to 8.0x LTM EBITDA. Multiplying ValueCo's terminal year EBITDA of $929.2 million by the 7.5x midpoint of this range provided a terminal value of $6,969 million (see Exhibit 3.50).

EXHIBIT 3.50 Exit Multiple Method

($ in millions)

Calculation of Terminal Value using EMM	
Terminal Year EBITDA (2017E)	$929.2
Exit Multiple	7.5x
Terminal Value	**$6,969.0**

= $EBITDA_{Terminal\ Year}$ × Exit Multiple
= $929.2 million × 7.5x

We then solved for the perpetuity growth rate implied by the exit multiple of 7.5x EBITDA. Given the terminal year FCF of $454.2 million and 10% midpoint of the selected WACC range, and adjusting for the use of a mid-year convention for the PGM terminal value, we calculated an implied perpetuity growth rate of 3% (see Exhibit 3.51).

EXHIBIT 3.51 Implied Perpetuity Growth Rate

($ in millions)

Implied Perpetuity Growth Rate	
Terminal Year Free Cash Flow (2017E)	$454.2
Discount Rate	10.0%
Terminal Value	$6,969.0
Implied Perpetuity Growth Rate	**3.0%**

= ((EMM Terminal Value × WACC) - $FCF_{Terminal\ Year}$ × $(1 + WACC)^{0.5}$) / (EMM Terminal Value + $FCF_{Terminal\ Year}$ × $(1 + WACC)^{0.5}$)
= (($6,969 million × 10%) - $454.2 million × $(1 + 10\%)^{0.5}$) / ($6,969 million + $454.2 million × $(1 + 10\%)^{0.5}$)

Perpetuity Growth Method   We selected a perpetuity growth rate range of 2% to 4% to calculate ValueCo's terminal value using the PGM. Using a perpetuity growth rate midpoint of 3%, WACC midpoint of 10%, and terminal year FCF of $454.2 million, we calculated a terminal value of $6,683.8 million for ValueCo (see Exhibit 3.52).

EXHIBIT 3.52   Perpetuity Growth Rate

($ in millions)

Calculation of Terminal Value using PGM	
Terminal Year Free Cash Flow (2017E)	$454.2
WACC	10.0%
Perpetuity Growth Rate	3.0%
Terminal Value	**$6,683.8**

= $FCF_{Terminal\ Year} \times (1 + \text{Perpetuity Growth Rate}) / (\text{WACC} - \text{Perpetuity Growth Rate})$
= $\$454.2 \text{ million} \times (1 + 3\%) / (10\% - 3\%)$

The terminal value of $6,683.8 million calculated using the PGM implied a 7.5x exit multiple, adjusting for year-end discounting using the EMM (see Exhibit 3.53). This is consistent with our assumptions using the EMM approach in Exhibit 3.50.

EXHIBIT 3.53   Implied Exit Multiple

($ in millions)

Implied Exit Multiple	
Terminal Value	$6,683.8
Terminal Year EBITDA (2017E)	929.2
WACC	10.0%
Implied Exit Multiple	**7.5x**

= $\text{PGM Terminal Value} \times (1 + \text{WACC})^{0.5} / \text{EBITDA}_{Terminal\ Year}$
= $\$6,683.8 \text{ million} \times (1 + 10\%)^{0.5} / \$929.2 \text{ million}$

Step V. Calculate Present Value and Determine Valuation

Calculate Present Value

ValueCo's projected annual FCF and terminal value were discounted to the present using the selected WACC midpoint of 10% (see Exhibit 3.54). We used a mid-year convention to discount projected FCF. For the terminal value calculation using the EMM, however, we used year-end discounting.

EXHIBIT 3.54 Present Value Calculation

($ in millions)

Present Value Calculation

$$= 1 / ((1 + WACC)^{(n - .05)})$$
$$= 1 / ((1 + 10\%)^{(4.5)})$$
Note: Mid-Year Convention applied

		Projection Period				
		2013	2014	2015	2016	2017
Unlevered Free Cash Flow		$353.3	$384.0	$410.0	$433.6	$454.2
WACC	10.0%					
Discount Period		0.5	1.5	2.5	3.5	4.5
Discount Factor		0.95	0.87	0.79	0.72	0.65
Present Value of Free Cash Flow		**$336.8**	**$332.8**	**$323.1**	**$310.6**	**$295.8**

= Unlevered FCF$_{2013E}$ × Discount Factor
= $336.8 million × 0.95

= Exit Year EBITDA × Exit Multiple
= $929.2 million × 7.5x

Terminal Value

Terminal Year EBITDA (2017E)	$929.2
Exit Multiple	7.5x
Terminal Value	**$6,969.0**
Discount Factor	0.62
Present Value of Terminal Value	**$4,327.2**

$$= 1 / ((1 + WACC)^n)$$
$$= 1 / ((1 + 10\%)^5)$$
Note: Mid-Year Convention not applied for Exit Multiple Method

Determine Valuation

Calculate Enterprise Value The results of the present value calculations for the projected FCF and terminal value were summed to produce an enterprise value of $5,926.4 million for ValueCo (see Exhibit 3.55). The enterprise value is comprised of $1,599.2 million from the present value of the projected FCF and $4,327.2 million from the present value of the terminal value. This implies that ValueCo's terminal value represents 73% of the enterprise value.

EXHIBIT 3.55 Enterprise Value

($ in millions)

Enterprise Value	
Present Value of Free Cash Flow	**$1,599.2**
Terminal Value	
Terminal Year EBITDA (2017E)	$929.2
Exit Multiple	7.5x
Terminal Value	**$6,969.0**
Discount Factor	0.62
Present Value of Terminal Value	**$4,327.2**
% of Enterprise Value	73.0%
Enterprise Value	**$5,926.4**

- Present Value of Free Cash Flow: = SUM (FCF$_{2013E-2017E}$, discounted at 10%) = SUM ($336.8 million : $295.8 million)
- Terminal Value: = Terminal Value × Discount Factor = $6,969 million × 0.62
- % of Enterprise Value: = PV of Terminal Value / Enterprise Value = $4,327.2 million / $5,926.4 million
- Enterprise Value: = PV of FCF$_{2013-2017}$ + PV of Terminal Value = $1,599.2 million + $4,327.2 million

Derive Equity Value We then calculated an implied equity value of $4,676.4 million for ValueCo by subtracting its net debt of $1,250 million ($1,500 million of debt − $250 million of cash) from enterprise value of $5,926.4 million (Exhibit 3.56). If ValueCo were a publicly traded company, we would then have divided the implied equity value by its fully diluted shares outstanding to determine an implied share price (see Exhibits 3.2 and 3.31).

EXHIBIT 3.56 Equity Value

($ in millions)

Implied Equity Value and Share Price	
Enterprise Value	$5,926.4
Less: Total Debt	(1,500.0)
Less: Preferred Stock	-
Less: Noncontrolling Interest	-
Plus: Cash and Cash Equivalents	250.0
Implied Equity Value	**$4,676.4**

= Enterprise Value - Total Debt + Cash and Cash Equivalents
= $5,926.4 million - $1,500 million + $250 million

DCF Output Page Exhibit 3.57 displays a typical DCF output page for ValueCo using the EMM.

EXHIBIT 3.57 ValueCo DCF Analysis Output Page

ValueCo Corporation
Discounted Cash Flow Analysis
($ in millions, fiscal year ending December 31)

Operating Scenario: 1
Mid-Year Convention: Y

Base

	Historical Period			CAGR	Projection Period					CAGR
	2009	2010	2011	('09 - '11)	2012	2013	2014	2015	2016	2017	('12 - '17)
Sales	$2,600.0	$2,900.0	$3,200.0	10.9%	$3,450.0	$3,708.8	$3,931.3	$4,127.8	$4,293.0	$4,421.7	5.1%
% growth	NA	11.5%	10.3%		7.8%	7.5%	6.0%	5.0%	4.0%	3.0%	
Cost of Goods Sold	1,612.0	1,769.0	1,920.0		2,070.0	2,225.3	2,358.8	2,476.7	2,575.8	2,653.0	
Gross Profit	$988.0	$1,131.0	$1,280.0	13.8%	$1,380.0	$1,483.5	$1,572.5	$1,651.1	$1,717.2	$1,768.7	5.1%
% margin	38.0%	39.0%	40.0%		40.0%	40.0%	40.0%	40.0%	40.0%	40.0%	
Selling, General & Administrative	496.6	551.0	608.0		655.0	704.1	746.4	783.7	815.0	839.5	
EBITDA	$491.4	$580.0	$672.0	16.9%	$725.0	$779.4	$826.1	$867.4	$902.1	$929.2	5.1%
% margin	18.9%	20.0%	21.0%		21.0%	21.0%	21.0%	21.0%	21.0%	21.0%	
Depreciation & Amortization	155.0	165.0	193.0		207.0	222.5	235.9	247.7	257.6	265.3	
EBIT	$336.4	$415.0	$479.0	19.3%	$518.0	$556.9	$590.3	$619.8	$644.6	$663.9	5.1%
% margin	12.9%	14.3%	15.0%		15.0%	15.0%	15.0%	15.0%	15.0%	15.0%	
Taxes	127.8	157.7	182.0		196.8	211.6	224.3	235.5	244.9	252.3	
EBIAT	$208.6	$257.3	$297.0	19.3%	$321.2	$345.2	$366.0	$384.3	$399.6	$411.6	5.1%
Plus: Depreciation & Amortization		165.0	193.0		207.0	222.5	235.9	247.7	257.6	265.3	
Less: Capital Expenditures		(116.0)	(144.0)		(155.3)	(166.9)	(176.9)	(185.8)	(193.2)	(199.0)	
Less: Inc./(Dec.) in Net Working Capital						(47.6)	(41.0)	(36.2)	(30.4)	(23.7)	
Unlevered Free Cash Flow						$353.3	$384.0	$410.0	$433.6	$454.2	
WACC	10.0%										
Discount Period						0.5	1.5	2.5	3.5	4.5	
Discount Factor						0.95	0.87	0.79	0.72	0.65	
Present Value of Free Cash Flow						$336.8	$332.8	$323.1	$310.6	$295.8	

Enterprise Value

Cumulative Present Value of FCF	$1,599.2
Terminal Value	
Terminal Year EBITDA (2017E)	$929.2
Exit Multiple	7.5x
Terminal Value	$6,969.0
Discount Factor	0.62
Present Value of Terminal Value	$4,327.2
% of Enterprise Value	73.0%
Enterprise Value	**$5,926.4**

Implied Equity Value and Share Price

Enterprise Value	$5,926.4
Less: Total Debt	(1,500.0)
Less: Preferred Stock	—
Less: Noncontrolling Interest	—
Plus: Cash and Cash Equivalents	250.0
Implied Equity Value	**$4,676.4**

Implied Perpetuity Growth Rate

Terminal Year Free Cash Flow (2017E)	$454.2
WACC	10.0%
Terminal Value	$6,969.0
Implied Perpetuity Growth Rate	**3.0%**

Implied EV/EBITDA

Enterprise Value	$5,926.4
LTM 9/30/2012 EBITDA	700.0
Implied EV/EBITDA	**8.5x**

Enterprise Value — Exit Multiple

WACC	6.5x	7.0x	7.5x	8.0x	8.5x
9.0%	5,561	5,863	6,165	6,467	6,769
9.5%	5,454	5,749	6,044	6,339	6,634
10.0%	5,349	5,638	**5,926**	6,215	6,503
10.5%	5,248	5,530	5,812	6,094	6,376
11.0%	5,149	5,425	5,700	5,976	6,252

Implied Perpetuity Growth Rate — Exit Multiple

WACC	6.5x	7.0x	7.5x	8.0x	8.5x
9.0%	1.1%	1.6%	2.1%	2.5%	2.8%
9.5%	1.5%	2.0%	2.5%	2.9%	3.3%
10.0%	2.0%	2.5%	**3.0%**	3.4%	3.7%
10.5%	2.4%	2.9%	3.4%	3.8%	4.2%
11.0%	2.9%	3.4%	3.9%	4.3%	4.7%

EXHIBIT 3.58 ValueCo Sensitivity Analysis

ValueCo Corporation
Sensitivity Analysis
($ in millions)

Enterprise Value

		6.5x	7.0x	7.5x	8.0x	8.5x
				Exit Multiple		
WACC	9.0%	5,561	5,863	6,165	6,467	6,769
	9.5%	5,454	5,749	6,044	6,339	6,634
	10.0%	5,349	5,638	**5,926**	6,215	6,503
	10.5%	5,248	5,530	5,812	6,094	6,376
	11.0%	5,149	5,425	5,700	5,976	6,252

Implied Equity Value

		6.5x	7.0x	7.5x	8.0x	8.5x
				Exit Multiple		
WACC	9.0%	4,311	4,613	4,915	5,217	5,519
	9.5%	4,204	4,499	4,794	5,089	5,384
	10.0%	4,099	4,388	**$4,676**	4,965	5,253
	10.5%	3,998	4,280	4,562	4,844	5,126
	11.0%	3,899	4,175	4,450	4,726	5,002

Implied Perpetuity Growth Rate

		6.5x	7.0x	7.5x	8.0x	8.5x
				Exit Multiple		
WACC	9.0%	1.1%	1.6%	2.1%	2.5%	2.8%
	9.5%	1.5%	2.0%	2.5%	2.9%	3.3%
	10.0%	2.0%	2.5%	**3.0%**	3.4%	3.7%
	10.5%	2.4%	2.9%	3.4%	3.8%	4.2%
	11.0%	2.9%	3.4%	3.9%	4.3%	4.7%

Implied Enterprise Value / LTM EBITDA

		6.5x	7.0x	7.5x	8.0x	8.5x
				Exit Multiple		
WACC	9.0%	7.9x	8.4x	8.8x	9.2x	9.7x
	9.5%	7.8x	8.2x	8.6x	9.1x	9.5x
	10.0%	7.6x	8.1x	**8.5x**	8.9x	9.3x
	10.5%	7.5x	7.9x	8.3x	8.7x	9.1x
	11.0%	7.4x	7.7x	8.1x	8.5x	8.9x

PV of Terminal Value % of Enterprise Value

		6.5x	7.0x	7.5x	8.0x	8.5x
				Exit Multiple		
WACC	9.0%	70.6%	72.1%	73.5%	74.7%	75.8%
	9.5%	70.3%	71.9%	73.2%	74.5%	75.6%
	10.0%	70.1%	71.6%	**73.0%**	74.3%	75.4%
	10.5%	69.9%	71.4%	72.8%	74.0%	75.2%
	11.0%	69.6%	71.2%	72.6%	73.8%	75.0%

Discounted Cash Flow Analysis

Perform Sensitivity Analysis

We then performed a series of sensitivity analyses on WACC and exit multiple for several key outputs, including enterprise value, equity value, implied perpetuity growth rate, implied EV/LTM EBITDA, and PV of terminal value as a percentage of enterprise value (see Exhibit 3.58).

We also sensitized key financial assumptions, such as sales growth rates and EBIT margins, to analyze the effects on enterprise value. This sensitivity analysis provided helpful perspective on our assumptions and enabled us to study the potential value creation or erosion resulting from outperformance or underperformance versus the Base Case financial projections. For example, as shown in Exhibit 3.59, an increase in ValueCo's annual sales growth rates and EBIT margins by 50 bps each results in an increase of approximately $179 million in enterprise value from $5,926 million to $6,105 million.

EXHIBIT 3.59   Sensitivity Analysis on Sales Growth Rates and EBIT Margins

		\\ Enterprise Value — Annual Sales Growth Inc. / (Dec.)				
		(1.0%)	(0.5%)	0.0%	0.5%	1.0%
Annual EBIT Margin Inc. / (Dec.)	(1.0%)	5,580	5,702	5,826	5,953	6,082
	(0.5%)	5,628	5,751	5,876	6,004	6,133
	0.0%	5,677	5,801	$5,926	6,054	6,185
	0.5%	5,726	5,850	5,976	6,105	6,236
	1.0%	5,775	5,899	6,027	6,156	6,288

After completing the sensitivity analysis, we proceeded to determine ValueCo's ultimate DCF valuation range. To derive this range, we focused on the shaded portion of the exit multiple / WACC data table (see top left corner of Exhibit 3.58). Based on an exit multiple range of 7.0x to 8.0x and a WACC range of 9.5% to 10.5%, we calculated an enterprise value range of approximately $5,530 million to $6,340 million for ValueCo.

We then added this range to our "football field" and compared it to the derived valuation ranges from our comparable companies analysis and precedent transactions analysis performed in Chapters 1 and 2 (see Exhibit 3.60).

EXHIBIT 3.60   ValueCo Football Field Displaying Comparable Companies, Precedent Transactions, and DCF Analysis

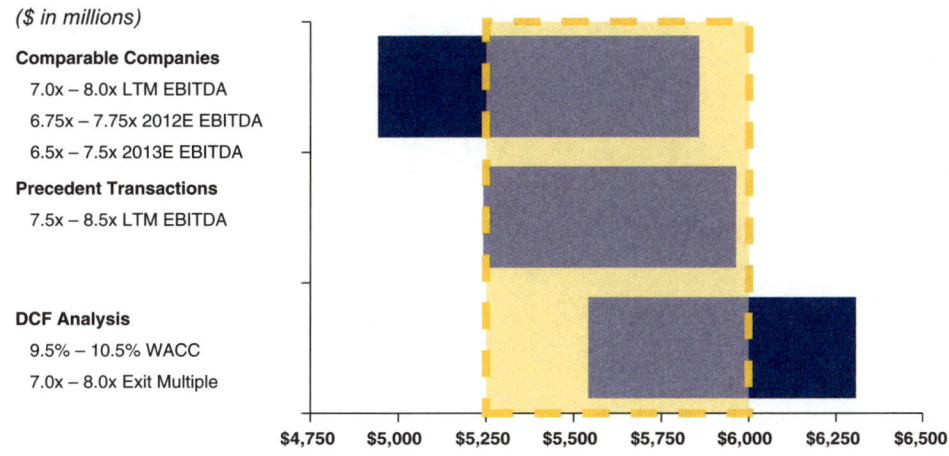

Bloomberg Appendix

APPENDIX 3.1 Reported Historical Figures and Consensus Estimates via Bloomberg Financial Analysis (FA<GO>)

BUY US Equity								
Buyer Corp								
In Millions	FY 2008	FY 2009	FY 2010	FY 2011	Current/LTM	FY 2012 Est	FY 2013 Est	
12 Months Ending	2008-12-31	2009-12-31	2010-12-31	2011-12-31	2012-09-30	2012-12-31	2013-12-31	
Market Cap	3,243.37	4,043.65	5,711.00	6,008.79	8,236.78			
- Cash & Equivalents	52.40	76.60	161.50	158.90	84.40			
+ Preferred & Other	63.50	56.70	57.70	63.50	63.50			
+ Total Debt	623.60	643.90	637.90	825.60	869.40			
Enterprise Value	3,878.07	4,667.65	6,245.10	6,738.99	9,085.28			
Revenue	3,115.30	2,826.20	3,116.30	3,377.90	3,656.90	3,758.27	4,093.55	
Growth %, YoY	18.32	-9.28	10.26	8.39	11.50	11.26	8.92	
Gross Profit	980.90	882.60	1,050.70	1,167.40	1,293.70	1,352.98	1,479.12	
Margin %	31.49	31.23	33.72	34.56	35.38	36.00	36.13	
EBITDA	674.50	594.70	672.60	746.30	808.20	857.90	955.30	
Margin %	21.65	21.04	21.58	22.09	22.10	22.83	23.34	
Net Income Before XO	346.50	257.00	218.50	414.00	441.60	481.20	549.20	
Margin %	11.12	9.09	7.01	12.26	12.08	12.80	13.42	
Adjusted EPS	2.32	2.08	2.42	2.99	3.47	3.49	4.00	
Growth %, YoY	49.84	-10.37	16.63	23.55	26.64	16.79	14.40	
Cash from Operations	307.60	321.40	354.50	381.30	415.90	576.75	692.52	
Capital Expenditures	-174.80	-161.20	-142.30	-189.50	-198.40	-235.67	-266.67	
Free Cash Flow	132.80	160.20	212.20	191.80	217.50	341.08	425.86	

APPENDIX 3.2 Bond Quote and Informational Overview from Bloomberg Bond Description Function (DES<GO>)

```
<HELP> for explanation.
BUYER CORP       BUY3.95 02/22-21   105.007/105.007  (3.29/3.29) TRAC
BUY 3.95 02/01/22 Corp      99) Feedback            Page 1/11  Description: Bond
                          94) Notes (NEW) ▶  95) Buy  96) Sell        97) Settings

21) Bond Description    22) Issuer Description

Pages                Issuer Information                            Identifiers
1) Bond Info         Name       BUYER CORP                          BB Number     EI8824886
2) Addtl Info        Industry   Chemicals                           CUSIP         302491AR6
3) Covenants         Security Information                           ISIN          US302491AR62
4) Guarantors        Mkt of Issue  US Domestic                     Bond Ratings
5) Bond Ratings      Country    US          Currency    USD        Moody's       Baa1
6) Identifiers       Rank       Sr Unsecured Series                 S&P           A-
7) Exchanges                                                        Composite     BBB+
8) Inv Parties       Coupon     3.95        Type        Fixed      Issuance & Trading
9) Fees, Restrict    Cpn Freq   S/A                                 Amt Issued/Outstanding
10) Schedules        Day Cnt    30/360      Iss Price   99.57500    USD           300,000.00 (M) /
11) Coupons          Maturity   02/01/2022                          USD           300,000.00 (M)
                     MAKE WHOLE @30 until 11/01/21/ CALL 11/01/21...  Min Piece/Increment
Quick Links          Issue Spread    205.00bp vs T 2 11/15/21                     2,000.00 / 1,000.00
32) ALLQ  Pricing    Calc Type  (1)STREET CONVENTION                Par Amount                1,000.00
33) QRD   Quote Recap Announcement Date       11/17/2011            Book Runner    CITI,MLPFS
34) TDH   Trade Hist Interest Accrual Date    11/22/2011            Reporting                    TRACE
35) CACS  Corp Action 1st Settle Date         11/22/2011
36) CF    Prospectus 1st Coupon Date          08/01/2012
37) CN    Sec News
38) HDS   Holders    CALL @ MAKE-WHOLE +30BP.

66) Send Bond
```

APPENDIX 3.3 U.S. Treasury Interpolated Benchmark Monitor (USTI<GO>)

	1) Libor Fixings	2) Yield Curve		3) Swap Curve			US Tsy Interpolated Benchmark Monitor			
Term	Description	Bid Yld	Ask Yld	Bid Chg	Swap Sprd	Bid Swap	Ask Swap	Bid Chg	last yield
1 mo	B 0 01/24/13	.061	.056	0.043	14.7	.208	.208	-0.0010	0.018
3 mo	B 0 03/28/13	.061	.051	0.018	24.4	.305	.305	-0.0010	0.043
6 mo	B 0 06/27/13	.117	.112	0.003	39.0	.506	.506	-0.0020	0.114
1 yr	B 0 12/12/13	.147	.142	0.007	17.0	.317	.337	-0.004	0.140
2 yr	T 0 1/8 12/31/14	.263	.259	0.014	12.8	.391	.396	-0.004	0.249
3 yr	T 0 1/4 12/15/15	.375	.373	0.022	12.3	.499	.502	-0.002	0.353
4 yr	(interpolated)	0.577	0.575	0.011	8.3	.660	.666	0.026	0.566
5 yr	T 0 3/4 12/31/17	.769	.768	0.045	10.8	.877	.880	0.027	0.724
6 yr	(interpolated)	1.010	1.008	0.057	10.1	1.111	1.114	0.019	0.953
7 yr	T 1 1/8 12/31/19	1.249	1.247	0.069	8.8	1.337	1.341	0.055	1.180
8 yr	(interpolated)	1.455	1.452	0.074	8.8	1.543	1.544	0.057	1.381
9 yr	(interpolated)	1.660	1.658	0.078	6.2	1.722	1.726	0.061	1.582
10 yr	T 1 5/8 11/15/22	1.839	1.837	0.081	4.5	1.884	1.888	0.045	1.758
15 yr	(interpolated)	2.149	2.147	0.086	28.9	2.438	2.444	0.130	2.063
20 yr	(interpolated)	2.451	2.449	0.090	22.4	2.675	2.679	0.086	2.361
25 yr	(interpolated)	2.753	2.751	0.094	4.5	2.798	2.798	0.096	2.659
30 yr	T 2 3/4 11/15/42	3.049	3.047	0.099	-17.8	2.871	2.875	0.068	2.950

APPENDIX 3.4 Historical Raw Beta and Adjusted Beta as Calculated by Bloomberg (BETA<GO>)

Item	Value
Raw BETA	1.416
Adjusted BETA	1.277
ALPHA(Intercept)	0.264
R^2(Correlation^2)	0.704
R(Correlation)	0.839
Std Dev of Error	2.255
Std Error of ALPHA	0.222
Std Error of BETA	0.091
t-Test	15.577
Significance	0.000
Last T-Value	-1.513
Last P-Value	0.067
Number of Points	104

Y = BUYER CORP
X = S&P 500 INDEX

* Last Observation

APPENDIX 3.5 Bloomberg WACC Analysis (WACC<GO>)

BUY US Equity	1) Create Report	2) Output to Excel	Weighted Average Cost of Capital
Buyer Corp		Period MR ▸ 2012 Q3	Filing MR

Cost of Capital – Current Market Value

	Weight	Cost	W × C
3) Equity	89.7%	13.2%	11.8%
4) Debt	10.3%	1.7%	0.2%
5) Preferred Equity	0.0%	0.0%	0.0%
WACC			12.0%

Capital Structure (Millions of USD)

Market Cap	7,608.9	89.7%
ST Debt	61.5	0.7%
LT Debt	807.9	9.5%
Pref. Eqty	0.0	0.0%
Total	8,478.3	100.0%

6) History

WACC ■ EVA ■ ROIC ■ EVA Spread

WACC 12.0237

Economic Value Added (Millions of USD)

7) Net Operating Profit	708.20
8) Cash Operating Taxes	235.26
NOPAT	472.94
9) Total Investment Capital	2,566.00
Capital Charge	308.53
Economic Value Added	164.41
ROIC	18.43%
EVA Spread	6.41%

PART Two

Leveraged Buyouts

CHAPTER 4

Leveraged Buyouts

A leveraged buyout (LBO) is the acquisition of a company, division, business, or collection of assets ("target") using debt to finance a large portion of the purchase price. The remaining portion of the purchase price is funded with an equity contribution by a financial sponsor ("sponsor"). LBOs are used by sponsors to acquire control of a broad range of businesses, including both public and private companies, as well as their divisions and subsidiaries. The sponsor's ultimate goal is to realize an acceptable return on its equity investment upon exit, typically through a sale or IPO of the target. Sponsors have historically sought a 20%+ annualized return and an investment exit within five years.

In a traditional LBO, debt has typically comprised 60% to 70% of the financing structure with equity comprising the remaining 30% to 40% (see Exhibit 4.12). The disproportionately high level of debt incurred by the target is supported by its projected free cash flow[1] and asset base, which enables the sponsor to contribute a small equity investment relative to the purchase price. The ability to leverage the relatively small equity investment is important for sponsors to achieve acceptable returns. The use of leverage provides the additional benefit of tax savings realized due to the tax deductibility of interest expense.

Companies with stable and predictable cash flow, as well as substantial assets, generally represent attractive LBO candidates due to their ability to support larger quantities of debt. Free cash flow is needed to service periodic interest payments and reduce the principal amount of debt over the life of the investment. In addition, a large tangible asset base increases the amount of *bank debt* available to the borrower (the least expensive source of debt financing) by providing greater comfort to lenders regarding the likelihood of principal recovery in the event of a bankruptcy. When the credit markets are particularly robust, however, credit providers are increasingly willing to focus more on cash flow generation and less on the size and quality of the target's asset base.

During the time from which the sponsor acquires the target until its exit ("investment horizon"), cash flow is used primarily to service and repay the principal amount of debt, thereby increasing the equity portion of the capital structure. At the same time, the sponsor aims to improve the financial performance of the target and grow the existing business (including through future "bolt-on" acquisitions), thereby increasing

---

[1] The "free cash flow" term ("levered free cash flow" or "cash available for debt repayment") used in LBO analysis differs from the "unlevered free cash flow" term used in DCF analysis as it includes the effects of leverage.

enterprise value and further enhancing potential returns. An appropriate LBO financing structure must balance the target's ability to service and repay debt with its need to use cash flow to manage and grow the business.

The successful closing of an LBO relies upon the sponsor's ability to obtain the requisite financing needed to acquire the target. Investment banks traditionally play a critical role in this respect, primarily as arrangers/underwriters of the debt used to fund the purchase price.[2] They typically compete with one another to provide a financing commitment for the sponsor's preferred financing structure in the form of legally binding letters ("financing" or "commitment" letters). The commitment letters promise funding for the debt portion of the purchase price in exchange for various fees and are subject to specific conditions, including the sponsor's contribution of an acceptable level of cash equity.[3]

The debt used in an LBO is raised through the issuance of various types of loans, securities, and other instruments that are classified based on their *security* status as well as their *seniority* in the capital structure. The condition of the prevailing debt capital markets plays a key role in determining leverage levels, as well as the cost of financing and key terms. The equity portion of the financing structure is usually sourced from a pool of capital ("fund") managed by the sponsor. Sponsors' funds range in size from tens of millions to tens of billions of dollars.

Due to the proliferation of private investment vehicles (e.g., private equity firms and hedge funds) and their considerable pools of capital, LBOs have become an increasingly large part of the capital markets and M&A landscape. Bankers who advise on LBO financings are tasked with helping to craft a financing structure that enables both the sponsor and debt investors to meet their respective investment objectives and return thresholds, while providing the target with sufficient financial flexibility and cushion needed to operate and grow the business. Investment banks also provide M&A advisory services to sponsors on LBO transactions. Furthermore, LBOs provide a multitude of subsequent opportunities for investment banks to provide their services after the close of the original transaction, most notably for future M&A activity, refinancing opportunities, and traditional exit events such as a sale of the target or an IPO.

This chapter provides an overview of the fundamentals of leveraged buyouts as depicted in the eight main categories shown in Exhibit 4.1.

---

[2]The term "investment bank" is used broadly to refer to financial intermediaries that perform corporate finance and M&A advisory services, as well as capital markets underwriting activities.
[3]Before they are agreed upon, these letters are typically highly negotiated among the sponsor, the banks providing the financing, and their respective legal counsels.

Leveraged Buyouts

EXHIBIT 4.1 LBO Fundamentals

- Key Participants
- Characteristics of a Strong LBO Candidate
- Economics of LBOs
- Primary Exit/Monetization Strategies
- LBO Financing: Structure
- LBO Financing: Primary Sources
- LBO Financing: Selected Key Terms
- LBO Financing: Determining Financing Structure

KEY PARTICIPANTS

This section provides an overview of the key participants in an LBO (see Exhibit 4.2).

EXHIBIT 4.2 Key Participants

- Financial Sponsors
- Investment Banks
- Bank and Institutional Lenders
- Bond Investors
- Target Management

Financial Sponsors

The term "financial sponsor" refers to traditional private equity (PE) firms, merchant banking divisions of investment banks, hedge funds, venture capital funds, and special purpose acquisition companies (SPACs), among other investment vehicles. PE firms, hedge funds, and venture capital funds raise the vast majority of their investment capital from third-party investors, which include public and corporate pension funds, insurance companies, endowments and foundations, sovereign wealth funds, and wealthy families/individuals. Sponsor partners and investment professionals may also invest their own money into the fund(s) or in specific investment opportunities.

Capital raised from third-party investors and the sponsor partners and investment professionals is organized into funds that are usually structured as limited partnerships. Limited partnerships are typically established as a finite-life investment vehicle with a specific total capital commitment, in which the general partner (GP, i.e., the sponsor) manages the fund on a day-to-day basis and the limited partners (LPs) serve as passive investors.[4] LPs subscribe to fund a specific portion of the total

---

[4] To compensate the GP for management of the fund, LPs typically pay 1% to 2% per annum on committed funds as a management fee. In addition, once the LPs have received the return of every dollar of committed capital plus the required investment return threshold, the sponsor typically receives a 20% "carry" on every dollar of investment profit ("carried interest").

fund's capital ("capital commitment"). These vehicles are considered "blind pools" in that the LPs subscribe to their capital commitment without specific knowledge of the investments that the sponsor plans to make.[5] However, sponsors are often limited in the amount of the fund's capital that can be invested in any particular business, typically no more than 10% to 20%.

Sponsors vary greatly in terms of fund size, focus, and investment strategy. The size of a sponsor's fund(s), which can range from tens of millions to tens of billions of dollars (based on its ability to raise capital), helps dictate its investment parameters. Some firms specialize in specific sectors (such as industrials or media, for example) while others focus on specific situations (such as distressed companies/turnarounds, roll-ups, or corporate divestitures). Many firms are simply generalists that look at a broad spectrum of opportunities across multiple industries and investment strategies. PE firms are staffed with investment professionals that fit their strategy, many of whom are former investment bankers or management consultants. They also typically employ (or engage the services of) operational professionals and industry experts, such as former CEOs and other company executives, who consult and advise the sponsor on specific transactions.

In evaluating an investment opportunity, the sponsor performs detailed due diligence on the target, often through an organized M&A sale process (see Chapter 6). Due diligence is the process of learning as much as possible about all aspects of the target (e.g., business, industry, financial, accounting, tax, legal, regulatory, and environmental) to discover, confirm, or discredit information critical to the sponsor's investment thesis. Detailed information on the target is typically stored in an online data room, such as those provided by Intralinks. Sponsors use due diligence findings to develop a financial model and support purchase price assumptions (including a preferred financing structure), often hiring accountants, consultants, and industry and other functional experts to assist in the process. Sponsors typically engage operating experts, many of whom are former senior industry executives, to assist in the due diligence process and potentially join the management team or board of directors of the acquired companies.

Investment Banks

Investment banks play a key role in LBOs, both as a provider of financing and as a strategic M&A advisor. Sponsors rely heavily on investment banks to help develop and market an optimal financing structure. They may also engage investment banks as buy-side M&A advisors in return for sourcing deals and/or for their expertise, relationships, and in-house resources. On the sell-side, sponsors typically engage bankers as M&A advisors (and potentially as *stapled financing* providers[6]) to market their portfolio companies to prospective buyers through an organized sale process.

Investment banks perform thorough due diligence on LBO targets (usually alongside their sponsor clients) and go through an extensive internal credit process in order to validate the target's business plan and underwrite a debt financing for the target. They must gain comfort with the target's ability to service a highly leveraged capital structure and their ability to market the debt financing to the appropriate investors. Investment banks

---

[5]LPs generally hold the capital they have committed to invest in a given fund until it is called by the GP in connection with a specific investment.
[6]The investment bank running an auction process (or sometimes a "partner" bank) may offer a pre-packaged financing structure, typically for prospective financial buyers, in support of the target being sold. This is commonly referred to as stapled financing ("staple"), as discussed in Chapter 6.

work closely with their sponsor clients to determine an appropriate financing structure for a particular transaction.[7] Once the sponsor chooses the preferred financing structure for an LBO (often a compilation of the best terms from proposals solicited from several banks), the deal team presents it to the bank's internal credit committee(s) for final approval.

Following credit committee approval, the investment banks are able to provide a financing commitment to support the sponsor's bid.[8] This commitment offers funding for the debt portion of the transaction under proposed terms and conditions (including worst case maximum interest rates ("caps") and structural flex[9]) in exchange for various fees[10] and roles.[11] The commitment letters are typically subject to specific conditions, including the sponsor's contribution of an acceptable level of cash equity and a minimum level of EBITDA for the target. This is also known as an *underwritten* financing, which traditionally has been required for LBOs due to the need to provide certainty of closing to the seller (including financing). These letters also typically provide for a marketing period during which the banks seek to syndicate their commitments to investors prior to the sponsor closing the transaction.

For the bank debt, each arranger[12] expects to hold a certain dollar amount of the revolving credit facility in its loan portfolio, while seeking to syndicate the remainder along with any term loan(s). As underwriters of the *high yield bonds* or *mezzanine debt*,[13] the investment banks attempt to sell the entire offering to investors without committing to hold any securities on their balance sheets. However, in an underwritten financing, the investment banks commit to provide a *bridge loan* for these securities to provide assurance that sufficient funding will be available to finance and close the deal even if the banks cannot sell the entire debt offering to investors.

---

[7] Alternatively, the banks may be asked to commit to a financing structure already developed by the sponsor.

[8] The financing commitment includes: a *commitment letter* for the bank debt and a bridge facility (to be provided by the lender in lieu of a bond financing if the capital markets are not available at the time the acquisition is consummated); an *engagement letter*, in which the sponsor engages the investment banks to underwrite the bonds on behalf of the issuer; and a *fee letter*, which sets forth the various fees to be paid to the investment banks in connection with the financing. Traditionally, in an LBO, the sponsor is required to provide certainty of financing to the seller and, therefore, pays for a bridge financing commitment even if it is unlikely that the bridge will be funded at the close of the acquisition.

[9] Allows the underwriter to modify the capital structure of the borrower/issuer during syndication, including key terms as well as allocations between classes of debt securities (e.g., secured vs. unsecured or operating company level ("OpCo") vs. holding company level ("HoldCo")).

[10] The fees associated with the commitment compensate the banks for their underwriting role and the risk associated with the pledge to fund the transaction in the event that a syndication to outside investors is not achievable.

[11] Investment banks compete for certain roles and associated titles in the debt syndicate. For example, investment banks typically covet the "Left-lead Bookrunner" role in a high yield bond underwriting, while peer banks are granted "Right-lead Bookrunner" or "Co-manager" titles. Roles and titles impact the amount of fees that an investment bank can earn as well as the influence that the investment bank has over the underwriting and selling process.

[12] The primary investment banks responsible for marketing the bank debt, including the preparation of marketing materials and running the syndication, are referred to as "Lead Arrangers" or "Bookrunners."

[13] The lead investment banks responsible for marketing the high yield bonds or mezzanine debt are referred to as "Bookrunners."

Bank and Institutional Lenders

Bank and institutional lenders are the capital providers for the bank debt in an LBO financing structure. Although there is often overlap between them, traditional bank lenders provide capital for revolvers and amortizing term loans, while institutional lenders provide capital for longer tenored, limited amortization term loans. Bank lenders typically consist of commercial banks, savings and loan institutions, finance companies, and the investment banks serving as arrangers. The institutional lender base is largely comprised of hedge funds, pension funds, mutual funds, insurance companies, and structured vehicles such as collateralized debt obligation funds (CDOs).[14]

Like investment banks, lenders perform due diligence and undergo an internal credit process before participating in an LBO financing. This involves analyzing the target's business and credit profile (with a focus on projected cash flow generation and credit statistics) to gain comfort that they will receive full future interest payments and principal repayment at maturity. Lenders also look to mitigate downside risk by requiring covenants and collateral coverage. Prior experience with a given company, sector, or financial sponsor is also factored into the decision to participate. To a great extent, however, lenders rely on the due diligence performed (and materials prepared) by the lead arrangers.

As part of their due diligence process, prospective lenders attend a group meeting known as a "bank meeting," which is organized by the lead arrangers.[15] In a bank meeting, the target's senior management team gives a detailed slideshow presentation about the company and its investment merits, followed by an overview of the debt offering by the lead arrangers and a Q&A session. At the bank meeting, prospective lenders receive a hard copy of the presentation, as well as a confidential information memorandum (CIM or "bank book") prepared by management and the lead arrangers.[16] As lenders go through their internal credit processes and make their final investment decisions, they conduct follow-up diligence that often involves requesting additional information and analysis from the company.

---

[14]CDOs are asset-backed securities ("securitized") backed by interests in pools of assets, usually some type of debt obligation. When the interests in the pool are loans, the vehicle is called a collateralized loan obligation (CLO). When the interests in the pool are bonds, the vehicle is called a collateralized bond obligation (CBO).

[15]For particularly large or complex transactions, the target's management may present to lenders on a one-on-one basis.

[16]The bank book is a comprehensive document that contains a detailed description of the transaction, investment highlights, company, and sector, as well as preliminary term sheets and historical and projected financials. In the event that publicly registered bonds are contemplated as part of the offering, two versions of the CIM are usually created—a public version and a private version (or private supplement). The public version, which excludes financial projections and forward-looking statements, is distributed to lenders who intend to purchase bonds or other securities that will eventually be registered with the SEC. The private version, on the other hand, includes financial projections as it is used by investors that intend to invest solely in the company's unregistered debt (i.e., bank debt). Both the bank meeting presentation and bank book are typically available to lenders through an online medium.

Bond Investors

Bond investors are the purchasers of the high yield bonds issued as part of the LBO financing structure. They are generally institutional investors, such as high yield mutual funds, hedge funds, pension funds, insurance companies, and CDOs.

As part of their investment assessment and decision-making process, bond investors attend one-on-one meetings, known as "roadshow presentations," during which senior executives present the investment merits of the company and the proposed transaction. A roadshow is typically a three to five-day process (depending on the size and scope of the transaction), where bankers from the lead underwriting institution (and generally an individual from the sponsor team) accompany the target's management on meetings with potential investors. These meetings may also be conducted as breakfasts or luncheons with groups of investors. The typical U.S. roadshow includes stops in the larger financial centers such as New York, Boston, Los Angeles, and San Francisco, as well as smaller cities throughout the country.[17,18]

Prior to the roadshow meeting, bond investors receive a preliminary offering memorandum (OM), which is a legal document containing much of the target's business, industry, and financial information found in the bank book. The preliminary OM, however, must satisfy a higher degree of legal scrutiny and disclosure (including risk factors[19]). Unlike bank debt, most bonds are eventually registered with the SEC (so they can be traded on an exchange) and are therefore subject to regulation under the Securities Act of 1933 and the Securities Exchange Act of 1934.[20] The preliminary OM also contains detailed information on the bonds, including a preliminary term sheet (excluding pricing) and a description of notes (DON).[21] Once the roadshow concludes and the bonds have been priced, the final terms are inserted into the document, which is then distributed to bond investors as the final OM.

Target Management

Management plays a crucial role in the marketing of the target to potential buyers (see Chapter 6) and lenders alike, working closely with the bankers on the preparation of marketing materials and financial information. Management also serves as the primary face of the company and must articulate the investment merits of the transaction to these constituents. Consequently, in an LBO, a strong management team can create tangible value by driving favorable financing terms and pricing, as well as providing sponsors with comfort to stretch on valuation.

From a structuring perspective, management typically holds a meaningful equity interest in the post-LBO company through "rolling" its existing equity or investing in the business alongside the sponsor at closing. Several layers of management typically

---

[17]For example, roadshow schedules often include stops in Philadelphia, Baltimore, Minneapolis, Milwaukee, Chicago, and Houston, as well as various cities throughout New Jersey and Connecticut, in accordance with where the underwriters believe there will be investor interest.
[18]European roadshows include primary stops in London, Paris, and Frankfurt, as well as secondary stops typically in Milan, Edinburgh, Zurich, and Amsterdam.
[19]A discussion of the most significant factors that make the offering speculative or risky.
[20]Laws that set forth requirements for companies that have issued securities listed on public exchanges, including registration and periodic disclosures of financial status, among others.
[21]The DON contains an overview of the material provisions of the bond indenture including key definitions, terms, and covenants.

also have the opportunity to participate (on a post-closing basis) in a stock option-based compensation package, generally tied to an agreed upon set of financial targets for the company. This structure provides management with meaningful economic incentives to improve the company's performance as they share in the value created. As a result, the interests of management and sponsor are aligned in pursuing superior performance. The broad-based equity incentive program outlined above is often a key differentiating factor versus a public company ownership structure.

Management Buyout An LBO originated and led by a target's existing management team is referred to as a management buyout (MBO). Often, an MBO is effected with the help of an equity partner, such as a financial sponsor, who provides capital support and access to debt financing through established investment banking relationships. The basic premise behind an MBO is that the management team believes it can create more value running the company on its own than under current ownership. The MBO structure also serves to eliminate the conflict between management and the board of directors/shareholders as owner-managers are able to run the company as they see fit.

Public company management may be motivated by the belief that the market is undervaluing the company, SEC and Sarbanes-Oxley (SOX)[22] compliance is too burdensome and costly (especially for smaller companies), and/or the company could operate more efficiently as a private entity. LBO candidates with sizeable management ownership are generally strong MBO candidates. Another common MBO scenario involves a buyout by the management of a division or subsidiary of a larger corporation who believe they can run the business more effectively when separated from the parent company.

CHARACTERISTICS OF A STRONG LBO CANDIDATE

Financial sponsors as a group are highly flexible investors that seek attractive investment opportunities across a broad range of sectors, geographies, and situations. While there are few steadfast rules, certain common traits emerge among traditional LBO candidates, as outlined in Exhibit 4.3. In addition, Bloomberg provides a screening tool to algorithmically identify potential LBO candidates using IBTI<GO> (see Appendix 4.1).

EXHIBIT 4.3 Characteristics of a Strong LBO Candidate

- Strong Cash Flow Generation
- Leading and Defensible Market Positions
- Growth Opportunities
- Efficiency Enhancement Opportunities
- Low Capex Requirements
- Strong Asset Base
- Proven Management Team

---

[22]The Sarbanes-Oxley Act of 2002 enacted substantial changes to the securities laws that govern public companies and their officers and directors in regards to corporate governance and financial reporting. Most notably, Section 404 of SOX requires public registrants to establish and maintain "Internal Controls and Procedures," which can consume significant internal resources, time, commitment, and expense.

During due diligence, the sponsor studies and evaluates an LBO candidate's key strengths and risks. Often, LBO candidates are identified among non-core or underperforming divisions of larger companies, neglected or troubled companies with turnaround potential, sponsor-owned businesses that have been held for an extended period, or companies in fragmented markets as platforms for a roll-up strategy.[23] In other instances, the target is simply a solidly performing company with a compelling business model, defensible competitive position, and strong growth opportunities. For a publicly traded LBO candidate, a sponsor may perceive the target as undervalued by the market or recognize opportunities for growth and efficiency not being exploited by current management. Regardless of the situation, the target only represents an attractive LBO opportunity if it can be purchased at a price and utilizing a financing structure that provides sufficient returns with a viable exit strategy.

Strong Cash Flow Generation

The ability to generate strong, predictable cash flow is critical for LBO candidates given the highly leveraged capital structure. Debt investors require a business model that demonstrates the ability to support periodic interest payments and debt principal repayment over the life of the loans and securities. Business characteristics that support the predictability of robust cash flow increase a company's attractiveness as an LBO candidate. For example, many strong LBO candidates operate in a mature or niche business with stable customer demand and end markets. They often feature a strong brand name, established customer base, and/or long-term sales contracts, all of which serve to increase the predictability of cash flow. Prospective financial sponsors and financing providers seek to confirm a given LBO candidate's cash flow generation potential during due diligence to gain comfort with the target management's projections. Cash flow projections are usually stress-tested (sensitized) based on historical volatility and potential future business and economic conditions to ensure the ability to support the LBO financing structure under challenging circumstances.

Leading and Defensible Market Positions

Leading and defensible market positions generally reflect entrenched customer relationships, brand name recognition, superior products and services, a favorable cost structure, and scale advantages, among other attributes. These qualities create barriers to entry and increase the stability and predictability of a company's cash flow. Accordingly, the sponsor spends a great deal of time during due diligence seeking assurance that the target's market positions are secure (and can potentially be expanded). Depending on the sponsor's familiarity with the sector, consultants may be hired to perform independent studies analyzing market share and barriers to entry.

---

[23]A roll-up strategy involves consolidating multiple companies in a given market or sector to create an entity with increased size, scale, and efficiency.

Growth Opportunities

Sponsors seek companies with growth potential, both organically and through potential future bolt-on acquisitions. Profitable top line growth at above-market rates helps drive outsized returns, generating greater cash available for debt repayment while also increasing EBITDA and enterprise value. Growth also enhances the speed and optionality for exit opportunities. For example, a strong growth profile is particularly important if the target is designated for an eventual IPO exit.

Companies with robust growth profiles have a greater likelihood of driving EBITDA "multiple expansion"[24] during the sponsor's investment horizon, which further enhances returns. Moreover, as discussed in Chapter 1, larger companies tend to benefit from their scale, market share, purchasing power, and lower risk profile, and are often rewarded with a premium valuation relative to smaller peers, all else being equal. In some cases, the sponsor opts not to maximize the amount of debt financing at purchase. This provides greater flexibility to pursue a growth strategy that may require future incremental debt to make acquisitions or build new facilities, for example.

Efficiency Enhancement Opportunities

While an ideal LBO candidate should have a strong fundamental business model, sponsors seek opportunities to improve operational efficiencies and generate cost savings. Traditional cost-saving measures include lowering corporate overhead, streamlining operations, introducing *lean manufacturing* and *Six Sigma* processes,[25] reducing headcount, rationalizing the supply chain, and implementing new management information systems. The sponsor may also seek to source new (or negotiate better) terms with existing suppliers and customers. These initiatives are a primary focus for the consultants and industry experts hired by the sponsor to assist with due diligence and assess the opportunity represented by establishing "best practices" at the target. Their successful implementation often represents substantial value creation that accrues to equity value at a multiple of each dollar saved (given an eventual exit).

At the same time, sponsors must be careful not to jeopardize existing sales or attractive growth opportunities by starving the business of necessary capital. Extensive cuts in marketing, capex, or research & development, for example, may hurt customer retention, new product development, or other growth initiatives. Such moves could put the company at risk of deteriorating sales and profitability or loss of market position.

Low Capex Requirements

All else being equal, low capex requirements enhance a company's cash flow generation capabilities. As a result, the best LBO candidates tend to have limited capital

---

[24]Selling the target for a higher multiple of EBITDA upon exit (i.e., purchasing the target for 7.0x EBITDA and selling it for 8.0x EBITDA).
[25]Lean manufacturing is a production practice and philosophy dedicated to eliminating waste, while Six Sigma is focused on improving output quality by identifying and eliminating defects and variability.

investment needs. However, a company with substantial capex requirements may still represent an attractive investment opportunity if it has a strong growth profile, high profit margins, and the business strategy is validated during due diligence.

During due diligence, the sponsor and its advisors focus on differentiating those expenditures deemed necessary to continue operating the business ("maintenance capex") from those that are discretionary ("growth capex"). Maintenance capex is capital required to sustain existing assets (typically PP&E) at their current output levels. Growth capex is used to purchase new assets, thereby expanding the existing asset base. In the event that economic conditions or operating performance decline, growth capex can potentially be reduced or eliminated.

Strong Asset Base

A strong asset base pledged as collateral against a loan benefits lenders by increasing the likelihood of principal recovery in the event of bankruptcy (and liquidation). This, in turn, increases their willingness to provide debt to the target. Strength is defined as size of the asset base (e.g., tangible assets as a percentage of total assets) as well as quality of the asset base. Accounts receivable and inventory are considered high quality assets given their liquidity. As opposed to long-term assets such as PP&E, they can be converted into cash easily and quickly.

The target's asset base is particularly important in the leveraged loan market, where the value of the assets helps dictate the amount of bank debt available (see "LBO Financing" sections for additional information). A strong asset base also tends to signify high barriers to entry because of the substantial capital investment required, which serves to deter new entrants in the target's markets. At the same time, a company with little or no assets can still be an attractive LBO candidate provided it generates sufficient cash flow.

Proven Management Team

A proven management team serves to increase the attractiveness (and value) of an LBO candidate. Talented management is critical in an LBO scenario given the need to operate under a highly leveraged capital structure with ambitious performance targets. Prior experience operating under such conditions, as well as success in integrating acquisitions or implementing restructuring initiatives, is highly regarded by sponsors.

For LBO candidates with strong management, the sponsor usually seeks to keep the existing team in place post-acquisition. It is customary for management to retain, invest, or be granted a meaningful equity stake so as to align their incentives under the new ownership structure with that of the sponsor. Alternatively, in those instances where the target's management is weak, sponsors seek to add value by making key changes to the existing team or installing a new team altogether to run the company. In either circumstance, a strong management team is crucial for driving company performance going forward and helping the sponsor meet its investment objectives.

ECONOMICS OF LBOs

Returns Analysis—Internal Rate of Return

Internal rate of return (IRR) is the primary metric by which sponsors gauge the attractiveness of a potential LBO, as well as the performance of their existing investments. IRR measures the total return on a sponsor's equity investment, including any additional equity contributions made, or dividends received, during the investment horizon. The IRR approach factors in the time value of money—for a given amount of cash proceeds at exit, a shorter exit timeline produces a higher IRR for the sponsor. In contrast, if the investment proceeds take longer to realize, the IRR will decrease.

IRR is defined as the discount rate that must be applied to the sponsor's cash outflows and inflows during the investment horizon in order to produce a net present value (NPV) of zero. Although the IRR calculation can be performed with a financial calculator or by using the IRR function in Microsoft Excel, it is important to understand the supporting math. Exhibit 4.4 displays the equation for calculating IRR, assuming a five-year investment horizon.

EXHIBIT 4.4 IRR Timeline

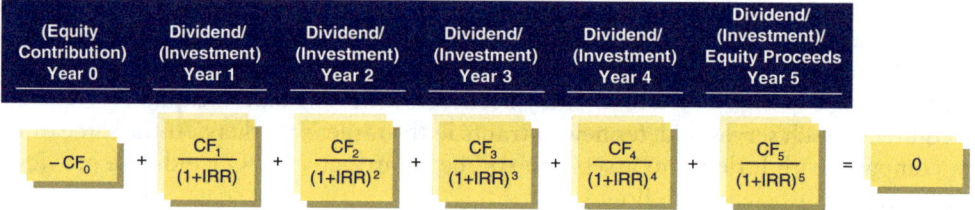

While multiple factors affect a sponsor's ultimate decision to pursue a potential acquisition, comfort with meeting acceptable IRR thresholds is critical. Sponsors typically target superior returns relative to alternative investments for their LPs, with a 20%+ threshold historically serving as a widely held "rule of thumb." This threshold, however, may increase or decrease depending on market conditions, the perceived risk of an investment, and other factors specific to the situation.

The primary IRR drivers include the target's projected financial performance,[26] purchase price, and financing structure (particularly the size of the equity contribution), as well as the exit multiple and year. As would be expected, a sponsor seeks to minimize the price paid and equity contribution while gaining a strong degree of confidence in the target's future financial performance and the ability to exit at a sufficient valuation.

In Exhibit 4.5, we assume that a sponsor contributes $300 million of equity (cash outflow) at the end of Year 0 as part of the LBO financing structure and receives equity proceeds upon sale of $1 billion (cash inflow) at the end of Year 5. This scenario produces an IRR of 27.2%, as demonstrated by the NPV of zero.

---

[26]Based on the sponsor's model (See Chapter 5).

Leveraged Buyouts

EXHIBIT 4.5 IRR Timeline Example
($ in millions)

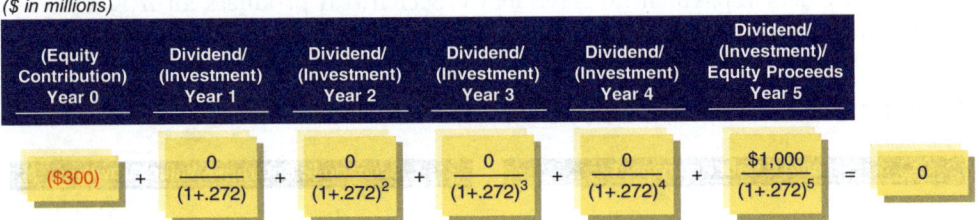

Returns Analysis—Cash Return

In addition to IRR, sponsors also examine returns on the basis of a multiple of their cash investment ("cash return"). For example, assuming a sponsor contributes $300 million of equity and receives equity proceeds of $1 billion at the end of the investment horizon, the cash return is 3.3x (assuming no additional investments or dividends during the period). However, unlike IRR, the cash return approach does not factor in the time value of money.

How LBOs Generate Returns

LBOs generate returns through a combination of debt repayment and growth in enterprise value. Exhibit 4.6 depicts how each of these scenarios independently increases equity value, assuming a sponsor purchases a company for $1 billion, using $700 million of debt financing (70% of the purchase price) and an equity contribution of $300 million (30% of the purchase price). In each scenario, the returns are equivalent on both an IRR and cash return basis.

Scenario I In Scenario I, we assume that the target generates cumulative free cash flow of $500 million, which is used to repay the principal amount of debt during the investment horizon. Debt repayment increases equity value on a dollar-for-dollar basis. Assuming the sponsor sells the target for $1 billion at exit, the value of the sponsor's equity investment increases from $300 million at purchase to $800 million even though there is no growth in the company's enterprise value. This scenario produces an IRR of 21.7% (assuming a five-year investment horizon) with a cash return of 2.7x.

Scenario II In Scenario II, we assume that the target does not repay any debt during the investment horizon. Rather, all cash generated by the target (after the payment of interest expense) is reinvested into the business, and the sponsor realizes 50% growth in enterprise value by selling the target for $1.5 billion after five years. This enterprise value growth can be achieved through EBITDA growth (e.g., organic growth, acquisitions, or streamlining operations) and/or achieving EBITDA multiple expansion.

As the debt represents a fixed claim on the business, the incremental $500 million of enterprise value accrues entirely to equity value. As in Scenario I, the value of the sponsor's equity investment increases from $300 million to $800 million, but this time without any debt repayment. Consequently, Scenario II produces an IRR and cash return equivalent to those in Scenario I (i.e., 21.7% and 2.7x, respectively).

EXHIBIT 4.6 How LBOs Generate Returns
($ in millions)

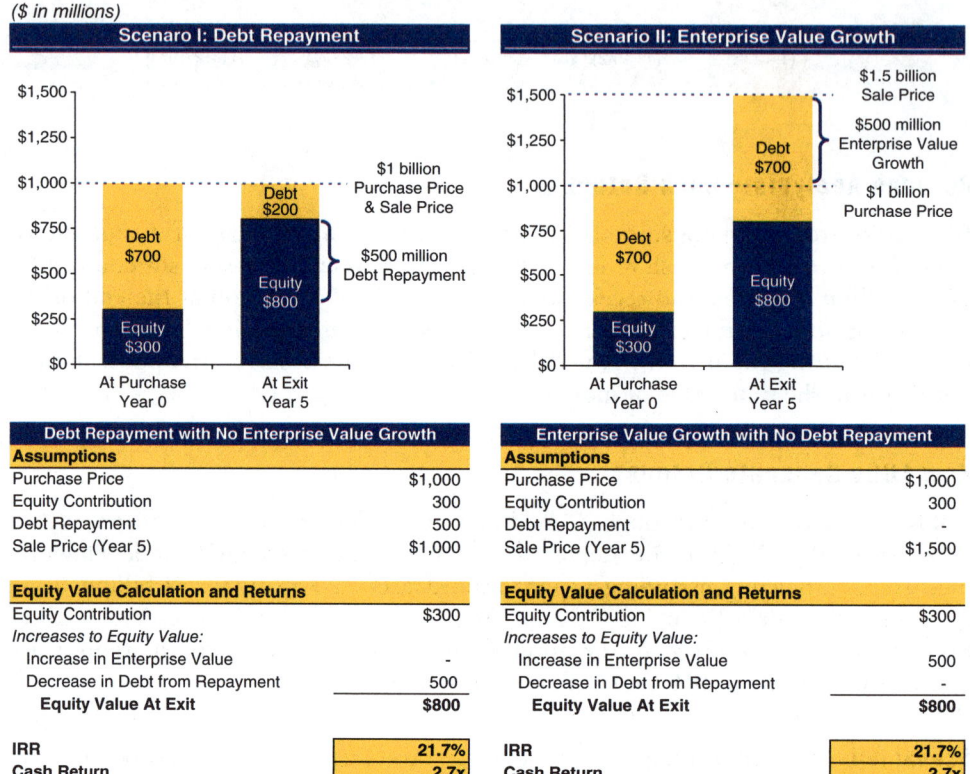

How Leverage Is Used to Enhance Returns

The concept of using leverage to enhance returns is fundamental to understanding LBOs. Assuming a fixed enterprise value at exit, using a higher percentage of debt in the financing structure (and a correspondingly smaller equity contribution) generates higher returns. Exhibit 4.7 illustrates this principle by analyzing comparative returns of an LBO financed with 30% debt versus an LBO financed with 70% debt. A higher level of debt provides the additional benefit of greater tax savings realized due to the tax deductibility of a higher amount of interest expense.

While increased leverage may be used to generate enhanced returns, there are certain clear trade-offs. As discussed in Chapter 3, higher leverage increases the company's risk profile (and probability of financial distress), limiting financial flexibility and making the company more susceptible to business or economic downturns.

EXHIBIT 4.7 How Leverage Is Used to Enhance Returns
($ in millions)

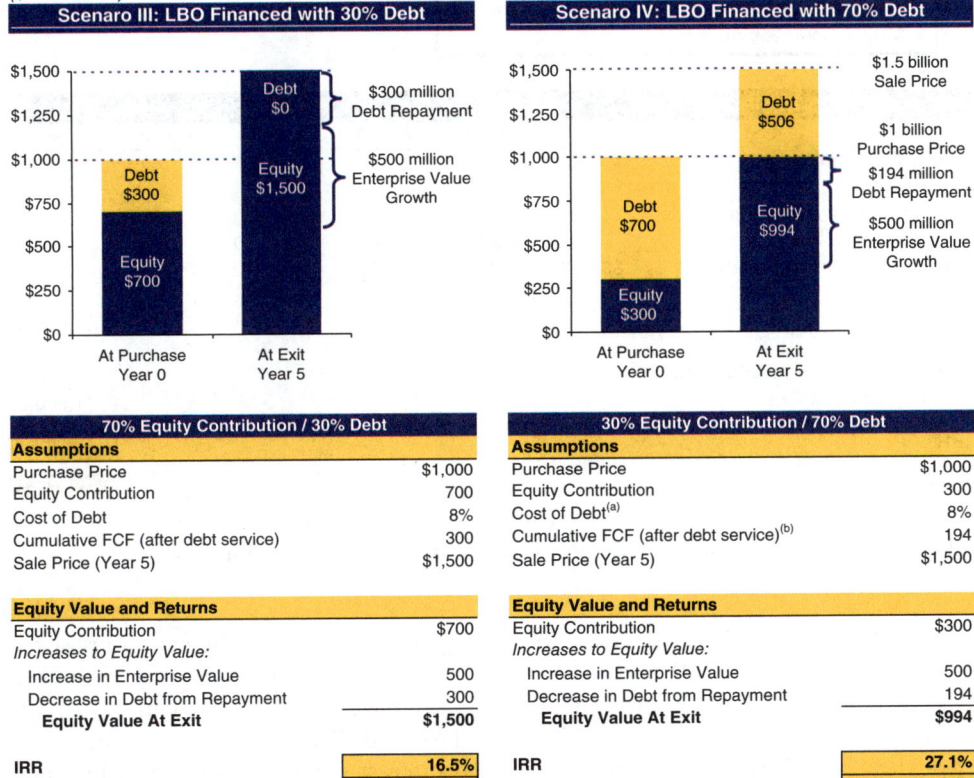

(a) In practice, the higher leverage in Scenario IV would require a higher blended cost of debt by investors versus Scenario III. For simplicity, we assume a constant cost of debt in this example.

(b) Reduced FCF in Scenario IV versus Scenario III reflects the incremental interest expense associated with the additional $400 million of debt, which results in less cash available for debt repayment.

Scenario III In Scenario III, we assume a sponsor purchases the target for $1 billion using $300 million of debt (30% of the purchase price) and contributing $700 million of equity (70% of the purchase price). After five years, the target is sold for $1.5 billion, thereby resulting in a $500 million increase in enterprise value ($1.5 billion sale price − $1 billion purchase price).

During the five-year investment horizon, we assume that the target generates annual free cash flow after the payment of interest expense of $60 million ($300 million on a cumulative basis), which is used for debt repayment. As shown in the timeline in Exhibit 4.8, the target completely repays the $300 million of debt by the end of Year 5.

By the end of the five-year investment horizon, the sponsor's original $700 million equity contribution is worth $1.5 billion as there is no debt remaining in the capital structure. This scenario generates an IRR of 16.5% and a cash return of approximately 2.1x after five years.

EXHIBIT 4.8 Scenario III Debt Repayment Timeline

> = Beginning Debt Balance$_{Year\ 1}$ - Free Cash Flow$_{Year\ 1}$
> = $300 million - $60 million

($ in millions)

Scenario III - 70% Equity / 30% Debt						
	Year 0	Year 1	Year 2	Year 3	Year 4	Year 5
Equity Contribution	($700.0)					
Total Debt, beginning balance		$300.0	$240.0	$180.0	$120.0	$60.0
Free Cash Flow$^{(a)}$		$60.0	$60.0	$60.0	$60.0	$60.0
Total Debt, ending balance	$300.0	$240.0	$180.0	$120.0	$60.0	-
Sale Price						$1,500.0
Less: Total Debt						(300.0)
Plus: Cumulative Free Cash Flow						300.0
Equity Value at Exit						$1,500.0
IRR						**16.5%**
Cash Return						**2.1x**

(a) Annual free cash flow is after interest expense on the $300 million of debt. Also known as levered free cash flow or cash available for debt repayment (see Chapter 5).

Scenario IV In Scenario IV, we assume that a sponsor buys the same target for $1 billion, but uses $700 million of debt (70% of the purchase price) and contributes $300 million of equity (30% of the purchase price). As in Scenario III, we assume the target is sold for $1.5 billion at the end of Year 5. However, annual free cash flow is reduced due to the incremental interest expense on the $400 million of additional debt.

As shown in Exhibit 4.9, under Scenario IV, the additional $400 million of debt ($700 million − $300 million) creates incremental interest expense of $32 million ($19.2 million after-tax) in Year 1. The after-tax incremental interest expense of $19.2 million is calculated as the $400 million difference multiplied by an 8% assumed cost of debt and then tax-effected at a 40% assumed marginal tax rate. For each year of the projection period, we calculate incremental interest expense as the difference between total debt (beginning balance) in Scenario III versus Scenario IV multiplied by 8% (4.8% after tax).

By the end of Year 5, the sponsor's original $300 million equity contribution is worth $994.3 million ($1.5 billion sale price − $505.7 million of debt remaining in the capital structure). This scenario generates an IRR of 27.1% and a cash return of approximately 3.3x after five years.

Leveraged Buyouts

EXHIBIT 4.9   Scenario IV Debt Repayment Timeline

> = Total Debt, beginning balance$_{Year\,5}$ - Free Cash Flow, ending$_{Year\,5}$
> = $542.5 million - $36.8 million

> = (Scenario IV Total Debt, beginning balance$_{Year\,1}$ -
>   Scenario III Total Debt, beginning balance$_{Year\,1}$) × Cost of Debt
> = ($700 million - $300 million) × 8%

($ in millions)

Scenario IV - 30% Equity / 70% Debt

	Year 0	Year 1	Year 2	Year 3	Year 4	Year 5
Equity Contribution	($300.0)					
Total Debt, beginning balance		$700.0	$659.2	$619.3	$580.4	$542.5
Free Cash Flow, beginning[a]		60.0	60.0	60.0	60.0	60.0
Incremental Interest Expense[b]		32.0	33.5	35.1	36.8	38.6
Interest Tax Savings		(12.8)	(13.4)	(14.1)	(14.7)	(15.4)
Free Cash Flow, ending		$40.8	$39.9	$38.9	$37.9	$36.8
Total Debt, ending balance	$700.0	$659.2	$619.3	$580.4	$542.5	$505.7

> = - Incremental Interest Expense$_{Year\,2}$ × Marginal Tax Rate
> = ($33.5) million × 40%

Sale Price	$1,500.0
Less: Total Debt	(700.0)
Plus: Cumulative Free Cash Flow	194.3
Equity Value at Exit	**$994.3**
IRR	**27.1%**
Cash Return	**3.3x**

[a] Post-debt service on the $300 million of debt in Scenario III.

[b] Employs a beginning year as opposed to an average debt balance approach to calculating interest expense (see Chapter 5).

PRIMARY EXIT/MONETIZATION STRATEGIES

Most sponsors aim to exit or monetize their investments within a five-year holding period in order to provide timely returns to their LPs. These returns are typically realized via a sale to another company (commonly referred to as a "strategic sale"), a sale to another sponsor, or an IPO. Sponsors may also extract a return prior to exit through a dividend recapitalization, which is the issuance of additional debt to pay shareholders a dividend. In addition, when the opportunity arises (e.g., during the 2008/2009 financial crisis), financial sponsors may opportunistically purchase the debt securities of their portfolio companies at a substantial discount to par.[27] These debt purchases may be made either directly by the issuer or by the sponsor. As markets normalize and these securities increase in price, the sponsors are able to realize an attractive return on their capital.

The ultimate decision regarding when to monetize an investment, however, depends on the performance of the target as well as prevailing market conditions. In some cases, such as when the target has performed particularly well or market conditions are favorable, the exit or monetization may occur within a year or two. Alternatively, the sponsor may be forced to hold an investment longer than desired as dictated by company performance or the market.

By the end of the investment horizon, ideally the sponsor has increased the target's EBITDA (e.g., through organic growth, acquisitions, and/or increased profitability) and reduced its debt, thereby substantially increasing the target's equity value. The sponsor also seeks to achieve multiple expansion upon exit. There are several strategies aimed at achieving a higher exit multiple, including an increase in the target's size and scale, meaningful operational improvements, a repositioning of the business toward more highly valued industry segments, an acceleration of the target's organic growth rate and/or profitability, and the accurate timing of a cyclical sector or economic upturn.

Below, we discuss the primary LBO exit/monetization strategies for financial sponsors.

Sale of Business

Traditionally, sponsors have sought to sell portfolio companies to strategic buyers, which typically represent the most attractive potential bidders due to their ability to realize synergies from the target and, therefore, pay a higher price. Strategic buyers may also benefit from a lower cost of capital and a lower return threshold. The proliferation of private equity funds, however, has made exits via a sale to another sponsor increasingly commonplace. Moreover, during robust debt financing markets, sponsors may be able to use high leverage levels and generous debt terms to support purchase prices competitive with (or even in excess of) those offered by strategic buyers.

---

[27] As permitted by the charter and mandate of the specific fund. Furthermore, such repurchases must be made in accordance with the specific debt instrument's credit agreement or indenture.

Initial Public Offering

In an IPO exit, the sponsor sells a portion of its shares in the target to the public. Post-IPO, the sponsor typically retains the largest single equity stake in the target with the understanding that a full exit will come through future follow-on equity offerings or an eventual sale of the company. Therefore, as opposed to an outright majority sale for control, an IPO generally affords the sponsor only a partial monetization of its investment. At the same time, the IPO provides the sponsor with a liquid market for its remaining equity investment while also preserving the opportunity to share in any future upside potential. Furthermore, depending on equity capital market conditions, an IPO may offer a compelling valuation premium to an outright sale.

Dividend Recapitalization

While not a true "exit strategy," a dividend recapitalization ("dividend recap") provides the sponsor with a viable option for monetizing a sizeable portion of its investment prior to exit. In a dividend recap, the target raises proceeds through the issuance of additional debt to pay shareholders a dividend. The incremental indebtedness may be issued in the form of an "add-on" to the target's existing credit facilities and/or bonds, a new security at the HoldCo level,[28] or as part of a complete refinancing of the existing capital structure. A dividend recap provides the sponsor with the added benefit of retaining 100% of its existing ownership position in the target, thus preserving the ability to share in any future upside potential and the option to pursue a sale or IPO at a future date. Depending on the size and number of dividends, the sponsor may be able to recoup all of (or more than) its initial equity investment.

Below Par Debt Repurchase

Many private equity firms have the flexibility to purchase the bank debt and high yield securities of their portfolio companies in the pursuit of acceptable risk-adjusted returns, either directly or through the issuer. As sponsors typically own a majority stake in the company and serve on the board of directors, they are well-positioned to evaluate the future prospects of the business, including its ability to service and eventually repay its indebtedness. This strategy is particularly attractive when the debt can be bought at distressed levels, which was relatively commonplace during the credit crisis of 2008 and 2009. In these instances, financial sponsors found opportunities to purchase debt instruments of their portfolio companies at significant discounts to par value. As market conditions improved and the financial performance of these companies rebounded, the debt instruments increased in price commensurately. This distressed debt strategy provides sponsors with an additional tool for generating returns from existing portfolio companies while still preserving future monetization opportunities via a refinancing, dividend, sale, or IPO.

---

[28]Debt incurrence and restricted payments covenants in the target's existing OpCo debt often substantially limit both incremental debt and the ability to pay a dividend to shareholders (see Exhibits 4.24 and 4.25). Therefore, dividend recaps frequently involve issuing a new security at the HoldCo, which is not subject to the existing OpCo covenants.

LBO FINANCING: STRUCTURE

In a traditional LBO, debt has typically comprised 60% to 70% of the financing structure, with the remainder of the purchase price funded by an equity contribution from a sponsor (or group of sponsors) and rolled/contributed equity from management. Given the inherently high leverage associated with an LBO, the various debt components of the capital structure are usually deemed non-investment grade, or rated 'Ba1' and below by Moody's Investor Service and 'BB+' and below by Standard and Poor's (see Chapter 1, Exhibit 1.23 for a ratings scale). The debt portion of the LBO financing structure may include a broad array of loans, securities, or other debt instruments with varying terms and conditions that appeal to different classes of investors.

We have grouped the primary types of LBO financing sources into the categories shown in Exhibit 4.10, corresponding to their relative ranking in the capital structure.

EXHIBIT 4.10 General Ranking of Financing Sources in an LBO Capital Structure

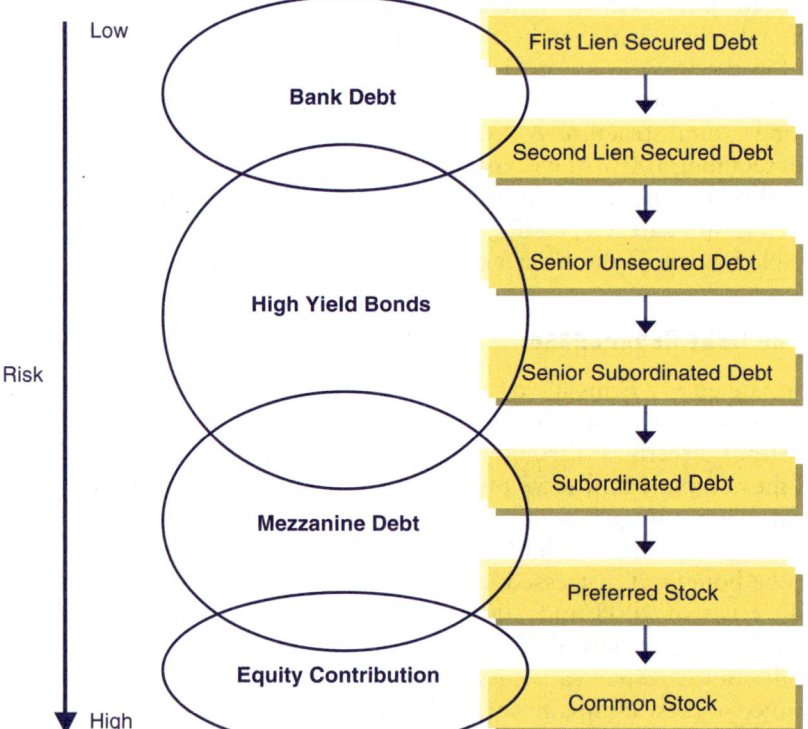

As a general rule, the higher a given debt instrument ranks in the capital structure hierarchy, the lower its risk and, consequently, the lower its cost of capital to the borrower/issuer. However, cost of capital tends to be inversely related to the flexibility permitted by the applicable debt instrument. For example, bank debt usually represents the least expensive form of LBO financing. At the same time, bank debt is secured by various forms of collateral and governed by *maintenance* covenants that require the borrower to "maintain" a designated credit profile through compliance with certain financial ratios (see Exhibit 4.24).

During the 2003 to 2012 period, the average LBO varied substantially in terms of leverage levels, purchase multiple, percentage of capital sourced from each class of debt, and equity contribution percentage. As shown in Exhibit 4.11, the average

LBO purchase price and leverage multiples (both senior-debt-to-EBITDA and total debt-to-EBITDA) increased dramatically during the 2002 to 2007 period. This was the result of changes in the prevailing capital markets conditions and investor landscape, including the proliferation of private investment vehicles (e.g., private equity funds and hedge funds) and structured credit vehicles such as CDOs.

EXHIBIT 4.11 Average LBO Purchase Price Breakdown 2003 – 2012

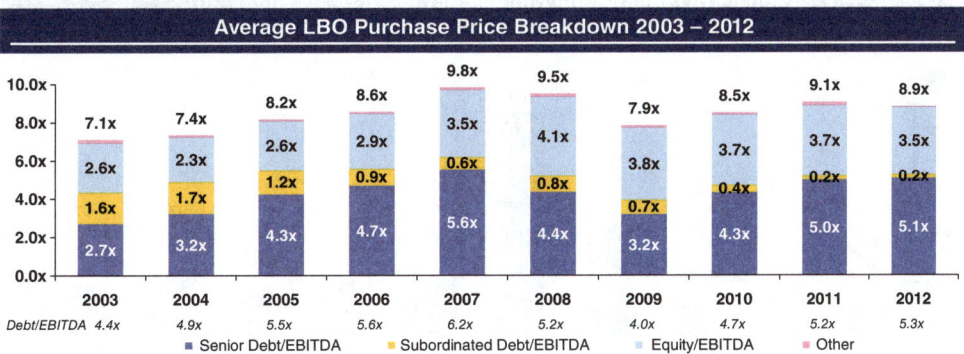

Source: Standard & Poor's Leveraged Commentary & Data Group
Note: 2008 includes deals committed to in 2007 (during the credit boom) that closed in 2008.
Senior debt includes bank debt, 2nd lien debt, senior secured notes, and senior unsecured notes. Subordinated debt includes senior and junior subordinated debt.
Equity includes HoldCo debt/seller notes, preferred stock, common stock, and rolled equity.
Other is cash and any other unclassified sources.

However, beginning in the second half of 2007, credit market conditions deteriorated dramatically due to the subprime mortgage crisis. As a result, lenders and debt investors became more cautious, and lending conditions became much tighter (less favorable) for borrowers. As shown in Exhibit 4.11, the average LBO leverage level decreased from 6.2x in 2007 to 4.0x in 2009. Correspondingly, the percentage of contributed equity in the average LBO increased from 31% to 46% during the same time period (see Exhibit 4.12). Including management rollover equity, the total equity consideration increased from 33% in 2007 to 51% in 2009.

EXHIBIT 4.12 Average Sources of LBO Proceeds 2003 – 2012

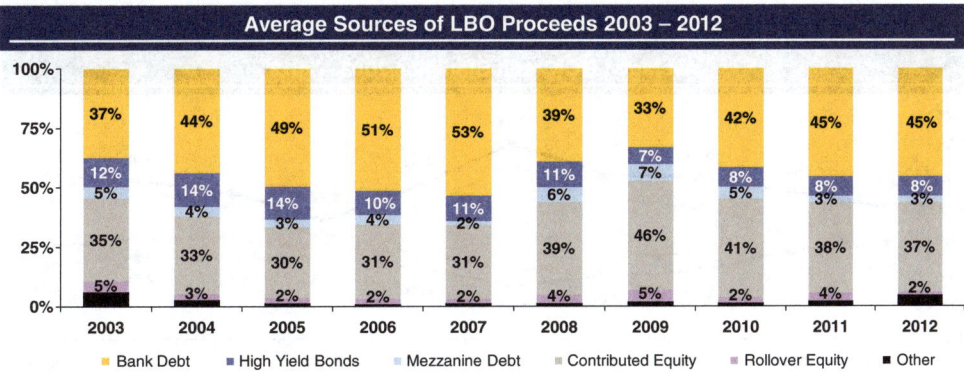

Source: Standard & Poor's Leveraged Commentary & Data Group
Note: Contributed equity includes HoldCo debt/seller notes, preferred stock, and common stock.

In addition, the LBO dollar volume and number of closed deals decreased considerably in 2008 and 2009 versus the unprecedented levels of 2006 and 2007, before beginning to recover in 2010 and 2011 (see Exhibit 4.13).

EXHIBIT 4.13 Global LBO Volume and Number of Closed Deals 2003 – 2012

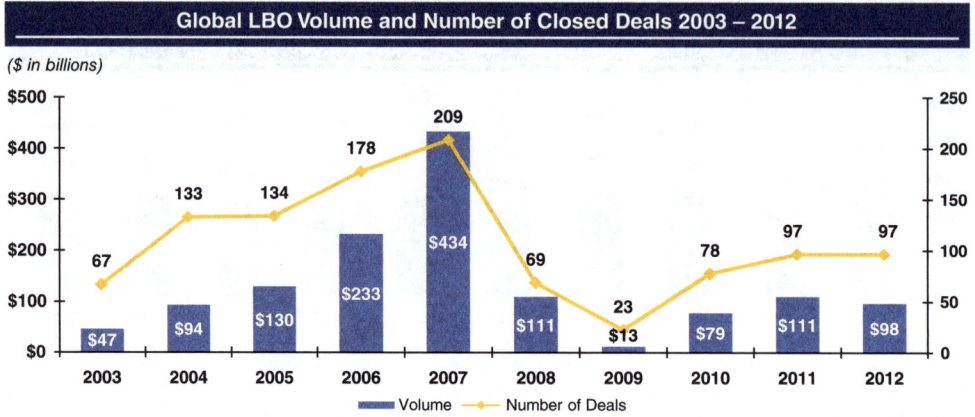

Source: Standard & Poor's Leveraged Commentary & Data Group

The average credit statistics for LBO transactions has fluctuated dramatically over the last decade. Beginning in 2003, the total debt-to-EBITDA multiple for the average LBO was 4.1x while the coverage ratio of (EBITDA – capex)-to-interest expense was 2.9x (see Exhibit 4.14). By 2007, these multiples reached peak levels of 6.1x and 1.7x, respectively, indicating extremely favorable conditions for borrowers/issuers. When credit conditions became tight in 2008 and 2009 during the credit crisis, credit statistics for LBO transactions became stronger (more favorable for lenders and debt investors and less favorable for borrowers/issuers). By 2010/2011, credit statistics reflected more normalized levels by historical standards.

EXHIBIT 4.14 Average LBO Credit Statistics 2003 – 2012

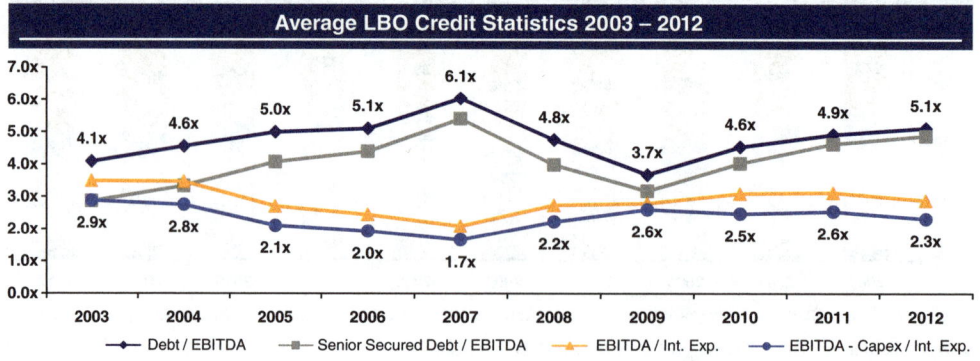

Source: Standard & Poor's Leveraged Commentary & Data Group

LBO FINANCING: PRIMARY SOURCES

Bank Debt

EXHIBIT 4.15 Bank Debt

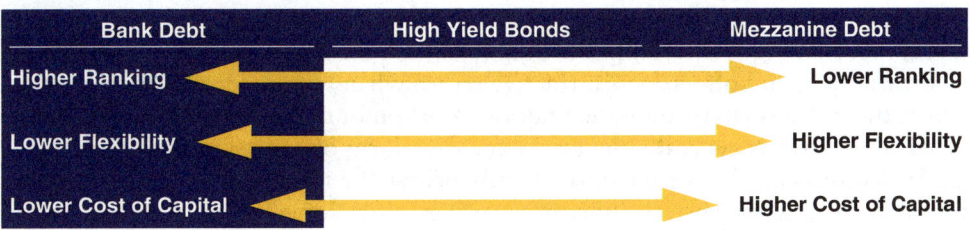

Bank debt is an integral part of the LBO financing structure, consistently serving as a substantial source of capital (as shown in Exhibit 4.12). Also referred to as "senior secured credit facilities," it is typically comprised of a revolving credit facility (which may be borrowed, repaid, and reborrowed) and one or more term loan tranches (which may not be reborrowed once repaid). The revolving credit facility may take the form of a traditional "cash flow" revolver[29] or an asset-based lending (ABL) facility.[30] Bank debt is issued in the private market and is therefore not subject to SEC regulations and disclosure requirements.[31] However, it has restrictive covenants that require the borrower to comply with certain provisions and financial tests throughout the life of the facility (see Exhibit 4.24).

Bank debt typically bears interest (payable on a quarterly basis) at a given benchmark rate, usually LIBOR or the Base Rate,[32] plus an applicable margin ("spread") based on the creditworthiness of the borrower (or quality of the asset base in the case of ABL facilities). This type of debt is often referred to as floating rate due to the fact that the borrowing cost varies in accordance with changes to the underlying benchmark rate. In addition, the spread may be adjusted downward (or upward) if it is tied to a performance-based grid based on the borrower's leverage ratio or credit ratings.

Revolving Credit Facility A traditional cash flow revolving credit facility ("revolver") is a line of credit extended by a bank or group of banks that permits the borrower to draw varying amounts up to a specified aggregate limit for a specified period of time. It is unique in that amounts borrowed can be freely repaid and reborrowed during the term of the facility, subject to agreed-upon conditions set forth in

---

[29] Lenders to the facility focus on the ability of the borrower to cover debt service by generating cash flow.

[30] Lenders to the facility focus on the liquidation value of the assets comprising the facility's borrowing base, typically accounts receivable and inventory (see Exhibit 4.16).

[31] As a private market instrument, bank debt is not subject to the Securities Act of 1933 and the Securities Exchange Act of 1934, which require periodic public reporting of financial and other information.

[32] Base Rate is most often defined as a rate equal to the higher of the prime rate or the Federal Funds rate plus 1/2 of 1%.

a credit agreement[33] (see Exhibit 4.24). The majority of companies utilize a revolver or equivalent lending arrangement to provide ongoing liquidity for seasonal working capital needs, capital expenditures, letters of credit (LC),[34] and other general corporate purposes. A revolver may also be used to fund a portion of the purchase price in an LBO, although it is usually undrawn at close.

Revolvers are typically arranged by one or more investment banks and then syndicated to a group of commercial banks and finance companies. To compensate lenders for making this credit line available to the borrower (which may or may not be drawn upon and offers a less attractive return when unfunded), a nominal annual commitment fee is charged on the undrawn portion of the facility.[35]

The revolver is generally the least expensive form of capital in the LBO financing structure, typically priced at, or slightly below, the term loan's spread. In return for the revolver's low cost, the borrower must sacrifice some flexibility. For example, lenders generally require a first priority security interest ("lien") on certain assets[36] of the borrower[37] (shared with the term loan facilities) and compliance with various covenants. The first lien provides lenders greater comfort by granting their debt claims a higher priority in the event of bankruptcy relative to obligations owed to second priority secured and unsecured creditors (see "Security"). The historical market standard for LBO revolvers has been a term ("tenor") of five to six years, with no scheduled reduction to the committed amount of such facilities prior to maturity.

Asset-Based Lending Facility An ABL facility is a type of revolving credit facility that is available to current asset-intensive companies. ABL facilities are secured by a first priority lien on all current assets (typically accounts receivable and inventory) of the borrower and may include a second priority lien on all other assets (typically PP&E). They are more commonly used by companies with sizeable accounts receivable and inventory and variable working capital needs that operate in seasonal or asset-intensive businesses. For example, ABL facilities are used by retailers, selected

---

[33] The legal contract between the borrower and its lenders that governs bank debt. It contains key definitions, terms, representations and warranties, covenants, events of default, and other protective provisions.

[34] An LC is a document issued to a specified beneficiary that guarantees payment by an "issuing" lender under the credit agreement. LCs reduce revolver availability.

[35] The fee is assessed on an ongoing basis and accrues daily, typically at an annualized rate up to 50 basis points (bps) depending on the creditworthiness of the borrower. For example, an undrawn $100 million revolver would typically have an annual commitment fee of 50 bps or $500,000 ($100 million × 0.50%). Assuming the average daily revolver usage (including the outstanding LC amounts) is $25 million, the annual commitment fee would be $375,000 (($100 million − $25 million) × 0.50%). For any drawn portion of the revolver, the borrower pays interest on that dollar amount at LIBOR or the Base Rate plus a spread. To the extent the revolver's availability is reduced by outstanding LCs, the borrower pays a fee on the dollar amount of undrawn outstanding LCs at the full spread, but does not pay LIBOR or the Base Rate. Banks may also be paid an *up-front fee* upon the initial closing of the revolver and term loan(s) to incentivize participation.

[36] For example, in the tangible and intangible assets of the borrower, including capital stock of subsidiaries.

[37] As well as its domestic subsidiaries (in most cases).

commodity producers and distributors (e.g., chemicals, forest products, and steel), manufacturers, and rental equipment businesses.

ABL facilities are subject to a *borrowing base* formula that limits availability based on "eligible" accounts receivable, inventory, and, in certain circumstances, fixed assets, real estate, or other more specialized assets of the borrower, all of which are pledged as collateral. The maximum amount available for borrowing under an ABL facility is capped by the size of the borrowing base at a given point in time or the committed amount of the facility, whichever is less. While the borrowing base formula varies depending on the individual borrower, a common example is shown in Exhibit 4.16.

EXHIBIT 4.16 ABL Borrowing Base Formula

ABL Borrowing Base = 85% × Eligible Accounts Receivable + 60%[a] × Eligible Inventory

[a] Based on 85% of appraised net orderly liquidation value (expected net proceeds if inventory is liquidated) as determined by a third party firm.

ABL facilities provide lenders with certain additional protections not found in traditional cash flow revolvers, such as periodic collateral reporting requirements and appraisals. In addition, the assets securing ABLs (such as accounts receivable and inventory) are typically easier to monetize and turn into cash in the event of bankruptcy. As such, the interest rate spread on an ABL facility is lower than that of a cash flow revolver for the same credit. Given their reliance upon a borrowing base as collateral, ABL facilities traditionally have only one "springing" financial covenant.[38] Traditional bank debt, by contrast, has multiple financial maintenance covenants restricting the borrower. The typical tenor of an ABL revolver is five years.

Term Loan Facilities

A term loan ("leveraged loan," when non-investment grade) is a loan with a specified maturity that requires principal repayment ("amortization") according to a defined schedule, typically on a quarterly basis. Like a revolver, a traditional term loan for an LBO financing is structured as a first lien debt obligation[39] and requires the borrower to maintain a certain credit profile through compliance with financial maintenance covenants contained in the credit agreement. Unlike a revolver, however, a term loan is fully funded on the date of closing and once principal is repaid, it cannot be reborrowed. Term loans are classified by an identifying letter such as "A," "B," "C," etc. in accordance with their lender base, amortization schedule, maturity date, and other terms.

---

[38] The traditional springing financial covenant is a fixed charge coverage ratio of 1.0x and is tested only if "excess availability" falls below a certain level (usually 10% to 15% of the ABL facility). Excess availability is equal to the lesser of the ABL facility or the borrowing base less, in each case, outstanding amounts under the facility.

[39] Often *pari passu* (or on an equal basis) with the revolver, which entitles term loan lenders to an equal right of repayment upon bankruptcy of the borrower.

Amortizing Term Loans "A" term loans ("Term Loan A" or "TLA") are commonly referred to as "amortizing term loans" because they typically require substantial principal repayment throughout the life of the loan.[40] Term loans with significant, annual required amortization are perceived by lenders as less risky than those with *de minimis* required principal repayments during the life of the loan due to their shorter average life. Consequently, TLAs are often the lowest priced term loans in the capital structure. TLAs are syndicated to commercial banks and finance companies together with the revolver and are often referred to as "pro rata" tranches because lenders typically commit to equal ("ratable") percentages of the revolver and TLA during syndication. TLAs in LBO financing structures typically have a term that ends simultaneously ("co-terminus") with the revolver.

Institutional Term Loans "B" term loans ("Term Loan B" or "TLB"), which are commonly referred to as "institutional term loans," are more prevalent than TLAs in LBO financings. They are typically larger in size than TLAs and sold to institutional investors (often the same investors who buy high yield bonds) rather than banks. The institutional investor class prefers non-amortizing loans with longer maturities and higher coupons. As a result, TLBs generally amortize at a nominal rate (e.g., 1% per annum) with a bullet payment at maturity.[41] TLBs are typically structured to have a longer term than the revolver and any TLA as bank lenders prefer to have their debt mature before the TLB. Hence, a tenor for TLBs of up to seven (or sometimes seven and one-half years) has historically been market standard for LBOs.

Second Lien Term Loans The prevalence of second lien term loans[42] to finance LBOs is generally a sign of a strong debt market, such as during the credit boom of the mid-2000s. A second lien term loan is a floating rate loan that is secured by a second priority security interest in the assets of the borrower. It ranks junior to the first priority security interest in the assets of the borrower benefiting a revolver, TLA, and TLB. In the event of bankruptcy (and liquidation), second lien lenders are entitled to repayment from the proceeds of collateral sales <u>after</u> such proceeds have first been applied to the claims of first lien lenders, but <u>prior to</u> any application to unsecured claims.[43] Unlike first lien term loans, second lien term loans generally do not amortize. Second lien term loans are typically structured to have a longer term than the first lien term loans as first lien lenders prefer to have their debt mature before the second lien term loan.

---

[40] A mandatory repayment schedule for a TLA issued at the end of 2012 with a six-year maturity might be structured as follows: 2013: 10%, 2014: 10%, 2015: 15%, 2016: 15%, 2017: 25%, 2018: 25%. Another example might be: 2013: 0%, 2014: 0%, 2015: 5%, 2016: 5%, 2017: 10%, 2018: 80%. The amortization schedule is typically set on a quarterly basis.

[41] A large repayment of principal at maturity that is standard among institutional term loans. A typical mandatory amortization schedule for a TLB issued at the end of 2012 with a seven-year maturity would be as follows: 2013: 1%, 2014: 1%, 2015: 1%, 2016: 1%, 2017: 1%, 2018: 1%, 2019: 94%. Like TLAs, the amortization schedule for B term loans is typically set on a quarterly basis. The sizeable 2019 principal repayment is referred to as a bullet.

[42] High yield bonds can also be structured with a security interest.

[43] Exact terms and rights between first and second lien lenders are set forth in an *intercreditor agreement*.

Leveraged Buyouts 211

For borrowers, second lien term loans offer an alternative to more traditional junior debt instruments, such as high yield bonds and mezzanine debt. As compared to traditional high yield bonds, for example, second lien term loans provide borrowers with superior prepayment optionality and no ongoing public disclosure requirements. They can also be issued in a smaller size than high yield bonds, which usually have a minimum issuance amount of $150+ million due to investors' desire for trading liquidity. Depending on the borrower and market conditions, second lien term loans may also provide a lower cost-of-capital. However, they typically carry the burden of financial covenants, albeit moderately less restrictive than first lien debt. For investors, which typically include hedge funds and CDOs, second lien term loans offer less risk (due to the secured status) than traditional unsecured high yield bonds while paying a higher coupon than first lien debt.

High Yield Bonds

EXHIBIT 4.17   High Yield Bonds

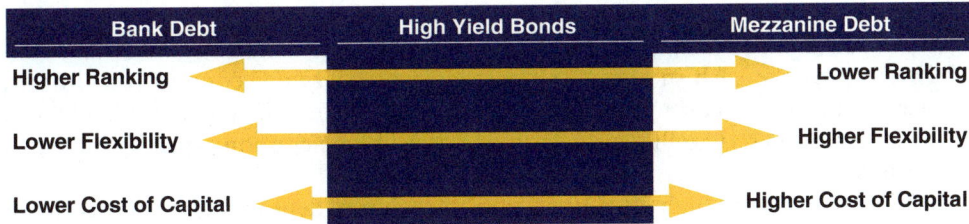

High yield bonds are non-investment grade debt securities that obligate the issuer to make interest payments to bondholders at regularly defined intervals (typically on a semiannual basis) and repay principal at a stated maturity date, usually seven to ten years after issuance. As opposed to term loans, high yield bonds are non-amortizing with the entire principal due as a bullet payment at maturity. Due to their junior, typically unsecured position in the capital structure, longer maturities, and less restrictive *incurrence* covenants as set forth in an indenture (see Exhibit 4.25),[44] high yield bonds feature a higher coupon than bank debt to compensate investors for the greater risk.

High yield bonds typically pay interest at a *fixed rate*, which is priced at issuance on the basis of a spread to a benchmark Treasury. As its name suggests, a fixed rate means that the interest rate is constant over the entire maturity. While high yield bonds may be structured with a floating rate coupon, this is not common for LBO financings. High yield bonds are typically structured as senior unsecured, senior subordinated, or, in certain circumstances, senior secured (first lien, second lien, or even third lien).

Traditionally, high yield bonds have been a mainstay in LBO financings. Used in conjunction with bank debt, high yield bonds enable sponsors to substantially increase leverage levels beyond those available in the leveraged loan market alone.

---

[44]The legal contract entered into by an issuer and corporate trustee (who acts on behalf of the bondholders) that defines the rights and obligations of the issuer and its creditors with respect to a bond issue. Similar to a credit agreement for bank debt, an indenture sets forth the covenants and other terms of a bond issue.

This permits sponsors to pay a higher purchase price and/or reduce the equity contribution. Furthermore, high yield bonds afford issuers greater flexibility than bank debt due to their less restrictive incurrence covenants (and absence of maintenance covenants), longer maturities, and lack of mandatory amortization. One offsetting factor, however, is that high yield bonds have non-call features (see Exhibit 4.23) that can negatively impact a sponsor's exit strategy.

Typically, high yield bonds are initially sold to qualified institutional buyers (QIBs)[45] through a private placement under Rule 144A of the Securities Act of 1933. They are then registered with the SEC within one year of issuance so that they can be traded on an open market. The private sale to QIBs expedites the initial sale of the bonds because SEC registration, which involves review of the registration statement by the SEC, can take several weeks or months. Once the SEC review of the documentation is complete, the issuer conducts an exchange offer pursuant to which investors exchange the unregistered bonds for registered securities. Post-registration, the issuer is subject to SEC disclosure requirements (e.g., the filing of 10-Ks, 10-Qs, 8-Ks, etc.).

During robust credit markets, companies have been able to issue bonds with atypical "issuer-friendly" provisions, such as a payment-in-kind (PIK) toggle. The PIK toggle allows an issuer to choose whether to pay interest "in-kind" (i.e., in the form of additional notes) or in cash. This optionality provides the issuer with the ability to preserve cash in times of challenging business or economic conditions, especially during the early years of the investment period when leverage is highest. If the issuer elects to pay PIK interest in lieu of cash, the coupon typically increases by 75 bps.

As bank debt and high yield bonds are the primary debt instruments used in an LBO financing, a comparison of the primary terms is shown in Exhibit 4.19.

Bridge Loans   A bridge loan facility ("bridge") is interim, committed financing provided to the borrower to "bridge" to the issuance of permanent capital, most often high yield bonds (the "take-out" securities). In an LBO, investment banks typically commit to provide funding for the bank debt and a bridge loan facility. The bridge usually takes the form of an unsecured term loan, which is only funded if the take-out securities cannot be issued and sold by the closing of the LBO.

Bridge loans are particularly important for LBO financings due to the sponsor's need to provide certainty of funding to the seller. The bridge financing gives comfort that the purchase consideration will be funded even in the event that market conditions for the take-out securities deteriorate between signing and closing of the transaction (subject to any conditions precedent to closing enumerated in the definitive agreement (see Chapter 6, Exhibit 6.9) or the commitment letter). If funded, the bridge loan can be replaced with the take-out securities at a future date, markets permitting.

In practice, however, the bridge loan is rarely intended to be funded, serving only as a financing of last resort. From the sponsor's perspective, the bridge loan is a

---

[45] As part of Rule 144A, the SEC created another category of financially sophisticated investors known as qualified institutional buyers, or QIBs. Rule 144A provides a safe harbor exemption from federal registration requirements for the resale of restricted securities to QIBs. QIBs generally are institutions or other entities that, in aggregate, own and invest (on a discretionary basis) at least $100 million in securities.

potentially costly funding alternative due to the additional fees required to be paid to the arrangers.[46] The interest rate on a bridge loan also typically increases periodically the longer it is outstanding until it hits the caps (maximum interest rate). The investment banks providing the bridge loan also hope that the bridge remains unfunded as it ties up capital and increases exposure to the borrower's credit. To mitigate the risk of funding a bridge, the lead arrangers often seek to syndicate all or a portion of the bridge loan commitment prior to the closing of the transaction.

Mezzanine Debt

EXHIBIT 4.18 Mezzanine Debt

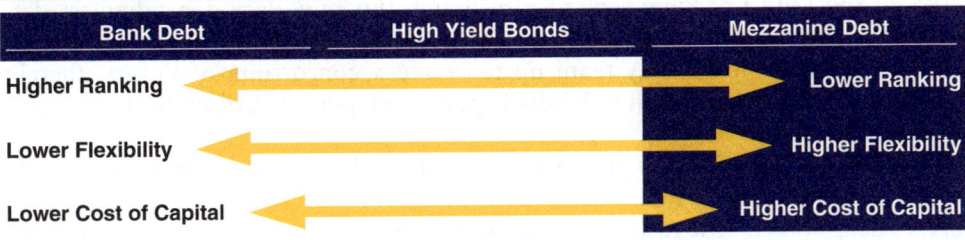

As its name suggests, mezzanine debt refers to a layer of capital that lies between traditional debt and equity. Mezzanine debt is a highly negotiated instrument between the issuer and investors that is tailored to meet the financing needs of the specific transaction and required investor returns. As such, mezzanine debt allows great flexibility in structuring terms conducive to issuer and investor alike.

For sponsors, mezzanine debt provides incremental capital at a cost below that of equity, which enables them to attain higher leverage levels and purchase price when alternative capital sources are inaccessible. For example, mezzanine debt may serve to substitute for, or supplement, high yield financing when markets are unfavorable or even inaccessible (e.g., for smaller companies whose size needs are below high yield bond market minimum thresholds). In the United States, it is particularly prevalent in middle market transactions.[47]

Typical investors include dedicated mezzanine funds, insurance companies, business development companies (BDCs), and hedge funds. For the investor, mezzanine debt offers a higher rate of return than traditional high yield bonds and can be structured to offer equity upside potential in the form of purchased equity or detachable warrants that are exchangeable into common stock of the issuer. The interest rate on mezzanine debt typically includes a combination of cash and non-cash PIK

---

[46] Investment banks are paid a commitment fee for arranging the bridge loan facility regardless of whether the bridge is funded. In the event the bridge is funded, the banks and lenders receive an additional *funding fee*. Furthermore, if the bridge remains outstanding after one year, the borrower also pays a *conversion fee*.

[47] In Europe, mezzanine debt is used to finance large as well as middle market transactions. It is typically structured as a floating rate loan (with a combination of cash and PIK interest) that benefits from a second or third lien on the same collateral benefiting the bank debt (of the same capital structure). U.S. mezzanine debt, on the other hand, is typically structured with a fixed rate coupon and is unsecured and oftentimes contractually subordinated (see Exhibit 4.21), thereby not benefiting from any security.

payments. Depending on available financing alternatives and market conditions, mezzanine investors typically target a "blended" return (including cash and non-cash components) in the low-to-mid teens (or higher) depending on market conditions. Maturities and terms for mezzanine debt may vary substantially, but tend to be similar to those for high yield bonds.[48]

Equity Contribution

The remaining portion of LBO funding comes in the form of an equity contribution by the financial sponsor and rolled/contributed equity by the target's management. The equity contribution percentage typically ranges from approximately 30% to 40% of the LBO financing structure, although this may vary depending on debt market conditions, the type of company, and the purchase multiple paid.[49] For large LBOs, several sponsors may team up to create a consortium of buyers, thereby reducing the amount of each individual sponsor's equity contribution (known as a "club deal").

The equity contribution provides a cushion for lenders and bondholders in the event that the company's enterprise value deteriorates as equity value is eliminated before debt holders lose recovery value. For example, if a sponsor contributes 30% equity to a given deal, lenders gain comfort that the value of the business would have to decline by more than 30% from the purchase price before their principal is jeopardized. Sponsors may also choose to "over-equitize" certain LBOs, such as when they plan to issue incremental debt at a future date to fund acquisitions or fund growth initiatives for the company.

Rollover/contributed equity by existing company management and/or key shareholders varies according to the situation, but often ranges from approximately 2% to 5% (or more) of the overall equity portion. Management equity rollover/contribution is usually encouraged by the sponsor in order to align incentives.

---

[48]However, if an LBO financing structure has both high yield bonds and mezzanine debt, the mezzanine debt will typically mature outside the high yield bonds, thereby reducing the risk to the more senior security.
[49]As previously discussed, the commitment papers for the debt financing are typically predicated on a minimum equity contribution by the sponsor.

EXHIBIT 4.19 Comparison of Bank Debt and High Yield Bonds

	Bank Debt	High Yield Bonds
Seniority	▪ Most senior debt in capital structure	▪ Subordinated to bank debt
Prepayability	▪ Prepayable (typically without penalty)	▪ Call protection or make-whole premium
Security	▪ Typically secured	▪ Typically unsecured
Coupon	▪ Floating interest rate	▪ Typically fixed rate coupon, but can be floating rate
	▪ Grid-based, depending on leverage metrics or ratings	▪ No change over life of bond / no change with improving or deteriorating credit
Ratings	▪ Not required, but typical	▪ Required (Moody's and S&P)
Investors	▪ Banks	▪ Fixed income/high yield mutual funds
	▪ CDOs/CLOs, prime rate funds and other institutions (Term Loan B)	▪ Hedge funds
		▪ Insurance companies
Syndication	▪ Bank or lenders' meetings	▪ Roadshow of 3–5 business days of meetings
	▪ 1–2 group meeting(s) with potential lenders	▪ Final Offering Memorandum printed after pricing
	▪ Two-week syndication process	▪ No SEC review of documentation prior to marketing
	▪ Distribution of confidential information memorandum	▪ Rule 144A private placement exception
	▪ One-week documentation process	▪ Closing and funding 3–5 days after the trade date
	▪ No SEC review, no registration	▪ Notes typically registered and exchanged into public bonds (registration rights) within 180–270 days following closing
Covenants	▪ Maintenance of a particular credit profile, tested on a quarterly basis	▪ Incurrence tests (no maintenance covenants), performance against covenants measured at incurrence of additional debt
	▪ Typical financial covenants include: maximum leverage (senior/total), minimum interest coverage, maximum capex	
	▪ Changes to credit agreement achieved through amendment/waiver process	

(Continued)

EXHIBIT 4.19 *(Continued)*

	Bank Debt	High Yield Bonds
Disclosure	<ul><li>May include non-public information</li><li>Reporting/information requirements determined by documentation</li><li>Information limited to existing lenders/syndicate</li></ul>	<ul><li>Public information only</li><li>SEC filing requirements</li><li>Information disseminated through investor conference calls</li><li>Research support is key for information flow</li></ul>
Trading	<ul><li>Liquid market for certain borrowers</li><li>Private market</li></ul>	<ul><li>Liquid market</li><li>Minimum new issue size typically $150+ million</li></ul>
Benefits	<ul><li>Lower cost than public debt</li><li>Lower underwriting fees</li><li>Fully pre-payable (low or no prepayment penalties)</li><li>Amendment process easier and less expensive</li><li>No public disclosure</li></ul>	<ul><li>Long-term fixed rate</li><li>Longer tenor (7–10 years)</li><li>No maintenance covenants</li><li>No amortization</li><li>Broadens investor profile</li><li>Access to large, liquid debt market</li><li>Ability to do further capital raises quickly</li><li>No pledge of collateral required</li></ul>
Considerations	<ul><li>Secured by collateral</li><li>Shorter tenor (5–7 years)</li><li>Limited market capacity</li><li>Maintenance covenants</li><li>Less flexibility to incur additional senior debt</li><li>Required amortization (may be minimal)</li></ul>	<ul><li>Higher cost than bank debt</li><li>Non-callable for specified period (4–5 years)</li><li>Often limits allowable bank/senior capacity</li><li>Higher underwriting fees than bank debt</li><li>Public disclosure of financial information</li></ul>

Leveraged Buyouts

LBO FINANCING: SELECTED KEY TERMS

Both within and across the broad categories of debt instruments used in LBO financings—which we group into bank debt, high yield bonds, and mezzanine debt—there are a number of key terms that affect risk, cost, flexibility, and investor base. As shown in Exhibit 4.20 and discussed in greater detail below, these terms include *security, seniority, maturity, coupon, call protection,* and *covenants*.

EXHIBIT 4.20 Summary of Selected Key Terms

Bank Debt	High Yield Bonds	Mezzanine Debt
Secured ←	Security	→ Unsecured
Senior ←	Seniority	→ Junior
Shorter ←	Maturity	→ Longer
Lower ←	Coupon	→ Higher
More Prepayability ←	Call Protection ←	Negotiated
More Restrictive ←	Covenants	→ Less Restrictive

Security

Security refers to the pledge of, or lien on, collateral that is granted by the borrower to the holders of a given debt instrument. Collateral represents assets, property, and/or securities pledged by a borrower to secure a loan or other debt obligation, which is subject to seizure and/or liquidation in the event of a default.[50] It can include accounts receivable, inventory, PP&E, intellectual property, and securities such as the common stock of the borrower/issuer and its subsidiaries. Depending upon the volatility of the target's cash flow, creditors may require higher levels of collateral coverage as protection.

Seniority

Seniority refers to the priority status of a creditor's claims against the borrower/issuer relative to those of other creditors. Generally, seniority is achieved through either *contractual* or *structural subordination*.

---

[50] In practice, in the event a material default is not waived by a borrower/issuer's creditors, the borrower/issuer typically seeks protection under Chapter 11 of the Bankruptcy Code to continue operating as a "going concern" while it attempts to restructure its financial obligations. During bankruptcy, while secured creditors are generally stayed from enforcing their remedies, they are entitled to certain protections and rights not provided to unsecured creditors (including the right to continue to receive interest payments). Thus, obtaining collateral is beneficial to a creditor even if it does not exercise its remedies to foreclose and sell that collateral.

Contractual Subordination Contractual subordination refers to the priority status of debt instruments at the same legal entity. It is established through *subordination provisions*, which stipulate that the claims of senior creditors must be satisfied in full before those of junior creditors (generally "senior" status is limited to bank lenders or similar creditors, not trade creditors[51]). In the case of subordinated bonds, the indenture contains the subordination provisions that are relied upon by the senior creditors as "third-party" beneficiaries.[52] Exhibit 4.21 provides an illustrative diagram showing the contractual seniority of multiple debt instruments.

EXHIBIT 4.21   Contractual Subordination

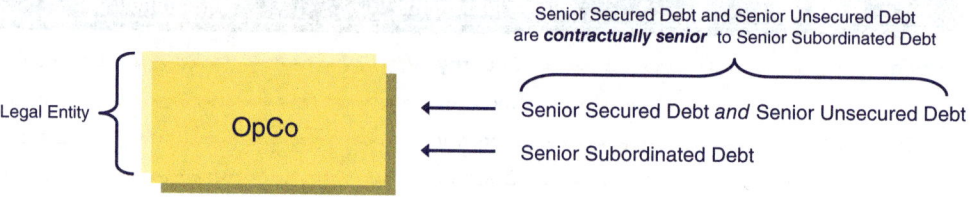

While both senior secured debt and senior unsecured debt have contractually equal debt claims (pari passu), senior secured debt may be considered "effectively" senior to the extent of the value of the collateral securing such debt.

Structural Subordination Structural subordination refers to the priority status of debt instruments at different legal entities within a company. For example, debt obligations at OpCo, where the company's assets are located, are structurally senior to debt obligations at HoldCo[53] so long as such HoldCo obligations do not benefit from a *guarantee* (credit support)[54] from OpCo. In the event of bankruptcy at OpCo, its obligations must be satisfied in full before a distribution or dividend can be made to its sole shareholder (i.e., HoldCo). Exhibit 4.22 provides an illustrative diagram showing the structural seniority of debt instruments at two legal entities.

---

[51]Suppliers and vendors owed money for goods and services provided to the company.
[52]When the transaction involves junior debt not governed by an indenture (e.g., privately placed second lien or mezzanine debt), the subordination provisions will generally be included in an *intercreditor agreement* with the senior creditors.
[53]A legal entity that owns all or a portion of the voting stock of another company/entity, in this case, OpCo.
[54]Guarantees provide credit support by one party for a debt obligation of a third party. For example, a subsidiary with actual operations and assets "guarantees" the debt, meaning that it agrees to use its cash and assets to pay debt obligations on behalf of HoldCo.

EXHIBIT 4.22 Structural Subordination

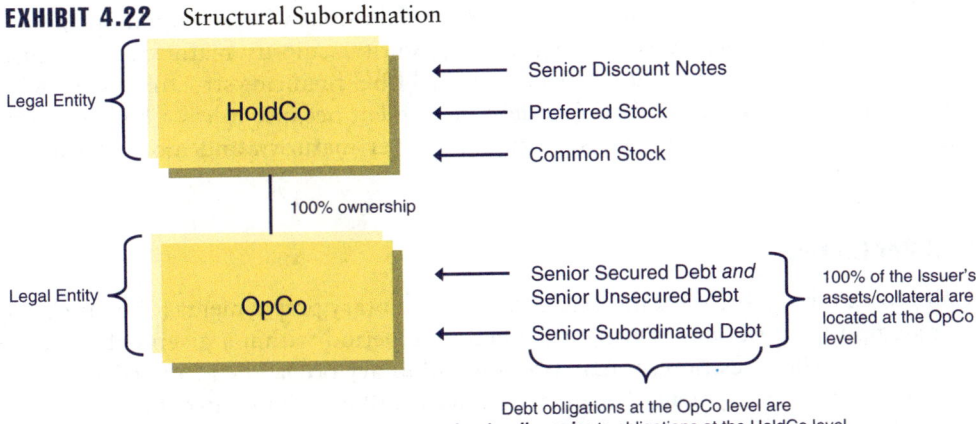

Maturity

The maturity ("tenor" or "term") of a debt obligation refers to the length of time the instrument remains outstanding until the full principal amount must be repaid. Shorter tenor debt is deemed less risky than debt with a longer maturity as it is required to be repaid earlier. Therefore, all else being equal, shorter tenor debt carries a lower cost of capital than longer tenor debt of the same credit.

In an LBO, various debt instruments with different maturities are issued to finance the debt portion of the transaction. Bank debt tends to have shorter maturities, often five to six years for revolvers and seven (or sometimes seven and one-half years) for institutional term loans. Historically, high yield bonds have had a maturity of seven to ten years. In an LBO financing structure comprising several debt instruments (e.g., a revolver, institutional term loans, and bonds), the revolver will mature before the institutional term loans, which, in turn, will mature before the bonds.

Coupon

Coupon refers to the annual interest rate ("pricing") paid on a debt obligation's principal amount outstanding. It can be based on either a floating rate (typical for bank debt) or a fixed rate (typical for bonds). Bank debt generally pays interest on a quarterly basis, while bonds generally pay interest on a semiannual basis. The bank debt coupon is typically based on a given benchmark rate, usually LIBOR or the Base Rate, plus a spread based on the credit of the borrower.[55] A high yield bond coupon, however, is generally priced at issuance on the basis of a spread to a benchmark Treasury.

---

[55]During the low interest rate environment that began in 2008, floors were often instituted on the LIBOR rate charged by lenders to borrowers. Credit facilities that include a LIBOR floor pay a coupon of LIBOR plus an applicable spread as long as LIBOR is above the stated floor level. If the current LIBOR is below the floor, the coupon is the floor level plus an applicable spread. For example, a term loan B with a coupon of L+400 bps and a 1.5% LIBOR floor would have a coupon of 5.5% as long as LIBOR remained below 150 bps. If LIBOR rose to 200 bps, the term loan would have a coupon of 6%. Pro rata term loans and ABL facilities typically do not have LIBOR floors.

There are a number of factors that affect a debt obligation's coupon, including the type of debt (and its investor class), ratings, security, seniority, maturity, covenants, and prevailing market conditions. In a traditional LBO financing structure, bank debt tends to be the lowest cost of capital debt instrument because it has a higher credit rating, first lien security, higher seniority, a shorter maturity, and more restrictive covenants than high yield bonds.

Call Protection

Call protection refers to certain restrictions on voluntary prepayments (of bank debt) or redemptions (of bonds) during a defined time period within a given debt instrument's term. These restrictions may prohibit voluntary prepayments or redemptions outright or require payment of a substantial fee ("call premium") in connection with any voluntary prepayment or redemption. Call premiums protect investors from having debt with an attractive yield refinanced long before maturity, thereby mitigating reinvestment risk in the event market interest rates decline.

Call protection periods are standard for high yield bonds. They are typically set at four years ("Non call-4" or "NC-4") for a seven/eight-year fixed rate bond and five years ("NC-5") for a ten-year fixed rate bond. The redemption of bonds prior to maturity requires the issuer to pay a premium in accordance with a defined call schedule as set forth in an indenture, which dictates call prices for set dates.[56]

A bond's call schedule and call prices depend on its term and coupon. Exhibit 4.23 displays a standard call schedule for: a) 8-year bond with an 8% coupon, and b) 10-year bond with a 10% coupon, both issued in 2012.[57]

EXHIBIT 4.23 Call Schedules

8-year, 8% Notes due 2020, NC-4			10-year, 10% Notes due 2022, NC-5		
Year	Formula	Call Price	Year	Formula	Call Price
2012 - 2015	Non-callable		2012 - 2015	Non-callable	
2016	Par plus 1/2 the coupon	$104.000	2016	Non-callable	
2017	Par plus 1/4 the coupon	$102.000	2017	Par plus 1/2 the coupon	$105.000
2018 +	Par	$100.000	2018	Par plus 1/3 the coupon	$103.333
-	-	-	2019	Par plus 1/6 the coupon	$101.667
-	-	-	2020 +	Par	$100.000

Traditional first lien bank debt has no call protection, meaning that the borrower can repay principal at any time without penalty. Other types of term loans, however,

---

[56] Redemption of bonds prior to the 1st call date requires the company to pay investors a premium, either defined in the indenture ("make-whole provision") or made in accordance with some market standard (typically a tender at the greater of par or Treasury Rate (T) + 50 bps). The tender premium calculation is based on the sum of the value of a bond's principal outstanding at the 1st call date (e.g., 105% of face value for a 10% coupon bond) plus the value of all interest payments to be received prior to the 1st call date from the present time, discounted at the Treasury Rate for an equivalent maturity plus 50 bps.

[57] High yield bonds also often feature an *equity clawback* provision, which allows the issuer to call a specified percentage of the outstanding bonds (typically 35%) with net proceeds from an equity offering at a price equal to par plus a premium equal to the coupon (e.g., 110% for a 10% coupon bond).

Leveraged Buyouts

such as those secured by a second lien, may have call protection periods, although terms vary depending on the loan.[58]

Covenants

Covenants are provisions in credit agreements and indentures intended to protect debt investors against the deterioration of the borrower/issuer's credit quality. They govern specific actions that may or may not be taken during the term of the debt obligation. Failure to comply with a covenant may trigger an event of default, which allows investors to accelerate the maturity of their debt unless amended or waived. There are three primary classifications of covenants: *affirmative*, *negative*, and *financial*.

While many of the covenants in credit agreements and indentures are similar in nature, a key difference is that traditional bank debt features financial maintenance covenants while high yield bonds have less restrictive incurrence covenants. As detailed in Exhibit 4.24, financial maintenance covenants require the borrower to "maintain" a certain credit profile at all times through compliance with certain financial ratios or tests on a quarterly basis. Financial maintenance covenants are also designed to limit the borrower's ability to take certain actions that may be adverse to lenders (e.g., making capital expenditures beyond a set amount), which allows the lender group to limit the financial risks taken by the borrower. Covenants are also designed to provide lenders with an early indication of financial distress.

Bank Debt Covenants Exhibit 4.24 displays typical covenants found in a credit agreement. With respect to financial maintenance covenants, the typical credit agreement contains two to three of these covenants. The required maintenance leverage ratios typically decrease ("step down") throughout the term of the loan. Similarly, the coverage ratios typically increase over time. This requires the borrower to improve its credit profile by repaying debt and/or growing cash flow in accordance with the financial projections it presents to lenders during syndication. "*Covenant-lite*" loans are a leveraged loan market convention that is prevalent during strong credit markets. As the name suggests, covenant-lite loans have covenant packages similar to those of high yield bonds, typically featuring incurrence covenants as opposed to quarterly financial maintenance covenants.

EXHIBIT 4.24 Bank Debt Covenants

Affirmative Covenants	Require the borrower and its subsidiaries to perform certain actions. Examples of standard affirmative covenants include:

- maintaining corporate existence and books and records
- regular financial reporting (e.g., supplying financial statements on a quarterly basis)
- maintaining assets, collateral, or other security
- maintaining insurance
- complying with laws
- paying taxes
- continuing in the same line of business

(Continued)

---

[58] For illustrative purposes, the call protection period for a second lien term loan may be structured as NC-1. At the end of one year, the loan would typically be prepayable at a price of $102, stepping down to $101 after two years, and then par after three years.

EXHIBIT 4.24 (Continued)

Negative Covenants	Limit the borrower's and its subsidiaries' ability to take certain actions (often subject to certain exceptions or "baskets").[a] Examples of negative covenants include:

- **limitations on debt** – limits the amount of debt that may be outstanding at any time
- **limitations on dividends and stock redemptions** – prevents cash from being distributed by the borrower to, or for the benefit of, equity holders
- **limitations on liens** – prevents pledge of assets as collateral
- **limitations on dispositions of assets** (including sales/leaseback transactions) – prevents the sale or transfer of assets in excess of an aggregate threshold
- **limitations on investments** – restricts the making of loans, acquisitions, and other investments (including joint ventures)
- **limitations on mergers and consolidations** – prohibits a merger or consolidation
- **limitations on prepayments of, and amendments to, certain other debt** – prohibits the prepayment of certain other debt or any amendments thereto in a manner that would be adverse to lenders
- **limitations on transactions with affiliates** – restricts the borrower and its subsidiaries from undertaking transactions with affiliated companies that may benefit the affiliate to the detriment of the borrower and its creditors[b]

Financial Maintenance Covenants	Require the borrower to maintain a certain credit profile through compliance with specified financial ratios or tests on a quarterly basis. Examples of financial maintenance covenants include:

- **maximum senior secured leverage ratio** – prohibits the ratio of senior secured debt-to-EBITDA for the trailing four quarters from exceeding a level set forth in a defined quarterly schedule
- **maximum total leverage ratio** – prohibits the ratio of total debt-to-EBITDA for the trailing four quarters from exceeding a level set in a defined quarterly schedule
- **minimum interest coverage ratio** – prohibits the ratio of EBITDA-to-interest expense for the trailing four quarters from falling below a set level as defined in a quarterly schedule
- **minimum fixed charge coverage ratio**[c] – prohibits the ratio of a measure of cash flow-to-fixed charges from falling below a set level (which may be fixed for the term of the bank debt or adjusted quarterly)
- **maximum annual capital expenditures** – prohibits the borrower and its subsidiaries from exceeding a set dollar amount of capital expenditures in any given year
- **minimum EBITDA** – requires the borrower to maintain a minimum dollar amount of EBITDA for the trailing four quarters as set forth in a defined quarterly schedule

[a] Baskets ("carve-outs") provide exceptions to covenants that permit the borrower/issuer to take specific actions (e.g., incur specific types and amounts of debt, make certain restricted payments, and sell assets up to a specified amount).

[b] Affiliate transactions must be conducted on an "arm's-length" basis (i.e., terms no less favorable than if the counterparty was unrelated).

[c] A fixed charge coverage ratio measures a borrower/issuer's ability to cover its fixed obligations, including debt interest and lease obligations. Although the definition may vary by credit agreement or indenture, fixed charges typically include interest expense, preferred stock dividends, and lease expenses (such as rent). The definition may be structured to include or exclude non-cash and capitalized interest.

Leveraged Buyouts

High Yield Bond Covenants Many of the covenants found in a high yield bond indenture are similar to those found in a bank debt credit agreement (see Exhibit 4.25). A key difference, however, is that the indenture contains incurrence covenants as opposed to maintenance covenants. Incurrence covenants prevent the issuer from taking specific actions (e.g., incurring additional debt, making certain investments, paying dividends) only in the event it is not in pro forma compliance with a "Ratio Test," or does not have certain "baskets" available to it at the time such action is taken. The Ratio Test is often a coverage test (e.g., a fixed charge coverage ratio), although it may also be structured as a leverage test (e.g., total debt-to-EBITDA) as is common for telecommunications/media companies.

EXHIBIT 4.25 High Yield Bond Covenants

High Yield Covenants	Principal covenants found in high yield bond indentures include:

- **limitations on additional debt** – ensures that the issuer cannot incur additional debt unless it is in pro forma compliance with the Ratio Test or otherwise permitted by a defined "basket"
- **limitations on restricted payments** – prohibits the issuer from making certain payments such as dividends, investments, and prepayments of junior debt except for a defined "basket" (subject to certain exceptions)[a]
- **limitations on liens** (generally senior subordinated notes allow unlimited liens on senior debt otherwise permitted to be incurred) – for senior notes, prohibits the issuer from granting liens on pari passu or junior debt without providing an equal and ratable lien in favor of the senior notes, subject to certain exceptions and/or compliance with a specified "senior secured leverage ratio"
- **limitations on asset sales** – prevents the issuer from selling assets without using net proceeds to reinvest in the business or reduce indebtedness (subject to certain exceptions)
- **limitations on transactions with affiliates** – see credit agreement definition
- **limitations on mergers, consolidations, or sale of substantially all assets** – prohibits a merger, consolidation, or sale of substantially all assets unless the surviving entity assumes the debt of the issuer and can incur $1.00 of additional debt under the Ratio Test
- **limitation on layering** (specific to indentures for senior subordinated notes) – prevents the issuer from issuing additional subordinated debt ("layering") which is senior to the existing issue
- **change of control put** (specific to indentures) – provides bondholders with the right to require the issuer to repurchase the notes at a premium of 101% of par in the event of a change in majority ownership of the company or sale of substantially all of the assets of the borrower and its subsidiaries

[a] The restricted payments basket is typically calculated as a small set dollar amount ("starting basket") plus 50% of cumulative consolidated net income of the issuer since issuance of the bonds, plus the amount of new equity issuances by the issuer since issuance of the bonds, plus cash from the sale of unrestricted subsidiaries (i.e., those that do not guarantee the debt).

Term Sheets

The key terms for the debt securities comprising an LBO financing structure are typically summarized in a one-page format, such as that shown in Exhibit 4.26 (bank debt) and Exhibit 4.28 (high yield bonds). Exhibits 4.27 and 4.29 provide explanations for the term sheet items.

EXHIBIT 4.26 Bank Debt Term Sheet

\multicolumn{2}{c}{Summary of Terms – Revolving Credit Facility and Term Loan}	
Borrower	ValueCo Corporation (the "Borrower")
Facilities	Revolving Credit Facility (the "Revolver") Term Loan B (the "Loan" and together, the "Credit Facilities")
Amount	Revolver: $250 million Loan: $2,150 million
Maturity	Revolver: 6 years Loan: 7 years
Coupon	Revolver: L+425 bps area Loan: L+450 bps area
LIBOR Floor	1.25 %
Assumed Ratings	B1 / B+
Security	Secured by first priority security interest in all assets of the Borrower and each of Borrower's direct and indirect domestic subsidiaries, including a pledge of 100% of stock of domestic subsidiaries and 65% of foreign subsidiaries
Ranking	The Credit Facilities will be a senior obligation of the Borrower and will rank pari passu in right of payment with any existing and future senior indebtedness of the Borrower, and senior to all existing and future subordinated indebtedness of the Borrower
Guarantees	All of the Borrower's direct and indirect domestic subsidiaries, whether currently existing or subsequently formed or acquired
Amortization	Revolver: None Loan: 1% per annum, with bullet at maturity
Commitment Fee	Revolver: 50 bps on the undrawn portion Loan: None
Mandatory Repayments	100% of asset sales, 100% of debt issuance, 50% of equity issuance, and 50% of excess cash flow, stepping down based on a leverage-based grid
Optional Repayments	Prepayable at any time without premium or penalty
Affirmative Covenants	Including but not limited to delivery of certified quarterly and audited annual financial statements, monthly management reports, reports to shareholders, notices of defaults, litigation, and other material events
Negative Covenants	Normal and customary for similar transactions of this nature, including, but not limited to, limitations on asset sales, acquisitions, indebtedness, capital expenditures, liens, and restricted payments
Financial Covenants	Maximum total leverage; minimum interest coverage; maximum capital expenditures
Events of Default	Including but not limited to nonpayment, breach of representations and covenants, cross-defaults, loss of lien on collateral, invalidity of guarantees, bankruptcy and insolvency events, judgments, and change of ownership or control

EXHIBIT 4.27 Explanation of Bank Debt Term Sheet

Summary of Terms – Revolving Credit Facility and Term Loan	
Borrower	Entity that is borrowing the funds
Facilities	Type of debt instruments
Amount	Principal amount of the facilities
Maturity	Timeframe in which the borrower must repay the unamortized principal
Coupon	Annual payment percentage on principal, expressed as a spread over LIBOR
LIBOR Floor	Minimum LIBOR rate paid by the borrower on the facilities, regardless of the current LIBOR
Assumed Ratings	Assumption regarding the debt instrument's credit ratings to be assigned by Moody's and Standard & Poor's
Security	Assets that become subject to seizure in default or foreclosure. These assets are registered, documented, and ranked
Ranking	Order in which the facilities are repaid in the event of default relative to the borrower's other debt instruments
Guarantees	Listing of other entities within the borrower's corporate structure that agree to satisfy its debt obligations
Amortization	Amount of principal owed above and beyond the recurring interest payments
Commitment Fee	Amount owed on the unborrowed amount of the facilities, which is paid for making the commitment available to the borrower
Mandatory Repayments	Obligations of the borrower to repay principal with cash raised from asset sales, debt or equity issuance, or excess cash flow generation
Optional Repayments	Provisions regarding premiums to be paid by the borrower in the event it decides to repay all or a portion of the facilities prior to maturity
Affirmative Covenants	Things the borrower promises to do
Negative Covenants	Things the borrower promises not to do
Financial Covenants	Financial performance metrics the borrower must maintain
Events of Default	Conditions under which the lender can demand immediate repayment of the facility

EXHIBIT 4.28 High Yield Bond Term Sheet

Summary of Terms – Senior Notes	
Issuer	ValueCo Corporation (the "Issuer")
Issue	Senior Notes (the "Notes")
Amount	$1,500 million
Maturity	8 years
Coupon	8.5% area
Assumed Ratings	B3 / B-
Security	None
Ranking	The Notes will be a senior obligation of the Issuer and will rank pari passu in right of payment with any existing and future senior indebtedness of the Issuer, and senior to all existing and future subordinated indebtedness of the Issuer
Guarantees	All of the Issuer's direct and indirect domestic subsidiaries, whether currently existing or subsequently formed or acquired
Optional Redemption	The Notes may be redeemed at the Issuer's option beginning 4 years from closing at a price of par plus premium, declining to par at the end of year 6
Equity Clawback	Within 3 years of the offering, the Issuer may repurchase up to 35% of the original principal amount of the Notes at a premium with the proceeds of an equity offering
Covenants	Standard incurrence-based high yield covenants, including limitations on: (i) debt incurrence; (ii) restricted payments; (iii) transactions with affiliates; (iv) asset sales; (v) subsidiary dividends; (vi) liens; (vii) consolidations, mergers and asset sales
Change of control	Upon a change of control, the Issuer will offer to repurchase the Notes at 101% of par

EXHIBIT 4.29 Explanation of High Yield Bond Term Sheet

Summary of Terms – Senior Notes	
Issuer	Same as "Borrower"
Issue	Type of debt offering
Amount	Same as bank debt
Maturity	Same as bank debt
Coupon	Same as bank debt, except it is typically a fixed rate
Assumed Ratings	Same as bank debt
Security	Same as bank debt
Ranking	Same as bank debt
Guarantees	Same as bank debt
Optional Redemption	The redemption of bonds prior to maturity requires the issuer to pay a premium in accordance with a defined call schedule as set forth in an indenture, which dictates call prices for set dates
Equity Clawback	Allows the issuer to repay up to 35% of the bond's principal with the proceeds from an IPO within a set time period. The prepayment penalty is typically set at par plus the coupon
Covenants	Prevents the issuer from taking specific actions (e.g., incurring additional debt, making certain investments, paying dividends) in the event it is not in pro forma compliance with a Ratio Test, or does not have certain "baskets" available to it at the time such action is taken
Change of control	Requires the issuer to make an offer to repurchase the bonds at 101% of principal amount in the event of a change in ownership of the company

LBO FINANCING: DETERMINING FINANCING STRUCTURE

As with valuation, determining the appropriate LBO financing structure involves a mix of art and science. This structuring exercise centers on fundamental company-specific cash flow, returns, and credit statistics analysis, as well as market conditions and precedent LBO deals. The fundamental analysis is akin to the DCF approach to intrinsic valuation, while market conditions and precedent LBO deals are similar to comparable companies and precedent transactions.

The ultimate LBO financing structure must balance the needs of the financial sponsor, debt investors, the company, and management, which are not necessarily aligned. For example, the sponsor often seeks to maximize leverage so as to generate the highest IRR. Lenders and bondholders, on the other hand, have an interest in limiting leverage as well as introducing covenants and other provisions to protect their principal. The company's best interests often reside with more moderate leverage from both a risk management and growth perspective. Meanwhile, depending on the situation, management is often both a meaningful shareholder aligned with the sponsor in the pursuit of maximum IRRs, as well as a caretaker of the company focused on mitigating risk and preserving flexibility.

Structuring an LBO is predicated on analyzing the target's cash flows and credit statistics, including leverage and coverage ratios as discussed in Chapter 1. This analysis centers on crafting a financing structure that provides high leverage while maintaining sufficient cushion and room to maneuver in a downside scenario. Target credit statistics vary substantially depending on sector, market conditions, and the company's individual credit profile (including size, market position, and profitability).

The target's sector plays a key role in determining the appropriate LBO structure, as reflected in total leverage, bank debt/high yield bond mix, and terms of the debt. Sector is directly relevant to the target's credit profile and ability to sustain an aggressive capital structure. For example, as shown in Exhibit 4.30, for highly cyclical industries, both the capital markets and rating agencies take a more conservative view towards leverage to help ensure the company is appropriately capitalized to withstand cycle troughs. On the other end of the spectrum, companies in sectors that have highly visible cash flows (especially those with subscription-based business models) are typically able to maintain a more highly leveraged capital structure. Of course, sector is only one aspect of the target's credit story. Within a given sector, there are multiple company-specific factors that can dramatically differentiate the risk profile of one company from another.

EXHIBIT 4.30 Illustrative Sector Leverage Dynamics

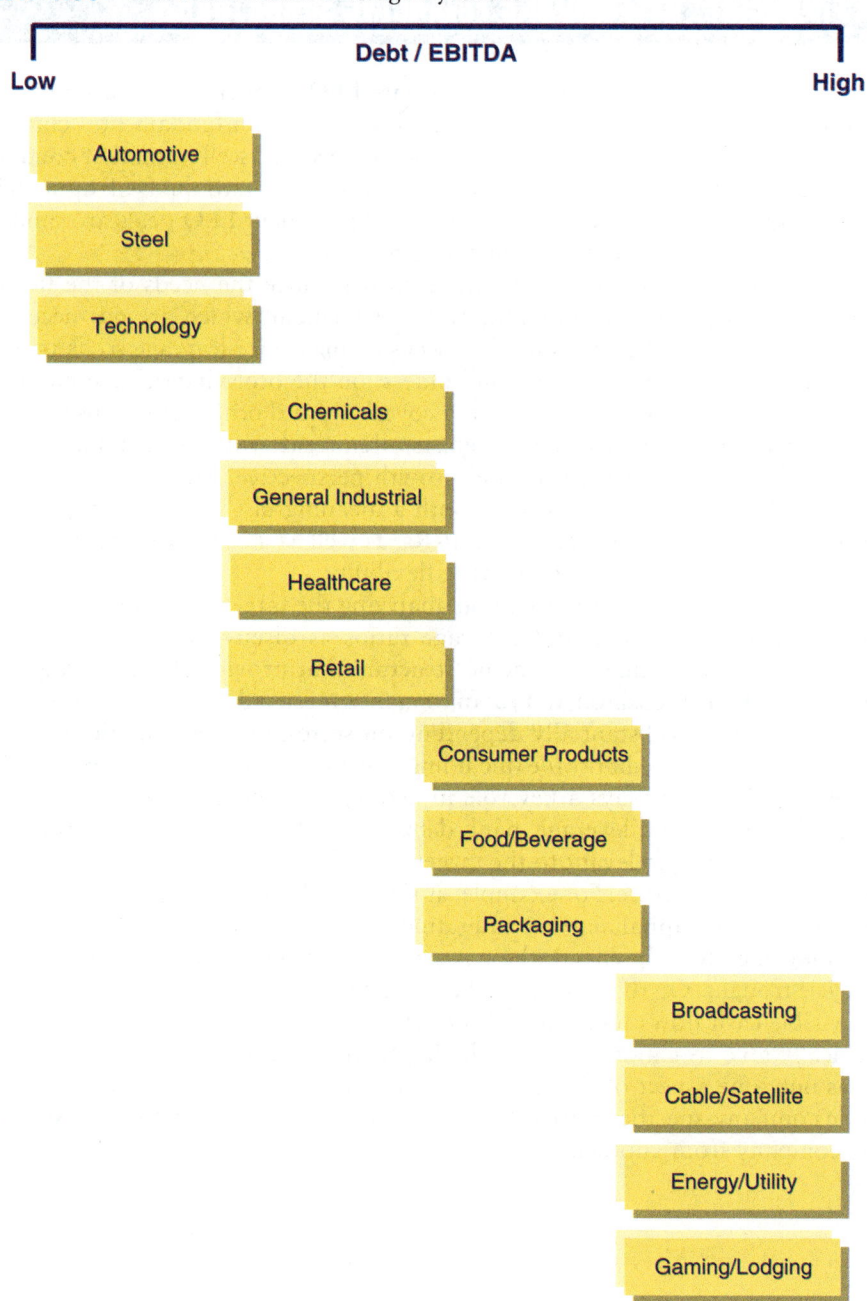

As with comparable companies and precedent transactions for valuation multiples, prevailing market conditions and precedent LBO deals play a critical role in determining leverage multiples and key financing terms. Leveraged finance professionals analyze recent LBO transactions to help determine what the market will bear in terms of financing structures for new deals. Recent LBOs in the target's sector are most relevant as well as deals of similar size and rating, as shown in Exhibit 4.31.

EXHIBIT 4.31 Recent LBO Transactions > $1 Billion Purchase Price

ValueCo Corporation
Recent LBO Transactions > $1 Billion Purchase Price
($ in millions)

Launch / Pricing	Borrower / Issuer	Size	Coupon	Description	Tenor	LIBOR Floor	Price	Yield	Moody's	S&P	Purchase Price	Sec.	Total	Equity	Sector	Sponsor
7/23/2012	C-town City	$400	L+175	ABL Revolver	5.0 year	-	-	-	B1	B	$2,700	4.1x	6.5x	32%	Retail	Damodaran Investment Partners
		$1,125	L+450	Term Loan B (Cov Lite)	7.0 year	1.25%	$99.000	6.000%	B1	B						
		$700	8.875%	Senior Notes	8.0 year	-	$100.000	8.875%	Caa1	CCC+						
	Owns, operates, and franchises specialty party goods stores in the United States and Puerto Rico
6/21/2012	Neren Industries	$350	L+450	Revolver	6.0 year	1.25%	$99.000	6.000%	B2	B	$8,075	3.0x	5.2x	35%	Chemicals	Domanski Capital
		$3,000	L+450	Term Loan B	7.0 year	1.25%	$99.000	6.000%	B2	B						
		$2,250	8.500%	Senior Notes	8.0 year	-	$100.000	10.000%	B3	B-						
	Specialty chemical company which supplies technologies and produces additives, ingredients, resins, and compounds
5/24/2012	Total Management	$125	L+550	Revolver	5.0 year	1.25%	$97.000	8.000%	B1	B+	$3,000	3.4x	5.4x	43%	Technology	Julis Capital Partners
		$1,050	L+550	Term Loan B	6.5 year	1.25%	$97.000	8.000%	B1	B+						
		$650	10.675%	Senior Notes	7.0 year	-	$99.350	10.789%	Caa1	CCC+						
	Provides cloud-based property management software for residential, commercial, and student housing property management companies
5/24/2012	Allan Builders Supply	$175	-	ABL Revolver	5.0 year	-	-	-	-	-	$1,430	3.1x	5.2x	30%	Industrials	Margo Equity Partners
		$600	L+525	Term Loan B (Cov Lite)	7.0 year	1.25%	$99.000	6.750%	B2	B						
		$1,000	10.000%	Senior Notes	8.0 year	-	$100.000	10.000%	B3	B-						
	Offers residential products that include shingles, tiles and specialty products, cement siding products, vinyl decking products, decorative stones, skylights, hatches, wood products, and accessories
4/15/2012	Whalen Inc.	$100	L+525	Revolver	6.0 year	1.25%	$99.000	6.750%	B2	B	$1,350	2.8x	4.4x	41%	Chemicals	The Hochberg Group
		$500	L+525	Term Loan B (Cov Lite)	7.0 year	1.25%	$99.000	6.750%	B2	B						
		$300	10.000%	Senior Notes	8.0 year	-	$100.000	10.000%	B3	B-						
	World's largest producer of alkylamines and derivatives
4/10/2012	JP Energy	$375	L+200	ABL Revolver	5.0 year	-	-	-	Ba3	BB-	$6,150	1.7x	3.5x	41%	Energy	J Harris & Company
		$800	L+525	Term Loan B (Cov Lite)	6.0 year	1.25%	$99.000	6.875%	Ba3	BB-						
		$800	6.875%	2nd Lien Notes	7.0 year	-	$100.000	6.875%	Ba3	BB-						
		$2,000	9.375%	Senior Notes	8.0 year	-	$100.000	9.375%	B2	B-						
	Engages in exploring for acquiring, developing, and producing oil and natural gas in North America
9/4/2011	Rughwani International	$175	L+500	Revolver	5.0 year	1.25%	$98.500	6.625%	Ba3	BB-	$4,340	2.7x	4.5x	42%	Chemicals	Eu-Han Capital
		$1,500	L+500	Term Loan B (Cov Lite)	7.0 year	1.25%	$98.500	6.625%	Ba3	BB-						
		$1,000	9.500%	Senior Notes	8.0 year	-	$100.000	9.500%	B3	B-						
	Supplies products for the manufacturing, construction, automotive, chemical processing, and other industries worldwide
8/17/2011	MashaCor	$100	L+575	Revolver	5.0 year	1.50%	$96.000	8.250%	Ba3	BB-	$1,725	3.9x	6.6x	42%	Healthcare	Grisha Capital
		$600	L+575	Term Loan B	7.0 year	1.50%	$96.000	8.250%	Ba3	BB-						
		$400	11.125%	Senior Notes	8.0 year	-	$98.715	11.375%	Caa1	B-						
	Manufactures reagents and systems used by hospitals, laboratories, and donor centers to detect and identify certain properties of the cell and serum components of blood prior to transfusion
6/24/2011	Ronie Industries	$110	L+525	Revolver	5.0 year	1.50%	$99.000	6.750%	Ba3	BB-	$2,615	3.9x	6.3x	43%	Industrials	D&R Ltd
		$920	L+525	Term Loan B	7.0 year	1.50%	$99.000	6.750%	Ba3	BB-						
		$575	10.500%	Senior Notes	8.0 year	-	$100.000	10.500%	B3	B-						
	Designs and manufactures injection molding equipment to the plastics industry worldwide
11/19/2010	Kamras Brands	$100	L+575	Revolver	5.0 year	1.50%	$96.000	8.250%	Ba3	BB-	$2,115	2.2x	3.9x	50%	Materials	Meisner Global Management
		$600	L+575	Term Loan B	7.0 year	1.50%	$96.000	8.250%	Ba3	BB-						
		$450	11.125%	Senior Notes	8.0 year	-	$98.715	11.375%	Caa1	B-						
	Manufactures and markets basic chemicals, vinyls, polymers, and fabricated building products
Mean											**$3,350**	**3.1x**	**5.2x**	**40%**		
Median											**$2,658**	**3.0x**	**5.2x**	**42%**		
High											**$8,075**	**4.1x**	**6.6x**	**50%**		
Low											**$1,350**	**1.7x**	**3.5x**	**30%**		

Source: Company filings

At the same time, current market conditions for bank debt and high yield bonds need to be closely monitored throughout the LBO process, especially as the commitment letters are finalized. The leveraged finance markets can be volatile with "market-clearing" terms often changing quickly, potentially rendering recent precedents meaningless. As shown in Exhibits 4.32 to 4.33 regarding historical issuance volumes and pricing, there are clear market windows where issuers have been able to take advantage of strong market conditions interspersed with more challenging periods. Even in the post-crisis 2010 – 2012 period, there have been dramatic fluctuations in the state of the leveraged loan and high yield markets as demonstrated by pricing volatility (see Exhibits 4.34 and 4.35).

At a given point in time, investment banking professionals look at new issue volumes, trading levels by ratings categories, and trading levels for comparable debt securities to determine the state of the markets. Once the initial financing structure is determined, it is run through the LBO model and sensitized to analyze IRRs and pro forma credit metrics, as discussed in Chapter 5. Adjustments are then made to fine-tune as appropriate.

EXHIBIT 4.32 Leveraged Loan New Issue Volume 2003 – 2012

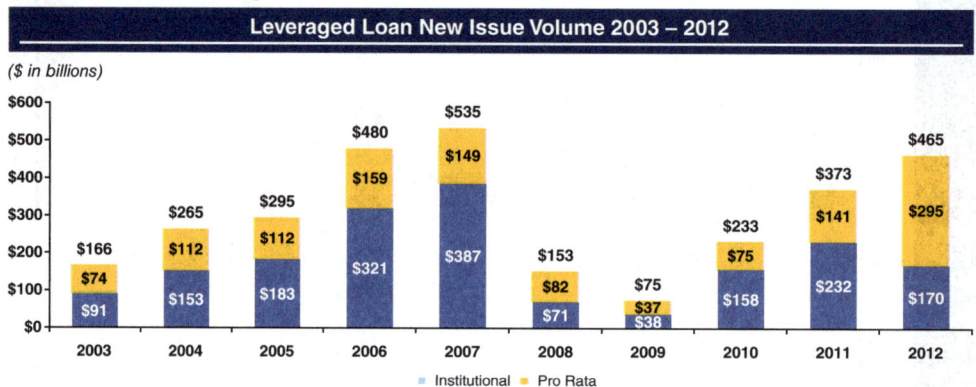

Source: Standard & Poor's Leveraged Commentary & Data Group

EXHIBIT 4.33 High Yield New Issue Volume 2003 – 2012

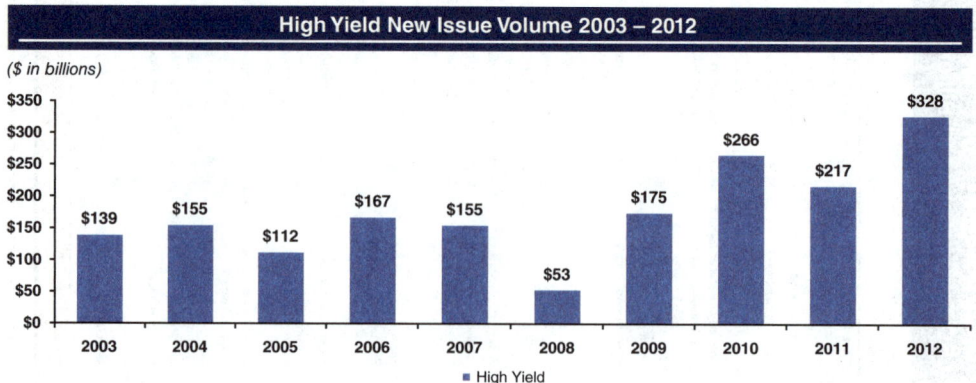

Source: Standard & Poor's Leveraged Commentary & Data Group

Leveraged Buyouts

EXHIBIT 4.34 Leveraged Loan Spreads by Ratings Category 2010 – 2012

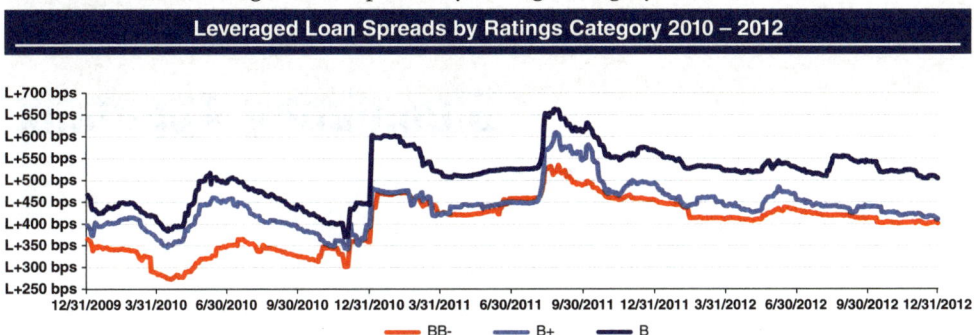

Source: Standard & Poor's Leveraged Commentary & Data Group

EXHIBIT 4.35 High Yield Index by Ratings Index 2010 – 2012

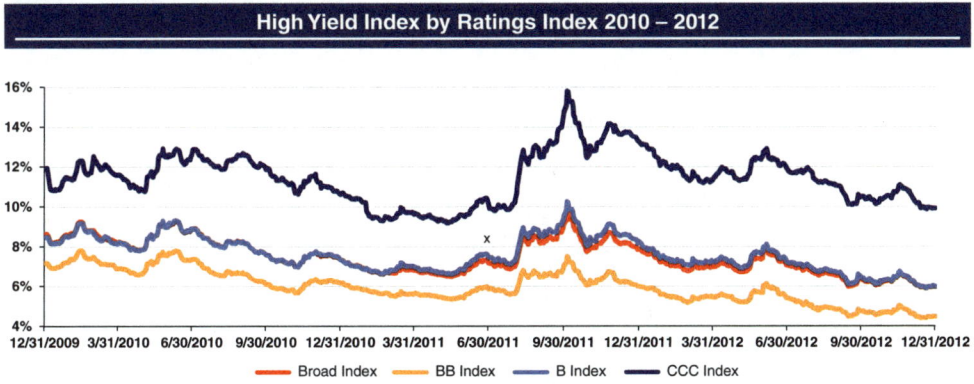

Source: Standard & Poor's Leveraged Commentary & Data Group

Bloomberg Appendix

APPENDIX 4.1 Bloomberg Screening Tool for LBO Candidates—Transaction Ideas (IBTI<GO>)

91) Export to Excel		92) Custom Screening (EQS)		99) Feedback		Transaction Ideas		
	Filter	Industry	Chemicals				24 securities in USD	
Themes		Company Name	EV/(EBITDA – Capex)	Market Cap	EV	Total Debt	Cash	
Refinancing								
3) Debt Maturity in FY		100) Company A	7.9	12.7B	12.4B	1.6B	2.3B	
4) Average Coupon		101) Company B	7.9	380.5M	689.7M	452.2M	143.0M	
5) Total Leverage		102) Company C	7.8	1.9B	2.4B	713.7M	165.2M	
		103) Company D	7.8	73.8B	99.0B	25.5B	13.7B	
M&A Targets		104) Company E	7.7	431.9M	350.8M	16.6M	70.7M	
6) EV / EBITDA		105) Company F	7.6	35.0B	36.7B	4.4B	2.7B	
7) EV / Cash Flow		106) Company G	7.6	14.0B	14.5B	2.0B	1.8B	
8) Price / Book		107) Company H	7.2	278.8M	640.1M	505.1M	154.9M	
		108) Company I	7.2	417.9M	569.3M	181.0M	27.9M	
Cash Balances		109) Company J	7.1	325.2M	303.7M	19.6M	41.9M	
9) Net Cash		110) Company K	6.7	966.1M	1.5B	636.9M	123.1M	
10) Cash / Debt		111) Company L	6.6	549.6M	353.2M	0.0	114.6M	
11) Cash / Mkt Cap		112) Company M	6.5	2.0B	2.2B	437.6M	110.9M	
		113) Company N	6.5	1.1B	809.9M	7.3M	425.2M	
Distressed		114) Company O	6.1	3.9B	4.3B	560.4M	200.3M	
12) 1 Yr Default Risk		115) Company P	6.0	844.1M	1.2B	363.5M	206.9M	
13) Abs. CDS Rate		116) Company Q	5.8	374.9M	1.3B	956.4M	29.7M	

90) Edit Screen Criteria

EV (M) between 300 and 1000000

EV / (EBITDA – Capex) between 0 - 8   1) Update   2) Restore

CHAPTER 5

LBO Analysis

LBO analysis is the core analytical tool used to assess financing structure, investment returns, and valuation in leveraged buyout scenarios. The same techniques can also be used to assess refinancing opportunities and restructuring alternatives for corporate issuers. LBO analysis is a more complex methodology than those previously discussed in this book as it requires specialized knowledge of financial modeling, leveraged debt capital markets, M&A, and accounting. At the center of an LBO analysis is a financial model (the "LBO model"), which is constructed with the flexibility to analyze a given target's performance under multiple financing structures and operating scenarios.

Financing Structure

On the debt financing side, the banker uses LBO analysis to help craft a viable financing structure for the target, which encompasses the amount and type of debt (including key terms outlined in Chapter 4) as well as an equity contribution from a financial sponsor. The model output enables the banker to analyze a given financing structure on the basis of cash flow generation, debt repayment, credit statistics, and investment returns over a projection period.

The analysis of an LBO financing structure is typically spearheaded by an investment bank's leveraged finance and capital market teams (along with a sector coverage team, collectively the "deal team"). The goal is to present a financial sponsor with tailored financing options that maximize returns while remaining marketable to investors. The financing structure must also provide the target with sufficient flexibility and cushion to run its business according to plan.

As discussed in Chapter 4, sponsors typically work closely with financing providers (e.g., investment banks) to determine the financing structure for a particular transaction. Once the sponsor chooses the preferred financing structure (often a compilation of the best terms from proposals solicited from several banks), the deal team presents it to the bank's internal credit committee(s) for approval. Following committee approval, the investment banks typically provide a financing commitment, which is then submitted to the seller and its advisor(s) as part of its final bid package (see Chapter 6).

Valuation

LBO analysis is also an essential component of an M&A toolset. It is used by sponsors, bankers, and other finance professionals to determine an implied valuation range for a given target in a potential LBO sale based on achieving acceptable returns. The valuation output is premised on key variables such as financial projections, purchase price, and financing structure, as well as exit multiple and year. Therefore, sensitivity analysis is performed on these key value drivers to produce a range of IRRs used to frame valuation for the target (see Exhibits 5.42 and 5.43). As discussed in Chapter 4, sponsors have historically used 20%+ IRRs to assess acquisition opportunities and determine valuation accordingly.

In an M&A sell-side advisory context, the banker conducts LBO analysis to assess valuation from the perspective of a financial sponsor. This provides the ability to set sale price expectations for the seller and guide negotiations with prospective buyers accordingly. Similarly, on buy-side engagements, the banker typically performs LBO analysis to help determine a purchase price range. For a strategic buyer, this analysis (along with those derived from other valuation methodologies) is used to frame valuation and bidding strategy by analyzing the price that a competing sponsor bidder might be willing to pay for the target.

The goal of this chapter is to provide a sound introduction to LBO analysis and its broad applications. While there are multiple approaches to performing this analysis (especially with regard to constructing the LBO model), we have designed the steps in Exhibit 5.1 to be as user-friendly as possible. We also perform an illustrative LBO analysis using ValueCo as our LBO target.

EXHIBIT 5.1 LBO Analysis Steps

Step I.	Locate and Analyze the Necessary Information
Step II.	Build the Pre-LBO Model
	a. Build Historical and Projected Income Statement through EBIT
	b. Input Opening Balance Sheet and Project Balance Sheet Items
	c. Build Cash Flow Statement through Investing Activities
Step III.	Input Transaction Structure
	a. Enter Purchase Price Assumptions
	b. Enter Financing Structure into Sources and Uses
	c. Link Sources and Uses to Balance Sheet Adjustments Columns
Step IV.	Complete the Post-LBO Model
	a. Build Debt Schedule
	b. Complete Pro Forma Income Statement from EBIT to Net Income
	c. Complete Pro Forma Balance Sheet
	d. Complete Pro Forma Cash Flow Statement
Step V.	Perform the LBO Analysis
	a. Analyze Financing Structure
	b. Perform Returns Analysis
	c. Determine Valuation
	d. Create Transaction Summary Page

Once the above steps are completed, all the essential outputs are linked to a transaction summary page that serves as the cover page of the LBO model (see Exhibit 5.2). This page allows the deal team to quickly review and spot-check the analysis and make adjustments to the purchase price, financing structure, operating assumptions,

ValueCo Corporation
Leveraged Buyout Analysis
($ in millions, fiscal year ending December 31)

Financing Structure: Structure 1
Operating Scenario: Base

Transaction Summary

	Sources of Funds						Uses of Funds			Purchase Price		Return Analysis	
	Amount	% of Total Sources	Multiple of EBITDA 9/30/2012	Cumulative	Pricing			Amount	% of Total Uses	Offer Price per Share	-	Exit Year	2017
Revolving Credit Facility	-	-%	-x	-x	L+425 bps	Purchase ValueCo Equity		$4,350.0	72.5%	Fully Diluted Shares	-	Entry Multiple	8.0x
Term Loan A	-	-%	-x	-x	NA	Repay Existing Debt		1,500.0	25.0%	Equity Purchase Price	$4,350.0	Exit Multiple	8.0x
Term Loan B	2,150.0	35.8%	3.1x	3.1x	L+450 bps	Tender / Call Premiums		20.0	0.3%	Plus: Existing Net Debt	1,250.0	IRR	20%
Term Loan C	-	-%	-x	3.1x	NA	Financing Fees		90.0	1.5%	**Enterprise Value**	**$5,600.0**	**Cash Return**	**2.5x**
2nd Lien	-	-%	-x	3.1x	NA	Other Fees and Expenses		40.0	0.7%				
Senior Notes	1,500.0	25.0%	2.1x	5.2x	8.500%							**Options**	
Senior Subordinated Notes	-	-%	-x	5.2x	NA					**Transaction Multiples**			
Equity Contribution	2,100.0	35.0%	3.0x	8.2x						Enterprise Value / Sales		**Financing Structure**	1
Rollover Equity	-	-%	-x	8.2x						LTM 9/30/2012	$3,385.0	**Operating Scenario**	1.7x
Cash on Hand	250.0	4.2%	0.4x	8.6x						2012E	3,450.0	**Cash Flow Sweep**	1.6x
Total Sources	**$6,000.0**	**100.0%**	**8.6x**			**Total Uses**		**$6,000.0**	**100.0%**	Enterprise Value / EBITDA		**Cash Balance**	
										LTM 9/30/2012	$700.0	**Average Interest**	8.0x
										2012E	725.0	**Financing Fees**	7.7x

Summary Financial Data

	Historical Period			LTM	Pro forma				Projection Period						
	2009	2010	2011	9/30/2012	2012	Year 1 2013	Year 2 2014	Year 3 2015	Year 4 2016	Year 5 2017	Year 6 2018	Year 7 2019	Year 8 2020	Year 9 2021	Year 10 2022
Sales	$2,600.0	$2,900.0	$3,200.0	$3,385.0	$3,450.0	$3,708.8	$3,931.3	$4,127.8	$4,293.0	$4,421.7	$4,554.4	$4,691.0	$4,831.8	$4,976.7	$5,126.0
% growth	NA	11.5%	10.3%	NA	7.8%	7.5%	6.0%	5.0%	4.0%	3.0%	3.0%	3.0%	3.0%	3.0%	3.0%
Gross Profit	$988.0	$1,131.0	$1,280.0	$1,350.0	$1,380.0	$1,483.5	$1,572.5	$1,651.1	$1,717.2	$1,768.7	$1,821.8	$1,876.4	$1,932.7	$1,990.7	$2,050.4
% margin	38.0%	39.0%	40.0%	39.9%	40.0%	40.0%	40.0%	40.0%	40.0%	40.0%	40.0%	40.0%	40.0%	40.0%	40.0%
EBITDA	$491.4	$580.0	$672.0	$700.0	$725.0	$779.4	$826.1	$867.4	$902.1	$929.2	$957.1	$985.8	$1,015.4	$1,045.8	$1,077.2
% margin	18.9%	20.0%	21.0%	20.7%	21.0%	21.0%	21.0%	21.0%	21.0%	21.0%	21.0%	21.0%	21.0%	21.0%	21.0%
Capital Expenditures	136.4	114.0	144.0	152.3	155.3	166.9	176.9	185.8	193.2	199.0	204.9	211.1	217.4	224.0	230.7
% sales	5.2%	3.9%	4.5%	4.5%	4.5%	4.5%	4.5%	4.5%	4.5%	4.5%	4.5%	4.5%	4.5%	4.5%	4.5%
Cash Interest Expense						246.6	233.7	218.7	201.7	182.8	163.6	141.2	128.9	128.9	128.9
Total Interest Expense						258.6	245.7	230.7	213.7	194.7	175.6	152.5	135.7	128.9	128.9
Free Cash Flow															
EBITDA						$779.4	$826.1	$867.4	$902.1	$929.2	$957.1	$985.8	$1,015.4	$1,045.8	$1,077.2
Less: Cash Interest Expense						(246.6)	(233.7)	(218.7)	(201.7)	(182.8)	(163.6)	(141.2)	(128.9)	(128.9)	(128.9)
Plus: Interest Income						-	-	-	-	-	-	-	1.1	3.2	5.4
Less: Income Taxes						(113.3)	(130.9)	(147.8)	(163.7)	(178.3)	(193.1)	(209.7)	(224.5)	(236.2)	(245.5)
Less: Capital Expenditures						(166.9)	(176.9)	(185.8)	(193.2)	(199.0)	(204.9)	(211.1)	(217.4)	(224.0)	(230.7)
Less: Increase in Net Working Capital						(47.6)	(41.0)	(36.2)	(30.1)	(23.7)	(24.4)	(25.1)	(25.9)	(26.7)	(27.5)
Free Cash Flow						**$204.9**	**$243.6**	**$278.9**	**$313.1**	**$345.5**	**$371.0**	**$398.7**	**$419.7**	**$433.3**	**$450.0**
Cumulative Free Cash Flow						204.9	448.5	727.4	1,040.6	1,386.1	1,757.1	2,155.8	2,575.4	3,008.8	3,458.8

Capitalization

Cash												$5.8	$425.4	$858.8	$1,308.8
Revolving Credit Facility															
Term Loan A															
Term Loan B						2,150.0	1,945.1	1,701.5	1,422.6	1,109.4	763.9	392.9	-	-	-
Term Loan C															
Existing Term Loan															
2nd Lien															
Other Debt															
Total Senior Secured Debt						**$2,150.0**	**$1,945.1**	**$1,701.5**	**$1,422.6**	**$1,109.4**	**$763.9**	**$392.9**	**-x**	**-x**	**-x**
Senior Notes						1,500.0	1,500.0	1,500.0	1,500.0	1,500.0	1,500.0	1,500.0	1,500.0	1,500.0	1,500.0
Total Senior Debt						**$3,650.0**	**$3,445.1**	**$3,201.5**	**$2,922.6**	**$2,609.4**	**$2,263.9**	**$1,892.9**	**$1,500.0**	**$1,500.0**	**$1,500.0**
Senior Subordinated Notes															
Total Debt						**$3,650.0**	**$3,445.1**	**$3,201.5**	**$2,922.6**	**$2,609.4**	**$2,263.9**	**$1,892.9**	**$1,500.0**	**$1,500.0**	**$1,500.0**
Shareholders' Equity						2,040.0	2,224.9	2,438.5	2,679.7	2,946.9	3,237.8	3,552.9	3,895.0	4,261.4	4,646.7	5,047.3
Total Capitalization						**$5,690.0**	**$5,670.0**	**$5,640.0**	**$5,602.3**	**$5,556.3**	**$5,501.7**	**$5,445.8**	**$5,395.0**	**$5,761.4**	**$6,146.7**	**$6,547.3**
% of Bank Debt Repaid						9.5%	20.9%	33.8%	48.4%	64.5%	81.7%	100.0%	100.0%	100.0%	100.0%

Credit Statistics

% Debt / Total Capitalization				64.1%		60.8%	56.8%	52.2%	47.0%	41.1%	34.8%	27.8%	26.0%	24.4%	22.9%
EBITDA / Cash Interest Expense				2.9x		3.2x	3.5x	4.0x	4.5x	5.1x	5.8x	7.0x	7.9x	8.1x	8.4x
(EBITDA - Capex) / Cash Interest Expense				2.3x		2.5x	2.8x	3.1x	3.5x	4.0x	4.6x	5.5x	6.2x	6.4x	6.6x
EBITDA / Total Interest Expense				2.7x		3.0x	3.4x	3.8x	4.2x	4.8x	5.5x	6.5x	7.5x	8.1x	8.4x
(EBITDA - Capex) / Total Interest Expense				2.2x		2.4x	2.6x	3.0x	3.3x	3.7x	4.3x	5.1x	5.9x	6.4x	6.6x
Senior Secured Debt / EBITDA				3.0x		2.5x	2.1x	1.6x	1.2x	0.8x	0.4x	-x	-x	-x	-x
Senior Debt / EBITDA				5.0x		4.4x	3.9x	3.4x	2.9x	2.4x	2.0x	1.5x	1.5x	1.4x	1.4x
Total Debt / EBITDA				5.0x		4.4x	3.9x	3.4x	2.9x	2.4x	2.0x	1.5x	1.5x	1.4x	1.4x
Net Debt / EBITDA				5.0x		4.4x	3.9x	3.4x	2.9x	2.4x	2.0x	1.5x	1.1x	0.6x	0.2x

EXHIBIT 5.2 LBO Model Transaction Summary Page

and other key inputs as necessary. It also includes the toggle cells that allow the banker to switch between various financing structures and operating scenarios, among other functions.[1] The fully completed model (including all assumptions pages) is shown in Exhibits 5.46 to 5.54.

STEP I. LOCATE AND ANALYZE THE NECESSARY INFORMATION

When performing LBO analysis, the first step is to collect, organize, and analyze all available information on the target, its sector, and the specifics of the transaction. In an organized sale process, the sell-side advisor provides such detail to prospective buyers, including financial projections that usually form the basis for the initial LBO model (see Chapter 6). This information is typically contained in a CIM, with additional information provided via a management presentation and data room, such as those provided by Intralinks (see Exhibit 6.7). For public targets, this information is supplemented by SEC filings, research reports, and other public sources as described in previous chapters.

In the absence of a CIM or supplemental company information (e.g., if the target is not being actively sold), the banker must rely upon public sources to perform preliminary due diligence and develop an initial set of financial projections. This task is invariably easier for a public company than a private company (see Chapter 3).

Regardless of whether there is a formal sale process, it is important for the banker to independently verify as much information as possible about the target and its sector. Public filings as well as equity and fixed income research on the target (if applicable) and its comparables are particularly important resources. In their absence, news runs, trade publications, and even a simple internet search on a given company or sector and its competitive dynamics may provide valuable information. Within an investment bank, the deal team also relies on the judgment and experience of its sector coverage bankers to provide insight on the target.

STEP II. BUILD THE PRE-LBO MODEL

In Step II, we provide detailed step-by-step instructions (see Exhibit 5.3) on how to build the standalone ("pre-LBO") operating model for our illustrative target company, ValueCo, assuming that the primary financial assumptions are obtained from a CIM. The pre-LBO model is a basic three-statement financial projection model (income statement, balance sheet, and cash flow statement) that initially excludes the effects of the LBO transaction. The incorporation of the LBO financing structure and the resulting pro forma effects are detailed in Steps III and IV.

---

[1]Toggles may also be created to activate the 100% cash flow sweep, cash balance sweep, average interest expense option, or other deal-specific toggles.

EXHIBIT 5.3 Pre-LBO Model Steps

> Step II(a): Build Historical and Projected Income Statement through EBIT
> Step II(b): Input Opening Balance Sheet and Project Balance Sheet Items
> Step II(c): Build Cash Flow Statement through Investing Activities

Step II(a): Build Historical and Projected Income Statement through EBIT

The banker typically begins the pre-LBO model by inputting the target's historical income statement information for the prior three-year period, if available. The historical income statement is generally only built through EBIT, as the target's prior annual interest expense and net income are not relevant given that the target will be recapitalized through the LBO. As with the DCF, historical financial performance should be shown on a pro forma basis for non-recurring items and recent events. This provides a normalized basis for projecting and analyzing future financial performance.

Management projections for sales through EBIT, as provided in the CIM, are then entered into an assumptions page (see Exhibit 5.52), which feeds into the projected income statement until other operating scenarios are developed/provided. This scenario is typically labeled as "Management Case." At this point, the line items between EBIT and earnings before taxes (EBT) are intentionally left blank, to be completed once a financing structure is entered into the model and a *debt schedule* is built (see Exhibit 5.29). In ValueCo's case, although it has an existing $1,000 million term loan and $500 million of senior notes (see Exhibit 5.5), it is not necessary to model the associated interest expense (or mandatory amortization) as it will be refinanced as part of the LBO transaction.

From a debt financing perspective, the projection period for an LBO model is typically set at seven to ten years so as to match the maturity of the longest tenured debt instrument in the capital structure.[2] A financial sponsor, however, may only use a five-year projection period in its internal LBO model so as to match its expectations for the anticipated investment horizon. As a CIM typically only provides five years of projected income statement data,[3] it is common for the banker to freeze the Year 5 growth rate and margin assumptions to frame the outer year projections (in the absence of specific guidance). As shown in ValueCo's pre-LBO income statement (Exhibit 5.4), we held Year 5 sales growth rate, gross margin, and EBITDA margin constant at 3%, 40%, and 21%, respectively, to drive projections in Years 6 through 10.

---

[2] A typical LBO model is built with the flexibility to accommodate a ten-year maturity, which is more common for senior subordinated notes and mezzanine financing. In this chapter, we assume the 8-year senior notes are refinanced at maturity.

[3] The length of the projection period provided in a CIM (or through another medium) may vary depending on the situation.

EXHIBIT 5.4 ValueCo Pre-LBO Income Statement

($ in millions, fiscal year ending December 31)

Income Statement

	Historical Period			LTM	Pro forma						Projection Period					
	2009	2010	2011	9/30/2012	2012	Year 1 2013	Year 2 2014	Year 3 2015	Year 4 2016	Year 5 2017	Year 6 2018	Year 7 2019	Year 8 2020	Year 9 2021	Year 10 2022
Sales	$2,600.0	$2,900.0	$3,200.0	$3,385.0	$3,450.0	$3,708.8	$3,931.3	$4,127.8	$4,293.0	$4,421.7	$4,554.4	$4,691.0	$4,831.8	$4,976.7	$5,126.0
% growth	NA	11.5%	10.3%	NA	7.8%	7.5%	6.0%	5.0%	4.0%	3.0%	3.0%	3.0%	3.0%	3.0%	3.0%
Cost of Goods Sold	1,612.0	1,769.0	1,920.0	2,035.0	2,070.0	2,225.3	2,358.8	2,476.7	2,575.8	2,653.0	2,732.6	2,814.6	2,899.1	2,986.0	3,075.6
Gross Profit	$988.0	$1,131.0	$1,280.0	$1,350.0	$1,380.0	$1,483.5	$1,572.5	$1,651.1	$1,717.2	$1,768.7	$1,821.8	$1,876.4	$1,932.7	$1,990.7	$2,050.4
% margin	38.0%	39.0%	40.0%	39.9%	40.0%	40.0%	40.0%	40.0%	40.0%	40.0%	40.0%	40.0%	40.0%	40.0%	40.0%
Selling, General & Administrative	496.6	551.0	608.0	650.0	655.0	704.1	746.4	783.7	815.0	839.5	864.7	890.6	917.3	944.9	973.2
% sales	19.1%	19.0%	19.0%	19.2%	19.0%	19.0%	19.0%	19.0%	19.0%	19.0%	19.0%	19.0%	19.0%	19.0%	19.0%
Other Expense / (Income)	-	-	-	-	-	-	-	-	-	-	-	-	-	-	-
EBITDA	$491.4	$580.0	$672.0	$700.0	$725.0	$779.4	$826.1	$867.4	$902.1	$929.2	$957.1	$985.8	$1,015.4	$1,045.8	$1,077.2
% margin	18.9%	20.0%	21.0%	20.7%	21.0%	21.0%	21.0%	21.0%	21.0%	21.0%	21.0%	21.0%	21.0%	21.0%	21.0%
Depreciation	116.0	121.5	145.0	150.0	155.3	166.9	176.9	185.8	193.2	199.0	204.9	211.1	217.4	224.0	230.7
Amortization	39.0	43.5	48.0	50.0	51.8	55.6	59.0	61.9	64.4	66.3	68.3	70.4	72.5	74.7	76.9
EBIT	$336.4	$415.0	$479.0	$500.0	$518.0	$556.9	$590.3	$619.8	$644.6	$663.9	$683.8	$704.3	$725.5	$747.2	$769.6
% margin	12.9%	14.3%	15.0%	14.8%	15.0%	15.0%	15.0%	15.0%	15.0%	15.0%	15.0%	15.0%	15.0%	15.0%	15.0%
Interest Expense															
Revolving Credit Facility															
Term Loan A															
Term Loan B															
Term Loan C															
Existing Term Loan															
2nd Lien															
Senior Notes															
Senior Subordinated Notes															
Commitment Fee on Unused Revolver															
Administrative Agent Fee															
Cash Interest Expense															
Amortization of Deferred Financing Fees															
Total Interest Expense															
Interest Income															
Net Interest Expense															
Earnings Before Taxes						556.9	590.3	619.8	644.6	663.9	683.8	704.3	725.5	747.2	769.6
Income Tax Expense						211.6	224.3	235.5	244.9	252.3	259.9	267.6	275.7	283.9	292.5
Net Income						$345.2	$366.0	$384.3	$399.6	$411.6	$424.0	$436.7	$449.8	$463.3	$477.2
% margin						9.3%	9.3%	9.3%	9.3%	9.3%	9.3%	9.3%	9.3%	9.3%	9.3%

TO BE CALCULATED

Income Statement Assumptions

	2009	2010	2011	LTM	Pro forma	Year 1	Year 2	Year 3	Year 4	Year 5	Year 6	Year 7	Year 8	Year 9	Year 10
Sales (% YoY growth)	NA	11.5%	10.3%	NA	7.8%	7.5%	6.0%	5.0%	4.0%	3.0%	3.0%	3.0%	3.0%	3.0%	3.0%
Cost of Goods Sold (% margin)	62.0%	61.0%	60.0%	60.1%	60.0%	60.0%	60.0%	60.0%	60.0%	60.0%	60.0%	60.0%	60.0%	60.0%	60.0%
SG&A (% sales)	19.1%	19.0%	19.0%	19.2%	19.0%	19.0%	19.0%	19.0%	19.0%	19.0%	19.0%	19.0%	19.0%	19.0%	19.0%
Other Expense / (Income) (% of sales)	- %	- %	- %	- %	- %	- %	- %	- %	- %	- %	- %	- %	- %	- %	- %
Depreciation (% of sales)	4.5%	4.2%	4.5%	4.4%	4.5%	4.5%	4.5%	4.5%	4.5%	4.5%	4.5%	4.5%	4.5%	4.5%	4.5%
Amortization (% of sales)	1.5%	1.5%	1.5%	1.5%	1.5%	1.5%	1.5%	1.5%	1.5%	1.5%	1.5%	1.5%	1.5%	1.5%	1.5%
Interest Income					0.5%	0.5%	0.5%	0.5%	0.5%	0.5%	0.5%	0.5%	0.5%	0.5%	0.5%
Tax Rate					38.0%	38.0%	38.0%	38.0%	38.0%	38.0%	38.0%	38.0%	38.0%	38.0%	38.0%

Additional Cases In addition to the Management Case, the deal team typically develops its own, more conservative operating scenario, known as the "Base Case." The Base Case is generally premised on management assumptions, but with adjustments made based on the deal team's independent due diligence, research, and perspectives.

The bank's internal credit committee(s) also requires the deal team to analyze the target's performance under one or more stress cases in order to gain comfort with the target's ability to service and repay debt during periods of duress. Sponsors perform similar analyses to test the durability of a proposed investment. These "Downside Cases" typically present the target's financial performance with haircuts to top line growth, margins, and potentially capex and working capital efficiency. As with the DCF model, a "toggle" function in the LBO model allows the banker to move from case to case without having to re-enter key financial inputs and assumptions. A separate toggle provides the ability to analyze different financing structures.

The operating scenario that the deal team ultimately uses to set covenants and market the transaction to investors is provided by the sponsor (the "Sponsor Case"). Sponsors use information gleaned from due diligence, industry experts, consulting studies, and research reports, as well as their own sector expertise to develop this case. The Sponsor Case, along with the sponsor's preferred financing structure (collectively, the "Sponsor Model"), is shared with potential underwriters as the basis for them to provide commitment letters.[4] The deal team then confirms both the feasibility of the Sponsor Case (based on its own due diligence and knowledge of the target and sector) and the marketability of the sponsor's preferred financing structure (by gaining comfort that there are buyers for the loans and securities given the proposed terms). This task is especially important because the investment banks are being asked to provide a commitment to a financing structure that may not come to market for several weeks or months (or potentially longer, depending on regulatory or other approvals required before the transaction can close).

---

[4]The timing for the sharing of the Sponsor Model depends on the specifics of the particular deal and the investment bank's relationship with the sponsor.

Step II(b): Input Opening Balance Sheet and Project Balance Sheet Items

The opening balance sheet (and potentially projected balance sheet data) for the target is typically provided in the CIM and entered into the pre-LBO model (see Exhibit 5.5, "Opening 2012" heading).[5] In addition to the traditional balance sheet accounts, new line items necessary for modeling the pro forma LBO financing structure are added, such as:

- financing fees (which are amortized) under long-term assets
- detailed line items for the new financing structure under long-term liabilities (e.g., the new revolver, term loan(s), and high yield bonds)

The banker must then build functionality into the model in order to input the new LBO financing structure. This is accomplished by inserting "adjustment" columns to account for the additions and subtractions to the opening balance sheet that result from the LBO (see Exhibits 5.5 and 5.15). The inputs for the adjustment columns, which bridge from the opening balance sheet to the pro forma closing balance sheet, feed from the *sources and uses* of funds in the transaction (see Exhibits 5.14 and 5.15). The banker also inserts a "pro forma" column, which nets the adjustments made to the opening balance sheet and serves as the starting point for projecting the target's post-LBO balance sheet throughout the projection period.

Prior to the entry of the LBO financing structure, the opening and pro forma closing balance sheets are identical. The target's basic balance sheet items—such as current assets, current liabilities, PP&E, other assets, and other long-term liabilities—are projected using the same methodologies discussed in Chapter 3. As with the assumptions for the target's projected income statement items, the banker enters the assumptions for the target's projected balance sheet items into the model through an assumptions page (see Exhibit 5.53), which feeds into the projected balance sheet. Projected debt repayment is not modeled at this point as the LBO financing structure has yet to be entered into the sources and uses of funds. For ValueCo, which has an existing $1,000 million term loan and $500 million of senior notes, we simply set the projection period debt balances equal to the opening balance amount (see Exhibit 5.5). At this stage, annual excess free cash flow[6] accrues to the ending cash balance for each projection year once the pre-LBO cash flow statement is completed (see Step II(c), Exhibits 5.9 and 5.10). This ensures that the model will balance once the three financial statements are fully linked.

Depending on the availability of information and need for granularity, the banker may choose to build a "short-form" LBO model that suffices for calculating debt repayment and performing a basic returns analysis. A short-form LBO model uses an abbreviated cash flow statement and debt schedule in place of a full balance sheet with working capital typically calculated as a percentage of sales. The construction of a traditional three-statement model, however, is recommended whenever possible so as to provide the most comprehensive analysis.

---

[5] If the banker is analyzing a public company as a potential LBO candidate outside of (or prior to) an organized sale process, the latest balance sheet data from the company's most recent 10-K or 10-Q is typically used.

[6] The "free cash flow" term used in an LBO analysis differs from that used in a DCF analysis as it includes the effects of leverage.

EXHIBIT 5.5 ValueCo Pre-LBO Balance Sheet

($ in millions, fiscal year ending December 31)

Balance Sheet

	Opening 2012	Adjustments +	Adjustments	Pro Forma 2012	Year 1 2013	Year 2 2014	Year 3 2015	Year 4 2016	Year 5 2017	Year 6 2018	Year 7 2019	Year 8 2020	Year 9 2021	Year 10 2022
Cash and Cash Equivalent	$250.0			$250.0					TO BE LINKED FROM CASH FLOW STATEMENT					
Accounts Receivable	450.0			450.0	483.8	512.8	538.4	560.0	576.7	594.1	611.9	630.2	649.1	668.6
Inventories	600.0			600.0	645.0	683.7	717.9	746.6	769.0	792.1	815.8	840.3	865.5	891.5
Prepaids and Other Current Assets	175.0			175.0	188.1	199.4	209.4	217.8	224.3	231.0	238.0	245.1	252.4	260.0
Total Current Assets	**$1,475.0**			**$1,475.0**	**$1,316.9**	**$1,395.9**	**$1,465.7**	**$1,524.3**	**$1,570.0**	**$1,617.1**	**$1,665.7**	**$1,715.6**	**$1,767.1**	**$1,820.1**
Property, Plant and Equipment, net	2,500.0			2,500.0	2,333.1	2,156.2	1,970.4	1,777.3	1,578.3	1,373.3	1,162.2	944.8	720.9	490.2
Goodwill	1,000.0			1,000.0	1,000.0	1,000.0	1,000.0	1,000.0	1,000.0	1,000.0	1,000.0	1,000.0	1,000.0	1,000.0
Intangible Assets	875.0			875.0	819.4	760.4	698.5	634.1	567.8	499.4	429.1	356.6	282.0	205.1
Other Assets	150.0			150.0	150.0	150.0	150.0	150.0	150.0	150.0	150.0	150.0	150.0	150.0
Deferred Financing Fees														
Total Assets	**$6,000.0**			**$6,000.0**	**$5,619.4**	**$5,462.5**	**$5,284.6**	**$5,085.7**	**$4,866.1**	**$4,639.9**	**$4,407.0**	**$4,167.0**	**$3,919.9**	**$3,665.4**
Accounts Payable	215.0			215.0	231.1	245.0	257.2	267.5	275.6	283.8	292.3	301.1	310.1	319.4
Accrued Liabilities	275.0			275.0	295.6	313.4	329.0	342.2	352.5	363.0	373.9	385.1	396.7	408.6
Other Current Liabilities	100.0			100.0	107.5	114.0	119.6	124.4	128.2	132.0	136.0	140.1	144.3	148.6
Total Current Liabilities	**$590.0**			**$590.0**	**$634.3**	**$672.3**	**$705.9**	**$734.2**	**$756.2**	**$778.9**	**$802.2**	**$826.3**	**$851.1**	**$876.6**
Revolving Credit Facility														
Term Loan A			TO BE											
Term Loan B			LINKED/											
Term Loan C			CALCULATED											
Existing Term Loan	1,000.		FROM		1,000.0	1,000.0	1,000.0	1,000.0	1,000.0	1,000.0	1,000.0	1,000.0	1,000.0	1,000.0
2nd Lien			SOURCES						TO BE LINKED FROM DEBT SCHEDULE					
Senior Notes			AND USES											
Existing Senior Notes	500.				500.0	500.0	500.0	500.0	500.0	500.0	500.0	500.0	500.0	500.0
Senior Subordinated Notes														
Other Debt														
Deferred Income Taxes	300.0			300.0	300.0	300.0	300.0	300.0	300.0	300.0	300.0	300.0	300.0	300.0
Other Long-Term Liabilities	110.0			110.0	110.0	110.0	110.0	110.0	110.0	110.0	110.0	110.0	110.0	110.0
Total Liabilities	**$2,500.0**			**$2,500.0**	**$2,544.3**	**$2,582.3**	**$2,615.9**	**$2,644.2**	**$2,666.2**	**$2,688.9**	**$2,712.2**	**$2,736.3**	**$2,761.1**	**$2,786.6**
Noncontrolling Interest														
Shareholders' Equity	3,500.			3,500.0	3,845.2	4,211.2	4,595.5	4,995.1	5,406.7	5,830.7	6,267.4	6,717.2	7,180.4	1,732.6
Total Shareholders' Equity	**$3,500.0**			**$3,500.0**	**$3,845.2**	**$4,211.2**	**$4,595.5**	**$4,995.1**	**$5,406.7**	**$5,830.7**	**$6,267.4**	**$6,717.2**	**$7,180.4**	**$1,732.6**
Total Liabilities and Equity	**$6,000.0**			**$6,000.0**	**$6,389.5**	**$6,793.5**	**$7,211.4**	**$7,639.3**	**$8,072.9**	**$8,519.6**	**$8,979.6**	**$9,453.5**	**$9,941.5**	**$4,519.3**
Balance Check	0.000			0.000										
Net Working Capital	635.0			635.0	682.6	723.6	759.8	790.2	813.9	838.3	863.4	889.3	916.0	943.5
(Increase) / Decrease in Net Working Capital					(47.6)	(41.0)	(36.2)	(30.4)	(23.7)	(24.4)	(25.1)	(25.9)	(26.7)	(27.5)

Balance Sheet Assumptions

Current Assets

Days Sales Outstanding (DSO)	47.6				47.6	47.6	47.6	47.6	47.6	47.6	47.6	47.6	47.6	47.6
Days Inventory Held (DIH)	105.8				105.8	105.8	105.8	105.8	105.8	105.8	105.8	105.8	105.8	105.8
Prepaid and Other Current Assets (% of sales)	5.1%				5.1%	5.1%	5.1%	5.1%	5.1%	5.1%	5.1%	5.1%	5.1%	5.1%

Current Liabilities

Days Payable Outstanding (DPO)	37.9				37.9	37.9	37.9	37.9	37.9	37.9	37.9	37.9	37.9	37.9
Accrued Liabilities (% of sales)	8.0%				8.0%	8.0%	8.0%	8.0%	8.0%	8.0%	8.0%	8.0%	8.0%	8.0%
Other Current Liabilities (% of sales)	2.9%				2.9%	2.9%	2.9%	2.9%	2.9%	2.9%	2.9%	2.9%	2.9%	2.9%

Notes:
- The ending cash balance for each year in the projection period is linked to the balance sheet from the cash flow statement once it is completed
- Prior to entry of capex assumptions, PP&E only reflects Depreciation
- Shareholders' equity is inflated until the financing structure is entered into the model
- Model will balance once the ending cash balance for each year in the projection period is linked from the cash flow statement

243

Step II(c): Build Cash Flow Statement through Investing Activities

The cash flow statement consists of three sections—operating activities, investing activities, and financing activities.

Operating Activities

Income Statement Links In building the cash flow statement, all the appropriate income statement items, including net income and non-cash expenses (e.g., D&A, amortization of deferred financing fees), must be linked to the operating activities section of the cash flow statement.

Net income is the first line item in the cash flow statement. It is initially inflated in the pre-LBO model as it excludes the pro forma interest expense and amortization of deferred financing fees associated with the LBO financing structure that have not yet been entered into the model. The amortization of deferred financing fees is a non-cash expense that is added back to net income in the post-LBO cash flow statement. Certain items, such as the annual projected D&A, do not change pro forma for the transaction.

EXHIBIT 5.6 Income Statement Links

($ in millions, fiscal year ending December 31)

Cash Flow Statement					Projection Period					
	Year 1 2013	Year 2 2014	Year 3 2015	Year 4 2016	Year 5 2017	Year 6 2018	Year 7 2019	Year 8 2020	Year 9 2021	Year 10 2022
Operating Activities										
Net Income	$345.2	$366.0	$384.3	$399.6	$411.6	$424.0	$436.7	$449.8	$463.3	$477.2
Plus: Depreciation	166.9	176.9	185.8	193.2	199.0	204.9	211.1	217.4	224.0	230.7
Plus: Amortization	55.6	59.0	61.9	64.4	66.3	68.3	70.4	72.5	74.7	76.9
Plus: Amortization of Financing Fees	TO BE LINKED FROM INCOME STATEMENT									

As shown in Exhibit 5.6, ValueCo's 2013E net income is $345.2 million, which is $160.3 million higher than the pro forma 2013E net income of $184.9 million after giving effect to the LBO financing structure (see Exhibit 5.31).

Balance Sheet Links Each YoY change to a balance sheet account must be accounted for by a corresponding addition or subtraction to the appropriate line item on the cash flow statement. As discussed in Chapter 3, an increase in an asset is a use of cash (represented by a negative value on the cash flow statement), and a decrease in an asset represents a source of cash. Similarly, an increase or decrease in a liability account represents a source or use of cash, respectively. The YoY changes in the target's projected working capital items are calculated in their corresponding line items in the operating activities section of the cash flow statement. These amounts do not change pro forma for the LBO transaction. The sum of the target's net income, non-cash expenses, changes in working capital items, and other items (as appropriate) provides the cash flow from operating activities amount.

As shown in Exhibit 5.7, ValueCo generates $520.1 million of cash flow from operating activities in 2013E before giving effect to the LBO transaction.

LBO Analysis

EXHIBIT 5.7 Balance Sheet Links

($ in millions, fiscal year ending December 31)

Cash Flow Statement

	\multicolumn{10}{c}{Projection Period}									
	Year 1 2013	Year 2 2014	Year 3 2015	Year 4 2016	Year 5 2017	Year 6 2018	Year 7 2019	Year 8 2020	Year 9 2021	Year 10 2022
Operating Activities										
Net Income	$345.2	$366.0	$384.3	$399.6	$411.6	$424.0	$436.7	$449.8	$463.3	$477.2
Plus: Depreciation	166.9	176.9	185.8	193.2	199.0	204.9	211.1	217.4	224.0	230.7
Plus: Amortization	55.6	59.0	61.9	64.4	66.3	68.3	70.4	72.5	74.7	76.9
Plus: Amortization of Financing Fees	\multicolumn{10}{c}{TO BE LINKED FROM INCOME STATEMENT}									
Changes in Working Capital Items										
(Inc.) / Dec. in Accounts Receivable	(33.8)	(29.0)	(25.6)	(21.5)	(16.8)	(17.3)	(17.8)	(18.4)	(18.9)	(19.5)
(Inc.) / Dec. in Inventories	(45.0)	(38.7)	(34.2)	(28.7)	(22.4)	(23.1)	(23.8)	(24.5)	(25.2)	(26.0)
(Inc.) / Dec. in Prepaid and Other Current Assets	(13.1)	(11.3)	(10.0)	(8.4)	(6.5)	(6.7)	(6.9)	(7.1)	(7.4)	(7.6)
Inc. / (Dec.) in Accounts Payable	16.1	13.9	12.2	10.3	8.0	8.3	8.5	8.8	9.0	9.3
Inc. / (Dec.) in Accrued Liabilities	20.6	17.7	15.7	13.2	10.3	10.6	10.9	11.2	11.6	11.9
Inc. / (Dec.) in Other Current Liabilities	7.5	6.5	5.7	4.8	3.7	3.8	4.0	4.1	4.2	4.3
(Inc.) / Dec. in Net Working Capital	(47.6)	(41.0)	(36.2)	(30.4)	(23.7)	(24.4)	(25.1)	(25.9)	(26.7)	(27.5)
Cash Flow from Operating Activities	$520.1	$560.9	$595.8	$626.8	$653.2	$672.8	$693.0	$713.8	$735.2	$757.3

Investing Activities Capex is typically the key line item under investing activities, although planned acquisitions or divestitures may also be captured in the "other investing activities" line item. Projected capex assumptions are typically sourced from the CIM and inputted into an assumptions page (see Exhibit 5.52) where they are linked to the cash flow statement. The target's projected net PP&E must incorporate the capex projections (added to PP&E) as well as those for depreciation (subtracted from PP&E). As discussed in Chapter 3, in the event that capex projections are not provided/available, the banker typically projects capex as a fixed percentage of sales at historical levels with appropriate adjustments for cyclical or non-recurring items.

The sum of the annual cash flows provided by operating activities and investing activities provides annual cash flow available for debt repayment, which is commonly referred to as free cash flow (see Exhibit 5.25).

EXHIBIT 5.8 Investing Activities

($ in millions, fiscal year ending December 31)

Cash Flow Statement

	\multicolumn{10}{c}{Projection Period}									
	Year 1 2013	Year 2 2014	Year 3 2015	Year 4 2016	Year 5 2017	Year 6 2018	Year 7 2019	Year 8 2020	Year 9 2021	Year 10 2022
Investing Activities										
Capital Expenditures	(166.9)	(176.9)	(185.8)	(193.2)	(199.0)	(204.9)	(211.1)	(217.4)	(224.0)	(230.7)
Other Investing Activities	-	-	-	-	-	-	-	-	-	-
Cash Flow from Investing Activities	($166.9)	($176.9)	($185.8)	($193.2)	($199.0)	($204.9)	($211.1)	($217.4)	($224.0)	($230.7)

As shown in Exhibit 5.8, we do not make any assumptions for ValueCo's other investing activities line item. Therefore, ValueCo's cash flow from investing activities amount is equal to capex in each year of the projection period.

Financing Activities The financing activities section of the cash flow statement is constructed to include line items for the (repayment)/drawdown of each debt instrument in the LBO financing structure. It also includes line items for dividends and equity issuance/(stock repurchase). These line items are initially left blank until the LBO financing structure is entered into the model (see Step III) and a detailed debt schedule is built (see Step IV(a)).

EXHIBIT 5.9 Financing Activities

($ in millions, fiscal year ending December 31)

Cash Flow Statement

	Year 1 2013	Year 2 2014	Year 3 2015	Year 4 2016	Year 5 2017	Year 6 2018	Year 7 2019	Year 8 2020	Year 9 2021	Year 10 2022
Financing Activities										
Revolving Credit Facility										
Term Loan A										
Term Loan B										
Term Loan C										
Existing Term Loan										
2nd Lien										
Senior Notes										
Senior Subordinated Notes										
Other Debt										
Dividends										
Equity Issuance / (Repurchase)										
Cash Flow from Financing Activities	-	-	-	-	-	-	-	-	-	-
Excess Cash for the Period	$353.3	$384.0	$410.0	$433.6	$454.2	$467.9	$481.9	$496.4	$511.3	$526.6
Beginning Cash Balance	250.0	603.3	987.2	1,397.2	1,830.9	2,285.1	2,753.0	3,234.9	3,731.2	4,242.5
Ending Cash Balance	**$603.3**	**$987.2**	**$1,397.2**	**$1,830.9**	**$2,285.1**	**$2,753.0**	**$3,234.9**	**$3,731.2**	**$4,242.5**	**$4,769.1**

Cash Flow Statement Assumptions

Capital Expenditures (% of sales)	4.5%	4.5%	4.5%	4.5%	4.5%	4.5%	4.5%	4.5%	4.5%	4.5%

TO BE LINKED FROM DEBT SCHEDULE

Excess Cash for the Period accrues to the Ending Cash Balance until the LBO financing structure is entered into the model and the debt schedule is built

The existing $250 million cash balance is pre-transaction and will ultimately be used as part of the financing structure

As shown in Exhibit 5.9, prior to giving effect to the LBO transaction, ValueCo's projected excess cash for the period accrues to the ending cash balance in each year of the projection period.

Cash Flow Statement Links to Balance Sheet Once the cash flow statement is built, the ending cash balance for each year in the projection period is linked to the cash and cash equivalents line item in the balance sheet, thereby fully linking the financial statements of the pre-LBO model.

EXHIBIT 5.10 Cash Flow Statement Links to Balance Sheet

($ in millions, fiscal year ending December 31)

Cash Flow Statement

	Year 1 2013	Year 2 2014	Year 3 2015	Year 4 2016	Year 5 2017	Year 6 2018	Year 7 2019	Year 8 2020	Year 9 2021	Year 10 2022
Excess Cash for the Period	$353.3	$384.0	$410.0	$433.6	$454.2	$467.9	$481.9	$496.4	$511.3	$526.6
Beginning Cash Balance	250.0	603.3	987.2	1,397.2	1,830.9	2,285.1	2,753.0	3,234.9	3,731.2	4,242.5
Ending Cash Balance	**$603.3**	**$987.2**	**$1,397.2**	**$1,830.9**	**$2,285.1**	**$2,753.0**	**$3,234.9**	**$3,731.2**	**$4,242.5**	**$4,769.1**

Balance Sheet

	Pro Forma 2012	Year 1 2013	Year 2 2014	Year 3 2015	Year 4 2016	Year 5 2017	Year 6 2018	Year 7 2019	Year 8 2020	Year 9 2021	Year 10 2022
Cash and Cash Equivalents	$250.0	$603.3	$987.2	$1,397.2	$1,830.9	$2,285.1	$2,753.0	$3,234.9	$3,731.2	$4,242.5	$4,769.1

= Ending Cash Balance$_{2013E}$ (from Cash Flow Statement)

LBO Analysis

As shown in Exhibit 5.10, in 2013E, ValueCo generates excess cash for the period of $353.3 million, which is added to the beginning cash balance of $250 million to produce an ending cash balance of $603.3 million.[7] This amount is linked to the 2013E cash and cash equivalents line item on the balance sheet.

At this point in the construction of the LBO model, the balance sheet should balance (i.e., total assets are equal to the sum of total liabilities and shareholders' equity) for each year in the projection period. If this is the case, then the model is functioning properly and the transaction structure can be entered into the sources and uses.

If the balance sheet does not balance, then the banker must revisit the steps performed up to this point and correct any input, linking, or calculation errors that are preventing the model from functioning properly. Common missteps include depreciation or capex not being properly linked to PP&E or changes in balance sheet accounts not being properly reflected in the cash flow statement.

STEP III. INPUT TRANSACTION STRUCTURE

EXHIBIT 5.11 Steps to Input the Transaction Structure

Step III(a):	Enter Purchase Price Assumptions
Step III(b):	Enter Financing Structure into Sources and Uses
Step III(c):	Link Sources and Uses to Balance Sheet Adjustments Columns

Step III(a): Enter Purchase Price Assumptions

A purchase price must be assumed for a given target in order to determine the supporting financing structure (debt and equity).

For the illustrative LBO of ValueCo (a private company), we assumed that a sponsor is basing its purchase price and financing structure on ValueCo's LTM 9/30/2012 EBITDA of $700 million and a year-end transaction close.[8] We also assumed a purchase multiple of 8.0x LTM EBITDA, which is consistent with the multiples paid for similar LBO targets (per the illustrative precedent transactions analysis performed in Chapter 2, see Exhibit 2.35). This results in an enterprise value of $5,600 million (prior to transaction-related fees and expenses) and an implied equity purchase price of $4,350 million after subtracting ValueCo's net debt of $1,250 million.

---

[7] The $250 million beginning cash balance in 2013E will ultimately be used as part of the financing structure.
[8] As ValueCo is private, we entered a "2" in the toggle cell for public/private target (see Exhibit 5.12).

EXHIBIT 5.12 Purchase Price Input Section of Assumptions Page 3 (see Exhibit 5.54) – Multiple of EBITDA

($ in millions)

Purchase Price	
Public / Private Target	**2**
Entry EBITDA Multiple	8.0x
LTM 9/30/2012 EBITDA	700.0
Enterprise Value	**$5,600.0**
Less: Total Debt	(1,500.0)
Less: Preferred Stock	-
Less: Noncontrolling Interest	-
Plus: Cash and Cash Equivalents	250.0
Equity Purchase Price	**$4,350.0**

Enter "1" for a public target
Enter "2" for a private target
*Our LBO model template automatically updates the labels and calculations for each selection (see Exhibit 5.13)

For a public company, the equity purchase price is calculated by multiplying the offer price per share by the target's fully diluted shares outstanding.[9] Net debt is then added to the equity purchase price to arrive at an implied enterprise value (see Exhibit 5.13).

EXHIBIT 5.13 Purchase Price Assumptions – Offer Price per Share

($ in millions, except per share data)

Purchase Price	
Public / Private Target	**1**
Offer Price per Share	$54.38
Fully Diluted Shares Outstanding	80.0
Equity Purchase Price	**$4,350.0**
Plus: Total Debt	1,500.0
Plus: Preferred Stock	-
Plus: Noncontrolling Interest	-
Less: Cash and Cash Equivalents	(250.0)
Enterprise Value	**$5,600.0**

---

[9]In this case, a "1" would be entered in the toggle cell for public/private target (see Exhibit 5.13).

Step III(b): Enter Financing Structure into Sources and Uses

A sources and uses table is used to summarize the flow of funds required to consummate a transaction. The *sources of funds* refer to the total capital used to finance an acquisition. The *uses of funds* refer to those items funded by the capital sources—in this case, the purchase of ValueCo's equity, the repayment of existing debt, and the payment of transaction fees and expenses, including the tender/call premiums on ValueCo's existing bonds. Regardless of the number and type of components comprising the sources and uses of funds, the sum of the sources of funds must equal the sum of the uses of funds.

We entered the sources and uses of funds for the multiple financing structures analyzed for the ValueCo LBO into an assumptions page (see Exhibits 5.14 and 5.54).

EXHIBIT 5.14   Financing Structures Input Section of Assumptions Page 3 (see Exhibit 5.54)

($ in millions)

Financing Structures

	Structure				
	1	2	3	4	5
Sources of Funds	Structure 1	Structure 2	Structure 3	Structure 4	Status Quo
Revolving Credit Facility Size	$250.0	$250.0	$250.0	$250.0	-
Revolving Credit Facility Draw	-	-	-	-	-
Term Loan A	-	500.0	-	-	-
Term Loan B	2,150.0	1,650.0	2,100.0	1,750.0	-
Term Loan C	-	-	-	-	-
2nd Lien	-	-	-	-	-
Senior Notes	1,500.0	1,500.0	700.0	1,000.0	-
Senior Subordinated Notes	-	-	700.0	1,000.0	-
Equity Contribution	2,100.0	2,100.0	2,250.0	2,250.0	-
Rollover Equity	-	-	-	-	-
Cash on Hand	250.0	250.0	250.0	-	-
Total Sources of Funds	$6,000.0	$6,000.0	$6,000.0	$6,000.0	-
Uses of Funds					
Equity Purchase Price	$4,350.0	$4,350.0	$4,350.0	$4,350.0	-
Repay Existing Bank Debt	1,500.0	1,500.0	1,500.0	1,500.0	-
Tender / Call Premiums	20.0	20.0	20.0	20.0	-
Financing Fees	90.0	90.0	90.0	90.0	-
Other Fees and Expenses	40.0	40.0	40.0	40.0	-
Total Uses of Funds	$6,000.0	$6,000.0	$6,000.0	$6,000.0	-

Sources of Funds   Structure 1 served as our preliminary proposed financing structure for the ValueCo LBO. As shown in Exhibit 5.14, it consists of:

- $2,150 million term loan B ("TLB")
- $1,500 million senior notes ("notes")
- $2,100 million equity contribution
- $250 million of cash on hand

This preliminary financing structure is comprised of senior secured leverage of 3.1x LTM EBITDA, total leverage of 5.2x, an equity contribution percentage of approximately 35%, and $250 million of ValueCo's cash on hand (see Exhibit 5.2).

We also contemplated a $250 million undrawn revolving credit facility ("revolver") as part of the financing. While not an actual source of funding for the ValueCo LBO, the revolver provides liquidity to fund anticipated seasonal working capital needs, issuance of letters of credit, and other cash uses at, or post, closing.

Uses of Funds   The uses of funds include:

- the purchase of ValueCo's equity for $4,350 million
- the repayment of ValueCo's existing $1,000 million term loan and $500 million senior notes
- the payment of total transaction fees and expenses of $150 million (consisting of financing fees of $90 million, tender/call premiums of $20 million, and other fees and expenses of $40 million)

The total sources and uses of funds are $6,000 million, which is $400 million higher than the implied enterprise value calculated in Exhibit 5.12. This is due to the payment of $150 million of total fees and expenses and the use of $250 million of cash on hand as a funding source.

Step III(c): Link Sources and Uses to Balance Sheet Adjustments Columns

Once the sources and uses of funds are entered into the model, each amount is linked to the appropriate cell in the adjustments columns adjacent to the opening balance sheet (see Exhibit 5.15). Any goodwill that is created, however, is calculated on the basis of equity purchase price and net identifiable assets[10] (see Exhibit 5.20). The equity contribution must also be adjusted to account for any transaction-related fees and expenses (other than financing fees) as well as tender/call premium fees that are expensed upfront.[11] These adjustments serve to bridge the opening balance sheet to the pro forma closing balance sheet, which forms the basis for projecting the target's balance sheet throughout the projection period.

EXHIBIT 5.15 Sources and Uses Links to Balance Sheet

($ in millions)

Sources of Funds			Uses of Funds		
Revolving Credit Facility	-		Purchase ValueCo Equity	$4,350.0	E
Term Loan B	2,150.0	A	Repay Existing Debt	1,500.0	F
Senior Notes	1,500.0	B	Tender / Call Premiums	20.0	G
Equity Contribution	2,100.0	C	Financing Fees	90.0	H
Cash on Hand	250.0	D	Other Fees and Expenses	40.0	I
Total Sources	**$6,000.0**		**Total Uses**	**$6,000.0**	

Balance Sheet	Opening 2012	Adjustments +	Adjustments −	Pro Forma 2012	
Cash and Cash Equivalents	$250.0		(250.0) D	-	
Accounts Receivable	450.0			450.0	
Inventories	600.0			600.0	
Prepaids and Other Current Assets	175.0			175.0	
Total Current Assets	**$1,475.0**			**$1,225.0**	
Property, Plant and Equipment, net	2,500.0			2,500.0	
Goodwill	1,000.0	1,850.0	(1,000.0)	1,850.0	= Equity Purchase Price
Intangible Assets	875.0			875.0	Less: Net Identifiable Assets
Other Assets	150.0			150.0	= $4,350 million − ($3,500 million − $1,000 million)
Deferred Financing Fees	-	90.0 H		90.0	
Total Assets	**$6,000.0**			**$6,690.0**	E
Accounts Payable	215.0			215.0	
Accrued Liabilities	275.0			275.0	
Other Current Liabilities	100.0			100.0	
Total Current Liabilities	**$590.0**			**$590.0**	
Revolving Credit Facility	-	A		-	
Term Loan A	-			-	
Term Loan B	-	2,150.0		2,150.0	
Term Loan C	-		F	-	
Existing Term Loan	1,000.0		(1,000.0)	-	
2nd Lien	-			-	
Senior Notes	-	B	F	-	
Existing Senior Notes	500.0		(500.0)	-	
Senior Subordinated Notes	-	1,500.0		1,500.0	
Other Debt	-			-	
Deferred Income Taxes	300.0			300.0	
Other Long-Term Liabilities	110.0			110.0	
Total Liabilities	**$2,500.0**			**$4,650.0**	
Noncontrolling Interest	-			-	
Shareholders' Equity	3,500.0	2,040.0	(3,500.0)	2,040.0	ValueCo's existing equity of $3,500 million is eliminated through the transaction and replaced with the sponsor's equity contribution
Total Shareholders' Equity	**$3,500.0**			**$2,040.0**	
Total Liabilities and Equity	**$6,000.0**			**$6,690.0**	
Balance Check	0.000			0.000	

= Equity Contribution − Tender / Call Premiums − Other Fees and Expenses
= $2,100 million − $20 million − $40 million

C   G   I

---

[10] Calculated as shareholders' equity less existing goodwill.
[11] In accordance with FAS 141(R), M&A transaction costs are expensed as incurred. Debt financing fees, however, continue to be treated as deferred costs and amortized over the life of the associated debt instruments.

Exhibit 5.16 provides a summary of the transaction adjustments to the opening balance sheet.

EXHIBIT 5.16 Balance Sheet Adjustments

Adjustments	
Additions	**Eliminations**
Assets	**Assets**
+ $1,850 million of Goodwill Created	− $250 million of Cash on Hand
+ $90 million of Financing Fees	− $1,000 million of Existing Goodwill
Liabilities	**Liabilities**
+ $2,150 million of Term Loan B	− $1,500 billion of Existing ValueCo Debt
+ $1,500 million of Senior Notes	
Shareholders' Equity	**Shareholders' Equity**
+ $2,100 million Sponsor Equity Contribution	− $3,500 million of ValueCo Shareholders' Equity
	− $20 million of Tender/Call Premiums
	− $40 million of Other Fees & Expenses

Sources of Funds Links The balance sheet links from the sources of funds to the adjustments columns are fairly straightforward. Each debt capital source corresponds to a like-named line item on the balance sheet and is linked as an addition in the appropriate adjustment column. For the equity contribution, however, the transaction-related fees and expenses as well as the tender/call premiums must be deducted in the appropriate cell during linkage. Any cash on hand used as part of the financing structure is subtracted from the existing cash balance.

Term Loan B, Senior Notes, and Equity Contribution As shown in Exhibit 5.17, in the ValueCo LBO, the new $2,150 million TLB, $1,500 million senior notes, and $2,100 million equity contribution ($2,040 million after deducting $20 million tender/call premiums and $40 million of other fees and expenses) were linked from the sources of funds to their corresponding line items on the balance sheet as an addition under the "+" adjustment column.

EXHIBIT 5.17 Term Loan B, Senior Notes, and Equity Contribution

($ in millions, fiscal year ending December 31)

Balance Sheet

	Opening 2012	Adjustments +	Adjustments −	Pro Forma 2012
Accounts Payable	215.0			215.0
Accrued Liabilities	275.0			275.0
Other Current Liabilities	100.0			100.0
Total Current Liabilities	**$590.0**			**$590.0**
Revolving Credit Facility	-			-
Term Loan B	-	2,150.0		2,150.0
Existing Term Loan	1,000.0			1,000.0
Existing Senior Notes	500.0			500.0
Senior Notes	-	1,500.0		1,500.0
Other Debt	300.0			300.0
Other Long-Term Liabilities	110.0			110.0
Total Liabilities	**$2,500.0**			**$6,150.0**
Noncontrolling Interest	-			-
Shareholders' Equity	3,500.0	2,040.0		5,540.0
Total Shareholders' Equity	**$3,500.0**			**$5,540.0**

= $2,100 million - $20 million - $40 million
= Equity Contribution - Tender / Call Premiums - Other Fees and Expenses

LBO Analysis

Cash on Hand   As shown in Exhibit 5.18, the $250 million use of cash on hand was linked from the sources of funds as a negative adjustment to the opening cash balance as it is used as a source of funding.

EXHIBIT 5.18   Cash on Hand

($ in millions, fiscal year ending December 31)

Balance Sheet	Opening 2012	Adjustments +	Adjustments −	Pro Forma 2012
Cash and Cash Equivalents	$250.0		(250.0)	−

Uses of Funds Links

Purchase ValueCo Equity   As shown in Exhibit 5.19, ValueCo's existing shareholders' equity of $3,500 million, which is included in the $4,350 million purchase price, was eliminated as a negative adjustment and replaced by the sponsor's equity contribution (less other fees and expenses and tender/call premiums).

EXHIBIT 5.19   Purchase ValueCo Equity

($ in millions, fiscal year ending December 31)

Balance Sheet	Opening 2012	Adjustments +	Adjustments −	Pro Forma 2012
Noncontrolling Interest	−			−
Shareholders' Equity	3,500.0	2,040.0	(3,500.0)	2,040.0
Total Shareholders' Equity	$3,500.0			$2,040.0

Goodwill Created   Goodwill is created from the excess amount paid for a target over its net identifiable assets. For the ValueCo LBO, it is calculated as the equity purchase price of $4,350 million less net identifiable assets of $2,500 million (shareholders' equity of $3,500 million less existing goodwill of $1,000 million). As shown in Exhibit 5.20, the net value of $1,850 million is linked to the adjustments column as an addition to the goodwill and intangible assets line item.[12] The goodwill created remains on the balance sheet (unamortized) over the life of the investment, but is tested annually for impairment.

---

[12] The allocation of the entire purchase price premium to goodwill is a simplifying assumption for the purposes of this analysis. In an actual transaction, the excess purchase price over the existing net identifiable assets is allocated to assets, such as PP&E and intangibles, as well as other balance sheet items, to reflect their fair market value at the time of the acquisition. The remaining excess purchase price is then allocated to goodwill. From a cash flow perspective, in a stock sale (see Chapter 7), there is no difference between allocating the entire purchase premium to goodwill as opposed to writing up other assets to fair market value. In an asset sale (see Chapter 7), however, there are differences in cash flows depending on the allocation of goodwill to tangible and intangible assets as the write-up is tax deductible.

EXHIBIT 5.20 Goodwill Created

($ in millions, fiscal year ending December 31)

Balance Sheet	Opening 2012	Adjustments +	Adjustments −	Pro Forma 2012
Property, Plant and Equipment, net	2,500.0			2,500.0
Goodwill & Intangible Assets	1,000.0	1,850.0	(1,000.0)	1,850.0

Calculation of Goodwill	
Equity Purchase Price	$4,350.0
Less: Net Identifiable Assets	(2,500.0)
Goodwill Created	**$1,850.0**

Repay Existing Debt ValueCo's existing $1,000 million term loan and $500 million of senior notes are assumed to be refinanced as part of the new LBO financing structure, which includes $3,650 million of total funded debt. As shown in Exhibit 5.21, this is performed in the model by linking the repayment of the existing term loan and senior notes directly from the uses of funds as a negative adjustment.

EXHIBIT 5.21 Repay Existing Debt

($ in millions, fiscal year ending December 31)

Balance Sheet	Opening 2012	Adjustments +	Adjustments −	Pro Forma 2012
Revolving Credit Facility	-			-
Term Loan B	-	2,150.0		2,150.0
Existing Term Loan	1,000.0		(1,000.0)	-
Senior Notes	-	1,500.0		1,500.0
Existing Senior Notes	500.0		(500.0)	-

Tender/Call Premiums As part of the transaction, we assumed ValueCo's existing senior notes have a change of control provision and are required to be refinanced as part of the LBO. For illustrative purposes, we assumed that ValueCo's existing $500 million 8% 8-year senior notes were issued approximately four years ago and, therefore, the call price after the first call date would be 104% of par (par plus ½ the coupon, see Chapter 4). As a result, ValueCo's existing senior notes require a premium of $20 million ($500 million × 4%) to be paid to existing note holders.

Financing Fees As opposed to M&A transaction-related fees and expenses, financing fees are a deferred expense and, as such, are not expensed immediately. Therefore, deferred financing fees are capitalized as an asset on the balance sheet, which means they are linked from the uses of funds as an addition to the corresponding line item (see Exhibit 5.22). The financing fees associated with each debt instrument are amortized on a straight line basis over the life of the obligation.[13] As previously discussed,

---

[13] Although financing fees are paid in full to the underwriters at transaction close, they are amortized in accordance with the tenor of the security for accounting purposes. Deferred financing

amortization is a non-cash expense and, therefore, must be added back to net income in the operating activities section of the model's cash flow statement in each year of the projection period.

For the ValueCo LBO, we calculated financing fees associated with the contemplated financing structure to be $90 million. Our illustrative calculation is based on fees of 1.5% for arranging the senior secured credit facilities (the revolver and TLB), 2.25% for underwriting the notes, 1.00% for committing to a bridge loan for the notes, and $5.3 million for other financing fees and expenses.[14] The left-lead arranger of a revolving credit facility typically serves as the "Administrative Agent"[15] and receives an annual administrative agent fee (e.g., $150,000), which is included in interest expense on the income statement.[16]

EXHIBIT 5.22 Financing Fees

($ in millions, fiscal year ending December 31)

Balance Sheet

	Opening 2012	Adjustments +	Adjustments −	Pro Forma 2012
Property, Plant and Equipment, net	2,500.0			2,500.0
Goodwill and Intangible Assets	1,000.0	1,850.0	(1,000.0)	1,850.0
Other Assets	150.0			150.0
Deferred Financing Fees	-	90.0		90.0
Total Assets	$6,000.0			$6,690.0

Calculation of Financing Fees

	Size	Fees (%)	Fees ($)
Revolving Credit Facility Size	$250.0	1.50%	$3.8
Term Loan B	2,150.0	1.50%	32.3
Senior Subordinated Notes	1,500.0	2.25%	33.8
Senior Subordinated Bridge Facility	1,500.0	1.00%	15.0
Other Financing Fees & Expenses			5.3
Total Financing Fees			**$90.0**

Other Fees and Expenses Other fees and expenses typically include payments for services such as M&A advisory (and potentially a sponsor deal fee), legal, accounting, and consulting, as well as other miscellaneous deal-related costs. For the ValueCo LBO, we estimated this amount to be $40 million. Within the context of the LBO sources and uses, this amount is netted upfront against the equity contribution.

---

fees from prior financing transactions are typically expensed when the accompanying debt is retired and show up as a one-time charge to the target's net income, thereby reducing retained earnings and shareholders' equity.

[14] Fees are dependent on the debt instrument, market conditions, and specific situation. The fees depicted are for illustrative purposes only.

[15] The bank that monitors the credit facilities including the tracking of lenders, handling of interest and principal payments, and associated back-office administrative functions.

[16] The fee for the first year of the facility is generally paid to the lead arranger at the close of the financing.

STEP IV. COMPLETE THE POST-LBO MODEL

EXHIBIT 5.23 Steps to Complete the Post-LBO Model

Step IV(a):	Build Debt Schedule
Step IV(b):	Complete Pro Forma Income Statement from EBIT to Net Income
Step IV(c):	Complete Pro Forma Balance Sheet
Step IV(d):	Complete Pro Forma Cash Flow Statement

Step IV(a): Build Debt Schedule

The debt schedule is an integral component of the LBO model, serving to layer in the pro forma effects of the LBO financing structure on the target's financial statements.[17] Specifically, the debt schedule enables the banker to:

- complete the pro forma income statement from EBIT to net income
- complete the pro forma long-term liabilities and shareholders' equity sections of the balance sheet
- complete the pro forma financing activities section of the cash flow statement

As shown in Exhibit 5.27, the debt schedule applies free cash flow to make mandatory and optional debt repayments, thereby calculating the annual beginning and ending balances for each debt tranche. The debt repayment amounts are linked to the financing activities section of the cash flow statement and the ending debt balances are linked to the balance sheet. The debt schedule is also used to calculate the annual interest expense for the individual debt instruments, which is linked to the income statement.

The debt schedule is typically constructed in accordance with the security and seniority of the loans, securities, and other debt instruments in the capital structure (i.e., beginning with the revolver, followed by term loan tranches, and bonds). As detailed in the following pages, we began the construction of ValueCo's debt schedule by entering the *forward LIBOR curve,* followed by the calculation of annual projected cash available for debt repayment (free cash flow). We then entered the key terms for each individual debt instrument in the financing structure (i.e., size, term, coupon, and mandatory repayments/amortization schedule, if any).

Forward LIBOR Curve For floating-rate debt instruments, such as revolving credit facilities and term loans, interest rates are typically based on LIBOR[18] plus a fixed spread. Therefore, to calculate their projected annual interest expense, the banker must first enter future LIBOR estimates for each year of the projection period. LIBOR for future

---

[17] In lieu of a debt schedule, some LBO model templates use formulas in the appropriate cells in the financing activities section of the cash flow statement and the interest expense line item(s) of the income statement to perform the same functions.

[18] 3-month LIBOR is generally used.

LBO Analysis

years is typically sourced from the Forward LIBOR Curve provided by Bloomberg (see Appendix 5.1).[19]

EXHIBIT 5.24 Forward LIBOR Curve

($ in millions, fiscal year ending December 31)

Debt Schedule											
					Projection Period						
	Pro forma 2012	Year 1 2013	Year 2 2014	Year 3 2015	Year 4 2016	Year 5 2017	Year 6 2018	Year 7 2019	Year 8 2020	Year 9 2021	Year 10 2022
Forward LIBOR Curve	0.25%	0.35%	0.50%	0.75%	1.00%	1.25%	1.50%	1.75%	2.00%	2.25%	2.50%

As shown in the forward LIBOR curve line item in Exhibit 5.24, LIBOR is expected to increase incrementally throughout the projection period from 35 bps in 2013E to 250 bps by 2022E.[20] The pricing spreads for the revolver and TLB are added to the forward LIBOR in each year of the projection period to calculate their annual interest rates. For example, the 2013E interest rate for ValueCo's revolver, which is priced at L+425 bps would be 4.6% (35 bps LIBOR + 425 bps spread). However, since we contemplate a LIBOR floor of 1.25%, the TLB bears interest at 5.5% until 2018E when LIBOR is expected to increase above 1.25% (see Exhibit 5.26).

Cash Available for Debt Repayment (Free Cash Flow) The annual projected cash available for debt repayment is the sum of the cash flows provided by operating and investing activities on the cash flow statement. It is calculated in a section beneath the forward LIBOR curve inputs. For each year in the projection period, this amount is first used to make mandatory debt repayments on the term loan tranches.[21] The remaining cash flow is used to make optional debt repayments, as calculated in the cash available for optional debt repayment line item (see Exhibit 5.25).

In addition to internally generated free cash flow, existing cash from the balance sheet may be used ("swept") to make incremental debt repayments (see cash from balance sheet line item in Exhibit 5.25). In ValueCo's case, however, there is no cash on the pro forma balance sheet at closing as it is used as part of the transaction funding. In the event the post-LBO balance sheet has a cash balance, the banker may choose to keep a constant minimum level of cash on the balance sheet throughout the projection period by inputting a dollar amount under the "MinCash" heading (see Exhibit 5.25).

As shown in Exhibit 5.25, pro forma for the LBO, ValueCo generates $371.8 million of cash flow from operating activities in 2013E. Netting out ($166.9) million of cash flow from investing activities results in cash available for debt repayment of $204.9 million. After satisfying the $21.5 million mandatory amortization of the TLB, ValueCo has $183.4 million of cash available for optional debt repayment.

---

[19] Bloomberg function: FWCV<GO> load the US Dollar Swaps (30/360) Security in the amber box, select the Implied Forwards tab, and enter "3 Mo" in the Interval box.

[20] Following the onset of the subprime mortgage crisis and the ensuing credit crunch, and the resulting rate cuts by the Federal Reserve, investors have insisted on "LIBOR floors" in many new bank deals. A LIBOR floor guarantees a minimum coupon for investors regardless of how low LIBOR falls. For example, a term loan priced at L+425 bps with a LIBOR floor of 125 bps will have a cost of capital of 5.5% even if the prevailing LIBOR is lower than 125 bps.

[21] Mandatory repayments are determined in accordance with each debt instrument's amortization schedule.

EXHIBIT 5.25 Cash Available for Debt Repayment (Free Cash Flow)

($ in millions, fiscal year ending December 31)

Debt Schedule

	Pro forma 2012	Year 1 2013	Year 2 2014	Year 3 2015	Year 4 2016	Year 5 2017	Year 6 2018	Year 7 2019	Year 8 2020	Year 9 2021	Year 10 2022
						Projection Period					
Forward LIBOR Curve	0.25%	0.35%	0.50%	0.75%	1.00%	1.25%	1.50%	1.75%	2.00%	2.25%	2.50%
Cash Flow from Operating Activities		$371.8	$420.5	$464.7	$506.3	$544.5	$575.9	$609.8	$637.1	$657.3	$680.7
Cash Flow from Investing Activities		(166.9)	(176.9)	(185.8)	(193.2)	(199.0)	(204.9)	(211.1)	(217.4)	(224.0)	(230.7)
Cash Available for Debt Repayment		**$204.9**	**$243.6**	**$278.9**	**$313.1**	**$345.5**	**$371.0**	**$398.7**	**$419.7**	**$433.3**	**$450.0**
Total Mandatory Repayments		(21.5)	(21.5)	(21.5)	(21.5)	(21.5)	(21.5)	(21.5)			
Cash From Balance Sheet	MinCash -	-	-	-	-	-	-	-	5.8	425.4	858.8
Cash Available for Optional Debt Repayment		**$183.4**	**$222.1**	**$257.4**	**$291.6**	**$324.0**	**$349.5**	**$377.2**	**$425.4**	**$858.8**	**$1,308.8**

= Cash Flow from Operating Activities$_{2013E}$ + Cash Flow from Investing Activities$_{2013E}$
= $371.8 million + ($166.9) million

= Mandatory Repayments on the Term Loan B, calculated as 1% x $2,150 million

= IF (Cash Balance toggle = 1, then sweep cash from the Balance Sheet less the Minimum Cash Balance, otherwise display 0)

= Cash Flow for Debt Repayment$_{2016E}$ − Total Mandatory Repayments$_{2016E}$
= $313.1 million + ($21.5) million

Revolving Credit Facility In the "Revolving Credit Facility" section of the debt schedule, the banker inputs the spread, term, and commitment fee associated with the facility (see Exhibit 5.26). The facility's size is linked from an assumptions page where the financing structure is entered (see Exhibits 5.14 and 5.54) and the beginning balance line item for the first year of the projection period is linked from the balance sheet. If no revolver draw is contemplated as part of the LBO financing structure, then the beginning balance is zero.

The revolver's drawdown/(repayment) line item feeds from the cash available for optional debt repayment line item at the top of the debt schedule. In the event the cash available for optional debt repayment amount is negative in any year (e.g., in a downside case), a revolver draw (or use of cash on the balance sheet, if applicable) is required. In the following period, the outstanding revolver debt is then repaid first from any positive cash available for optional debt repayment (i.e., once mandatory repayments are satisfied).

In connection with the ValueCo LBO, we contemplated a $250 million revolver, which is priced at L+425 bps with a 1.25% LIBOR floor and a term of six years. The revolver is assumed to be undrawn at the close of the transaction and remains undrawn throughout the projection period. Therefore, no interest expense is incurred. ValueCo, however, must pay an annual commitment fee of 50 bps on the undrawn portion of the revolver, translating into an expense of $1.25 million ($250 million × 0.50%) per year (see Exhibit 5.26).[22] This amount is included in interest expense on the income statement, together with the annual administrative agent fee of $150,000.

Term Loan Facility In the "Term Loan Facility" section of the debt schedule, the banker inputs the spread, term, and mandatory repayment schedule associated with the facility (see Exhibit 5.27). The facility's size is linked from the sources and uses of funds on the transaction summary page (see Exhibit 5.46). For the ValueCo LBO, we contemplated a $2,150 million TLB with a coupon of L+450 bps, LIBOR floor of 1.25%, and a term of seven years.

Mandatory Repayments (Amortization) Unlike a revolving credit facility, which only requires repayment at the maturity date of all the outstanding advances, a term loan facility is fully funded at close and has a set amortization schedule as defined in the corresponding credit agreement. While amortization schedules vary per term loan tranche, the standard for TLBs is 1% amortization per year on the principal amount of the loan with a bullet payment of the loan balance at maturity.[23]

As noted in Exhibit 5.27 under the repayment schedule line item, ValueCo's new TLB requires an annual 1% amortization payment equating to $21.5 million ($2,150 million × 1%).

---

[22]To the extent the revolver is used, the commitment expense will decline, and ValueCo will be charged interest on the amount of the revolver draw at L+425 bps / 1.25% LIBOR floor.
[23]Credit agreements typically also have a provision requiring the borrower to prepay term loans in an amount equal to a specified percentage (and definition) of excess cash flow and in the event of specified asset sales and issuances of certain debt or equity.

EXHIBIT 5.26 Revolving Credit Facility Section of Debt Schedule

($ in millions, fiscal year ending December 31)

Debt Schedule

	Pro forma 2012	Year 1 2013	Year 2 2014	Year 3 2015	Year 4 2016	Year 5 2017	Year 6 2018	Year 7 2019	Year 8 2020	Year 9 2021	Year 10 2022
						Projection Period					
Forward LIBOR Curve	0.25%	0.35%	0.50%	0.75%	1.00%	1.25%	1.50%	1.75%	2.00%	2.25%	2.50%
Cash Flow from Operating Activities		$371.8	$420.5	$464.7	$506.3	$544.5	$575.9	$609.8	$637.1	$657.3	$680.7
Cash Flow from Investing Activities		(166.9)	(176.9)	(185.8)	(193.2)	(199.0)	(204.9)	(211.1)	(217.4)	(224.0)	(230.7)
Cash Available for Debt Repayment		**$204.9**	**$243.6**	**$278.9**	**$313.1**	**$345.5**	**$371.0**	**$398.7**	**$419.7**	**$433.3**	**$450.0**
Total Mandatory Repayments		(21.5)	(21.5)	(21.5)	(21.5)	(21.5)	(21.5)	(21.5)			
Cash From Balance Sheet	MinCash	-	-	-	-	-	-	-	5.8	425.4	858.8
Cash Available for Optional Debt Repayment		**$183.4**	**$222.1**	**$257.4**	**$291.6**	**$324.0**	**$349.5**	**$377.2**	**$425.4**	**$858.8**	**$1,308.8**

Revolving Credit Facility

Revolving Credit Facility Size	$250.0										
Spread	4.250%										
LIBOR Floor	1.250%										
Term	6 years										
Commitment Fee on Unused Portion	0.50%										
Beginning Balance		-	-	-	-	-	-	-	-	-	-
Drawdown/(Repayment)		-	-	-	-	-	-	-	-	-	-
Ending Balance		-	-	-	-	-	-	-	-	-	-
Interest Rate		5.50%	5.50%	5.50%	5.50%	5.50%	5.75%	6.00%	6.25%	6.50%	6.75%
Interest Expense		-	-	-	-	-	-	-	-	-	-
Commitment Fee		1.3	1.3	1.3	1.3	1.3	1.3	1.3	1.3	1.3	1.3
Administrative Agent Fee		0.2	0.2	0.2	0.2	0.2	0.2	0.2	0.2	0.2	0.2

= IF (LIBOR floor is greater than LIBOR $_{2013E}$,
then use LIBOR floor, otherwise use LIBOR$_{2013E}$) + Spread
= IF (1.25% > 0.35%, 1.25%, 0.35%) + 4.25%

= Ending Balance from Prior Year

= Ending Revolver Balance from Pro Forma 2012E Balance Sheet

= Commitment Fee on Unused Portion x (Revolver Capacity - (Average of Beginning Balance$_{2021E}$ and Ending Balance$_{2021E}$))
= 0.50% x $250 million

= IF (Cash Available for Optional Debt Repayment$_{2022E}$ > 0, then sweep the negative value of the minimum of (Cash Available for Optional Debt Repayment$_{2022E}$ vs. the Beginning Balance$_{2022E}$), otherwise sweep the negative value of the minimum of (Cash Available for Optional Debt Repayment$_{2022E}$ vs. 0))

= IF (Cash Available for Optional Debt Repayment$_{2022E}$ > 0, -MIN(Cash Available for Optional Debt Repayment$_{2022E}$, $0.0), -MIN(Cash Available for Optional Debt Repayment$_{2022E}$, 0))

EXHIBIT 5.27 Term Loan Facility Section of Debt Schedule

($ in millions, fiscal year ending December 31)

Debt Schedule

	Pro forma 2012	Year 1 2013	Year 2 2014	Year 3 2015	Year 4 2016	Year 5 2017	Projection Period Year 6 2018	Year 7 2019	Year 8 2020	Year 9 2021	Year 10 2022
Forward LIBOR Curve	0.25%	0.35%	0.50%	0.75%	1.00%	1.25%	1.50%	1.75%	2.00%	2.25%	2.50%
Cash Flow from Operating Activities		$371.8	$420.5	$464.7	$506.3	$544.5	$575.9	$609.8	$637.1	$657.3	$680.7
Cash Flow from Investing Activities		(166.9)	(176.9)	(185.8)	(193.2)	(199.0)	(204.9)	(211.1)	(217.4)	(224.0)	(230.7)
Cash Available for Debt Repayment		**$204.9**	**$243.6**	**$278.9**	**$313.1**	**$345.5**	**$371.0**	**$398.7**	**$419.7**	**$433.3**	**$450.0**
Total Mandatory Repayments	MinCash	(21.5)	(21.5)	(21.5)	(21.5)	(21.5)	(21.5)	(21.5)	-	-	-
Cash From Balance Sheet	-								5.8	425.4	858.8
Cash Available for Optional Debt Repayment		**$183.4**	**$222.1**	**$257.4**	**$291.6**	**$324.0**	**$349.5**	**$377.2**	**$425.4**	**$858.8**	**$1,308.8**

Term Loan B Facility

Size	$2,150.0										
Spread	4.500%										
LIBOR Floor	1.250%										
Term	7 years										
Repayment Schedule	1.0% Per Annum, Bullet at Maturity										
Beginning Balance		$2,150.0	$1,945.1	$1,701.5	$1,422.6	$1,109.4	$763.9	$392.9	-	-	-
Mandatory Repayments		(21.5)	(21.5)	(21.5)	(21.5)	(21.5)	(21.5)	(21.5)	-	-	-
Optional Repayments		(183.4)	(222.1)	(257.4)	(291.6)	(324.0)	(349.5)	(371.4)	-	-	-
Ending Balance		**$1,945.1**	**$1,701.5**	**$1,422.6**	**$1,109.4**	**$763.9**	**$392.9**	-	-	-	-
Interest Rate		5.75%	5.75%	5.75%	5.75%	5.75%	6.00%	6.25%	6.50%	6.75%	7.00%
Interest Expense		117.7	104.8	89.8	72.8	53.9	34.7	12.3	-	-	-

= Interest Rate$_{2013E}$ x Average(Beginning Balance$_{2013E}$:Ending Balance$_{2013E}$)
= 5.75% x Average of $2,150 million and $1,945.1 million

= Ending Term Loan B Balance from Pro Forma 2012E Balance Sheet

= The negative of the minimum of (Cash Flow Available for Optional Debt Repayment$_{2015E}$ vs. Beginning Balance$_{2015E}$ + Mandatory Amortization$_{2015E}$)
= -MIN ($257.4 million : $1,701.5 million + ($21.5) million)

= IF (Beginning Balance$_{2018E}$ is greater than 0 and greater than 1% of the principal amount, then subtract 1% Mandatory Amortization on the principal amount of the Term Loan B, otherwise display $0.0)
= IF ($763.9 million > 0 and > 1% x $2,150 million, then 1% x $2,150 million, otherwise $0.0)

Optional Repayments A typical LBO model employs a "100% cash flow sweep" that assumes all cash generated by the target after making mandatory debt repayments is applied to the optional repayment of outstanding prepayable debt (typically bank debt). For modeling purposes, bank debt is generally repaid in the following order: revolver balance, term loan A, term loan B, etc.[24]

From a credit risk management perspective, ideally the target generates sufficient cumulative free cash flow during the projection period to repay the term loan(s) within their defined maturities. In some cases, however, the borrower may not be expected to repay the entire term loan balance within the proposed tenor and will instead face refinancing risk as the debt matures.

As shown in Exhibit 5.27, in 2013E, ValueCo is projected to generate cash available for debt repayment of $204.9 million. Following the mandatory TLB principal repayment of $21.5 million, ValueCo has $183.4 million of excess free cash flow remaining. These funds are used to make optional debt repayments on the TLB, which is prepayable without penalty. Hence, the beginning year balance of $2,150 million is reduced to an ending balance of $1,945.1 million following the combined mandatory and optional debt repayments.

Interest Expense The banker typically employs an average interest expense approach in determining annual interest expense in an LBO model. This methodology accounts for the fact that bank debt is repaid throughout the year rather than at the beginning or end of the year. Annual average interest expense for each debt tranche is calculated by multiplying the average of the beginning and ending debt balances in a given year by its corresponding interest rate.

As shown in Exhibit 5.27, in 2013E, ValueCo's TLB has a beginning balance of $2,150 million and ending balance of $1,945.1 million. Using the average debt approach, this implies interest expense of $117.7 million for the TLB in 2013E (($2,150 million + $1,945.1 million)/2) × 5.75%). The $117.7 million of interest expense is linked from the debt schedule to the income statement under the corresponding line item for TLB interest expense.

Senior Notes In the "Senior Notes" section of the debt schedule, the banker inputs the coupon and term associated with the security (see Exhibit 5.28). As with the TLB, the principal amount of the notes is linked from the sources and uses of funds on the transaction summary page (see Exhibit 5.46). Unlike traditional bank debt, high yield bonds are not prepayable without penalty and do not have a mandatory repayment schedule prior to the bullet payment at maturity. As a result, the model does not assume repayment of the high yield bonds prior to maturity and the beginning and ending balances for each year in the projection period are equal.

---

[24]Some credit agreements give credit to the borrower for voluntary repayments on a go-forward basis and/or may require pro rata repayment of certain tranches.

LBO Analysis

EXHIBIT 5.28 Senior Notes Section of Debt Schedule

($ in millions, fiscal year ending December 31)

Debt Schedule		Projection Period									
	Pro forma 2012	Year 1 2013	Year 2 2014	Year 3 2015	Year 4 2016	Year 5 2017	Year 6 2018	Year 7 2019	Year 8 2020	Year 9 2021	Year 10 2022
Senior Notes											
Size	$1,500.0										
Coupon	8.500%										
Term	8 years										
Beginning Balance		$1,500.0	$1,500.0	$1,500.0	$1,500.0	$1,500.0	$1,500.0	$1,500.0	$1,500.0	$1,500.0	$1,500.0
Repayment		-	-	-	-	-	-	-	-	-	-
Ending Balance		$1,500.0	$1,500.0	$1,500.0	$1,500.0	$1,500.0	$1,500.0	$1,500.0	$1,500.0	$1,500.0	$1,500.0
Interest Expense		127.5	127.5	127.5	127.5	127.5	127.5	127.5	127.5	127.5	127.5

= Coupon on Senior Notes × Principal Amount
= 8.5% × $1,500 million

For the ValueCo LBO, we contemplated a senior notes issuance of $1,500 million with an 8.5% coupon and a maturity of eight years.[25] The notes are the longest-tenored debt instrument in the financing structure. As the notes do not amortize and there is no optional repayment due to the call protection period (standard in high yield bonds), annual interest expense is simply $127.5 million ($1,500 million × 8.5%).

The completed debt schedule is shown in Exhibit 5.29.

---

[25]The notes are assumed to be refinanced at maturity.

EXHIBIT 5.29 Debt Schedule

($ in millions, fiscal year ending December 31)

Debt Schedule

	Pro forma 2012	Year 1 2013	Year 2 2014	Year 3 2015	Year 4 2016	Year 5 2017	Year 6 2018	Year 7 2019	Year 8 2020	Year 9 2021	Year 10 2022
Forward LIBOR Curve	0.25%	0.35%	0.50%	0.75%	1.00%	1.25%	1.50%	1.75%	2.00%	2.25%	2.50%
Cash Flow from Operating Activities		$371.8	$420.5	$464.7	$506.3	$544.5	$575.9	$609.8	$637.1	$657.3	$680.7
Cash Flow from Investing Activities		(166.9)	(176.9)	(185.8)	(193.2)	(199.0)	(204.9)	(211.1)	(217.4)	(224.0)	(230.7)
Cash Available for Debt Repayment		**$204.9**	**$243.6**	**$278.9**	**$313.1**	**$345.5**	**$371.0**	**$398.7**	**$419.7**	**$433.3**	**$450.0**
Total Mandatory Repayments	MinCash	(21.5)	(21.5)	(21.5)	(21.5)	(21.5)	(21.5)	(21.5)			
Cash From Balance Sheet	—								5.8	425.4	858.8
Cash Available for Optional Debt Repayment		**$183.4**	**$222.1**	**$257.4**	**$291.6**	**$324.0**	**$349.5**	**$377.2**	**$425.4**	**$858.8**	**$1,308.8**

Revolving Credit Facility

Revolving Credit Facility Size	$250.0										
Spread	4.250%										
LIBOR Floor	1.250%										
Term	6 years										
Commitment Fee on Unused Portion	0.50%										
Beginning Balance		—	—	—	—	—	—	—	—	—	—
Drawdown/(Repayment)		—	—	—	—	—	—	—	—	—	—
Ending Balance		—	—	—	—	—	—	—	—	—	—
Interest Rate		5.50%	5.50%	5.50%	5.50%	5.50%	5.75%	6.00%	6.25%	6.50%	6.75%
Interest Expense		—	—	—	—	—	—	—	—	—	—
Commitment Fee		1.3	1.3	1.3	1.3	1.3	1.3	1.3	1.3	1.3	1.3
Administrative Agent Fee		0.2	0.2	0.2	0.2	0.2	0.2	0.2	0.2	0.2	0.2

Term Loan B Facility

Size	$2,150.0										
Spread	4.500%										
LIBOR Floor	1.250%										
Term	7 years										
Repayment Schedule	1.0% Per Annum, Bullet at Maturity										
Beginning Balance		$2,150.0	$1,945.1	$1,701.5	$1,422.6	$1,109.4	$763.9	$392.9	—	—	—
Mandatory Repayments		(21.5)	(21.5)	(21.5)	(21.5)	(21.5)	(21.5)	(21.5)	—	—	—
Optional Repayments		(183.4)	(222.1)	(257.4)	(291.6)	(324.0)	(349.5)	(371.4)	—	—	—
Ending Balance		**$1,945.1**	**$1,701.5**	**$1,422.6**	**$1,109.4**	**$763.9**	**$392.9**	—	—	—	—
Interest Rate		5.75%	5.75%	5.75%	5.75%	5.75%	6.00%	6.25%	6.50%	6.75%	7.00%
Interest Expense		117.7	104.8	89.8	72.8	53.9	34.7	12.3			

Senior Notes

Size	$1,500.0										
Coupon	8.500%										
Term	8 years										
Beginning Balance		$1,500.0	$1,500.0	$1,500.0	$1,500.0	$1,500.0	$1,500.0	$1,500.0	$1,500.0	$1,500.0	$1,500.0
Repayment		—	—	—	—	—	—	—	—	—	—
Ending Balance		**$1,500.0**	**$1,500.0**	**$1,500.0**	**$1,500.0**	**$1,500.0**	**$1,500.0**	**$1,500.0**	**$1,500.0**	**$1,500.0**	**$1,500.0**

Step IV(b): Complete Pro Forma Income Statement from EBIT to Net Income

The calculated average annual interest expense for each loan, bond, or other debt instrument in the capital structure is linked from the completed debt schedule to its corresponding line item on the income statement (see Exhibit 5.30).[26]

EXHIBIT 5.30 Pro Forma Projected Income Statement—EBIT to Net Income

($ in millions, fiscal year ending December 31)

Income Statement	Pro forma 2012	Year 1 2013	Year 2 2014	Year 3 2015	Year 4 2016	Year 5 2017	Year 6 2018	Year 7 2019	Year 8 2020	Year 9 2021	Year 10 2022
EBIT	$518.0	$556.9	$590.3	$619.8	$644.6	$663.9	$683.8	$704.3	$725.5	$747.2	$769.6
% margin	15.0%	15.0%	15.0%	15.0%	15.0%	15.0%	15.0%	15.0%	15.0%	15.0%	15.0%
Interest Expense											
Revolving Credit Facility	-	-	-	-	-	-	-	-	-	-	-
Term Loan A	-	-	-	-	-	-	-	-	-	-	-
Term Loan B	123.6	117.7	104.8	89.8	72.8	53.9	34.7	12.3	-	-	-
Term Loan C	-	-	-	-	-	-	-	-	-	-	-
Existing Term Loan	-	-	-	-	-	-	-	-	-	-	-
2nd Lien	-	-	-	-	-	-	-	-	-	-	-
Senior Notes	127.5	127.5	127.5	127.5	127.5	127.5	127.5	127.5	127.5	127.5	127.5
Senior Subordinated Notes	-	-	-	-	-	-	-	-	-	-	-
Commitment Fee on Unused Revolver	1.3	1.3	1.3	1.3	1.3	1.3	1.3	1.3	1.3	1.3	1.3
Administrative Agent Fee	0.2	0.2	0.2	0.2	0.2	0.2	0.2	0.2	0.2	0.2	0.2
Cash Interest Expense	$252.5	$246.6	$233.7	$218.7	$201.7	$182.8	$163.6	$141.2	$128.9	$128.9	$128.9
Amortization of Deferred Financing Fees	12.0	12.0	12.0	12.0	12.0	12.0	12.0	11.4	6.8	-	-
Total Interest Expense	$264.5	$258.6	$245.7	$230.7	$213.7	$194.7	$175.6	$152.5	$135.7	$128.9	$128.9
Interest Income	-	-	-	-	-	-	-	(0.0)	(1.1)	(3.2)	(5.4)
Net Interest Expense		$258.6	$245.7	$230.7	$213.7	$194.7	$175.6	$152.5	$134.6	$125.7	$123.5
Earnings Before Taxes		298.2	344.5	389.1	430.9	469.2	508.2	551.8	590.9	621.5	646.2
Income Tax Expense		113.3	130.9	147.8	163.7	178.3	193.1	209.7	224.5	236.2	245.5
Net Income	$184.9	$213.6	$241.2	$267.2	$290.9	$315.1	$342.1	$366.4	$385.4	$400.6	
% margin		5.0%	5.4%	5.8%	6.2%	6.6%	6.9%	7.3%	7.6%	7.7%	7.8%

Cash Interest Expense Cash interest expense refers to a company's actual cash interest and associated financing-related payments in a given year. It is the sum of the average interest expense for each cash-pay debt instrument plus the commitment fee on the unused portion of the revolver and the administrative agent fee. As shown in Exhibit 5.30, ValueCo is projected to have $246.6 million of cash interest expense in 2013E. This amount decreases to $128.9 million by the end of the projection period after the bank debt is repaid.

Total Interest Expense Total interest expense is the sum of cash and non-cash interest expense, most notably the amortization of deferred financing fees, which is linked from an assumptions page (see Exhibit 5.54). The amortization of deferred financing fees, while technically not interest expense, is included in total interest expense as it is a financial charge. In a capital structure with a PIK instrument, the non-cash interest portion would also be included in total interest expense and added back to cash flow from operating activities on the cash flow statement. As shown in Exhibit 5.30, ValueCo has non-cash deferred financing fees of $12 million in

---

[26]At this point, a circular reference centering on interest expense has been created in the model. Interest expense is used to calculate net income and determine cash available for debt repayment and ending debt balances, which, in turn, are used to calculate interest expense. The spreadsheet must be set up to perform the circular calculation (in Microsoft Excel) by selecting Tools, Options, clicking on the "Calculation" tab, checking the box next to "Iteration," and setting the "Maximum iterations" field to 1000 (see Exhibit 3.30).

2013E. These fees are added to the 2013E cash interest expense of $246.6 million to sum to $258.6 million of total interest expense.

Net Interest Expense Net interest expense is calculated by subtracting interest income received on cash held on a company's balance sheet from its total interest expense. In the ValueCo LBO, however, until 2019E (Year 7), when all prepayable debt is repaid and cash begins to build on the balance sheet, there is no interest income as the cash balance is zero. In 2020E, ValueCo is expected to earn interest income of $1.1 million,[27] which is netted against total interest expense of $135.7 million to produce net interest expense of $134.6 million.

Net Income To calculate ValueCo's net income for 2013E, we subtracted net interest expense of $258.6 million from EBIT of $556.9 million, which resulted in earnings before taxes of $298.2 million. We then multiplied EBT by ValueCo's marginal tax rate of 38% to produce tax expense of $113.3 million, which was netted out of EBT to calculate net income of $184.9 million.

Net income for each year in the projection period is linked from the income statement to the cash flow statement as the first line item under operating activities. It also feeds into the balance sheet as an addition to shareholders' equity in the form of retained earnings.

The completed pro forma income statement is shown in Exhibit 5.31.

---

[27]Assumes a 0.5% interest rate earned on cash (using an average balance method), which is indicative of a short-term money market instrument.

EXHIBIT 5.31 Pro Forma ValueCo Income Statement

($ in millions, fiscal year ending December 31)

Income Statement

	Historical Period			LTM	Pro forma	Projection Period									
	2009	2010	2011	9/30/2012	2012	Year 1 2013	Year 2 2014	Year 3 2015	Year 4 2016	Year 5 2017	Year 6 2018	Year 7 2019	Year 8 2020	Year 9 2021	Year 10 2022
Sales	$2,600.0	$2,900.0	$3,200.0	$3,385.0	$3,450.0	$3,708.8	$3,931.3	$4,127.8	$4,293.0	$4,421.7	$4,554.4	$4,691.0	$4,831.8	$4,976.7	$5,126.0
% growth	NA	11.5%	10.3%	NA	7.8%	7.5%	6.0%	5.0%	4.0%	3.0%	3.0%	3.0%	3.0%	3.0%	3.0%
Cost of Goods Sold	1,612.0	1,769.0	1,920.0	2,035.0	2,070.0	2,225.3	2,358.8	2,476.7	2,575.8	2,653.0	2,732.6	2,814.6	2,899.1	2,986.0	3,075.6
Gross Profit	$988.0	$1,131.0	$1,280.0	$1,350.0	$1,380.0	$1,483.5	$1,572.5	$1,651.1	$1,717.2	$1,768.7	$1,821.8	$1,876.4	$1,932.7	$1,990.7	$2,050.4
% margin	38.0%	39.0%	40.0%	39.9%	40.0%	40.0%	40.0%	40.0%	40.0%	40.0%	40.0%	40.0%	40.0%	40.0%	40.0%
Selling, General & Administrative	496.6	551.0	608.0	650.0	655.0	704.1	746.4	783.7	815.0	839.5	864.7	890.6	917.3	944.9	973.2
% sales	19.1%	19.0%	19.0%	19.2%	19.0%	19.0%	19.0%	19.0%	19.0%	19.0%	19.0%	19.0%	19.0%	19.0%	19.0%
Other Expense / (Income)															
EBITDA	$491.4	$580.0	$672.0	$700.0	$725.0	$779.4	$826.1	$867.4	$902.1	$929.2	$957.1	$985.8	$1,015.4	$1,045.8	$1,077.2
% margin	18.9%	20.0%	21.0%	20.7%	21.0%	21.0%	21.0%	21.0%	21.0%	21.0%	21.0%	21.0%	21.0%	21.0%	21.0%
Depreciation	116.0	121.5	145.0	150.0	155.3	166.9	176.9	185.8	193.2	199.0	204.9	211.1	217.4	224.0	230.7
Amortization	39.0	43.5	48.0	50.0	51.8	55.6	59.0	61.9	64.4	66.3	68.3	70.4	72.5	74.7	76.9
EBIT	$336.4	$415.0	$479.0	$500.0	$518.0	$556.9	$590.3	$619.8	$644.6	$663.9	$683.8	$704.3	$725.5	$747.2	$769.6
% margin	12.9%	14.3%	15.0%	14.8%	15.0%	15.0%	15.0%	15.0%	15.0%	15.0%	15.0%	15.0%	15.0%	15.0%	15.0%
Interest Expense															
Revolving Credit Facility															
Term Loan A															
Term Loan B						123.6	104.8	89.8	72.8	53.9	34.7	12.3			
Term Loan C															
Existing Term Loan															
2nd Lien															
Senior Notes						127.5	127.5	127.5	127.5	127.5	127.5	127.5	127.5	127.5	127.5
Senior Subordinated Notes															
Commitment Fee on Unused Revolver						1.3	1.3	1.3	1.3	1.3	1.3	1.3	1.3	1.3	1.3
Administrative Agent Fee						0.2	0.2	0.2	0.2	0.2	0.2	0.2	0.2	0.2	0.2
Cash Interest Expense						$252.5	$233.7	$218.7	$201.7	$182.8	$163.6	$141.2	$128.9	$128.9	$128.9
Amortization of Deferred Financing Fees						12.0	12.0	12.0	12.0	12.0	12.0	11.4	6.8		
Total Interest Expense						$264.5	$245.7	$230.7	$213.7	$194.7	$175.6	$152.5	$135.7	$128.9	$128.9
Interest Income												(0.0)	(1.1)	(3.2)	(5.4)
Net Interest Expense						$258.6	$245.7	$230.7	$213.7	$194.7	$175.6	$152.5	$134.6	$125.7	$123.5
Earnings Before Taxes						298.2	344.5	389.1	430.9	469.2	508.2	551.8	590.9	621.5	646.2
Income Tax Expense						113.3	130.9	147.8	163.7	178.3	193.1	209.7	224.5	236.2	245.5
Net Income						$184.9	$213.6	$241.2	$267.2	$290.9	$315.1	$342.1	$366.4	$385.4	$400.6
% margin						5.0%	5.4%	5.8%	6.2%	6.6%	6.9%	7.3%	7.6%	7.7%	7.8%
Income Statement Assumptions															
Sales (% YoY growth)	NA	11.5%	10.3%	NA	7.8%	7.5%	6.0%	5.0%	4.0%	3.0%	3.0%	3.0%	3.0%	3.0%	3.0%
Cost of Goods Sold (% margin)	62.0%	61.0%	60.0%	60.1%	60.0%	60.0%	60.0%	60.0%	60.0%	60.0%	60.0%	60.0%	60.0%	60.0%	60.0%
SG&A (% sales)	19.1%	19.0%	19.0%	19.2%	19.0%	19.0%	19.0%	19.0%	19.0%	19.0%	19.0%	19.0%	19.0%	19.0%	19.0%
Other Expense / (Income) (% of sales)	-%	-%	-%	-%	-%	-%	-%	-%	-%	-%	-%	-%	-%	-%	-%
Depreciation (% of sales)	4.5%	4.2%	4.5%	4.4%	4.5%	4.5%	4.5%	4.5%	4.5%	4.5%	4.5%	4.5%	4.5%	4.5%	4.5%
Amortization (% of sales)	1.5%	1.5%	1.5%	1.5%	1.5%	1.5%	1.5%	1.5%	1.5%	1.5%	1.5%	1.5%	1.5%	1.5%	1.5%
Interest Income					0.5%	0.5%	0.5%	0.5%	0.5%	0.5%	0.5%	0.5%	0.5%	0.5%	0.5%
Tax Rate					38.0%	38.0%	38.0%	38.0%	38.0%	38.0%	38.0%	38.0%	38.0%	38.0%	38.0%

Step IV(c): Complete Pro Forma Balance Sheet

Liabilities The balance sheet is completed by linking the year-end balances for each debt instrument directly from the debt schedule. The remaining non-current and non-debt liabilities, captured in the other long-term liabilities line item, are generally held constant at the prior year level in the absence of specific management guidance.

As shown in Exhibit 5.32, during the projection period, ValueCo's $2,150 million TLB is completely repaid by 2019E. ValueCo's $1,500 million senior notes, on the other hand, remain outstanding. In addition, we held the 2012E deferred income taxes and other long-term liabilities amount constant at $300 million and $110 million, respectively, for the length of the projection period.

EXHIBIT 5.32 Pro Forma Total Liabilities Section of Balance Sheet

($ in millions, fiscal year ending December 31)

Balance Sheet	Opening 2012	Adjustments +	Adjustments -	Pro Forma 2012	Year 1 2013	Year 2 2014	Year 3 2015	Year 4 2016	Year 5 2017	Year 6 2018	Year 7 2019	Year 8 2020	Year 9 2021	Year 10 2022
Accounts Payable	215.0			215.0	231.1	245.0	257.2	267.5	275.6	283.8	292.3	301.1	310.1	319.4
Accrued Liabilities	275.0			275.0	295.6	313.4	329.0	342.2	352.5	363.0	373.9	385.1	396.7	408.6
Other Current Liabilities	100.0			100.0	107.5	114.0	119.6	124.4	128.2	132.0	136.0	140.1	144.3	148.6
Total Current Liabilities	**$590.0**			**$590.0**	**$634.3**	**$672.3**	**$705.9**	**$734.2**	**$756.2**	**$778.9**	**$802.2**	**$826.3**	**$851.1**	**$876.6**
Revolving Credit Facility	-			-	-	-	-	-	-	-	-	-	-	-
Term Loan B	-	2,150.0		2,150.0	1,945.1	1,701.5	1,422.6	1,109.4	763.9	392.9	-	-	-	-
Existing Term Loan	1,000.0		(1,000.0)	-	-	-	-	-	-	-	-	-	-	-
Senior Notes	-	1,500.0		1,500.0	1,500.0	1,500.0	1,500.0	1,500.0	1,500.0	1,500.0	1,500.0	1,500.0	1,500.0	1,500.0
Existing Senior Notes	500.0		(500.0)	-	-	-	-	-	-	-	-	-	-	-
Deferred Income Taxes	300.0			300.0	300.0	300.0	300.0	300.0	300.0	300.0	300.0	300.0	300.0	300.0
Other Long-Term Liabilities	110.0			110.0	110.0	110.0	110.0	110.0	110.0	110.0	110.0	110.0	110.0	110.0
Total Liabilities	**$2,500.0**			**$4,650.0**	**$4,489.4**	**$4,283.8**	**$4,038.5**	**$3,753.6**	**$3,430.1**	**$3,081.8**	**$2,712.2**	**$2,736.3**	**$2,761.1**	**$2,786.6**

Shareholders' Equity Pro forma net income, which has now been calculated for each year in the projection period, is added to the prior year's shareholders' equity as retained earnings.

As shown in Exhibit 5.33, at the end of 2012E pro forma for the LBO, ValueCo has $2,040 million of shareholders' initial equity (representing the sponsor's equity contribution less other fees and expenses). To calculate 2013E shareholders' equity, we added the 2013E net income of $184.9 million, which summed to $2,224.9 million.

EXHIBIT 5.33 Pro Forma Total Shareholders' Equity Section of Balance Sheet

($ in millions, fiscal year ending December 31)

Balance Sheet	Opening 2012	Adjustments +	Adjustments -	Pro Forma 2012	Year 1 2013	Year 2 2014	Year 3 2015	Year 4 2016	Year 5 2017	Year 6 2018	Year 7 2019	Year 8 2020	Year 9 2021	Year 10 2022
Shareholders' Equity	3,500.0	2,040.0	(3,500.0)	2,040.0	2,224.9	2,438.5	2,679.7	2,946.9	3,237.8	3,552.9	3,895.0	4,261.4	4,646.7	5,047.3
Total Shareholders' Equity	**$3,500.0**			**$2,040.0**	**$2,224.9**	**$2,438.5**	**$2,679.7**	**$2,946.9**	**$3,237.8**	**$3,552.9**	**$3,895.0**	**$4,261.4**	**$4,646.7**	**$5,047.3**
Total Liabilities and Equity	**$6,000.0**			**$6,690.0**	**$6,714.3**	**$6,722.3**	**$6,718.2**	**$6,700.5**	**$6,667.9**	**$6,634.7**	**$6,607.2**	**$6,997.7**	**$7,407.8**	**$7,834.0**

= Shareholders' Equity$_{2012E}$ + Net Income$_{2013E}$
= $2,040 million + $184.9 million

The completed pro forma balance sheet is shown in Exhibit 5.34.

EXHIBIT 5.34 Pro Forma ValueCo Balance Sheet

($ in millions, fiscal year ending December 31)

Balance Sheet

	Opening 2012	Adjustments +	Adjustments −	Pro Forma 2012	Year 1 2013	Year 2 2014	Year 3 2015	Year 4 2016	Year 5 2017	Year 6 2018	Year 7 2019	Year 8 2020	Year 9 2021	Year 10 2022
Cash and Cash Equivalents	$250.0		(250.0)	$-	$-	$-	$-	$-	$-	$-	$5.8	$425.4	$858.8	$1,308.8
Accounts Receivable	450.0			450.0	483.8	512.8	538.4	560.0	576.7	594.1	611.9	630.2	649.1	668.6
Inventories	600.0			600.0	645.0	683.7	717.9	746.6	769.0	792.1	815.8	840.3	865.5	891.5
Prepaids and Other Current Assets	175.0			175.0	188.1	199.4	209.4	217.8	224.3	231.0	238.0	245.1	252.4	260.0
Total Current Assets	**$1,475.0**			**$1,225.0**	**$1,316.9**	**$1,395.9**	**$1,465.7**	**$1,524.3**	**$1,570.0**	**$1,617.1**	**$1,671.4**	**$2,141.1**	**$2,625.8**	**$3,128.9**
Property, Plant and Equipment, net	2,500.0			2,500.0	2,500.0	2,500.0	2,500.0	2,500.0	2,500.0	2,500.0	2,500.0	2,500.0	2,500.0	2,500.0
Goodwill	1,000.0	1,850.0	(1,000.0)	1,850.0	1,850.0	1,850.0	1,850.0	1,850.0	1,850.0	1,850.0	1,850.0	1,850.0	1,850.0	1,850.0
Intangible Assets	875.0			875.0	819.4	760.4	698.5	634.1	567.8	499.4	429.1	356.6	282.0	205.1
Other Assets	150.0			150.0	150.0	150.0	150.0	150.0	150.0	150.0	150.0	150.0	150.0	150.0
Deferred Financing Fees	-	90.0		90.0	78.0	66.0	54.1	42.1	30.1	18.1	6.7	-	-	-
Total Assets	**$6,000.0**			**$6,690.0**	**$6,714.3**	**$6,722.3**	**$6,718.2**	**$6,700.5**	**$6,667.9**	**$6,634.7**	**$6,607.2**	**$6,997.7**	**$7,407.8**	**$7,834.0**
Accounts Payable	215.0			215.0	231.1	245.0	257.2	267.5	275.6	283.8	292.3	301.1	310.1	319.4
Accrued Liabilities	275.0			275.0	295.6	313.4	329.0	342.2	352.5	363.0	373.9	385.1	396.7	408.6
Other Current Liabilities	100.0			100.0	107.5	114.0	119.6	124.4	128.2	132.0	136.0	140.1	144.3	148.6
Total Current Liabilities	**$590.0**			**$590.0**	**$634.3**	**$672.3**	**$705.9**	**$734.2**	**$756.2**	**$778.9**	**$802.2**	**$826.3**	**$851.1**	**$876.6**
Revolving Credit Facility	-			-	-	-	-	-	-	-	-	-	-	-
Term Loan A	-			-	-	-	-	-	-	-	-	-	-	-
Term Loan B	-	2,150.0		2,150.0	1,945.1	1,701.5	1,422.6	1,109.4	763.9	392.9	-	-	-	-
Term Loan C	-			-	-	-	-	-	-	-	-	-	-	-
Existing Term Loan	1,000.0		(1,000.0)	-	-	-	-	-	-	-	-	-	-	-
2nd Lien	-			-	-	-	-	-	-	-	-	-	-	-
Senior Notes	-	1,500.0		1,500.0	1,500.0	1,500.0	1,500.0	1,500.0	1,500.0	1,500.0	1,500.0	1,500.0	1,500.0	1,500.0
Existing Senior Notes	500.0		(500.0)	-	-	-	-	-	-	-	-	-	-	-
Senior Subordinated Notes	-			-	-	-	-	-	-	-	-	-	-	-
Other Debt	-			-	-	-	-	-	-	-	-	-	-	-
Deferred Income Taxes	300.0			300.0	300.0	300.0	300.0	300.0	300.0	300.0	300.0	300.0	300.0	300.0
Other Long-Term Liabilities	110.0			110.0	110.0	110.0	110.0	110.0	110.0	110.0	110.0	110.0	110.0	110.0
Total Liabilities	**$2,500.0**			**$4,650.0**	**$4,489.4**	**$4,283.8**	**$4,038.5**	**$3,753.6**	**$3,430.1**	**$3,081.8**	**$2,712.2**	**$2,736.3**	**$2,761.1**	**$2,786.6**
Noncontrolling Interest	-			-	-	-	-	-	-	-	-	-	-	-
Shareholders' Equity	3,500.0	2,040.0	(3,500.0)	2,040.0	2,224.9	2,438.5	2,679.7	2,946.9	3,237.8	3,552.9	3,895.0	4,261.4	4,646.7	5,047.3
Total Shareholders' Equity	**$3,500.0**			**$2,040.0**	**$2,224.9**	**$2,438.5**	**$2,679.7**	**$2,946.9**	**$3,237.8**	**$3,552.9**	**$3,895.0**	**$4,261.4**	**$4,646.7**	**$5,047.3**
Total Liabilities and Equity	**$6,000.0**			**$6,690.0**	**$6,714.3**	**$6,722.3**	**$6,718.2**	**$6,700.5**	**$6,667.9**	**$6,634.7**	**$6,607.2**	**$6,997.7**	**$7,407.8**	**$7,834.0**
Balance Check	0.000			0.000	0.000	0.000	0.000	0.000	0.000	0.000	0.000	0.000	0.000	0.000
Net Working Capital	635.0			635.0	682.6	723.6	759.8	790.2	813.9	838.3	863.4	889.3	916.0	943.5
(Increase) / Decrease in Net Working Capital					(47.6)	(41.0)	(36.2)	(30.4)	(23.7)	(24.4)	(25.1)	(25.9)	(26.7)	(27.5)

Balance Sheet Assumptions

Current Assets

Days Sales Outstanding (DSO)	47.6			47.6	47.6	47.6	47.6	47.6	47.6	47.6	47.6	47.6	47.6	47.6
Days Inventory Held (DIH)	105.8			105.8	105.8	105.8	105.8	105.8	105.8	105.8	105.8	105.8	105.8	105.8
Prepaid and Other Current Assets (% of sales)	5.1%			5.1%	5.1%	5.1%	5.1%	5.1%	5.1%	5.1%	5.1%	5.1%	5.1%	5.1%

Current Liabilities

Days Payable Outstanding (DPO)	37.9			37.9	37.9	37.9	37.9	37.9	37.9	37.9	37.9	37.9	37.9	37.9
Accrued Liabilities (% of sales)	8.0%			8.0%	8.0%	8.0%	8.0%	8.0%	8.0%	8.0%	8.0%	8.0%	8.0%	8.0%
Other Current Liabilities (% of sales)	2.9%			2.9%	2.9%	2.9%	2.9%	2.9%	2.9%	2.9%	2.9%	2.9%	2.9%	2.9%

Step IV(d): Complete Pro Forma Cash Flow Statement

To complete the cash flow statement, the mandatory and optional repayments for each debt instrument, as calculated in the debt schedule, are linked to the appropriate line items in the financing activities section and summed to produce the annual repayment amounts. The annual pro forma beginning and ending cash balances are then calculated accordingly.

In 2013E, ValueCo is projected to generate $204.9 million of free cash flow. This amount is first used to satisfy the $21.5 million mandatory TLB amortization with the remaining cash used to make an optional repayment of $183.4 million. As shown in Exhibit 5.35, these combined actions are linked to the TLB line item in the financing activities section of the cash flow statement as a $204.9 million use of cash in 2013E.

EXHIBIT 5.35 Pro Forma Financing Activities Section of Cash Flow Statement

($ in millions, fiscal year ending December 31)

Cash Flow Statement				Projection Period						
	Year 1 2013	Year 2 2014	Year 3 2015	Year 4 2016	Year 5 2017	Year 6 2018	Year 7 2019	Year 8 2020	Year 9 2021	Year 10 2022
Financing Activities										
Revolving Credit Facility	-	-	-	-	-	-	-	-	-	-
Term Loan B	(204.9)	(243.6)	(278.9)	(313.1)	(345.5)	(371.0)	(392.9)	-	-	-
Existing Term Loan	-	-	-	-	-	-	-	-	-	-
Senior Notes	-	-	-	-	-	-	-	-	-	-
Dividends	-	-	-	-	-	-	-	-	-	-
Equity Issuance / (Repurchase)	-	-	-	-	-	-	-	-	-	-
Cash Flow from Financing Activities	($204.9)	($243.6)	($278.9)	($313.1)	($345.5)	($371.0)	($392.9)	-	-	-
Excess Cash for the Period	-	-	-	-	-	-	$5.8	$419.7	$433.3	$450.0
Beginning Cash Balance	-	-	-	-	-	-	-	5.8	425.4	858.8
Ending Cash Balance	-	-	-	-	-	-	$5.8	$425.4	$858.8	$1,308.8
Cash Flow Statement Assumptions										
Capital Expenditures (% of sales)	4.5%	4.5%	4.5%	4.5%	4.5%	4.5%	4.5%	4.5%	4.5%	4.5%

= Mandatory Repayments$_{2013E}$
+ Optional Repayments$_{2013E}$
= ($21.5) million + ($183.4) million

As we assumed a 100% cash flow sweep, cash does not build on the balance sheet until the bank debt is fully repaid. Hence, ValueCo's ending cash balance line item remains constant at zero until 2019E when the TLB is completely paid down.[28] As shown in Exhibit 5.10, the ending cash balance for each year in the projection period links to the balance sheet.

The completed pro forma cash flow statement is shown in Exhibit 5.36.

---

[28] While a cash balance of zero may be unrealistic from an operating perspective, it is a relatively common modeling convention.

EXHIBIT 5.36 Pro Forma ValueCo Cash Flow Statement

($ in millions, fiscal year ending December 31)

Cash Flow Statement

	Year 1 2013	Year 2 2014	Year 3 2015	Year 4 2016	Projection Period Year 5 2017	Year 6 2018	Year 7 2019	Year 8 2020	Year 9 2021	Year 10 2022
Operating Activities										
Net Income	$184.9	$213.6	$241.2	$267.2	$290.9	$315.1	$342.1	$366.4	$385.4	$400.6
Plus: Depreciation	166.9	176.9	185.8	193.2	199.0	204.9	211.1	217.4	224.0	230.7
Plus: Amortization	55.6	59.0	61.9	64.4	66.3	68.3	70.4	72.5	74.7	76.9
Plus: Amortization of Financing Fees	12.0	12.0	12.0	12.0	12.0	12.0	11.4	6.8	-	-
Changes in Working Capital Items										
(Inc.) / Dec. in Accounts Receivable	(33.8)	(29.0)	(25.6)	(21.5)	(16.8)	(17.3)	(17.8)	(18.4)	(18.9)	(19.5)
(Inc.) / Dec. in Inventories	(45.0)	(38.7)	(34.2)	(28.7)	(22.4)	(23.1)	(23.8)	(24.5)	(25.2)	(26.0)
(Inc.) / Dec. in Prepaid and Other Current Assets	(13.1)	(11.3)	(10.0)	(8.4)	(6.5)	(6.7)	(6.9)	(7.1)	(7.4)	(7.6)
Inc. / (Dec.) in Accounts Payable	16.1	13.9	12.2	10.3	8.0	8.3	8.5	8.8	9.0	9.3
Inc. / (Dec.) in Accrued Liabilities	20.6	17.7	15.7	13.2	10.3	10.6	10.9	11.2	11.6	11.9
Inc. / (Dec.) in Other Current Liabilities	7.5	6.5	5.7	4.8	3.7	3.8	4.0	4.1	4.2	4.3
(Inc.) / Dec. in Net Working Capital	(47.6)	(41.0)	(36.2)	(30.4)	(23.7)	(24.4)	(25.1)	(25.9)	(26.7)	(27.5)
Cash Flow from Operating Activities	**$371.8**	**$420.5**	**$464.7**	**$506.3**	**$544.5**	**$575.9**	**$609.8**	**$637.1**	**$657.3**	**$680.7**
Investing Activities										
Capital Expenditures	(166.9)	(176.9)	(185.8)	(193.2)	(199.0)	(204.9)	(211.1)	(217.4)	(224.0)	(230.7)
Other Investing Activities	-	-	-	-	-	-	-	-	-	-
Cash Flow from Investing Activities	**($166.9)**	**($176.9)**	**($185.8)**	**($193.2)**	**($199.0)**	**($204.9)**	**($211.1)**	**($217.4)**	**($224.0)**	**($230.7)**
Financing Activities										
Revolving Credit Facility	-	-	-	-	-	-	-	-	-	-
Term Loan B	(204.9)	(243.6)	(278.9)	(313.1)	(345.5)	(371.0)	(392.9)	-	-	-
Existing Term Loan	-	-	-	-	-	-	-	-	-	-
Senior Notes	-	-	-	-	-	-	-	-	-	-
Dividends	-	-	-	-	-	-	-	-	-	-
Equity Issuance / (Repurchase)	-	-	-	-	-	-	-	-	-	-
Cash Flow from Financing Activities	**($204.9)**	**($243.6)**	**($278.9)**	**($313.1)**	**($345.5)**	**($371.0)**	**($392.9)**	-	-	-
Excess Cash for the Period	-	-	-	-	-	-	$5.8	$419.7	$433.3	$450.0
Beginning Cash Balance	-	-	-	-	-	-	-	5.8	425.4	858.8
Ending Cash Balance	-	-	-	-	-	-	**$5.8**	**$425.4**	**$858.8**	**$1,308.8**
Cash Flow Statement Assumptions										
Capital Expenditures (% of sales)	4.5%	4.5%	4.5%	4.5%	4.5%	4.5%	4.5%	4.5%	4.5%	4.5%

STEP V. PERFORM LBO ANALYSIS

EXHIBIT 5.37 Steps to Perform LBO Analysis

Step V(a):	Analyze Financing Structure
Step V(b):	Perform Returns Analysis
Step V(c):	Determine Valuation
Step V(d):	Create Transaction Summary Page

Once the LBO model is fully linked and tested, it is ready for use to evaluate various financing structures, gauge the target's ability to service and repay debt, and measure the sponsor's investment returns and other financial effects under multiple operating scenarios. This analysis, in turn, enables the banker to determine an appropriate valuation range for the target.

Step V(a): Analyze Financing Structure

A central part of LBO analysis is the crafting of an optimal financing structure for a given transaction. From an underwriting perspective, this involves determining whether the target's financial projections can support a given leveraged financing structure under various business and economic conditions. The use of realistic and defensible financial projections is critical to assessing whether a given financial structure is viable.

A key credit risk management concern for the underwriters centers on the target's ability to service its annual interest expense and repay all (or a substantial portion) of its bank debt within the proposed tenor. The primary credit metrics used to analyze the target's ability to support a given capital structure include variations of the leverage and coverage ratios outlined in Chapter 1 (e.g., debt-to-EBITDA, debt-to-total capitalization, and EBITDA-to-interest expense). Exhibit 5.38 displays a typical output summarizing the target's key financial data as well as pro forma capitalization and credit statistics for each year in the projection period. This output is typically shown on a transaction summary page (see Exhibit 5.46).

For the ValueCo LBO, we performed our financing structure analysis on the basis of our Base Case financial projections (see Step II) and assumed transaction structure (see Step III). Pro forma for the LBO, ValueCo has a total capitalization of $5,690 million, comprised of the $2,150 million TLB, $1,500 million senior notes, and $2,040 million of shareholders' equity (the equity contribution less other fees and expenses). This capital structure represents total leverage of 5.2x LTM 9/30/2012 EBITDA of $700 million, including senior secured leverage of 3.1x (5.0x 2012E total leverage and 3.0x senior secured leverage). At these levels, ValueCo has a debt-to-total capitalization of 64.1%, EBITDA-to-interest expense of 2.7x and (EBITDA – capex)-to-interest expense of 2.2x at close.

As would be expected for a company that is projected to grow EBITDA, generate sizeable free cash flow, and repay debt, ValueCo's credit statistics improve significantly over the projection period. By the end of 2019E, ValueCo's TLB is completely repaid as total leverage decreases to 1.5x and senior secured leverage is reduced to zero. In addition, ValueCo's debt-to-total capitalization decreases to 27.8% and EBITDA-to-interest expense increases to 6.5x.

EXHIBIT 5.38 Summary Financial Data, Capitalization, and Credit Statistics

($ in millions, fiscal year ending December 31)

Summary Financial Data

	LTM 9/30/2012	Pro forma 2012	Year 1 2013	Year 2 2014	Year 3 2015	Year 4 2016	Year 5 2017	Year 6 2018	Year 7 2019	Year 8 2020	Year 9 2021	Year 10 2022
Sales	$3,385.0	$3,450.0	$3,708.8	$3,931.3	$4,127.8	$4,293.0	$4,421.7	$4,554.4	$4,691.0	$4,831.8	$4,976.7	$5,126.0
% growth	NA	7.8%	7.5%	6.0%	5.0%	4.0%	3.0%	3.0%	3.0%	3.0%	3.0%	3.0%
Gross Profit	$1,350.0	$1,380.0	$1,483.5	$1,572.5	$1,651.1	$1,717.2	$1,768.7	$1,821.8	$1,876.4	$1,932.7	$1,990.7	$2,050.4
% margin	39.9%	40.0%	40.0%	40.0%	40.0%	40.0%	40.0%	40.0%	40.0%	40.0%	40.0%	40.0%
EBITDA	$700.0	$725.0	$779.4	$826.1	$867.4	$902.1	$929.2	$957.1	$985.8	$1,015.4	$1,045.8	$1,077.2
% margin	20.7%	21.0%	21.0%	21.0%	21.0%	21.0%	21.0%	21.0%	21.0%	21.0%	21.0%	21.0%
Capital Expenditures	152.3	155.3	166.9	176.9	185.8	193.2	199.0	204.9	211.1	217.4	224.0	230.7
% sales	4.5%	4.5%	4.5%	4.5%	4.5%	4.5%	4.5%	4.5%	4.5%	4.5%	4.5%	4.5%
Cash Interest Expense		252.5	246.6	233.7	218.7	201.7	182.8	163.6	141.2	128.9	128.9	128.9
Total Interest Expense		264.5	258.6	245.7	230.7	213.7	194.7	175.6	152.5	135.7	128.9	128.9
Free Cash Flow												
EBITDA			$779.4	$826.1	$867.4	$902.1	$929.2	$957.1	$985.8	$1,015.4	$1,045.8	$1,077.2
Less: Cash Interest Expense			(246.6)	(233.7)	(218.7)	(201.7)	(182.8)	(163.6)	(141.2)	(128.9)	(128.9)	(128.9)
Plus: Interest Income									0.0	1.1	3.2	5.4
Less: Income Taxes			(113.3)	(130.9)	(147.8)	(163.7)	(178.3)	(193.1)	(209.7)	(224.5)	(236.2)	(245.5)
Less: Capital Expenditures			(166.9)	(176.9)	(185.8)	(193.2)	(199.0)	(204.9)	(211.1)	(217.4)	(224.0)	(230.7)
Less: Increase in Net Working Capital			(47.6)	(41.0)	(36.2)	(30.4)	(23.7)	(24.4)	(25.1)	(25.9)	(26.7)	(27.5)
Free Cash Flow			$204.9	$243.6	$278.9	$313.1	$345.5	$371.0	$398.7	$419.7	$433.3	$450.0
Cumulative Free Cash Flow			204.9	448.5	727.4	1,040.6	1,386.1	1,757.1	2,155.8	2,575.4	3,008.8	3,458.8

Capitalization

	Pro forma 2012	Year 1 2013	Year 2 2014	Year 3 2015	Year 4 2016	Year 5 2017	Year 6 2018	Year 7 2019	Year 8 2020	Year 9 2021	Year 10 2022
Cash								$5.8	$425.4	$858.8	$1,308.8
Revolving Credit Facility	-	-	-	-	-	-	-	-	-	-	-
Term Loan A	-	-	-	-	-	-	-	-	-	-	-
Term Loan B	2,150.0	1,945.1	1,701.5	1,422.6	1,109.4	763.9	392.9	-	-	-	-
Term Loan C	-	-	-	-	-	-	-	-	-	-	-
Existing Term Loan	-	-	-	-	-	-	-	-	-	-	-
2nd Lien	-	-	-	-	-	-	-	-	-	-	-
Other Debt	-	-	-	-	-	-	-	-	-	-	-
Total Senior Secured Debt	$2,150.0	$1,945.1	$1,701.5	$1,422.6	$1,109.4	$763.9	$392.9	-	-	-	-
Senior Notes	1,500.0	1,500.0	1,500.0	1,500.0	1,500.0	1,500.0	1,500.0	1,500.0	1,500.0	1,500.0	1,500.0
Total Senior Debt	$3,650.0	$3,445.1	$3,201.5	$2,922.6	$2,609.4	$2,263.9	$1,892.9	$1,500.0	$1,500.0	$1,500.0	$1,500.0
Senior Subordinated Notes	-	-	-	-	-	-	-	-	-	-	-
Total Debt	$3,650.0	$3,445.1	$3,201.5	$2,922.6	$2,609.4	$2,263.9	$1,892.9	$1,500.0	$1,500.0	$1,500.0	$1,500.0
Shareholders' Equity	2,040.0	2,224.9	2,438.5	2,679.7	2,946.9	3,237.8	3,552.9	3,895.0	4,261.4	4,646.7	5,047.3
Total Capitalization	$5,690.0	$5,670.0	$5,640.0	$5,602.3	$5,556.3	$5,501.7	$5,445.8	$5,395.0	$5,761.4	$6,146.7	$6,547.3
% of Bank Debt Repaid	-	9.5%	20.9%	33.8%	48.4%	64.5%	81.7%	100.0%	100.0%	100.0%	100.0%

In Year 7, 100% of ValueCo's bank debt is repaid

Credit Statistics

	Pro forma 2012	Year 1 2013	Year 2 2014	Year 3 2015	Year 4 2016	Year 5 2017	Year 6 2018	Year 7 2019	Year 8 2020	Year 9 2021	Year 10 2022
% Debt / Total Capitalization	64.1%	60.8%	56.8%	52.2%	47.0%	41.1%	34.8%	27.8%	26.0%	24.4%	22.9%
EBITDA / Cash Interest Expense	2.9x	3.2x	3.5x	4.0x	4.5x	5.1x	5.8x	7.0x	7.9x	8.1x	8.4x
(EBITDA - Capex) / Cash Interest Expense	2.3x	2.5x	2.8x	3.1x	3.5x	4.0x	4.6x	5.5x	6.2x	6.4x	6.6x
EBITDA / Total Interest Expense	2.7x	3.0x	3.4x	3.8x	4.2x	4.8x	5.5x	6.5x	7.5x	8.1x	8.4x
(EBITDA - Capex) / Total Interest Expense	2.2x	2.4x	2.6x	3.0x	3.3x	3.7x	4.3x	5.1x	5.9x	6.4x	6.6x
Senior Secured Debt / EBITDA	3.0x	2.5x	2.1x	1.6x	1.2x	0.8x	0.4x	- x	- x	- x	- x
Senior Debt / EBITDA	5.0x	4.4x	3.9x	3.4x	2.9x	2.4x	2.0x	1.5x	1.5x	1.4x	1.4x
Total Debt / EBITDA	5.0x	4.4x	3.9x	3.4x	2.9x	2.4x	2.0x	1.5x	1.5x	1.4x	1.4x
Net Debt / EBITDA	5.0x	4.4x	3.9x	3.4x	2.9x	2.4x	2.0x	1.5x	1.1x	0.6x	0.2x

273

Step V(b): Perform Returns Analysis

After analyzing the contemplated financing structure from a debt repayment and credit statistics perspective, the banker determines whether it provides sufficient returns to the sponsor given the proposed purchase price and equity contribution. As discussed in Chapter 4, sponsors have historically sought 20%+ IRRs in assessing acquisition opportunities. If the implied returns are too low, both the purchase price and financing structure need to be revisited.

IRRs are driven primarily by the target's projected financial performance, the assumed purchase price and financing structure (particularly the size of the equity contribution), and the assumed exit multiple and year (assuming a sale). Although a sponsor may realize a monetization or exit through various strategies and timeframes (see Chapter 4, "Primary Exit/Monetization Strategies"), a traditional LBO analysis contemplates a full exit via a sale of the entire company in five years.

Return Assumptions In a traditional LBO analysis, it is common practice to conservatively assume an exit multiple equal to (or below) the entry multiple.

EXHIBIT 5.39 Calculation of Enterprise Value and Equity Value at Exit

($ in millions)

Calculation of Exit Enterprise Value and Equity Value (assumes 8.0x exit multiple and 2017E exit year)	
	Year 5 2017
2017E EBITDA	$929.2
Exit EBITDA Multiple	8.0x
Enterprise Value at Exit	**$7,433.7**
Less: Net Debt	
Revolving Credit Facility	-
Term Loan B	763.9
Senior Notes	1,500.0
Total Debt	**$2,263.9**
Less: Cash and Cash Equivalents	-
Net Debt	**$2,263.9**
Equity Value at Exit	**$5,169.7**

As shown in Exhibit 5.39, for ValueCo's LBO analysis, we assumed that the sponsor exits in 2017E (Year 5) at a multiple of 8.0x EBITDA, which is equal to the entry multiple. In 2017E, ValueCo is projected to generate EBITDA of $929.2 million, translating into an implied enterprise value of $7,433.7 million at an exit multiple of 8.0x EBITDA. Cumulative debt repayment over the period is $1,386.1 million (2012E TLB beginning balance of $2,150 million less 2017E ending balance of $763.9 million), leaving ValueCo with projected 2017E debt of $2,263.9 million. This debt amount, which is

LBO Analysis

equal to net debt given the zero cash balance, is subtracted from the enterprise value of $7,433.7 million to calculate an implied equity value of $5,169.7 million in the exit year.

IRR and Cash Return Calculations Assuming no additional cash inflows (dividends to the sponsor) or outflows (additional investment by the sponsor) during the investment period, IRR and cash return are calculated on the basis of the sponsor's initial equity contribution (outflow) and the assumed equity proceeds at exit (inflow). This concept is illustrated in the timeline shown in Exhibit 5.40.

EXHIBIT 5.40 Investment Timeline

($ in millions)

	Pro forma 2012	Year 1 2013	Year 2 2014	Year 3 2015	Year 4 2016	Year 5 2017
Initial Equity Investment	($2,100.0)	-	-	-	-	-
Dividends / (Investment)	-	-	-	-	-	-
Equity Value at Exit	-	-	-	-	-	5,169.7
Total	($2,100.0)	-	-	-	-	$5,169.7
IRR	20%					
Cash Return	2.5x					

= IRR (Initial Equity Investment : Equity Value at Exit)
= IRR (-$2,100 million : $5,169.7 million)

= Equity Value at Exit / Initial Equity Investment
= $5,169.7 million / $2,100 million

The initial equity contribution represents a cash outflow for the sponsor. Hence, it is shown as a negative value on the timeline, as would any additional equity investment by the sponsor, whether for acquisitions or other purposes. On the other hand, cash distributions to the sponsor, such as proceeds received at exit or dividends received during the investment period, are shown as positive values on the timeline.

For the ValueCo LBO, we assumed no cash inflows or outflows during the investment period other than the initial equity contribution and anticipated equity proceeds at exit. Therefore, we calculated an IRR of approximately 20% and a cash return of 2.5x based on $2,100 million of initial contributed equity and $5,169.7 million of equity proceeds in 2017E.

Returns at Various Exit Years In Exhibit 5.41, we calculated IRR and cash return assuming an exit at the end of each year in the projection period using the fixed 8.0x EBITDA exit multiple. As we progress through the projection period, equity value increases due to the increasing EBITDA and decreasing net debt. Therefore, the cash return increases as it is a function of the fixed initial equity investment and increasing equity value at exit. As the timeline progresses, however, IRR decreases in accordance with the declining growth rates and the time value of money.

EXHIBIT 5.41 Returns at Various Exit Years

($ in millions, fiscal year ending December 31)

Returns Analysis

		Pro forma 2012	Year 1 2013	Year 2 2014	Year 3 2015	Year 4 2016	Year 5 2017	Projection Period Year 6 2018	Year 7 2019	Year 8 2020	Year 9 2021	Year 10 2022
Entry EBITDA Multiple	8.0x											
Initial Equity Investment		$2,100.0										
EBITDA			$779.4	$826.1	$867.4	$902.1	$929.2	$957.1	$985.8	$1,015.4	$1,045.8	$1,077.2
Exit EBITDA Multiple	8.0x											
Enterprise Value at Exit			$6,235.0	$6,609.1	$6,939.6	$7,217.1	$7,433.7	$7,656.7	$7,886.4	$8,123.0	$8,366.6	$8,617.6
Less: Net Debt												
Revolving Credit Facility			—	—	—	—	—	—	—	—	—	—
Term Loan A			1,945.1	1,701.5	1,422.6	1,109.4	763.9	392.9	—	—	—	—
Term Loan B			—	—	—	—	—	—	—	—	—	—
Term Loan C			—	—	—	—	—	—	—	—	—	—
Existing Term Loan			—	—	—	—	—	—	—	—	—	—
2nd Lien			—	—	—	—	—	—	—	—	—	—
Senior Notes			1,500.0	1,500.0	1,500.0	1,500.0	1,500.0	1,500.0	1,500.0	1,500.0	1,500.0	1,500.0
Senior Subordinated Notes			—	—	—	—	—	—	—	—	—	—
Other Debt			—	—	—	—	—	—	—	—	—	—
Total Debt			$3,445.1	$3,201.5	$2,922.6	$2,609.4	$2,263.9	$1,892.9	$1,500.0	$1,500.0	$1,500.0	$1,500.0
Less: Cash and Cash Equivalents			—	—	—	—	—	—	5.8	425.4	858.8	1,308.8
Net Debt			$3,445.1	$3,201.5	$2,922.6	$2,609.4	$2,263.9	$1,892.9	$1,494.2	$1,074.6	$641.2	$191.2
Equity Value at Exit			$2,789.9	$3,407.6	$4,017.0	$4,607.7	$5,169.7	$5,763.7	$6,392.1	$7,048.4	$7,725.4	$8,426.4
Cash Return			1.3x	1.6x	1.9x	2.2x	2.5x	2.7x	3.0x	3.4x	3.7x	4.0x

	Year 1 2013	Year 2 2014	Year 3 2015	Year 4 2016	Year 5 2017	Year 6 2018	Year 7 2019	Year 8 2020	Year 9 2021	Year 10 2022
Initial Equity Investment	($2,100.0)	($2,100.0)	($2,100.0)	($2,100.0)	($2,100.0)	($2,100.0)	($2,100.0)	($2,100.0)	($2,100.0)	($2,100.0)
Equity Proceeds	$2,789.9	$3,407.6	$4,017.0	$4,607.7	$5,169.7	$5,763.7	$6,392.1	$7,048.4	$7,725.4	$8,426.4
IRR	32.9%	27.4%	24.1%	21.7%	19.7%	18.3%	17.2%	16.3%	15.6%	14.9%

LBO Analysis

IRR Sensitivity Analysis Sensitivity analysis is critical for analyzing IRRs and framing LBO valuation. IRR can be sensitized for several key value drivers, such as entry and exit multiple, exit year, leverage level, and equity contribution percentage, as well as key operating assumptions such as growth rates and margins (see Chapter 3, Exhibit 3.59).

As shown in Exhibit 5.42, for the ValueCo LBO, we assumed a fixed leverage level of 5.2x LTM 9/30/2012 EBITDA of $700 million and a 2017E exit year, while sensitizing entry and exit multiples. For our IRR analysis, we focused on entry and exit multiple combinations that produced an IRR in the 20% area, assuming an equity contribution comfortably within the range of 25% to 40%.

EXHIBIT 5.42 IRR Sensitivity Analysis – Entry and Exit Multiples

Enterprise Value	Equity Contribution	Entry Multiple	IRR - Assuming Exit in 2017E — Exit Multiple						
			7.00x	7.25x	7.50x	7.75x	8.00x	8.25x	8.50x
$4,900.0	26.4%	7.00x	24.8%	26.2%	27.4%	28.7%	29.9%	31.0%	32.1%
5,075.0	28.8%	7.25x	21.9%	23.2%	24.5%	25.7%	26.8%	28.0%	29.0%
5,250.0	31.0%	7.50x	19.4%	20.6%	21.9%	23.1%	24.2%	25.3%	26.3%
5,425.0	33.0%	7.75x	17.1%	18.4%	19.6%	20.7%	21.8%	22.9%	24.0%
5,600.0	35.0%	8.00x	15.1%	16.3%	17.5%	18.6%	19.7%	20.8%	21.8%
5,775.0	36.8%	8.25x	13.3%	14.5%	15.6%	16.8%	17.8%	18.9%	19.9%
5,950.0	38.6%	8.50x	11.6%	12.8%	13.9%	15.0%	16.1%	17.1%	18.1%

For example, an 8.0x entry and exit multiple provides an IRR of approximately 20% while requiring a 35% equity contribution given the proposed leverage. Toward the higher end of the range, an 8.25x entry and exit multiple yields an IRR of 18.9% while requiring an equity contribution of 36.8%. Toward the low end of the range, a 7.25x entry and exit multiple provides an IRR of 23.2% while requiring a 28.8% equity contribution.

It is also common to perform sensitivity analysis on a combination of exit multiples and exit years. As shown in Exhibit 5.43, we assumed fixed total leverage and entry multiples of 5.2x and 8.0x LTM 9/30/2012 EBITDA, respectively, and examined the resulting IRRs for a range of exit years from 2015E to 2019E and exit multiples from 7.0x to 9.0x.

EXHIBIT 5.43 IRR Sensitivity Analysis – Exit Multiple and Exit Year

		IRR - Assuming 8.0x Entry Multiple — Exit Year				
		2015	2016	2017	2018	2019
	7.0x	14.5%	15.3%	15.1%	14.8%	14.5%
Exit	7.5x	19.5%	18.6%	17.5%	16.6%	15.9%
Multiple	8.0x	24.1%	21.7%	19.7%	18.3%	17.2%
	8.5x	28.5%	24.6%	21.8%	19.9%	18.5%
	9.0x	32.5%	27.3%	23.8%	21.4%	19.7%

Step V(c): Determine Valuation

As previously discussed, sponsors base their valuation of an LBO target in large part on their comfort with realizing acceptable returns at a given purchase price. This analysis assumes a given set of financial projections, purchase price, and financing structure, as well as exit multiple and year. At the same time, sponsors are guided by the other valuation methodologies discussed in this book.

LBO analysis is also informative for strategic buyers by providing perspective on the price a competing sponsor bidder might be willing to pay for a given target in an organized sale process. This data point allows strategic buyers to frame their bids accordingly. As a result, the banker is expected to employ LBO analysis as a valuation technique while serving as an M&A advisor in both buy-side and sell-side situations.

Traditionally, the valuation implied by LBO analysis is toward the lower end of a comprehensive analysis when compared to other methodologies, particularly precedent transactions and DCF analysis. This is largely due to the constraints imposed by an LBO, including leverage capacity, credit market conditions, and the sponsor's own IRR hurdles. Furthermore, strategic buyers are typically able to realize synergies from the target, thereby enhancing their ability to earn a targeted return on their invested capital at a higher purchase price. However, during robust debt financing environments, such as during the credit boom of the mid-2000s, sponsors have been able to compete with strategic buyers on purchase price. The multiples paid in LBO transactions during this period were supported by the use of a high proportion of low-cost debt in the capital structure, translating into a relatively lower overall cost of capital for the target.

EXHIBIT 5.44 ValueCo Football Field Displaying Comparable Companies, Precedent Transactions, DCF Analysis, and LBO Analysis

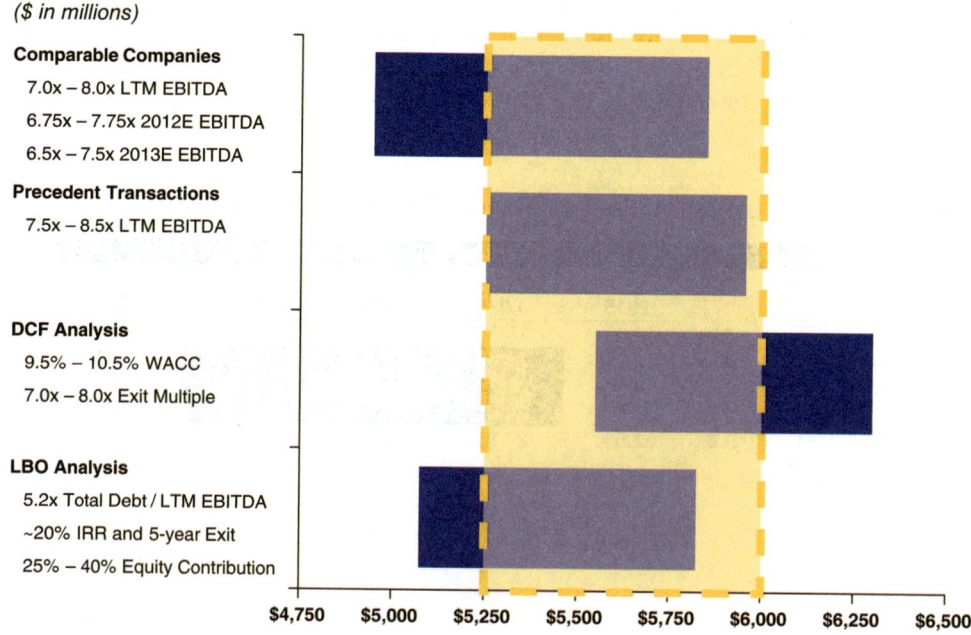

As with the DCF, the implied valuation range for ValueCo was derived from sensitivity analysis output tables (see Exhibit 5.42). For the ValueCo LBO, we focused on a range of entry and exit multiples that produced IRRs in the 20% area, given an equity contribution comfortably within the range of 25% to 40%. This approach led us to determine a valuation range of 7.25x to 8.25x LTM 9/30/2012 EBITDA, or approximately $5,075 million to $5,775 million (see Exhibit 5.44).

Step V(d): Create Transaction Summary Page

Once the LBO model is fully functional, all the essential model outputs are linked to a transaction summary page (see Exhibit 5.46). This page provides an overview of the LBO analysis in a user-friendly format, typically displaying the sources and uses of funds, acquisition multiples, summary returns analysis, and summary financial data, as well as projected capitalization and credit statistics. This format allows the deal team to quickly review and spot-check the analysis and make adjustments to the purchase price, financing structure, operating assumptions, and other key inputs as necessary.

The transaction summary page also typically contains the toggle cells that allow the banker to switch among various financing structures and operating scenarios, as well as activate other functionality. The outputs on this page (and throughout the entire model) change accordingly as the toggle cells are changed.

ILLUSTRATIVE LBO ANALYSIS FOR VALUECO

The following pages display the full LBO model for ValueCo based on the step-by-step approach outlined in this chapter. Exhibit 5.45 lists these pages, which are shown in Exhibits 5.46 to 5.54.

EXHIBIT 5.45 LBO Model Pages

LBO Model
I. Transaction Summary
II. Income Statement
III. Balance Sheet
IV. Cash Flow Statement
V. Debt Schedule
VI. Returns Analysis
Assumptions Pages
I. Assumptions Page 1—Income Statement and Cash Flow Statement
II. Assumptions Page 2—Balance Sheet
III. Assumptions Page 3—Financing Structures and Fees

EXHIBIT 5.46 ValueCo LBO Transaction Summary

ValueCo Corporation
Leveraged Buyout Analysis
($ in millions, fiscal year ending December 31)

Financing Structure: Structure 1
Operating Scenario: Base

Transaction Summary

Sources of Funds	Amount	% of Total Sources	Multiple of EBITDA 9/30/2012	Cumulative	Pricing
Revolving Credit Facility	-	-%	-x	-x	L+425 bps
Term Loan A	-	-%	-x	-x	NA
Term Loan B	2,150.0	35.8%	3.1x	3.1x	L+450 bps
Term Loan C	-	-%	-x	3.1x	NA
2nd Lien	-	-%	-x	3.1x	NA
Senior Notes	1,500.0	25.0%	2.1x	5.2x	8.500%
Senior Subordinated Notes	-	-%	-x	5.2x	NA
Equity Contribution	2,100.0	35.0%	3.0x	8.2x	
Rollover Equity	-	-%	-x	8.2x	
Cash on Hand	250.0	4.2%	0.4x	8.6x	
Total Sources	**$6,000.0**	**100.0%**	**8.6x**		

Uses of Funds	Amount	% of Total Uses
Purchase ValueCo Equity	$4,350.0	72.5%
Repay Existing Debt	1,500.0	25.0%
Tender / Call Premiums	20.0	0.3%
Financing Fees	90.0	1.5%
Other Fees and Expenses	40.0	0.7%
Total Uses	**$6,000.0**	**100.0%**

Purchase Price

Offer Price per Share	-
Fully Diluted Shares	-
Equity Purchase Price	**$4,350.0**
Plus: Existing Net Debt	1,250.0
Enterprise Value	**$5,600.0**

Transaction Multiples
Enterprise Value / Sales		
LTM 9/30/2012	$3,385.0	1.7x
2012E	3,450.0	1.6x
Enterprise Value / EBITDA		
LTM 9/30/2012	$700.0	8.0x
2012E	725.0	7.7x

Return Analysis

Exit Year	-
Entry Multiple	8.0x
Exit Multiple	8.0x
IRR	20%
Cash Return	2.5x

Options
- Financing Structure
- Operating Scenario
- Cash Flow Sweep
- Cash Balance
- Average Interest
- Financing Fees

Summary Financial Data

	Historical Period			LTM	Pro forma	Projection Period									
	2009	2010	2011	9/30/2012	2012	Year 1 2013	Year 2 2014	Year 3 2015	Year 4 2016	Year 5 2017	Year 6 2018	Year 7 2019	Year 8 2020	Year 9 2021	Year 10 2022
Sales	$2,600.0	$2,900.0	$3,200.0	$3,385.0	$3,450.0	$3,708.8	$3,931.3	$4,127.8	$4,293.0	$4,421.7	$4,554.4	$4,691.0	$4,831.8	$4,976.7	$5,126.0
% growth	NA	11.5%	10.3%	NA	7.8%	7.5%	6.0%	5.0%	4.0%	3.0%	3.0%	3.0%	3.0%	3.0%	3.0%
Gross Profit	$988.0	$1,131.0	$1,280.0	$1,350.0	$1,380.0	$1,483.5	$1,572.5	$1,651.1	$1,717.2	$1,768.7	$1,821.8	$1,876.4	$1,932.7	$1,990.7	$2,050.4
% margin	38.0%	39.0%	40.0%	39.9%	40.0%	40.0%	40.0%	40.0%	40.0%	40.0%	40.0%	40.0%	40.0%	40.0%	40.0%
EBITDA	$491.4	$580.0	$672.0	$700.0	$725.0	$779.4	$826.1	$867.4	$902.1	$929.2	$957.1	$985.8	$1,015.4	$1,045.8	$1,077.2
% margin	18.9%	20.0%	21.0%	20.7%	21.0%	21.0%	21.0%	21.0%	21.0%	21.0%	21.0%	21.0%	21.0%	21.0%	21.0%
Capital Expenditures	136.4	114.0	144.0	152.3	155.3	166.9	176.9	185.8	193.2	199.0	204.9	211.1	217.4	224.0	230.7
% sales	5.2%	3.9%	4.5%	4.5%	4.5%	4.5%	4.5%	4.5%	4.5%	4.5%	4.5%	4.5%	4.5%	4.5%	4.5%
Cash Interest Expense					252.5	246.6	233.7	218.7	201.7	182.8	163.6	141.2	128.9	128.9	128.9
Total Interest Expense					264.5	258.6	245.7	230.7	213.7	194.7	175.6	152.5	135.7	128.9	128.9
Free Cash Flow															
EBITDA						$779.4	$826.1	$867.4	$902.1	$929.2	$957.1	$985.8	$1,015.4	$1,045.8	$1,077.2
Less: Cash Interest Expense						(246.6)	(233.7)	(218.7)	(201.7)	(182.8)	(163.6)	(141.2)	(128.9)	(128.9)	(128.9)
Plus: Interest Income						-	-	-	-	-	-	-	1.1	3.2	5.4
Less: Income Taxes						(113.3)	(130.9)	(147.8)	(163.7)	(178.3)	(193.1)	(209.7)	(224.5)	(236.2)	(245.5)
Less: Capital Expenditures						(166.9)	(176.9)	(185.8)	(193.2)	(199.0)	(204.9)	(211.1)	(217.4)	(224.0)	(230.7)
Less: Increase in Net Working Capital						(47.6)	(41.0)	(36.2)	(30.4)	(23.7)	(24.4)	(25.1)	(25.9)	(26.7)	(27.5)
Free Cash Flow						**$204.9**	**$243.6**	**$278.9**	**$313.1**	**$345.5**	**$371.0**	**$398.7**	**$419.7**	**$433.3**	**$450.0**
Cumulative Free Cash Flow						204.9	448.5	727.4	1,040.6	1,386.1	1,757.1	2,155.8	2,575.4	3,008.8	3,458.8

Capitalization

	9/30/2012	Pro forma 2012	Year 1 2013	Year 2 2014	Year 3 2015	Year 4 2016	Year 5 2017	Year 6 2018	Year 7 2019	Year 8 2020	Year 9 2021	Year 10 2022
Cash										$5.8	$425.4	$858.8	$1,308.8
Revolving Credit Facility													
Term Loan A													
Term Loan B		2,150.0	1,945.1	1,701.5	1,422.6	1,109.4	763.9	392.9	-	-	-	-
Term Loan C													
Existing Term Loan													
2nd Lien													
Other Debt													
Total Senior Secured Debt	$2,150.0	$1,945.1	$1,701.5	$1,422.6	$1,109.4	$763.9	$392.9	-	-	-	-	
Senior Notes		1,500.0	1,500.0	1,500.0	1,500.0	1,500.0	1,500.0	1,500.0	1,500.0	1,500.0	1,500.0	1,500.0
Total Senior Debt	$3,650.0	$3,445.1	$3,201.5	$2,922.6	$2,609.4	$2,263.9	$1,892.9	$1,500.0	$1,500.0	$1,500.0	$1,500.0	
Senior Subordinated Notes													
Total Debt	$3,650.0	$3,445.1	$3,201.5	$2,922.6	$2,609.4	$2,263.9	$1,892.9	$1,500.0	$1,500.0	$1,500.0	$1,500.0	
Shareholders' Equity		2,040.0	2,224.9	2,438.5	2,679.7	2,946.9	3,237.8	3,552.9	3,895.0	4,261.4	4,646.7	5,047.3
Total Capitalization	$5,690.0	$5,670.0	$5,640.0	$5,602.3	$5,556.3	$5,501.7	$5,445.8	$5,395.0	$5,761.4	$6,146.7	$6,547.3	
% of Bank Debt Repaid		9.5%	20.9%	33.8%	48.4%	64.5%	81.7%	100.0%	100.0%	100.0%	100.0%	100.0%

Credit Statistics

	9/30/2012	Pro forma 2012	Year 1 2013	Year 2 2014	Year 3 2015	Year 4 2016	Year 5 2017	Year 6 2018	Year 7 2019	Year 8 2020	Year 9 2021	Year 10 2022
% Debt / Total Capitalization	64.1%	60.8%	56.8%	52.2%	47.0%	41.1%	34.8%	27.8%	26.0%	24.4%	22.9%	
EBITDA / Cash Interest Expense	2.9x	3.2x	3.5x	4.0x	4.5x	5.1x	5.8x	7.0x	7.9x	8.1x	8.4x	
(EBITDA - Capex) / Cash Interest Expense	2.3x	2.5x	2.8x	3.1x	3.5x	4.0x	4.6x	5.5x	6.2x	6.4x	6.6x	
EBITDA / Total Interest Expense	2.7x	3.0x	3.4x	3.8x	4.2x	4.8x	5.5x	6.5x	7.5x	8.1x	8.4x	
(EBITDA - Capex) / Total Interest Expense	2.2x	2.4x	2.6x	3.0x	3.3x	3.7x	4.3x	5.1x	5.9x	6.4x	6.6x	
Senior Secured Debt / EBITDA	3.0x	2.5x	2.1x	1.6x	1.2x	0.8x	0.4x	-x	-x	-x	-x	
Senior Debt / EBITDA	5.0x	4.4x	3.9x	3.4x	2.9x	2.4x	2.0x	1.5x	1.5x	1.5x	1.4x	
Total Debt / EBITDA	5.0x	4.4x	3.9x	3.4x	2.9x	2.4x	2.0x	1.5x	1.5x	1.5x	1.4x	
Net Debt / EBITDA	5.0x	4.4x	3.9x	3.4x	2.9x	2.4x	2.0x	1.5x	1.5x	1.1x	0.6x	0.2x

EXHIBIT 5.47 ValueCo LBO Income Statement

($ in millions, fiscal year ending December 31)

Income Statement

	Historical Period			LTM 9/30/2012	Pro forma 2012	Projection Period									
	2009	2010	2011			Year 1 2013	Year 2 2014	Year 3 2015	Year 4 2016	Year 5 2017	Year 6 2018	Year 7 2019	Year 8 2020	Year 9 2021	Year 10 2022
Sales	$2,600.0	$2,900.0	$3,200.0	$3,385.0	$3,450.0	$3,708.8	$3,931.3	$4,127.8	$4,293.0	$4,421.7	$4,554.4	$4,691.0	$4,831.8	$4,976.7	$5,126.0
% growth	NA	11.5%	10.3%	NA	7.8%	7.5%	6.0%	5.0%	4.0%	3.0%	3.0%	3.0%	3.0%	3.0%	3.0%
Cost of Goods Sold	1,612.0	1,769.0	1,920.0	2,035.0	2,070.0	2,225.3	2,358.8	2,476.7	2,575.8	2,653.0	2,732.6	2,814.6	2,899.1	2,986.0	3,075.6
Gross Profit	$988.0	$1,131.0	$1,280.0	$1,350.0	$1,380.0	$1,483.5	$1,572.5	$1,651.1	$1,717.2	$1,768.7	$1,821.8	$1,876.4	$1,932.7	$1,990.7	$2,050.4
% margin	38.0%	39.0%	40.0%	39.9%	40.0%	40.0%	40.0%	40.0%	40.0%	40.0%	40.0%	40.0%	40.0%	40.0%	40.0%
Selling, General & Administrative	496.6	551.0	608.0	650.0	655.0	704.1	746.4	783.7	815.0	839.5	864.7	890.6	917.3	944.9	973.2
% sales	19.1%	19.0%	19.0%	19.2%	19.0%	19.0%	19.0%	19.0%	19.0%	19.0%	19.0%	19.0%	19.0%	19.0%	19.0%
Other Expense / (Income)	-	-	-	-	-	-	-	-	-	-	-	-	-	-	-
EBITDA	$491.4	$580.0	$672.0	$700.0	$725.0	$779.4	$826.1	$867.4	$902.1	$929.2	$957.1	$985.8	$1,015.4	$1,045.8	$1,077.2
% margin	18.9%	20.0%	21.0%	20.7%	21.0%	21.0%	21.0%	21.0%	21.0%	21.0%	21.0%	21.0%	21.0%	21.0%	21.0%
Depreciation	116.0	121.5	145.0	150.0	155.3	166.9	176.9	185.8	193.2	199.0	204.9	211.1	217.4	224.0	230.7
Amortization	39.0	43.5	48.0	50.0	51.8	55.6	59.0	61.9	64.4	66.3	68.3	70.4	72.5	74.7	76.9
EBIT	$336.4	$415.0	$479.0	$500.0	$518.0	$556.9	$590.3	$619.8	$644.6	$663.9	$683.8	$704.3	$725.5	$747.2	$769.6
% margin	12.9%	14.3%	15.0%	14.8%	15.0%	15.0%	15.0%	15.0%	15.0%	15.0%	15.0%	15.0%	15.0%	15.0%	15.0%
Interest Expense															
Revolving Credit Facility						-	-	-	-	-	-	-	-	-	-
Term Loan A						-	-	-	-	-	-	-	-	-	-
Term Loan B						117.7	104.8	89.8	72.8	53.9	34.7	12.3	-	-	-
Term Loan C						-	-	-	-	-	-	-	-	-	-
Existing Term Loan						-	-	-	-	-	-	-	-	-	-
2nd Lien						-	-	-	-	-	-	-	-	-	-
Senior Notes					127.5	127.5	127.5	127.5	127.5	127.5	127.5	127.5	127.5	127.5	127.5
Senior Subordinated Notes					-	-	-	-	-	-	-	-	-	-	-
Commitment Fee on Unused Revolver					1.3	1.3	1.3	1.3	1.3	1.3	1.3	1.3	1.3	1.3	1.3
Administrative Agent Fee					0.2	0.2	0.2	0.2	0.2	0.2	0.2	0.2	0.2	0.2	0.2
Cash Interest Expense					$252.5	$246.6	$233.7	$218.7	$201.7	$182.8	$163.6	$141.2	$128.9	$128.9	$128.9
Amortization of Deferred Financing Fees					12.0	12.0	12.0	12.0	12.0	12.0	12.0	12.0	11.4	6.8	-
Total Interest Expense					$264.5	$258.6	$245.7	$230.7	$213.7	$194.7	$175.6	$152.5	$135.7	$128.9	$128.9
Interest Income						-	-	-	-	-	-	(0.0)	(1.1)	(3.2)	(5.4)
Net Interest Expense						$258.6	$245.7	$230.7	$213.7	$194.7	$175.6	$152.5	$134.6	$125.7	$123.5
Earnings Before Taxes						298.2	344.5	389.1	430.9	469.2	508.2	551.8	590.9	621.5	646.2
Income Tax Expense						113.3	130.9	147.8	163.7	178.3	193.1	209.7	224.5	236.2	245.5
Net Income						$184.9	$213.6	$241.2	$267.2	$290.9	$315.1	$342.1	$366.4	$385.4	$400.6
% margin						5.0%	5.4%	5.8%	6.2%	6.6%	6.9%	7.3%	7.6%	7.7%	7.8%

Income Statement Assumptions

Sales (% YoY growth)	NA	11.5%	10.3%	NA	7.8%	7.5%	6.0%	5.0%	4.0%	3.0%	3.0%	3.0%	3.0%	3.0%	3.0%
Cost of Goods Sold (% margin)	62.0%	61.0%	60.0%	60.1%	60.0%	60.0%	60.0%	60.0%	60.0%	60.0%	60.0%	60.0%	60.0%	60.0%	60.0%
SG&A (% sales)	19.1%	19.0%	19.0%	19.2%	19.0%	19.0%	19.0%	19.0%	19.0%	19.0%	19.0%	19.0%	19.0%	19.0%	19.0%
Other Expense / (Income) (% of sales)	-%	-%	-%	-%	-%	-%	-%	-%	-%	-%	-%	-%	-%	-%	-%
Depreciation (% of sales)	4.5%	4.2%	4.5%	4.4%	4.5%	4.5%	4.5%	4.5%	4.5%	4.5%	4.5%	4.5%	4.5%	4.5%	4.5%
Amortization (% of sales)	1.5%	1.5%	1.5%	1.5%	1.5%	1.5%	1.5%	1.5%	1.5%	1.5%	1.5%	1.5%	1.5%	1.5%	1.5%
Interest Income						0.5%	0.5%	0.5%	0.5%	0.5%	0.5%	0.5%	0.5%	0.5%	0.5%
Tax Rate					38.0%	38.0%	38.0%	38.0%	38.0%	38.0%	38.0%	38.0%	38.0%	38.0%	38.0%

EXHIBIT 5.48 ValueCo LBO Balance Sheet

($ in millions, fiscal year ending December 31)

Balance Sheet

	Opening 2012	Adjustments −	Adjustments +	Pro Forma 2012	Year 1 2013	Year 2 2014	Year 3 2015	Year 4 2016	Year 5 2017	Year 6 2018	Year 7 2019	Year 8 2020	Year 9 2021	Year 10 2022
Cash and Cash Equivalents	$250.0	(250.0)			$5.8						$5.8	$425.4	$858.8	$1,308.8
Accounts Receivable	450.0			450.0	483.8	512.8	538.4	560.0	576.7	594.1	611.9	630.2	649.1	668.6
Inventories	600.0			600.0	645.0	683.7	717.9	746.6	769.0	792.1	815.8	840.3	865.5	891.5
Prepaids and Other Current Assets	175.0			175.0	188.1	199.4	209.4	217.8	224.3	231.0	238.0	245.1	252.4	260.0
Total Current Assets	**$1,475.0**			**$1,225.0**	**$1,316.9**	**$1,395.9**	**$1,465.7**	**$1,524.3**	**$1,570.0**	**$1,617.1**	**$1,671.4**	**$2,141.1**	**$2,625.8**	**$3,128.9**
Property, Plant and Equipment, net	2,500.0			2,500.0	2,500.0	2,500.0	2,500.0	2,500.0	2,500.0	2,500.0	2,500.0	2,500.0	2,500.0	2,500.0
Goodwill	1,000.0	(1,000.0)	1,850.0	1,850.0	1,850.0	1,850.0	1,850.0	1,850.0	1,850.0	1,850.0	1,850.0	1,850.0	1,850.0	1,850.0
Intangible Assets	875.0			875.0	819.4	760.4	698.5	634.1	567.8	499.4	429.1	356.6	282.0	205.1
Other Assets	150.0			150.0	150.0	150.0	150.0	150.0	150.0	150.0	150.0	150.0	150.0	150.0
Deferred Financing Fees			90.0	90.0	78.0	66.0	54.1	42.1	30.1	18.1	6.7			
Total Assets	**$6,000.0**			**$6,690.0**	**$6,714.3**	**$6,722.3**	**$6,718.2**	**$6,700.5**	**$6,667.9**	**$6,634.7**	**$6,607.2**	**$6,997.7**	**$7,407.8**	**$7,834.0**
Accounts Payable	215.0			215.0	231.1	245.0	257.2	267.5	275.6	283.8	292.3	301.1	310.1	319.4
Accrued Liabilities	275.0			275.0	295.6	313.4	329.0	342.2	352.5	363.0	373.9	385.1	396.7	408.6
Other Current Liabilities	100.0			100.0	107.5	114.0	119.6	124.4	128.2	132.0	136.0	140.1	144.3	148.6
Total Current Liabilities	**$590.0**			**$590.0**	**$634.3**	**$672.3**	**$705.9**	**$734.2**	**$756.2**	**$778.9**	**$802.2**	**$826.3**	**$851.1**	**$876.6**
Revolving Credit Facility														
Term Loan A														
Term Loan B			2,150.0	2,150.0	1,945.1	1,701.5	1,422.6	1,109.4	763.9	392.9				
Term Loan C														
Existing Term Loan		(1,000.0)												
2nd Lien	1,000.0													
Senior Notes			1,500.0	1,500.0	1,500.0	1,500.0	1,500.0	1,500.0	1,500.0	1,500.0	1,500.0	1,500.0	1,500.0	1,500.0
Existing Senior Notes	500.0	(500.0)												
Senior Subordinated Notes														
Other Debt	300.0			300.0	300.0	300.0	300.0	300.0	300.0	300.0	300.0	300.0	300.0	300.0
Deferred Income Taxes	110.0			110.0	110.0	110.0	110.0	110.0	110.0	110.0	110.0	110.0	110.0	110.0
Other Long-Term Liabilities														
Total Liabilities	**$2,500.0**			**$4,650.0**	**$4,489.4**	**$4,283.8**	**$4,038.5**	**$3,753.6**	**$3,430.1**	**$3,081.8**	**$2,712.2**	**$2,736.3**	**$2,761.1**	**$2,786.6**
Noncontrolling Interest														
Shareholders' Equity	3,500.0	(3,500.0)	2,040.0	2,040.0	2,224.9	2,438.5	2,679.7	2,946.9	3,237.8	3,552.9	3,895.0	4,261.4	4,646.7	5,047.3
Total Shareholders' Equity	**$3,500.0**			**$2,040.0**	**$2,224.9**	**$2,438.5**	**$2,679.7**	**$2,946.9**	**$3,237.8**	**$3,552.9**	**$3,895.0**	**$4,261.4**	**$4,646.7**	**$5,047.3**
Total Liabilities and Equity	**$6,000.0**			**$6,690.0**	**$6,714.3**	**$6,722.3**	**$6,718.2**	**$6,700.5**	**$6,667.9**	**$6,634.7**	**$6,607.2**	**$6,997.7**	**$7,407.8**	**$7,834.0**
Balance Check				0.000	0.000	0.000	0.000	0.000	0.000	0.000	0.000	0.000	0.000	0.000
Net Working Capital	635.0			635.0	682.6	723.6	759.8	790.2	813.9	838.3	863.4	889.3	916.0	943.5
(Increase) / Decrease in Net Working Capital					(47.6)	(41.0)	(36.2)	(30.4)	(23.7)	(24.4)	(25.1)	(25.9)	(26.7)	(27.5)

Balance Sheet Assumptions

Current Assets														
Days Sales Outstanding (DSO)	47.6				47.6	47.6	47.6	47.6	47.6	47.6	47.6	47.6	47.6	47.6
Days Inventory Held (DIH)	105.8				105.8	105.8	105.8	105.8	105.8	105.8	105.8	105.8	105.8	105.8
Prepaid and Other Current Assets (% of sales)	5.1%				5.1%	5.1%	5.1%	5.1%	5.1%	5.1%	5.1%	5.1%	5.1%	5.1%
Current Liabilities														
Days Payable Outstanding (DPO)	37.9				37.9	37.9	37.9	37.9	37.9	37.9	37.9	37.9	37.9	37.9
Accrued Liabilities (% of sales)	8.0%				8.0%	8.0%	8.0%	8.0%	8.0%	8.0%	8.0%	8.0%	8.0%	8.0%
Other Current Liabilities (% of sales)	2.9%				2.9%	2.9%	2.9%	2.9%	2.9%	2.9%	2.9%	2.9%	2.9%	2.9%

EXHIBIT 5.49 ValueCo LBO Cash Flow Statement

($ in millions, fiscal year ending December 31)

Cash Flow Statement

	Year 1 2013	Year 2 2014	Year 3 2015	Year 4 2016	Year 5 2017	Year 6 2018	Year 7 2019	Year 8 2020	Year 9 2021	Year 10 2022
Operating Activities										
Net Income	$184.9	$213.6	$241.2	$267.2	$290.9	$315.1	$342.1	$366.4	$385.4	$400.6
Plus: Depreciation	166.9	176.9	185.8	193.2	199.0	204.9	211.1	217.4	224.0	230.7
Plus: Amortization	55.6	59.0	61.9	64.4	66.3	68.3	70.4	72.5	74.7	76.9
Plus: Amortization of Financing Fees	12.0	12.0	12.0	12.0	12.0	12.0	11.4	6.8	-	-
Changes in Working Capital Items										
(Inc.) / Dec. in Accounts Receivable	(33.8)	(29.0)	(25.6)	(21.5)	(16.8)	(17.3)	(17.8)	(18.4)	(18.9)	(19.5)
(Inc.) / Dec. in Inventories	(45.0)	(38.7)	(34.2)	(28.7)	(22.4)	(23.1)	(23.8)	(24.5)	(25.2)	(26.0)
(Inc.) / Dec. in Prepaid and Other Current Assets	(13.1)	(11.3)	(10.0)	(8.4)	(6.5)	(6.7)	(6.9)	(7.1)	(7.4)	(7.6)
Inc. / (Dec.) in Accounts Payable	16.1	13.9	12.2	10.3	8.0	8.3	8.5	8.8	9.0	9.3
Inc. / (Dec.) in Accrued Liabilities	20.6	17.7	15.7	13.2	10.3	10.6	10.9	11.2	11.6	11.9
Inc. / (Dec.) in Other Current Liabilities	7.5	6.5	5.7	4.8	3.7	3.8	4.0	4.1	4.2	4.3
(Inc.) / Dec. in Net Working Capital	(47.6)	(41.0)	(36.2)	(30.4)	(23.7)	(24.4)	(25.1)	(25.9)	(26.7)	(27.5)
Cash Flow from Operating Activities	**$371.8**	**$420.5**	**$464.7**	**$506.3**	**$544.5**	**$575.9**	**$609.8**	**$637.1**	**$657.3**	**$680.7**
Investing Activities										
Capital Expenditures	(166.9)	(176.9)	(185.8)	(193.2)	(199.0)	(204.9)	(211.1)	(217.4)	(224.0)	(230.7)
Other Investing Activities	-	-	-	-	-	-	-	-	-	-
Cash Flow from Investing Activities	**($166.9)**	**($176.9)**	**($185.8)**	**($193.2)**	**($199.0)**	**($204.9)**	**($211.1)**	**($217.4)**	**($224.0)**	**($230.7)**
Financing Activities										
Revolving Credit Facility	-	-	-	-	-	-	-	-	-	-
Term Loan A	(204.9)	(243.6)	(278.9)	(313.1)	(345.5)	(371.0)	(392.9)	-	-	-
Term Loan B	-	-	-	-	-	-	-	-	-	-
Term Loan C	-	-	-	-	-	-	-	-	-	-
Existing Term Loan	-	-	-	-	-	-	-	-	-	-
2nd Lien	-	-	-	-	-	-	-	-	-	-
Senior Notes	-	-	-	-	-	-	-	-	-	-
Senior Subordinated Notes	-	-	-	-	-	-	-	-	-	-
Other Debt	-	-	-	-	-	-	-	-	-	-
Dividends	-	-	-	-	-	-	-	-	-	-
Equity Issuance / (Repurchase)	-	-	-	-	-	-	-	-	-	-
Cash Flow from Financing Activities	**($204.9)**	**($243.6)**	**($278.9)**	**($313.1)**	**($345.5)**	**($371.0)**	**($392.9)**	-	-	-
Excess Cash for the Period	-	-	-	-	-	-	$5.8	$419.7	$433.3	$450.0
Beginning Cash Balance	-	-	-	-	-	-	-	5.8	425.4	858.8
Ending Cash Balance	-	-	-	-	-	-	**$5.8**	**$425.4**	**$858.8**	**$1,308.8**

Cash Flow Statement Assumptions

Capital Expenditures (% of sales)	4.5%	4.5%	4.5%	4.5%	4.5%	4.5%	4.5%	4.5%	4.5%	4.5%

EXHIBIT 5.50 ValueCo LBO Debt Schedule

($ in millions, fiscal year ending December 31)

Debt Schedule

	Pro forma 2012	Year 1 2013	Year 2 2014	Year 3 2015	Year 4 2016	Year 5 2017	Projection Period Year 6 2018	Year 7 2019	Year 8 2020	Year 9 2021	Year 10 2022
Forward LIBOR Curve	0.25%	0.35%	0.50%	0.75%	1.00%	1.25%	1.50%	1.75%	2.00%	2.25%	2.50%
Cash Flow from Operating Activities		$371.8	$420.5	$464.7	$506.3	$544.5	$575.9	$609.8	$637.1	$657.3	$680.7
Cash Flow from Investing Activities		(166.9)	(176.9)	(185.8)	(193.2)	(199.0)	(204.9)	(211.1)	(217.4)	(224.0)	(230.7)
Cash Available for Debt Repayment		**$204.9**	**$243.6**	**$278.9**	**$313.1**	**$345.5**	**$371.0**	**$398.7**	**$419.7**	**$433.3**	**$450.0**
Total Mandatory Repayments		(21.5)	(21.5)	(21.5)	(21.5)	(21.5)	(21.5)	(21.5)			
Cash From Balance Sheet	MinCash								5.8		
Cash Available for Optional Debt Repayment	—	**$183.4**	**$222.1**	**$257.4**	**$291.6**	**$324.0**	**$349.5**	**$377.2**	**$425.4**	**$858.8**	**$1,308.8**

Revolving Credit Facility

Revolving Credit Facility Size	$250.0											
Spread	4.250%											
LIBOR Floor	1.250%											
Term	6 years											
Commitment Fee on Unused Portion	0.50%											
Beginning Balance		—	—	—	—	—	—	—	—	—	—
Drawdown/(Repayment)		—	—	—	—	—	—	—	—	—	—
Ending Balance		—	—	—	—	—	—	—	—	—	—
Interest Rate		5.50%	5.50%	5.50%	5.50%	5.50%	5.75%	6.00%	6.25%	6.50%	6.75%
Interest Expense		—	—	—	—	—	—	—	—	—	—
Commitment Fee		1.3	1.3	1.3	1.3	1.3	1.3	1.3	1.3	1.3	1.3
Administrative Agent Fee		0.2	0.2	0.2	0.2	0.2	0.2	0.2	0.2	0.2	0.2

Term Loan B Facility

Size	$2,150.0											
Spread	4.500%											
LIBOR Floor	1.250%											
Term	7 years											
Repayment Schedule	1.0% Per Annum, Bullet at Maturity											
Beginning Balance		$2,150.0	$1,945.1	$1,701.5	$1,422.6	$1,109.4	$763.9	$392.9	—	—	—
Mandatory Repayments		(21.5)	(21.5)	(21.5)	(21.5)	(21.5)	(21.5)	(21.5)	—	—	—
Optional Repayments		(183.4)	(222.1)	(257.4)	(291.6)	(324.0)	(349.5)	(371.4)	—	—	—
Ending Balance		**$1,945.1**	**$1,701.5**	**$1,422.6**	**$1,109.4**	**$763.9**	**$392.9**	—	—	—	—
Interest Rate		5.75%	5.75%	5.75%	5.75%	5.75%	6.00%	6.25%	6.50%	6.75%	7.00%
Interest Expense		117.7	104.8	89.8	72.8	53.9	34.7	12.3	—	—	—

Senior Notes

Size	$1,500.0											
Coupon	8.500%											
Term	8 years											
Beginning Balance		$1,500.0	$1,500.0	$1,500.0	$1,500.0	$1,500.0	$1,500.0	$1,500.0	$1,500.0	$1,500.0	$1,500.0
Repayment		—	—	—	—	—	—	—	—	—	—
Ending Balance		**$1,500.0**	**$1,500.0**	**$1,500.0**	**$1,500.0**	**$1,500.0**	**$1,500.0**	**$1,500.0**	**$1,500.0**	**$1,500.0**	**$1,500.0**
Interest Expense		127.5	127.5	127.5	127.5	127.5	127.5	127.5	127.5	127.5	127.5

EXHIBIT 5.51 ValueCo LBO Returns Analysis

($ in millions, fiscal year ending December 31)

Returns Analysis

		Pro forma 2012	Year 1 2013	Year 2 2014	Year 3 2015	Year 4 2016	Year 5 2017	Year 6 2018	Year 7 2019	Year 8 2020	Year 9 2021	Year 10 2022
Entry EBITDA Multiple	8.0x											
Initial Equity Investment		$2,100.0										
EBITDA			$779.4	$826.1	$867.4	$902.1	$929.2	$957.1	$985.8	$1,015.4	$1,045.8	$1,077.2
Exit EBITDA Multiple	8.0x											
Enterprise Value at Exit			$6,235.0	$6,609.1	$6,939.6	$7,217.1	$7,433.7	$7,656.7	$7,886.4	$8,123.0	$8,366.6	$8,617.6
Less: Net Debt												
Revolving Credit Facility			-	-	-	-	-	-	-	-	-	-
Term Loan A			1,945.1	1,701.5	1,422.6	1,109.4	763.9	392.9	-	-	-	-
Term Loan B			-	-	-	-	-	-	-	-	-	-
Term Loan C			-	-	-	-	-	-	-	-	-	-
Existing Term Loan			-	-	-	-	-	-	-	-	-	-
2nd Lien			-	-	-	-	-	-	-	-	-	-
Senior Notes			1,500.0	1,500.0	1,500.0	1,500.0	1,500.0	1,500.0	1,500.0	1,500.0	1,500.0	1,500.0
Senior Subordinated Notes			-	-	-	-	-	-	-	-	-	-
Other Debt			-	-	-	-	-	-	-	-	-	-
Total Debt			$3,445.1	$3,201.5	$2,922.6	$2,609.4	$2,263.9	$1,892.9	$1,500.0	$1,500.0	$1,500.0	$1,500.0
Less: Cash and Cash Equivalents			-	-	-	-	-	-	5.8	425.4	858.8	1,308.8
Net Debt			$3,445.1	$3,201.5	$2,922.6	$2,609.4	$2,263.9	$1,892.9	$1,494.2	$1,074.6	$641.2	$191.2
Equity Value at Exit			$2,789.9	$3,407.6	$4,017.0	$4,607.7	$5,169.7	$5,763.7	$6,392.1	$7,048.4	$7,725.4	$8,426.4
Cash Return			1.3x	1.6x	1.9x	2.2x	2.5x	2.7x	3.0x	3.4x	3.7x	4.0x

	Year 1 2013	Year 2 2014	Year 3 2015	Year 4 2016	Year 5 2017	Year 6 2018	Year 7 2019	Year 8 2020	Year 9 2021	Year 10 2022
Initial Equity Investment	($2,100.0)	($2,100.0)	($2,100.0)	($2,100.0)	($2,100.0)	($2,100.0)	($2,100.0)	($2,100.0)	($2,100.0)	($2,100.0)
Equity Proceeds	$2,789.9	$3,407.6	$4,017.0	$4,607.7	$5,169.7	$5,763.7	$6,392.1	$7,048.4	$7,725.4	$8,426.4
IRR	32.9%	27.4%	24.1%	21.7%	19.7%	18.3%	17.2%	16.3%	15.6%	14.9%

IRR - Assuming Exit in 2017E

	Exit Multiple				
	7.0x	7.5x	8.0x	8.5x	9.0x
Entry Multiple 7.0x	24.8%	27.4%	29.9%	32.1%	34.2%
7.5x	19.4%	21.9%	24.2%	26.3%	28.4%
8.0x	15.1%	17.5%	19.7%	21.8%	23.8%
8.5x	11.6%	13.9%	16.1%	18.1%	20.0%
9.0x	8.7%	10.9%	13.0%	15.0%	16.8%

IRR - Assuming 8.0x Entry Multiple

	Exit Year				
	2015	2016	2017	2018	2019
Exit Multiple 7.0x	14.5%	15.3%	15.1%	14.8%	14.5%
7.5x	19.5%	18.6%	17.5%	16.6%	15.9%
8.0x	24.1%	21.7%	19.7%	18.3%	17.2%
8.5x	28.5%	24.6%	21.8%	19.9%	18.5%
9.0x	32.5%	27.3%	23.8%	21.4%	19.7%

EXHIBIT 5.52 ValueCo LBO Assumptions Page 1

Assumptions Page 1 - Income Statement and Cash Flow Statement

		Year 1 2013	Year 2 2014	Year 3 2015	Year 4 2016	Year 5 2017	Year 6 2018	Year 7 2019	Year 8 2020	Year 9 2021	Year 10 2022
Income Statement Assumptions											
Sales (% growth)											
Base	1	7.5%	6.0%	5.0%	4.0%	3.0%	3.0%	3.0%	3.0%	3.0%	3.0%
Sponsor	2	7.5%	6.0%	5.0%	4.0%	3.0%	3.0%	3.0%	3.0%	3.0%	3.0%
Management	3	10.0%	8.0%	6.0%	4.0%	3.0%	3.0%	3.0%	3.0%	3.0%	3.0%
Downside 1	4	12.0%	10.0%	8.0%	6.0%	4.0%	4.0%	4.0%	4.0%	4.0%	4.0%
Downside 2	5	5.0%	4.0%	3.0%	3.0%	3.0%	3.0%	3.0%	3.0%	3.0%	3.0%
		2.0%	2.0%	2.0%	2.0%	2.0%	2.0%	2.0%	2.0%	2.0%	2.0%
Cost of Goods Sold (% sales)											
Base	1	60.0%	60.0%	60.0%	60.0%	60.0%	60.0%	60.0%	60.0%	60.0%	60.0%
Sponsor	2	60.0%	60.0%	60.0%	60.0%	60.0%	60.0%	60.0%	60.0%	60.0%	60.0%
Management	3	59.0%	59.0%	59.0%	59.0%	59.0%	59.0%	59.0%	59.0%	59.0%	59.0%
Downside 1	4	61.0%	61.0%	61.0%	61.0%	61.0%	61.0%	61.0%	61.0%	61.0%	61.0%
Downside 2	5	62.0%	62.0%	62.0%	62.0%	62.0%	62.0%	62.0%	62.0%	62.0%	62.0%
SG&A (% sales)											
Base	1	19.0%	19.0%	19.0%	19.0%	19.0%	19.0%	19.0%	19.0%	19.0%	19.0%
Sponsor	2	19.0%	19.0%	19.0%	19.0%	19.0%	19.0%	19.0%	19.0%	19.0%	19.0%
Management	3	18.0%	18.0%	18.0%	18.0%	18.0%	18.0%	18.0%	18.0%	18.0%	18.0%
Downside 1	4	18.0%	18.0%	18.0%	18.0%	18.0%	18.0%	18.0%	18.0%	18.0%	18.0%
Downside 2	5	20.0%	20.0%	20.0%	20.0%	20.0%	20.0%	20.0%	20.0%	20.0%	20.0%
		21.0%	21.0%	21.0%	21.0%	21.0%	21.0%	21.0%	21.0%	21.0%	21.0%
Depreciation (% sales)											
Base	1	4.5%	4.5%	4.5%	4.5%	4.5%	4.5%	4.5%	4.5%	4.5%	4.5%
Sponsor	2	4.5%	4.5%	4.5%	4.5%	4.5%	4.5%	4.5%	4.5%	4.5%	4.5%
Management	3	4.5%	4.5%	4.5%	4.5%	4.5%	4.5%	4.5%	4.5%	4.5%	4.5%
Downside 1	4	4.5%	4.5%	4.5%	4.5%	4.5%	4.5%	4.5%	4.5%	4.5%	4.5%
Downside 2	5	4.5%	4.5%	4.5%	4.5%	4.5%	4.5%	4.5%	4.5%	4.5%	4.5%
Amortization (% sales)											
Base	1	1.5%	1.5%	1.5%	1.5%	1.5%	1.5%	1.5%	1.5%	1.5%	1.5%
Sponsor	2	1.5%	1.5%	1.5%	1.5%	1.5%	1.5%	1.5%	1.5%	1.5%	1.5%
Management	3	1.5%	1.5%	1.5%	1.5%	1.5%	1.5%	1.5%	1.5%	1.5%	1.5%
Downside 1	4	1.5%	1.5%	1.5%	1.5%	1.5%	1.5%	1.5%	1.5%	1.5%	1.5%
Downside 2	5	1.5%	1.5%	1.5%	1.5%	1.5%	1.5%	1.5%	1.5%	1.5%	1.5%
Cash Flow Statement Assumptions											
Capital Expenditures (% sales)											
Base	1	4.5%	4.5%	4.5%	4.5%	4.5%	4.5%	4.5%	4.5%	4.5%	4.5%
Sponsor	2	4.5%	4.5%	4.5%	4.5%	4.5%	4.5%	4.5%	4.5%	4.5%	4.5%
Management	3	4.5%	4.5%	4.5%	4.5%	4.5%	4.5%	4.5%	4.5%	4.5%	4.5%
Downside 1	4	5.0%	5.0%	5.0%	5.0%	5.0%	5.0%	5.0%	5.0%	5.0%	5.0%
Downside 2	5	5.0%	5.0%	5.0%	5.0%	5.0%	5.0%	5.0%	5.0%	5.0%	5.0%

EXHIBIT 5.53 ValueCo LBO Assumptions Page 2

Assumptions Page 2 - Balance Sheet

		Year 1 2013	Year 2 2014	Year 3 2015	Year 4 2016	Projection Period Year 5 2017	Year 6 2018	Year 7 2019	Year 8 2020	Year 9 2021	Year 10 2022
Current Assets											
Days Sales Outstanding (DSO)											
Base	1	47.6	47.6	47.6	47.6	47.6	47.6	47.6	47.6	47.6	47.6
Sponsor	2	47.6	47.6	47.6	47.6	47.6	47.6	47.6	47.6	47.6	47.6
Management	3	47.6	47.6	47.6	47.6	47.6	47.6	47.6	47.6	47.6	47.6
Downside 1	4	50.0	50.0	50.0	50.0	50.0	50.0	50.0	50.0	50.0	50.0
Downside 2	5	55.0	55.0	55.0	55.0	55.0	55.0	55.0	55.0	55.0	55.0
Days Inventory Held (DIH)											
Base	1	105.8	105.8	105.8	105.8	105.8	105.8	105.8	105.8	105.8	105.8
Sponsor	2	105.8	105.8	105.8	105.8	105.8	105.8	105.8	105.8	105.8	105.8
Management	3	105.8	105.8	105.8	105.8	105.8	105.8	105.8	105.8	105.8	105.8
Downside 1	4	110.0	110.0	110.0	110.0	110.0	110.0	110.0	110.0	110.0	110.0
Downside 2	5	115.0	115.0	115.0	115.0	115.0	115.0	115.0	115.0	115.0	115.0
Prepaids and Other Current Assets (% sales)											
Base	1	5.1%	5.1%	5.1%	5.1%	5.1%	5.1%	5.1%	5.1%	5.1%	5.1%
Sponsor	2	5.1%	5.1%	5.1%	5.1%	5.1%	5.1%	5.1%	5.1%	5.1%	5.1%
Management	3	5.1%	5.1%	5.1%	5.1%	5.1%	5.1%	5.1%	5.1%	5.1%	5.1%
Downside 1	4	5.1%	5.1%	5.1%	5.1%	5.1%	5.1%	5.1%	5.1%	5.1%	5.1%
Downside 2	5	5.1%	5.1%	5.1%	5.1%	5.1%	5.1%	5.1%	5.1%	5.1%	5.1%
Current Liabilities											
Days Payable Outstanding (DPO)											
Base	1	37.9	37.9	37.9	37.9	37.9	37.9	37.9	37.9	37.9	37.9
Sponsor	2	37.9	37.9	37.9	37.9	37.9	37.9	37.9	37.9	37.9	37.9
Management	3	37.9	37.9	37.9	37.9	37.9	37.9	37.9	37.9	37.9	37.9
Downside 1	4	35.0	35.0	35.0	35.0	35.0	35.0	35.0	35.0	35.0	35.0
Downside 2	5	30.0	30.0	30.0	30.0	30.0	30.0	30.0	30.0	30.0	30.0
Accrued Liabilities (% sales)											
Base	1	8.0%	8.0%	8.0%	8.0%	8.0%	8.0%	8.0%	8.0%	8.0%	8.0%
Sponsor	2	8.0%	8.0%	8.0%	8.0%	8.0%	8.0%	8.0%	8.0%	8.0%	8.0%
Management	3	8.0%	8.0%	8.0%	8.0%	8.0%	8.0%	8.0%	8.0%	8.0%	8.0%
Downside 1	4	8.0%	8.0%	8.0%	8.0%	8.0%	8.0%	8.0%	8.0%	8.0%	8.0%
Downside 2	5	8.0%	8.0%	8.0%	8.0%	8.0%	8.0%	8.0%	8.0%	8.0%	8.0%
Other Current Liabilities (% sales)											
Base	1	2.9%	2.9%	2.9%	2.9%	2.9%	2.9%	2.9%	2.9%	2.9%	2.9%
Sponsor	2	2.9%	2.9%	2.9%	2.9%	2.9%	2.9%	2.9%	2.9%	2.9%	2.9%
Management	3	2.9%	2.9%	2.9%	2.9%	2.9%	2.9%	2.9%	2.9%	2.9%	2.9%
Downside 1	4	2.9%	2.9%	2.9%	2.9%	2.9%	2.9%	2.9%	2.9%	2.9%	2.9%
Downside 2	5	2.9%	2.9%	2.9%	2.9%	2.9%	2.9%	2.9%	2.9%	2.9%	2.9%

EXHIBIT 5.54 ValueCo LBO Assumptions Page 3

($ in millions, fiscal year ending December 31)

Assumptions Page 3 - Financing Structures and Fees

Financing Structures

Sources of Funds	Structure 1	Structure 2	Structure 3	Structure 4	Structure 5 Status Quo
Revolving Credit Facility Size	$250.0	$250.0	$250.0	$250.0	-
Revolving Credit Facility Draw	-	-	-	-	-
Term Loan A	-	500.0	-	-	-
Term Loan B	2,150.0	1,650.0	2,100.0	1,750.0	-
Term Loan C	-	-	-	-	-
2nd Lien	-	-	-	-	-
Senior Notes	1,500.0	1,500.0	700.0	1,000.0	-
Senior Subordinated Notes	-	-	700.0	1,000.0	-
Equity Contribution	2,100.0	2,100.0	2,250.0	2,250.0	-
Rollover Equity	250.0	250.0	250.0	-	-
Cash on Hand	-	-	-	-	-
Total Sources of Funds	**$6,000.0**	**$6,000.0**	**$6,000.0**	**$6,000.0**	-

Uses of Funds					
Equity Purchase Price	$4,350.0	$4,350.0	$4,350.0	$4,350.0	-
Repay Existing Bank Debt	1,500.0	1,500.0	1,500.0	1,500.0	-
Tender / Call Premiums	20.0	20.0	20.0	20.0	-
Financing Fees	90.0	90.0	90.0	90.0	-
Other Fees and Expenses	40.0	40.0	40.0	40.0	-
Total Uses of Funds	**$6,000.0**	**$6,000.0**	**$6,000.0**	**$6,000.0**	-

Financing Fees

	Structure 1		
	Size	Fees (%)	($)
Revolving Credit Facility Size	$250.0	1.500%	$3.8
Term Loan A	-	1.500%	-
Term Loan B	2,150.0	1.500%	32.3
Term Loan C	-	1.500%	-
2nd Lien	-	2.250%	-
Senior Notes	1,500.0	2.250%	33.8
Senior Subordinated Notes	-	2.250%	-
Senior Bridge Facility	1,500.0	1.000%	15.0
Senior Subordinated Bridge Facility	-	1.000%	-
Other Financing Fees & Expenses			5.3
Total Financing Fees			**$90.0**

Purchase Price

Public / Private Target		2
Entry EBITDA Multiple		8.0x
LTM 9/30/2012 EBITDA		700.0
Enterprise Value		**$5,600.0**
Less: Total Debt		(1,500.0)
Less: Preferred Stock		-
Less: Noncontrolling Interest		-
Plus: Cash and Cash Equivalents		250.0
Equity Purchase Price		**$4,350.0**

Calculation of Fully Diluted Shares Outstanding

Offer Price per Share			
Basic Shares Outstanding			
Plus: Shares from In-the-Money Options			
Less: Shares Repurchased			
Net New Shares from Options			
Plus: Shares from Convertible Securities			
Fully Diluted Shares Outstanding			

Options/Warrants	Number of Shares	Exercise Price	In-the-Money Shares
Tranche 1	-	-	-
Tranche 2	-	-	-
Tranche 3	-	-	-
Tranche 4	-	-	-
Tranche 5	-	-	-
Total	-		-

Convertible Securities	Amount	Conversion Price	Conversion Ratio	New Shares	Proceeds
Issue 1	-		-	-	-
Issue 2	-		-	-	-
Issue 3	-		-	-	-
Issue 4	-		-	-	-
Issue 5	-		-	-	-
Total				-	-

Amortization of Financing Fees

	Term	Year 1 2013	Year 2 2014	Year 3 2015	Year 4 2016	Year 5 2017	Year 6 2018	Year 7 2019	Year 8 2020	Year 9 2021	Year 10 2022
Revolving Credit Facility Size	6	$0.6	$0.6	$0.6	$0.6	$0.6	$0.6	-	-	-	-
Term Loan A	7	4.6	4.6	4.6	4.6	4.6	4.6	4.6	-	-	-
Term Loan B		-	-	-	-	-	-	-	-	-	-
Term Loan C		-	-	-	-	-	-	-	-	-	-
2nd Lien	8	4.2	4.2	4.2	4.2	4.2	4.2	4.2	4.2	-	-
Senior Notes		-	-	-	-	-	-	-	-	-	-
Senior Subordinated Notes	8	1.9	1.9	1.9	1.9	1.9	1.9	1.9	1.9	-	-
Senior Bridge Facility		-	-	-	-	-	-	-	-	-	-
Senior Subordinated Bridge Facility	8	0.7	0.7	0.7	0.7	0.7	0.7	0.7	0.7	-	-
Other Financing Fees & Expenses		-	-	-	-	-	-	-	-	-	-
Annual Amortization		**$12.0**	**$12.0**	**$12.0**	**$12.0**	**$12.0**	**$12.0**	**$11.4**	**$6.8**	-	-

Bloomberg Appendix

APPENDIX 5.1 Bloomberg Forward Analysis of 3 Month Libor Projections (FWCV<GO>)

US Dollar Swaps (30/360, S/A) Curve

Date	Spot	Projection
03/30/2013	0.2829	0.2942
06/28/2013	0.2939	0.3272
09/30/2013	0.3081	0.3574
12/30/2013	0.3218	0.4015
03/31/2014	0.3382	0.4469
06/30/2014	0.3581	0.5103
09/30/2014	0.3818	0.5746
12/30/2014	0.4070	0.6506
03/30/2015	0.4344	0.7253
06/30/2015	0.4654	0.8181
09/30/2015	0.4995	0.9174
12/30/2015	0.5355	1.0517
03/30/2016	0.5764	1.2732
06/30/2016	0.6286	1.3717
09/30/2016	0.6806	1.4687
12/30/2016	0.7312	1.7079
03/30/2017	0.7890	1.8370
06/30/2017	0.8499	1.9479
09/29/2017	0.9097	2.0567
12/29/2017	0.9686	2.2597

PART Three

Mergers & Acquisitions

CHAPTER 6

Sell-Side M&A

The sale of a company, division, business, or collection of assets ("target") is a major event for its owners (shareholders), management, employees, and other stakeholders. It is an intense, time-consuming process with high stakes, usually spanning several months. Consequently, the seller typically hires an investment bank and its team of trained professionals ("sell-side advisor") to ensure that key objectives are met and a favorable result is achieved. In many cases, a seller turns to its bankers for a comprehensive financial analysis of the various strategic alternatives available to the target. These include a sale of all or part of the business, a recapitalization, an initial public offering, or a continuation of the status quo.

Once the decision to sell has been made, the sell-side advisor seeks to achieve the optimal mix of value maximization, speed of execution, and certainty of completion among other deal-specific considerations for the selling party. Accordingly, it is the sell-side advisor's responsibility to identify the seller's priorities from the onset and craft a tailored sale process. If the seller is largely indifferent toward confidentiality, timing, and potential business disruption, the advisor may consider running a *broad auction* reaching out to as many potential interested parties as reasonably possible. This process, which is relatively neutral toward prospective buyers, is designed to maximize competitive dynamics and heighten the probability of finding the one buyer willing to offer the best value.

Alternatively, if speed, confidentiality, a particular transaction structure, and/or cultural fit are a priority for the seller, then a *targeted auction*, where only a select group of potential buyers are approached, or even a *negotiated sale* with a single party, may be more appropriate. Generally, an auction requires more upfront organization, marketing, process points, and resources than a negotiated sale with a single party. Consequently, this chapter focuses primarily on the auction process.

From an analytical perspective, a sell-side assignment requires the deal team to perform a comprehensive valuation of the target using those methodologies discussed in this book. In addition, in order to assess the potential purchase price that specific public strategic buyers may be willing to pay for the target, merger consequences analysis is performed with an emphasis on accretion/(dilution) and balance sheet effects (see Chapter 7). These valuation analyses are used to frame the seller's price expectations, select the final buyer list, set guidelines for the range of acceptable bids, evaluate offers received, and ultimately guide negotiations of the final purchase price. Furthermore, for public targets (and certain private targets, depending on the situation) the sell-side advisor or an additional investment bank may be called upon to provide a fairness opinion.

In discussing the process by which companies are bought and sold in the marketplace, we provide greater context to the topics discussed earlier in this book. In a sale process, theoretical valuation methodologies are ultimately tested in the market based on what a buyer will actually pay for the target (see Exhibit 6.1). An effective sell-side advisor seeks to push the buyer(s) toward, or through, the upper endpoint of the implied valuation range for the target. On a fundamental level, this involves properly positioning the business and tailoring the sale process accordingly to maximize its value.

AUCTIONS

An auction is a staged process whereby a target is marketed to multiple prospective buyers ("buyers" or "bidders"). A well-run auction is designed to have a substantial positive impact on value (both price and terms) received by the seller due to a variety of factors related to the creation of a competitive environment. This environment encourages bidders to put forth their best offer on both price and terms, and helps increase speed of execution by encouraging quick action by buyers.

An auction provides a level of comfort that the market has been tested as well as a strong indicator of inherent value (supported by a fairness opinion, if required). At the same time, the auction process may have potential drawbacks, including information leakage into the market from bidders, negative impact on employee morale, possible collusion among bidders, reduced negotiating leverage once a "winner" is chosen (thereby encouraging re-trading[1]), and "taint" in the event of a failed auction. In addition, certain prospective buyers may decide not to participate in a broad auction given their reluctance to commit serious time and resources to a situation where they may perceive a relatively low likelihood of winning.

A successful auction requires significant dedicated resources, experience, and expertise. Upfront, the deal team establishes a solid foundation through the preparation of compelling marketing materials, identification of potential deal issues, coaching of management, and selection of an appropriate group of prospective buyers. Once the auction commences, the sell-side advisor is entrusted with running as effective a process as possible. This involves the execution of a wide range of duties and functions in a tightly coordinated manner.

To ensure a successful outcome, investment banks commit a team of bankers that is responsible for the day-to-day execution of the transaction. Auctions also require significant time and attention from key members of the target's management team, especially on the production of marketing materials and facilitation of buyer due diligence (e.g., management presentations, site visits, data room population, and responses to specific buyer inquiries). It is the deal team's responsibility, however, to alleviate as much of this burden from the management team as possible.

In the later stages of an auction, a senior member of the sell-side advisory team typically negotiates directly with prospective buyers with the goal of encouraging them to put forth their best offer. As a result, sellers seek investment banks with extensive negotiation experience, sector expertise, and buyer relationships to run these auctions.

---

[1]Refers to the practice of replacing an initial bid with a lower one at a later date.

EXHIBIT 6.1 Valuation Paradigm

Implied Valuation Range				Actual Price Paid
Comparable Companies Analysis	Precedent Transactions Analysis	Discounted Cash Flow Analysis	Leveraged Buyout Analysis	M&A Sale Process

Description

- **Comparable Companies Analysis**: Valuation based on the current trading multiples of peer companies
- **Precedent Transactions Analysis**: Valuation based on the multiples paid for peer companies in past M&A transactions
- **Discounted Cash Flow Analysis**: Valuation based on the present value of projected free cash flow
- **Leveraged Buyout Analysis**: Valuation based on the price a financial sponsor would likely pay
- **M&A Sale Process**: Determines the ultimate price a buyer is willing to pay

Common Value Drivers

- Sector performance and outlook
- Company performance
  - size, margins and growth profile
  - historical and projected financial performance
- Company positioning
  - market share
  - ability to differentiate products/services
  - quality of management
- General economic and financing market conditions

Unique Value Drivers

Comparable Companies Analysis
- Relative performance to peer companies

Precedent Transactions Analysis
- M&A market conditions
- Deal specific situation
- Premium paid for control
- Level of synergies

Discounted Cash Flow Analysis
- Free cash flow
- Cost of capital
- Terminal value

Leveraged Buyout Analysis
- Credit market conditions
- Free cash flow
- Ability to leverage
- Debt repayment
- Cost of capital
- Required returns

M&A Sale Process
- Process dynamics
  - auction vs. negotiated sale
  - number of parties in process
  - level of information disclosure
  - "trophy"/must own asset
- Buyer appetite
  - strategic vs. sponsor
  - desire/ability to pay
  - amount needed to "win"
- Pro forma impact to buyer
  - financial effects
  - pro forma leverage
  - returns thresholds

There are two primary types of auctions—broad and targeted.

- *Broad Auction:* As its name implies, a broad auction maximizes the universe of prospective buyers approached. This may involve contacting dozens of potential bidders, comprising both strategic buyers (potentially including direct competitors) and financial sponsors. By casting as wide a net as possible, a broad auction is designed to maximize competitive dynamics, thereby increasing the likelihood of finding the best possible offer. This type of process typically involves more upfront organization and marketing due to the larger number of buyer participants in the early stages of the process. It is also more difficult to maintain confidentiality as the process is susceptible to leakage to the public (including customers, suppliers, and competitors), which, in turn, can increase the potential for business disruption.[2]

- *Targeted Auction:* A targeted auction focuses on a few clearly defined buyers that have been identified as having a strong strategic fit and/or desire, as well as the financial capacity, to purchase the target. This process is more conducive to maintaining confidentiality and minimizing business disruption to the target. At the same time, there is greater risk of "leaving money on the table" by excluding a potential bidder that may be willing to pay a higher price.

Exhibit 6.2 provides a summary of the potential advantages and disadvantages of each process.

EXHIBIT 6.2 Advantages and Disadvantages of Broad and Targeted Auctions

	Broad	Targeted
Advantages	- Heightens competitive dynamics - Maximizes probability of achieving maximum sale price - Helps to ensure that all likely bidders are approached - Limits potential buyers' negotiating leverage - Enhances board's comfort that it has satisfied its fiduciary duty to maximize value	- Higher likelihood of preserving confidentiality - Reduces business disruption - Reduces the potential of a failed auction by signaling a desire to select a "partner" - Maintains perception of competitive dynamics - Serves as a "market check" for board to meet its fiduciary duties
Disadvantages	- Difficult to preserve confidentiality - Highest business disruption risk - Some prospective buyers decline participation in broad auctions - Unsuccessful outcome can create perception of undesirable asset - Industry competitors may participate just to gain access to sensitive information	- Potentially excludes non-obvious, but credible, buyers - Potential to leave "money on the table" if certain buyers excluded - Lesser degree of competition - May afford buyers more leverage in negotiations - Provides less market data on which board can rely to satisfy its fiduciary duties

---

[2] In some circumstances, the auction is actually made public by the seller to encourage all interested buyers to come forward and state their interest in the target.

Auction Structure

The traditional auction is structured as a two-round bidding process that generally spans from three to six months (or longer) from the decision to sell until the signing of a definitive purchase/sale agreement ("definitive agreement") with the winning bidder (see Exhibit 6.3). The timing of the post-signing ("closing") period depends on a variety of factors not specific to an auction, such as regulatory approvals and/or third-party consents, financing, and shareholder approval. The entire auction process consists of multiple stages and discrete milestones within each of these stages. There are numerous variations within this structure that allow the sell-side advisor to customize, as appropriate, for a given situation.

ORGANIZATION AND PREPARATION

- Identify Seller Objectives and Determine Appropriate Sale Process
- Perform Sell-Side Advisor Due Diligence and Preliminary Valuation Analysis
- Select Buyer Universe
- Prepare Marketing Materials
- Prepare Confidentiality Agreement

Identify Seller Objectives and Determine Appropriate Sale Process

At the onset of an auction, the sell-side advisor works with the seller to identify its objectives, determine the appropriate sale process to conduct, and develop a process roadmap. The advisor must first gain a clear understanding of the seller's priorities so as to tailor the process accordingly. Perhaps the most basic decision is how many prospective buyers to approach (i.e., whether to run a broad or targeted auction).

As previously discussed, while a broad auction may be more appealing to a seller in certain circumstances, a targeted auction may better satisfy certain "softer" needs, such as speed to transaction closing, heightened confidentiality, a tailored transaction structure, and less risk of business disruption. Furthermore, the target's board of directors must also take into account its fiduciary duties in deciding whether to conduct a broad or targeted auction.[3] At this point, the deal team drafts a detailed process timeline and roadmap, including target dates for significant milestones, such as launch, receipt of initial and final bids, contract signing, and deal closing.

---

[3]In Delaware (which generally sets the standards upon which many states base their corporate law), when the sale of control or the break-up of a company has become inevitable, the directors have the duty to obtain the highest price reasonably available. There is no statutory or judicial "blueprint" for an appropriate sale or auction process. Directors enjoy some latitude in this regard, so long as the process is designed to satisfy the directors' duties by ensuring that they have reasonably informed themselves about the company's value.

EXHIBIT 6.3 Stages of an Auction Process

Stages of an Auction Process

Organization and Preparation	First Round	Second Round	Negotiations	Closing
■ Identify seller objectives and determine appropriate sale process ■ Perform sell-side advisor due diligence and preliminary valuation analysis ■ Select buyer universe ■ Prepare marketing materials ■ Prepare confidentiality agreement	■ Contact prospective buyers ■ Negotiate and execute confidentiality agreements with interested parties ■ Distribute CIM and initial bid procedures letter ■ Prepare management presentation ■ Set up data room ■ Prepare stapled financing package (if applicable) ■ Receive initial bids and select buyers to proceed to second round	■ Conduct management presentations ■ Facilitate site visits ■ Provide data room access ■ Distribute final bid procedures letter and draft definitive agreement ■ Receive final bids	■ Evaluate final bids ■ Negotiate with preferred buyer(s) ■ Select winning bidder ■ Render fairness opinion (if required) ■ Receive board approval and execute definitive agreement ("signing")	■ Obtain necessary approvals ■ Financing and closing
2 – 4 weeks	4 – 6 weeks	6 – 8 weeks	2 – 4 weeks (may include a third "mini round")	4 – 8 weeks +

Perform Sell-Side Advisor Due Diligence and Preliminary Valuation Analysis

Sale process preparation begins with extensive due diligence on the part of the sell-side advisor. This typically kicks off with an in-depth session with target management. The sell-side advisor must have a comprehensive understanding of the target's business and the management team's vision prior to drafting marketing materials and communicating with prospective buyers. Due diligence facilitates the advisor's ability to properly position the target and articulate its investment merits. It also allows for the identification of potential buyer concerns on issues ranging from growth sustainability, margin trends, and customer concentration to environmental matters, contingent liabilities, and labor relations.

A key portion of sell-side diligence centers on ensuring that the advisor understands and provides perspective on the assumptions that drive management's financial model. This diligence is particularly important as the model forms the basis for the valuation work that will be performed by prospective buyers. Therefore, the sell-side advisor must approach the target's financial projections from a buyer's perspective and gain comfort with the numbers, trends, and key assumptions driving them.

An effective sell-side advisor understands the valuation methodologies that buyers will use in their analysis (e.g., comparable companies, precedent transactions, DCF analysis, and LBO analysis) and performs this work beforehand to establish a valuation range benchmark. For specific public buyers, accretion/(dilution) analysis and balance sheet effects are also performed to assess their ability to pay. Ultimately, however, the target's implied valuation based on these methodologies needs to be weighed against market appetite. Furthermore, the actual value received in a transaction must be assessed on the basis of structure and terms, in addition to price.

In the event a stapled financing package is being provided, a separate financing deal team is formed (either at the sell-side advisor's institution or another bank) to begin conducting due diligence in parallel with the sell-side team. Their analysis is used to craft a generic pre-packaged financing structure to support the purchase of the target.[4] The initial financing package terms are used as guideposts to derive an implied LBO analysis valuation.

Select Buyer Universe

The selection of an appropriate group of prospective buyers, and compilation of corresponding contact information, is a critical part of the organization and preparation stage. At the extreme, the omission or inclusion of a potential buyer (or buyers) can mean the difference between a successful or failed auction. Sell-side advisors are selected in large part on the basis of their sector knowledge, including their relationships with, and insights on, prospective buyers. Correspondingly, the deal team is

---

[4]Ultimately, buyers who require financing to complete a deal will typically work with multiple banks to ensure they are receiving the most favorable financing package (debt quantum, pricing, and terms) available in the market.

expected to both identify the appropriate buyers and effectively market the target to them.

In a broad auction, the buyer list typically includes a mix of strategic buyers and financial sponsors. The sell-side advisor evaluates each buyer on a broad range of criteria pertinent to its likelihood and ability to acquire the target at an acceptable value. When evaluating strategic buyers, the banker looks first and foremost at strategic fit, including potential synergies. Financial capacity or "ability to pay"—which is typically dependent on size, balance sheet strength, access to financing, and risk appetite—is also closely scrutinized. Other factors play a role in assessing potential strategic bidders, such as cultural fit, M&A track record, existing management's role going forward, relative and pro forma market position (including antitrust concerns), and effects on existing customer and supplier relationships. Bankers can use a variety of Bloomberg functions to identify potential strategic buyers (examples include: Bloomberg Industries (BI<GO>), M&A Analysis (MA<GO>), Industry Classification Browser (ICS<GO>), Supply Chain (SPLC<GO>), Equity Screening (EQS<GO>), Private Company Screening (PSCR<GO>, see Appendix 6.1) and Transaction Ideas (IBTI<GO>)).

When evaluating potential financial sponsor buyers, key criteria include investment strategy/focus, sector expertise, fund size,[5] track record, fit within existing investment portfolio, fund life cycle,[6] and ability to obtain financing. As part of this process, the deal team looks for sponsors with existing portfolio companies that may serve as an attractive combination candidate for the target. In many cases, a strategic buyer is able to pay a higher price than a sponsor due to the ability to realize synergies and a lower cost of capital. Depending on the prevailing capital markets conditions, a strategic buyer may also present less financing risk than a sponsor. The Bloomberg Private Equity suite of functions (PEFS<GO>) provides search tools to identify potential financial sponsors meeting any criteria a banker may specify (see Appendix 6.2).

Once the sell-side advisor has compiled a list of prospective buyers, it presents them to the seller for final sign-off.

Prepare Marketing Materials

Marketing materials often represent the first formal introduction of the target to prospective buyers. They are essential for sparking buyer interest and creating a favorable first impression. Effective marketing materials present the target's investment highlights in a succinct manner, while also providing supporting evidence and basic operational, financial, and other essential business information. The two main marketing documents for the first round of an auction process are the teaser and confidential information memorandum (CIM). The sell-side advisors take the lead on producing these materials with substantial input from management. Legal counsel also reviews these documents, as well as the management presentation, for various potential legal concerns (e.g., antitrust[7]).

---

[5]Refers to the total size of the fund as well as remaining equity available for investment.

[6]As set forth in the agreement between the fund's general partners (GPs) and limited partners (LPs), refers to how long the fund will be permitted to seek investments prior to entering a harvest and distribution phase.

[7]Typically, counsel closely scrutinizes any discussion of a business combination (i.e., in a strategic transaction) as marketing materials will be subjected to scrutiny by antitrust authorities in connection with their regulatory review.

Teaser The teaser is the first marketing document presented to prospective buyers. It is designed to inform buyers and generate sufficient interest for them to do further work and potentially submit a bid. The teaser is generally a brief one- or two-page synopsis of the target, including a company overview, investment highlights, and summary financial information. It also contains contact information for the bankers running the sell-side process so that interested parties may respond.

Teasers vary in terms of format and content in accordance with the target, sector, sale process, advisor, and potential seller sensitivities. For public companies, Regulation FD concerns govern the content of the teaser (i.e., no material non-public information) as well as the nature of the buyer contacts themselves.[8] Exhibit 6.4 displays an illustrative teaser template as might be presented to prospective buyers.

EXHIBIT 6.4 Sample Teaser

Confidential Information Memorandum The CIM is a detailed written description of the target (often 50+ pages) that serves as the primary marketing document for the target in an auction. The deal team, in collaboration with the target's management, spends significant time and resources drafting the CIM before it is deemed ready for distribution to prospective buyers. In the event the seller is a financial sponsor (e.g., selling a portfolio company), the sponsor's investment professionals typically also provide input.

---

[8]The initial buyer contact or teaser can put a public company "in play" and may constitute the selective disclosure of material information (i.e., that the company is for sale).

Like teasers, CIMs vary in terms of format and content depending on situation-specific circumstances. There are, however, certain generally accepted guidelines for content, as reflected in Exhibit 6.5. The CIM typically contains an executive summary,

EXHIBIT 6.5 Confidential Information Memorandum Table of Contents

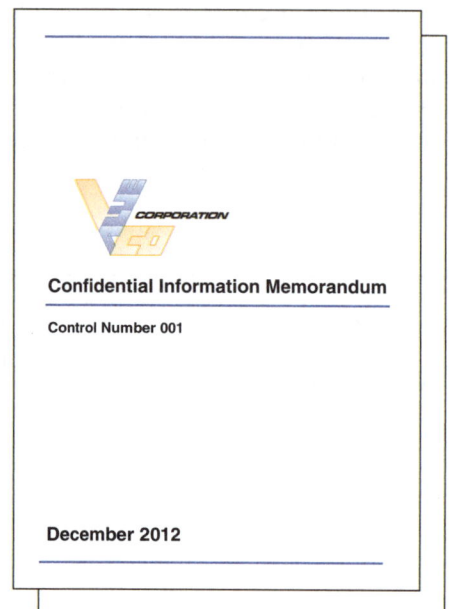

investment considerations, and detailed information about the target, as well as its sector, customers and suppliers (often presented on an anonymous basis), operations, facilities, management, and employees. A modified version of the CIM may be prepared for designated strategic buyers, namely competitors with whom the seller may be concerned about sharing certain sensitive information.

Financial Information The CIM contains a detailed financial section presenting historical and projected financial information with accompanying narrative explaining both past and expected future performance (MD&A). This data forms the basis for the preliminary valuation analysis performed by prospective buyers.

Consequently, the deal team spends a great deal of time working with the target's CFO, treasurer, and/or finance team (and division heads, as appropriate) on the CIM's financial section. This process involves normalizing the historical financials (e.g., for acquisitions, divestitures, and other one-time and/or extraordinary items) and crafting an accompanying MD&A. The sell-side advisor also helps develop a set of projections, typically five years in length, as well as supporting assumptions and narrative. Given the importance of the projections in framing valuation, prospective buyers subject them to intense scrutiny. Therefore, the sell-side advisor must gain sufficient comfort that the numbers are realistic and defensible in the face of potential buyer skepticism.

In some cases, the CIM provides additional financial information to help guide buyers toward potential growth/acquisition scenarios for the target. For example, the sell-side advisor may work with management to compile a list of potential acquisition opportunities for inclusion in the CIM (typically on an anonymous basis), including their incremental sales and EBITDA contributions. This information is designed to provide potential buyers with perspective on the potential upside represented by using the target as a growth platform so they can craft their bids accordingly.

Prepare Confidentiality Agreement

A confidentiality agreement (CA) is a legally binding contract between the target and prospective buyers that governs the sharing of confidential company information. The CA is typically drafted by the target's counsel and distributed to prospective buyers along with the teaser, with the understanding that the receipt of more detailed information is conditioned on execution of the CA.

A typical CA includes provisions governing the following:

- *Use of information* – states that all information furnished by the seller, whether oral or written, is considered proprietary information and should be treated as confidential and used solely to make a decision regarding the proposed transaction

- *Term* – designates the time period during which the confidentiality restrictions remain in effect[9]

- *Permitted disclosures* – outlines under what limited circumstances the prospective buyer is permitted to disclose the confidential information provided; also prohibits disclosure that the two parties are in negotiations

- *Return of confidential information* – mandates the return or destruction of all provided documents once the prospective buyer exits the process

- *Non-solicitation/no hire* – prevents prospective buyers from soliciting to hire (or hiring) target employees for a designated time period

- *Standstill agreement*[10] – for public targets, precludes prospective buyers from making unsolicited offers or purchases of the target's shares, or seeking to control/influence the target's management, board of directors, or policies

- *Restrictions on clubbing* – prevents prospective buyers from collaborating with each other or with outside financial sponsors/equity providers without the prior consent of the target (in order to preserve a competitive environment)

---

[9]Typically one-to-two years for financial sponsors and potentially longer for strategic buyers.
[10]May also be crafted as a separate legal document outside of the CA.

FIRST ROUND

- Contact Prospective Buyers
- Negotiate and Execute Confidentiality Agreements with Interested Parties
- Distribute Confidential Information Memorandum and Initial Bid Procedures Letter
- Prepare Management Presentation
- Set up Data Room
- Prepare Stapled Financing Package (if applicable)
- Receive Initial Bids and Select Buyers to Proceed to Second Round

Contact Prospective Buyers

The first round begins with the contacting of prospective buyers, which marks the formal launch of the auction process. This typically takes the form of a scripted phone call to each prospective buyer by a senior member of the sell-side advisory deal team (either an M&A banker or the coverage banker that maintains the relationship with the particular buyer), followed by the delivery of the teaser and CA.[11] The sell-side advisor generally keeps a detailed record of all interactions with prospective buyers, called a *contact log*, which is used as a tool to monitor a buyer's activity level and provide a record of the process.

Negotiate and Execute Confidentiality Agreement with Interested Parties

Upon receipt of the CA, a prospective buyer presents the document to its legal counsel for review. In the likely event there are comments, the buyer's counsel and seller's counsel negotiate the CA with input from their respective clients. Following execution of the CA, the sell-side advisor is legally able to distribute the CIM and *initial bid procedures letter* to a prospective buyer.[12]

Distribute Confidential Information Memorandum and Initial Bid Procedures Letter

Prospective buyers are typically given several weeks to review the CIM,[13] study the target and its sector, and conduct preliminary financial analysis prior to submitting their initial non-binding bids. During this period, the sell-side advisor maintains a

---

[11] In some cases, the CA must be signed prior to receipt of any information, including the teaser, depending on seller sensitivity.

[12] Calls are usually commenced one-to-two weeks prior to the CIM being printed to allow sufficient time for the negotiation of CAs. Ideally, the sell-side advisor prefers to distribute the CIMs simultaneously to provide all prospective buyers an equal amount of time to consider the investment prior to the bid due date.

[13] Each CIM is given a unique control number that is used to track each party that receives a copy.

dialogue with the prospective buyers, often providing additional color, guidance, and materials, as appropriate, on a case-by-case basis.

Depending on their level of interest, prospective buyers may also engage investment banks (as M&A buy-side advisors and/or financing providers), other external financing sources, and consultants at this stage. Buy-side advisors play an important role in helping their client, whether a strategic buyer or a financial sponsor, assess the target from a valuation perspective and determine a competitive initial bid price. Financing sources help assess both the buyer's and target's ability to support a given capital structure and provide their clients with data points on amounts, terms, and availability of financing. This financing data is used to help frame the valuation analysis performed by the buyer. Consultants provide perspective on key business and market opportunities, as well as potential risks and areas of operational improvement for the target.

Initial Bid Procedures Letter The initial bid procedures letter, which is typically sent out to prospective buyers following distribution of the CIM, states the date and time by which interested parties must submit their written, non-binding preliminary indications of interest ("first round bids"). It also defines the exact information that should be included in the bid, such as:

- Indicative purchase price (typically presented as a range) and form of consideration (cash vs. stock mix)[14]
- Key assumptions to arrive at the stated purchase price
- Structural and other considerations
- Information on financing sources
- Treatment of management and employees
- Timing for completing a deal and diligence that must be performed
- Key conditions to signing and closing
- Required approvals
- Buyer contact information

---

[14]For acquisitions of private companies, buyers are typically asked to bid assuming the target is both cash and debt free.

Prepare Management Presentation

The management presentation is typically structured as a slideshow with accompanying hardcopy handout. The sell-side advisor takes the lead on preparing these materials with substantial input from management. In parallel, the sell-side advisor works with the management team to determine the speaker lineup for the presentation, as well as key messages, and the preparation of answers for likely questions. Depending on the management team, the rehearsal process for the presentations ("dry runs") may be intense and time-consuming. The management presentation slideshow needs to be completed by the start of the second round when the actual meetings with buyers begin.

The presentation format generally maps to that of the CIM, but is more crisp and concise. It also tends to contain an additional level of detail, analysis, and insight more conducive to an interactive session with management and later-stage due diligence. A typical management presentation outline is shown in Exhibit 6.6.

EXHIBIT 6.6 Sample Management Presentation Outline

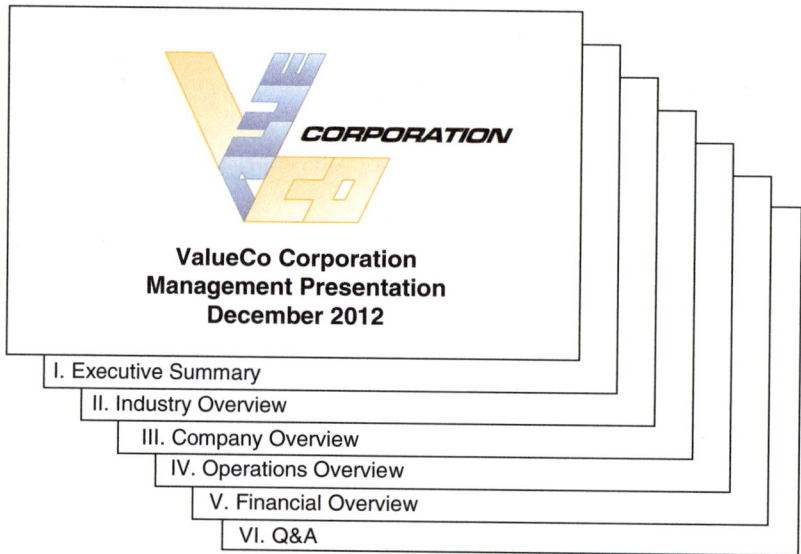

Set up Data Room

The data room serves as the hub for the buyer due diligence that takes place in the second round of the process. It is a location, typically online, where comprehensive, detailed information about the target is stored, catalogued, and made available to pre-screened bidders.[15] A well-organized data room facilitates buyer due diligence, helps keep the sale process on schedule, and inspires confidence in bidders. While most data rooms follow certain basic guidelines, they may vary greatly in terms of content and accessibility depending on the company and confidentiality concerns.

Data rooms, such as those provided by Intralinks, generally contain a broad base of essential company information, documentation, and analyses. In essence, the data room is designed to provide a comprehensive set of information relevant for buyers to make an informed investment decision about the target, such as detailed financial reports, industry reports, and consulting studies. It also contains detailed company-specific information such as customer and supplier lists, labor contracts, purchase contracts, description and terms of outstanding debt, lease and pension contracts, and environmental compliance certification (see Exhibit 6.7). At the same time, the content must reflect any concerns over sharing sensitive data for competitive reasons.[16]

The data room also allows the buyer (together with its legal counsel, accountants, and other advisors) to perform more detailed confirmatory due diligence prior to consummating a transaction. This due diligence includes reviewing charters/bylaws, outstanding litigation, regulatory information, environmental reports, and property deeds, for example. It is typically conducted only after a buyer has decided to seriously pursue the acquisition.

The sell-side bankers work closely with the target's legal counsel and selected employees to organize, populate, and manage the data room. While the data room is continuously updated and refreshed with new information throughout the auction, the aim is to have a basic data foundation in place by the start of the second round. Access to the data room is typically granted to those buyers that move forward after first round bids, prior to, or coinciding with, their attendance at the management presentation.

---

[15] Prior to the establishment of web-based data retrieval systems, data rooms were physical locations (i.e., offices or rooms, usually housed at the target's law firm) where file cabinets or boxes containing company documentation were set up. Today, however, most data rooms are online sites where buyers can view all the necessary documentation remotely. Among other benefits, the online process facilitates the participation of a greater number of prospective buyers as data room documents can be reviewed simultaneously by different parties. They also enable the seller to customize the viewing, downloading, and printing of various data and documentation for specific buyers.

[16] Sensitive information (e.g., customer, supplier, and employment contracts, or profitability metrics by product/customer/location) is generally withheld from competitor bidders until later in the process.

EXHIBIT 6.7 Intralinks Data Room Document Index

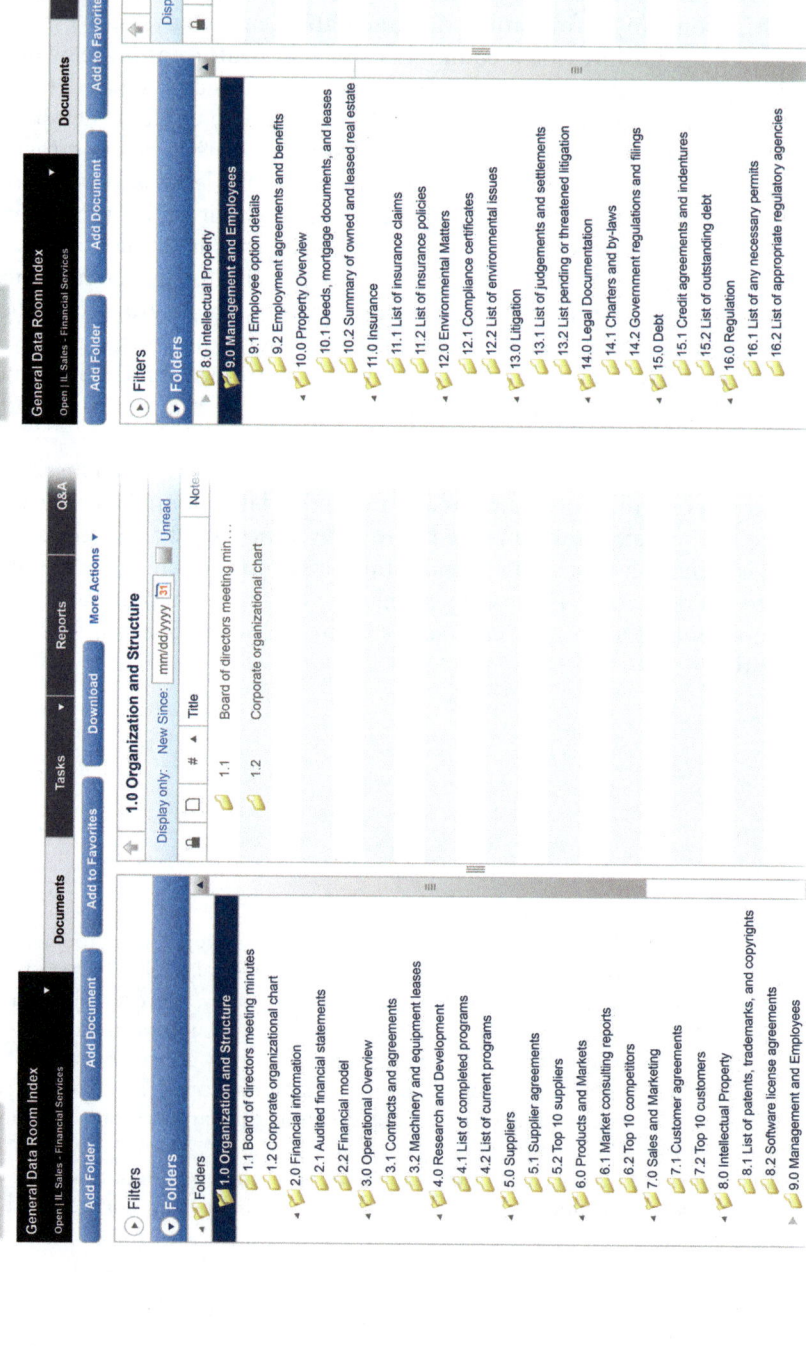

Prepare Stapled Financing Package

The investment bank running the auction process (or sometimes a "partner" bank) may prepare a "pre-packaged" financing structure in support of the target being sold. The staple is targeted toward financial sponsor buyers and is typically only provided for private companies.[17] Although prospective buyers are not required to use the staple, historically it has positioned the sell-side advisor to play a role in the deal's financing. Often, however, buyers seek their own financing sources to match or "beat" the staple. Alternatively, certain buyers may choose to use less leverage than provided by the staple.

To avoid a potential conflict of interest, the investment bank running the M&A sell-side sets up a separate financing team distinct from the sell-side advisory team to run the staple process. This financing team is tasked with providing an objective assessment of the target's leverage capacity. They conduct due diligence and financial analysis separately from (but often in parallel with) the M&A team and craft a viable financing structure that is presented to the bank's internal credit committee for approval. This financing package is then presented to the seller for sign-off, after which it is offered to prospective buyers as part of the sale process.

The basic terms of the staple are typically communicated verbally to buyers in advance of the first round bid date so they can use that information to help frame their bids. Staple term sheets and/or actual financing commitments are not provided until later in the auction's second round, prior to submission of final bids. Those investment banks without debt underwriting capabilities (e.g., middle market or boutique investment banks) may pair up with a partner bank capable of providing a staple, if requested by the client.

While buyers are not obligated to use the staple, it is designed to send a strong signal of support from the sell-side bank and provide comfort that the necessary financing will be available to buyers for the acquisition. The staple may also compress the timing between the start of the auction's second round and signing of a definitive agreement by eliminating duplicate buyer financing due diligence. To some extent, the staple may serve to establish a valuation floor for the target by setting a leverage level that can be used as the basis for extrapolating a purchase price. For example, a staple offering debt financing equal to 5x LTM EBITDA with a 30% minimum equity contribution would imply a purchase price of approximately 7.25x LTM EBITDA.

Receive Initial Bids and Select Buyers to Proceed to Second Round

On the first round bid date, the sell-side advisor receives the initial indications of interest from prospective buyers. Over the next few days, the deal team conducts a thorough analysis of the bids received, assessing indicative purchase price as well as key deal terms and other stated conditions. There may also be dialogue with certain buyers at this point, typically focused on seeking clarification on key bid points.

An effective sell-side advisor is able to discern which bids are "real" (i.e., less likely to be re-traded). Furthermore, it may be apparent that certain bidders are simply trying to get a free look at the target without any serious intent to consummate a transaction. As previously discussed, the advisor's past deal experience, specific sector expertise, and knowledge of the given buyer universe is key in this respect.

---

[17] In re Del Monte Foods Company Shareholders Litigation, C.A. No. 6027-VCL (Del. Ch. Feb. 14, 2011), the court held that the advice the public target's board received from its sell-side M&A advisor was conflicted given that the bank was also offering financing to the buyer.

Once this analysis is completed, the bid information is summarized and presented to the seller along with a recommendation on which buyers to invite to the second round (see Exhibit 6.8 for sample graphical presentation of purchase price ranges from bidders). The final decision regarding which buyers should advance, however, is made by the seller in consultation with its advisors.

Valuation Perspectives – Strategic Buyers vs. Financial Sponsors As discussed in Chapters 4 and 5, financial sponsors use LBO analysis and the implied IRRs and cash returns, together with guidance from the other methodologies discussed in this book, to frame their purchase price range. The CIM financial projections and an initial assumed financing structure (e.g., a staple, if provided, or indicative terms from a financing provider) form the basis for the sponsor in formulating a first round bid. The sell-side advisor performs its own LBO analysis in parallel to assess the sponsor bids.

While strategic buyers also rely on the fundamental methodologies discussed in this book to establish a valuation range for a potential acquisition target, they typically employ additional techniques. For example, public strategics use accretion/(dilution) analysis to measure the pro forma effects of the transaction on EPS, assuming a given purchase price and financing structure. Therefore, the sell-side advisor performs similar analysis in parallel to determine the maximum price a given buyer may be willing to pay. This requires making assumptions regarding each specific acquirer's financing mix and cost, as well as synergies.

EXHIBIT 6.8 First Round Bids Summary

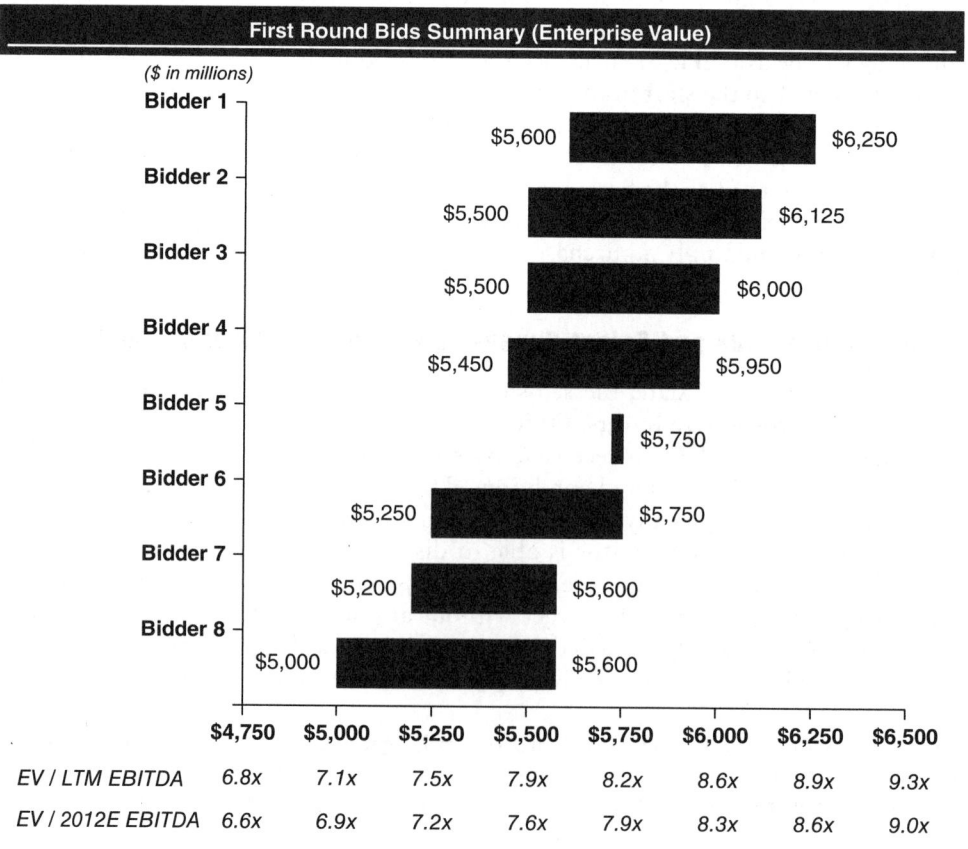

SECOND ROUND

- Conduct Management Presentations
- Facilitate Site Visits
- Provide Data Room Access
- Distribute Final Bid Procedures Letter and Draft Definitive Agreement
- Receive Final Bids

The second round of the auction centers on facilitating the prospective buyers' ability to conduct detailed due diligence and analysis so they can submit strong, final (and ideally) binding bids by the set due date. The diligence process is meant to be exhaustive, typically spanning several weeks, depending on the target's size, sector, geographies, and ownership. The length and nature of the diligence process often differs based on the buyer's profile. A strategic buyer that is a direct competitor of the target, for example, may already have in-depth knowledge of the business and therefore focus on a more limited scope of company-specific information.[18] For a financial sponsor that is unfamiliar with the target and its sector, however, due diligence may take longer. As a result, sponsors often seek professional advice from hired consultants, operational advisors, and other industry experts to assist in their due diligence.

The sell-side advisor plays a central role during the second round by coordinating management presentations and facility site visits, monitoring the data room, and maintaining regular dialogue with prospective buyers. During this period, each prospective buyer is afforded time with senior management, a cornerstone of the due diligence process. The buyers also comb through the target's data room, visit key facilities, conduct follow-up diligence sessions with key company officers, and perform detailed financial and industry analyses. Prospective buyers are given sufficient time to complete their due diligence, secure financing, craft a final bid price and structure, and submit a markup of the draft definitive agreement. At the same time, the sell-side advisor seeks to maintain a competitive atmosphere and keep the process moving by limiting the time available for due diligence, access to management, and ensuring bidders move in accordance with the established schedule.

Conduct Management Presentations

The management presentation typically marks the formal kickoff of the second round, often spanning a full business day. At the presentation, the target's management team presents each prospective buyer with a detailed overview of the company. This involves an in-depth discussion of topics ranging from basic business, industry, and financial information to competitive positioning, future strategy, growth opportunities, synergies (if appropriate), and financial projections. The core team presenting typically consists of the target's CEO, CFO, and key division heads or other operational

---

[18]Due diligence in these instances may be complicated by the need to limit the prospective buyers' access to highly sensitive information that the seller is unwilling to provide.

executives, as appropriate. The presentation is intended to be interactive with Q&A encouraged and expected. It is customary for prospective buyers to bring their investment banking advisors and financing sources, as well as industry and/or operational consultants, to the management presentation so they can conduct their due diligence in parallel and provide insight.

The management presentation is often the buyer's first meeting with management. Therefore, this forum represents a unique opportunity to gain a deeper understanding of the business and its future prospects directly from the individuals who know the company best. Furthermore, the management team itself typically represents a substantial portion of the target's value proposition and is therefore a core diligence item. The presentation is also a chance for prospective buyers to gain a sense of "fit" between themselves and management.

Facilitate Site Visits

Site visits are an essential component of buyer due diligence, providing a firsthand view of the target's operations. Often, the management presentation itself takes place at, or near, a key company facility and includes a site visit as part of the agenda. Prospective buyers may also request visits to multiple sites to better understand the target's business and assets. The typical site visit involves a guided tour of a key target facility, such as a manufacturing plant, distribution center, and/or sales office. The guided tours are generally led by the local manager of the given facility, often accompanied by a sub-set of senior management and a member of the sell-side advisory team. They tend to be highly interactive as key buyer representatives, together with their advisors and consultants, use this opportunity to ask detailed questions about the target's operations. In many cases, the seller does not reveal the true purpose of the site visit as employees outside a selected group of senior managers are often unaware a sale process is underway.

Provide Data Room Access

In conjunction with the management presentation and site visits, prospective buyers are provided access to the data room. As outlined in Exhibit 6.7, the data room contains detailed information about all aspects of the target (e.g., business, financial, accounting, tax, legal, insurance, environmental, information technology, and property). Serious bidders dedicate significant resources to ensure their due diligence is as thorough as possible. They often enlist a full team of accountants, attorneys, consultants, and other functional specialists to conduct a comprehensive investigation of company data. Through rigorous data analysis and interpretation, the buyer seeks to identify the key opportunities and risks presented by the target, thereby framing the acquisition rationale and investment thesis. This process also enables the buyer to identify those outstanding items and issues that should be satisfied prior to submitting a formal bid and/or specifically relating to the seller's proposed definitive agreement.

Some online data rooms allow users to download documents, while others only permit screenshots (that may or may not be printable). Similarly, for physical data rooms, some sellers allow photocopying of documents, while others may only permit transcription. Data room access may be tailored to individual bidders or even specific members of the bidder teams (e.g., limited to legal counsel only). For example, strategic buyers that compete directly with the target may be restricted from viewing sensitive competitive information (e.g., customer and supplier contracts), at least until the later stages when the preferred bidder is selected. The sell-side advisor monitors data room access throughout the process, including the viewing of specific items. This enables them to track buyer interest and activity, draw conclusions, and take action accordingly.

As prospective buyers pore through the data, they identify key issues, opportunities, and risks that require follow-up inquiry. The sell-side advisor plays an active role in this respect, channeling follow-up due diligence requests to the appropriate individuals at the target and facilitating an orderly and timely response.

Distribute Final Bid Procedures Letter and Draft Definitive Agreement

During the second round, the *final bid procedures letter* is distributed to the remaining prospective buyers often along with the draft definitive agreement. As part of their final bid package, prospective buyers submit a markup of the draft definitive agreement together with a cover letter detailing their proposal in response to the items outlined in the final bid procedures letter.

Final Bid Procedures Letter Similar to the initial bid procedures letter in the first round, the final bid procedures letter outlines the exact date and guidelines for submitting a final, legally binding bid package. As would be expected, however, the requirements for the final bid are more stringent, including:

- Purchase price details, including the exact dollar amount of the offer and form of purchase consideration (e.g., cash versus stock)[19]

- Markup of the draft definitive agreement provided by the seller in a form that the buyer would be willing to sign

- Evidence of committed financing and information on financing sources

- Attestation to completion of due diligence (or very limited confirmatory due diligence required)

- Attestation that the offer is binding and will remain open for a designated period of time

- Required regulatory approvals and timeline for completion

- Board of directors approvals (if appropriate)

- Estimated time to sign and close the transaction

- Buyer contact information

---

[19]Like the initial bid procedures letter, for private targets, the buyer is typically asked to bid assuming the target is both cash and debt free. If the target is a public company, the bid will be expressed on a per share basis.

Definitive Agreement The definitive agreement is a legally binding contract between a buyer and seller detailing the terms and conditions of the sale transaction. In an auction, the first draft is prepared by the seller's legal counsel in collaboration with the seller and its bankers. It is distributed to prospective buyers (and their legal counsel) during the second round—often toward the end of the diligence process. The buyer's counsel then provides specific comments on the draft document (largely informed by the buyer's second round diligence efforts) and submits it as part of the final bid package.

Ideally, the buyer is required to submit a form of revised definitive agreement that it would be willing to sign immediately if the bid is accepted. Often, the buyer's and seller's legal counsel pre-negotiate certain terms in an effort to obtain the most definitive, least conditional revised definitive agreement possible prior to submission to the seller. This aids the seller in evaluating the competing contract terms. Sometimes, however, a prospective buyer refuses to devote legal resources to a specific markup of the definitive agreement until it is informed it has won the auction, instead simply providing an "issues list" in the interim. This can be risky for the seller because it may encourage re-trading on contract terms or tougher negotiations on the agreement after a prospective buyer is identified as the leading or "winning bidder."

Definitive agreements involving public and private companies differ in terms of content, although the basic format of the document is the same, containing an overview of the transaction structure/deal mechanics, representations and warranties, pre-closing commitments (including covenants), closing conditions, termination provisions, and indemnities (if applicable),[20] as well as associated disclosure schedules and exhibits.[21] Exhibit 6.9 provides an overview of some of the key sections of a definitive agreement.

Receive Final Bids

Upon conclusion of the second round, prospective buyers submit their final bid packages to the sell-side advisor by the date indicated in the final bid procedures letter. These bids are expected to be final with minimal conditionality, or "outs," such as the need for additional due diligence or firming up of financing commitments. In practice, the sell-side advisor works with viable buyers throughout the second round to firm up their bids as much as possible before submission.

---

[20] Indemnities are generally only included for the sale of private companies or divisions/assets of public companies.
[21] Frequently, the seller's disclosure schedules, which qualify the representations and warranties made by the seller in the definitive agreement and provide other vital information to making an informed bid, are circulated along with the draft definitive agreement.

EXHIBIT 6.9 Key Sections of a Definitive Agreement

Definitive Agreement Summary	
Transaction Structure/Deal Mechanics	<ul><li>Transaction structure (e.g., merger, stock sale, asset sale)[a]</li><li>Price and terms (e.g., form of consideration, earn-outs, adjustment to price)</li><li>Treatment of the target's stock and options (if a merger)</li><li>Identification of assets and liabilities being transferred (if an asset deal)</li></ul>
Representations and Warranties	<ul><li>The buyer and seller make representations ("reps") to each other about their ability to engage in the transaction, and the seller makes reps about the target's business. In a stock-for-stock transaction, the buyer also makes reps about its own business. Examples include:<ul><li>financial statements must fairly present the current financial position</li><li>no material adverse changes (MACs)[b]</li><li>all material contracts have been disclosed</li><li>availability of funds (usually requested from a financial sponsor)</li></ul></li><li>Reps and warranties serve several purposes:<ul><li>assist the buyer in due diligence</li><li>help assure the buyer it is getting what it thinks it is paying for</li><li>baseline for closing condition (see "bring-down" condition below)</li><li>baseline for indemnification</li></ul></li></ul>
Pre-Closing Commitments (Including Covenants)	<ul><li>Assurances that the target will operate in the ordinary course between signing and closing, and will not take value-reducing actions or change the business. Examples include:<ul><li>restrictions on paying special dividends</li><li>restrictions on making capital expenditures in excess of an agreed budget</li></ul></li><li>In some circumstances, one party may owe a termination fee ("breakup fee") to the other party. Examples include:<ul><li>the buyer and seller may agree on a maximum level of compromise that the buyer is required to accept from regulatory authorities before it is permitted to walk away from the deal</li></ul></li></ul>
Other Agreements	<ul><li>"No-shop" and other deal protections</li><li>Treatment of employees post-closing</li><li>Tax matters (such as the allocation of pre-closing and post-closing taxes within the same tax year)</li><li>Commitment of the buyer to obtain third-party financing, if necessary, and of the seller to cooperate in obtaining such financing</li></ul>

(Continued)

EXHIBIT 6.9 (*Continued*)

	Definitive Agreement Summary
Closing Conditions	■ A party is not required to close the transaction unless the conditions to such party's obligations are satisfied.(c) Key conditions include: – accuracy of the other party's reps and warranties as of the closing date (known as the "bring-down" condition)(d) – compliance by the other party with all of its affirmative covenants – receipt of antitrust clearance and other regulatory approvals – receipt of shareholder approval, if required – absence of injunction
Termination Provisions	■ Circumstances under which one party may terminate the agreement rather than complete the deal. Examples include: – failure to obtain regulatory or shareholder approvals – permanent injunction (i.e., a court order blocking the deal) – seller exercises fiduciary termination (i.e., the right to take a better offer) – deal has not closed by specified outside date ("drop dead date") ■ Mutual commitment for the buyer and seller to use their "best efforts" to consummate the transaction, including obtaining regulatory approvals – if the seller terminates the deal to take a better offer, the seller pays a breakup fee to the buyer – if the seller terminates because the buyer can not come up with financing, the buyer may owe a breakup fee to the seller
Indemnification	■ Typically, in private deals only (public shareholders do not provide indemnities in public deals), the parties will indemnify each other for breaches of the representations and warranties. As a practical matter, it is usually the buyer that is seeking indemnity from the seller.(e) For example: – The seller represents that it has no environmental liability. However, post-closing, a $100 million environmental problem is discovered. If the buyer had an indemnification against environmental liabilities, the seller would be required to pay the buyer $100 million (less any negotiated "deductible"). ■ Indemnification rights are often limited in several respects: – time during which a claim can be made – cap on maximum indemnity – losses that the buyer must absorb before making a claim (a deductible)

(*Continued*)

EXHIBIT 6.9   (*Continued*)

(a) An acquisition of a company can be effected in several different ways, depending on the particular tax, legal, and other preferences. In a basic merger transaction, the acquirer and target merge into one surviving entity. More often, a subsidiary of the acquirer is formed, and that subsidiary merges with the target (with the resulting merged entity becoming a wholly-owned subsidiary of the acquirer). In a basic stock sale transaction, the acquirer (or a subsidiary thereof) acquires 100% of the capital stock (or other equity interests) of the target. In a basic asset sale transaction, the acquirer (or a subsidiary thereof) purchases all, or substantially all, of the assets of the target and, depending on the situation, may assume all, or some of, the liabilities of the target associated with the acquired assets. In an asset sale, the target survives the transaction and may choose to either continue operations or dissolve after distributing the proceeds from the sale to its equity holders.

(b) Also called material adverse effect (MAE). This is a highly negotiated provision in the definitive agreement, which may permit a buyer to avoid closing the transaction in the event that a substantial adverse situation is discovered after signing or a detrimental post-signing event occurs that affects the target. As a practical matter, it has proven difficult for buyers in recent years to establish that a MAC has occurred such that the buyer is entitled to terminate the deal.

(c) Receipt of financing is usually not a condition to closing, although this may be subject to change in accordance with market conditions.

(d) The representations usually need to be true only to some forgiving standard, such as "true in all material respects" or, more commonly: "true in all respects except for such inaccuracies that, taken together, do not amount to a material adverse effect." Material adverse effect, one of the most negotiated provisions in the entire agreement, has been interpreted by the courts to mean, in most circumstances, a very significant problem that is likely to be lasting rather than short-term.

(e) As the buyer only makes very limited reps and warranties in the definitive agreement, it is rare that any indemnification payments are ever paid by a buyer to a seller.

NEGOTIATIONS

- Evaluate Final Bids
- Negotiate with Preferred Buyer(s)
- Select Winning Bidder
- Render Fairness Opinion (if required)
- Receive Board Approval and Execute Definitive Agreement

Evaluate Final Bids

The sell-side advisor works together with the seller and its legal counsel to conduct a thorough analysis of the price, structure, and conditionality of the final bids. Purchase price is assessed within the context of the first round bids and the target's recent financial performance, as well as the valuation work performed by the sell-side advisors. The deemed binding nature of each final bid, or lack thereof, is also carefully weighed in assessing its strength. For example, a bid with a superior headline offer price, but significant conditionality, may be deemed weaker than a firmer bid at a lower price. Once this analysis is completed, the seller selects a preferred party or parties with whom to negotiate a definitive agreement.

Negotiate with Preferred Buyer(s)

Often, the sell-side advisor recommends that the seller negotiates with two (or more) parties, especially if the bid packages are relatively close and/or there are issues with the higher bidder's markup of the definitive agreement. Skillful negotiation on the part of the sell-side advisor at this stage can meaningfully improve the final bid terms. While tactics vary broadly, the advisor seeks to maintain a level playing field so as not to advantage one bidder over another and maximize the competitiveness of the final stage of the process. During these final negotiations, the advisor works intensely with the bidders to clear away any remaining confirmatory diligence items (if any) while firming up key terms in the definitive agreement (including price), with the goal of driving one bidder to differentiate itself.

Select Winning Bidder

The sell-side advisor and legal counsel negotiate a final definitive agreement with the winning bidder, which is then presented to the target's board of directors for approval. Not all auctions result in a successful sale. The seller normally reserves the right to reject any and all bids as inadequate at every stage of the process. Similarly, each prospective buyer has the right to withdraw from the process at any time prior to the execution of a binding definitive agreement. An auction that fails to produce a sale is commonly referred to as a "busted" or "failed" process.

Render Fairness Opinion

In response to a proposed offer for a public company, the target's board of directors typically requires a fairness opinion to be rendered as one item for their consideration before making a recommendation on whether to accept the offer and approve the execution of a definitive agreement. For public companies selling divisions or subsidiaries, a fairness opinion may be requested by the board of directors depending on the size and scope of the business being sold. The board of directors of a private company may also require a fairness opinion to be rendered in certain circumstances, especially if the stock of the company is broadly held (i.e., there are a large number of shareholders).

As the name connotes, a fairness opinion is a letter opining on the "fairness" (from a financial point of view) of the consideration offered in a transaction. The opinion letter is supported by detailed analysis and documentation providing an overview of the sale process run (including number of parties contacted and range of bids received), as well as an objective valuation of the target. The valuation analysis typically includes comparable companies, precedent transactions, DCF analysis, and LBO analysis (if applicable), as well as other relevant industry and share price performance benchmarking analyses, including premiums paid (if the target is publicly traded). The supporting analysis also contains a summary of the target's financial performance, including both historical and projected financials, along with key drivers and assumptions on which the valuation is based. Relevant industry information and trends supporting the target's financial assumptions and projections may also be included.

Prior to the delivery of the fairness opinion to the board of directors, the sell-side advisory team must receive approval from its internal fairness opinion committee.[22] In a public deal, the fairness opinion and supporting analysis is publicly disclosed and described in detail in the relevant SEC filings (see Chapter 2). Once rendered, the fairness opinion is one consideration for the target's board of directors as they exercise their broader business judgment seeking to fulfill their fiduciary duties with respect to the proposed transaction.

Receive Board Approval and Execute Definitive Agreement

Once the seller's board of directors votes to approve the deal, the definitive agreement is executed by the buyer and seller. A formal transaction announcement agreed to by both parties is made with key deal terms disclosed depending on the situation (see Chapter 2). The two parties then proceed to satisfy all of the closing conditions to the deal, including regulatory and shareholder approvals.

---

[22] Historically, the investment bank serving as sell-side advisor to the target has typically rendered the fairness opinion. This role was supported by the fact that the sell-side advisor was best positioned to opine on the offer on the basis of its extensive due diligence and intimate knowledge of the target, the process conducted, and detailed financial analyses already performed. In recent years, however, the ability of the sell-side advisor to objectively evaluate the target has come under increased scrutiny. This line of thinking presumes that the sell-side advisor has an inherent bias toward consummating a transaction when a significant portion of the advisor's fee is based on the closing of the deal and/or if a stapled financing is provided by the advisor's firm to the winning bidder. As a result, some sellers hire a separate investment bank/boutique to render the fairness opinion from an "independent" perspective that is not contingent on the closing of the transaction.

CLOSING

- Obtain Necessary Approvals
- Financing and Closing

Obtain Necessary Approvals

Regulatory Approval The primary regulatory approval requirement for the majority of U.S. M&A transactions is made in accordance with the Hart-Scott-Rodino Antitrust Improvements Act of 1976 (the "HSR Act").[23] Depending on the size of the transaction, the HSR Act requires both parties to an M&A transaction to file respective notifications and report forms with the Federal Trade Commission (FTC) and Antitrust Division of the Department of Justice (DOJ). Companies with significant foreign operations may require approval from comparable foreign regulatory authorities such as the Competition Bureau (Canada) and European Commission (European Union).

The HSR filing is typically made directly following the execution of a definitive agreement. If there are minimal or no antitrust concerns, the parties can consummate the transaction after a 30-day (15-day in the case of tender offers) waiting period has been observed (unless the regulator agrees to shorten this period). Transactions with complex antitrust issues can take considerably longer to clear or may result in a deal not closing because one or more agencies challenge the deal or require undesirable conditions to be met (e.g., the divestiture of a line of business).

Shareholder Approval

One-Step Merger In a "one-step" merger transaction for public companies, target shareholders vote on whether to approve or reject the proposed transaction at a formal shareholder meeting pursuant to relevant state law. Prior to this meeting, a proxy statement is distributed to shareholders describing the transaction, parties involved, and other important information.[24] U.S. public acquirers listed on a major exchange may also need to obtain shareholder approval if stock is being offered as a form of consideration and the new shares issued represent over 20% of the acquirer's pre-deal common shares outstanding. Shareholder approval is typically determined by a majority vote, or 50.1% of the voting stock. Some companies, however, may have corporate charters, or are incorporated in states, that require higher approval levels for certain events, including change of control transactions.

---

[23] Depending on the industry (e.g., banking, insurance, and telecommunications), other regulatory approvals may be necessary.

[24] For public companies, the SEC requires that a proxy statement includes specific information as set forth in Schedule 14A. These information requirements, as relevant in M&A transactions, generally include a summary term sheet, background of the transaction, recommendation of the board(s), fairness opinion(s), summary financial and pro forma data, and the definitive agreement, among many other items either required or deemed pertinent for shareholders to make an informed decision on the transaction.

In a one-step merger, the timing from the signing of a definitive agreement to closing may take as little as six weeks, but often takes longer (perhaps three or four months) depending on the size and complexity of the transaction. Typically, the main driver of the timing is the SEC's decision on whether to comment on the public disclosure documents. If the SEC decides to comment on the public disclosure, it can often take six weeks or more to receive comments, respond, and obtain the SEC's approval of the disclosure (sometimes, several months). Additionally, regulatory approvals, such as antitrust, banking, or insurance, can impact the timing of the closing.[25]

Following the SEC's approval, the documents are mailed to shareholders and a meeting is scheduled to approve the deal, which typically adds a month or more to the timetable. Certain transactions, such as a management buyout or a transaction in which the buyer's shares are being issued to the seller (and, therefore, registered with the SEC), increase the likelihood of an SEC review.

Two-Step Tender Process Alternatively, a public acquisition can be structured as a "two-step" tender offer[26] on either a negotiated or unsolicited basis, followed by a merger. In Step I of the two-step process, the tender offer is made directly to the target's public shareholders with the target's approval pursuant to a definitive agreement.[27] The tender offer is conditioned, among other things, on sufficient acceptances to ensure that the buyer will acquire a majority (or supermajority, as appropriate) of the target's shares within 20 business days of launching the offer. If the buyer only succeeds in acquiring a majority (or supermajority, as appropriate) of the shares in the tender offer, it would then have to complete the shareholder meeting and approval mechanics in accordance with a "one-step" merger (with approval assured because of the buyer's majority ownership). However, if the requisite threshold of tendered shares is reached as designed (typically 90%), the acquirer can subsequently consummate a back-end "short form" merger (Step II) to squeeze out the remaining public shareholders without needing to obtain shareholder approval.

In a squeeze out scenario, the entire process can be completed much quicker than in a one-step merger. If the requisite level of shares are tendered, the merger becomes effective shortly afterward (e.g., the same day or within a couple of days). In total, the transaction can be completed in as few as five weeks. However, if the buyer needs to access the public capital markets to finance the transaction, the timing advantage of a tender offer would most likely be lost as such transactions typically take approximately 75 to 90 days to arrange post-signing.

---

[25] Large transactions in highly regulated industries, such as telecommunications, can often take more than a year to close because of the lengthy regulatory review.
[26] A tender offer is an offer to purchase shares for cash. An acquirer can also effect an exchange offer, pursuant to which the target's shares are exchanged for shares of the acquirer.
[27] Although the tender offer documents are also filed with the SEC and subject to its scrutiny, as a practical matter, the SEC's comments on tender offer documents rarely interfere with, or extend, the timing of the tender offer.

Financing and Closing

In parallel with obtaining all necessary approvals and consents as defined in the definitive agreement, the buyer proceeds to source the necessary capital to fund and close the transaction. This financing process timing may range from relatively instantaneous (e.g., the buyer has necessary cash-on-hand or revolver availability) to several weeks or months for funding that requires access to the capital markets (e.g., bank, bond, and/or equity financing). In the latter scenario, the buyer begins the marketing process for the financing following the signing of the definitive agreement so as to be ready to fund expeditiously once all of the conditions to closing in the definitive agreement are satisfied. The acquirer may also use bridge financing to fund and close the transaction prior to raising permanent debt or equity capital. Once the financing is received and conditions to closing in the definitive agreement are met, the transaction is funded and closed.

Deal Toys   Upon closing of a deal, it is customary for the analyst or associate from the lead investment bank to design a "deal toy," such as those provided by The Corporate Presence, Inc., the global leader in the custom design and manufacturing of deal toys. The deal toy is meant to commemorate the transaction and is typically presented to the client management team at a closing dinner event.

NEGOTIATED SALE

While auctions have become increasingly prevalent with the proliferation of private equity activity, a substantial portion of M&A activity is conducted through negotiated transactions. In contrast to an auction, a negotiated sale centers on a direct dialogue with a single prospective buyer. In a negotiated sale, the seller understands that it may have less leverage than in an auction where the presence of multiple bidders throughout the process creates competitive tension. Therefore, the seller and buyer typically reach agreement upfront on key deal terms such as price, structure, and governance matters (e.g., board of directors / management composition).

Negotiated sales are particularly compelling in situations involving a natural strategic buyer with clear synergies and strategic fit. As discussed in Chapter 2, synergies enable the buyer to justify paying a purchase price higher than that implied by a target's standalone valuation. For example, when synergies are added to the existing cash flows in a DCF analysis, they increase the implied valuation accordingly. Similarly, for a multiples-based approach, such as precedent transactions, adding the expected annual run-rate synergies to an earnings metric in the denominator serves to decrease the implied multiple paid.

A negotiated sale is often initiated by the buyer, whether as the culmination of months or years of research, direct discussion between buyer and seller executives, or as a move to preempt an auction ("preemptive bid"). The groundwork for a negotiated sale typically begins well in advance of the actual process. The buyer often engages the seller (or vice versa, as the case may be) on an informal basis with an eye toward assessing the situation. These phone calls or meetings generally involve a member of the prospective buyer's senior management directly communicating with a member of the target's senior management. Depending on the outcome of these initial discussions, the two parties may choose to execute a CA to facilitate the exchange of additional information necessary to further evaluate the potential transaction.

In many negotiated sales, the banker plays a critical role as the idea generator and/or intermediary before a formal process begins. For example, a proactive banker might propose ideas to a client on potential targets with accompanying thoughts and analysis on strategic benefits, valuation, financing structure, pro forma financial effects, and approach tactics. Ideally, the banker has contacts on the target's board of directors or with the target's senior management and can arrange an introductory meeting between key buyer and seller principals. The banker also plays an important role in advising on tactical points at the initial stage, such as timing and script for introductory conversations.

Many of the key negotiated sale process points mirror those of an auction, but on a compressed timetable. The sell-side advisory team still needs to conduct extensive due diligence on the target, position the target's story, understand and provide perspective on management's projection model, anticipate and address buyer concerns, and prepare selected marketing materials (e.g., management presentation). The sell-side advisory team must also set up and monitor a data room and coordinate access to management, site visits, and follow-up due diligence. Furthermore, throughout the process, the sell-side advisor is responsible for regular interface with the prospective buyer, including negotiating key deal terms. As a means of keeping pressure on the buyer and discouraging a re-trade (as well as contingency planning), the sell-side advisor may preserve the threat of launching an auction in the event the two parties cannot reach an agreement.

In some cases, a negotiated sale may move faster than an auction as much of the upfront preparation, buyer contact, and marketing is bypassed. This is especially true if a strategic buyer is in the same business as the target, requiring less sector and company-specific education and thereby potentially accelerating to later stage due diligence. A negotiated sale process is typically more flexible than an auction process and can be customized as there is only a single buyer involved. However, depending on the nature of the buyer and seller, as well as the size, profile, and type of transaction, a negotiated sale can be just as intense as an auction. Furthermore, the upfront process during which key deal terms are agreed upon by both sides may be lengthy and contested, requiring multiple iterations over an extended period of time.

In a negotiated sale, ideally the seller realizes fair and potentially full value for the target while avoiding the potential risks and disadvantages of an auction. As indicated in Exhibit 6.10, these may include business disruption, confidentiality breaches, and potential issues with customers, suppliers, and key employees, as well as the potential stigma of a failed process. The buyer, for its part, avoids the time and risk of a process that showcases the target to numerous parties, potentially including competitors.

EXHIBIT 6.10 Advantages and Disadvantages of a Negotiated Sale

	Negotiated Sale
Advantages	<ul><li>Highest degree of confidentiality</li><li>Generally less disruptive to business than an auction; flexible deal timeline/deadlines</li><li>Typically fastest timing to signing</li><li>Minimizes "taint" perception if negotiations fail</li><li>May be the only basis on which a particular buyer will participate in a sale process</li></ul>
Disadvantages	<ul><li>Limits seller negotiating leverage and competitive tension</li><li>Potential to leave "money on the table" if other buyers would have been willing to pay more</li><li>Still requires significant management time to satisfy buyer due diligence needs</li><li>Depending on buyer, may require sharing of sensitive information with competitor without certainty of transaction close</li><li>Provides less market data on which the target's board of directors can rely to satisfy itself that value has been maximized</li></ul>

Bloomberg Appendix

APPENDIX 6.1 Bloomberg Private Company Screening (PSCR<GO>)

Private Company Screening

2) Tools   3) Feedback

Screening Criteria

Sector/Industry	<Search>	Revenue Any USD
Location	<Search>	Employee Count Any
Name/Description	<Partial Search>	Private Equity Backed

Selected Criteria   4) Modify All Criteria

Location United States ✕   PE Backed Yes ✕   Sector/Industry Chemicals ✕

15 out of 66 matching companies   66 companies

1) Click to view all search results

Name	Industry	Revenue (USD) ↑	Employees	State
11) Private Company A	Specialty Chemicals	5.2B	5,300	OH
12) Private Company B	Specialty Chemicals	2.6B	4,750	OH
13) Private Company C	Specialty Chemicals	728.8M	2,500	CO
14) Private Company D	Specialty Chemicals	*444.2M	4,965	WA
15) Private Company E	Specialty Chemicals	183.7M	1,148	SC
16) Private Company F	Specialty Chemicals	*144.2M	2,038	PA
17) Private Company G	Specialty Chemicals	132.0M	2,000	OH
18) Private Company H	Agricultural Chemicals	*109.6M	1,018	NJ
19) Private Company I	Specialty Chemicals	54.8M	564	IL
20) Private Company J	Basic & Diversified Ch...	*53.6M	460	PA
21) Private Company K	Basic & Diversified Ch...	*48.1M	250	FL
22) Private Company L	Specialty Chemicals	*46.0M	198	TX
23) Private Company M	Specialty Chemicals	39.0M	350	MA
24) Private Company N	Specialty Chemicals	35.4M	550	PA
25) Private Company O	Specialty Chemicals	*33.8M	500	AZ

* Estimated Revenue

APPENDIX 6.2 Bloomberg Private Equity Fund Search (PEFS<GO>)

1) Tools	2) Export to Excel	3) Feedback			Private Equity Fund Search
Screening Criteria					4) Hide Criteria
Name	<Add>		Industry Focus	<Add>	Size (USD) <Add>
Strategy	<Add>		Region Focus	<Add>	Net IRR <Add>
Status	<Add>		Vintage Year	1980 - 2012	Holdings <Add>
Screening Results					5) Delete Criteria
Region Focus	North America	X Vintage	1980-2012	X Name	Lee Equity* X
Apollo*	X Carlyle*	X Fund Strategy	Buyout	X	
					15 Funds

	Fund	General Partner	Vintage↑	Size (USD)	Status	Net IRR
11)	Carlyle US Equity Opportunity Fund LP	Carlyle Group LP/The	2011	1.1B	Investing	--
12)	Apollo Investment Fund VII LP	Apollo Global Management LLC	2008	14.7B	Investing	22.6
13)	Lee Equity Partners Fund LP	Lee Equity Partners LLC	2008	2.5B	Investing	.8
14)	Carlyle Partners V LP	Carlyle Group LP/The	2007	13.7B	Investing	9.9
15)	Carlyle Partners IV LP	Carlyle Group LP/The	2005	7.9B	Harvesting	11.4
16)	Apollo Investment Fund VI LP	Apollo Global Management LLC	2005	10.2B	Harvesting	9.2
17)	Carlyle Management Group Partners...	Carlyle Group LP/The	2002	590.0M	Liquidated	--
18)	Apollo Investment Fund V LP	Apollo Global Management LLC	2001	3.7B	Liquidated	38.4
19)	Carlyle Partners III LP	Carlyle Group LP/The	2000	3.9B	Liquidated	22.7
20)	Apollo Investment Fund IV LP	Apollo Global Management LLC	1998	3.6B	Liquidated	7.6
21)	Carlyle Partners II LP	Carlyle Group LP/The	1996	1.3B	Liquidated	25.4
22)	Apollo Investment Fund III LP	Apollo Global Management LLC	1995	1.5B	Liquidated	10.9
23)	Apollo Investment Fund II LP	Apollo Global Management LLC	1992	500.0M	Liquidated	--
24)	Apollo Investment Fund LP	Apollo Global Management LLC	1990	400.0M	Liquidated	--
25)	Carlyle Partners I LP	Carlyle Group LP/The	1990	100.0M	Liquidated	--

CHAPTER 7

Buy-Side M&A

Mergers and acquisitions ("M&A") is a catch-all phrase for the purchase, sale, and combination of companies, their subsidiaries and assets. M&A facilitates a company's ability to continuously grow, evolve, and re-focus in accordance with ever-changing market conditions, industry trends, and shareholder demands. In strong economic times, M&A activity tends to increase as company management confidence is high and financing is readily available. Buyers seek to allocate excess cash, out-maneuver competitors, and take advantage of favorable capital markets conditions, while sellers look to opportunistically monetize their holdings or exit non-strategic businesses. In more difficult times, M&A activity typically slows down as financing becomes more expensive and buyers focus on their core business, as well as fortifying their balance sheet. At the same time, sellers are hesitant to "cash out" when facing potentially lower valuations and the fear of "selling at the bottom."

M&A transactions, including LBOs, tend to be the highest profile part of investment banking activity, with larger, "big name" deals receiving a great deal of media attention. For the companies and key executives involved, the decision to buy, sell, or combine with another company is usually a transformational event. On both sides of the transaction, the buyer and seller seek an optimal result in terms of value, deal terms, structure, timing, certainty, and other key considerations for shareholders and stakeholders. This requires extensive analysis, planning, resources, expense, and expertise. As a result, depending on the size and complexity of the transaction, both buyers and sellers typically enlist the services of an investment bank.[1]

M&A advisory assignments are core to investment banking, traditionally representing a substantial portion of the firm's annual corporate finance revenues. In addition, most M&A transactions require financing on the part of the acquirer through the issuance of debt and/or equity, which, in turn, represents additional opportunities for investment banks. An investment banking advisory assignment for a company seeking to buy another company, or part thereof, is referred to as a "buy-side" assignment.

The high stakes involved in M&A transactions elevate the role of the banker, who is at the forefront of the negotiations and decision-making process. While senior company management and the Board of Directors play a crucial role in the

---

[1]Larger corporations may have internal M&A or business development teams that execute certain transactions without an advisor. For most public company M&A transactions, however, investment banks are hired to advise on both the buy-side and sell-side.

transaction, they typically defer to the banker as a hired expert on key deal issues, such as valuation, financing, deal structure, process, timing, and tactics. As a result, expectations are extremely high for bankers to make optimal decisions in a timely manner on behalf of their clients.

On buy-side advisory engagements, the core analytical work centers on the construction of a detailed financial model that is used to assess valuation, financing structure, and financial impact to the acquirer ("merger consequences analysis").[2] The banker also advises on key process tactics and strategy, and plays the lead role in interfacing with the seller and its advisor(s). This role is particularly important in a competitive bidding process, where the buy-side adviser is trusted with outmaneuvering other bidders while not exceeding the client's ability to pay. Consequently, bankers are typically chosen for their prior deal experience, negotiating skills, and deal-making ability, in addition to technical expertise, sector knowledge, and relationships.

For day-to-day execution, an appointed member(s) of the investment banking advisory team liaises with a point person(s) at the client company (e.g., a key executive or someone from its corporate development group). The client point person is charged with corralling internal resources as appropriate to ensure a smooth and timely process. This involves facilitating access to key company officers and information, as well as synthesizing input from various internal parties. Company input is essential for performing merger consequences analysis, including determining synergies and conducting EPS accretion/(dilution) and balance sheet effects.

This chapter seeks to provide essential buy-side analytical tools, including both qualitative aspects such as buyer motivations and strategies, as well as technical financial and valuation assessment tools.

BUYER MOTIVATION

The decision to buy another company (or assets of another company) is driven by numerous factors, including the desire to grow, improve, and/or expand an existing business platform. In many instances, growth through an acquisition represents a cheaper, faster, and less risky option than building a business from scratch. *Greenfielding* a new facility, expanding into a new geographic region, and/or moving into a new product line or distribution channel is typically more risky, costly, and time-consuming than buying an existing company with an established business model, infrastructure, and customer base. Successful acquirers are capable of fully integrating newly purchased companies quickly and efficiently with minimal disruption to the existing business.

Acquisitions typically build upon a company's core business strengths with the goal of delivering growth and enhanced profitability to provide higher returns to shareholders. They may be undertaken directly within an acquirer's existing product lines, geographies, or other core competencies (often referred to as "bolt-on acquisitions"), or represent an extension into new focus areas. For acquisitions within core competencies, acquirers seek value creation opportunities from combining the

---

[2]Merger consequences analysis calculates the pro forma effects of a given transaction on the acquirer, including impact on key financial metrics such as earnings and credit statistics.

businesses, such as cost savings and enhanced growth initiatives. At the same time, acquirers need to be mindful of abiding by anti-trust legislation that prevents them from gaining too much share in a given market, thereby creating potential monopoly effects and restraining competition.

Synergies

Synergies refer to expected cost savings, growth opportunities, and other financial benefits that occur as a result of the combination of two companies. They represent one of the primary value enhancers for M&A transactions, especially when targeting companies in core or related businesses. This notion that "two plus two can equal five" helps support premiums paid and shareholder enthusiasm for a given M&A opportunity. The size and degree of likelihood for realizing potential synergies plays an important role in framing purchase price, often representing the difference between meeting or falling short of internal investment return thresholds and shareholder expectations. Similarly, in a competitive bidding process, those acquirers who expect to realize substantial synergies can typically afford to pay more than those who lack them. As a result, strategic acquirers have traditionally been able to outbid financial sponsors in organized sale processes.

Due to their critical role in valuation and potential to make or break a deal, bankers on buy-side assignments need to understand the nature and magnitude of the expected synergies. Successful acquirers typically have strong internal M&A or business development teams who work with company operators to identify and quantify synergy opportunities, as well as craft a feasible integration plan. The buy-side deal team must ensure that these synergies are accurately reflected in the financial model and M&A analysis, as well as in communication to the public markets.

Upon announcement of a material acquisition, public acquirers typically provide the investor community with guidance on expected synergies. Depending on the situation, investors afford varying degrees of credit for these announced synergies, which can be reflected in the acquirer's post-announcement share price. Post-acquisition, appointed company officers are entrusted with garnering the proper resources internally and overseeing successful integration. The successful and timely delivery of expected synergies is extremely important for the acquirer and, in particular, the executive management team. Failure to achieve them can result in share price decline as well as weakened support for future acquisitions from shareholders, creditors, and rating agencies.

While there has been a mixed degree of success across companies and sectors in terms of the successful realization of synergies, certain patterns have emerged. For example, synergies tend to be greater, and the degree of success higher, when acquirers buy targets in the same or closely-related businesses. In these cases, the likelihood of overlap and redundancy is greater and acquirers can leverage their intimate knowledge of the business and market dynamics to achieve greater success. In addition, cost synergies, which are easily quantifiable (such as headcount reduction and facility consolidation), tend to have a higher likelihood of success than revenue synergies.[3] Consequently, cost synergies are typically rewarded by the market via stock price

---

[3]According to *McKinsey Quarterly* (Scott A. Christofferson, Robert S. McNish, and Diane Sias, "Where Mergers Go Wrong," May 2004).

appreciation. Other synergies may include tangible financial benefits such as adopting the target's net operating losses (NOLs) for tax purposes,[4] or a lower cost of capital due to the increased size, diversification, and market share of the combined entity.

Cost Synergies

On the cost side, traditional synergies include headcount reduction, consolidation of overlapping facilities, and the ability to buy key inputs at lower prices due to increased purchasing power. Following the combination of two companies, there is no need for two CEOs, two CFOs, two accounting departments, two marketing departments, or two information technology platforms. Similarly, acquirers seek opportunities to close redundant corporate, manufacturing, distribution, and sales facilities in order to trim costs without sacrificing the ability to sustain and grow sales.

Increased size enhances a company's ability to leverage its fixed cost base (e.g., administrative overhead, marketing and advertising expenses, manufacturing and sales facilities, and sales force) across existing and new products, as well as to obtain better terms from suppliers due to larger volume orders, also known as "purchasing synergies." This provides for *economies of scale*, which refers to the notion that larger companies are able to produce and sell more units at a lower cost per unit than smaller competitors. Increased size also lends towards *economies of scope*, which allows for the allocation of common resources across multiple products and geographies. Another common cost synergy is the adoption of "best practices" whereby either the acquirer's or target's systems and processes are implemented globally by the combined company.

Revenue Synergies

Revenue synergies refer to the enhanced sales growth opportunities presented by the combination of businesses. A typical revenue synergy is the acquirer's ability to sell the target's products though its own distribution channels without cannibalizing existing acquirer or target sales. For example, an acquirer might seek to leverage its strong retail presence by purchasing a company with an expanded product line but no retail distribution, thereby broadening its product offering through the existing retail channel. Alternatively, a company that sells its core products primarily through large retailers might seek to acquire a target that sells through the professional or contractor channel so as to expand its paths to market. An additional revenue synergy occurs when the acquirer leverages the target's technology, geographic presence, or know-how to enhance or expand its existing product or service offering.

Revenues synergies tend to be more speculative than cost synergies. As a result, valuation and M&A analysis typically incorporate conservative assumptions (if any) regarding revenue synergies. Such synergies, however, represent tangible upside that may be factored into the acquirer's ultimate bid price. Investors and lenders also tend to view revenue synergies more skeptically than cost synergies, affording them less credit in their pro forma earnings projections.

---

[4]An NOL is created when a company's tax-deductible expenses exceed its taxable income for a taxable year, thereby resulting in negative taxable income. NOLs can be used to offset future tax payments (carryforward) as well as historical tax payments (carryback).

ACQUISITION STRATEGIES

Companies are guided by a variety of acquisition strategies in their pursuit of growth and enhanced profitability. The two most common frameworks for viewing acquisition strategies are *horizontal* and *vertical integration*. Horizontal integration is the acquisition of a company at the same level of the value chain as the acquirer. Vertical integration occurs when a company either expands upstream in the supply chain by acquiring an existing or potential supplier, or downstream by acquiring an existing or potential customer. Alternatively, some companies make acquisitions in relatively unrelated business areas, an acquisition strategy known as *conglomeration*. In so doing, they compile a portfolio of disparate businesses under one management team, typically with the goal of providing an attractive investment vehicle for shareholders while diversifying risk.

Horizontal Integration

Horizontal integration involves the purchase of a business that expands the acquirer's geographic reach, product lines, services, or distribution channels. In this type of transaction, the acquirer seeks to realize both economies of scale and scope due to the ability to leverage a fixed cost base and know-how for greater production efficiencies as well as product and geographic diversification. InBev's purchase of Anheuser-Busch in 2008 is a high profile example of a deal featuring both economies of scale and scope.

This category of acquisitions often results in significant cost synergies from eliminating redundancies and leveraging the acquirer's existing infrastructure and overhead. In addition, the acquirer's increased size typically affords greater leverage with suppliers and customers, with the former providing greater purchasing power and the latter providing greater pricing power. A horizontal acquisition strategy typically also provides synergy opportunities from leveraging each respective company's distribution network, customer base, and technologies. There are, however, potential risks to a horizontal integration strategy, including anti-trust issues and negative revenue synergies in the event certain existing customers take their business elsewhere post-transaction.

A thoughtful horizontal integration strategy tends to produce higher synergy realization and shareholder returns than acquisitions of relatively unrelated businesses. While the acquirer's internal M&A team or operators take the lead on formulating synergy estimates, bankers are often called upon to provide input. For example, as discussed in Chapter 2, bankers research and calculate synergies for similar deals that have been consummated in a given sector, both in terms of types and size. This serves as a sanity check on the client's estimates, while providing an indication of potential market expectations.

Vertical Integration

Vertical integration seeks to provide a company with cost efficiencies and potential growth opportunities by affording control over key components of the supply chain. When companies move upstream to purchase their suppliers, it is known as *backward integration*; conversely, when they move downstream to purchase their customers, it is known as *forward integration*. Exhibit 7.1 displays the "nuts-and-bolts" of a typical supply chain. In addition, Bloomberg provides analysis of a company's supply chain via function: SPLC<GO> (see Appendix 7.1).

EXHIBIT 7.1 Supply Chain Structure

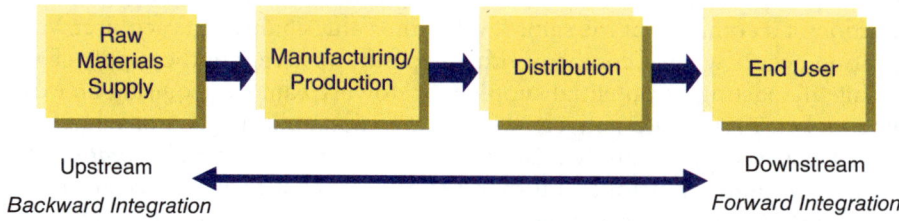

An automobile original equipment manufacturer (OEM) moving upstream to acquire an axle manufacturer or steel producer is an example of backward integration. An example of forward integration would involve an OEM moving downstream to acquire a distributor.

Vertical integration is motivated by a multitude of potential advantages, including increased control over key raw materials and other essential inputs, the ability to capture upstream or downstream profit margins, improved supply chain coordination, and moving closer to the end user to "own" the customer relationship. Owning the means of production or distribution potentially enables a company to service its customers faster and more efficiently. It also affords greater control over the finished product and its delivery, which helps ensure high quality standards and customer satisfaction.

At the same time, vertical integration can pose business and financial risks to those moving up or down the value chain. By moving supply in-house, for example, companies risk losing the benefits of choosing from a broad group of suppliers, which may limit product variety, innovation, and the ability to source as competitively as possible on price. A fully integrated structure also presents its own set of management and logistical hurdles, as well as the potential for channel conflict with customers. Furthermore, the financial return and profitability metrics for upstream and downstream businesses tend to differ, which may create pressure to separate them over time. At its core, however, perhaps the greatest challenge for successfully implementing a vertical integration strategy is that the core competencies for upstream and downstream activities tend to be fundamentally different. For example, distribution requires a distinctly different operating model and skill set than manufacturing, and vice versa. As companies broaden their scope, it becomes increasingly difficult to remain a "best-in-class" operator in multiple competencies.

Conglomeration

Conglomeration refers to a strategy that brings together companies that are generally unrelated in terms of products and services provided under one corporate umbrella. Conglomerates tend to be united in their business approach and use of best practices, as well as the ability to leverage a common management team, infrastructure, and balance sheet to benefit a broad range of businesses. A conglomeration strategy also seeks to benefit from portfolio diversification benefits while affording the flexibility to opportunistically invest in higher growth segments.

Two of the largest and most well-known conglomerates are General Electric ("GE") and Berkshire Hathaway ("Berkshire"). GE operates a variety of businesses in several sectors including aerospace, energy, financial and insurance services, healthcare, and transportation. Like GE, Berkshire is engaged in a number of diverse business activities including insurance, apparel, building products, chemicals, energy, general industrial, retail, and transportation. Investors in GE and Berkshire believe that management competency, business practices, philosophy, and investment strategies at these companies add tangible value. The "GE Way," for example, was viewed for years as a superior method for operating companies and delivering superior shareholder returns.

FORM OF FINANCING

This section focuses on common forms of financing for corporate M&A transactions (i.e., for strategic buyers), as opposed to LBOs. Form of financing refers to the sourcing of internal and/or external capital used as consideration to fund an M&A transaction. Successful M&A transactions depend on the availability of sufficient funds, which typically take the form of cash on hand, debt, and equity.

The form of financing directly drives certain parts of merger consequences analysis, such as earnings accretion/(dilution) and pro forma credit statistics, thereby affecting the amount an acquirer is willing to or can afford to pay for the target. Similarly, the sellers may have a preference for a certain type of consideration (e.g., cash over stock) that may affect their perception of value. The form of financing available to an acquirer is dependent upon several factors, including its size, balance sheet, and credit profile. External factors, such as capital markets and macroeconomic conditions, also play a key role.

The acquirer typically chooses among the available sources of funds based on a variety of factors, including cost of capital, balance sheet flexibility, rating agency considerations, and speed and certainty to close the transaction. In terms of cost, cash on hand and debt financing are often viewed as equivalent,[5] and both are cheaper than equity. On the other hand, equity provides greater flexibility by virtue of the fact that it does not have mandatory cash coupon and principal repayments nor restrictive covenants. It is also viewed more favorably by the rating agencies.

Bankers play an important role in advising companies on their financing options and optimal structure in terms of type of securities, leverage levels, cost, and flexibility. They are guided by in-depth analysis of the acquirer's pro forma projected cash flows, accretion/(dilution), and balance sheet effects (credit statistics). Ultimately, the appropriate financing mix depends on the optimal balance of all of the above considerations, as reflected in merger consequences analysis.

---

[5] A company's use of cash on hand is typically assumed to be the opportunity cost of issuing debt. Using cash and financing with external debt are equivalent on a net debt basis.

Cash on Hand

The use of cash on hand pertains to strategic buyers that employ excess cash on their balance sheet to fund acquisitions. Nominally, it is the cheapest form of acquisition financing as its cost is simply the foregone interest income earned on the cash, which is minimal in a low interest rate environment. In practice, however, companies tend to view use of cash in terms of the opportunity cost of raising external debt as cash can theoretically be used to repay existing debt. As a general rule, companies do not rely upon the maintenance of a substantial cash position (also referred to as a "war chest") to fund sizeable acquisitions.[6] Instead, they tend to access the capital markets when attractive acquisition opportunities are identified. Furthermore, a large portion of a company's cash position may be held outside of the U.S. and face substantial tax repatriation expenses, thereby limiting its availability for domestic M&A opportunities. From a credit perspective, raising new debt and using existing cash are equivalent on a net debt basis, although new debt increases total leverage ratios as well as interest expense.

Debt Financing

Debt financing refers to the issuance of new debt or use of revolver availability to partially, or fully, fund an M&A transaction. The primary sources of debt financing include new or existing revolving credit facilities, term loans, bonds, and, for investment grade companies, commercial paper.

- A *revolving credit facility* is essentially a line of credit extended by a bank or group of banks that permits the borrower to draw varying amounts up to a specified limit for a specified period of time. It may be predicated on the company's cash flows (also known as a cash flow revolver) or asset base (also known as an asset-based lending (ABL) facility).

- A *term loan* is a loan for a specific period of time that requires principal repayment ("amortization") according to a defined schedule, typically on a quarterly basis. Revolvers and term loans bear interest on a quarterly basis at a floating rate, based on an underlying benchmark (typically LIBOR), plus an applicable margin.

- A *bond* or *note* is a security that obligates the issuer to pay bondholders interest payments at regularly defined intervals (typically cash payments on a semi-annual basis at a fixed rate) and repay the entire principal at a stated maturity date.

- *Commercial paper* is a short-term (typically less than 270 days), unsecured corporate debt instrument issued by investment-grade companies for near-term use, such as inventory, accounts payable, and other short-term assets or liabilities including acquisitions. It is typically issued as a zero coupon instrument at a discount, like T-bills, meaning that the spread between the purchase price and face value (discount) is the amount of interest received by the investor.

---

[6]Certain companies may retain cash war chests as part of their corporate and financial strategy for pursuing growth opportunities, including M&A. Examples include large-cap public companies such as Apple, Microsoft, Google, and ExxonMobil.

As discussed in Chapter 3, we estimate a company's cost of debt through a variety of methods depending on the company, its capitalization, and credit profile. The all-in cost of debt must be viewed on a tax-effected basis as interest payments are tax deductible. While debt is cheaper than equity in terms of required return by investors, acquirers are constrained with regard to the amount of debt they can incur in terms of covenants, market permissiveness, and credit ratings, as well as balance sheet flexibility considerations.

Equity Financing

Equity financing refers to a company's use of its stock as acquisition currency. An acquirer can either offer its own stock directly to target shareholders as purchase consideration or offer cash proceeds from an equity offering. Offering equity to the shareholders as consideration eliminates the contingency that could arise as a result of attempting to issue shares in the open market. While equity is more expensive to the issuer than debt financing,[7] it is a mainstay of M&A financing particularly for large-scale public transactions. For a merger of equals (MOE) M&A transaction, the consideration is typically all-stock and the premium received by the sellers is small relative to a takeover premium.

Equity financing provides issuers with greater flexibility as there are no mandatory cash interest payments (dividends are discretionary),[8] no principal repayment, and no covenants. In the event that a public company issues 20% or greater of its outstanding shares in a transaction, it will need to obtain shareholder approval as required by stock exchange rules, which adds time and uncertainty to the financing process. This can prove to be an impediment for the acquirer in terms of providing speed and certainty in funding and closing the transaction to the seller.

As would be expected, acquirers are more inclined to use equity when their share price is high, both on an absolute basis and relative to that of the target. From a target company perspective, shareholders may find stock compensation attractive provided that the acquirer's shares are perceived to have upside potential (including synergies from the contemplated deal). Furthermore, tax-sensitive shareholders may prefer equity provided they can defer the capital gain. More commonly, however, target shareholders view equity as a less desirable form of compensation than cash. Acquirer share price volatility during the period from announcement of the deal until consummation adds uncertainty about the exact economics to be received by target shareholders. Similarly, the target's Board of Directors and shareholders must gain comfort with the value embedded in the acquirer's stock and the pro forma entity going forward, which requires due diligence.

---

[7]Although debt has a higher cash cost than equity, it is considered cheaper because equity investors require a higher rate of return than debt equity investors to compensate for the higher risk (see Chapter 4).

[8]Companies are not required to pay dividends, and many do not. Dividends on common stock are typically paid in cash (as opposed to stock) and have substantially lower yields than traditional debt. Dividend payments, unlike interest payments, are not tax deductible to the issuer.

Debt vs. Equity Financing Summary—Acquirer Perspective

Exhibit 7.2 provides a high-level summary of the relative benefits to the issuer of using either debt or equity financing.

EXHIBIT 7.2 Debt vs. Equity Financing Summary—Acquirer Perspective

	Greater Benefits to the Issuer	
	Debt	**Equity**
EPS Accretion	✓	
Cost of Capital	✓	
Tax Deductible	✓	
Return on Equity	✓	
Balance Sheet Flexibility		✓
No Mandatory Cash Payments		✓
Credit Rating Considerations		✓
Lack of Covenants		✓

DEAL STRUCTURE

As with form of financing, detailed valuation and merger consequences analysis requires the banker to make initial assumptions regarding deal structure. Deal structure pertains to how the transaction is legally structured, such as a Stock Sale (including a 338(h)(10) Election) or an Asset Sale. Like form of financing, deal structure directly affects buyer and seller perspectives on value. For the buyer, it is a key component in valuation and merger consequences analysis, and therefore affects willingness and ability to pay. For the seller, it can have a direct impact on after-tax proceeds.

Stock Sale

A stock sale is the most common form of M&A deal structure, particularly for a C Corporation (also known as a "C Corp"). A C Corp is a corporation that is taxed separately from its shareholders (i.e., at the corporate level only as opposed to the shareholder level). S Corps, LLCs or other partnerships, by contrast, are conduit entities in which corporate earnings are passed on directly to shareholders and therefore not taxed at the corporate level.[9] C Corps comprise the vast majority of public companies and hence receive most of the focus in this chapter.

A stock sale involves the acquirer purchasing the target's stock from the company's shareholders for some form of consideration. From a tax perspective, in the event that target shareholders receive significant equity consideration in the acquirer, their capital gain is generally deferred. On the other hand, in the event they receive cash, a capital gain is triggered. The extent to which a capital gains tax is triggered is

---

[9] There are restrictions on the number of shareholders in an S Corp as well as who can own shares in an S Corp.

dependent upon whether the shareholder is taxable (e.g., an individual) or non-taxable (e.g., a pension fund).

In a stock sale, the target ceases to remain in existence post-transaction, becoming a wholly-owned subsidiary of the acquirer. This means that the acquirer assumes all of the target's past, present, and future known and unknown liabilities, in addition to the assets. In this sense, a stock sale is the cleanest form of transaction from the seller's perspective, eliminating all tail liabilities.

As part of the deal negotiations, however, the acquirer may receive representations ("reps") and warranties, indemnifications associated with these reps and warranties, or other concessions to alleviate the risk of certain liabilities. In a public company transaction, the reps and warranties do not survive closing. In a private company transaction with a limited number of shareholders, however, the reps and warranties typically survive closing with former shareholders providing indemnification to the acquirer (see Chapter 6). This affords the acquirer legal recourse against former shareholders in the event the reps and warranties prove untrue.

Goodwill In modeling a stock sale transaction for financial accounting (GAAP) purposes, in the event the purchase price exceeds the net identifiable assets[10] of the target, the excess is first allocated to the target's tangible and identifiable intangible assets, which are "written-up" to their fair market value. As their respective names connote, tangible assets refer to "hard" assets such as PP&E and inventory, while intangibles refer to items such as customer lists, non-compete contracts, copyrights, and patents.

These tangible and intangible asset write-ups are reflected in the acquirer's pro forma GAAP balance sheet. They are then depreciated and amortized, respectively, over their useful lives, thereby reducing after-tax GAAP earnings. For modeling purposes, simplifying assumptions are typically made regarding the amount of the write-ups to the target's tangible and intangible assets before the receipt of more detailed information.

In a stock sale, the transaction-related depreciation and amortization is not deductible for tax purposes. Neither buyer nor seller pays taxes on the "gain" on the GAAP asset write-up. Therefore, from an IRS tax revenue generation standpoint, the buyer should not be allowed to reap future tax deduction benefits from this accounting convention. From an accounting perspective, this difference between book and tax is resolved through the creation of a *deferred tax liability (DTL)* on the balance sheet (where it often appears as deferred income taxes). The DTL is calculated as the amount of the write-up multiplied by the company's tax rate (see Exhibit 7.3).

---

[10]Refer to shareholders' equity less existing goodwill.

EXHIBIT 7.3 Calculation of Deferred Tax Liability

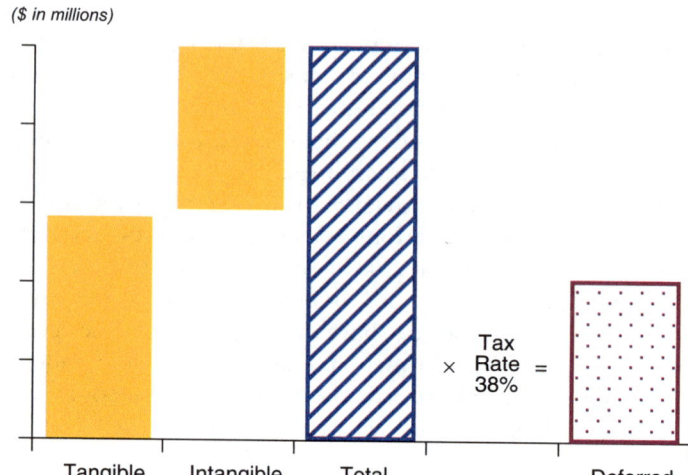

Goodwill is calculated as the purchase price minus the target's net identifiable assets minus allocations to the target's tangible and intangible assets, plus the DTL. Exhibit 7.4 displays a graphical representation of the calculation of goodwill, including the asset write-up and DTL adjustments.

EXHIBIT 7.4 Calculation of Goodwill

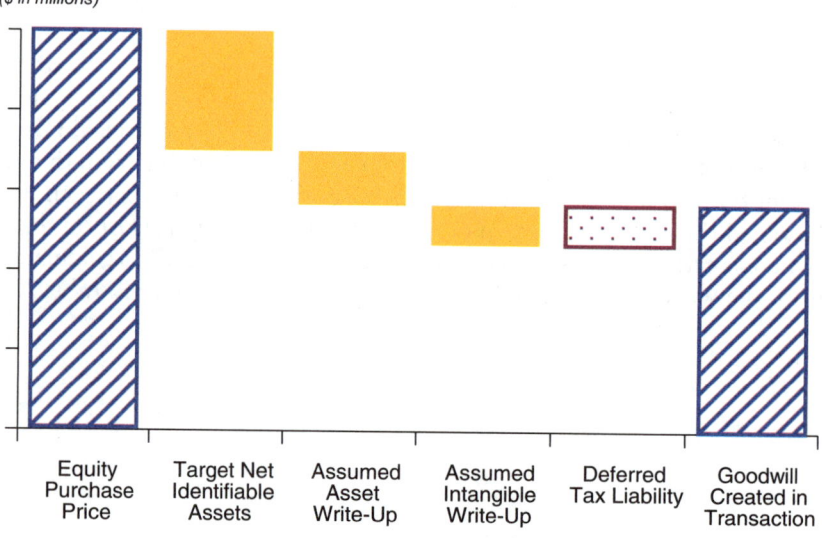

Once calculated, goodwill is added to the assets side of the acquirer's balance sheet and tested annually for impairment, with certain exceptions. While goodwill is no longer amortized in the U.S., impairment could result in a "write-down" to book value, which would result in a one-time charge to the acquirer's earnings.

Deferred Tax Liability (DTL) The DTL is created due to the fact that the target's written-up assets are depreciated on a GAAP book basis but not for tax purposes. Therefore, while the depreciation expense is netted out from pre-tax income on the GAAP income statement, the company does not receive cash benefits from the tax shield. In other words, the perceived tax shield on the book depreciation exists for accounting purposes only. In reality, the company must pay cash taxes on the pre-tax income amount before the deduction of transaction-related depreciation and amortization expense.

The DTL line item on the balance sheet remedies this accounting difference between book basis and tax basis. It serves as a reserve account that is reduced annually by the amount of the taxes associated with the new transaction-related depreciation and amortization (i.e., the annual depreciation and amortization amounts multiplied by the company's tax rate). This annual tax payment is a real use of cash and runs through the company's statement of cash flows.

Asset Sale

An asset sale refers to an M&A transaction whereby an acquirer purchases all or some of the target's assets. Under this structure, the target legally remains in existence post-transaction, which means that the buyer purchases specified assets and assumes certain liabilities. This can help alleviate the buyer's risk, especially when there may be substantial unknown contingent liabilities.[11] From the seller's perspective, however, this is often less attractive than a stock sale where liabilities are transferred as part of the deal and the seller is absolved from all liabilities, including potential contingent liabilities. For reasons explained in greater detail below, a complete asset sale for a public company is a rare event.

An asset sale may provide certain tax benefits for the buyer in the event it can "step up" the tax basis of the target's acquired assets to fair market value, as reflected in the purchase price. The stepped-up portion is depreciable and/or amortizable on a tax deductible basis over the assets' useful life for both GAAP book and tax purposes. This results in real cash benefits for the buyer during the stepped-up depreciable period.

In Exhibit 7.5, we assume a target is acquired for $2 billion and its assets are written up by $1,500 million ($2,000 million purchase price – $500 million asset basis) and, for illustrative purposes, depreciated over 15 years (the actual depreciation of the step-up is determined by the tax code depending on the asset type). This results in annual depreciation expense of $100 million, which we multiply by the acquirer's marginal tax rate of 38% to calculate an annual tax shield of $38 million. Using a 10% discount rate, we calculate a present value of $289 million for these future cash flows.

The seller's decision regarding an asset sale versus a stock sale typically depends on a variety of factors that frequently result in a preference for a stock deal, especially for C Corps. The most notable issue for the seller and its shareholders is the risk of double taxation in the event the target is liquidated in order to distribute the sale proceeds to its shareholders (as is often the case).

---

[11]Potential liabilities that may be incurred by a company in the future based on the outcome of certain events (e.g., the outcome of litigation).

EXHIBIT 7.5 Present Value of Annual Tax Savings for Asset Write-Up for Buyer

= Asset Step-Up / Amortization Period = Annual Depreciation × Corporate Tax Rate
= $1,500 million / 15 years   = $100 million × 38%

($ in millions)

Assumptions

Purchase Price	$2,000	
Asset Basis	500	Marginal Tax Rate — 38%
Asset Step-Up	**$1,500**	Annual Tax Savings — $38
Amortization Period	15 yrs	Discount Rate — 10%
Annual Depreciation	$100	

$= 1/(1 + WACC)^n$
$= 1/(1 + 10\%)^1$

$=$ Annual Tax Savings × Discount Factor$_n$
$=$ $38 million × 0.83

Year	1	2	3	4	5	6	7	8	9	10	11	12	13	14	15
Annual Tax Savings	$38	$38	$38	$38	$38	$38	$38	$38	$38	$38	$38	$38	$38	$38	$38
Discount Factor	0.91	0.83	0.75	0.68	0.62	0.56	0.51	0.47	0.42	0.39	0.35	0.32	0.29	0.26	0.24
Present Value	**$34.5**	**$31.4**	**$28.5**	**$26.0**	**$23.6**	**$21.5**	**$19.5**	**$17.7**	**$16.1**	**$14.7**	**$13.3**	**$12.1**	**$11.0**	**$10.0**	**$9.1**

Present Value of Annual Tax Savings $289.0

= Sum of Present Value of Annual Tax Savings
= SUM ($34.5 million : $9.1 million)

The first level of taxation occurs at the corporate level, where taxes on the gain upon sale of the assets are paid at the corporate income rate. The second level of taxation takes place upon distribution of proceeds to shareholders in the form of a capital gains tax on the gain in the appreciation of their stock.

The upfront double taxation to the seller in an asset sale tends to outweigh the tax shield benefits to the buyer, which are realized over an extended period of time. Hence, as discussed above, stock deals are the most common structure for C Corps. This phenomenon is demonstrated in Exhibit 7.6, where the seller's net proceeds are $1,775 million in a stock sale vs. $1,290.5 million in an asset sale, a difference of $484.5 million. This $484.5 million additional upfront tax burden greatly outweighs the $289 million tax benefits for the buyer in an asset sale.

EXHIBIT 7.6 Deal Structures—Stock Sale vs. Asset Sale

($ in millions)

Assumptions

Purchase Price	$2,000.0	Amortization Period	15 yrs
Stock Basis	500.0	Marginal Tax Rate	38%
Asset Basis	500.0	Capital Gains Rate	15%

Deal Structure

	Stock Sale	Asset Sale
Purchase Price	$2,000.0	$2,000.0
Gain on Sale		
Corporate Level	-	$1,500.0
Taxes (38%)	-	(570.0)
Shareholder Level	$1,500.0	$930.0
Taxes (15%)	(225.0)	(139.5)
Seller Net Proceeds	$1,775.0	$1,290.5

Stock Sale Shareholder Level:
= Purchase Price - Stock Basis
= $2 billion - $500 million

Asset Sale Corporate Level:
= Corporate Level Gain x Marginal Tax Rate
= $1.5 billion x 38%

Asset Sale Shareholder Level (basis line):
= Purchase Price - Asset Basis
= $2 billion - $500 million

Stock Sale Seller Net Proceeds:
= Purchase Price - Shareholder Level Taxes
= $2 billion - $225 million

Asset Sale Shareholder Taxes:
= Shareholder Level Gain x Capital Gains Rate
= $930 million x 15%

Asset Sale Seller Net Proceeds:
= Purchase Price - Corporate & Shareholder Level Taxes
= $2 billion - $570 million - $139.5 million

Buyer Cost

	Stock Sale	Asset Sale
Purchase Price	$2,000.0	$2,000.0
Tax Benefits	-	(289.0)
Net Purchase Price	$2,000.0	$1,711.0

= Present Value of Buyer's Annual Tax Savings from Exhibit 7.5

Buyer Tax Basis (post-transaction)

	Stock Sale	Asset Sale
Stock	$2,000.0	-
Asset	500.0	2,000.0
Asset Tax Basis Step-up	-	1,500.0

= Purchase Price - Asset Basis
= $2 billion - $500 million

In deciding upon an asset sale or stock sale from a pure after-tax proceeds perspective, the seller also considers the tax basis of its assets (also known as "inside basis") and stock (also known as "outside basis"). In the event the company has a lower inside basis than outside basis, which is commonplace, the result is a larger gain upon sale. This would further encourage the seller to eschew an asset sale in favor of a stock sale due to the larger tax burden. As a result, asset sales are most attractive for subsidiary sales when the parent company seller has significant losses or other tax attributes to shield the corporate-level tax. This eliminates double taxation for the seller while affording the buyer the tax benefits of the step-up.

An asset sale often presents problematic practical considerations in terms of the time, cost, and feasibility involved in transferring title in the individual assets. This is particularly true for companies with a diverse group of assets, including various licenses and contracts, in multiple geographies. In a stock sale, by contrast, title to all the target's assets is transferred indirectly through the transfer of stock to the new owners.

Stock Sales Treated as Asset Sales for Tax Purposes

Section 338 Election

In accordance with Section 338 of the Internal Revenue Code, an acquirer may choose to treat the purchase of the target's stock as an asset sale for tax purposes. This enables the acquirer to write up the assets to their fair market value and receive the tax benefits associated with the depreciation and amortization of the asset step-up. Consequently, a 338 transaction is often referred to as a stock sale that is treated as an asset sale. In a 338 election, however, the acquirer typically assumes the additional tax burden associated with the deemed sale of the target's assets. As a result, a 338 election is extremely rare for the sale of a C Corp.

338(h)(10) Election

A more common derivation of the 338 election is the joint 338(h)(10) election, so named because it must be explicitly consented to by both the buyer and seller. As with an asset sale, this structure is commonly used when the target is a subsidiary of a parent corporation. In a subsidiary sale, the parent typically pays taxes on the gain on sale at the corporate tax rate regardless of whether it is a stock sale, asset sale, or 338(h)(10) election.

The 338(h)(10) election provides all the buyer tax benefits of an asset sale but without the practical issues around the transfer of individual asset titles previously discussed. Therefore, properly structured, the 338(h)(10) election creates an optimal outcome for both buyer and seller. In this scenario, the buyer is willing to pay the seller a higher price in return for acquiescing to a 338(h)(10) election, which affords tax benefits to the buyer from the asset step-up that results in the creation of tax-deductible depreciation and amortization. This results in a lower after-tax cost for the acquirer and greater after-tax proceeds for the seller. The Internal Revenue Code requires that the 338(h)(10) be a joint election by both the buyer and seller, and therefore forces both parties to work together to maximize the value.

The ability to utilize a 338(h)(10) election often stems from the fact that a subsidiary's outside basis is generally greater than its inside basis. This occurs because a subsidiary's assets are depreciated over time, which is not the case with its stock basis. In the event that the subsidiary or business has been purchased recently, the stock basis may be particularly high relative to its inside basis. Therefore, the taxable capital gain amount is often lower for a stock sale than an asset sale.

In a subsidiary sale through a 338(h)(10) election, the corporate seller is not subject to double taxation as long as it does not distribute the proceeds from the sale to shareholders. Instead, the seller is taxed only once at the corporate level on the gain on sale. As shown in Exhibit 7.7, Seller Net Proceeds are $1,430 million in both the subsidiary stock sale and 338(h)(10) election scenarios. In the 338(h)(10) election scenario, however, the buyer's Net Purchase Price of $1,711 million is significantly lower due to the $289 million tax benefit.

In this scenario, the buyer has a meaningful incentive to increase its bid in order to convince the seller to agree to a 338(h)(10) election. As shown in the Buyer Breakeven column in Exhibit 7.7, the buyer is willing to pay up to $2,358 million before the tax benefits of the deal are outweighed by the additional purchase price. At the same time, the seller gains $0.62 (1 – 38% marginal tax rate) on each additional dollar the buyer is willing to pay. This provides strong incentive to consent to the 338(h)(10) election as purchase price is increased. At the breakeven purchase price of $2,358 million, the seller receives Net Proceeds of $1,652 million.

EXHIBIT 7.7 Comparison of Subsidiary Acquisition Structures

($ in millions)

Assumptions				
Purchase Price	$2,000.0	Amortization Period		15 yrs
Stock Basis	500.0	Marginal Tax Rate		38%
Asset Basis	500.0	Capital Gains Rate		15%

Split Difference = (Purchase Price for 338(h)(10) + Purchase Price for Buyer Breakeven) / 2
= ($2,000 million + $2,358 million) / 2

Deal Structure	Subsidiary Stock Sale	338(h)(10) Election	Buyer Breakeven	Split Difference
Purchase Price	$2,000.0	$2,000.0	$2,358.0	$2,179.0
Gain on Sale				
Corporate Level	$1,500.0	$1,500.0	$1,858.0	$1,679.0
Taxes (38%)	(570.0)	(570.0)	(706.0)	(638.0)
Seller Net Proceeds	$1,430.0	$1,430.0	$1,652.0	$1,541.0
Buyer Cost				
Purchase Price	$2,000.0	$2,000.0	$2,358.0	$2,179.0
Tax Benefits	-	(289.0)	(358.0)	(323.5)
Net Purchase Price	$2,000.0	$1,711.0	$2,000.0	$1,855.5
Buyer Tax Basis (post-transaction)				
Stock	$2,000.0	$2,000.0	$2,358.0	$2,179.0
Asset	500.0	2,000.0	2,358.0	2,179.0
Asset Tax Basis Step-up	-	1,500.0	1,858.0	1,679.0

In the Split Difference column, we show a scenario in which the buyer and seller share the tax benefit, which is a more typical 338(h)(10) election outcome. Here, we assume the buyer pays a purchase price of $2,179 million, which is the midpoint between a purchase price of $2,000 million and the buyer breakeven bid of $2,358 million. At the Split Difference purchase price, both buyer and seller are better off than in a stock deal at $2,000 million. The seller receives net proceeds of $1,541 million and the buyer's net purchase price is $1,855.5 million.

In those cases where the target's inside basis is significantly lower than its outside basis, the seller needs to be compensated for the higher tax burden in the form of a higher purchase price or else it will not agree to the 338(h)(10) election. At the same time, as demonstrated above, the acquirer has a ceiling purchase price above which it is economically irrational to increase its purchase price, represented by the incremental value of the tax benefits. Therefore, depending on the target's inside stock basis and the incremental value of the tax benefit, the buyer and seller may not be able to reach an agreement.

A comparison of selected key attributes for the various deal structures is shown in Exhibit 7.8.

EXHIBIT 7.8 Summary of Primary Deal Structures

Summary of Primary Deal Structures			
	Stock Sale	Asset Sale (Sub)	338(h)(10) Election (Sub)
Shareholders are Sellers	✓		
Corporate Entity is Seller		✓	✓
Double Taxation Potential[a]		✓	✓
Seller Transfers All Assets & Liabilities	✓		✓
Execution Simplicity	✓		✓
Asset Step-Up for Accounting Purposes	✓	✓	✓
Asset Step-Up for Tax Purposes		✓	✓
Common for Large Public Companies	✓		
Common for Subsidiary Sales	✓	✓	✓

[a] Double taxation for subsidiary sale only occurs in the event sale proceeds are distributed to shareholders.

BUY-SIDE VALUATION

Valuation analysis is central to framing the acquirer's view on purchase price. The primary methodologies used to value a company—namely, comparable companies, precedent transactions, DCF, and LBO analysis—form the basis for this exercise. These techniques provide different approaches to valuation, with varying degrees of overlap. The results of these analyses are typically displayed on a graphic known as a "football field" for easy comparison and analysis. For the comprehensive M&A buy-side valuation analysis performed in this chapter, we reference our prior valuation work for ValueCo in Chapters 1–5. *For this chapter, however, we assume ValueCo is a public company.*

Buy-Side M&A

A comprehensive buy-side M&A valuation analysis also typically includes analysis at various prices (AVP) and contribution analysis (typically used in stock-for-stock deals). AVP, also known as a valuation matrix, displays the implied multiples paid at a range of transaction values and offer prices (for public targets) at set intervals. Contribution analysis examines the financial "contributions" made by acquirer and target to the pro forma entity prior to any transaction adjustments.

Football Field

As previously discussed, a "football field," so named for its resemblance to a U.S. football playing field, is a commonly used visual aid for displaying the valuation ranges derived from the various methodologies. For public companies, the football field also typically includes the target's 52-week trading range, along with a premiums paid range in line with precedent transactions in the given sector (e.g., 25%–40%). The football field may also reference the valuation implied by a range of target prices from equity research reports.

Once completed, the football field is used to help fine-tune the final valuation range, typically by analyzing the overlap of the multiple valuation methodologies, as represented by the bars in the graphic below. As would be expected, certain methodologies receive greater emphasis depending on the situation. This valuation range is then tested and analyzed within the context of merger consequences analysis in order to determine the ultimate bid price. Exhibit 7.9 displays an illustrative enterprise value football field for ValueCo.

EXHIBIT 7.9 ValueCo Football Field for Enterprise Value

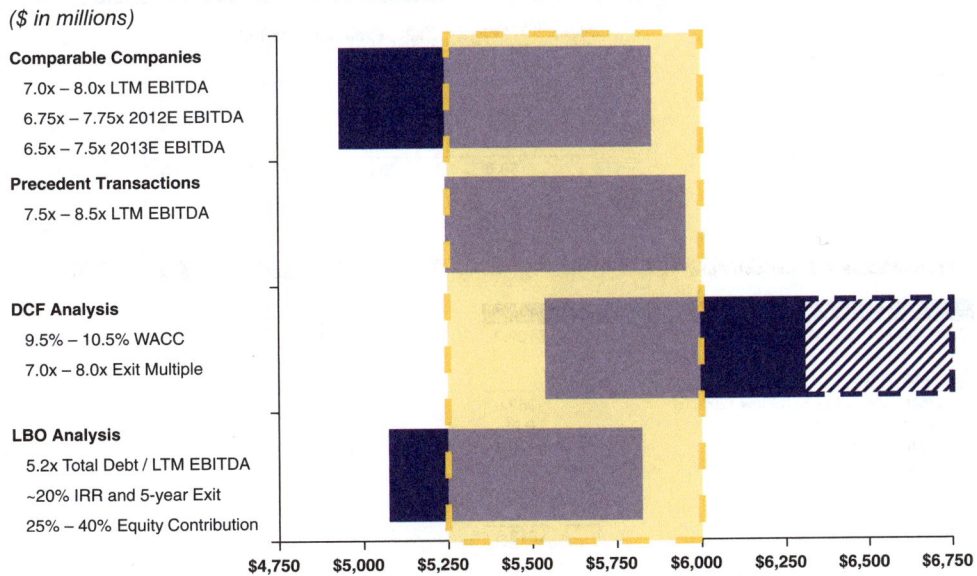

Note: Diagonal-shaded bar represents present value of potential synergies (see Exhibit 7.10).

As discussed in Chapter 3, the DCF typically provides the highest valuation, primarily due to the fact that it is based on management projections, which tend to be optimistic, especially in M&A sell-side situations. We have also layered in the present value of $100 million potential synergies (see dotted line bar above), assuming the acquirer is a strategic buyer. This additional value is calculated by discounting the projected after-tax synergies to the present using the target's WACC (see Exhibit 7.10).

Precedent transactions, which typically include a control premium and/or synergies, tend to follow the DCF in the valuation hierarchy, followed by comparable companies. This hierarchy, however, is subject to market conditions and therefore not universally true. Traditionally, LBO analysis, which serves as a proxy for what a financial sponsor might be willing to pay for the target, has been used to establish a minimum price that a strategic buyer must bid to be competitive. As discussed in Chapter 4, however, while the valuation implied by LBO analysis is constrained by achievable leverage levels and target returns, strong debt markets and other factors may drive a superior LBO analysis valuation.

Based on the football field in Exhibit 7.9, we extrapolate a valuation range for ValueCo of $5,250 million to $6,000 million, which implies an EV/LTM EBITDA multiple range of approximately 7.5x to 8.5x LTM EBITDA of $700 million. This range can be tightened and/or stressed upwards or downwards depending on which valuation methodology (or methodologies) the banker deems most indicative.

EXHIBIT 7.10 DCF Analysis—Present Value of Expected Synergies

($ in millions, except per share data)

Synergy Valuation

			Projection Period			
Mid-Year Convention	Y	2013	2014	2015	2016	2017
Cost Savings		$100.0	$100.0	$100.0	$100.0	$100.0
Cost Associated with Synergies		(100.0)	(100.0)	(50.0)	0.0	0.0
Pre-Tax Synergies		$0.0	$0.0	$50.0	$100.0	$100.0
Taxes		0.0	0.0	(19.0)	(38.0)	(38.0)
Free Cash Flow		$0.0	$0.0	$31.0	$62.0	$62.0
WACC	10.0%					
Discount Period		0.5	1.5	2.5	3.5	4.5
Discount Factor		0.95	0.87	0.79	0.72	0.65
Present Value of Free Cash Flow		-	-	$24.4	$44.4	$40.4

Present Value of Synergies

Cumulative Present Value of FCF	$109.2
Terminal Value	
Terminal Year Free Cash Flow (2017E)	$62.0
Perpetuity Growth Rate	0.0%
Terminal Value	$620.0
Discount Factor	0.65
Present Value of Terminal Value	$403.8
Total Synergy Value	**$513.0**
Fully Diluted Shares Outstanding	80.0
Implied Equity Value	**$6.41**

Buy-Side M&A

Exhibit 7.11 displays an illustrative share price football field for ValueCo. Here we layer in the target's 52-week trading range, a 35% premium to the target's 3-month trading range, and a range of target prices from equity research reports. This analysis yields an implied share price range of $52.50 to $60.00 for ValueCo.

EXHIBIT 7.11 ValueCo Football Field for Share Price

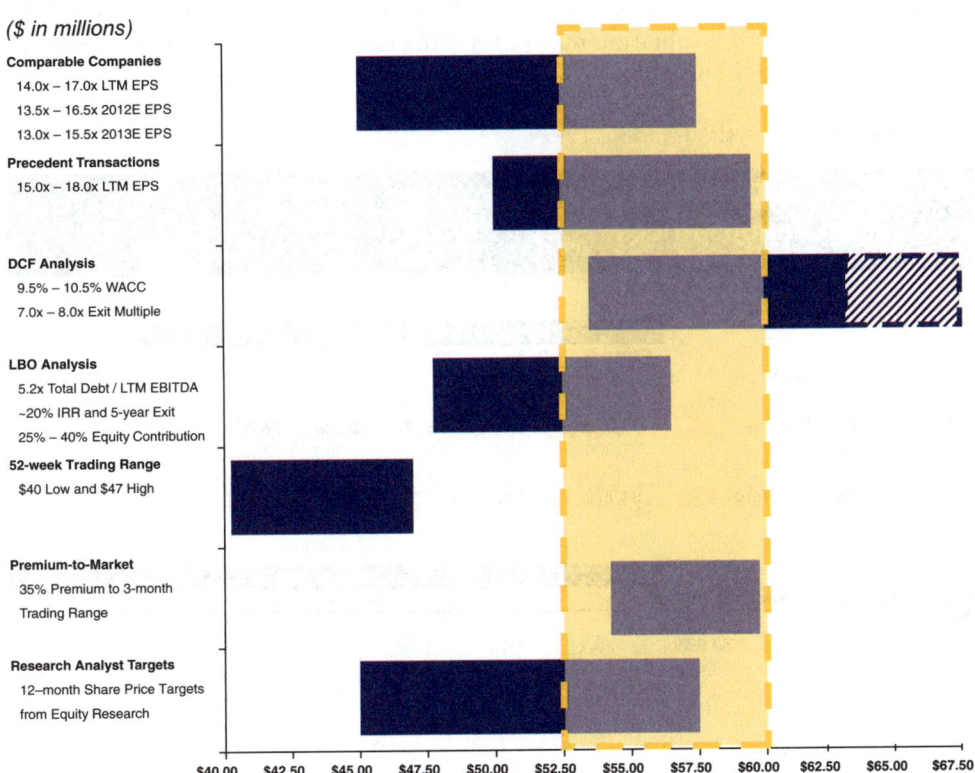

Analysis at Various Prices

Buy-side M&A valuation analysis typically employs analysis at various prices (AVP) to help analyze and frame valuation. Also known as a valuation matrix, AVP displays the implied multiples paid at a range of offer prices (for public targets) and transaction values at set intervals. The multiple ranges derived from Comparable Companies and Precedent Transactions are referenced to provide perspective on whether the contemplated purchase price is in line with the market and precedents. Exhibit 7.12 shows an example of a valuation matrix for ValueCo assuming a current share price of $43.50 and premiums from 25% to 45%.

EXHIBIT 7.12 Analysis at Various Prices

ValueCo Corporation
Analysis at Various Prices
($ in millions, except per share data)

		\multicolumn{5}{c}{Premium to Current Stock Price}				
		Current	25%	30%	35%	40%	45%
Implied Offer Price per Share		$43.50	$54.38	$56.55	$58.73	$60.90	$63.08
Fully Diluted Shares Outstanding		79.7	79.9	80.0	80.0	80.1	80.1
Implied Offer Value		**$3,468**	**$4,347**	**$4,523**	**$4,700**	**$4,877**	**$5,053**
Plus: Total Debt		1,500	1,500	1,500	1,500	1,500	1,500
Less: Cash and Cash Equivalents		(250)	(250)	(250)	(250)	(250)	(250)
Implied Transaction Value		**$4,718**	**$5,597**	**$5,773**	**$5,950**	**$6,127**	**$6,303**

		\multicolumn{6}{c}{Valuation Multiples}	
Implied Transaction Value Multiples								
Sales	Metrics							BuyerCo
LTM	$3,385	1.4x	1.7x	1.7x	1.8x	1.8x	1.9x	1.8x
2012E	3,450	1.4x	1.6x	1.7x	1.7x	1.8x	1.8x	1.7x
2013E	3,709	1.3x	1.5x	1.6x	1.6x	1.7x	1.7x	1.6x
EBITDA								
LTM	$700	6.7x	8.0x	8.2x	8.5x	8.8x	9.0x	8.0x
2012E	725	6.5x	7.7x	8.0x	8.2x	8.5x	8.7x	7.8x
2013E	779	6.1x	7.2x	7.4x	7.6x	7.9x	8.1x	7.3x
EBIT								
LTM	$500	9.4x	11.2x	11.5x	11.9x	12.3x	12.6x	9.1x
2012E	518	9.1x	10.8x	11.1x	11.5x	11.8x	12.2x	8.8x
2013E	557	8.5x	10.1x	10.4x	10.7x	11.0x	11.3x	8.2x
Implied Offer Price Multiples								
EPS	Metrics							
LTM	$3.22	13.5x	16.9x	17.6x	18.2x	18.9x	19.6x	13.9x
2012E	3.36	12.9x	16.2x	16.8x	17.5x	18.1x	18.8x	13.5x
2013E	3.71	11.7x	14.6x	15.2x	15.8x	16.4x	17.0x	12.5x

For a public company, the valuation matrix starts with a "premiums paid" header, which serves as the basis for calculating implied offer value. The premiums to the current stock price are typically shown for a range consistent with historical premiums paid (e.g., 25% to 45%) in increments of 5% or 10%, although this range can be shortened or extended depending on the situation.

The offer price at given increments is multiplied by the implied number of fully diluted shares outstanding at that price in order to calculate implied offer value. As the incremental offer price increases, so too may the amount of fully diluted shares outstanding in accordance with the treasury stock method (see Chapter 1, Exhibit 1.7). Furthermore, as discussed in Chapter 2, in an M&A scenario, the target's fully diluted shares outstanding typically reflect all *outstanding* in-the-money stock options as opposed to only *exercisable* options. This is due to the fact that most stock options contain a provision whereby they become exercisable upon a change-of-control if they are in-the-money.

Once the implied offer values are calculated, net debt is then added in order to obtain the implied transaction values. For example, at a 35% premium to the assumed current share price of $43.50 per share, the offer value for ValueCo's equity is $4,700 million. After adding net debt of $1,250 million, this equates to an enterprise value of $5,950 million. The enterprise value/EBITDA multiples at a 35% premium are 8.5x and 8.2x on an LTM and 2012E basis, respectively. At the same 35% premium, the respective LTM and 2012E offer price/EPS multiples are 18.2x and 17.5x, respectively.

Contribution Analysis

Contribution analysis depicts the financial "contributions" that each party makes to the pro forma entity in terms of sales, EBITDA, EBIT, net income, and equity value, typically expressed as a percentage. This analysis is most commonly used in stock-for-stock transactions. In Exhibit 7.13, we show the relative contributions for BuyerCo and ValueCo for a variety of key metrics.

The calculation of each company's contributed financial metrics is relatively straightforward as no transaction-related adjustments are made to the numbers. For public companies, equity value is also a simple calculation, including the premium paid by the acquirer. For private company targets, equity value needs to be calculated based on an assumed purchase price and net debt. While technically not a "valuation technique," this analysis allows the banker to assess the relative valuation of each party. In theory, if both companies' financial metrics are valued the same, the pro forma ownership would be equivalent to the contribution analysis.

EXHIBIT 7.13 Contribution Analysis

ValueCo Corporation
Contribution Analysis
($ in millions, except per share data)

	BuyerCo	ValueCo	Pro Forma Combined	Contribution (%) BuyerCo	Contribution (%) ValueCo
Enterprise Value					
Sales					
LTM	$6,560	$3,385	$9,945	66.0%	34.0%
2012E	6,756	3,450	10,206	66.2%	33.8%
2013E	7,229	3,709	10,937	66.1%	33.9%
EBITDA					
LTM	$1,443	$700	$2,143	67.3%	32.7%
2012E	1,486	725	2,211	67.2%	32.8%
2013E	1,590	779	2,370	67.1%	32.9%
Enterprise Value					
Current	$11,600	$4,718	$16,318	71.1%	28.9%
25% Premium	11,600	5,597	17,197	67.5%	32.5%
35% Premium	11,600	5,950	17,550	66.1%	33.9%
45% Premium	11,600	6,303	17,903	64.8%	35.2%
Equity Value					
Net Income					
LTM	$705	$258	$962	73.2%	26.8%
2012E	728	269	997	73.0%	27.0%
2013E	787	297	1,084	72.6%	27.4%
Equity Value					
Current	$9,800	$3,468	$13,268	73.9%	26.1%
25% Premium	9,800	4,347	14,147	69.3%	30.7%
35% Premium	9,800	4,700	14,500	67.6%	32.4%
45% Premium	9,800	5,053	14,853	66.0%	34.0%

MERGER CONSEQUENCES ANALYSIS

Merger consequences analysis enables strategic buyers to fine-tune the ultimate purchase price, financing mix, and deal structure. As the name suggests, it involves examining the pro forma impact of a given transaction on the acquirer. Merger consequences analysis measures the impact on EPS in the form of accretion/(dilution) analysis, as well as credit statistics through balance sheet effects. It requires key assumptions regarding purchase price and target company financials, as well as form of financing and deal structure. The sections below outline each of the components of merger consequences analysis in greater detail, assuming that ValueCo Corporation ("ValueCo") is acquired by a strategic buyer, BuyerCo Enterprises ("BuyerCo"), through a stock sale.

The M&A model (or "merger model") that facilitates merger consequences analysis is a derivation of the LBO model that we construct in detail in Chapter 5. For merger consequences analysis, we first construct standalone operating models (income statement, balance sheet, and cash flow statement) for both the target and acquirer. These models are then combined into one pro forma financial model that incorporates various transaction-related adjustments. The purchase price assumptions for the deal as well as the sources and uses of funds are then inputted into the model (see Exhibits 7.29 to 7.48 for the fully completed model).

The transaction summary page in Exhibit 7.14 displays the key merger consequences analysis outputs as linked from the merger model. These outputs include purchase price assumptions, sources and uses of funds, premium paid and exchange ratio, summary financial data, pro forma capitalization and credit statistics, accretion/(dilution) analysis, and implied acquisition multiples. As with the transaction summary page for LBO Analysis in Chapter 5, this format allows the deal team to quickly review and spot-check the analysis and make adjustments to purchase price, financing mix, operating assumptions, and other key inputs as necessary.

Purchase Price Assumptions

Based on the valuation analysis performed in Exhibits 7.9 through 7.12, as well as the outputs from Chapters 1–3 and 5, we assume BuyerCo is offering $58.73 for each share of ValueCo common stock. This represents a 35% premium to the company's current share price of $43.50. At a $58.73 offer price, we calculate fully diluted shares outstanding of approximately 80 million for ValueCo, which implies an equity purchase price of $4,700 million. Adding net debt of $1,250 million, we calculate an enterprise value of $5,950 million, or 8.5x LTM EBITDA of $700 million (see Exhibit 7.14).

The 8.5x LTM EBITDA purchase price multiple is 0.5x higher than the 8.0x LTM EBITDA multiple under the LBO scenario shown in Chapter 5. BuyerCo is able to pay a higher price in part due to its ability to extract $100 million in annual run-rate synergies from the combination. In fact, on a synergy-adjusted basis, BuyerCo is only paying 7.4x LTM EBITDA for ValueCo.

EXHIBIT 7.14 Merger Consequences Analysis Transaction Summary Page

BuyerCo Acquisition of ValueCo
Merger Consequences Analysis
($ in millions, fiscal year ending December 31)

Financing Structure: **Structure 1**
Operating Scenario: **Base**

Transaction Summary

Sources of Funds	Amount	% of Total Sources	Multiple of Pro Forma EBITDA 2012	Cumulative	Pricing
Revolving Credit Facility	-	-%	-x	-x	L+350 bps
Term Loan A	-	-%	-x	-x	NA
Term Loan B	2,200.0	34.6%	1.0x	1.0x	L+375 bps
Term Loan C	-	-%	-x	1.0x	NA
2nd Lien	-	-%	-x	1.0x	NA
Senior Notes	1,500.0	23.6%	0.6x	1.6x	7.500%
Senior Subordinated Notes	-	-%	-x	1.6x	NA
Issuance of Common Stock	2,350.0	37.0%	1.0x	2.6x	
Cash on Hand	300.0	4.7%	0.1x	2.7x	
Other	-	-%	-x	2.6x	
Total Sources	**$6,350.0**	**100.0%**		**2.7x**	

Uses of Funds	Amount	% of Total Uses
Purchase ValueCo Equity	$4,700.0	74.0%
Repay Existing Debt	1,500.0	23.6%
Tender / Call Premiums	20.0	0.3%
Transaction Fees	40.0	0.6%
Debt Financing Fees	90.0	1.4%
Total Uses	**$6,350.0**	**100.0%**

Premium Paid & Exchange Ratio	
ValueCo Current Share Price	$43.50
Offer Price per Share	$58.73
Premium Paid	35%
BuyerCo Current Share Price	$70.00
Exchange Ratio	0.8x

Purchase Price	
Offer Price per Share	$58.73
Fully Diluted Shares	80.0
Equity Purchase Price	**$4,700.0**
Plus: Existing Net Debt	1,250.0
Enterprise Value	**$5,950.0**

Acquisition Structure for Equity	
Stock Consideration for Equity	50%
Transaction Debt Raised	$3,700.0
% of ValueCo Enterprise Value	62%
Acquisition Type	Stock Sale
Year 1 Synergies	$100
	Options
Financing Structure	1
Operating Scenario	1
Cash Flow Sweep	1
Cash Balance	(400.0)
Average Interest	1
Financing Fees	$11,600.0

Valuation Summary

	Target	Acquirer
Company Name	ValueCo	BuyerCo
Ticker	VLCO	BUY
Current Share Price (12/20/2012)	$43.50	$70.00
Premium to Current Share Price	35%	
Offer Price per Share	$58.73	
Fully Diluted Shares	80.0	140.0
Equity Value	$4,700.0	$9,800.0
Plus: Total Debt	1,500.0	2,200.0
Plus: Preferred Equity	-	-
Plus: Noncontrolling Interest	-	-
Less: Cash and Equivalents	(250.0)	(400.0)
Enterprise Value	$5,950.0	$11,600.0

Transaction Multiples

	Metric	Multiple	Metric	Multiple	Metric	Multiple
Enterprise Value / LTM EBITDA	$700.0	8.5x			$1,443.1	8.0x
Enterprise Value / 2012E EBITDA	725.0	8.2x			1,486.3	7.8x
Enterprise Value / 2013E EBITDA	779.4	7.6x			1,590.3	7.3x
Equity Value / 2012E Net Income	$268.8	17.5x			$728.5	13.5x
Equity Value / 2013E Net Income	297.0	15.8x			786.8	12.5x

Pro Forma Combined Financial Summary

	Pro Forma 2012	1 2013	2 2014	3 2015	4 2016	5 2017
Sales	$10,205.8	$10,937.5	$11,593.7	$12,173.4	$12,660.3	$13,040.1
% growth	8.2%	7.2%	6.0%	5.0%	4.0%	3.0%
Gross Profit	$3,947.2	$4,230.4	$4,484.2	$4,708.4	$4,896.8	$5,043.7
% margin	38.7%	38.7%	38.7%	38.7%	38.7%	38.7%
EBITDA	$2,311.3	$2,469.7	$2,611.9	$2,737.5	$2,843.0	$2,925.3
% margin	22.6%	22.6%	22.5%	22.5%	22.5%	22.4%
Interest Expense	374.8	348.6	296.3	270.3	270.3	270.3
Net Income	$945.2	$1,043.3	$1,148.7	$1,231.4	$1,289.5	$1,336.0
% margin	9.3%	9.5%	9.9%	10.1%	10.2%	10.2%
Fully Diluted Shares	173.6	173.6	173.6	173.6	173.6	173.6
Diluted EPS	**$5.45**	**$6.01**	**$6.62**	**$7.09**	**$7.43**	**$7.70**
Cash Flow from Operating Activities	1,387.9	1,528.0	1,641.8	1,729.6	1,803.6	
Less: Capital Expenditures	(383.8)	(406.8)	(427.1)	(444.2)	(457.5)	
Free Cash Flow	**$1,004.2**	**$1,121.2**	**$1,214.6**	**$1,285.4**	**$1,346.0**	
Senior Secured Debt	2,200.0	1,095.8	0.0	0.0	0.0	0.0
Senior Debt	5,900.0	4,795.8	3,700.0	3,700.0	3,700.0	3,700.0
Total Debt	5,900.0	4,795.8	3,700.0	3,700.0	3,700.0	3,700.0
Cash & Equivalents	350.0	250.0	275.4	1,490.0	2,775.4	4,121.5

Credit Statistics

	BuyerCo 2012	Pro Forma 2012	1 2013	2 2014	3 2015	4 2016	5 2017
EBITDA / Interest Expense	10.3x	6.2x	7.1x	8.8x	10.1x	10.5x	10.8x
(EBITDA - Capex) / Interest Expense	8.9x	5.2x	6.0x	7.4x	8.5x	8.9x	9.1x
Senior Secured Debt / EBITDA	-x	1.0x	0.4x	-x	-x	-x	-x
Senior Debt / EBITDA	1.5x	2.6x	1.9x	1.4x	1.4x	1.3x	1.3x
Total Debt / EBITDA	1.5x	2.6x	1.8x	1.4x	1.4x	1.3x	1.3x
Net Debt / EBITDA	1.2x	2.4x	1.8x	1.3x	0.8x	0.3x	(0.1x)
Debt / Total Capitalization	47.0%	55.3%	45.2%	34.7%	31.1%	28.1%	25.5%

Accretion / (Dilution) Analysis

	Pro Forma 2012	1 2013	2 2014	3 2015	4 2016	5 2017
BuyerCo Standalone Diluted EPS	$5.20	$5.62	$6.01	$6.36	$6.66	$6.89
ValueCo Standalone Diluted EPS	$3.36	$3.71	$4.08	$4.44	$4.70	$4.86
Pro Forma Combined Diluted EPS	$5.45	$6.01	$6.62	$7.09	$7.43	$7.70
Accretion / (Dilution) - $	$0.25	$0.39	$0.61	$0.74	$0.77	$0.81
Accretion / (Dilution) - %	4.7%	7.0%	10.1%	11.6%	11.6%	11.7%
Accretive / Dilutive	Accretive	Accretive	Accretive	Accretive	Accretive	Accretive
Breakeven Pre-Tax Synergies / (Cushion)	($59)	($109)	($170)	($206)	($217)	($225)

Pro Forma Ownership

	Shares	Ownership
Existing BuyerCo Shareholders	140.0	80.7%
Former ValueCo Shareholders	33.6	19.3%
Pro Forma Fully Diluted Shares	**173.6**	**100.0%**

Annual EPS Accretion / (Dilution) Sensitivity Analysis - Premium Paid

Offer Price	Premium	2012	2013	2014	2015	2016
$54.38	25%	7.3%	9.5%	12.4%	13.6%	13.7%
$56.55	30%	6.0%	8.2%	11.2%	12.6%	12.6%
$58.73	35%	4.7%	7.0%	10.1%	11.6%	11.6%
$60.90	40%	3.5%	5.7%	8.9%	10.5%	10.6%
$63.08	45%	2.2%	4.5%	7.7%	9.4%	9.7%

2013E EPS Accretion / (Dilution) Sensitivity Analysis - Premium Paid & Consideration Mix

		% Stock Consideration Mix				
Offer Price	Premium	0%	25%	50%	75%	100%
$54.38	25%	25.0%	16.5%	9.5%	6.4%	1.3%
$56.55	30%	24.1%	15.3%	8.2%	5.0%	(0.1%)
$58.73	35%	23.2%	14.2%	7.0%	3.7%	(1.5%)
$60.90	40%	22.2%	13.1%	5.7%	2.4%	(2.9%)
$63.08	45%	21.3%	11.9%	4.5%	1.1%	(4.2%)

356

EXHIBIT 7.15   Purchase Price Assumptions

($ in millions, except per share data)

Purchase Price Assumptions	Amount	Multiple w/o Synergies	Multiple w/Synergies
ValueCo Current Share Price	$43.50		
Premium to Current Share Price	35%		
Offer Price per Share	**$58.73**	18.2x	14.7x
Fully Diluted Shares Outstanding	80.0		
Equity Purchase Price	**$4,700.0**		
Plus: Total Debt	1,500.0		
Less: Cash and Cash Equivalents	(250.0)		
Enterprise Value	**$5,950.0**	8.5x	7.4x
LTM EPS		$3.22	$4.00
LTM EBITDA		$700.0	$800.0

Sources of Funds   Assuming a 50% stock / 50% cash consideration offered to ValueCo shareholders, the sources of funds include:

- $2,350 million of stock (50% of $4,700 million equity purchase price for ValueCo), or 33.6 million shares ($2,350 million / BuyerCo share price of $70.00)
- $2,200 million of term loan B
- $1,500 million of senior notes
- $300 million of cash on hand (including $50 million of existing BuyerCo cash)

Uses of Funds   The uses of funds include:

- the purchase of ValueCo's equity for $4,700 million
- the repayment of ValueCo's existing $1,000 million term loan and $500 million senior notes
- the payment of total fees and expenses of $150 million, consisting of: i) M&A advisory and other transaction fees of $40 million, ii) debt financing fees of $90 million, and iii) tender/call premiums of $20 million[12]

The sources and uses of funds table is summarized in Exhibit 7.16 (excerpt from the transaction summary page) together with implied multiples of the pro forma combined entity through the capital structure and key debt terms.

---

[12] M&A advisory fees and other transaction fees, as well as tender/call premiums are expensed upfront and netted from proceeds to the acquirer. As discussed in Chapter 5, debt financing fees are amortized over the life of the loans and securities.

EXHIBIT 7.16   Sources and Uses of Funds

($ in millions)

	Sources of Funds				
		% of Total	Multiple of Pro Forma EBITDA		
	Amount	Sources	2012	Cumulative	Pricing
Revolving Credit Facility[a]	-	- %	- x	- x	L+350 bps
Term Loan A	-	- %	- x	- x	NA
Term Loan B[a]	2,200.0	34.6%	1.0x	1.0x	L+375 bps
Term Loan C	-	- %	- x	1.0x	NA
2nd Lien	-	- %	- x	1.0x	NA
Senior Notes	1,500.0	23.6%	0.6x	1.6x	7.500%
Senior Subordinated Notes	-	- %	- x	1.6x	NA
Issuance of Common Stock	2,350.0	37.0%	1.0x	2.6x	
Cash on Hand	300.0	4.7%	0.1x	2.7x	
Other	-	- %	- x	2.6x	
Total Sources	**$6,350.0**	**100.0%**	**2.7x**	**2.7x**	

	Uses of Funds	
	Amount	% of Total Uses
Purchase ValueCo Equity	$4,700.0	74.0%
Repay Existing Debt	1,500.0	23.6%
Tender / Call Premiums	20.0	0.3%
Debt Financing Fees	90.0	1.4%
Transaction Fees	40.0	0.6%
Total Uses	**$6,350.0**	**100.0%**

[a] Revolver size of $500 million. Revolver and term loan B coupons include 1% LIBOR floor.

Goodwill Created

Once the sources and uses of funds are inputted into the model, goodwill is calculated (see Exhibit 7.17). For the purchase of ValueCo by BuyerCo, we introduce additional complexities in calculating goodwill versus LBO Analysis in Chapter 5. Here, we assume a write-up of the target's tangible and intangible assets, as well as a deferred tax liability (DTL).

Goodwill is calculated by first subtracting ValueCo's net identifiable assets of $2,500 million ($3,500 million shareholders' equity − $1,000 million existing goodwill) from the equity purchase price of $4,700 million, which results in an allocable purchase price premium of $2,200 million. Next, we subtract the combined write-ups of ValueCo's tangible and intangible assets of $550 million from the allocable purchase price premium (based on a 15% write-up for the tangible assets and a 10% write-up for the intangible assets). Given this is a stock deal, we then add the deferred tax liability of $209 million, which is calculated as the sum of the asset write-ups multiplied by BuyerCo's marginal tax rate of 38%. The net value of these adjustments of $1,859 million is added to BuyerCo's existing goodwill.

Buy-Side M&A

EXHIBIT 7.17 Calculation of Goodwill Created

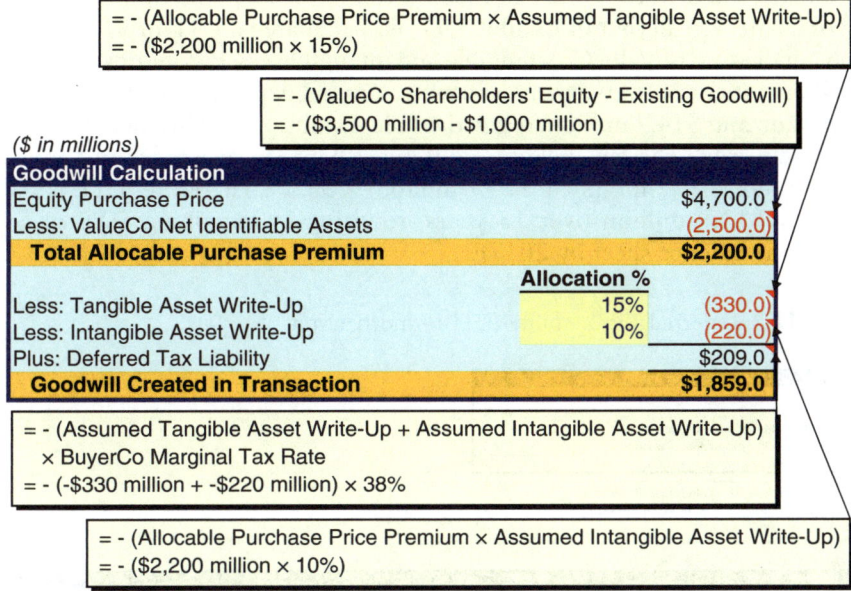

Annual Depreciation & Amortization from Write-Ups The assumed write-ups of ValueCo's tangible and intangible assets are linked to the adjustments columns in the balance sheet and increase the value of PP&E and intangible assets, respectively. As shown in Exhibit 7.18, these additions to the balance sheet are amortized over a defined period—in this case, we assume 15 years for both the tangible and intangible write-ups. This creates additional annual PP&E depreciation and intangible amortization of $22 million and $14.7 million, respectively.

EXHIBIT 7.18 Annual Depreciation and Amortization from Write-Ups

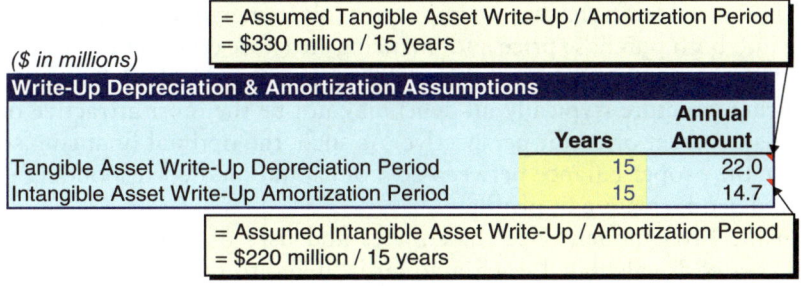

Deferred Tax Liability In Exhibit 7.19, we demonstrate how the DTL is created on the balance sheet in the Deferred Income Taxes line item and amortized over the course of its life. Recall that in Exhibit 7.17, we calculated a DTL of $209 million by multiplying the sum of ValueCo's tangible and intangible asset write-ups by BuyerCo's marginal tax rate of 38%. We then determined annual depreciation and amortization of $22 million and $14.7 million, respectively, in Exhibit 7.18. This incremental D&A is not tax deductible, thereby creating a difference between cash taxes and book taxes of $13.9 million (($22 million + $14.7 million) × 38%). Therefore, DTL is reduced annually by $13.9 million over 15 years, resulting in remaining DTL of $539.3 million on the balance sheet by 2017E.

EXHIBIT 7.19 Deferred Tax Liability (DTL) Amortization

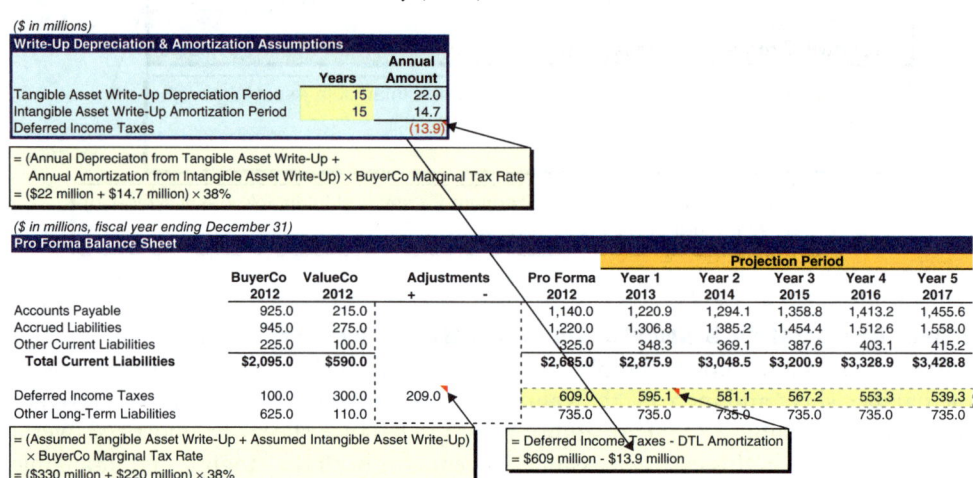

Balance Sheet Effects

Balance sheet considerations play an important role in merger consequences analysis, factoring into both purchase price and financing structure considerations. They must be carefully analyzed in conjunction with EPS accretion/(dilution). The most accretive financing structure (typically all debt) may not be the most attractive or viable from a balance sheet or credit perspective. As such, the optimal financing structure must strike the proper balance between cost of capital (and corresponding earnings impact) and pro forma credit profile.

As in the LBO model, once the sources and uses of funds are finalized and goodwill created is calculated, each amount is linked to the appropriate cell in the adjustments columns adjacent to the opening balance sheet (see Exhibit 7.20). These adjustments, combined with the sum of the acquirer and target balance sheet items, serve to bridge the opening balance sheet to the pro forma closing balance sheet. After these balance sheet transaction adjustments are made, we calculate the pro forma credit statistics and compare them to the pre-transaction standalone metrics.

Buy-Side M&A

EXHIBIT 7.20 Links to Balance Sheet

($ in millions)

Sources of Funds			Uses of Funds		
Revolving Credit Facility	-		Purchase ValueCo Equity	$4,700.0	E
Term Loan B	2,200.0	A	Repay Existing Debt	1,500.0	F
Senior Notes	1,500.0	B	Tender / Call Premiums	20.0	G
Issuance of Common Stock	2,350.0	C	Debt Financing Fees	90.0	H
Cash on Hand	300.0	D	Transaction Fees	40.0	I
Total Sources	**$6,350.0**		**Total Uses**	**$6,350.0**	

Goodwill Calculation		
Equity Purchase Price	$4,700.0	E
Less: ValueCo Net Identifiable Assets	(2,500.0)	
Total Allocable Purchase Premium	**$2,200.0**	
	Allocation %	
Less: Tangible Asset Write-Up	15%	(330.0) J
Less: Intangible Asset Write-Up	10%	(220.0) K
Plus: Deferred Tax Liability		209.0 L
Goodwill Created in Transaction		**$1,859.0**

Balance Sheet

	BuyerCo 2012	ValueCo 2012	Adjustments +	Adjustments -	Pro Forma 2012
Cash and Cash Equivalents	$400.0	$250.0		(300.0) D	$350.0
Accounts Receivable	1,000.0	450.0			1,450.0
Inventories	1,225.0	600.0			1,825.0
Prepaids and Other Current Assets	525.0	175.0			700.0
Total Current Assets	**$3,150.0**	**$1,475.0**			**$4,325.0**
Property, Plant and Equipment, net	2,500.0	2,500.0	330.0 J		5,330.0
Goodwill	575.0	1,000.0	1,859.0	(1,000.0)	2,434.0
Intangible Assets	825.0	875.0	220.0		1,920.0
Other Assets	450.0	150.0	K		600.0
Deferred Financing Fees	-	-	90.0 H		90.0
Total Assets	**$7,500.0**	**$6,000.0**			**$14,699.0**
Accounts Payable	925.0	215.0			1,140.0
Accrued Liabilities	945.0	275.0			1,220.0
Other Current Liabilities	225.0	100.0			325.0
Total Current Liabilities	**$2,095.0**	**$590.0**			**$2,685.0**
Revolving Credit Facility	-	-		F	-
ValueCo Term Loan	-	1,000.0	A	(1,000.0)	-
New Term Loan B	-	-	2,200.0		2,200.0
BuyerCo Senior Notes	2,200.0	-		F	2,200.0
ValueCo Senior Notes	-	500.0	B	(500.0)	-
New Senior Notes	-	-	1,500.0		1,500.0
Deferred Income Taxes	100.0	300.0	209.0		609.0
Other Long-Term Liabilities	625.0	110.0	L		735.0
Total Liabilities	**$5,020.0**	**$2,500.0**			**$9,929.0**
Noncontrolling Interests	-	-			-
Shareholders' Equity	2,480.0	3,500.0	2,290.0	(3,500.0)	4,770.0
Total Shareholders' Equity	**$2,480.0**	**$3,500.0**			**$4,770.0**
Total Liabilities and Equity	**$7,500.0**	**$6,000.0**			**$14,699.0**
Balance Check	0.000	0.000			0.000

= - (Issuance of Common Stock - Tender/Call Premiums - Transaction Expenses)
= - ($2,350 million - $20 million - $40 million)

C   G   I

Balance Sheet Adjustments Exhibit 7.21 provides a summary of the transaction adjustments to the opening balance sheet.

EXHIBIT 7.21 Balance Sheet Adjustments

Adjustments	
Additions	**Eliminations**
Assets	**Assets**
+ $1,859 million of Goodwill Created	− $1,000 million of Existing ValueCo Goodwill
+ $330 million from Tangible Asset Write-Up	− $300 million of Cash on Hand
+ $220 million from Intangible Asset Write-Up	
+ $90 million of Deferred Financing Fees	
Liabilities	**Liabilities**
+ $2,220 million of Term Loan B	− $1,500 million of Existing ValueCo Debt
+ $1,500 million of Senior Notes	
+ $209 million of Deferred Tax Liabilities	
Shareholders' Equity	**Shareholders' Equity**
+ $2,350 million from Issuance of BuyerCo Stock	− $3,500 million of ValueCo Shareholders' Equity
	− $40 million of Transaction Fees & Expenses
	− $20 million of Tender/Call Premiums

Strategic acquirers tend to prioritize the maintenance of target credit ratings, which directly affect their cost of capital as well as general investor perception of the company. Some companies may also require a minimum credit rating for operating purposes or covenant compliance. Consequently, companies often pre-screen potential acquisitions and proposed financing structures with the rating agencies to gain comfort that a given credit rating will be received or maintained. The ultimate financing structure often reflects this rating agency feedback, which may result in the company increasing the equity portion of the financing despite an adverse effect on pro forma earnings.

The balance sheet effects analysis centers on analyzing the acquirer's capital structure and credit statistics pro forma for the transaction. It is driven primarily by purchase price and the sources of financing.

Credit Statistics As discussed in Chapters 1 and 4, the most widely used credit statistics are grouped into leverage ratios (e.g., debt-to-EBITDA and debt-to-total-capitalization) and coverage ratios (e.g., EBITDA-to-interest expense). The rating agencies tend to establish target ratio thresholds for companies that correspond to given ratings categories. These ratings methodologies and requirements are made available to issuers who are expected to manage their balance sheets accordingly. Therefore, acquirers are often guided by the desire to maintain key target ratios in crafting their M&A financing structure.

As shown in Exhibit 7.22, assuming a 50% stock/50% cash consideration offered to ValueCo shareholders, BuyerCo's credit statistics weaken slightly given the incremental debt raise. Pro forma for the deal, BuyerCo's debt-to-EBITDA increases from 1.5x to 2.6x while debt-to-total capitalization of 47% increases to 55.3%. By the end of 2013E, however, the pro forma entity deleverages to below 2.0x and further decreases to 1.4x by the end of 2014E (in line with BuyerCo's pre-transaction leverage). Similarly, by the end of 2013E, debt-to-total capitalization reaches 45.2%, which is slightly lower than the pre-transaction level.

At the same time, EBITDA-to-interest expense decreases from 10.3x pre-deal to 7.1x by the end of 2013E while capex-adjusted coverage decreases from 8.9x to 6.0x. These coverage ratios return to roughly pre-transaction levels by 2015E-2016E. Therefore, the pro forma combined entity has a moderately weaker credit profile than that of standalone BuyerCo. Within a relatively short time period, however, BuyerCo's credit profile returns to target levels. BuyerCo's use of significant equity as a funding source, combined with the synergies from the combination with ValueCo, helps to maintain credit ratios within an acceptable range.

Given the borderline nature of these pro forma credit statistics, BuyerCo may consider the use of more equity to ensure there is no ratings downgrade. As previously discussed, however, this typically has a negative impact on income statement effects, such as EPS accretion/(dilution). In order to assess these situations, it is common to sensitize the acquirer's pro forma credit statistics for key inputs such as purchase price and financing mix. In Exhibit 7.22, we sensitize key credit statistics (i.e., debt-to-EBITDA and EBITDA-to-interest expense) for purchase price and finance mix.

EXHIBIT 7.22 Capitalization and Credit Statistics Analysis

($ in millions, fiscal year ending December 31)

Capitalization

	BuyerCo 2012	ValueCo 2012	Adjustments +	Adjustments –	Pro forma 2012	1 2013	2 2014	3 2015	4 2016	5 2017
Cash	$400.0	$250.0		(300.0)	$350.0	$250.0	$275.4	$1,490.0	$2,775.4	$4,121.5
Revolving Credit Facility	-	-			-	-	-	-	-	-
ValueCo Term Loan	-	1,000.0		(1,000.0)	-	-	-	-	-	-
New Term Loan B	-	-	2,200.0		2,200.0	1,095.8	-	-	-	-
Other Debt	-	-			-	-	-	-	-	-
Total Senior Secured Debt	-	$1,000.0			$2,200.0	$1,095.8	-	-	-	-
BuyerCo Senior Notes	2,200.0	-			2,200.0	2,200.0	2,200.0	2,200.0	2,200.0	2,200.0
ValueCo Senior Notes	-	500.0		(500.0)	-	-	-	-	-	-
New Senior Notes	-	-	1,500.0		1,500.0	1,500.0	1,500.0	1,500.0	1,500.0	1,500.0
Total Senior Debt	$2,200.0	$1,500.0			$5,900.0	$4,795.8	$3,700.0	$3,700.0	$3,700.0	$3,700.0
Senior Subordinated Notes	-	-			-	-	-	-	-	-
Total Debt	$2,200.0	$1,500.0			$5,900.0	$4,795.8	$3,700.0	$3,700.0	$3,700.0	$3,700.0
Shareholders' Equity	2,480.0	3,500.0	2,290.0	(3,500.0)	4,770.0	5,813.3	6,962.0	8,193.4	9,482.9	10,818.9
Total Capitalization	$4,680.0	$5,000.0			$10,670.0	$10,609.1	$10,662.0	$11,893.4	$13,182.9	$14,518.9
% of Bank Debt Repaid						50.2%	100.0%	100.0%	100.0%	100.0%

Credit Statistics

	BuyerCo 2012	ValueCo 2012			Pro forma 2012	1 2013	2 2014	3 2015	4 2016	5 2017
EBITDA	$1,486.3	$725.0			$2,311.3	$2,469.7	$2,611.9	$2,737.5	$2,843.0	$2,925.3
Capital Expenditures	202.7	155.3		100.0	357.9	383.8	406.8	427.1	444.2	457.5
Interest Expense	144.4	85.9		144.5	374.8	348.6	296.3	270.3	270.3	270.3
EBITDA / Interest Expense	10.3x	8.4x			6.2x	7.1x	8.8x	10.1x	10.5x	10.8x
(EBITDA - Capex) / Interest Expense	8.9x	6.6x			5.2x	6.0x	7.4x	8.5x	8.9x	9.1x
Senior Secured Debt / EBITDA	- x	1.4x			1.0x	0.4x	- x	- x	- x	- x
Senior Debt / EBITDA	1.5x	2.1x			2.6x	1.9x	1.4x	1.4x	1.3x	1.3x
Total Debt / EBITDA	1.5x	2.1x			2.6x	1.9x	1.4x	1.4x	1.3x	1.3x
Net Debt / EBITDA	1.2x	1.7x			2.4x	1.8x	1.3x	0.8x	0.3x	(0.1x)
% Debt / Total Capitalization	47.0%	30.0%			55.3%	45.2%	34.7%	31.1%	28.1%	25.5%

Debt / EBITDA

Premium Paid		% Stock Consideration Mix			
	0%	25%	50%	75%	100%
25%	3.4x	3.0x	2.5x	2.0x	1.5x
30%	3.5x	3.0x	2.5x	2.0x	1.5x
35%	3.6x	3.1x	**2.6x**	2.0x	1.5x
40%	3.7x	3.1x	2.6x	2.0x	1.5x
45%	3.7x	3.2x	2.6x	2.1x	1.5x

EBITDA / Interest Expense

Premium Paid		% Stock Consideration Mix			
	0%	25%	50%	75%	100%
25%	4.9x	5.5x	6.3x	8.7x	11.0x
30%	4.8x	5.4x	6.2x	8.6x	11.0x
35%	4.7x	5.3x	**6.2x**	8.6x	11.0x
40%	4.6x	5.2x	6.1x	8.5x	11.0x
45%	4.5x	5.2x	6.0x	8.4x	11.0x

Accretion/(Dilution) Analysis

Accretion/(dilution) analysis measures the effects of a transaction on a potential acquirer's earnings, assuming a given financing structure. It centers on comparing the acquirer's earnings per share (EPS) pro forma for the transaction versus on a stand-alone basis. If the pro forma combined EPS is lower than the acquirer's standalone EPS, the transaction is said to be *dilutive*; conversely, if the pro forma EPS is higher, the transaction is said to be *accretive*.

A rule of thumb for 100% stock transactions is that when an acquirer purchases a target with a lower P/E, the acquisition is accretive. This concept is intuitive—when a company pays a lower multiple for the target's earnings than the multiple at which its own earnings trade, the transaction is de facto accretive. Conversely, transactions where an acquirer purchases a higher P/E target are de facto dilutive. Sizable synergies, however, may serve to offset this financial convention and result in such acquisitions being accretive. Transaction-related expenses such as depreciation and amortization, on the other hand, have the opposite effect.

Acquirers target accretive transactions as they create value for their shareholders due to the fact that the market usually responds favorably. Ideally, acquirers seek immediate earnings accretion although certain transactions may not be accretive on "day one." Rather, they are longer-term strategic moves focused on creating value for shareholders over time. For this reason, as well as the fact that equity markets in general are forward-looking, accretion/(dilution) analysis focuses on EPS effects for future years. Therefore, accretion/(dilution) analysis captures the target's future expected performance, including growth prospects, synergies, and other combination effects with the acquirer.

Accretion/(dilution) analysis is usually a key screening mechanism for potential acquirers. As a general rule, acquirers do not pursue transactions that are dilutive over the foreseeable earnings projection period due to the potential destructive effects on shareholder value. There may be exceptions in certain situations, however. For example, a rapidly growing business with an accelerated earnings ramp-up in the relatively distant future years may eventually yield accretive results that do not show up in a typical two-year earnings projection time horizon.

The key drivers for accretion/(dilution) are purchase price, acquirer and target projected earnings, synergies, and form of financing, most notably the debt/equity mix and cost of debt. The calculations must also reflect transaction-related effects pertaining to deal structure, such as the write-up of tangible and intangible assets. As would be expected, maximum accretive effects are served by negotiating as low a purchase price as possible, sourcing the cheapest form of financing, choosing the optimal deal structure, and identifying significant achievable synergies.

Exhibit 7.23 is a graphical depiction of the accretion/(dilution) calculation, which in this case begins by summing the EBIT of the acquirer and target, including synergies. An alternative approach would begin by combining the acquirer's and target's EPS and then making the corresponding tax-effected adjustments.

Transaction expenses related to M&A advisory and financing fees may also be factored into accretion/(dilution) analysis. As discussed in Chapter 4, M&A advisory fees are typically expensed upfront while debt financing fees are amortized over the life of the security. In many cases, however, transaction fees are treated as non-recurring items and excluded from accretion/(dilution) analysis, which is the approach we adopt in our analysis.

The EPS accretion/(dilution) analysis calculation in Exhibit 7.23 consists of the following ten steps:

I. Enter the acquirer's standalone projected operating income (EBIT)

II. Add the target's standalone projected operating income (EBIT)

III. Add expected synergies from the transaction for the projection period

IV. Subtract transaction-related depreciation and amortization expenses (typically associated with writing up the target's tangible and intangible assets)

V. Subtract the acquirer's existing interest expense

VI. Subtract the incremental interest expense associated with the new transaction debt to calculate pro forma earnings before taxes[13]

VII. Subtract the tax expense at the acquirer's tax rate to arrive at pro forma combined net income

VIII. In the event stock is used as a portion, or all, of the purchase price, add the new shares issued as part of the transaction to the acquirer's existing fully diluted shares outstanding

IX. Divide pro forma net income by the pro forma fully diluted shares outstanding to arrive at pro forma combined EPS[14]

X. Compare pro forma EPS with the acquirer's standalone EPS to determine whether the transaction is accretive or dilutive

---

[13] The target's existing debt is either assumed to be refinanced as part of the new transaction debt or is kept in place with the corresponding interest expense unchanged.

[14] For all-debt financed transactions, there are no adjustments to shares outstanding.

EXHIBIT 7.23 Accretion/(Dilution) Calculation from EBIT to EPS

($ in millions, except per share data)

Step I	Acquirer EBIT
Step II	Target EBIT
Step III	Synergies
Step IV	Depreciation Write-Up / Amortization Write-Up
Step V	Acquirer Standalone Interest Exp.
Step VI	Additional Acquisition Interest Exp.
Step VII	Income Taxes
	Pro Forma Net Income
Step VIII	÷ (Acquirer Fully Diluted Shares Outstanding + New Shares Issued in Transaction)
Step IX	Pro Forma EPS
Step X	Standalone EPS

Legend: Acquirer, Target, Combined

367

In Exhibits 7.24 through 7.26, we conduct accretion/(dilution) analysis for BuyerCo's illustrative acquisition of ValueCo for three scenarios: I) 50% stock/50% cash, II) 100% cash, and III) 100% stock. In each of these scenarios, we utilize the purchase price assumptions in Exhibit 7.15, namely an offer price per share of $58.73, representing an equity purchase price of $4,700 million and enterprise value of $5,950 million. We also assume the deal is structured as a stock sale.

Acquisition Scenarios—I) 50% Stock / 50% Cash; II) 100% Cash; and III) 100% Stock

Scenario I: 50% Stock / 50% Cash   In scenario I, a 50% stock/50% cash consideration mix is offered by BuyerCo to ValueCo shareholders. This serves as our base case scenario as shown on the transaction summary page in Exhibit 7.15. Public companies making sizeable acquisitions often use a combination of debt and equity financing to fund a given acquisition.

In Exhibit 7.24, 2013E pro forma EBIT of $2,066.4 million is calculated by combining BuyerCo's and ValueCo's EBIT plus expected synergies of $100 million. Transaction-related depreciation and amortization expenses of $36.7 million from the write-up of ValueCo's tangible and intangible assets ($22 million + $14.7 million) are then deducted. BuyerCo's existing interest expense of $140.6 million and the incremental interest expense of $206.4 million from the acquisition debt (including refinancing ValueCo's debt) are also subtracted. The resulting earnings before taxes of $1,682.7 million is then tax-effected at BuyerCo's marginal tax rate of 38% to calculate pro forma combined net income of $1,043.3 million.

In calculating pro forma EPS, BuyerCo's 140 million shares outstanding are increased by the additional 33.6 million shares issued in connection with the acquisition. Pro forma EPS of $6.01 is determined by dividing net income of $1,043.3 million by 173.6 million total shares outstanding. Hence, the transaction is accretive by 7% on the basis of 2013E EPS. Excluding synergies, however, the transaction is only accretive by 0.5% (see Exhibit 7.27). In Exhibit 7.24, the bottom section shows the pre-tax synergies necessary to make the transaction breakeven (i.e., neither accretive nor dilutive). In the event the transaction is dilutive in a given year, this analysis determines the amount of pre-tax synergies necessary to make pro forma EPS neutral to standalone EPS. Similarly, in the event the transaction is accretive, the analysis determines the synergy cushion before the transaction becomes dilutive.

Buy-Side M&A **369**

EXHIBIT 7.24 Scenario I: 50% Stock / 50% Cash Consideration

= BuyerCo EBIT$_{2013E}$ + ValueCo EBIT$_{2013E}$ + Synergies
= $1,409.6 million + $556.9 million + $100 million

= Tangible Asset Write-up / Depreciation Period
= $330 million / 15 years

= Intangible Asset Write-up / Amortization Period
= $220 million / 15 years

($ in millions, except per share data)

Accretion / (Dilution) Analysis - 50% Stock / 50% Cash Consideration

	Pro forma 2012	1 2013	2 2014	3 2015	4 2016	5 2017
BuyerCo EBIT	$1,317.4	$1,409.6	$1,494.2	$1,568.9	$1,631.6	$1,680.6
ValueCo EBIT	518.0	556.9	590.3	619.8	644.6	663.9
Synergies	100.0	100.0	100.0	100.0	100.0	100.0
Pro Forma Combined EBIT (pre-transaction)	**$1,935.4**	**$2,066.4**	**$2,184.4**	**$2,288.7**	**$2,376.2**	**$2,444.5**
Depreciation from Write-Up	22.0	22.0	22.0	22.0	22.0	22.0
Amortization from Write-Up	14.7	14.7	14.7	14.7	14.7	14.7
Pro Forma Combined EBIT	**$1,898.7**	**$2,029.8**	**$2,147.8**	**$2,252.0**	**$2,339.5**	**$2,407.8**
Standalone Net Interest Expense	142.4	140.6	137.0	133.0	128.9	124.5
Incremental Net Interest Expense	230.9	206.4	158.0	132.8	130.8	128.6
Earnings Before Taxes	**$1,525.4**	**$1,682.7**	**$1,852.8**	**$1,986.1**	**$2,079.9**	**$2,154.8**
Income Tax Expense @ 38.0%	579.7	639.4	704.0	754.7	790.4	818.8
Pro Forma Combined Net Income	**$945.8**	**$1,043.3**	**$1,148.7**	**$1,231.4**	**$1,289.5**	**$1,336.0**
BuyerCo Standalone Net Income	**$728.5**	**$786.8**	**$841.5**	**$890.2**	**$931.7**	**$964.8**
Standalone Fully Diluted Shares Outstanding	140.0	140.0	140.0	140.0	140.0	140.0
Net New Shares Issued in Transaction	33.6	33.6	33.6	33.6	33.6	33.6
Pro Forma Fully Diluted Shares Outstanding	**173.6**	**173.6**	**173.6**	**173.6**	**173.6**	**173.6**
Pro Forma Combined Diluted EPS	$5.45	$6.01	$6.62	$7.09	$7.43	$7.70
BuyerCo Standalone Diluted EPS	5.20	5.62	6.01	6.36	6.66	6.89
Accretion / (Dilution) - $		**$0.25**	**$0.39**	**$0.61**	**$0.74**	**$0.77**	**$0.81**
Accretion / (Dilution) - %		**4.7%**	**7.0%**	**10.1%**	**11.6%**	**11.6%**	**11.7%**
Accretive / Dilutive		Accretive	Accretive	Accretive	Accretive	Accretive	Accretive
Included Pre-Tax Synergies		$100.0	$100.0	$100.0	$100.0	$100.0	$100.0
Additional Pre-Tax Synergies to Breakeven		(68.7)	(109.5)	(170.1)	(205.9)	(216.8)	(225.5)
Required Synergies to Breakeven / (Cushion)		**$31.3**	**($9.5)**	**($70.1)**	**($105.9)**	**($116.8)**	**($125.5)**

= Pro Forma Net Income$_{2013E}$ / Pro Forma Fully Diluted Shares$_{2013E}$
= $1,043.3 million / 173.6 million

= BuyerCo Standalone Net Income$_{2014E}$ / Standalone Fully Diluted Shares
= $841.5 million / 140.0 million

= Pro Forma Combined Diluted EPS$_{2015E}$ - BuyerCo Standalone Diluted EPS$_{2015E}$
= $7.09 - $6.36

= Pro Forma Combined Diluted EPS$_{2016E}$ / BuyerCo Standalone Diluted EPS$_{2016E}$ - 1
= $7.43 / $6.66 - 1

= - (EPS Accretion/(Dilution)$_{2017E}$ x Pro Forma Fully Diluted Shares) / (1 - Tax Rate)
= - ($0.81 x 173.6 million / (1 - 38%)

Scenario II: 100% Cash Scenario II demonstrates an illustrative accretion/(dilution) analysis assuming ValueCo shareholders receive 100% cash consideration. As shown in Exhibit 7.25, 2013E pro forma EBIT of $2,029.8 million after transaction-related adjustments is calculated in the same manner as Scenario I. However, interest expense is $120 million higher given the financing structure includes $2,350 million of additional debt to fund the $4,700 million equity purchase price for ValueCo. As a result, pro forma 2013E net income is $968.9 million vs. $1,043.3 million in Scenario I.

Pro forma 2013E EPS of $6.92 (vs. $6.01 in Scenario I) is calculated by dividing pro forma net income of $968.9 million by BuyerCo's fully diluted shares outstanding of 140 million. As the consideration received by ValueCo shareholders is 100% cash, no new shares are issued in connection with the transaction. Hence, as shown in Exhibit 7.25, the transaction is accretive by 23.2% on the basis of 2013E EPS, versus 7% in the 50% stock/50% cash scenario. From a balance sheet effects perspective, however, this financing mix is less attractive. Pro forma leverage in the all cash scenario is 3.6x vs. 2.6x in Scenario I (see Exhibit 7.22), which significantly weakens BuyerCo's credit profile and likely results in a credit ratings downgrade.

EXHIBIT 7.25 Scenario II: 100% Cash Consideration

($ in millions, except per share data)

Accretion / (Dilution) Analysis - 100% Cash Consideration						
		\multicolumn{6}{c}{Projection Period}					
	Pro forma 2012	1 2013	2 2014	3 2015	4 2016	5 2017
BuyerCo EBIT	$1,317.4	$1,409.6	$1,494.2	$1,568.9	$1,631.6	$1,680.6
ValueCo EBIT	518.0	556.9	590.3	619.8	644.6	663.9
Synergies	100.0	100.0	100.0	100.0	100.0	100.0
Pro Forma Combined EBIT (pre-transaction)	**$1,935.4**	**$2,066.4**	**$2,184.4**	**$2,288.7**	**$2,376.2**	**$2,444.5**
Depreciation from Write-Up	22.0	22.0	22.0	22.0	22.0	22.0
Amortization from Write-Up	14.7	14.7	14.7	14.7	14.7	14.7
Pro Forma Combined EBIT	**$1,898.7**	**$2,029.8**	**$2,147.8**	**$2,252.0**	**$2,339.5**	**$2,407.8**
Standalone Net Interest Expense	142.4	140.6	137.0	133.0	128.9	124.5
Incremental Net Interest Expense	349.2	326.4	280.8	232.3	179.0	148.5
Earnings Before Taxes	**$1,407.1**	**$1,562.8**	**$1,730.0**	**$1,886.7**	**$2,031.7**	**$2,134.9**
Income Tax Expense @ 38.0%	534.7	593.8	657.4	716.9	772.0	811.2
Pro Forma Combined Net Income	**$872.4**	**$968.9**	**$1,072.6**	**$1,169.7**	**$1,259.6**	**$1,323.6**
BuyerCo Standalone Net Income	**$728.5**	**$786.8**	**$841.5**	**$890.2**	**$931.7**	**$964.8**
Standalone Fully Diluted Shares Outstanding	140.0	140.0	140.0	140.0	140.0	140.0
Net New Shares Issued in Transaction	0.0	0.0	0.0	0.0	0.0	0.0
Pro Forma Fully Diluted Shares Outstanding	**140.0**	**140.0**	**140.0**	**140.0**	**140.0**	**140.0**
Pro Forma Combined Diluted EPS	$6.23	$6.92	$7.66	$8.36	$9.00	$9.45
BuyerCo Standalone Diluted EPS	5.20	5.62	6.01	6.36	6.66	6.89
Accretion / (Dilution) - $	**$1.03**	**$1.30**	**$1.65**	**$2.00**	**$2.34**	**$2.56**
Accretion / (Dilution) - %	**19.8%**	**23.2%**	**27.5%**	**31.4%**	**35.2%**	**37.2%**
Accretive / Dilutive	*Accretive*	*Accretive*	*Accretive*	*Accretive*	*Accretive*	*Accretive*
Included Pre-Tax Synergies	$100.0	$100.0	$100.0	$100.0	$100.0	$100.0
Additional Pre-Tax Synergies to Breakeven	(232.1)	(293.8)	(372.8)	(450.8)	(528.9)	(578.7)
Required Synergies to Breakeven / (Cushion)	**($132.1)**	**($193.8)**	**($272.8)**	**($350.8)**	**($428.9)**	**($478.7)**

Scenario III: 100% Stock Scenario III demonstrates an illustrative accretion/(dilution) analysis assuming ValueCo shareholders receive 100% stock consideration. As shown in Exhibit 7.26, total interest expense of $180.8 million in 2013E is the lowest of the three scenarios given no incremental debt issuance (beyond the refinancing of ValueCo's existing net debt). As a result, pro forma net income of $1,146.4 million is the highest. However, given the need to issue 67.1 million shares (twice the amount in Scenario I), pro forma 2013E EPS is $5.53 vs. $5.62 on a standalone basis. Hence, the transaction is dilutive by 1.5%, versus 7% accretive and 23.2% accretive in Scenarios I and II, respectively.

EXHIBIT 7.26 Scenario III: 100% Stock Consideration

($ in millions, except per share data)

Accretion / (Dilution) Analysis - 100% Stock Consideration	Pro forma 2012	Projection Period				
		1 2013	2 2014	3 2015	4 2016	5 2017
BuyerCo EBIT	$1,317.4	$1,409.6	$1,494.2	$1,568.9	$1,631.6	$1,680.6
ValueCo EBIT	518.0	556.9	590.3	619.8	644.6	663.9
Synergies	100.0	100.0	100.0	100.0	100.0	100.0
Pro Forma Combined EBIT (pre-transaction)	**$1,935.4**	**$2,066.4**	**$2,184.4**	**$2,288.7**	**$2,376.2**	**$2,444.5**
Depreciation from Write-Up	22.0	22.0	22.0	22.0	22.0	22.0
Amortization from Write-Up	14.7	14.7	14.7	14.7	14.7	14.7
Pro Forma Combined EBIT	**$1,898.7**	**$2,029.8**	**$2,147.8**	**$2,252.0**	**$2,339.5**	**$2,407.8**
Standalone Net Interest Expense	142.4	140.6	137.0	133.0	128.9	124.5
Incremental Net Interest Expense	66.9	40.2	10.7	6.6	4.2	1.6
Earnings Before Taxes	**$1,689.4**	**$1,849.0**	**$2,000.1**	**$2,112.4**	**$2,206.5**	**$2,281.7**
Income Tax Expense @ 38.0%	642.0	702.6	760.0	802.7	838.5	867.1
Pro Forma Combined Net Income	**$1,047.4**	**$1,146.4**	**$1,240.0**	**$1,309.7**	**$1,368.0**	**$1,414.7**
BuyerCo Standalone Net Income	**$728.5**	**$786.8**	**$841.5**	**$890.2**	**$931.7**	**$964.8**
Standalone Fully Diluted Shares Outstanding	140.0	140.0	140.0	140.0	140.0	140.0
Net New Shares Issued in Transaction	67.1	67.1	67.1	67.1	67.1	67.1
Pro Forma Fully Diluted Shares Outstanding	**207.1**	**207.1**	**207.1**	**207.1**	**207.1**	**207.1**
Pro Forma Combined Diluted EPS	$5.06	$5.53	$5.99	$6.32	$6.60	$6.83
BuyerCo Standalone Diluted EPS	5.20	5.62	6.01	6.36	6.66	6.89
Accretion / (Dilution) - $		($0.15)	($0.09)	($0.02)	($0.04)	($0.05)	($0.06)
Accretion / (Dilution) - %		(2.8%)	(1.5%)	(0.4%)	(0.6%)	(0.8%)	(0.9%)
Accretive / Dilutive		Dilutive	Dilutive	Dilutive	Dilutive	Dilutive	Dilutive
Included Pre-Tax Synergies		$100.0	$100.0	$100.0	$100.0	$100.0	$100.0
Additional Pre-Tax Synergies to Breakeven		49.1	28.6	8.0	12.1	17.0	20.7
Required Synergies to Breakeven / (Cushion)		**$149.1**	**$128.6**	**$108.0**	**$112.1**	**$117.0**	**$120.7**

Sensitivity Analysis Given the prominence of accretion/(dilution) analysis in the ultimate M&A decision, it is critical to perform sensitivity analysis. The most commonly used inputs for this exercise are purchase price, financing consideration (% stock and % cash), and amount of synergies. The data tables in Exhibit 7.27 show three different EPS accretion/(dilution) sensitivity analysis output tables:

I. Projection year and premium paid from 25% to 45%, assuming fixed 50% stock/50% cash mix and annual synergies of $100 million. *Accretion decreases as purchase price is increased.*

II. Consideration mix from 0% to 100% stock and premium paid from 25% to 45%, assuming annual synergies of $100 million. *Accretion increases in accordance with a higher proportion of debt financing and a lower offer price.*

III. Pre-tax synergies from $0 million to $200 million and premium paid from 25% to 45%, assuming fixed 50% stock / 50% cash mix. *Maximum accretive results are achieved by increasing synergies and decreasing offer price.*

EXHIBIT 7.27 Accretion / (Dilution) Sensitivity Analysis

Annual EPS Accretion / (Dilution) Sensitivity Analysis - Premium Paid

Offer Price	Premium	2012	2013	2014	2015	2016
$54.38	25%	7.3%	9.5%	12.4%	13.6%	13.7%
$56.55	30%	6.0%	8.2%	11.2%	12.6%	12.6%
$58.73	35%	4.7%	7.0%	10.1%	11.6%	11.6%
$60.90	40%	3.5%	5.7%	8.9%	10.5%	10.6%
$63.08	45%	2.2%	4.5%	7.7%	9.4%	9.7%

2013E EPS Accretion / (Dilution) Sensitivity Analysis - Premium Paid & Consideration Mix

Offer Price	Premium	0%	25%	50%	75%	100%
$54.38	25%	25.0%	16.5%	9.5%	6.4%	1.3%
$56.55	30%	24.1%	15.3%	8.2%	5.0%	(0.1%)
$58.73	35%	23.2%	14.2%	7.0%	3.7%	(1.5%)
$60.90	40%	22.2%	13.1%	5.7%	2.4%	(2.9%)
$63.08	45%	21.3%	11.9%	4.5%	1.1%	(4.2%)

2013E EPS Accretion / (Dilution) Sensitivity Analysis - Premium Paid & Synergies

Offer Price	Premium	$0	$50	$100	$150	$200
$54.38	25%	2.9%	6.2%	9.5%	12.7%	16.0%
$56.55	30%	1.7%	5.0%	8.2%	11.5%	14.7%
$58.73	35%	0.5%	3.7%	7.0%	10.2%	13.4%
$60.90	40%	(0.7%)	2.5%	5.7%	8.9%	12.1%
$63.08	45%	(1.8%)	1.3%	4.5%	7.7%	10.9%

ILLUSTRATIVE MERGER CONSEQUENCES ANALYSIS FOR THE BUYERCO / VALUECO TRANSACTION

The following pages display the full M&A model for BuyerCo's acquisition of ValueCo based on this chapter's discussion. Exhibit 7.28 lists these pages, which are shown in Exhibits 7.29 to 7.48.

EXHIBIT 7.28   M&A Model Pages

M&A Model	
I.	Transaction Summary
II.	Pro Forma Combined Income Statement
III.	Pro Forma Combined Balance Sheet
IV.	Pro Forma Combined Cash Flow Statement
V.	Pro Forma Combined Debt Schedule
VI.	Capitalization and Credit Statistics
VII.	Accretion / (Dilution) Analysis
VIII.	Assumptions Page—Transaction Adjustments, Financing Structures, & Fees

BuyerCo Standalone Model	
IX.	BuyerCo Income Statement
X.	BuyerCo Balance Sheet
XI.	BuyerCo Cash Flow Statement
XII.	BuyerCo Debt Schedule
XIII.	BuyerCo Assumptions Page 1—Income Statement and Cash Flow Statement
XIV.	BuyerCo Assumptions Page 2—Balance Sheet

ValueCo Standalone Model	
XV.	ValueCo Income Statement
XVI.	ValueCo Balance Sheet
XVII.	ValueCo Cash Flow Statement
XVIII.	ValueCo Debt Schedule
XIX.	ValueCo Assumptions Page 1—Income Statement and Cash Flow Statement
XX.	ValueCo Assumptions Page 2—Balance Sheet

EXHIBIT 7.29 Merger Consequences Analysis Transaction Summary Page

BuyerCo Acquisition of ValueCo
Merger Consequences Analysis
($ in millions, fiscal year ending December 31)

Financing Structure: **Structure 1**
Operating Scenario: **Base**

Transaction Summary

Sources of Funds

	Amount	% of Total Sources	Multiple of Pro Forma EBITDA 2012	Cumulative	Pricing
Revolving Credit Facility	-	- %	- x	- x	L+350 bps
Term Loan A	-	- %	- x	- x	NA
Term Loan B	2,200.0	34.6%	1.0x	1.0x	L+375 bps
Term Loan C	-	- %	- x	1.0x	NA
2nd Lien	-	- %	- x	1.0x	NA
Senior Notes	1,500.0	23.6%	0.6x	1.6x	7.500%
Senior Subordinated Notes	-	- %	- x	1.6x	NA
Issuance of Common Stock	2,350.0	37.0%	1.0x	2.6x	
Cash on Hand	300.0	4.7%	0.1x	2.7x	
Other	-	- %	- x	2.7x	
Total Sources	**$6,350.0**	**100.0%**	**2.7x**	**2.7x**	

Uses of Funds

	Amount	% of Total Uses
Purchase ValueCo Equity	$4,700.0	74.0%
Repay Existing Debt	1,500.0	23.6%
Tender / Call Premiums	20.0	0.3%
Transaction Fees	40.0	0.6%
Debt Financing Fees	90.0	1.4%
Total Uses	**$6,350.0**	**100.0%**

Premium Paid & Exchange Ratio

ValueCo Current Share Price	$43.50
Offer Price per Share	$58.73
Premium Paid	**35%**
BuyerCo Current Share Price	$70.00
Exchange Ratio	0.8x

Purchase Price

Offer Price per Share	$58.73
Fully Diluted Shares	80.0
Equity Purchase Price	**$4,700.0**
Plus: Existing Net Debt	1,250.0
Enterprise Value	**$5,950.0**

Acquisition Structure & Synergies

Stock Consideration for Equity	50%
Transaction Debt Raised	$3,700.0
% of ValueCo Enterprise Value	62%
Acquisition Type	Stock Sale
Year 1 Synergies	$100
	Options
Financing Structure	1
Operating Scenario	1
Cash Flow Sweep	1
Cash Balance	
Average Interest	
Financing Fees	

Valuation Summary

	Target		Acquirer
Company Name	ValueCo		BuyerCo
Ticker	VLCO		BUY
Current Share Price (12/20/2012)	$43.50		$70.00
Premium to Current Share Price	35%		
Offer Price per Share	$58.73		
Fully Diluted Shares	80.0		140.0
Equity Value	**$4,700.0**		**$9,800.0**
Plus: Total Debt	1,500.0		2,200.0
Plus: Preferred Equity	-		-
Plus: Noncontrolling Interest	-		-
Less: Cash and Equivalents	(250.0)		(400.0)
Enterprise Value	**$5,950.0**		**$11,600.0**

Transaction Multiples

	Target		Acquirer	
	Metric	Multiple	Metric	Multiple
Enterprise Value / LTM EBITDA	$700.0	8.5x	$1,443.1	8.0x
Enterprise Value / 2012E EBITDA	725.0	8.2x	1,486.3	7.8x
Enterprise Value / 2013E EBITDA	779.4	7.6x	1,590.3	7.3x
Equity Value / 2012E Net Income	$268.8	17.5x	$728.5	13.5x
Equity Value / 2013E Net Income	297.0	15.8x	786.8	12.5x

Pro Forma Ownership

	Shares	Ownership
Existing BuyerCo Shareholders	140.0	80.7%
Former ValueCo Shareholders	33.6	19.3%
Pro Forma Fully Diluted Shares	**173.6**	**100.0%**

Pro Forma Combined Financial Summary

	Pro Forma 2012	1 2013	2 2014	3 2015	4 2016	5 2017
Sales	$10,205.8	$10,937.5	$11,593.7	$12,173.4	$12,660.3	$13,040.1
% growth	8.2%	7.2%	6.0%	5.0%	4.0%	3.0%
Gross Profit	$3,947.2	$4,230.4	$4,484.2	$4,708.4	$4,896.8	$5,043.7
% margin	38.7%	38.7%	38.7%	38.7%	38.7%	38.7%
EBITDA	**$2,311.3**	**$2,469.7**	**$2,611.9**	**$2,737.5**	**$2,843.0**	**$2,925.3**
% margin	22.6%	22.6%	22.5%	22.5%	22.5%	22.4%
Interest Expense	374.8	348.6	296.3	270.3	270.3	270.3
Net Income	$945.8	$1,043.3	$1,148.7	$1,231.4	$1,289.5	$1,336.0
% margin	9.3%	9.5%	9.9%	10.1%	10.2%	10.2%
Fully Diluted Shares	173.6	173.6	173.6	173.6	173.6	173.6
Diluted EPS	**$5.45**	**$6.01**	**$6.62**	**$7.09**	**$7.43**	**$7.70**
Cash Flow from Operating Activities	1,387.9	1,528.0	1,641.8	1,729.6	1,803.6	
Less: Capital Expenditures	(363.8)	(406.8)	(427.1)	(444.2)	(457.5)	
Free Cash Flow	**$1,004.2**	**$1,121.2**	**$1,214.6**	**$1,285.4**	**$1,346.0**	
Senior Secured Debt	2,200.0	0.0	0.0	0.0	0.0	0.0
Senior Debt	5,900.0	4,795.8	3,700.0	3,700.0	3,700.0	3,700.0
Total Debt	5,900.0	4,795.8	3,700.0	3,700.0	3,700.0	3,700.0
Cash & Equivalents	350.0	250.0	275.4	1,490.0	2,775.4	4,121.5

Credit Statistics

	BuyerCo 2012	Pro Forma 2012	1 2013	2 2014	3 2015	4 2016	5 2017
EBITDA / Interest Expense	10.3x	6.2x	7.1x	8.8x	10.1x	10.5x	10.8x
(EBITDA - Capex) / Interest Expense	8.9x	5.2x	6.0x	7.4x	8.5x	8.9x	9.1x
Senior Secured Debt / EBITDA	- x	1.0x	0.4x	- x	- x	- x	- x
Senior Debt / EBITDA	1.5x	2.6x	1.9x	1.4x	1.4x	1.3x	1.3x
Total Debt / EBITDA	1.5x	2.6x	1.9x	1.4x	1.4x	1.3x	1.3x
Net Debt / EBITDA	1.2x	2.4x	1.8x	1.3x	0.8x	0.3x	(0.1x)
Debt / Total Capitalization	47.0%	55.3%	45.2%	34.7%	31.1%	28.1%	25.5%

Accretion / (Dilution) Analysis

	BuyerCo 2012	Pro Forma 2012	1 2013	2 2014	3 2015	4 2016	5 2017
BuyerCo Standalone Diluted EPS	$5.20		$5.62	$6.01	$6.36	$6.66	$6.89
ValueCo Standalone Diluted EPS	$3.36		$3.71	$4.08	$4.44	$4.70	$4.86
Pro Forma Combined Diluted EPS	$5.45		$6.01	$6.62	$7.09	$7.43	$7.70
Accretion / (Dilution) - $	**$0.25**		**$0.39**	**$0.61**	**$0.74**	**$0.77**	**$0.81**
Accretion / (Dilution) - %	**4.7%**		**7.0%**	**10.1%**	**11.6%**	**11.6%**	**11.7%**
Accretive / Dilutive	Accretive		Accretive	Accretive	Accretive	Accretive	Accretive
Breakeven Pre-Tax Synergies / (Cushion)	($69)		($109)	($170)	($206)	($217)	($225)

Annual EPS Accretion / (Dilution) Sensitivity Analysis - Premium Paid

Offer Price	Premium	25%	30%	35%	40%	45%
$54.38	25%	7.3%	6.0%	4.7%	3.5%	2.2%
$56.55	30%	9.5%	8.2%	7.0%	5.7%	4.5%
$58.73	35%	11.2%	10.1%	8.9%	7.7%	
$60.90	40%	12.4%	11.2%	10.1%	8.9%	7.7%
$63.08	45%	13.6%	12.6%	11.6%	10.5%	9.4%

Year: 2012 | 2013 | 2014 | 2015 | 2016

2013E EPS Accretion / (Dilution) Sensitivity Analysis - Premium Paid & Consideration Mix

		% Stock Consideration Mix				
Offer Price	Premium	0%	25%	50%	75%	100%
$54.38	25%	25.0%	16.5%	9.5%	6.4%	1.3%
$56.55	30%	24.1%	15.3%	8.2%	5.0%	(0.1%)
$58.73	35%	23.2%	14.2%	7.0%	3.7%	(1.5%)
$60.90	40%	22.2%	13.1%	5.7%	2.4%	(2.9%)
$63.08	45%	21.3%	11.9%	4.5%	1.1%	(4.2%)

EXHIBIT 7.30 Pro Forma Income Statement

($ in millions, except per share data, fiscal year ending December 31)

Pro Forma Income Statement

	Historical Period			LTM 9/30/2012	Pro Forma 2012	Year 1 2013	Year 2 2014	Projection Period Year 3 2015	Year 4 2016	Year 5 2017
	2009	2010	2011							
BuyerCo Sales	$4,771.7	$5,484.7	$6,232.6	$6,559.6	$6,755.8	$7,228.7	$7,662.4	$8,045.5	$8,367.4	$8,618.4
ValueCo Sales	2,600.0	2,900.0	3,200.0	3,385.0	3,450.0	3,708.8	3,931.3	4,127.8	4,293.0	4,421.7
Total Sales	**$7,371.7**	**$8,384.7**	**$9,432.6**	**$9,944.6**	**$10,205.8**	**$10,937.5**	**$11,593.7**	**$12,173.4**	**$12,660.3**	**$13,040.1**
% growth	NA	13.7%	12.5%	NA	8.2%	7.2%	6.0%	5.0%	4.0%	3.0%
BuyerCo COGS	$3,053.9	$3,455.4	$3,864.2	$4,067.0	$4,188.6	$4,481.8	$4,750.7	$4,988.2	$5,187.8	$5,343.4
ValueCo COGS	1,612.0	1,769.0	1,920.0	2,035.0	2,070.0	2,225.3	2,358.8	2,476.7	2,575.8	2,653.0
Total COGS	**$4,665.9**	**$5,224.4**	**$5,784.2**	**$6,102.0**	**$6,258.8**	**$6,707.0**	**$7,109.5**	**$7,464.9**	**$7,763.5**	**$7,996.4**
% sales	63.3%	62.3%	61.3%	61.4%	61.3%	61.3%	61.3%	61.3%	61.3%	61.3%
BuyerCo Gross Profit	$1,717.8	$2,029.3	$2,368.4	$2,492.6	$2,567.2	$2,746.9	$2,911.7	$3,057.3	$3,179.6	$3,275.0
ValueCo Gross Profit	988.0	1,131.0	1,280.0	1,350.0	1,380.0	1,483.5	1,572.5	1,651.1	1,717.2	1,768.7
Total Gross Profit	**$2,705.8**	**$3,160.3**	**$3,648.4**	**$3,842.6**	**$3,947.2**	**$4,230.4**	**$4,484.2**	**$4,708.4**	**$4,896.8**	**$5,043.7**
% margin	36.7%	37.7%	38.7%	38.6%	38.7%	38.7%	38.7%	38.7%	38.7%	38.7%
BuyerCo SG&A	$811.2	$905.0	$997.2	$1,049.5	$1,080.9	$1,156.6	$1,226.0	$1,287.3	$1,338.8	$1,378.9
ValueCo SG&A	496.6	551.0	608.0	650.0	655.0	704.1	746.4	783.7	815.0	839.5
Total SG&A	**$1,307.8**	**$1,456.0**	**$1,605.2**	**$1,699.5**	**$1,735.9**	**$1,860.7**	**$1,972.4**	**$2,071.0**	**$2,153.8**	**$2,218.4**
% sales	17.7%	17.4%	17.0%	17.1%	17.0%	17.0%	17.0%	17.0%	17.0%	17.0%
BuyerCo EBITDA	$906.6	$1,124.4	$1,371.2	$1,443.1	$1,486.3	$1,590.3	$1,685.7	$1,770.0	$1,840.8	$1,896.0
ValueCo EBITDA	491.4	580.0	672.0	700.0	725.0	779.4	826.1	867.4	902.1	929.2
Synergies					100.0	100.0	100.0	100.0	100.0	100.0
Total EBITDA	**$1,398.0**	**$1,704.4**	**$2,043.2**	**$2,243.1**	**$2,311.3**	**$2,469.7**	**$2,611.9**	**$2,737.5**	**$2,843.0**	**$2,925.3**
% margin	19.0%	20.3%	21.7%	22.6%	22.6%	22.6%	22.5%	22.5%	22.5%	22.4%
BuyerCo Depreciation					135.1	144.6	153.2	160.9	167.3	172.4
BuyerCo Amortization					33.8	36.1	38.3	40.2	41.8	43.1
ValueCo Depreciation					155.3	166.9	176.9	185.8	193.2	199.0
ValueCo Amortization					51.8	55.6	59.0	61.9	64.4	66.3
Depreciation on Tangible Asset Write-up					22.0	22.0	22.0	22.0	22.0	22.0
Amortization on Intangible Asset Write-up					14.7	14.7	14.7	14.7	14.7	14.7
EBIT					**$1,898.7**	**$2,029.8**	**$2,147.8**	**$2,252.0**	**$2,339.5**	**$2,407.8**
% margin					18.6%	18.6%	18.5%	18.5%	18.5%	18.5%
Interest Expense										
Revolving Credit Facility					-	-	-	-	-	-
New Term Loan B					104.5	78.3	26.0	-	-	-
BuyerCo Senior Notes					143.0	143.0	143.0	143.0	143.0	143.0
New Senior Notes					112.5	112.5	112.5	112.5	112.5	112.5
Commitment Fee on Unused Revolver					2.5	2.5	2.5	2.5	2.5	2.5
Administrative Agent Fee					0.2	0.2	0.2	0.2	0.2	0.2
Cash Interest Expense					**$362.7**	**$336.4**	**$284.2**	**$258.2**	**$258.2**	**$258.2**
Amortization of Deferred Financing Fees					12.2	12.2	12.2	12.2	12.2	12.2
Total Interest Expense					**$374.8**	**$348.6**	**$296.3**	**$270.3**	**$270.3**	**$270.3**
Interest Income					(1.5)	(1.5)	(1.3)	(4.4)	(10.7)	(17.2)
Net Interest Expense					**$373.3**	**$347.1**	**$295.0**	**$265.9**	**$259.6**	**$253.1**
Earnings Before Taxes					$1,525.4	$1,682.7	$1,852.8	$1,986.1	$2,079.9	$2,154.8
Plus: Non-Tax Deductible Depreciation					22.0	22.0	22.0	22.0	22.0	22.0
Plus: Non-Tax Deductible Amortization					14.7	14.7	14.7	14.7	14.7	14.7
Taxable Income					**$1,562.1**	**$1,719.4**	**$1,889.4**	**$2,022.8**	**$2,116.6**	**$2,191.4**
Current Income Tax Expense					593.6	653.4	718.0	768.7	804.3	832.7
Deferred Tax Expense					(13.9)	(13.9)	(13.9)	(13.9)	(13.9)	(13.9)
Net Income					**$945.8**	**$1,043.3**	**$1,148.7**	**$1,231.4**	**$1,289.5**	**$1,336.0**
% margin					9.3%	9.5%	9.9%	10.1%	10.2%	10.2%
Diluted Shares Outstanding					173.6	173.6	173.6	173.6	173.6	173.6
Diluted EPS					**$5.45**	**$6.01**	**$6.62**	**$7.09**	**$7.43**	**$7.70**
% growth						10.3%	10.1%	7.2%	4.7%	3.6%
BuyerCo Marginal Tax Rate					38.0%	38.0%	38.0%	38.0%	38.0%	38.0%
Effective Tax Rate					38.9%	38.8%	38.8%	38.7%	38.7%	38.6%

375

EXHIBIT 7.31 Pro Forma Balance Sheet

($ in millions, fiscal year ending December 31)

Pro Forma Balance Sheet

	Standalone		Adjustments		Pro Forma	Projection Period				
	BuyerCo 2012	ValueCo 2012	+	–	Pro Forma 2012	Year 1 2013	Year 2 2014	Year 3 2015	Year 4 2016	Year 5 2017
Cash and Cash Equivalents	$400.0	$250.0		(300.0)	$350.0	$250.0	$275.4	$1,490.0	$2,775.4	$4,121.5
Accounts Receivable	1,000.0	450.0			1,450.0	1,553.8	1,647.0	1,729.3	1,798.5	1,852.5
Inventories	1,225.0	600.0			1,825.0	1,955.8	2,073.1	2,176.7	2,263.8	2,331.7
Prepaids and Other Current Assets	525.0	175.0			700.0	749.9	794.9	834.6	868.0	894.0
Total Current Assets	**$3,150.0**	**$1,475.0**			**$4,325.0**	**$4,509.4**	**$4,790.4**	**$6,230.7**	**$7,705.7**	**$9,199.7**
Property, Plant and Equipment, net	2,500.0	2,500.0	330.0		5,330.0	5,380.3	5,434.9	5,493.4	5,555.0	5,619.2
Goodwill	575.0	1,000.0	1,859.0	(1,000.0)	2,434.0	2,434.0	2,434.0	2,434.0	2,434.0	2,434.0
Intangible Assets	825.0	875.0	220.0		1,920.0	1,813.6	1,701.6	1,584.8	1,463.9	1,339.8
Other Assets	450.0	150.0			600.0	600.0	600.0	600.0	600.0	600.0
Deferred Financing Fees	–	–	90.0		90.0	77.8	65.7	53.5	41.4	29.2
Total Assets	**$7,500.0**	**$6,000.0**			**$14,699.0**	**$14,815.1**	**$15,026.6**	**$16,396.4**	**$17,800.1**	**$19,222.0**
Accounts Payable	925.0	215.0			1,140.0	1,220.9	1,294.1	1,358.8	1,413.2	1,455.6
Accrued Liabilities	945.0	275.0			1,220.0	1,306.8	1,385.2	1,454.4	1,512.6	1,558.0
Other Current Liabilities	225.0	100.0			325.0	348.3	369.1	387.6	403.1	415.2
Total Current Liabilities	**$2,095.0**	**$590.0**			**$2,685.0**	**$2,875.9**	**$3,048.5**	**$3,200.9**	**$3,328.9**	**$3,428.8**
Revolving Credit Facility	–	–			–	–	–	–	–	–
ValueCo Term Loan	–	–	1,000.0		1,000.0	1,095.8	–	–	–	–
New Term Loan B	–	–		(1,000.0)	–	–	–	–	–	–
BuyerCo Senior Notes	2,200.0	–			2,200.0	2,200.0	2,200.0	2,200.0	2,200.0	2,200.0
ValueCo Senior Notes	–	500.0		(500.0)	–	–	–	–	–	–
New Senior Notes	–	–	1,500.0		1,500.0	1,500.0	1,500.0	1,500.0	1,500.0	1,500.0
Deferred Income Taxes	100.0	300.0	209.0		609.0	595.1	581.1	567.2	553.3	539.3
Other Long-Term Liabilities	625.0	110.0			735.0	735.0	735.0	735.0	735.0	735.0
Total Liabilities	**$5,020.0**	**$2,500.0**			**$9,929.0**	**$9,001.8**	**$8,064.6**	**$8,203.1**	**$8,317.2**	**$8,403.1**
Noncontrolling Interest	–	–			–	–	–	–	–	–
Shareholders' Equity	2,480.0	3,500.0	2,290.0	(3,500.0)	4,770.0	5,813.3	6,962.0	8,193.4	9,482.9	10,818.9
Total Shareholders' Equity	**$2,480.0**	**$3,500.0**			**$4,770.0**	**$5,813.3**	**$6,962.0**	**$8,193.4**	**$9,482.9**	**$10,818.9**
Total Liabilities and Equity	**$7,500.0**	**$6,000.0**			**$14,699.0**	**$14,815.1**	**$15,026.6**	**$16,396.4**	**$17,800.1**	**$19,222.0**
Balance Check	0.000	0.000			0.000	0.000	0.000	0.000	0.000	0.000
Net Working Capital	655.0	635.0			1,290.0	1,383.5	1,466.5	1,539.8	1,601.4	1,649.4
(Increase) / Decrease in Net Working Capital						(93.5)	(83.0)	(73.3)	(61.6)	(48.0)

Balance Sheet Ratios

Current Assets

	BuyerCo 2012	ValueCo 2012			Pro Forma 2012	Year 1 2013	Year 2 2014	Year 3 2015	Year 4 2016	Year 5 2017
Days Sales Outstanding (DSO)	54.0	47.6			51.9	51.9	51.9	51.9	51.9	51.9
Days Inventory Held (DIH)	106.7	105.8			106.8	106.4	106.4	106.4	106.4	106.4
Prepaid and Other Current Assets (% of sales)	7.8%	5.1%			5.1%	6.9%	6.9%	6.9%	6.9%	6.9%

Current Liabilities

	BuyerCo 2012	ValueCo 2012			Pro Forma 2012	Year 1 2013	Year 2 2014	Year 3 2015	Year 4 2016	Year 5 2017
Days Payable Outstanding (DPO)	80.6	37.9			66.5	66.4	66.4	66.4	66.4	66.4
Accrued Liabilities (% of sales)	14.0%	8.0%			12.0%	11.9%	11.9%	11.9%	11.9%	11.9%
Other Current Liabilities (% of sales)	3.3%	4.8%			3.2%	3.2%	3.2%	3.2%	3.2%	3.2%

EXHIBIT 7.32 Pro Forma Cash Flow Statement

($ in millions, fiscal year ending December 31)

Pro Forma Cash Flow Statement

	Year 1 2013	Year 2 2014	Projection Period Year 3 2015	Year 4 2016	Year 5 2017
Operating Activities					
Net Income	$1,043.3	$1,148.7	$1,231.4	$1,289.5	$1,336.0
Plus: Depreciation	311.5	330.2	346.7	360.5	371.3
Plus: Amortization	91.8	97.3	102.1	106.2	109.4
Plus: Depreciation on Tangible Assets Write-up	22.0	22.0	22.0	22.0	22.0
Plus: Amortization on Intangible Assets Write-up	14.7	14.7	14.7	14.7	14.7
Plus: Amortization of Financing Fees	12.2	12.2	12.2	12.2	12.2
Changes in Working Capital Items					
(Inc.) / Dec. in Accounts Receivable	(103.8)	(93.2)	(82.3)	(69.2)	(54.0)
(Inc.) / Dec. in Inventories	(130.8)	(117.3)	(103.7)	(87.1)	(67.9)
(Inc.) / Dec. in Prepaid and Other Current Assets	(49.9)	(45.0)	(39.7)	(33.4)	(26.0)
Inc. / (Dec.) in Accounts Payable	80.9	73.3	64.7	54.4	42.4
Inc. / (Dec.) in Accrued Liabilities	86.8	78.4	69.3	58.2	45.4
Inc. / (Dec.) in Other Current Liabilities	23.3	20.9	18.5	15.5	12.1
(Inc.) / Dec. in Net Working Capital	(93.5)	(83.0)	(73.3)	(61.6)	(48.0)
Inc. / (Dec.) in Deferred Taxes	(13.9)	(13.9)	(13.9)	(13.9)	(13.9)
Cash Flow from Operating Activities	**$1,387.9**	**$1,528.0**	**$1,641.8**	**$1,729.6**	**$1,803.6**
Investing Activities					
Capital Expenditures	(383.8)	(406.8)	(427.1)	(444.2)	(457.5)
Other Investing Activities	—	—	—	—	—
Cash Flow from Investing Activities	**($383.8)**	**($406.8)**	**($427.1)**	**($444.2)**	**($457.5)**
Financing Activities					
Revolving Credit Facility	(1,104.2)	(1,095.8)	—	—	—
New Term Loan B Facility	—	—	—	—	—
BuyerCo Senior Notes	—	—	—	—	—
New Senior Notes	—	—	—	—	—
Equity Issuance / (Repurchase)	—	—	—	—	—
Cash Flow from Financing Activities	**($1,104.2)**	**($1,095.8)**	**—**	**—**	**—**
Excess Cash for the Period	(100.0)	$25.4	$1,214.6	$1,285.4	$1,346.0
Beginning Cash Balance	350.0	250.0	275.4	1,490.0	2,775.4
Ending Cash Balance	**$250.0**	**$275.4**	**$1,490.0**	**$2,775.4**	**$4,121.5**
Capital Expenditures (% of sales)	3.5%	3.5%	3.5%	3.5%	3.5%

EXHIBIT 7.33 Pro Forma Debt Schedule

($ in millions, fiscal year ending December 31)

Pro Forma Debt Schedule

	Pro forma 2012	Year 1 2013	Year 2 2014	Year 3 2015	Year 4 2016	Year 5 2017
Projection Period						
Forward LIBOR Curve	0.25%	0.35%	0.50%	0.75%	1.00%	1.25%
Cash Flow from Operating Activities		$1,387.9	$1,528.0	$1,641.8	$1,729.6	$1,803.6
Cash Flow from Investing Activities		(383.8)	(406.8)	(427.1)	(444.2)	(457.5)
Cash Available for Debt Repayment		$1,004.2	$1,121.2	$1,214.6	$1,285.4	$1,346.0
Total Mandatory Repayments	MinCash	(22.0)	(22.0)	-	-	-
Cash From Balance Sheet	250.0	100.0	(0.0)	25.4	1,240.0	2,525.4
Cash Available for Optional Debt Repayment		$1,082.2	$1,099.2	$1,240.0	$2,525.4	$3,871.5

Revolving Credit Facility

Revolving Credit Facility Size	$500.0					
Spread	3.500%					
LIBOR Floor	1.000%					
Term	6 years					
Commitment Fee on Unused Portion	0.50%					
Beginning Balance		-	-	-	-	-
Drawdown/(Repayment)		-	-	-	-	-
Ending Balance		-	-	-	-	-
Interest Rate		4.50%	4.50%	4.50%	4.50%	4.75%
Interest Expense		-	-	-	-	-
Commitment Fee		2.5	2.5	2.5	2.5	2.5
Administrative Agent Fee		0.2	0.2	0.2	0.2	0.2

New Term Loan B Facility

Size	$2,200.0					
Spread	3.750%					
LIBOR Floor	1.000%					
Term	7 years					
Repayment Schedule	1.0% Per Annum, Bullet at Maturity					
Beginning Balance		$2,200.0	$1,095.8	-	-	-
Mandatory Repayments		(22.0)	(22.0)	-	-	-
Optional Repayments		(1,082.2)	(1,073.8)	-	-	-
Ending Balance		$1,095.8	-	-	-	-
Interest Rate		4.75%	4.75%	4.75%	4.75%	5.00%
Interest Expense		78.3	26.0	-	-	-

BuyerCo Existing Senior Notes

Size	$2,200.0					
Coupon	6.500%					
Term	8 years					
Beginning Balance		$2,200.0	$2,200.0	$2,200.0	$2,200.0	$2,200.0
Repayment		-	-	-	-	-
Ending Balance		$2,200.0	$2,200.0	$2,200.0	$2,200.0	$2,200.0
Interest Expense		143.0	143.0	143.0	143.0	143.0

New Senior Notes

Size	$1,500.0					
Coupon	7.500%					
Term	8 years					
Beginning Balance		$1,500.0	$1,500.0	$1,500.0	$1,500.0	$1,500.0
Repayment		-	-	-	-	-
Ending Balance		$1,500.0	$1,500.0	$1,500.0	$1,500.0	$1,500.0
Interest Expense		112.5	112.5	112.5	112.5	112.5

EXHIBIT 7.34 Pro Forma Capitalization and Credit Statistics

($ in millions, fiscal year ending December 31)

Capitalization

	BuyerCo 2012	ValueCo 2012	Adjustments +	Adjustments −	Pro forma 2012	Projection Period 1 2013	2 2014	3 2015	4 2016	5 2017
Cash	$400.0	$250.0		(300.0)	$350.0	$250.0	$275.4	$1,490.0	$2,775.4	$4,121.5
Revolving Credit Facility	-	-			-	-	-	-	-	-
ValueCo Term Loan	-	1,000.0		(1,000.0)	-	-	-	-	-	-
New Term Loan B	-	-	2,200.0		2,200.0	1,095.8	-	-	-	-
Other Debt	-	-			-	-	-	-	-	-
Total Senior Secured Debt	-	**$1,000.0**			**$2,200.0**	**$1,095.8**	-	-	-	-
BuyerCo Senior Notes	2,200.0	-			2,200.0	2,200.0	2,200.0	2,200.0	2,200.0	2,200.0
ValueCo Senior Notes	-	500.0		(500.0)	-	-	-	-	-	-
New Senior Notes	-	-	1,500.0		1,500.0	1,500.0	1,500.0	1,500.0	1,500.0	1,500.0
Total Senior Debt	**$2,200.0**	**$1,500.0**			**$5,900.0**	**$4,795.8**	**$3,700.0**	**$3,700.0**	**$3,700.0**	**$3,700.0**
Senior Subordinated Notes	-	-			-	-	-	-	-	-
Total Debt	**$2,200.0**	**$1,500.0**			**$5,900.0**	**$4,795.8**	**$3,700.0**	**$3,700.0**	**$3,700.0**	**$3,700.0**
Shareholders' Equity	2,480.0	3,500.0	2,290.0	(3,500.0)	4,770.0	5,813.3	6,962.0	8,193.4	9,482.9	10,818.9
Total Capitalization	**$4,680.0**	**$5,000.0**			**$10,670.0**	**$10,609.1**	**$10,662.0**	**$11,893.4**	**$13,182.9**	**$14,518.9**
% of Bank Debt Repaid						50.2%	100.0%	100.0%	100.0%	100.0%

Credit Statistics

	BuyerCo 2012	ValueCo 2012			Pro forma 2012	1 2013	2 2014	3 2015	4 2016	5 2017
EBITDA	$1,486.3	$725.0		100.0	$2,311.3	$2,469.7	$2,611.9	$2,737.5	$2,843.0	$2,925.3
Capital Expenditures	202.7	155.3			357.9	383.8	406.8	427.1	444.2	457.5
Interest Expense	144.4	85.9		144.5	374.8	348.6	296.3	270.3	270.3	270.3
EBITDA / Interest Expense	10.3x	8.4x			6.2x	7.1x	8.8x	10.1x	10.5x	10.8x
(EBITDA - Capex) / Interest Expense	8.9x	6.6x			5.2x	6.0x	7.4x	8.5x	8.9x	9.1x
Senior Secured Debt / EBITDA	- x	1.4x			1.0x	0.4x	- x	- x	- x	- x
Senior Debt / EBITDA	1.5x	2.1x			2.6x	1.9x	1.4x	1.4x	1.3x	1.3x
Total Debt / EBITDA	1.5x	2.1x			2.6x	1.9x	1.4x	1.4x	1.3x	1.3x
Net Debt / EBITDA	1.2x	1.7x			2.4x	1.8x	1.3x	0.8x	0.3x	(0.1x)
% Debt / Total Capitalization	47.0%	30.0%			55.3%	45.2%	34.7%	31.1%	28.1%	25.5%

Debt / EBITDA — % Stock Consideration Mix

Premium Paid	0%	25%	50%	75%	100%
25%	3.4x	3.0x	2.5x	2.0x	1.5x
30%	3.5x	3.0x	2.5x	2.0x	1.5x
35%	3.6x	3.1x	2.6x	2.0x	1.5x
40%	3.7x	3.1x	2.6x	2.0x	1.5x
45%	3.7x	3.2x	2.6x	2.1x	1.5x

EBITDA / Interest Expense — % Stock Consideration Mix

Premium Paid	0%	25%	50%	75%	100%
25%	4.9x	5.5x	6.3x	8.7x	11.0x
30%	4.8x	5.4x	6.2x	8.6x	11.0x
35%	4.7x	5.3x	6.2x	8.6x	11.0x
40%	4.6x	5.2x	6.1x	8.5x	11.0x
45%	4.5x	5.2x	6.0x	8.4x	11.0x

EXHIBIT 7.35 Accretion / (Dilution) Analysis

($ in millions, except per share data)
Accretion / (Dilution) Analysis - 50% Stock / 50% Cash

	Pro forma 2012	1 2013	2 2014	3 2015	4 2016	5 2017
BuyerCo EBIT	$1,317.4	$1,409.6	$1,494.2	$1,568.9	$1,631.6	$1,680.6
ValueCo EBIT	518.0	556.9	590.3	619.8	644.6	663.9
Synergies	100.0	100.0	100.0	100.0	100.0	100.0
Pro Forma Combined EBIT (pre-deal structure)	**$1,935.4**	**$2,066.4**	**$2,184.4**	**$2,288.7**	**$2,376.2**	**$2,444.5**
Depreciation from Write-Up	22.0	22.0	22.0	22.0	22.0	22.0
Amortization from Write-Up	14.7	14.7	14.7	14.7	14.7	14.7
Pro Forma Combined EBIT	**$1,898.7**	**$2,029.8**	**$2,147.8**	**$2,252.0**	**$2,339.5**	**$2,407.8**
Standalone Net Interest Expense	142.4	140.6	137.0	133.0	128.9	124.5
Incremental Net Interest Expense	230.9	206.4	158.0	132.8	130.8	128.6
Earnings Before Taxes	**$1,525.4**	**$1,682.7**	**$1,852.8**	**$1,986.1**	**$2,079.9**	**$2,154.8**
Income Tax Expense @ 38.0%	579.7	639.4	704.0	754.7	790.4	818.8
Pro Forma Combined Net Income	**$945.8**	**$1,043.3**	**$1,148.7**	**$1,231.4**	**$1,289.5**	**$1,336.0**
BuyerCo Standalone Net Income	$728.5	$786.8	$841.5	$890.2	$931.7	$964.8
Standalone Fully Diluted Shares Outstanding	140.0	140.0	140.0	140.0	140.0	140.0
Net New Shares Issued in Transaction	33.6	33.6	33.6	33.6	33.6	33.6
Pro Forma Fully Diluted Shares Outstanding	173.6	173.6	173.6	173.6	173.6	173.6
Pro Forma Combined Diluted EPS	**$5.45**	**$6.01**	**$6.62**	**$7.09**	**$7.43**	**$7.70**
BuyerCo Standalone Diluted EPS	**5.20**	**5.62**	**6.01**	**6.36**	**6.66**	**6.89**
Accretion / (Dilution) - $	$0.25	$0.39	$0.61	$0.74	$0.77	$0.81
Accretion / (Dilution) - %	4.7%	7.0%	10.1%	11.6%	11.6%	11.7%
Accretive / Dilutive	Accretive	Accretive	Accretive	Accretive	Accretive	Accretive
Included Pre-Tax Synergies	$100.0	$100.0	$100.0	$100.0	$100.0	$100.0
Additional Pre-Tax Synergies to Breakeven	(68.7)	(109.5)	(170.1)	(205.9)	(216.8)	(225.5)
Required Synergies to Breakeven / (Cushion)	**$31.3**	**($9.5)**	**($70.1)**	**($105.9)**	**($116.8)**	**($125.5)**

Annual EPS Accretion / (Dilution) Sensitivity Analysis - Premium Paid

Offer Price	Premium	2012	2013	2014	2015	2016
$54.38	25%	7.3%	9.5%	12.4%	13.6%	13.7%
$56.55	30%	6.0%	8.2%	11.2%	12.6%	12.6%
$58.73	35%	4.7%	7.0%	10.1%	11.6%	11.6%
$60.90	40%	3.5%	5.7%	8.9%	10.5%	10.6%
$63.08	45%	2.2%	4.5%	7.7%	9.4%	9.7%

Breakeven Synergies Sensitivity Analysis

Offer Price	Premium	$0	$50	$100	$150	$200
$54.38	25%	2.9%	6.2%	9.5%	12.7%	16.0%
$56.55	30%	1.7%	5.0%	8.2%	11.5%	14.7%
$58.73	35%	0.5%	3.7%	7.0%	10.2%	13.4%
$60.90	40%	(0.7%)	2.5%	5.7%	8.9%	12.1%
$63.08	45%	(1.8%)	1.3%	4.5%	7.7%	10.9%

2012E EPS Accretion / (Dilution) Sensitivity Analysis - Premium Paid & Consideration Mix

		% Stock Consideration Mix				
Offer Price	Premium	0%	25%	50%	75%	100%
$54.38	25%	25.0%	16.5%	9.5%	6.4%	1.3%
$56.55	30%	24.1%	15.3%	8.2%	5.0%	(0.1%)
$58.73	35%	23.2%	14.2%	7.0%	3.7%	(1.5%)
$60.90	40%	22.2%	13.1%	5.7%	2.4%	(2.9%)
$63.08	45%	21.3%	11.9%	4.5%	1.1%	(4.2%)

Breakeven Synergies Sensitivity Analysis

		Pre-Tax Synergies Required to Breakeven				
Offer Price	Premium	2012	2013	2014	2015	2016
$54.38	25%	($4)	($47)	($105)	($139)	($151)
$56.55	30%	$14	($28)	($88)	($122)	($134)
$58.73	35%	$31	($9)	($70)	($106)	($117)
$60.90	40%	$49	$9	($51)	($88)	($100)
$63.08	45%	$67	$28	($31)	($70)	($83)

EXHIBIT 7.36 Assumptions Page

($ in millions, fiscal year ending December 31)
Assumptions Page - Transaction Adjustments, Financing Structures, and Fees

Financing Structures

Sources of Funds	Structure 1	Structure 2	Structure 3	Structure 4	Status Quo 5
Revolving Credit Facility Size	$500.0	$500.0	$500.0	$500.0	
Revolving Credit Facility Draw	-	-	-	-	
Term Loan A	2,200.0	1,175.0	500.0	-	
Term Loan B	-	-	850.0	-	
Term Loan C	-	-	-	-	
2nd Lien	-	-	-	-	
Senior Notes	1,500.0	2,825.0	2,000.0	4,000.0	
Senior Subordinated Notes	-	-	-	-	
Issuance of Common Stock	2,350.0	2,350.0	2,350.0	2,350.0	
Cash on Hand	300.0	-	650.0	-	
Other	-	-	-	-	
Total Sources of Funds	**$6,350.0**	**$6,350.0**	**$6,350.0**	**$6,350.0**	

Uses of Funds	Structure 1	Structure 2	Structure 3	Structure 4	Status Quo 5
Equity Purchase Price	$4,700.0	$4,700.0	$4,700.0	$4,700.0	
Repay Existing Bank Debt	1,500.0	1,500.0	1,500.0	1,500.0	
Tender / Call Premiums	20.0	20.0	20.0	20.0	
Debt Financing Fees	90.0	90.0	90.0	90.0	
Transaction and Other Fees	40.0	40.0	40.0	40.0	
	-	-	-	-	
	-	-	-	-	
Total Uses of Funds	**$6,350.0**	**$6,350.0**	**$6,350.0**	**$6,350.0**	

Purchase Price

Public / Private Target — 1

Offer Price per Share	$58.73
Fully Diluted Shares Outstanding	80.0
Equity Purchase Price	**$4,700.0**
Plus: Total Debt	1,500.0
Plus: Preferred Securities	-
Plus: Noncontrolling Interest	-
Less: Cash and Cash Equivalents	(250.0)
Enterprise Value	**$5,950.0**

Goodwill Calculation

Equity Purchase Price	$4,700.0
Less: ValueCo Net Identifiable Assets	(2,500.0)
Total Allocable Purchase Premium	**$2,200.0**

	Allocation %	
Less: Tangible Asset Write-Up	15%	(330.0)
Less: Intangible Asset Write-Up	10%	(220.0)
Plus: Deferred Tax Liability		209.0
Goodwill Created in Transaction		**$1,859.0**

Write-Up Depreciation & Amortization Assumptions

	Years	Annual Amount
Tangible Asset Write-Up Depreciation Period	15	22.0
Intangible Asset Write-Up Amortization Period	15	14.7
Deferred Income Taxes		(13.9)

Financing Fees

	Structure 1	Size	Fees (%)	Fees ($)
Revolving Credit Facility Size		$500.0	1.500%	$7.5
Term Loan A		2,200.0	1.500%	33.0
Term Loan B		-	1.500%	-
Term Loan C		-	1.500%	-
2nd Lien		-	2.250%	-
Senior Notes		1,500.0	2.250%	33.8
Senior Subordinated Notes		-	2.250%	-
Senior Bridge Facility		1,500.0	1.000%	15.0
Senior Subordinated Bridge Facility		-	1.000%	-
Other Financing Fees & Expenses			1.000%	0.8
Total Financing Fees				**$90.0**

Amortization of Financing Fees

	Term	Year 1 2013	Year 2 2014	Year 3 2015	Year 4 2016	Year 5 2017
Revolving Credit Facility Size	6	$1.3	$1.3	$1.3	$1.3	$1.3
Term Loan A	7	4.7	4.7	4.7	4.7	4.7
Term Loan B		-	-	-	-	-
Term Loan C		-	-	-	-	-
2nd Lien	8	4.2	4.2	4.2	4.2	4.2
Senior Notes						
Senior Subordinated Notes	8	1.9	1.9	1.9	1.9	1.9
Senior Bridge Facility						
Senior Subordinated Bridge Facility						
Other Financing Fees & Expenses	8	0.1	0.1	0.1	0.1	0.1
Annual Amortization		**$12.2**	**$12.2**	**$12.2**	**$12.2**	**$12.2**

ValueCo Fully Diluted Shares Outstanding

Basic Shares Outstanding		79.726
Plus: Shares from In-the-Money Options		1.500
Less: Shares Repurchased		(1.192)
Net New Shares from Options		**0.308**
Plus: Shares from Convertible Securities		-
Fully Diluted Shares Outstanding		**80.034**

Options/Warrants

Tranche	Number of Shares	Exercise Price	In-the-Money Shares	Proceeds
Tranche 1	1.000	$45.00	1.000	$45.0
Tranche 2	0.500	50.00	0.500	25.0
Tranche 3	-	-	-	-
Tranche 4	-	-	-	-
Tranche 5	-	-	-	-
Total	**1.500**		**1.500**	**$70.0**

BuyerCo Fully Diluted Shares Outstanding

Basic Shares Outstanding		139.982
Plus: Shares from In-the-Money Options		0.250
Less: Shares Repurchased		(0.232)
Net New Shares from Options		**0.018**
Plus: Shares from Convertible Securities		-
Fully Diluted Shares Outstanding		**140.000**

Options/Warrants

Tranche	Number of Shares	Exercise Price	In-the-Money Shares	Proceeds
Tranche 1	0.250	$65.00	0.250	$16.3
Tranche 2	0.750	75.00	-	-
Tranche 3	-	-	-	-
Tranche 4	-	-	-	-
Tranche 5	-	-	-	-
Total	**1.000**		**0.250**	**$16.3**

Synergies

	Year 1 2013	Year 2 2014	Year 3 2015	Year 4 2016	Year 5 2017
Revenue	-	-	-	-	-
Cost Savings	100.0	100.0	100.0	100.0	100.0
Capex	-	-	-	-	-

EXHIBIT 7.37 BuyerCo Standalone Income Statement

BuyerCo Enterprises
Standalone Income Statement
($ in millions, fiscal year ending December 31)

	Historical Period						LTM		Projection Period				
	2009	2010	2011	YTD 9/30/2011	YTD 9/30/2012	2012	9/30/2012	Year 1 2013	Year 2 2014	Year 3 2015	Year 4 2016	Year 5 2017
Sales	$4,771.7	$5,484.7	$6,232.6	$4,611.6	$4,938.6	$6,755.8	$6,559.6	$7,228.7	$7,662.4	$8,045.5	$8,367.4	$8,618.4
% growth	NA	14.9%	13.6%	NA	7.1%	8.4%	NA	7.0%	6.0%	5.0%	4.0%	3.0%
Cost of Goods Sold	3,053.9	3,455.4	3,864.2	2,859.2	3,061.9	4,188.6	4,067.0	4,481.8	4,750.7	4,988.2	5,187.8	5,343.4
Gross Profit	$1,717.8	$2,029.3	$2,368.4	$1,752.4	$1,876.7	$2,567.2	$2,492.6	$2,746.9	$2,911.7	$3,057.3	$3,179.6	$3,275.0
% margin	36.0%	37.0%	38.0%	38.0%	38.0%	38.0%	38.0%	38.0%	38.0%	38.0%	38.0%	38.0%
Selling, General & Administrative	811.2	905.0	997.2	737.9	790.2	1,080.9	1,049.5	1,156.6	1,226.0	1,287.3	1,338.8	1,378.9
% sales	17.0%	16.5%	16.0%	16.0%	16.0%	16.0%	16.0%	16.0%	16.0%	16.0%	16.0%	16.0%
Other Expense / (Income)												
EBITDA	$906.6	$1,124.4	$1,371.2	$1,014.6	$1,086.5	$1,486.3	$1,443.1	$1,590.3	$1,685.7	$1,770.0	$1,840.8	$1,896.0
% margin	19.0%	20.5%	22.0%	22.0%	22.0%	22.0%	22.0%	22.0%	22.0%	22.0%	22.0%	22.0%
Depreciation	95.4	109.7	124.7	92.2	98.8	135.1	131.2	144.6	153.2	160.9	167.3	172.4
Amortization	23.9	27.4	31.2	23.1	24.7	33.8	32.8	36.1	38.3	40.2	41.8	43.1
EBIT	$787.3	$987.2	$1,215.4	$899.3	$963.0	$1,317.4	$1,279.1	$1,409.6	$1,494.2	$1,568.9	$1,631.6	$1,680.6
% margin	16.5%	18.0%	19.5%	19.5%	19.5%	19.5%	19.5%	19.5%	19.5%	19.5%	19.5%	19.5%
Interest Expense												
Revolving Credit Facility												
Term Loan A												
Term Loan B												
Term Loan C												
Existing Term Loan												
2nd Lien												
Senior Notes												
Senior Subordinated Notes						143.0	143.0	143.0	143.0	143.0	143.0	143.0
Commitment Fee on Unused Revolver						1.3	1.3	1.3	1.3	1.3	1.3	1.3
Administrative Agent Fee						0.2	0.2	0.2	0.2	0.2	0.2	0.2
Total Interest Expense						$144.4	$144.4	$144.4	$144.4	$144.4	$144.4	$144.4
Interest Income						(2.0)	(2.0)	(3.8)	(7.4)	(11.4)	(15.5)	(19.9)
Net Interest Expense						$142.4	$142.4	$140.6	$137.0	$133.0	$128.9	$124.5
Earnings Before Taxes						1,175.0	1,136.7	1,269.0	1,357.2	1,435.8	1,502.8	1,556.1
Income Tax Expense						446.5	432.0	482.2	515.7	545.6	571.1	591.3
Net Income						$728.5	$704.8	$786.8	$841.5	$890.2	$931.7	$964.8
% margin						10.8%	10.7%	10.9%	11.0%	11.1%	11.1%	11.2%
Diluted Shares Outstanding						140.0	140.0	140.0	140.0	140.0	140.0	140.0
Diluted EPS						$5.20	$5.03	$5.62	$6.01	$6.36	$6.66	$6.89

Income Statement Assumptions

Sales (% YoY growth)	NA	14.9%	13.6%	(26.0%)	7.1%	8.4%	NA	7.0%	6.0%	5.0%	4.0%	3.0%
Cost of Goods Sold (% margin)	64.0%	63.0%	62.0%	62.0%	62.0%	62.0%	62.0%	62.0%	62.0%	62.0%	62.0%	62.0%
SG&A (% sales)	17.0%	16.5%	16.0%	16.0%	16.0%	16.0%	16.0%	16.0%	16.0%	16.0%	16.0%	16.0%
Other Expense / (Income) (% of sales)	- %	- %	- %	- %	- %	- %	- %	- %	- %	- %	- %	- %
Depreciation & Amortization (% of sales)	2.0%	2.0%	2.0%	2.0%	2.0%	2.0%	2.0%	2.0%	2.0%	2.0%	2.0%	2.0%
Amortization (% of sales)	0.5%	0.5%	0.5%	0.5%	0.5%	0.5%	0.5%	0.5%	0.5%	0.5%	0.5%	0.5%
Interest Income												
Tax Rate						38.0%	38.0%	38.0%	38.0%	38.0%	38.0%	38.0%

EXHIBIT 7.38 BuyerCo Standalone Balance Sheet

($ in millions, fiscal year ending December 31)

BuyerCo Standalone Balance Sheet

		Projection Period				
	2012	Year 1 2013	Year 2 2014	Year 3 2015	Year 4 2016	Year 5 2017
Cash and Cash Equivalents	$400.0	$1,104.8	$1,865.9	$2,678.7	$3,537.4	$4,434.8
Accounts Receivable	1,000.0	1,070.0	1,134.2	1,190.9	1,238.5	1,275.7
Inventories	1,225.0	1,310.8	1,389.4	1,458.9	1,517.2	1,562.7
Prepaids and Other Current Assets	525.0	561.8	595.5	625.2	650.2	669.7
Total Current Assets	**$3,150.0**	**$4,047.3**	**$4,984.9**	**$5,953.7**	**$6,943.4**	**$7,942.9**
Property, Plant and Equipment, net	2,500.0	2,572.3	2,648.9	2,729.4	2,813.0	2,899.2
Goodwill	575.0	575.0	575.0	575.0	575.0	575.0
Intangible Assets	825.0	788.9	750.5	710.3	668.5	625.4
Other Assets	450.0	450.0	450.0	450.0	450.0	450.0
Deferred Financing Fees	-	-	-	-	-	-
Total Assets	**$7,500.0**	**$8,433.4**	**$9,409.4**	**$10,418.4**	**$11,449.9**	**$12,492.6**
Accounts Payable	925.0	989.8	1,049.1	1,101.6	1,145.7	1,180.0
Accrued Liabilities	945.0	1,011.2	1,071.8	1,125.4	1,170.4	1,205.5
Other Current Liabilities	225.0	240.8	255.2	268.0	278.7	287.0
Total Current Liabilities	**$2,095.0**	**$2,241.7**	**$2,376.1**	**$2,495.0**	**$2,594.8**	**$2,672.6**
Revolving Credit Facility	-	-	-	-	-	-
Term Loan A	-	-	-	-	-	-
Term Loan B	-	-	-	-	-	-
Term Loan C	-	-	-	-	-	-
Existing Term Loan	-	-	-	-	-	-
2nd Lien	-	-	-	-	-	-
Senior Notes	2,200.0	2,200.0	2,200.0	2,200.0	2,200.0	2,200.0
Senior Subordinated Notes	-	-	-	-	-	-
Other Debt	-	-	-	-	-	-
Deferred Income Taxes	100.0	100.0	100.0	100.0	100.0	100.0
Other Long-Term Liabilities	625.0	625.0	625.0	625.0	625.0	625.0
Total Liabilities	**$5,020.0**	**$5,166.7**	**$5,301.1**	**$5,420.0**	**$5,519.8**	**$5,597.6**
Noncontrolling Interest	-	-	-	-	-	-
Shareholders' Equity	2,480.0	3,266.8	4,108.2	4,998.4	5,930.2	6,895.0
Total Shareholders' Equity	**$2,480.0**	**$3,266.8**	**$4,108.2**	**$4,998.4**	**$5,930.2**	**$6,895.0**
Total Liabilities and Equity	**$7,500.0**	**$8,433.4**	**$9,409.4**	**$10,418.4**	**$11,449.9**	**$12,492.6**
Balance Check	0.000	0.000	0.000	0.000	0.000	0.000
Net Working Capital	655.0	700.9	742.9	780.0	811.2	835.6
(Increase) / Decrease in Net Working Capital		(45.9)	(42.1)	(37.1)	(31.2)	(24.3)

Balance Sheet Assumptions

Current Assets

	2012	2013	2014	2015	2016	2017
Days Sales Outstanding (DSO)	54.0	54.0	54.0	54.0	54.0	54.0
Days Inventory Held (DIH)	106.7	106.7	106.7	106.7	106.7	106.7
Prepaid and Other Current Assets (% of sales)	7.8%	7.8%	7.8%	7.8%	7.8%	7.8%

Current Liabilities

	2012	2013	2014	2015	2016	2017
Days Payable Outstanding (DPO)	80.6	80.6	80.6	80.6	80.6	80.6
Accrued Liabilities (% of sales)	14.0%	14.0%	14.0%	14.0%	14.0%	14.0%
Other Current Liabilities (% of sales)	3.3%	3.3%	3.3%	3.3%	3.3%	3.3%

EXHIBIT 7.39 BuyerCo Standalone Cash Flow Statement

($ in millions, fiscal year ending December 31)

BuyerCo Standalone Cash Flow Statement					
	Projection Period				
	Year 1 2013	Year 2 2014	Year 3 2015	Year 4 2016	Year 5 2017
Operating Activities					
Net Income	$786.8	$841.5	$890.2	$931.7	$964.8
Plus: Depreciation & Amortization	144.6	153.2	160.9	167.3	172.4
Plus: Amortization	36.1	38.3	40.2	41.8	43.1
Changes in Working Capital Items					
(Inc.) / Dec. in Accounts Receivable	(70.0)	(64.2)	(56.7)	(47.6)	(37.2)
(Inc.) / Dec. in Inventories	(85.8)	(78.6)	(69.5)	(58.4)	(45.5)
(Inc.) / Dec. in Prepaid and Other Current Assets	(36.8)	(33.7)	(29.8)	(25.0)	(19.5)
Inc. / (Dec.) in Accounts Payable	64.8	59.4	52.5	44.1	34.4
Inc. / (Dec.) in Accrued Liabilities	66.2	60.7	53.6	45.0	35.1
Inc. / (Dec.) in Other Current Liabilities	15.8	14.4	12.8	10.7	8.4
(Inc.) / Dec. in Net Working Capital	(45.9)	(42.1)	(37.1)	(31.2)	(24.3)
Cash Flow from Operating Activities	**$921.6**	**$991.0**	**$1,054.2**	**$1,109.7**	**$1,155.9**
Investing Activities					
Capital Expenditures	(216.9)	(229.9)	(241.4)	(251.0)	(258.6)
Other Investing Activities	-	-	-	-	-
Cash Flow from Investing Activities	**($216.9)**	**($229.9)**	**($241.4)**	**($251.0)**	**($258.6)**
Financing Activities					
Revolving Credit Facility	-	-	-	-	-
Term Loan A	-	-	-	-	-
Term Loan B	-	-	-	-	-
Term Loan C	-	-	-	-	-
Existing Term Loan	-	-	-	-	-
2nd Lien	-	-	-	-	-
Senior Notes	-	-	-	-	-
Senior Subordinated Notes	-	-	-	-	-
Other Debt	-	-	-	-	-
Dividends	-	-	-	-	-
Equity Issuance / (Repurchase)	-	-	-	-	-
Cash Flow from Financing Activities	**-**	**-**	**-**	**-**	**-**
Excess Cash for the Period	$704.8	$761.1	$812.9	$858.7	$897.4
Beginning Cash Balance	400.0	1,104.8	1,865.9	2,678.7	3,537.4
Ending Cash Balance	**$1,104.8**	**$1,865.9**	**$2,678.7**	**$3,537.4**	**$4,434.8**
Cash Flow Statement Assumptions					
Capital Expenditures (% of sales)	3.0%	3.0%	3.0%	3.0%	3.0%

Buy-Side M&A

EXHIBIT 7.40 BuyerCo Standalone Debt Schedule

($ in millions, fiscal year ending December 31)

BuyerCo Standalone Debt Schedule

	Pro forma 2012	Year 1 2013	Year 2 2014	Year 3 2015	Year 4 2016	Year 5 2017
				Projection Period		
Forward LIBOR Curve	0.25%	0.35%	0.50%	0.75%	1.00%	1.25%
Cash Flow from Operating Activities		$921.6	$991.0	$1,054.2	$1,109.7	$1,155.9
Cash Flow from Investing Activities		(216.9)	(229.9)	(241.4)	(251.0)	(258.6)
Cash Available for Debt Repayment		$704.8	$761.1	$812.9	$858.7	$897.4
Total Mandatory Repayments	MinCash	-	-	-	-	-
Cash From Balance Sheet	100.0	300.0	1,004.8	1,765.9	2,578.7	3,437.4
Cash Available for Optional Debt Repayment		$1,004.8	$1,765.9	$2,578.7	$3,437.4	$4,334.8

Revolving Credit Facility

Revolving Credit Facility Size	$250.0					
Spread	2.500%					
LIBOR Floor	1.000%					
Term	6 years					
Commitment Fee on Unused Portion	0.50%					
Beginning Balance		-	-	-	-	-
Drawdown/(Repayment)		-	-	-	-	-
Ending Balance		-	-	-	-	-
Interest Rate		3.50%	3.50%	3.50%	3.50%	3.75%
Interest Expense		-	-	-	-	-
Commitment Fee		1.3	1.3	1.3	1.3	1.3
Administrative Agent Fee		0.2	0.2	0.2	0.2	0.2

Term Loan B Facility

Size	-					
Spread	2.750%					
LIBOR Floor	1.000%					
Term	7 years					
Repayment Schedule	1.0% Per Annum, Bullet at Maturity					
Beginning Balance		-	-	-	-	-
Mandatory Repayments		-	-	-	-	-
Optional Repayments		-	-	-	-	-
Ending Balance		-	-	-	-	-
Interest Rate		3.75%	3.75%	3.75%	3.75%	4.00%
Interest Expense		-	-	-	-	-

Senior Notes

Size	$2,200.0					
Coupon	6.500%					
Term	8 years					
Beginning Balance		$2,200.0	$2,200.0	$2,200.0	$2,200.0	$2,200.0
Repayment		-	-	-	-	-
Ending Balance		$2,200.0	$2,200.0	$2,200.0	$2,200.0	$2,200.0
Interest Expense		143.0	143.0	143.0	143.0	143.0

EXHIBIT 7.41 BuyerCo Standalone Assumptions Page 1

BuyerCo Standalone Assumptions Page 1 - Income Statement and Cash Flow Statement

		Projection Period				
		Year 1 2013	Year 2 2014	Year 3 2015	Year 4 2016	Year 5 2017
Income Statement Assumptions						
Sales (% growth)		7.0%	6.0%	5.0%	4.0%	3.0%
Base	1	7.0%	6.0%	5.0%	4.0%	3.0%
Upside	2	10.0%	8.0%	6.0%	4.0%	3.0%
Management	3	12.0%	10.0%	8.0%	6.0%	4.0%
Downside 1	4	5.0%	4.0%	3.0%	3.0%	3.0%
Downside 2	5	2.0%	2.0%	2.0%	2.0%	2.0%
Cost of Goods Sold (% sales)		62.0%	62.0%	62.0%	62.0%	62.0%
Base	1	62.0%	62.0%	62.0%	62.0%	62.0%
Upside	2	62.0%	62.0%	62.0%	62.0%	62.0%
Management	3	61.0%	61.0%	61.0%	61.0%	61.0%
Downside 1	4	63.0%	63.0%	63.0%	63.0%	63.0%
Downside 2	5	64.0%	64.0%	64.0%	64.0%	64.0%
SG&A (% sales)		16.0%	16.0%	16.0%	16.0%	16.0%
Base	1	16.0%	16.0%	16.0%	16.0%	16.0%
Upside	2	15.0%	15.0%	15.0%	15.0%	15.0%
Management	3	15.0%	15.0%	15.0%	15.0%	15.0%
Downside 1	4	18.0%	18.0%	18.0%	18.0%	18.0%
Downside 2	5	20.0%	20.0%	20.0%	20.0%	20.0%
Depreciation (% sales)		2.0%	2.0%	2.0%	2.0%	2.0%
Base	1	2.0%	2.0%	2.0%	2.0%	2.0%
Upside	2	2.0%	2.0%	2.0%	2.0%	2.0%
Management	3	2.0%	2.0%	2.0%	2.0%	2.0%
Downside 1	4	2.0%	2.0%	2.0%	2.0%	2.0%
Downside 2	5	2.0%	2.0%	2.0%	2.0%	2.0%
Amortization (% sales)		0.5%	0.5%	0.5%	0.5%	0.5%
Base	1	0.5%	0.5%	0.5%	0.5%	0.5%
Upside	2	0.5%	0.5%	0.5%	0.5%	0.5%
Management	3	0.5%	0.5%	0.5%	0.5%	0.5%
Downside 1	4	0.5%	0.5%	0.5%	0.5%	0.5%
Downside 2	5	0.5%	0.5%	0.5%	0.5%	0.5%
Cash Flow Statement Assumptions						
Capital Expenditures (% sales)		3.0%	3.0%	3.0%	3.0%	3.0%
Base	1	3.0%	3.0%	3.0%	3.0%	3.0%
Upside	2	3.0%	3.0%	3.0%	3.0%	3.0%
Management	3	3.0%	3.0%	3.0%	3.0%	3.0%
Downside 1	4	3.0%	3.0%	3.0%	3.0%	3.0%
Downside 2	5	3.0%	3.0%	3.0%	3.0%	3.0%

EXHIBIT 7.42 BuyerCo Standalone Assumptions Page 2

BuyerCo Standalone Assumptions Page 2 - Balance Sheet

		Projection Period				
		Year 1 2013	Year 2 2014	Year 3 2015	Year 4 2016	Year 5 2017
Current Assets						
Days Sales Outstanding (DSO)		54.0	54.0	54.0	54.0	54.0
Base	1	54.0	54.0	54.0	54.0	54.0
Upside	2	54.0	54.0	54.0	54.0	54.0
Management	3	54.0	54.0	54.0	54.0	54.0
Downside 1	4	56.0	56.0	56.0	56.0	56.0
Downside 2	5	58.0	58.0	58.0	58.0	58.0
Days Inventory Held (DIH)		106.7	106.7	106.7	106.7	106.7
Base	1	106.7	106.7	106.7	106.7	106.7
Upside	2	106.7	106.7	106.7	106.7	106.7
Management	3	106.7	106.7	106.7	106.7	106.7
Downside 1	4	110.0	110.0	110.0	110.0	110.0
Downside 2	5	115.0	115.0	115.0	115.0	115.0
Prepaids and Other Current Assets (% sales)		7.8%	7.8%	7.8%	7.8%	7.8%
Base	1	7.8%	7.8%	7.8%	7.8%	7.8%
Upside	2	7.8%	7.8%	7.8%	7.8%	7.8%
Management	3	7.8%	7.8%	7.8%	7.8%	7.8%
Downside 1	4	7.8%	7.8%	7.8%	7.8%	7.8%
Downside 2	5	7.8%	7.8%	7.8%	7.8%	7.8%
Current Liabilities						
Days Payable Outstanding (DPO)		80.6	80.6	80.6	80.6	80.6
Base	1	80.6	80.6	80.6	80.6	80.6
Upside	2	80.6	80.6	80.6	80.6	80.6
Management	3	80.6	80.6	80.6	80.6	80.6
Downside 1	4	77.0	77.0	77.0	77.0	77.0
Downside 2	5	75.0	75.0	75.0	75.0	75.0
Accrued Liabilities (% sales)		14.0%	14.0%	14.0%	14.0%	14.0%
Base	1	14.0%	14.0%	14.0%	14.0%	14.0%
Upside	2	14.0%	14.0%	14.0%	14.0%	14.0%
Management	3	14.0%	14.0%	14.0%	14.0%	14.0%
Downside 1	4	14.0%	14.0%	14.0%	14.0%	14.0%
Downside 2	5	14.0%	14.0%	14.0%	14.0%	14.0%
Other Current Liabilities (% sales)		3.3%	3.3%	3.3%	3.3%	3.3%
Base	1	3.3%	3.3%	3.3%	3.3%	3.3%
Upside	2	3.3%	3.3%	3.3%	3.3%	3.3%
Management	3	3.3%	3.3%	3.3%	3.3%	3.3%
Downside 1	4	3.3%	3.3%	3.3%	3.3%	3.3%
Downside 2	5	3.3%	3.3%	3.3%	3.3%	3.3%

EXHIBIT 7.43 ValueCo Standalone Income Statement

ValueCo Corporation
Standalone Income Statement
($ in millions, fiscal year ending December 31)

	Historical Period								Projection Period				
	2009	2010	2011	YTD 9/30/2011	YTD 9/30/2012	LTM 9/30/2012	2012	Year 1 2013	Year 2 2014	Year 3 2015	Year 4 2016	Year 5 2017
Sales	$2,600.0	$2,900.0	$3,200.0	$2,400.0	$2,585.0	$3,385.0	$3,450.0	$3,708.8	$3,931.3	$4,127.8	$4,293.0	$4,421.7
% growth	NA	11.5%	10.3%	NA	7.7%	NA	7.8%	7.5%	6.0%	5.0%	4.0%	3.0%
Cost of Goods Sold	1,612.0	1,769.0	1,920.0	1,440.0	1,555.0	2,035.0	2,070.0	2,225.3	2,358.8	2,476.7	2,575.8	2,653.0
Gross Profit	$988.0	$1,131.0	$1,280.0	$960.0	$1,030.0	$1,350.0	$1,380.0	$1,483.5	$1,572.5	$1,651.1	$1,717.2	$1,768.7
% margin	38.0%	39.0%	40.0%	40.0%	39.8%	39.9%	40.0%	40.0%	40.0%	40.0%	40.0%	40.0%
Selling, General & Administrative	496.6	551.0	608.0	443.0	485.0	650.0	655.0	704.1	746.4	783.7	815.0	839.5
% sales	19.1%	19.0%	19.0%	18.5%	18.8%	19.2%	19.0%	19.0%	19.0%	19.0%	19.0%	19.0%
Other Expense / (Income)	-	-	-	-	-	-	-	-	-	-	-	-
EBITDA	$491.4	$580.0	$672.0	$517.0	$545.0	$700.0	$725.0	$779.4	$826.1	$867.4	$902.1	$929.2
% margin	18.9%	20.0%	21.0%	21.5%	21.1%	20.7%	21.0%	21.0%	21.0%	21.0%	21.0%	21.0%
Depreciation & Amortization	116.0	121.5	145.0	110.0	115.0	150.0	155.3	166.9	176.9	185.8	193.2	199.0
Amortization	39.0	43.5	48.0	33.0	35.0	50.0	51.8	55.6	59.0	61.9	64.4	66.3
EBIT	$336.4	$415.0	$479.0	$374.0	$395.0	$500.0	$518.0	$556.9	$590.3	$619.8	$644.6	$663.9
% margin	12.9%	14.3%	15.0%	15.6%	15.3%	14.8%	15.0%	15.0%	15.0%	15.0%	15.0%	15.0%
Interest Expense												
Revolving Credit Facility						-	-	-	-	-	-	-
Term Loan A						-	-	-	-	-	-	-
Term Loan B						45.0	45.0	38.1	23.5	7.9	-	-
Term Loan C						-	-	-	-	-	-	-
Existing Term Loan						-	-	-	-	-	-	-
2nd Lien						-	-	-	-	-	-	-
Senior Notes						40.0	40.0	40.0	40.0	40.0	40.0	40.0
Senior Subordinated Notes						-	-	-	-	-	-	-
Commitment Fee on Unused Revolver						0.8	0.8	0.8	0.8	0.8	0.8	0.8
Administrative Agent Fee						0.2	0.2	0.2	0.2	0.2	0.2	0.2
Total Interest Expense						$85.9	$85.9	$79.0	$64.4	$48.8	$40.9	$40.9
Interest Income						(1.5)	(1.5)	(1.3)	(1.3)	(1.3)	(2.4)	(4.5)
Net Interest Expense						$84.4	$84.4	$77.8	$63.2	$47.5	$38.5	$36.4
Earnings Before Taxes						415.6	433.6	479.1	527.1	572.3	606.1	627.5
Income Tax Expense						157.9	164.8	182.0	200.3	217.5	230.3	238.5
Net Income						$257.7	$268.8	$297.0	$326.8	$354.8	$375.8	$389.1
% margin						7.6%	7.8%	8.0%	8.3%	8.6%	8.8%	8.8%
Diluted Shares Outstanding						80.0	80.0	80.0	80.0	80.0	80.0	80.0
Diluted EPS						$3.22	$3.36	$3.71	$4.08	$4.44	$4.70	$4.86

Income Statement Assumptions

	2009	2010	2011	YTD 9/30/2011	YTD 9/30/2012	LTM 9/30/2012	2012	Year 1 2013	Year 2 2014	Year 3 2015	Year 4 2016	Year 5 2017
Sales (% YoY growth)	NA	11.5%	10.3%	NA	7.7%	NA	7.8%	7.5%	6.0%	5.0%	4.0%	3.0%
Cost of Goods Sold (% margin)	62.0%	61.0%	60.0%	60.0%	60.2%	60.1%	60.0%	60.0%	60.0%	60.0%	60.0%	60.0%
SG&A (% sales)	19.1%	19.0%	19.0%	18.5%	18.8%	19.2%	19.0%	19.0%	19.0%	19.0%	19.0%	19.0%
Other Expense / (Income) (% of sales)	- %	- %	- %	- %	- %	- %	- %	- %	- %	- %	- %	- %
Depreciation & Amortization (% of sales)	4.5%	4.2%	4.5%	4.6%	4.4%	4.4%	4.5%	4.5%	4.5%	4.5%	4.5%	4.5%
Amortization (% of sales)	1.5%	1.5%	1.5%	1.4%	1.4%	1.5%	1.5%	1.5%	1.5%	1.5%	1.5%	1.5%
Interest Income							0.6%	0.5%	0.5%	0.5%	0.5%	0.5%
Tax Rate						38.0%	38.0%	38.0%	38.0%	38.0%	38.0%	38.0%

EXHIBIT 7.44 ValueCo Standalone Balance Sheet

($ in millions, fiscal year ending December 31)

ValueCo Standalone Balance Sheet

		Projection Period				
	2012	Year 1 2013	Year 2 2014	Year 3 2015	Year 4 2016	Year 5 2017
Cash and Cash Equivalents	$250.0	$250.0	$250.0	$280.4	$690.2	$1,121.9
Accounts Receivable	450.0	483.8	512.8	538.4	560.0	576.7
Inventories	600.0	645.0	683.7	717.9	746.6	769.0
Prepaids and Other Current Assets	175.0	188.1	199.4	209.4	217.8	224.3
Total Current Assets	**$1,475.0**	**$1,566.9**	**$1,645.9**	**$1,746.1**	**$2,214.5**	**$2,691.9**
Property, Plant and Equipment, net	2,500.0	2,500.0	2,500.0	2,500.0	2,500.0	2,500.0
Goodwill	1,000.0	1,000.0	1,000.0	1,000.0	1,000.0	1,000.0
Intangible Assets	875.0	819.4	760.4	698.5	634.1	567.8
Other Assets	150.0	150.0	150.0	150.0	150.0	150.0
Deferred Financing Fees	-	-	-	-	-	-
Total Assets	**$6,000.0**	**$6,036.2**	**$6,056.3**	**$6,094.6**	**$6,498.6**	**$6,909.7**
Accounts Payable	215.0	231.1	245.0	257.2	267.5	275.6
Accrued Liabilities	275.0	295.6	313.4	329.0	342.2	352.5
Other Current Liabilities	100.0	107.5	114.0	119.6	124.4	128.2
Total Current Liabilities	**$590.0**	**$634.3**	**$672.3**	**$705.9**	**$734.2**	**$756.2**
Revolving Credit Facility	-	-	-	-	-	-
Term Loan A						
Term Loan B	1,000.0	695.0	350.2	-	-	-
Term Loan C						
Existing Term Loan						
2nd Lien						
Senior Notes	500.0	500.0	500.0	500.0	500.0	500.0
Senior Subordinated Notes	-	-	-	-	-	-
Other Debt						
Deferred Income Taxes	300.0	300.0	300.0	300.0	300.0	300.0
Other Long-Term Liabilities	110.0	110.0	110.0	110.0	110.0	110.0
Total Liabilities	**$2,500.0**	**$2,239.2**	**$1,932.5**	**$1,615.9**	**$1,644.2**	**$1,666.2**
Noncontrolling Interest	-	-	-	-	-	-
Shareholders' Equity	3,500.0	3,797.0	4,123.8	4,478.7	4,854.4	5,243.5
Total Shareholders' Equity	**$3,500.0**	**$3,797.0**	**$4,123.8**	**$4,478.7**	**$4,854.4**	**$5,243.5**
Total Liabilities and Equity	**$6,000.0**	**$6,036.2**	**$6,056.3**	**$6,094.6**	**$6,498.6**	**$6,909.7**
Balance Check	0.000	0.000	0.000	0.000	0.000	0.000
Net Working Capital	635.0	682.6	723.6	759.8	790.2	813.9
(Increase) / Decrease in Net Working Capital		(47.6)	(41.0)	(36.2)	(30.4)	(23.7)

Balance Sheet Assumptions

Current Assets

Days Sales Outstanding (DSO)	47.6	47.6	47.6	47.6	47.6	47.6
Days Inventory Held (DIH)	105.8	105.8	105.8	105.8	105.8	105.8
Prepaid and Other Current Assets (% of sales)	5.1%	5.1%	5.1%	5.1%	5.1%	5.1%

Current Liabilities

Days Payable Outstanding (DPO)	37.9	37.9	37.9	37.9	37.9	37.9
Accrued Liabilities (% of sales)	8.0%	8.0%	8.0%	8.0%	8.0%	8.0%
Other Current Liabilities (% of sales)	2.9%	2.9%	2.9%	2.9%	2.9%	2.9%

EXHIBIT 7.45 ValueCo Standalone Cash Flow Statement

($ in millions, fiscal year ending December 31)

ValueCo Standalone Cash Flow Statement

	Year 1 2013	Year 2 2014	Year 3 2015	Year 4 2016	Year 5 2017
Operating Activities					
Net Income	$297.0	$326.8	$354.8	$375.8	$389.1
Plus: Depreciation & Amortization	166.9	176.9	185.8	193.2	199.0
Plus: Amortization	55.6	59.0	61.9	64.4	66.3
Changes in Working Capital Items					
(Inc.) / Dec. in Accounts Receivable	(33.8)	(29.0)	(25.6)	(21.5)	(16.8)
(Inc.) / Dec. in Inventories	(45.0)	(38.7)	(34.2)	(28.7)	(22.4)
(Inc.) / Dec. in Prepaid and Other Current Assets	(13.1)	(11.3)	(10.0)	(8.4)	(6.5)
Inc. / (Dec.) in Accounts Payable	16.1	13.9	12.2	10.3	8.0
Inc. / (Dec.) in Accrued Liabilities	20.6	17.7	15.7	13.2	10.3
Inc. / (Dec.) in Other Current Liabilities	7.5	6.5	5.7	4.8	3.7
(Inc.) / Dec. in Net Working Capital	(47.6)	(41.0)	(36.2)	(30.4)	(23.7)
Cash Flow from Operating Activities	**$471.9**	**$521.7**	**$566.3**	**$603.0**	**$630.7**
Investing Activities					
Capital Expenditures	(166.9)	176.9)	(185.8)	(193.2)	(199.0)
Other Investing Activities	-	-	-	-	-
Cash Flow from Investing Activities	**($166.9)**	**($176.9)**	**($185.8)**	**($193.2)**	**($199.0)**
Financing Activities					
Revolving Credit Facility	-	-	-	-	-
Term Loan A	-	-	-	-	-
Term Loan B	(305.0)	(344.8)	(350.2)	-	-
Term Loan C	-	-	-	-	-
Existing Term Loan	-	-	-	-	-
2nd Lien	-	-	-	-	-
Senior Notes	-	-	-	-	-
Senior Subordinated Notes	-	-	-	-	-
Other Debt	-	-	-	-	-
Dividends	-	-	-	-	-
Equity Issuance / (Repurchase)	-	-	-	-	-
Cash Flow from Financing Activities	**($305.0)**	**($344.8)**	**($350.2)**	**-**	**-**
Excess Cash for the Period	-	-	$30.4	$409.8	$431.7
Beginning Cash Balance	250.0	250.0	250.0	280.4	690.2
Ending Cash Balance	**$250.0**	**$250.0**	**$280.4**	**$690.2**	**$1,121.9**
Cash Flow Statement Assumptions					
Capital Expenditures (% of sales)	4.5%	4.5%	4.5%	4.5%	4.5%

EXHIBIT 7.46 ValueCo Standalone Debt Schedule

($ in millions, fiscal year ending December 31)

ValueCo Standalone Debt Schedule

	Pro forma 2012	Year 1 2013	Year 2 2014	Year 3 2015	Year 4 2016	Year 5 2017
				Projection Period		
Forward LIBOR Curve	0.25%	0.35%	0.50%	0.75%	1.00%	1.25%
Cash Flow from Operating Activities		$471.9	$521.7	$566.3	$603.0	$630.7
Cash Flow from Investing Activities		(166.9)	(176.9)	(185.8)	(193.2)	(199.0)
Cash Available for Debt Repayment		**$305.0**	**$344.8**	**$380.6**	**$409.8**	**$431.7**
Total Mandatory Repayments	MinCash	(10.0)	(10.0)	(10.0)	-	-
Cash From Balance Sheet	250.0	-	-	-	30.4	440.2
Cash Available for Optional Debt Repayment		**$295.0**	**$334.8**	**$370.6**	**$440.2**	**$871.9**

Revolving Credit Facility

Revolving Credit Facility Size	$150.0					
Spread	3.250%					
LIBOR Floor	1.000%					
Term	6 years					
Commitment Fee on Unused Portion	0.50%					
Beginning Balance		-	-	-	-	-
Drawdown/(Repayment)		-	-	-	-	-
Ending Balance		**-**	**-**	**-**	**-**	**-**
Interest Rate		4.25%	4.25%	4.25%	4.25%	4.50%
Interest Expense		-	-	-	-	-
Commitment Fee		0.8	0.8	0.8	0.8	0.8
Administrative Agent Fee		0.2	0.2	0.2	0.2	0.2

Term Loan B Facility

Size	$1,000.0					
Spread	3.500%					
LIBOR Floor	1.000%					
Term	7 years					
Repayment Schedule	1.0% Per Annum, Bullet at Maturity					
Beginning Balance		$1,000.0	$695.0	$350.2	-	-
Mandatory Repayments		(10.0)	(10.0)	(10.0)	-	-
Optional Repayments		(295.0)	(334.8)	(340.2)	-	-
Ending Balance		**$695.0**	**$350.2**	**-**	**-**	**-**
Interest Rate		4.50%	4.50%	4.50%	4.50%	4.75%
Interest Expense		38.1	23.5	7.9	-	-

Senior Notes

Size	$500.0					
Coupon	8.000%					
Term	8 years					
Beginning Balance		$500.0	$500.0	$500.0	$500.0	$500.0
Repayment		-	-	-	-	-
Ending Balance		**$500.0**	**$500.0**	**$500.0**	**$500.0**	**$500.0**
Interest Expense		40.0	40.0	40.0	40.0	40.0

EXHIBIT 7.47 ValueCo Standalone Assumptions Page 1

ValueCo Standalone Assumptions Page 1 - Income Statement and Cash Flow Statement

		Projection Period				
		Year 1 2013	Year 2 2014	Year 3 2015	Year 4 2016	Year 5 2017
Income Statement Assumptions						
Sales (% growth)		7.5%	6.0%	5.0%	4.0%	3.0%
Base	1	7.5%	6.0%	5.0%	4.0%	3.0%
Upside	2	10.0%	8.0%	6.0%	4.0%	3.0%
Management	3	12.0%	10.0%	8.0%	6.0%	4.0%
Downside 1	4	5.0%	4.0%	3.0%	3.0%	3.0%
Downside 2	5	2.0%	2.0%	2.0%	2.0%	2.0%
Cost of Goods Sold (% sales)		60.0%	60.0%	60.0%	60.0%	60.0%
Base	1	60.0%	60.0%	60.0%	60.0%	60.0%
Upside	2	60.0%	60.0%	60.0%	60.0%	60.0%
Management	3	59.0%	59.0%	59.0%	59.0%	59.0%
Downside 1	4	61.0%	61.0%	61.0%	61.0%	61.0%
Downside 2	5	62.0%	62.0%	62.0%	62.0%	62.0%
SG&A (% sales)		19.0%	19.0%	19.0%	19.0%	19.0%
Base	1	19.0%	19.0%	19.0%	19.0%	19.0%
Upside	2	18.0%	18.0%	18.0%	18.0%	18.0%
Management	3	18.0%	18.0%	18.0%	18.0%	18.0%
Downside 1	4	20.0%	20.0%	20.0%	20.0%	20.0%
Downside 2	5	21.0%	21.0%	21.0%	21.0%	21.0%
Depreciation (% sales)		4.5%	4.5%	4.5%	4.5%	4.5%
Base	1	4.5%	4.5%	4.5%	4.5%	4.5%
Upside	2	4.5%	4.5%	4.5%	4.5%	4.5%
Management	3	4.5%	4.5%	4.5%	4.5%	4.5%
Downside 1	4	4.5%	4.5%	4.5%	4.5%	4.5%
Downside 2	5	4.5%	4.5%	4.5%	4.5%	4.5%
Amortization (% sales)		1.5%	1.5%	1.5%	1.5%	1.5%
Base	1	1.5%	1.5%	1.5%	1.5%	1.5%
Upside	2	1.5%	1.5%	1.5%	1.5%	1.5%
Management	3	1.5%	1.5%	1.5%	1.5%	1.5%
Downside 1	4	1.5%	1.5%	1.5%	1.5%	1.5%
Downside 2	5	1.5%	1.5%	1.5%	1.5%	1.5%
Cash Flow Statement Assumptions						
Capital Expenditures (% sales)		4.5%	4.5%	4.5%	4.5%	4.5%
Base	1	4.5%	4.5%	4.5%	4.5%	4.5%
Upside	2	4.5%	4.5%	4.5%	4.5%	4.5%
Management	3	4.5%	4.5%	4.5%	4.5%	4.5%
Downside 1	4	5.0%	5.0%	5.0%	5.0%	5.0%
Downside 2	5	5.0%	5.0%	5.0%	5.0%	5.0%

EXHIBIT 7.48 ValueCo Standalone Assumptions Page 2

ValueCo Standalone Assumptions Page 2 - Balance Sheet

		Projection Period				
		Year 1 2013	Year 2 2014	Year 3 2015	Year 4 2016	Year 5 2017
Current Assets						
Days Sales Outstanding (DSO)		47.6	47.6	47.6	47.6	47.6
Base	1	47.6	47.6	47.6	47.6	47.6
Upside	2	47.6	47.6	47.6	47.6	47.6
Management	3	47.6	47.6	47.6	47.6	47.6
Downside 1	4	50.0	50.0	50.0	50.0	50.0
Downside 2	5	55.0	55.0	55.0	55.0	55.0
Days Inventory Held (DIH)		105.8	105.8	105.8	105.8	105.8
Base	1	105.8	105.8	105.8	105.8	105.8
Upside	2	105.8	105.8	105.8	105.8	105.8
Management	3	105.8	105.8	105.8	105.8	105.8
Downside 1	4	110.0	110.0	110.0	110.0	110.0
Downside 2	5	115.0	115.0	115.0	115.0	115.0
Prepaids and Other Current Assets (% sales)		5.1%	5.1%	5.1%	5.1%	5.1%
Base	1	5.1%	5.1%	5.1%	5.1%	5.1%
Upside	2	5.1%	5.1%	5.1%	5.1%	5.1%
Management	3	5.1%	5.1%	5.1%	5.1%	5.1%
Downside 1	4	5.1%	5.1%	5.1%	5.1%	5.1%
Downside 2	5	5.1%	5.1%	5.1%	5.1%	5.1%
Current Liabilities						
Days Payable Outstanding (DPO)		37.9	37.9	37.9	37.9	37.9
Base	1	37.9	37.9	37.9	37.9	37.9
Upside	2	37.9	37.9	37.9	37.9	37.9
Management	3	37.9	37.9	37.9	37.9	37.9
Downside 1	4	35.0	35.0	35.0	35.0	35.0
Downside 2	5	30.0	30.0	30.0	30.0	30.0
Accrued Liabilities (% sales)		8.0%	8.0%	8.0%	8.0%	8.0%
Base	1	8.0%	8.0%	8.0%	8.0%	8.0%
Upside	2	8.0%	8.0%	8.0%	8.0%	8.0%
Management	3	8.0%	8.0%	8.0%	8.0%	8.0%
Downside 1	4	8.0%	8.0%	8.0%	8.0%	8.0%
Downside 2	5	8.0%	8.0%	8.0%	8.0%	8.0%
Other Current Liabilities (% sales)		2.9%	2.9%	2.9%	2.9%	2.9%
Base	1	2.9%	2.9%	2.9%	2.9%	2.9%
Upside	2	2.9%	2.9%	2.9%	2.9%	2.9%
Management	3	2.9%	2.9%	2.9%	2.9%	2.9%
Downside 1	4	2.9%	2.9%	2.9%	2.9%	2.9%
Downside 2	5	2.9%	2.9%	2.9%	2.9%	2.9%

Bloomberg Appendix

APPENDIX 7.1 Bloomberg Supply Chain Analysis (SPLC<GO>)

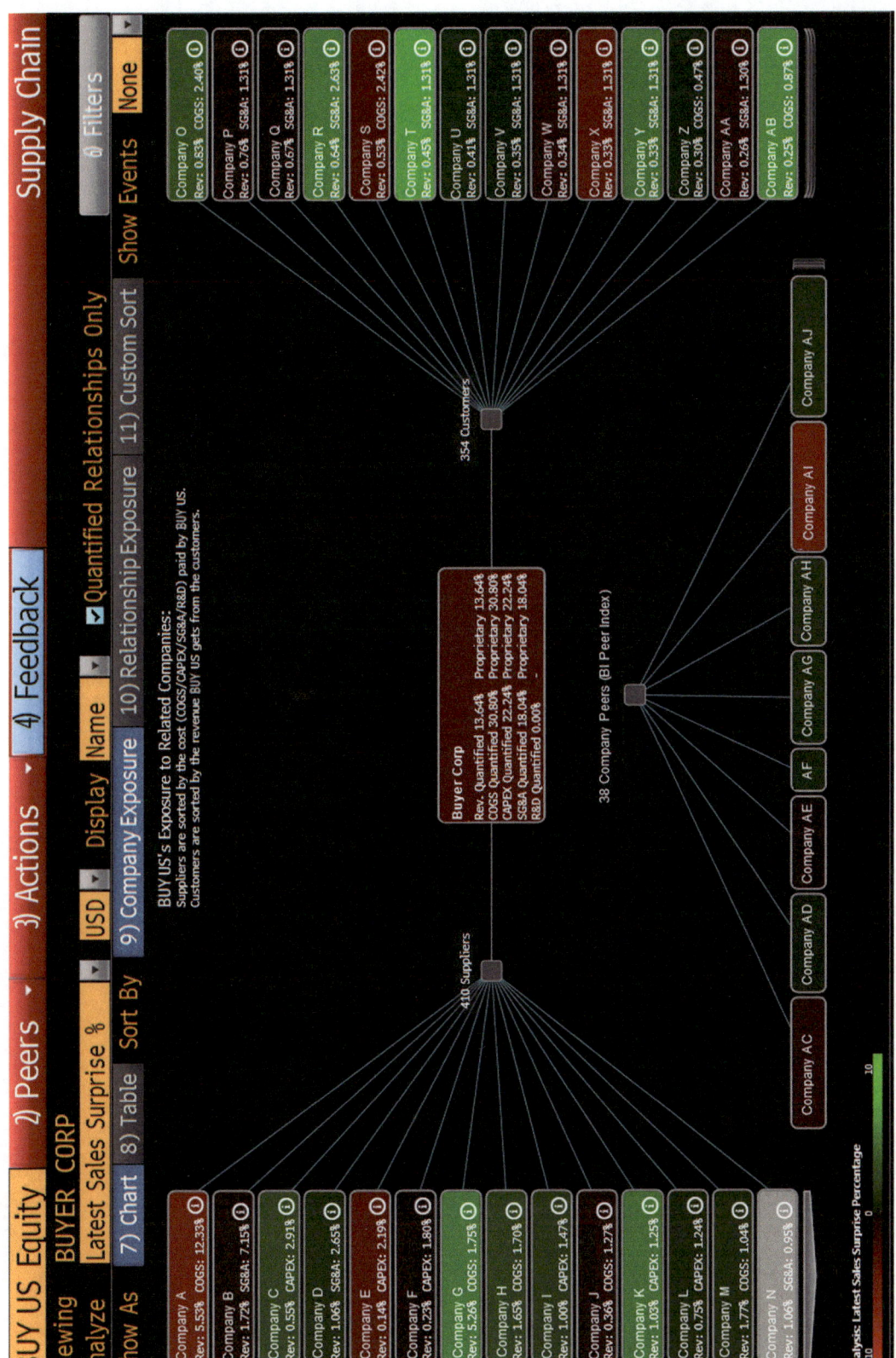

Afterword

Prior to co-founding Apollo Global Management, LLC, I began my Wall Street career at Drexel Burnham Lambert. It was there, as a member of their Mergers and Acquisitions team, that I honed my technical skills and financial knowledge while working long hours on many high profile deals. I know what it takes to master these skills and how critical they are to succeeding in the current market environment. Today, I look for these same abilities in the associates we recruit at Apollo. It gives me great confidence that many from the new generation of future financial leaders learned their corporate finance fundamentals with the help of Rosenbaum and Pearl and their best-selling book, *Investment Banking*.

I have personally been involved in the successful execution of hundreds of M&A and LBO transactions over the past 25 years and I recommend this book to advisors, financiers, practitioners, and anyone else interested in investment transactions. Rosenbaum and Pearl have created a comprehensive, yet highly accessible, written guide to the core skills of the successful investment professional, with a particular emphasis on valuation analysis.

We live in an uncertain and volatile world where market conditions, credit availability, and deal structure can change quickly with little or no warning. With numerous unknowns and potential challenges at every turn, we are grounded by what we can control—namely, solid fundamental analysis, financial discipline, rigorous due diligence, and sound judgment. At Apollo, these variables are key cornerstones for valuing companies, creating long-term equity value and delivering industry-leading returns for our investors. Therefore, I support Rosenbaum and Pearl's book, *Investment Banking*, and its work on the fundamentals of valuation and transaction-related finance.

JOSHUA HARRIS
Co-Founder and Managing Partner
Apollo Global Management, LLC

Bibliography and Recommended Reading

Almeida, Heitor, and Thomas Philippon. "The Risk-Adjusted Cost of Financial Distress." *Journal of Finance* 62 (2007): 2557–2586.

Alti, Aydogan. "How Persistent Is the Impact of Market Timing on Capital Structure?" *Journal of Finance* 61 (2006): 1681–1710.

Altman, Edward I., ed. *The High-Yield Debt Market: Investment Performance and Economic Impact*. New York: Beard Books, 1998.

Andrade, Gregor, and Steven Kaplan. "How Costly is Financial (Not Economic) Distress? Evidence from Highly Leveraged Transactions that Became Distressed." *Journal of Finance* 53 (1998): 1443–1493.

Baginski, Stephen P., and John M. Hassell. *Management Decisions and Financial Accounting Reports*. 2nd ed. Mason, OH: South-Western College Publishing, 2004.

Bahnson, Paul R., Brian P. McAllister, and Paul B.W. Miller. "Noncontrolling In-terest: Much More Than a Name Change." *Journal of Accountancy* (2008).

Baker, Malcolm, and Jeffrey Wurgler. "Market Timing and Capital Structure." *Journal of Finance* 57 (2002): 1–32.

Barnhill, Theodore, Jr., Mark Shenkman, and William Maxwell. *High Yield Bonds: Market Structure, Valuation, and Portfolio Strategies*. New York: McGraw-Hill, 1999.

Barr, Alistair. "Big Leveraged Buyouts Won't Return for Year or More: Lee Equity." *MarketWatch*, April 8, 2008.

Bierman, Harold, Jr. *Private Equity: Transforming Public Stock Into Private Equity to Create Value*. Hoboken, NJ: John Wiley & Sons, 2003.

Boot, Arnoud W. A., Radhakrishnan Goplan, and Anjan V. Thakor. "Market Liquidity, Investor Participation, and Managerial Autonomy: Why Do Firms Go Private?" *Journal of Finance* 63 (2008): 2013–2059.

Bruner, Robert F. *Applied Mergers and Acquisitions*. Hoboken, NJ: John Wiley & Sons, 2004.

Calamos, John P. *Convertible Securities: The Latest Instruments, Portfolio Strategies, and Valuation Analysis*. Rev. ed. New York: McGraw-Hill, 1998.

Carey, Dennis, Robert J. Aiello, Michael D. Watkins, Robert G. Eccles, and Alfred Rappaport. *Harvard Business Review on Mergers & Acquisitions*. Boston: Harvard Business School Press, 2001.

Carney, William J. *Corporate Finance: Principles and Practice.* New York: Foundation Press, 2004.

Carney, William J. *Mergers and Acquisitions: Case and Materials.* New York: Foundation Press, 2000.

Chava, Sudheer, and Michael R. Roberts. "How Does Financing Impact Investment? The Role of Debt Covenants." *Journal of Finance* 63 (2008): 2085–2121.

Chisholm, Andrew. *An Introduction to Capital Markets: Products, Strategies, Participants.* West Sussex, UK: John Wiley & Sons, 2002.

Clements, Philip J., and Philip W. Wisler. *The Standard & Poor's Guide to Fairness Opinions.* New York: McGraw-Hill, 2005.

Copeland, Tom, Tim Koller, Marc Goedhart, and David Wessels. *Valuation: Measuring and Managing the Value of Companies.* 4th ed. Hoboken, NJ: John Wiley & Sons, 2005.

Damodaran, Aswath. *Damodaran on Valuation: Security Analysis for Investment and Corporate Finance.* 2nd ed. Hoboken, NJ: John Wiley & Sons, 2006.

Damodaran, Aswath. *Investment Valuation: Tools and Techniques for Determining the Value of Any Asset.* 2nd ed. New York: John Wiley & Sons, 2002.

Datta, Sudip, Mai Iskandar-Datta, and Kartik Raman. "Managerial Stock Ownership and the Maturity Structure of Corporate Debt." *Journal of Finance* 60 (2005): 2333–2350.

Downes, John, and Jordan Elliot Goodman. *Dictionary of Finance and Investment Terms.* 7th ed. Hauppauge, NY: Barron's Educational Series, 2006.

Ergungor, O. Emre. "Dividends." Federal Reserve Bank of Cleveland, Economic Commentary. 2004.

Evans, Frank C., and David M. Bishop. *Valuation for M&A: Building Value in Private Companies.* New York: John Wiley & Sons, 2001.

Fabozzi, Frank J. *The Handbook of Fixed Income Securities.* 6th ed. New York: McGraw-Hill, 2000.

Fama, Eugene F., and Kenneth R. French. "The Value Premium and the CAPM." *Journal of Finance* 61 (2006): 2163–2185.

Fang, Lily Hua. "Investment Bank Reputation and the Price and Quality of Underwriting Services." *Journal of Finance* 60 (2005): 2729–2761.

Feldman, Stanley J. *Principles of Private Firm Valuation.* Hoboken, NJ: John Wiley & Sons, 2005.

Ferguson, Joy. "LBOs Sponsor-to-Sponsor Deals Raise Eyebrows." *High Yield Report*, August 9, 2004.

Frankel, Michael E. S. *Mergers and Acquisitions Basics: The Key Steps of Acquisitions, Divestitures, and Investments.* Hoboken, NJ: John Wiley & Sons, 2005.

Gaughan, Patrick A. *Mergers, Acquisitions, and Corporate Restructurings.* 4th ed. Hoboken, NJ: John Wiley & Sons, 2007.

Gaughan, Patrick A. *Mergers: What Can Go Wrong and How to Prevent It.* Hoboken, NJ: John Wiley & Sons, 2005.

Gilson, Stuart. "Transactions Costs and Capital Structure Choice: Evidence from Financially Distressed Firms." *Journal of Finance* 52 (1997): 161–196.

Goetzmann, William N., and Roger G. Ibbotson. *The Equity Risk Premium: Essays and Explorations*. New York: Oxford University Press, 2006.

Graham, John R. "How Big Are the Tax Benefits of Debt?" *Journal of Finance* 55 (2000): 1901–1941.

Greenwald, Bruce C. N., Judd Kahn, Paul D. Sonkin, and Michael van Biema. *Value Investing: From Graham to Buffett and Beyond*. Hoboken, NJ: John Wiley & Sons, 2004.

Grinblatt, Mark, and Sheridan Titman. *Financial Markets and Corporate Strategy*. New York: McGraw-Hill, 2008.

Gu, Zhaoyang, and Ting Chen. "Analysts' Treatment of Nonrecurring Items in Street Earnings." Carnegie Mellon University (2004): 1–52.

Haas, Jeffrey J. *Corporate Finance in a Nutshell*. St. Paul, MN: Thomson West, 2003.

Hennessy, Christopher A., and Toni M. Whited. "Debt Dynamics." *Journal of Finance* 60 (2005): 1129–1165.

Hooke, Jeffrey C. *M&A: A Practical Guide to Doing the Deal*. New York: John Wiley & Sons, 1996.

Ibbotson, Roger G., and Rex Sinquefield. *Ibbotson SBBI 2008 Valuation Yearbook*. Chicago: Morningstar, 2007.

Kaback, Hoffer. "Behind the Art of M&A with Bruce Wasserstein." *Directors & Boards*, Spring 1999.

Kaplan, Steven N., and Antoinette Schoar. "Private Equity Performance: Returns, Persistence, and Capital Flows." *Journal of Finance* 60 (2005): 1791–1823.

Kieso, Donald E., Jerry J. Weygandt, and Terry D. Warfield. *Intermediate Accounting*. 12th ed. Hoboken, NJ: John Wiley & Sons, 2007.

Kisgen, Darren J. "Credit Ratings and Capital Structure." *Journal of Finance* 61 (2006): 1035–1072.

Koons, Cynthia. "Strong Loan Market Allowing Riskier Debt." *MarketWatch*, February 14, 2007.

Lajoux, Alexandra Reed. *The Art of M&A Integration: A Guide to Merging Resources, Processes, and Responsibilities*. 2nd ed. New York: McGraw-Hill, 2005.

Lajoux, Alexandra Reed, and Charles M. Elson. *The Art of M&A: Financing and Refinancing*. New York: McGraw-Hill, 1999.

Lajoux, Alexandra Reed, and H. Peter Nesvold. *The Art of M&A Structuring: Techniques for Mitigating Financial, Tax, and Legal Risk*. New York: McGraw-Hill, 2004.

Lajoux, Alexandra Reed, and J. Fred Weston. *The Art of M&A Due Diligence*. New York: McGraw-Hill, 2000.

Latham & Watkins. *The Book of Jargon*. New York: June 2008.

Leary, Mark T., and Michael R. Roberts. "Do Firms Rebalance Their Capital Structure?" *Journal of Finance* 60 (2005): 2575–2619.

Leland, Hayne E. "Corporate Debt Value, Bond Covenants, and Optimal Capital Structure." *Journal of Finance* 49 (1994): 1213–1252.

Leland, Hayne E. "Financial Synergies and the Optimal Scope of the Firm: Implications for Mergers, Spinoffs, and Structured Finance." *Journal of Finance* 62 (2007): 765–808.

Lerner, Josh, Felda Hardymon, and Ann Leamon. *Venture Capital and Private Equity: A Casebook*. Hoboken, NJ: John Wiley & Sons, 2007.

Liaw, K. Thomas. *The Business of Investment Banking: A Comprehensive Overview*. Hoboken, NJ: John Wiley & Sons, 2005.

Liaw, K. Thomas. *Capital Markets*. Mason, OH: Thomson South-Western, 2003.

Luo, Yuanzhi. "Do Insiders Learn from Outsiders? Evidence from Mergers and Acquisitions." *Journal of Finance* 60 (2005): 1951–1982.

Marren, Joseph H. *Mergers & Acquisitions: A Valuation Handbook*. New York: McGraw-Hill, 1992.

Metrick, Andrew, and Ayako Yasuda. "The Economics of Private Equity Funds.," (Working paper, Yale University). February 22, 2007.

Miller, Hazel (Orrick, Herrington & Sutcliffe LLP). "2005: Another Strong Year for the Financing of LBOs." *Financier Worldwide*, February 2006.

Mitchell, Mark, Todd Pulvino, and Erik Stafford. "Price Pressure around Mergers." *Journal of Finance* 60 (2004): 31–63.

McCafferty, Joseph. "The Buyout Binge." *CFO Magazine*, April 1, 2007.

Oesterle, Dale A. *Mergers and Acquisitions in a Nutshell*. St. Paul, MN: Thomson West, 2006.

Pereiro, Luis E. *Valuation of Companies in Emerging Markets*. New York: John Wiley & Sons, 2002.

Pratt, Shannon P. *Business Valuation Discounts and Premiums*. New York: John Wiley & Sons, 2001.

Pratt, Shannon P., and Roger J. Grabowski. *Cost of Capital: Estimation and Applications*. 3rd ed. Hoboken, NJ: John Wiley & Sons, 2008.

Rajan, Arvind, Glen McDermott, and Ratul Roy. *The Structured Credit Handbook*. Hoboken, NJ: John Wiley & Sons, 2007.

Reed, Stanley Foster, Alexandra Lajoux, and H. Peter Nesvold. *The Art of M&A: A Merger Acquisition Buyout Guide*. 4th ed. New York: McGraw-Hill, 2007.

Rickertsen, Rick, and Robert E. Gunther. *Buyout: The Insider's Guide to Buying Your Own Company*. New York: AMACOM, 2001.

Rhodes-Kropf, Matthew, and S. Viswanathan. "Market Valuation and Merger Waves." *Journal of Finance* 59 (2004): 2685–2718.

Rosenbloom, Arthur H., ed. *Due Diligence for Global Deal Making: The Definitive Guide to Cross-Border Mergers and Acquisitions (M&A), Joint Ventures, Financings, and Strategic Alliances*. Princeton: Bloomberg Press, 2002.

Rubino, Robert, and Timothy Shoyer. "Why Today's Borrowers & Investors Lean Toward Second Liens." *Bank Loan Report*, March 8, 2004.

Ross, Stephen A., Randolph W. Westerfield, and Jeffrey Jaffe. *Corporate Finance*. 6th ed. New York: McGraw-Hill, 2002.

Salter, Malcolm S., and Joshua N. Rosenbaum. *OAO Yukos Oil Company*. Boston: Harvard Business School Publishing, 2001.

Schneider, Arnold. *Managerial Accounting: Manufacturing and Service Applications*. 5th ed. Mason, OH: Cengage Learning, 2009.

Schwert, G. William. "Hostility in Takeovers: In the Eyes of the Beholder?" *Journal of Finance* 55 (2000): 2599–2640.

Scott, David L. *Wall Street Words: An A to Z Guide to Investment Terms for Today's Investor*. 3rd ed. Boston: Houghton Mifflin, 2003.

Siegel, Jeremy J. *Stocks for the Long Run*. 4th ed. New York: McGraw-Hill, 2007.

Sherman, Andrew J., and Milledge A. Hart. *Mergers & Acquisitions From A to Z*. 2nd ed. New York: AMACOM, 2006.

Slee, Robert T. "Business Owners Choose a Transfer Value." *Journal of Financial Planning* 17, no. 6 (2004): 86–91.

Slee, Robert T. *Private Capital Markets: Valuation, Capitalization, and Transfer of Private Business Interests*. Hoboken, NJ: John Wiley & Sons, 2004.

Standard and Poor's/Leveraged Commentary & Data. *A Guide to the Loan Market*. October 2007.

Standard and Poor's/Leveraged Commentary & Data. *High Yield Bond Market Primer*. 2007.

Strebulaev, Ilya A. "Do Tests of Capital Structure Theory Mean What They Say?" *Journal of Finance* 62 (2007): 1747–1787.

Thompson, Samuel C., Jr. *Business Planning for Mergers and Acquisitions: Corporate, Securities, Tax, Antitrust, International, and Related Aspects*. 3rd ed. Durham, NC: Carolina Academic Press, 2007.

Wasserstein, Bruce. *Big Deal: Mergers and Acquisitions in the Digital Age*. New York: Warner Books, 2001.

White, Gerald I., Ashwinpaul C. Sondhi, and Dov Fried. *The Analysis and Use of Financial Statements*. 3rd ed. New York: John Wiley & Sons, 2002.

Yago, Glenn, and Susanne Trimbath. *Beyond Junk Bonds: Expanding High Yield Markets*. New York: Oxford University Press, 2003.

Yasuda, Ayako. "Do Bank Relationships Affect the Firm's Underwriter Choice in the Corporate-Bond Underwriting Market?" *Journal of Finance* 60 (2005): 1259–1292.

Index

A

ability to pay, 83, 203, 297, 301–302, 332, 340
ABL facility. *See* asset based lending facility
accelerated depreciation, 136
accountants, 188, 309, 314
accounting, 13, 27, 34–35, 44, 47, 188, 235, 254–255, 314, 334, 341, 343, 348
accounts payable, 134, 137–138, 140, 338
accounts receivable, 137–139, 195, 207–209, 217
accretion/(dilution) analysis, 301, 312, 355, 365–366, 368, 370–372
accretive, 360, 365–366, 368, 370–372
accrued liabilities, 137–138, 140, 161
acquisition currency, 88, 339
acquisition-driven growth, 21
acquisition financing, 88–90, 93, 338
adjusted income statement, 46, 64, 68, 116–117
adjustments
   balance sheet, 242, 250–255, 268, 357–362
   capital expenditures, 245
   capital structure changes, 35–36
   management projections, 132, 239, 241
   mid-year convention, 169
   non-recurring items, 24–25, 44–46, 64–65, 92, 115–117, 131, 245, 366
   purchase price and financing structure, 238, 279
   recent events, 25, 46, 92, 131
   synergies, 92, 104–105
   year-end discounting, 170
administrative agent, 255
administrative agent fee, 255, 259, 265
advisor, 87, 90, 92, 188, 235, 238, 278, 295–296, 299–302, 304–306, 308–313, 315–316, 320–321, 325–326
affiliate, 91, 222
affirmative covenants, 221, 318
all-cash transaction, 89, 98, 113
amortization
   acquisition-related, 37, 48
   intangible assets, of, 135–136
   deferred financing fees, of, 244, 254, 265
   term loan, 209–210, 259, 261, 270
   schedule, for term loans, 209–210, 259. *See also* depreciation & amortization (D&A)
amortizing term loans, 209–210. *See also* term loan A
analysis at various prices (AVP), 349, 352
announcement
   earnings, 23, 25–26, 42, 44, 57
   transaction, 46, 85, 92, 95, 99, 100–104, 109, 110–111, 113, 118, 321, 333
annual report. *See* Form 10-K
antitrust, 302, 318, 322–323
arranger, 186, 189–190, 213, 256
asset base, 39, 137, 185, 192, 195
asset based lending (ABL) facility, 207–209
asset sale,
   gains on, 44, 64–65, 116
   limitations on, 223
   losses on, 44
   term loan prepayment, 259
   transaction, 253, 317, 319

attorneys, 314
AVP, *See* analysis at various prices
auction, 88–89, 106, 108, 188, 295–324. *See also* broad auction and targeted auction

B

back-end short form merger, 323
balance sheet, 24–25, 27, 35, 46, 62
  in LBO analysis, 238, 242–245, 251–255, 268–269, 283
bank book, 190–191
bank debt, 185, 189–191, 204, 216, 219, 231, 262–263, 270, 272
bank lenders, 190, 210, 218
bank meeting, 190
bankruptcy, 35, 185, 195, 208–210, 217–218
barriers to entry, 193, 195
Base Case, 4, 132, 157–159, 161, 175, 241, 272, 274
Base Rate, 207–208, 219
basic shares outstanding, 24–25, 27, 30–33, 56, 59–61, 114, 154
basket, 222–223
benchmarking analysis
  comparable companies analysis, 13, 15, 21–22, 25, 28, 43, 50–51, 57, 65, 69–75
  precedent transactions analysis, 85, 96, 106, 119
benchmark rate. *See* LIBOR and Base Rate
Berkshire Hathaway, 337
beta (β), 144–148, 165–166
  relevering, 147, 166
  unlevering, 146–147, 165
bidders. *See* prospective buyers
bidding strategy, 236
Bloomberg, 15–18, 23–27, 49, 75–81, 84, 87, 93, 122–124, 131, 143, 145–146, 148, 176–181, 192, 232–233, 257, 290–291, 302, 327–329, 336, 394–395
board approval, 300, 315, 320–321
board of directors, 91, 94, 110, 192, 299, 305, 320–321, 325–326
bond investors, 191

book value
  assets, 135–136
  equity, 251, 253–254, 341–342, 358–359
bookrunners, 189
borrower, 21, 185, 204, 207–231, 259, 262
borrowing base, 207, 209
breakage costs, 35
breakeven pre-tax synergies, 368
breakup fee, 317–318
bridge loans, 189, 212–213, 255
bring-down provision, 317–319
broad auction, 295–296, 298–299, 302
  advantages and disadvantages, 298
business disruption, 35, 295, 298–299, 326
business profile, 18–20, 22, 106
buy-side advisory, 132, 186, 188, 236, 278, 307, 331–393

C

C Corp, 340–341, 345–346
CA. *See* confidentiality agreement
CAGR. *See* compound annual growth rate
calendarization of financial data, 15, 28, 43–44, 53
calendar year, 23, 43, 47, 152
call date, 143, 220
call premium, 220
call price, 143, 220
call protection, 217, 220–221, 263
call schedule, 143, 220
callable bond, 143
capex. *See* capital expenditures
capital asset pricing model (CAPM), 144–148, 165–166
capital expenditures (capex), 24, 27, 48, 65, 117, 125, 127, 156, 208, 241, 245, 247. *See also* growth capex and maintenance capex
  in coverage ratios, 41, 67, 272
  in free cash flow, 131, 133, 135–137, 157, 160–161
  in leverage ratios, 40

Index

limitations on, 221–222, 317
low requirements, for LBOs, 192, 194–195
projection of, 137, 161
capital markets, 41, 186, 337
  conditions, 20, 88, 107–108, 186, 189, 297, 302
  transactions, 25–26, 57, 324
capital structure, 13, 35–38, 47, 127, 131, 156, 164, 185
  effects of changes in, 36
  LBO financing, 185–186, 188, 193, 195, 199–200, 203–204, 210–211, 213, 227, 239, 256, 265, 272, 278, 307. *See also* financing structure
  optimal capital structure, 142–143
  target capital structure, for WACC, 141–144, 146–147, 164–167
capitalization, 141–142, 164, 272, 279
capitalization ratio, 40–41, 66–67, 142, 164, 272
CAPM. *See* capital asset pricing model
caps, 189, 213
cash and stock transaction, 98, 101
cash available for debt repayment, 127, 185, 194, 199–200, 256–257, 262, 265
cash flow generation, 48, 54, 143, 185, 190, 192–195, 197–198, 199–200, 235, 262
cash flow statement 25, 27, 36–37, 44, 65, 117, 135, 137
  in LBO analysis, 238, 244–247, 255–257, 265–266, 270, 284
cash flow sweep, 238, 262, 270
cash interest expense, 265
cash on hand, 139–140
  funding source, 250, 252, 324, 357, 362
cash return, 197–201, 275
CDO. *See* collateralized debt obligation funds
certainty of closing/completion, 89, 189, 295, 326, 337, 339
change of control, 96, 223, 322, 353

closest comparables, 14–15, 50–51, 56, 69, 165
closing, of transaction, 99, 113, 189, 191, 212–213, 250, 257, 299–300, 307, 317, 319, 321-324
closing conditions, 316, 318–319, 321, 324
club deal, 214
clubbing, 305
COGS. *See* cost of goods sold
collar, 99
collateral, 195, 204, 209–210, 213, 217–219, 221–222
collateral coverage, 190, 217
collateralized debt obligation (CDO) funds, 190, 205, 211
commitment fee, 208, 213, 259, 265
commitment letter, 186, 189, 212, 241
commodity, 20, 133, 208–209
common stock, 30, 32, 204, 213, 217, 339
comparable companies analysis, 13–81, 83–85, 87, 96, 102, 106–107, 121, 125, 128, 132, 142, 149, 152, 155–157, 165, 169, 175, 278, 297, 301, 321.
  key pros and cons, 54
Competition Bureau, 322
competitors, 14, 18, 22, 55, 126, 130, 147, 298, 304, 326, 334
compound annual growth rate (CAGR), 38, 68, 157
confidential information memorandum (CIM), 55, 126, 130, 190, 238–239, 242, 245, 300, 302–308, 312
  sample, 304
confidentiality agreement (CA), 102, 299–300, 305–306, 325
  provisions, 305
conglomeration, 335–337
consensus estimates, 23, 26, 39, 46, 51, 56–57, 67–68, 132–134, 136, 157, 159–160.

consultants, 188, 193–194, 307, 313–314
contact log, 306
contractual subordination, 218
contribution analysis, 349, 353
control premium, 83, 89, 350
conversion price, 32–34
convertible securities, 30–34, 46, 60
corporate finance, 186
corporate website, 17–18, 24, 26, 57, 93, 111
cost of capital 127, 145, 202–204, 207, 211, 213, 219–220, 257, 278, 297, 302. *See also* weighted average cost of capital (WACC)
cost of debt, 34, 141–144, 164, 167, 200, 339, 365
cost of equity, 141–148, 165–167. *See also* capital asset pricing model (CAPM)
cost of good sold (COGS), 36–37, 135, 138–140
  non-recurring items in , 64–65
  projection of, 133–134, 159
cost structure, 20, 193
coupon, 32–33, 143–144, 210–213, 217, 219–220, 256–257, 259, 262–263, 337–338
covenant-lite loans, 221
covenants, 190–191, 203, 207–208, 211, 217, 220–223, 241, 337, 339–340
  incurrence, 211, 221, 223
  in definitive agreements, 316–318
  maintenance, 204, 209, 212, 221–223
coverage ratios. *See* interest coverage
credit agreement, 207–209, 211, 221–223, 259
credit committee, 189, 235, 241, 311
credit crunch, 88–89, 107, 125, 257
credit markets, 89, 185
credit profile, 18, 21–22, 28, 40–41, 143, 190, 204, 209, 221–222, 227, 337, 360, 363

credit ratings, 26–28, 41–42, 57, 143–144, 207, 339–340, 362
  ratings scales, 42
credit statistics, 65–67, 143, 190, 235, 272, 274, 279, 332, 337, 355, 360, 362–363
cultural fit, 295, 302
current assets, 137–140, 161, 208, 242
current liabilities, 137–140, 161, 242
current report. *See* Form 8-K
current stub, 42, 65
current yield, 143, 164
customers, 18–20, 24, 55, 126, 130, 157, 194, 298, 304, 326, 335–336
cyclical sectors, 18, 131, 133, 149, 202, 227
cyclicality, 106–108, 127, 134, 143, 148, 245

D

D&A. *See* depreciation & amortization
data room, 55, 238, 296, 300, 306, 309–310, 313– 315, 325
  general index, 310
days inventory held (DIH), 139, 157, 161
days payable outstanding (DPO), 140, 157, 161
days sales outstanding (DSO), 139–140, 157, 161
DCF. *See* discounted cash flow analysis
D/E. *See* debt-to-equity
deal dynamics, 84, 88–89, 92, 106, 108, 119
deal terms, 22, 92, 95, 321, 325–326, 331
deal toys, 324
debt capital markets, 143, 186, 235
debt repayment, 193, 197–200, 235, 242, 256, 274, 297
debt schedule, 239, 242, 245, 256–264, 270, 285
debt securities, 17, 84, 90–91, 93, 130, 211

Index

debt-to-EBITDA, 40–41, 66, 222–223, 272
debt-to-equity (D/E), 146–147, 164–167
debt-to-total capitalization, 40–41, 66–67, 142, 164, 272
DEF14A. *See* proxy statement
default, 42, 143, 208, 217, 221
deferred financing fees, 244, 254–255, 265
deferred tax liability (DTL), 341–342, 358, 360
definitive agreement, 90, 92, 95, 99, 109, 119, 212, 299–300, 311, 313–316, 319–324
   key sections, 317–319
DEFM14A. *See* merger proxy
Delaware, 299
Department of Justice (DOJ), 322
depreciation, 135–136, 245, 247
depreciation & amortization (D&A), 36–37, 48, 65, 135–137, 160, 244, 360
   projection of, 135–137, 160
description of notes, 191
DIH, *See* days inventory held
dilutive, 31–34, 365–366, 368 371
discount factor, 128, 151–152
   with mid-year convention, 152, 171
   with year-end discounting, 151
discount rate, 125, 127–128, 141, 151–152, 155, 196 . *See also* weighted average cost of capital (WACC)
discounted cash flow (DCF) analysis, 22, 53–54, 125–181, 185, 242, 278, 301, 321, 325
   key pros and cons, 156
distressed companies, 188
distribution channels, 18–20, 55, 83
dividend recapitalization, 202–203
dividend yield, 21, 28, 40, 66
DOJ. *See* Department of Justice
Downside Case, 132, 241, 259
DPO. *See* days payable outstanding
DSO. *See* days sales outstanding
due diligence, 126, 188, 190, 193–194, 238, 241, 296, 300–301, 308–311, 313–317, 321, 325–326, 339,
DTL. *See* deferred tax liability

E

earnings before interest after taxes (EBIAT), 21, 39, 135, 137–138, 161
earnings before interest and taxes (EBIT), 20–21, 27, 37–38, 353, 365–366
   projection of, 134, 160
earnings before interest, taxes, depreciation and amortization (EBITDA), 20–21, 27, 36–38, 353
   projection of, 134, 159–160
earnings call transcript, 17, 57, 126, 130
earnings per share (EPS), 21, 24–25, 27, 33, 37, 39, 45, 47, 57, 65, 67–68, 102–103, 106, 312, 355, 365–366, 372
EBIAT. *See* earnings before interest after taxes
EBIT. *See* earnings before interest and taxes
EBITDA. *See* earnings before interest, taxes, depreciation and amortization
economies of scale, 334–335
economies of scope, 334–335
EDGAR. *See* Electronic Data Gathering, Analysis, and Retrieval system
effective tax rate, 135
Electronic Data Gathering, Analysis, and Retrieval system (EDGAR), 24
EMM. *See* exit multiple method
end markets, 18–19, 24, 55, 83, 130, 193
end-of-year discounting. *See* year-end discounting

endowments, 187
engagement letter, 189
enterprise value, 13, 15, 20, 22, 28, 47–48, 67, 74, 96, 102–103, 108–109, 111, 125, 128, 153–154, 172, 175, 185–186, 194, 214, 248
   at exit, in LBO, 197–201, 274
   calculation of, 35–36, 59–63, 96, 102, 113–115
   implied, 52–53, 74, 121, 247, 250
enterprise value multiples, 35, 47–49, 67–68, 103
enterprise value-to-EBIT (EV/EBIT), 47–48, 67–68, 103, 117
enterprise value-to-EBITDA (EV/EBITDA), 13, 15, 47–48, 51–52, 67–68, 74, 85, 103, 106, 117, 121, 169
enterprise value-to-sales (EV/sales), 47–48, 67–68, 103, 117
EPS. *See* earnings per share
equity contribution, 185, 196–201, 204, 212, 214, 235, 250–252, 255, 268, 272, 274–275, 277–279, 311
equity investors, 21, 40, 142, 144
equity purchase price, 96, 247, 251, 253, 342, 358
equity research analysts, 22, 39, 46, 68
equity research reports, 22–23, 25, 27, 55–57, 102, 105, 111, 126, 130, 132–133
equity risk premium, 145. *See also* market risk premium
equity sweetener, 30
equity value, 15, 20, 22, 26, 28, 35, 47, 49, 67, 102, 175, 197–200, 202, 214, 353
   at exit, in LBO, 194, 197–201, 274–275
   calculation of, 28, 30–34, 59–61, 96–102, 111, 114
   implied, 52–53, 96, 115, 128, 153–154, 172
equity value multiples, 47, 49, 103. *See also* price-to-earnings (P/E) ratio

equity-linked securities. *See* convertible securities
European Commission (European Union), 322
EV/EBIT. *See* enterprise value-to-EBIT
EV/EBITDA. *See* enterprise value-to-EBITDA
EV/sales. *See* enterprise value-to-sales
exchange offer, 91, 94, 212, 324
exercisable, 30–31, 96, 114
exercise price, 30–33, 52, 60–61
exit multiple, 149–150, 155–156, 170, 175, 196, 202, 274–275, 277
   implied, 150, 170, 236
exit multiple method (EMM), 127, 149–150, 152, 169–172
exit strategies, 193, 202–203, 212, 274
exit year, 196, 236, 274–275, 277
expenses, 37, 44–45, 127, 131, 135, 140, 222
   financing, 254
   non-cash, 37, 136, 244, 255, 265
   transaction, 249–255, 268, 272

F

face value, 34, 144, 220
fair market value, 253
fairness opinion, 22, 90–91, 110, 295–296, 300, 320–321
   screening for comparable companies, 22, 55
   screening for comparable acquisitions, 87
FASB. *See* Financial Accounting Standards Board
FCF. *See* free cash flow
Federal Funds rate, 207
federal taxes, 45, 135
Federal Trade Commission (FTC), 322
fee letter, 189
fiduciary duties, 298–299, 321
fiduciary termination, 318
final bid package, 235, 315–316
final bid procedures letter, 300, 315–316
final bids, 299–300, 311, 316, 320

Financial Accounting Standards Board (FASB), 34
financial covenants, 211. *See also* maintenance covenants
financial distress, 35, 40–41, 142, 198, 221
financial information services, 24–26, 44, 56
financial profile, 18, 20–22, 28, 50, 55, 74, 83, 106, 130
financial sponsors, 88, 108, 185–195, 199–201, 214, 235–236, 239, 241, 247, 274–275, 278, 300, 302–303, 305, 307, 312–313, 317
financial statistics, 13–15, 20–21, 23, 25, 28, 38, 40, 47–48, 50–51, 55–57, 65, 84–85, 90, 92, 102–103, 106–107, 111, 119, 132
financing structure, 185–190, 193, 196, 198, 204–206, 208, 210, 214, 219, 235–239, 241–247, 249–250, 255–256, 259, 263, 278–279, 311–312, 325, 332, 360, 362–363, 365
   analysis of, 272–274
   pre-packaged, 301, 311
firm value, 35
first lien, 204, 208–212, 220–221
first priority interest. *See* first lien
first round, of auction, 300, 302, 306–312, 315, 320
fiscal year, 24, 42–43, 46
Fitch Ratings, 22–23, 26, 41
fixed charge coverage ratio, 209, 222–223
fixed charges, 222
fixed costs, 37, 134
fixed exchange ratio, 98–101
fixed price. *See* floating exchange ratio
fixed rate, 211, 213, 219–220
fixed value, 98, 101
floating exchange ratio, 98–101
floating rate, 207, 210–213, 219, 256
football field, 74, 121, 175, 278, 349
Form 8-K, 17, 23–27, 42, 46, 57, 92–95, 109, 113, 126, 130, 212
Form S-4, 46, 91, 93–95. *See also* registration statement
Form 10-K, 17, 23–27, 31–32, 39, 42–44, 56–57, 63, 65, 91–92, 94, 111, 114–115, 117, 130, 137, 242
Form 10-Q. *See* pages for Form 10-K
forward LIBOR curve, 256–257
forward multiples, 67–68, 74
free cash flow (FCF), 125–130, 148–150, 152, 156–160, 169, 171–172, 185, 197–200, 242, 256–257, 262, 270, 272, 297
   calculation of, 131
   projection of, 131–140, 161–163
friendly (deal), 88, 108
FTC. *See* Federal Trade Commission
fully diluted shares outstanding, 28–33, 52, 60–61, 96, 98–99, 102, 114, 153, 248, 353, 366
fund (pool of capital), 186–188, 302

G

GAAP. *See* generally accepted accounting principles
General Electric, 337
general partner (GP), 187, 302
generally accepted accounting principles (GAAP), 27, 32, 36, 135, 341, 343
geography, 18, 20, 23, 87
goodwill, 136, 251–253, 341–342, 358
goodwill created, 251–253, 341–342, 358
goodwill impairment, 44, 136
GP. *See* general partner
greenfielding, 332
gross margin, 36–37, 133–134, 159, 239
gross profit, 20–21, 24, 27–28, 36
   projection of, 133–134, 159
growth capex, 194–195
growth profile, 18, 21, 28, 38, 130, 194–195, 297
growth rates, 15, 20–21, 28, 38–39, 50, 68, 125, 127–128, 131, 133, 155–158, 175, 275
guarantees, 208, 218–219, 223

H

Hart-Scott-Rodino Antitrust Improvements Act of 1976 (HSR Act), 322
hedge funds, 186–187, 190, 205, 211, 213
high yield bonds, 93, 189, 191, 204–206, 209–216, 219–221, 223, 242, 262
historical financial data/performance, 21, 23, 28, 38–39, 55, 63, 68, 92, 111, 131–138, 157–161, 163, 190, 193, 239, 297, 304, 321, 334
holding company (HoldCo), 203, 205, 218–219
horizontal integration, 335
hostile (deal), 88–89
HSR Act. See Hart-Scott-Rodino Antitrust Improvements Act of 1976

I

Ibbotson, 145, 147, 165
if-converted method, 31–33
in-the-money, 30–33, 60–61, 96, 114, 153, 353
income statement, 15, 25, 27, 34–38, 45–46, 57, 63–65, 68, 115–117, 135–137, 157
   in LBO analysis, 239–242, 244, 255–256, 259, 262–263, 265–266, 282
incurrence covenants, 211, 221, 223
indemnification, 317–319, 341
indenture, 143, 191, 211, 218, 220, 222–223
industry, 18, 191, 202, 298, 313, 321–322. See also sector
information statement, 94
initial bid procedures letter, 300, 306–308, 315
initial bids, 297, 306, 311
initial public offering (IPO), 13, 125, 185–186, 194, 202–203
initiating coverage reports, 22, 25, 133
insolvency, 35, 142
institutional investors, 210
institutional lenders, 187, 190
institutional term loans, 210, 219. See also term loan B
intangible assets, 135–136, 208, 253, 341–342, 358–359, 365–366
interest coverage, 41, 222
interest expense, in LBO analysis, 265–267
interest income, 266
internal rate of return (IRR), 196–201, 275–279
Intralinks, 55, 188, 238, 309–310
intrinsic valuation analysis, 13
intrinsic value, 125
inventory, 44–45, 64, 134, 137, 139, 161, 207–208, 217
investment banks, 18, 22, 31, 87, 145, 185–190, 192, 208, 212, 235, 241, 295–296, 307, 311, 321, 331–332
investment decisions, 13, 125, 190, 309
investment grade, 42
investment horizon, 185, 194–197, 199–201, 239
investor presentations, 17–18, 22–23, 126, 130
IPO. See initial public offering
IRR. See internal rate of return
issuer, 17, 30, 32–34, 41, 46, 91, 94, 189, 204, 211–233

J

joint proxy/registration statement, 91
joint ventures, 222
junior (ranking), 205, 210–211, 217–218, 223

L

large-cap, 338
last twelve months (LTM), 15, 23, 28, 40–43, 46–47, 51–53, 56, 63–68, 74, 85, 102–107, 117–119, 149, 152, 157, 169, 175, 247, 250, 277–278, 311, 350
layering, 223
LBO. See leveraged buyouts

LBO analysis, 22, 53, 128, 185, 235–291, 297, 301, 312, 321.
LC. *See* letters of credit
lease, 37, 222, 309
legal counsel, 302, 305–306, 309, 316, 320
letters of credit (LC), 208, 250
leverage levels, 186, 202–206, 211, 277, 311, 337
leverage ratios, 28, 40, 207, 221–233, 338, 363
leveraged buyouts (LBO), 185–233.
leveraged loan, 195, 209, 211. *See also* bank debt
levered beta, 144, 146
  predicted, 59, 165
levered free cash flow, 127, 185, 200. *See also* cash available for debt repayment
liabilities, long-term, 242, 256, 268
LIBOR. *See* London Interbank Offered Rate
LIBOR floor, 257
limited partnership (LPs), 187, 196, 202, 302
liquidity, 139–140, 208, 250
London Interbank Offered Rate (LIBOR), 164, 256
long-term growth rate, 38–39, 133
LPs. *See* limited partnership
LTM. *See* last twelve months

M

M&A. *See* mergers & acquisitions
MAC/MAE. *See* material adverse change/effect
maintenance capex, 195
maintenance covenants, 204, 209, 212, 221–222
make-whole provision, 220
management buyout (MBO), 192, 323
Management Case, 132, 156, 239
management discussion & analysis (MD&A), 24, 44, 57, 111, 117, 130, 137, 304
management presentation, 55, 238, 300, 302, 306, 308–309, 313–314, 325

sample, 308
mandatory amortization/repayment, 212, 239, 256–257, 259, 270, 337
marginal tax rate, 45, 59, 65, 131, 135, 141, 144, 146, 161, 165, 200, 266, 343, 358, 360
margins, 15, 21, 28, 37, 47, 50, 125, 127–128, 131, 134, 155–156, 159, 175, 195, 241, 277, 297, 336
market capitalization, 30, 147, 166. *See also* equity value
market conditions, 13, 54–55, 83, 88, 106–108, 119, 196, 202–203, 211–214, 220, 255, 278, 297, 319, 350
marketing materials, 189, 191, 296, 299–300, 302–305. *See also* confidential information memorandum (CIM) and teaser
market risk premium, 144–145, 165–166
market share, 36, 50, 133, 193–194, 297, 334
market value, 40, 125, 141, 146, 165, 341, 343
material adverse change/effect (MAC/MAE), 317, 319
maturity, 190, 208–212, 217, 219–221, 239, 259, 262, 338
MBO. *See* management buyout
MD&A. *See* management discussion & analysis
merchant banking, 187
merger, 222–223, 317, 319. *See also* one-step merger and two-step tender process
merger of equals (MOE), 89, 339
mergers & acquisitions (M&A) transaction, 22, 25, 46, 83–84, 92–94, 297
merger proxy (PREM14A/DEFM14A), 22, 90, 94, 110
mezzanine debt/financing, 30, 189, 204, 211, 213–214
mid-cap, 166

mid-year convention/discounting, 150–152, 169, 171
minority interest, 35. See also noncontrolling interest
MOE. See merger of equals
Moody's Investors Service, 22–23, 26, 41, 57, 204
monetization, 202–203, 274
multiples. See trading multiples and transaction multiples

N

NAICS. See North American Industry Classification System
NASDAQ, 90
NC. See non-callable
negative covenants, 222–223
negotiated sale, 88, 295, 297, 325–326
    advantages and disadvantages, 326
negotiations, 139, 236, 295–296, 298, 300, 305–306, 316, 319–321, 326, 331, 341, 365
net debt, 35, 39–40, 52–53, 62, 65–67, 96, 102, 115, 153, 172, 247, 275, 337, 353
net income, 15, 20, 24, 27–28, 33, 35, 37–39, 44–46, 52, 102–103, 106, 117, 223, 239, 224–225, 255, 265–266, 268, 366
net income margin, 28, 38, 47
net interest expense, 266
net operating loss (NOL), 334
net operating profit after taxes (NPOAT) 21, 39, 135. See also EBIAT
net present value (NPV), 196–197. See also present value
net share settlement (NSS), 31, 34
net working capital (NWC), 125, 135
    projection of, 137–140, 161–163
New York Stock Exchange, 90
non-callable, 220
noncontrolling interest, 35, 40, 102, 153
non-investment grade, 41–42, 204, 209–210. See also high yield bonds

non-recurring items, 15, 24–25, 28, 39, 57, 111, 366
    adjusting for, 44–46, 53, 64–65, 92, 103, 115–117, 131, 239, 245
non-solicitation, 305
NOL. See net operating loss
NOPAT. See net operating profit after taxes
normalized basis/level, 44–45, 55, 103, 127, 131, 133, 149, 239, 303
North American Industry Classification System (NAICS), 23, 55
notes to the financials, 45, 57, 111, 135
NPV. See net present value
NSS. See net share settlement
NWC. See net working capital

O

offer price per share, 96, 98–104, 109–110, 113, 248
offer price per share-to-LTM EPS, 103, 106–107, 117–118
Offer to Purchase, 91
offer value, 96, 320. See also equity purchase price
offering memorandum, 191
one-step merger, 90, 322–323
operating company (OpCo), 203, 218–219
operating income/profit, 36, 134
operating scenarios, 134, 235, 238–239, 272, 279
options. See stock options
organic growth, 21, 194, 197, 202–203
organization and preparation stage, of auction, 300–306
out-of-the-money, 32, 61, 96
outliers, 15, 26, 50–51, 69, 85, 106

P

par value, 34, 143, 164, 220, 223
parent company, 92, 192, 346
pari passu, 209, 218, 223
payment-in-kind (PIK) interest, 212–214, 265

Index

PE firms. *See* private equity firms
P/E ratio. *See* price-to-earnings ratio
P/FCF. *See* price-to-free cash flow
pension contracts, 309
pension funds, 187, 190
performance drivers, 126, 128, 130–131, 157
peripheral comparables, 15, 51
permitted disclosures, 305
perpetuity growth method (PGM), 127, 148–150, 152, 169–170
perpetuity growth rate, 128, 149–150, 155, 169–170
   implied, 150, 169, 175
PGM. *See* perpetuity growth method
PIK. *See* payment-in-kind
PP&E. *See* property, plant, and equipment
PRE14A. *See* proxy statement
precedent transactions analysis, 22, 53, 83–124, 128, 155, 175, 247, 278, 297, 301, 321, 325, 349–350, 352.
   key pros and cons, 107
pre-closing commitments, 316–317
preemptive bid, 325
preferred stock, 35, 40, 102, 153, 204–205, 222
PREM14A. *See* merger proxy
premium paid, 83, 85, 89, 96, 102–104, 107–108, 110–111, 118, 121, 297
prepaid expenses, 137, 140, 161
prepayments, 211, 220, 222–223
present value, 125, 127–128, 141, 148, 151, 156, 171, 297
press release excerpts
   all-cash transaction, 98, 110
   announced synergies, 105
   cash and stock transaction, 101
   floating exchange ratio, 101
   fixed exchange ratio, 100
press releases, 15, 17, 23–24, 26–27, 42, 46, 57, 60, 66, 92–93, 95, 104, 109, 113
price-to-earnings (P/E) ratio, 13, 47, 51–53, 67, 103, 118

price-to-free cash flow (FCF), 49
prime rate, 207
prior stub, 42
priority status, 208, 217
private acquirers, 92–93
private equity (PE) firms, 187
privately held companies, 17
private placement. *See* Rule 144A
private targets, 22, 90, 93, 295, 315
pro forma
   accretion/(dilution) analysis, 301, 312, 355, 365–372
   balance sheet, 46, 242, 244, 251, 253, 256, 266–268, 341–343, 359–362
   cash flow statement, 256–257, 270–271
   compliance, 223
   income statement, 256, 265–267
   financial data, 25, 36, 46, 90–92, 238–239, 244, 272, 297, 322, 325, 355
products (and services), 18–20, 36–37, 55, 130, 139, 193, 297
profitability, 15, 18, 21, 28, 36–37, 48, 50, 65, 69, 126, 134, 202–203, 335–336
projection period, 125, 127, 131–138, 140, 142, 148–152, 156–161, 200, 235, 239, 242, 245–247, 251, 255–256, 259, 262–263, 266, 268, 270, 272, 274–275, 365–366
property, plant, and equipment (PP&E), 135–136, 195, 208, 217, 244–247, 253, 341, 359
pro-rata
   bank debt, 209
   repayment, 262
prospective buyers, 18, 89, 188, 193, 236, 238, 295–296, 298, 300–307, 311, 313–316, 320, 325
prospectus (424B), 32, 46. *See also* registration statement
proxy statement, 22, 25, 27, 31, 55, 90–94, 110, 114, 322
public acquirers, 84, 90–93, 104, 108, 322, 333

public targets, 90–91, 94, 102–103, 109, 238, 295, 305, 349, 352
publicly traded companies, 17, 125, 130, 132, 153, 172, 193
purchase consideration, 88–96, 98–101, 111, 113, 212, 315, 339
purchase price, 22, 46, 83–84, 88–91, 93, 102, 104–105, 110, 185–186, 188, 196–197, 199, 202–206, 208, 212, 214, 236, 253, 274, 278–279, 295, 307, 311–312, 315, 320, 325, 333, 338, 341–343, 348, 352, 355, 360, 365–366
   assumptions, 247–248
purchase/sale agreement, 25, 90, 299. *See also* definitive agreement

Q
qualified institutional buyers (QIBs), 91, 212
quarterly report. *See* Form 10-Q

R
ranking
   capital structure, 204, 207, 211, 213, 362
   relative to peers, 15, 50
rating agencies, 22–23, 27, 41, 57, 337, 363. *See also* Fitch Ratings, Moody's, and S&P
Ratio Test, 223
redemptions, 220, 222
refinanced, 46, 96, 220, 239, 254, 366
refinancing, 102, 186, 203, 262
registration statement, 46, 91–95, 212
Regulation FD (fair disclosure), 17, 25, 303
regulatory approvals, 299, 315, 317–318, 322
reinvestment risk, 220
reported income statement, 44–45, 63
reporting period, 24, 46–47, 130
representations and warranties, 208, 316–319
restricted payments, 203, 222–223
restructuring charges, 44, 64–65
restructurings, 13, 83, 125, 195, 235

return on assets (ROA), 21, 28, 39, 66
return on equity (ROE), 21, 28, 39, 65
return on invested capital (ROIC), 21, 28, 39, 65
return on investment (ROI), 21, 28, 39, 65–66
revenues, 19, 132. *See* also sales
revolver availability, 208, 324, 338
revolving credit facilities (revolver), 143, 190, 207–211, 219, 242, 250, 255–257, 259, 262, 265, 338
risk-free rate, 144–145, 165–166
ROA. *See* return on assets
roadshow, 191
ROE. *See* return on equity
ROI. *See* return on investment
ROIC. *See* return on invested capital
rolled equity, 204–205, 214
roll-up, 188, 193
Rule 144A, 91, 212
Rule 424, 46

S
S Corp, 340
sale process, 18, 25, 55, 89–90, 102, 132, 188, 238, 242, 278, 295–329, 333.
sales, 20, 27, 36
   projection of, 133, 159
Sarbanes-Oxley Act of 2002 (SOX), 192
scale, 21, 36, 131, 193–194, 202
Schedule 13E-3, 91–92, 94
Schedule 14A. *See* proxy statement
Schedule 14D-9, 91, 94
Schedule TO, 91, 94
screening
   for comparable companies, 22–23, 55–56
   for comparable acquisitions, 87–89, 108
SEC. *See* Securities and Exchange Commission
SEC filings, 15, 17–18, 23–26, 37, 39, 46, 56–57, 60, 92–95, 102, 109, 126, 130, 157, 238, 321

Index

second lien, 204, 208, 210–211, 218, 221
second lien term loans, 210–211
second priority interest. *See* second lien
second round, of auction, 299–311, 313–316
section 338, 346
sector, 13, 17–25, 28, 37, 49, 51, 54–55, 74, 84, 87, 106, 108, 119, 125–127, 137–138, 143, 149, 157, 188, 193, 202, 238, 241, 297, 302–303, 306, 313, 333, 335, 349
sector coverage, 235, 238
sector-specific multiples, 47, 49
Securities Act of 1933, 91, 191, 207, 212
Securities and Exchange Commission (SEC), 15
Securities Exchange Act of 1934, 15, 191, 207
security, 186, 208, 217, 256, 338, 366
selling, general & administrative (SG&A), 37–38, 135
  projection of, 133–134, 159
sell-side advisory, 132, 188, 236, 238, 278, 295–296, 299–302, 304–313, 315–321, 325–326
senior (ranking), 52, 214–218, 223
senior secured, 40, 207, 211, 218–219, 222, 250, 255, 272. *See also* first lien and second lien
senior subordinated, 204, 211, 218–219, 223, 262–263
senior unsecured, 204, 211, 218–219
seniority, 186, 217–220, 256
sensitivity analysis
  DCF analysis, 125, 128, 149, 155–156, 167–168, 174–175
  LBO analysis, 236, 277–279
  M&A analysis, 372
SG&A. *See* selling, general & administrative
share price, 26–27, 30–34, 40, 47–48, 52, 57, 61, 66–67, 96, 98–100, 103–104, 118–119, 128
  accretion/(dilution) analysis, 355, 357
  implied, 52, 153–154, 172, 351

performance benchmarking, 321
systematic risk, 144
unaffected, 102–104, 111, 118
shareholder approval, 299, 318, 321–324, 339
shareholder vote, 90, 94
shareholders' equity, 21, 27, 35, 39, 65–66, 247, 252–256, 266, 268, 272, 341, 358
short-form LBO model, 242
SIC. *See* Standard Industrial Classification system
size, of company, 15, 17–18, 20–21, 23, 28, 47–48, 50–51, 69, 92, 108, 143, 147, 193, 202, 297, 302, 313, 322, 326, 337
  key financial data, 36–41
  market valuation, 28–35
size premium (SP), 147, 166
small-cap, 69, 74
sources and uses of funds, 242, 247, 249–252, 255, 259, 279, 355, 357–358, 360
sovereign wealth funds, 187
SOX. *See* Sarbanes-Oxley Act of 2002
SP. *See* size premium
S&P. *See* Standard & Poor's
S&P 500, 146
SPACs. *See* special purpose acquisition companies
special dividends, 317
special purpose acquisition companies (SPACs), 187
Sponsor Case/Model, 241
sponsors. *See* financial sponsors
spreading, 14
  comparable companies, 15, 25, 28–49, 57–67
  precedent transactions, 84–85, 90, 93–105, 111–118
springing financial covenant, 209
standalone, 104, 238, 312, 325, 355, 360, 365–366
Standard & Poor's (S&P), 22, 23, 26, 41, 57, 204
Standard & Poor's Leveraged Commentary & Data Group, 205–206, 230–231

Standard Industrial Classification (SIC) system, 23, 55
standstill agreement, 305
stapled financing, 188, 300–301, 306, 311
state law, 90, 322
steady state, 127, 131–132, 134, 136, 148
stock-for-stock transaction, 98–101, 317
stock options, 24, 27, 30–33, 52, 56, 59–60, 92, 96, 114, 153, 317, 353
stock price. *See* share price
stock sale, 253, 317, 319, 340–343, 345–347
straight-line depreciation, 136
strategic alternatives, 104, 111, 118, 295
strategic buyer, 83, 88–89, 104, 108, 202, 236, 278, 295–296, 302–305, 307, 312–313, 315, 325–326, 337–338, 350, 355
strategic fit, 298, 302, 325
strike price. *See* exercise price
structural protections, 99
structural subordination, 217–219
stub period, 159
subordination provisions, 218
subprime mortgage crisis, 205, 257
sub-sector, 15, 17–19, 51
sum of the parts, 141
suppliers, 19, 37, 126, 130, 140, 157, 194, 298, 302, 304, 309, 315, 326, 334–336
syndication, 189, 210, 221
synergies, 83, 85, 89, 92, 96, 99, 102, 104–105, 111, 202, 278, 297, 302, 313, 325, 332–336, 350, 365–366, 372
systematic risk, 144, 146

T

tangible assets, 136, 208, 253, 341, 358
tangible value, 104, 191, 337
target management, 187, 191–192, 195, 214, 296, 302–303, 305, 313
targeted auction, 295–296, 298–299, 309
advantages and disadvantages, 298
tax basis, 343, 346
tax deductibility, 142, 185, 198, 253, 334, 339, 343
tax expense, 37, 45
projection of, 135, 161
tax regime, 13, 37
taxable event, 98
T-bills, 144
T-bonds, 144
teaser, 303–306
tender premium, 220
tender offers, 91, 93–94, 322–323
tenor. *See* maturity
term. *See* maturity
term loan A, 210, 262
term loan B, 210, 250–251, 262, 357
term loan facilities, 209–210
terminal value, 125–128, 130, 133, 140, 148–152, 156–157, 169–171, 175, 297
terminal year, 127, 133, 148–150, 169
termination fee. *See* breakup fee
termination provisions, 316, 318
terms, of LBO financing, 191, 217–226
third lien, 210–211, 213
tiering, 15, 21, 51, 147
time value of money, 151, 197, 275
T-notes, 144
toggle cells/function, 132, 238, 241, 247, 279
total interest expense, 265–266
trading comps. *See* comparable companies analysis
trading liquidity, 21, 211
trading multiples, 13–15, 21, 25, 28, 43, 47, 50–51, 57, 65, 67–68, 297
terminal value, 149–150, 152, 169
trailing multiples, 67
trailing twelve months (TTM). *See* last twelve months
transaction comps. *See* precedent transactions analysis
transaction multiples, 83–85, 90, 92–93, 102, 105–107, 111, 117–118

transaction rationale, 92, 109
transaction structure, 247, 272, 295, 316–317
transaction value, 102
treasury stock method (TSM), 31–32, 34, 52, 60, 114
triggering event, 25
TSM. *See* treasury stock method
two-step tender process, 323

U

underwriters, 186, 189, 191, 241, 254, 272
underwritten financing, 189
undrawn, 208, 250, 259
unlevered beta, 146–147, 165–166
unlevered free cash flow, 149, 185
unsecured, 211, 217
unsecured claims, 210
unsecured creditors, 208, 217
unsecured term loan, 212
unsystematic risk, 144
useful life, 135–136
uses of funds. *See* sources and uses of funds

V

valuation
  implied by EV/EBITDA, 52
  implied by P/E, 52–53
  comparable companies, determination in, 15–17, 51–53, 74
  precedent transactions, determination in, 85, 106, 121
  DCF analysis, determination in, 127–128, 153–155, 171–175
  LBO analysis, determination in, 278–279
valuation analysis, in sale process, 299–300, 304, 307, 321

valuation floor, 311
valuation matrix, 349, 352–353
valuation paradigm, 297
value maximization, 89, 295, 298
variable costs, 37, 134
venture capital funds, 187
vertical integration, 335–336
vesting period, 30

W

WACC. *See* weighted average cost of capital
Wall Street, 13, 37, 146, 159
warrants, 24, 27, 30–32, 56, 59–60, 92, 96, 114, 153, 213
weighted average cost of debt, 143
weighted average cost of capital (WACC), 125–127, 130, 141–152, 155–156, 164, 167–169, 171, 175, 350
weighted average exercise (strike) price, 31, 52, 60–61, 96, 114
working capital. *See* net working capital (NWC)
write-down, 44–46, 342
write-up, 253, 341–342, 358–360, 365

Y

year-end discounting, 151–152, 170–171
year-over-year (YoY)
  balance sheet accounts, changes in, 244
  growth rates, 159
  NWC, changes in, 138, 161, 244
year-to-date (YTD), 24, 42, 56, 115
yield-to-call (YTC), 143
yield-to-worst call (YTW), 143

KNOW YOUR UNIVERSE

//

BLOOMBERG FOR INVESTMENT BANKING

Investment bankers demand timely and complete information on the companies and industries they cover. The Bloomberg Professional® service puts powerful data, news and analysis in context. Track key developments in your coverage universe, generate transaction ideas for conversations with clients and get the latest on company fundamentals, industry research and precedent transactions – the information that matters to you.

Whether you're in the office or on the road, Bloomberg puts the information you need at your fingertips.

To learn more or to arrange a demonstration, please visit
bloomberg.com/investmentbanking
or call +1 212 318 2000.

Bloomberg

Work smarter

More than a virtual data room

Learn how to get deals done faster: intralinks.com/Dealspace

the corporate presence

The Leader in Financial Deal Toys!

For the most creative, memorable and effective Lucites to commemorate deals, look to the proven experts: The Corporate Presence.

With more than 30 years of experience, The Corporate Presence provides in-person service in key global locations and leads the industry in the design and manufacture of Lucites for investment banks worldwide.

NEW YORK 48 Wall Street 24th Floor New York, NY 10005 T: +1 212 989 6446 F: +1 917 677 8444

www.cpresence.com   info@cpresence.com

More great resources to help you master investment banking and valuation

Welcome to the No. 1 knowledge center for M&A and capital markets professionals, professors, and students. It includes the deepest educational ancillaries and self-study tools anywhere, including a comprehensive workbook and detailed valuation models, as well as focus notes for those learning on the go.

Get started at www.rosenbaumandpearl.com

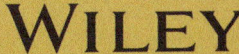